# BLACK HISTORY EXTRAVAGANZA

# HONORING DR. BEN-JOCHANNAN

# BY

# FREDERICK MONDERSON

**ISBN - 9781610230520**
**LCCN - 201900721**

In the Tribute to Professor George Simmonds, "Unsung Hero," Dr. Fred Monderson sat at the feet of his heroes, Brother X, Michael Carter, Dr. Leonard Jeffries, El Hombre Brath, Dr. Lewis, Prof. George Simmonds, Dr. ben-Jochannan, Sister Camille Yarbrough, among others.

**Black History Extravaganza.** Dr. Yosef Alfredo Antonio Ben-Jochannan, Author, educator, historian, publisher, Egyptologist, archaeologist and African nationalist who showed us the "Light."

**Black History Extravaganza - Photo -** The Gods in sail.

**Black History Extravaganza.** Dr. John Henrik Clarke, Author, educator, Sovereignist, African Nationalist, Emeritus Professor, Hunter College, CUNY; he insisted African history must be written by African scholars and "Failure is not an option!"

**Black History Extravaganza**. One of many African images defaced throughout Egypt; high-up and in most significant locations in existential spiritual, religious and artistic data because this image betrays representation of the ancient Egyptians in the African mold.

## ABOUT THE AUTHOR

Dr. Frederick Monderson is a retired college professor and school teacher who taught **African History** in the City University of New York and **American History and Government** in the New York public schools. He has written some 1000 articles in the New York Black Press, **Daily Challenge**, **Afro Times** and **New American** newspapers. In this venture, Monderson lends his expertise as a historian, Egyptologist, journalist and author of several books including *Ladies in the House*; *Michael Jackson: The Last Dance*; *50 on Point*; *Barack Obama: Ready, Fit to Lead*; *Barack Obama: Master of Washington D.C.*; *Obama: Master and Commander* and *Obama: The Journey Completed*; *Sonny Carson:*

*The Final Triumph* (5 Volumes); *Black Nationalism: Alive and Well*; *Black Nationalism: Still Alive and Well*; *Guyana: Land of Beauty and Many Waters*; and on Ancient Egypt *Seven Letters to Mike Tyson on Egyptian Temples*; *10 Poems Praising Great Blacks for Mike Tyson*; *Research Essays on Ancient Egypt*; *Temple of Karnak: The Majestic Architecture of Ancient Kemet*; *Where are the Kamite Kings?*; *Abydos and Osiris*; *Temple of Luxor*; *Medinet Habu: Mortuary Temple of Rameses III*; *The Quintessential Book on Ancient Egypt: "Holy Land"* (A Tour Guide Novel on Egypt); *Hatshepsut's Temple at Deir el Bahari*; *Intrigue Through Time (An Egyptian Resurrection)*, a Novel on Ancient Egypt); *The Majesty of Egyptian Gods and Temples* (a book of Egyptian Poems); *Egypt Essays on Ancient Kemet; The Ramesseum: Mortuary Temple of Rameses II*; *The Colonnade: Then and Now*; *Reflections on Ancient Kemet*; *Grassroots View of Ancient Egypt*; *Glory of the Ancestors: 19 Letters to O.J. Simpson on Ancient African History*; and *Celebrating Dr. Ben-Jochannan*; *Into the Egyptian Mind*; *African Nationalist Poetry and Prose*; *More Woman, More Power*; *Reflections on Ancient Egypt - Book One*; *Reflections on Ancient Egypt - Book Two*; *Black History Everyday - Part One*; *Black History Everyday - Part Two*; *Let's Liberate the Temple*; and more. A student of the esteemed Dr. Yosef ben-Jochannan, Dr. Monderson conducts tours to Egypt.

For Tour information, Contact Orleane Brooks-Williams at Nostrand Travel, 730 Nostrand Avenue, Brooklyn, New York 11216. Phone Number 718-756-5300. Next Tour of Egypt is July 13-July 27, 2018.

fredsegypt.com@fredsegypt.com
SuMonPublishers.com@SuMonPublishers.com
BlackEgyptbooks.com@BlackEgyptbooks.com

**Black History Extravaganza**. Gil Noble of ABC's "**Like It Is**" celebrated 30 years on television enlightening several generations of African-Americans with his consistent and tremendously educational program, was honored in Harem at Harriet Tubman's School by Elombe Brathe with Dr. Ben-Jochannan in attendance as was Mr. Gil Noble, Dr. John Henrik and Sister Sybil William-Clarke, Sonny and Mae Carson, Congressman Charles Rangel, Dr. Lewis and wife, Councilwoman Una Clarke and education activist Jitu Weusi, among others.

**Black History Extravaganza**. Old Glory in Red, White and Blue!

**Black History Extravaganza**. With his wife besides him, this New Kingdom Nobleman stands before Gods in his tomb at Thebes.

# DR. BEN-JOCHANNAN AS TEACHER
## By
## Dr. Fred Monderson

In his lengthy career as historian, researcher, Egyptologist, writer, publisher and lecturer, but most especially teacher, Dr. Ben-Jochannan admonished his students to not simply research but dig deeply to locate and reveal pertinent historical, cultural, even religious facts and features of the Nile Valley experience. In this, he emphasized the understanding and practice of Ma'at, a profound philosophical and social idea and tool. That is, so that African people will go from strength to strength and generation to generation knowing even more about the great body of knowledge ancient African minds bequeathed the world. After all, the philosophic and religious exhilir Ma'at is about righteousness, truth and justice being applied in every situation of the human experience. In that meaningful journey, among his many admonitions, Dr. Ben charged young and thinking Africans get knowledge, seek understanding of this wonderful experience as they search for and expose the truth.

Particularly, he insisted, when researching the topic of ancient Egypt especially, he emphasized "get the oldest materials you can find and work from there." Just as substantive, Gary Byrd, the New York City radio personality for his part insisted, "The information you don't have could kill you," so get everything available. Equally too, Dr. Ben encouraged visits to Egypt, then challenged the many thousands he showed the way by bringing them to Egypt, and importantly laying down the gauntlet by asking pointedly "Now that you have come to Egypt, seen what you have seen, what are you going to do with the knowledge?" As such, and seeking ongoing positive outcomes in that intellectual and culturally transformative environment he constantly invoked a mantra of "Publish or Perish."

Even more important, the master-teacher implored, seek out the most significant facts and even nuances of the ancient culture so that each one can teach one. His admonition was to encourage and empower African people to advance along a continuum armed with an intellectual awareness that can rightly challenge falsity with unadulterated facts.

In arming oneself for combat in the zones of spiritual and intellectual warfare relative where and to whom Egypt belongs, even who actually owns the heritage, the legacy, a potent tool is knowledge of the sources of historical references that record the esoteric evidence as revealed and must now be made manifest.

From the earliest times of the Predynastic period **Slate Palettes** have served as a beginning pictographic record but the **Narmer Palette** and the **Narmer Macehead** culminated this process of enlightenment particularly because they center upon a historic individual and underscore an event that divides time in initiating new standards in all walks of human experience. The **Turin Canon**, **Palermo Stone**, **Westcar Papyrus** and **Abusir Papyrus** are important and ground-breaking as literary sources that chronicle the early history of the culture in which later evidence substantially corroborated these early records.

**Black History Extravaganza**. Ankh, the Egyptian Symbol of Life, complemented by Ma'at, whose practice emphasized, Justice, Truth and Righteousness, are both powerful African symbols of Good.

In times when Egyptian society had achieved full maturity, the **Karnak Tablet** of Thutmose III's *Akh Menu* festival temple, the

**Abydos Tablet** or List of Seti I, the **Second Abydos List** of his son, Rameses II from their temples at Abydos and the **Sakkara Tomb List** of the noble Tenroy, substantially provided the names of the monarchs of the great periods of Egyptian history. As the earliest of the above sources were in their formative stages, the **Pyramid Texts**, **Coffin Texts** and later **Book of the Dead** or **Per-M-Hru** established an unbroken continuum of religious beliefs dating to prehistoric times designed to ensure survivability of the king in the next life and ultimately came to incorporate the aspirations of nobles and even common folks in what became the democratization of the afterlife. However, while religious data, mortuary and worship, chronicled a great deal of Egyptian beliefs in this world and the next, intellectual activities in the realms of science, education, medicine, art and architectural building practices and much more create and chronicle the great flowering of Egyptian, Nile Valley, African culture. What is significant, extant evidence at Edfu temple of Horus reflects the beliefs that takes the reader back to mythological times when the potent cosmological ideas were being forged and formed in the emerging creative African mind chronicling the activities of the gods. It is laughable when Caucasians are credited with being the creators of Egyptian civilization, much of which were laid down by the Anu, Black people, who founded Heliopolis as a place replete with intellectual activities and worship in establishing the doctrines of Ra. Thus and that being so, these foreigners should, perhaps, be given credit for "re-inventing the African wheel." Let us not forget, Mosso in The Foundation of Mediterranean Civilization indicated these "Asiatics never penetrated the Nile valley nor the Aegean areas." This should have been known early, yet no attempts were made to correct the falsity which to this day pervades.

**Black History Extravaganza**. How convenient the face is defaced! Nevertheless, this **Table of Offerings** is designed to give the deceased all good things in the **Afterlife**, for a well-deserved life of goodness in service to the Gods and fellowman.

There were other sources that provide evidence of their rulers and their times; the **Biennial Cattle Count** has been used to measure wealth but also the number of years of an individual king's reign. The forward motion of time we are so much accustomed to did not apply to an individual's period of rule which began upon his assumption of rule and ended when he or she died, abdicated or was forcefully overthrown. Time sort of "stood still" until his successor assumed ruler-ship and then the cycle began again. In the Middle Kingdom, the Co-Regency bridged this gap. Thus, the "cattle count," often depicted in colorful illustration was one way of reckoning time and providing evidence of a king's reign. But there were other measures by which the names of individuals and their times were being recorded. As early as the first dynasty stone became a workable material, first for lining the floor of tombs and then for hard areas as thresholds, door posts, windows, etc., in homes under heavy wear. As such, the art of quarrying of stone reached a high state of perfection and thus, stone quarries became famous down through dynastic history.

Workers and kings left their names and messages at quarries such as **Wady Maghara** where limestone was mined; **Hat Nub** provided alabaster; and the **Aswan Quarries** were known for red granite, where these sites all became "blackboards" upon which kings and their officials added to the early record of history. Still, there were the **Rock lands at Toma in Nubia** as well as a number of "decrees" even "hymns of praise" to the king, even the gods, that have served to provide information of a historical nature. Last but certainly not least, the **Heb Sed Festival** celebrated initially after 30 years of rule was established by Unification from evidence provided at Hierakonpolis. Practiced through the age even before the Step-Pyramid, this festival has provided a wealth of information in its corollary adjunct to all forms of record keeping. Certainly the Sun Temples at Abusir, of which there were six but only two were discovered and cleared, provide evidence of the **Heb Sed Fes**tival. Adding more to the idea of historical sources we can add, among other references, **Royal Decrees** and the **Elephantine Archives of Sixth Dynasty Nomarchs** at Elephantine is another.

**Nile Marks** throughout the country especially at Aswan and Semna in Nubia are also significant in providing evidence of Nile Valley history. Naturally the **Census** is a credible source but so too **Graffiti inscriptions at Wady Hammamat** in the Eastern Desert as well as across the river in the Western Desert, both in Southern Upper Egypt. Finally, let us not forget those Old and Middle Kingdom **Instructions of Ptahhotep** and **Kagenmi**; and certainly the **Tale of Ipuwer** who decried the state of events in the First Intermediate Period. This and more Dr. Ben-Jochannan very early and consistently helped identify, and instructed his students to study and encouraged their further learning by visiting Egypt for hands-on edification.

**Black History Extravaganza**. How refreshing it is that the people come out to pay their respects to one who has "Talked the Talk" and "Walked the Talk;" "Talked the Walk," and "Walked the Talk" of African People's Enlightenment, Liberation and Empowerment and bequeathed a powerful and enduring body of work for progeny to purchase, read, digest and gain knowledge for the journey.

**Black History Extravaganza.** When the Anubi come to pay homage, it is well-deserved for service to all humanity having challenged the oppressor and pointed out distortion and omission.

**Black History Extravaganza.** Once the deceased undergoes the Ceremony of **Opening the Mouth**, therein declared "True of Voice" at the Judgment, he can then sail in the "Boat of the Gods."

# BLACK HISTORY EXTRAVAGANZA HONORING DR. BEN-JOCHANNAN

|     | PREFACE | 2 |
| --- | --- | --- |
| I. | INTRODUCTION | 12 |
| II. | WISDOM OF THE ANCIENT EGYPTIANS | 38 |
| III. | TRIBUTE TO DR. BEN-JOCHANNAN | 66 |
| IV. | DR. BEN-JOCHANNAN'S LETTER ENDORSING FRED MONDERSON | 90 |
| V. | DR. YOSEF BEN-JOCHANNAN'S RECOGNIZING DR. FREDERICK MONDERSON | 93 |
| VI. | THE AWESOME EGYPTIAN TEMPLE | 95 |
| VII. | WHO WERE THE ANCIENT EGYPTIANS? | 138 |
| VIII. | THE ARCHAEOLOGY OF EGYPT | 245 |
| IX. | THE ART OF ANCIENT EGYPT | 332 |
| X. | ARCHITECTURE OF ANCIENT EGYPT | 433 |
| XI. | THE RELIGION OF ANCIENT EGYPT I | 486 |
| XII. | THE HISTORY OF EGYPT I | 609 |
| XIII. | THE RELIGION OF EGYPT II | 640 |
| XIV. | THE HISTORY OF EGYPT II | 643 |
| XV. | CONCLUSIONS and REFERENCES | 742 |

# FREDERICK MONDERSON

## PREFACE
## BY
## DR. FRED MONDERSON

Throughout his lengthy activist life, Dr. Yosef A.A. ben-Jochannan has not simply defended African peoples' moral and spiritual capabilities, their humanistic nature, the indisputable and divinely inspired attributes of the African female, the artistic and cultural creativity that created an unbelievable heritage but he has importantly encouraged intellectual development through vigorous and resolute research and publication. To wit, his mantra has been "Publish or Perish!" Through vigorous research in search of truth, he has sought to develop "intellectual autonomy" as part of problem solving armament to help young people especially to "decode their environment" and meet the social, economic and even civil and human rights challenges they will continue to face as life goes on.

As such, in this treatise **BLACK HISTORY EXTRAVAGANZA: HONORING DR. BEN-JOCHANNAN**, we not simply recognize and praise his work among Africans worldwide but offer scholarship in the areas he for so long highlighted to his students, viz., art, architecture, temple, religion, history, etc., to provide some form of continuity to his work but also to establish a point of departure for research purposes to young minds to seriously engage in the grand strategy of African historiographic reconstruction.

First and foremost, we need be reminded and young scholars need to be informed when it comes to foundations upon which African civilizations bequeathed knowledge, viz., science, philosophy, religious belief and practice and the imponderables of law, government, medicine, etc., we must remember, the Nile Valley through Ethiopia, Nubia and Egypt schooled the world. In examining this reality, the evidence is clear:

# BLACK HISTORY EXTRAVAGANZA
# HONORING DR. BEN-JOCHANNAN

**Black History Extravaganza - Photo -** Osiris enthroned and holding Whip and Scepter.

# FREDERICK MONDERSON

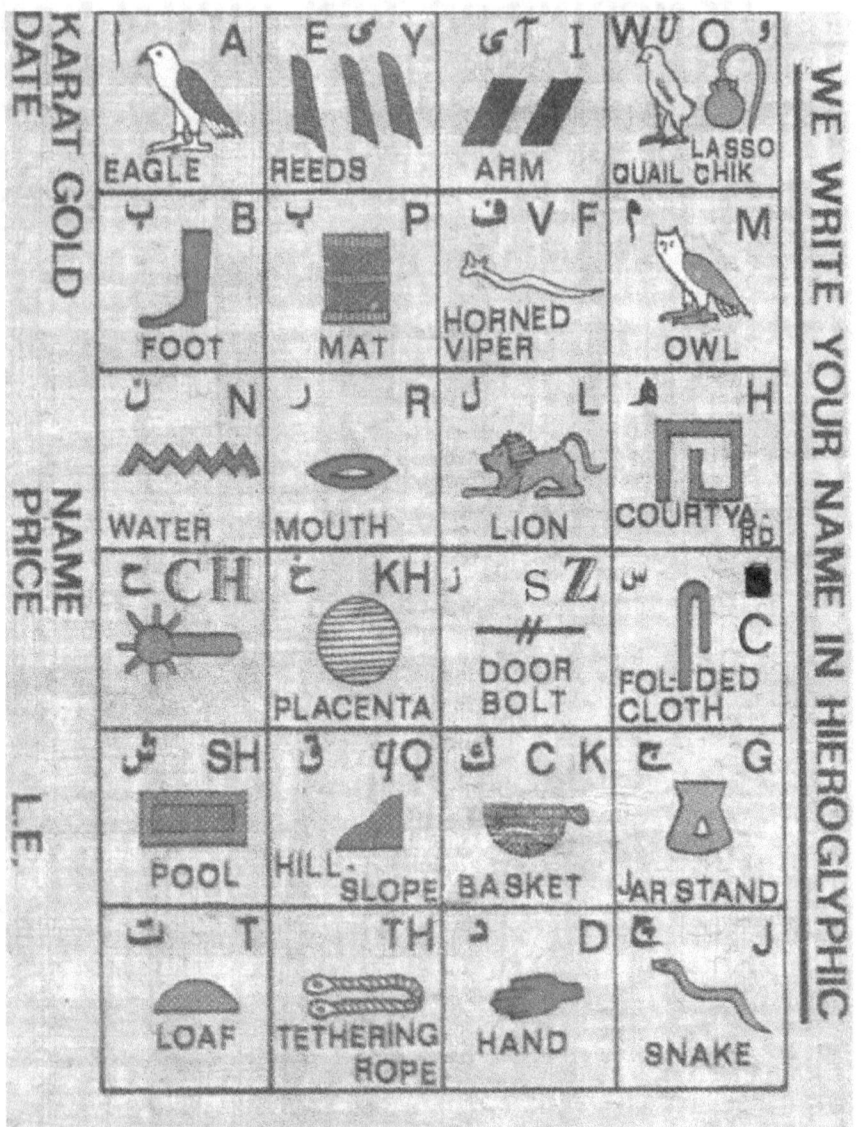

**Black History Extravaganza - Photo -** The Egyptian Alphabet which allows anyone to write their name in Hieroglyphs.

1.   Dr. Cheikh Anta Diop has boldly asserted and eruditely demonstrated, **Ancient Egypt was a Black Civilization** and any whites who came there were latecomers.

# BLACK HISTORY EXTRAVAGANZA HONORING DR. BEN-JOCHANNAN

2.　　Dr. John Henrik Clarke has forever insisted, "African people must write African history" with a view to correcting distortions and falsity, given, "The people who preached racism colonized history" and "When Europe colonized the world, she colonized the world's knowledge," particularly because "Europe's claim to ancient Egypt is not based on logic."

3.　　Dr. Leonard James advised his students, "Search for and root out distortion then include omissions systematically implanted" by racist European and American historiography, and especially because, "The existential data contradicts the symbolic representation."

4.　　Dr. Yosef Ben-Jochannan, beyond his credible admonitions advised, "When doing research on Ancient Egypt, get the oldest material you can find and work from there." This is particularly so important since, "Not only has the West hijacked Egypt," these days practically every modern book on Egypt written in the West essentially begins with a chapter on this ancient civilization instead of previously on Greece and Rome. In this strategically ingrained yet false strategy, much of Africa is falsely impregnated with Caucasian types, and the Africans have totally disappeared. So much so, as Dr. Diop has argued, perhaps mocking Herman Junker's "First Appearance of the Negro in the Nile Valley (*Journal of Egyptian Archaeology* 1921) he stated: "In Junker's and similarly others," in creating "the true Negro, has made all the other Negroes of the world fake Negroes."

More important, in their attempt to "hide the ancient Egyptians" in "plain sight," practically every image, both male and female; wherever noticed as still surviving, whether in temple, tomb, or civic structure, the facial features have been defaced. However, while this feature is a marked reality in practically every museum in Europe and America, it is not so generally in Egyptian museums. After all, to support "Doctoring in European museum basements," the argument is made, falsely, that it is; "because the Mummy's brains were generally extracted through the nostrils, then the statues' noses had to be broken." How sad:

# FREDERICK MONDERSON

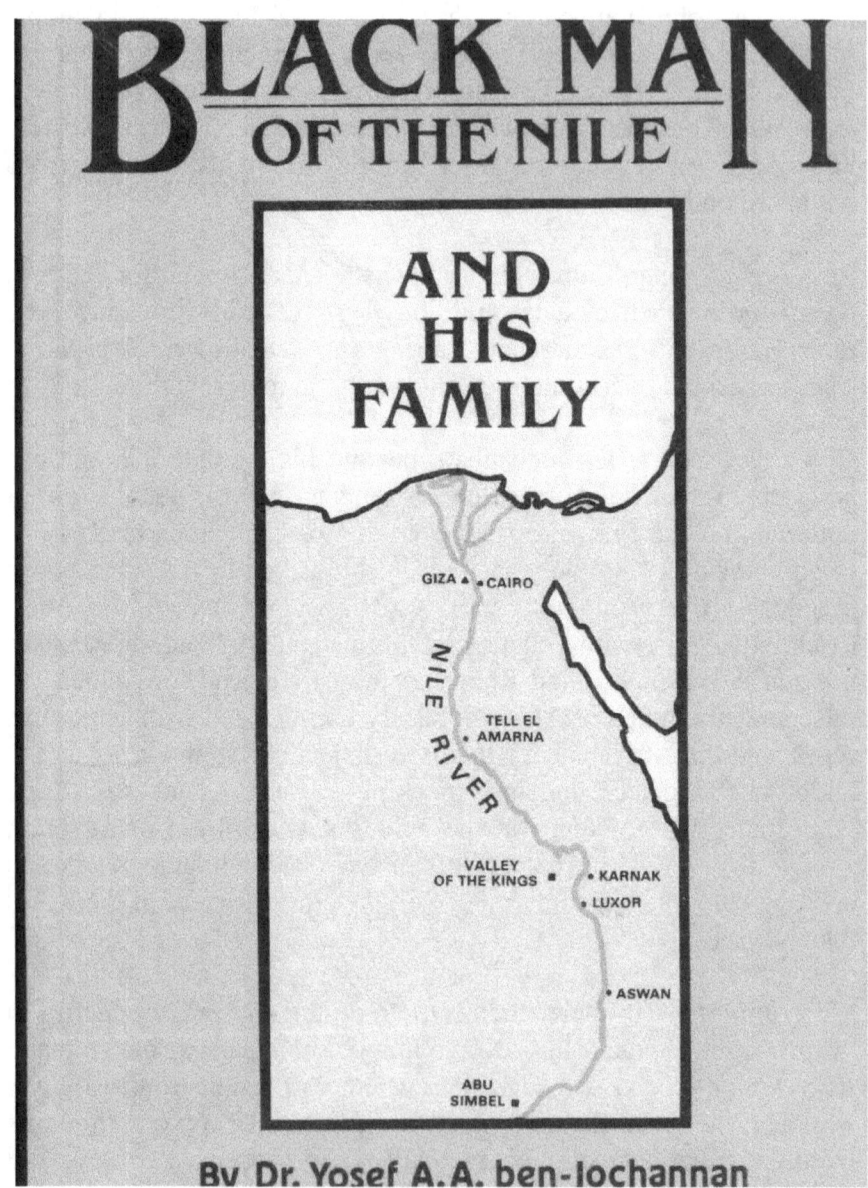

Black History Extravaganza - Dr. Ben's Book - **Black Man of the Nile and His Family.**

# BLACK HISTORY EXTRAVAGANZA
# HONORING DR. BEN-JOCHANNAN

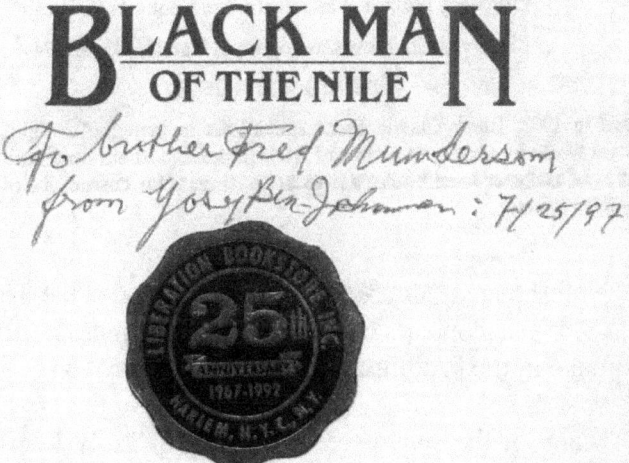

**Black History Extravaganza -** Dr. Ben's Book **- Black Man of the Nile -** Autographed to Brother Fred Monderson 7-25-1997.

# FREDERICK MONDERSON

**Black History Extravaganza - Photo -** Khepre wearing Menat.

1.  Neferhotep's "double statue" found under the Third Pylon at Karnak Temple, deposited there in ancient times, is displayed in a photo image in the Wadjit; and its nose is not broken.

2.  Many of the statues recovered 1904-05 by Legrain from the "Cachette Court" at Karnak deposited in Roman times and many now on display at the Antiquities Museum in Cairo, these noses are not so disfigured. Several in Luxor Museum are of the same disposition.

3.  The image of "Alexander the Great, described as "so Greek," on the outer western face of the sanctuary wall at Luxor Temple which he rebuilt is not disfigured, though Min's "creative organ" nearby is blackened from being "touched."

4.  At Kom Ombo, the Graeco-Roman temple, on a back wall in the blazing sun and in full public glare, the images of the female figures there not so defaced.

# BLACK HISTORY EXTRAVAGANZA
# HONORING DR. BEN-JOCHANNAN

5. At Philae Temple of Isis, just to the right on entering the Dromos, on a south wall of the Temple of Harendotus, the first encountered of three temples fronted by the Eastern Colonnade, again in public glare, these images of Greco-Roman female features are beautiful but not defaced or disfigured in any way.

6. Whether it is Seti I's surviving statue at the Temple of Sesebi dedicated to the Theban Triad of Amon, Mut and Khonsu, that Rameses II helped construct placing a statue of himself there, the one at Gerf Hussein "carved in the rather heavy, powerful style sometimes employed in Nubian Art;" or, the two displayed from the Temple of "Amon who hears petitions" at East Karnak, also known as "the place where Rameses hears petitions," these latter two statues as depicted in Emily Teeter's *Religion and Ritual in Ancient Egypt* (Cambridge University Press, 2011: 81) are so crafted "in the Negro mold" and unlike the plastic image displayed in a Berlin of the supposed "classic Rameses II statue" underscore the problem. Strange that these two and the one at Sesebi have, so far, escaped the destructive hand of modern purveyors of distortion and destruction. Perhaps the reason is only the hardy tourist dares to venture this far into Karnak and the out of the way Sesebi Temple.

More important, however, in further examining distortion of this subject matter and culture, Teeter's statement context (2011: 4) while in general an examination of the Egyptian mind, more specifically it goes the notion of misrepresentation. In this, she states: "To the Egyptians, a representation of an object was a counter-image - an actual substitute for the object portrayed. The statue of an individual, for example, had the potential to be imbued with the spirit of that person and to serve as his or her eternal double and surrogate. Statues were an essential part of mortuary cults because Egyptians believed that a person could not exist in the afterlife unless his image - in the form of a statue - was preserved among the living. The sculptures that now fill museum galleries, most of them carefully incised with the name of the deceased, were those eternal images that perpetuated the memory of the dead. This was a practical and stunningly simple solution to immortality - as long as the individual was remembered on earth, that person had not died." How then could the person agree to have his or her statue disfigured when he wanted to have all parts of his body and personality united for effective use in the Afterlife?

**Black History Extravaganza - Photo -** The disappearing "Eyes of Horus" are very evident here.

**Black History Extravaganza - Photo -** Sailing boat with cabin, individuals and a priest in leopard skin.

# BLACK HISTORY EXTRAVAGANZA
# HONORING DR. BEN-JOCHANNAN

**Black History Extravaganza - Photo -** Remains of two of four colossal statues at the entrance of Rameses II's Abu Simbel Temple, in Nubia. The head of this one on the right lies on the ground below.

**Black History Extravaganza - Photo -** Remains of the other two colossal statues at the entrance of Rameses II's Abu Simbel Temple, in Nubia.

# FREDERICK MONDERSON

## I  INTRODUCTION
### By
### Dr. Fred Monderson

Egyptian art and architecture have been, perhaps, the most fascinating invention emanating from the mind and creative efforts of the African man. Whether religious, mortuary, domestic, civic or military forms, Egyptian architecture as a Nile Valley creation has endured, set standards and been most innovative in its cultural and intellectual growth enabling and benefitting mankind's pageantry of progress. However, while its various modes have been tremendously beneficial to the outward posture of human endeavor, religious architecture has penetrated the inner man, influencing and directing his soul and psychic being. Even more, because of man's inherent desire to interact with cosmic and divine forces, whether in praise or mortuary architecture, no other field has so influenced the alpha and omega experience of the emergent human spirit. Thus, from his earliest intellectual and religious consciousness, Churchward says some 300,000 years, man has enjoyed "sweet communion with deity" and this interaction has been so significant in humanity's psychological and spiritual pageantry it has laid the basis for and innovated particularly in creative art and architecture and in many an associated field benefiting the march of development along the historical continuum of mankind's journey. This experience, therefore, made the Nile Valley African the first universal physical, cultural, religious and spiritual personality. Therefore, and significantly, we can thank Dr. Yosef A.A. Ben-Jochannan for un-muddling this reality and placing the African in his proper perspective as central to this undertaking. So much so, African descendants now have a better and fuller grasp of this phenomenal fact and better understanding the existential data contradicts especially the currently projected symbolic representation.

# BLACK HISTORY EXTRAVAGANZA HONORING DR. BEN-JOCHANNAN

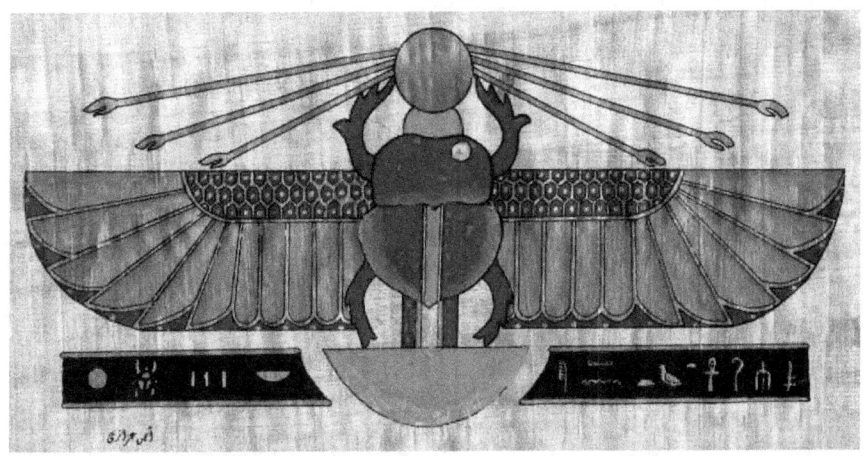

**Black History Extravaganza - Papyrus -** A winged-Khepre (Scarabaeus) standing on Heb greets the Sun-disk whose hands reach outward.

In his many years of writing, teaching and carrying people to Egypt. Dr. Ben-Jochannan has always insisted his students pay attention to architectural features, especially in temples and the Hypostyle Hall in Karnak temple particularly has been significant not simply for its role in processional ritual but as stepping stone into understanding the divine space entrancing the "Holy of Holies." We have come to realize, in emergence of man's religious consciousness along the Valley of the Nile, religious architecture was born to shelter and protect the divine essence that contacted and contracted with the ancient African being. In actuality, divinity insisted, you protect and worship me and I will benefit your spirit and creativity to bring you joy, happiness and industry beyond your greatest expectations. According to the New Kingdom *Instructions of Ani*, it's been said of the god, "Song, dance and incense are his foods. Receiving protestations are his wealth." As such, then, temple or religious architecture was born to house the deity who could be invoked to manifest his presence among humanity. In that manifestation, many points of divine contact were established of which the temple became the principal loci or place of interaction. As established belief holds, the first architects were priests who were instructed to build the temple

# FREDERICK MONDERSON

as a place to shelter the divine force where his adherents could worship and ritualize such essence.

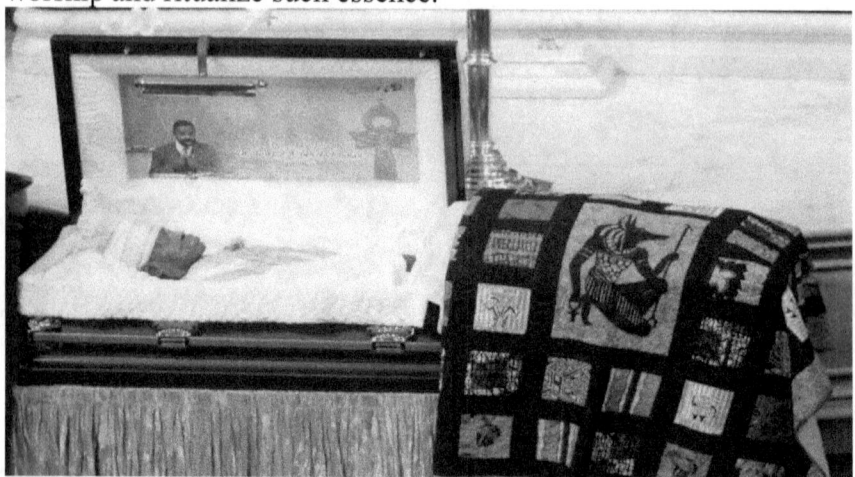

**Black History Extravaganza - Photo -** In historic and magisterial fashion, Dr. Ben-Jochannan **Lies in State** in Abyssinia Baptist Church in Harlem, as he is about to make his transition as a revered ancestor. Anubis is prominent on his funerary quilt.

**Black History Extravaganza - Photo -** Professor James Small, **Master of Ceremony** and in full Sem-priest regalia wearing the lion-skin cloak of a Sem-Priest prepares to administer the "Opening of the Mouth Ceremony" intended to restore the voice, limbs and legs of Dr. Yosef Ben-Jochannan for his eternal existence as a revered ancestor.

# BLACK HISTORY EXTRAVAGANZA HONORING DR. BEN-JOCHANNAN

Because of the structure of the monarchial society with a king, a "Servant of the God" or priests and other citizenry, the first two enjoyed an access to divinity not shared by the last. Therefore, as the Egyptian belief system has shown, the gods first ruled Egypt, the Demi-gods, manes and then the king, later pharaoh, was a direct descendant and heir to the throne they vacated. This meant the king, regarded as the "Son of God," was himself a god on earth and can and did have access to his father and brother gods upon whose strength and powers he could draw. However, while his holy person enjoyed a divine aura and spiritual potency, wherever he was could be considered holy; yet it was only in the temple he could invoke and worship his god in which a ritual was created for this purpose.

Just as today we call God by a multitude of names, so too disparate groups of these early Africans worshipped their own separate god but based on the same principle recognizing a universal and beneficent father god. In time, the god's earthly representatives, called theologians, sorted the disparities and fused the various strands of divine worship into a syncretism establishing a harmony throughout a hierarchical structure that enabled all to be part of the conjoined whole enabling them to enjoy the blessing of the divine beneficence.

**Black History Extravaganza - Photo -** Abu Simbel Temple of Rameses II. Legs of two seated colossal with figures of female relatives of the king and other images of this magnificent work of art.

# FREDERICK MONDERSON

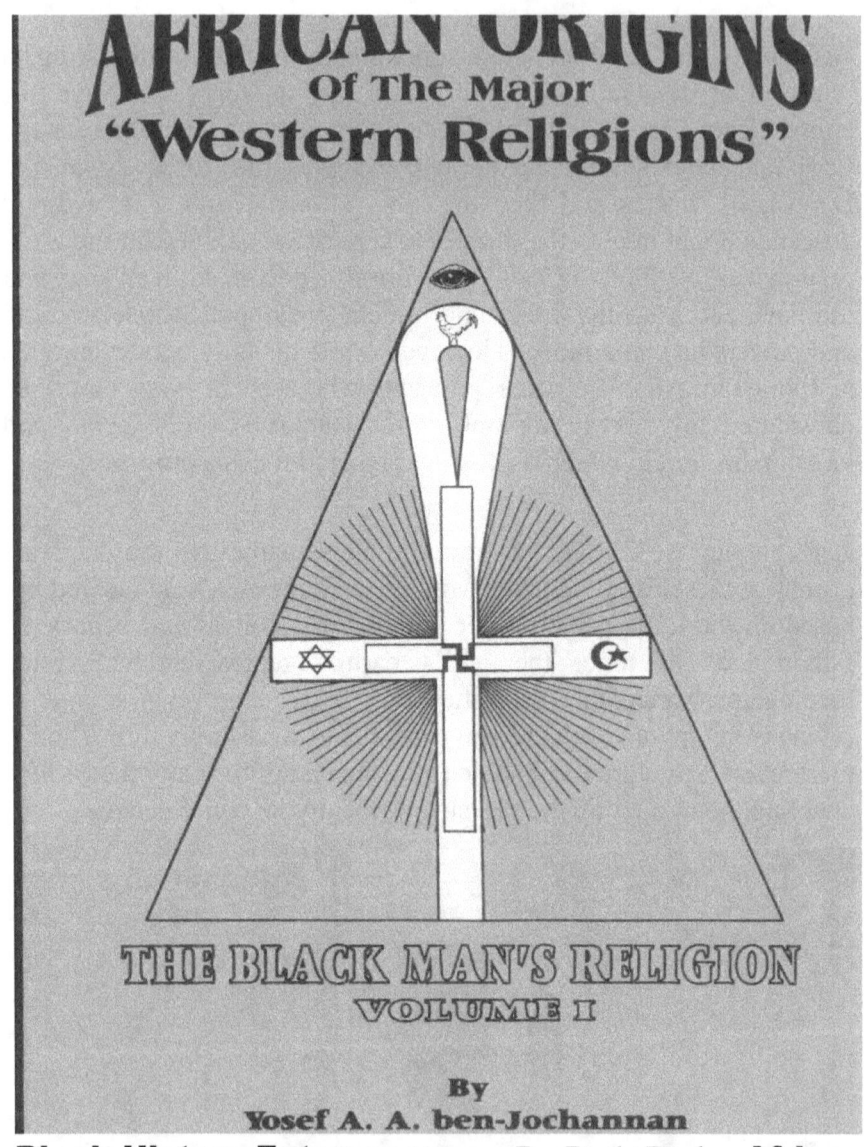

**Black History Extravaganza -** Dr. Ben's Book **- African Origins of the Major "Western Religions" - The Black Man's Religion - Volume I.**

# BLACK HISTORY EXTRAVAGANZA
# HONORING DR. BEN-JOCHANNAN

Yosef ben-Jochannan is a master teacher with a forceful command of ancient and contemporary history. He uses wit, humor, and common sense to accent history and expose historical distortions. Currently retired, but still active, Dr. Ben has taught on the faculty of colleges and universities in the United States and abroad. He is a former Senior Lecturer, Faculty of Languages, Al Azhar University (Arab Republic of Egypt), and for many years served as Adjunct Professor of History and Egyptology at Cornell University's Africana Studies and Research Center.

Photo credit: Baba El Zulu / Ujamaa School

## *African Origins Of The Major "Western Religions"*

For more than five decades Yosef ben-Jochannan—researcher, author, lecturer—has led what has now become a mass effort to emphasize African contributions to the world. *African Origins Of The Major "Western Religions,"* first published in 1970, continues to be one of Dr. Ben's most thought-provoking works. This critical examination of the history, beliefs and myths, which are the foundation of Judaism, Christianity, and Islam, remains instructive and fresh. By highlighting the African influences and roots of these religions, Dr. Ben reveals an untold history that many would prefer to forget.

The Black Classic Press edition of *African Origins Of The Major "Western Religions"* is a facsimile edition, with an added index and extended bibliography.

BLACK CLASSIC PRESS
www.blackclassicbooks.com

ISBN-13 978-0-933121-29-4
ISBN-10 0-933121-29-6  $24.95

**Black History Extravaganza** - Dr. Ben's Book - **African Origins of the Major "Western Religions" - The Black Man's Religion Volume I (Back Cover).**

# FREDERICK MONDERSON

Sacred Egyptian texts representing the codification of oral beliefs reaching back into the remotest millennia indicated there was a time when nothing existed in this universe. Conversely, Theophile Obenga in *African Philosophy: The Pharaonic Period* - 2780-330 B.C., argue, the Egyptian believed a prior universe existed before this current universe. Yet, from this nothingness the divine essence emerged from watery matter and became manifest, first creating everything including man and giving specific instructions on how things were to be, particularly as it related to shelter for his divine essence. In *The World of the Pharaohs: A Complete Guide to Ancient Egypt*, Christine Hobson (1987: 128) explained what she calls "The First Occasion." As stated, she wrote: "There was once a time, Egyptian legend said, when the earth was filled with a watery emptiness, without shape. From these waters, called Nun, there emerged a mound of land, and upon this mound, all that exists came into being. According to which group of priests told the story, either a plant emerged that served as a perch for the first life, the falcon Horus; or a lotus plant grew and blossomed, from which the sun emerged. The outpouring of energy that created mankind on this, called the 'First Occasion,' was revered by the Egyptian as the tangible manifestation of divine power. The first temple came into existence on this mound in the form of an outer enclosure wall, designed to separate the god and its power from everything outside. Inside, a reed mat shelter was placed over the very source of creation - the perch or plant - to protect it and mark it as being sacred." As such, "every Egyptian temple" was "built as a copy of the first temple" encouraging the god to return to earth lured by the familiarity of the structure.

Theophile Obenga, on the other hand, referring to the Coffin Text, an offshoot of the Pyramid Texts, in *African Philosophy: The Pharaonic Period*: 2780-330 B.C. mentions four major acts of "Ra the creator, who emerged from Nwn in the primal period of creation." In regards to Ra:

"First, he created the air, giving all living beings breath throughout their time on earth. The gaseous envelope covering he earth, the atmosphere., is simply the air we breathe wherever we are in the world, the four winds, namely south, north, east and west. Ancient

# BLACK HISTORY EXTRAVAGANZA HONORING DR. BEN-JOCHANNAN

Egyptian tradition promised the blessed dead 'the gentle breath of the north wind.'"

**Black History Extravaganza - Photo -** Empty Ceramic cartouche (above) and below male figures in various attitudes of work experience with the Supervisor shown in larger scale.

# FREDERICK MONDERSON

"Ra's second act was to create the waters: The Nile with its freight of loam, the lakes of the countryside, the sea, all the bodies of beneficial water. The spectacular rise of the Nile (the great flood) in the month of July was a cosmic event, essential for the life of the country, a blessing to the administrator as much as to the humble peasant."

"Ra's third accomplishment was the institution of equality and fraternity between humans (each man his brother0. Evil (*isfit*) in the world is imputed to humans themselves, as free beings. There is a transcendent order, but humans, thus individualized, can obey or disobey it. Here the heart, *ib*, symbolizes the seat of liberty, the locus of the guiding principle of our behavior. To this faculty, the Greek Stoic philosophers gave the name hegemonicon. At one stroke, 'God' is rendered innocent of human evil. The heart, as the inner core of the human subject, expresses the ontological and the logical nature of being. This makes striving to do his or her work without necessarily taking orders from an external power. We are bonded to our ancestors in solidarity: we are part of our society; still, we are individually responsible for what we do. Here we see the ancient Egyptians, two thousand years before this era began, clearly asserting human equality and fraternity, moral freedom, human will, and the accountability for our actions as individuals."

"Ra's fourth accomplishment involved the use of liquid essences. Using water, sperm, sweat, saliva and tears, the demiurge created all the various forms of nature: humans, animals, everything that lives."

In a desert state, water and its uses are extremely important as shown in its uses as follows, in:

1. The Pool of Life;

2. The Pool of Earu;

3. The Waters of Kher-Eha;

# BLACK HISTORY EXTRAVAGANZA
# HONORING DR. BEN-JOCHANNAN

4. The Cool Pool or Stream of Nun is where Piankhi the Ethiopian washed his face on way to Heliopolis where he was to be recognized as the Son of the Sun-god.

5. The Water of Life and Good Fortune is what washed the living Pharaoh;

6. Upon birth, the infant who will become Pharaoh was washed by the "Sun-God;"

7. As actual pharaoh, he was washed at the Ceremony of Coronation;

8. Pharaoh was washed or purified when he entered the temple to perform the ritual. This was also called the Baptism;

9. The dead pharaoh was washed by Atum in Heliopolis as the Book of Breathings indicates as he hurried to the place where the gods are born.

10. The dead pharaoh was washed upon his arrival in the heavenly abode, so that his presence would be as a pure one.

**Black History Extravaganza - Photo -** The Nubian village of **Daboud** between Aswan and Luxor, Dr. Ben-Jochannan's most favorite place in all of Upper Egypt.

# FREDERICK MONDERSON

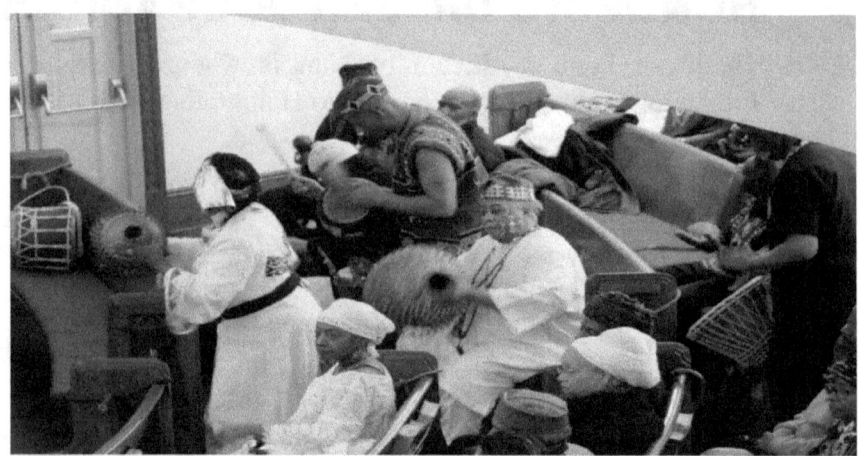

**Black History Extravaganza - Photo -** At the funeral for Dr. Ben-Jochannan, I observed this musician in white with green hat and thought, "If Dr. Ben finally made it to heaven, the energy and dedication this individual demonstrated with his musical instrument, this may have been the man responsible for the successful transition."

**Black History Extravaganza - Photo -** Dates on a tree before the Temple of Seti I at Kurneh on the West Bank at Luxor or Thebes.

# BLACK HISTORY EXTRAVAGANZA
# HONORING DR. BEN-JOCHANNAN

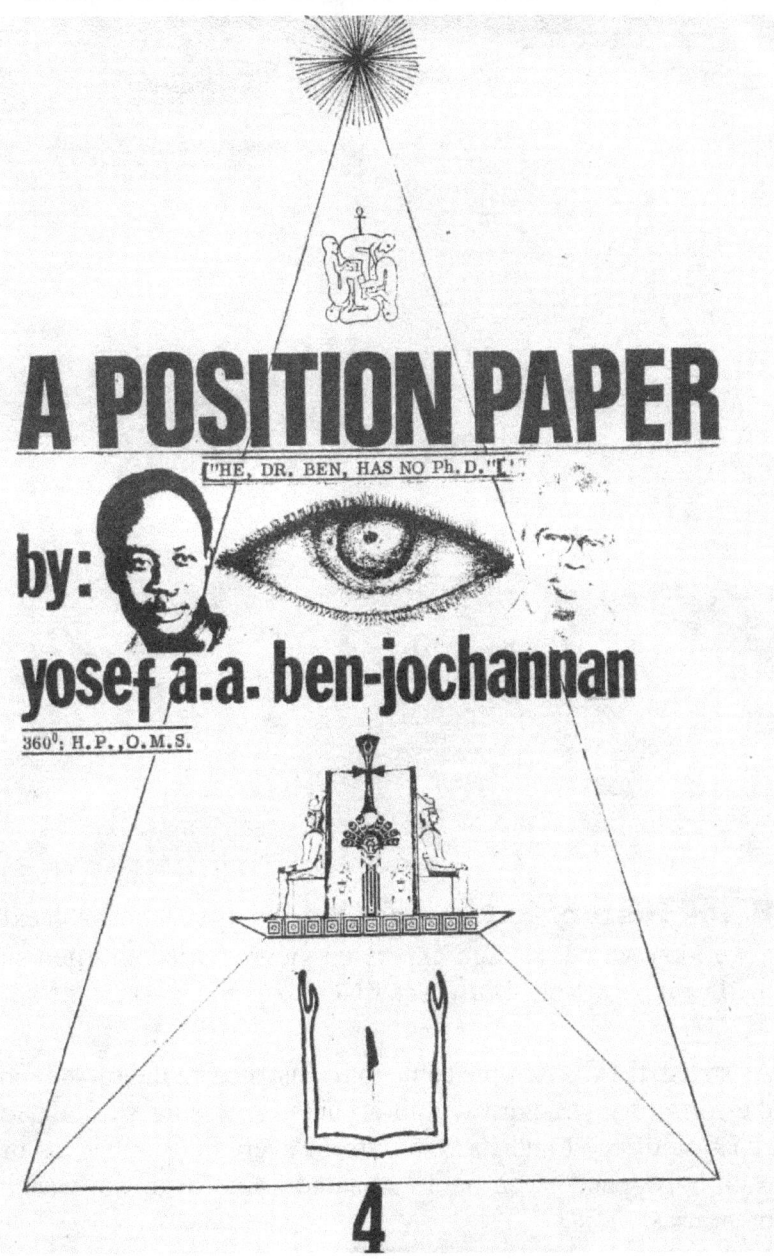

**Black History Extravaganza** - Dr. Ben's Book - **A Position Paper.**

# FREDERICK MONDERSON

This Position Paper is dedicated to those who respect the natural intelligence of our African life-source with, or without, title. And to my Father and Mother for making me realize that my "education" began in HEAVEN - My Mother's Sacred and Most Holy Womb.

by:

Yosef A. A. ben-Jochannan, 360° H. P.
Adjunct Associate Professor of History, Malcolm-King College, Harlem, New York City, N.Y.

Published by Yosef A.A. ben-Jochannan
209 West 125th Street, Suite 213A-213B, New York City, New York 10027

Former Adjunct Professor of History and Egyptology, Africana Studies and Research Center, Cornell University, Ithaca, N.Y.

[From: "Sports Today", Ching Chow ®]

Copyright © 1985 C.C./A.D., New York, N.Y. by Yosef A.A. ben-Jochannan. All rights reserved. No part of this monogram may be reproduced in any form whatsoever without the expressly written consent of the author or his representatives. Front Cover design included in this Copyright: God Amen-Ra emerging from the House Of Fire as His Son of the Sun's Eye Of Horus survey they Defensive Art of the Throne and Pharaohs' Ka and Feather of Truth, etc., etc., etc., eternally.

**Black History Extravaganza** - Dr. Ben-Jochannan expresses a well-known but seldom expressed view of wisdom often stated in the Local New York *Daily News* Newspaper.

As stated, the first temple came into existence on the sacred mound in the form of a structure within an outer enclosure wall, designed to separate the god and its power from everything outside. Similarly, each holy space had a pool or Sacred Lake for use in washing and other uses.

From this early time the god's shelter, made of the flimsiest material, served to invoke the divine presence and as time passed more durable material was used to build the temple. Contrary to muddle as to who

# BLACK HISTORY EXTRAVAGANZA
# HONORING DR. BEN-JOCHANNAN

were the ancient Egyptians the earliest surviving examples of Egyptian temples date to one for the god Min at Koptos in Upper Egypt. Another on the Island of Elephantine, Aswan, stood at Egypt's southern border. God Min, a Black god, and the island of Elephantine were more closely linked to inner Africa. However, two interesting points are raised in the above scenarios. Addressing this controversy presented here has been the life's work of Dr. Ben-Jochannan.

The Englishman Flinders Petrie, the "father of modern archaeology" found large intact pre-dynastic statues of God Min painted black at his temple in the city of Koptos. These are now safely preserved in the confines of the Ashmolean Museum, Oxford University town. In the rush to falsely claim foreign origin of the ancient Egyptians scholars first discounted the statues' age assigning them to the Fourth Dynasty of the Old Kingdom. Next the god's statues were said to be of Mesopotamian origin from whence the Caucasian originators of Egyptian civilization supposedly began. Yet, the first contradiction seems these Caucasians were painting their important god statues black! Now, as with the 11$^{th}$ Dynasty king Mentuhotep II whose statue was found in his temple at Deir el Bahari and the 18$^{th}$ Dynasty statues of King Tutankhamon they were both said to only be painted black for the funeral service. Thus, Min's statue as god was not dead and being the first represented the prototype for "painted statues." Therefore, the false argument of being "painted for the funerary ceremony" cannot stand logical scrutiny. In *The Royal Mummies* (1905) G. Elliot Smith who examined the mummies indicated they were often covered with a black, bitumen substance as a preservative overcoat but the mummy's color ranging from brown to black, never white, could be observed underneath. Now, Min was a living god and no need to have camouflaged his color. In addition, one of Mentuhotep's Queens Kemsit was painted black in her tomb yet she was called a Negress but her husband who, painted black was said to be so for the funeral service! Again, while the two guardian statues of Tutankhamon, in the Cairo Museum are also painted black, yet wearing royal regalia, on a wall in the Hall of Tutankhamon the king is also shown as a bronze sphinx trampling other Africans painted black yet called Negro! Still, the king is said to be neither Negro nor black! As Prof. John H. Clarke

# FREDERICK MONDERSON

said "Europeans claim the heritage of ancient Egypt but use no logic!" As such, we recognize Dr. Leonard James' teachings that "The existential data contradicts the symbolic representation."

**Black history Extravaganza - Photo -** Dr. Leonard Jeffries seems to be saying something very powerfully profound to his friend and colleague as he bids him farewell and good-bye for the journey to prepare a place for us, "Who are yet to die!"

**Black History Extravaganza - Tomb of Nakht -** Workers busy at work. Notice their knives

# BLACK HISTORY EXTRAVAGANZA
## HONORING DR. BEN-JOCHANNAN

**Black History Extravaganza** - Dr. Ben's Book - **A Chronology of the Bible.**

# FREDERICK MONDERSON

# A Chronology of the Bible

Yosef ben-Jochannan (affectionately known as Dr. Ben) is a master teacher with a forceful command of ancient and contemporary history. He uses wit, humor, and common sense to accent history and expose historical distortions. Dr. Ben has taught on the faculty of colleges and universities in the United States and abroad. His most recent assignment was as Senior Lecturer, Faculty of Languages, Al Azhar University (Arab Republic of Egypt). Prior to that, he served as Adjunct Professor of History and Egyptology at Cornell University's Africana Studies & Research Center.

Among the many books written by Dr. Ben, *A Chronology of the Bible* (first published in 1972) is perhaps his most popular work. Originally prepared at the request of a group of Harlem-based ministers, *Chronology* documents the African origins of Judaism, Christianity, and Islam. Dr. Ben traces significant influences, developments, and people that have shaped and provided the foundation for the holy books used in these religions.

We are republishing *A Chronology of the Bible* in response to the constant demand from our readers for this little pamphlet. The BCP edition has been typeset and minimally edited to maintain the integrity and flavor of the original edition. The last entry in the *Chronology* is for 1973. Dr. Ben is presently working on the revised edition that will include versions of the Bible that have been published in subsequent years.

Order from your local bookseller or directly from:

**Black Classic Press**
**P. O. Box 13414**
**Baltimore, MD 21203**
**www.blackclassicbooks.com**

Include $5.00 shipping for the first book and $.50 for each additional title ordered. Credit card orders call: 1-800-476-8870

**Black History Extravaganza** - Dr. Ben's Book - **A Chronology of the Bible (Back Cover).**

# BLACK HISTORY EXTRAVAGANZA HONORING DR. BEN-JOCHANNAN

But there is logic, of a twisted nature. Again, in pinpointing how the existential data contradicts the symbolic representation, I submit the following:

1. A prevailing presentation today is that Mentuhotep II is painted black for the funeral ceremony. W.L. Nash in *Proceedings of the Society of Biblical Archaeology* (1901: 291) stated: "The crown was painted red, the face and body black. The eyeballs white and the tunic white." On the other hand, in *The Art and Architecture of Ancient Egypt* (1959) W. Stephenson Smith simply wrote, Mentuhotep had "Black flesh."

2. We know two wooden statues in royal attire stood before Tutankhamon's burial chamber. These too were said to be "painted for the funeral ceremony." Also, "though the king looks black, he is not Nubian."

**Black History Extravaganza - Photo -** The lower portions of the two-left side seated colossal statues, showing female and other figures at the feet.

# FREDERICK MONDERSON

**Black History Extravaganza - Photo -** The lower portions of the two-right side seated colossal statues, showing female and other figures at the feet.

3.  The notorious A.E.P. Weigall, in *Flights into Antiquity* has a chapter entitled, "Exploits of a Nigger King" where he exhibits a photograph of a white woman and said this was the Queen of Sheba. However, in "A New Egyptian Discovery" in the *Century Magazine* Vol. 78 (1909: 289-97) on p. 295 we read: "In all directions broken figures of the gods were lying, and two defaced wooden statues of the king were all over thrown beside the sarcophagus." Sounds familiar?

4.  G. Elliot Smith, who examined many mummies for the Egyptian government especially *The Royal Mummies* (1912) indicated a "Black resinous material coating was placed over the mummy," but in places one could still see the "Brown skin" that was also attributed to Rameses II and in the 1820 *Gentleman's Magazine* article we note the "brown mummy" as late as "Roman times." Again, the existential data contradicts the symbolic representation.

# BLACK HISTORY EXTRAVAGANZA
# HONORING DR. BEN-JOCHANNAN

**Black History Extravaganza - Photo -** Drumming musicians in the street provide exhilarating and melodic music for the moment and to wish the revered elder the very best as he transitions to meet his great compatriots among the Black Pantheon.

**Black History Extravaganza - Photo -** Representation of four bulls, perhaps as part of a cattle reckoning.

# FREDERICK MONDERSON

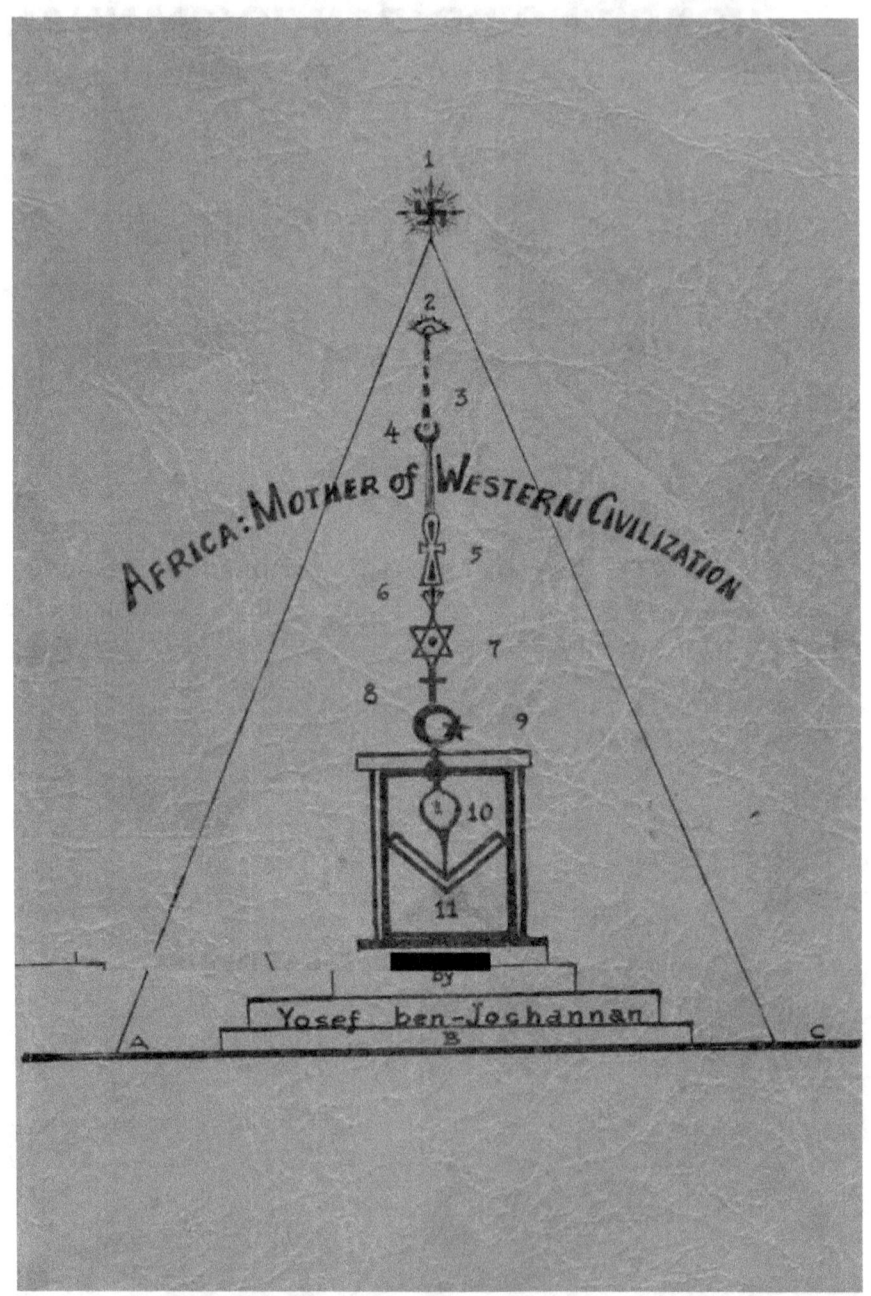

**Black History Extravaganza -** Dr. Ben's Book **- Africa: Mother of Western Civilization.**

# BLACK HISTORY EXTRAVAGANZA
# HONORING DR. BEN-JOCHANNAN

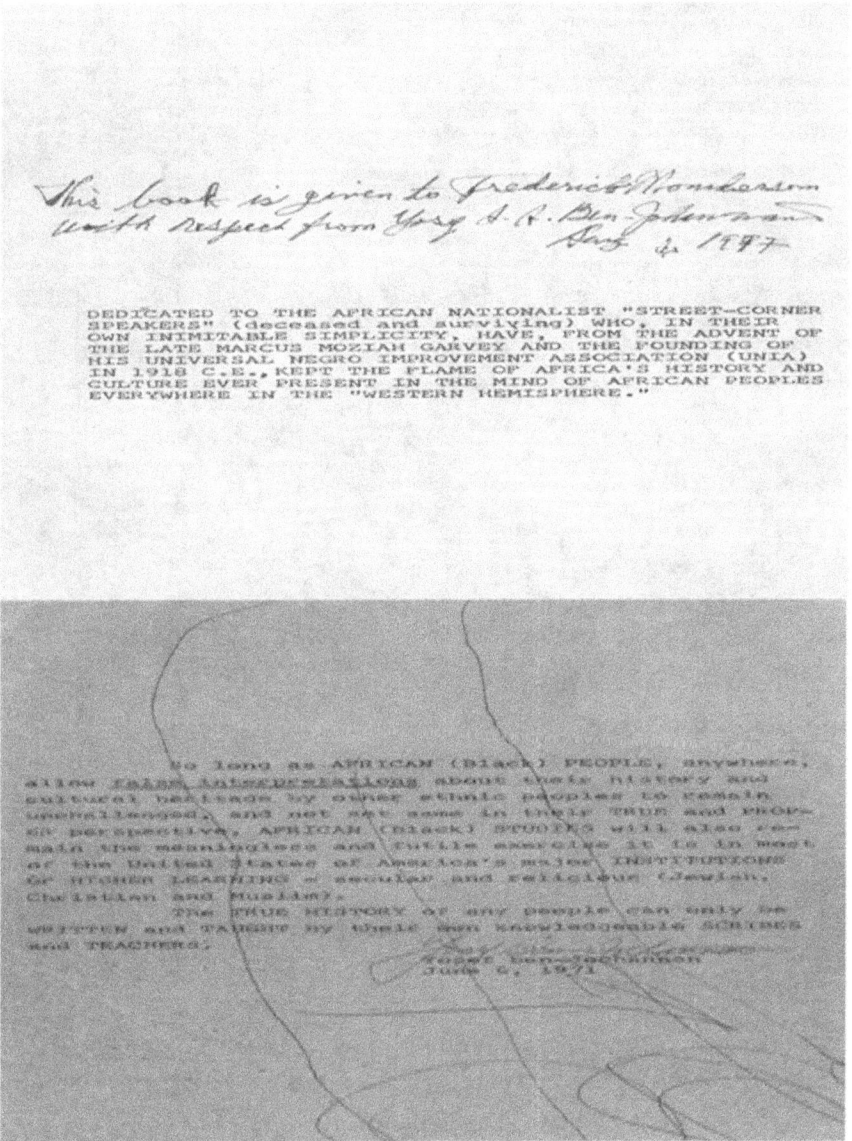

**Black History Extravaganza** - Dr. Ben's Book - **Africa: Mother of Western Civilization** – Overleaf of the Cover page "Dedication" and Back Cover. **Note - Signed** - "This book is given to Frederick Monderson with respect from Yosef A.A. Ben-Jochannan, August 4, 1997."

# FREDERICK MONDERSON

Relief of Horus and Isis ( Kalabsha temple )

**Black History Extravaganza - Photo - Papyrus -** Relief of Horus and Isis enthroned as depicted at Kalabsha Temple.

In a recent book of the last decade entitled **Black Genesis**, two authors Bauval and Brophy discuss a people who occupied the region of Nabta Playa from the earliest times, c. 7500 to about 3500 B.C. They were the "first scientists" who mapped the heavens, created a calendar, were agriculturalists and pastoralists who first began

# BLACK HISTORY EXTRAVAGANZA HONORING DR. BEN-JOCHANNAN

worshipping the "cow goddess." When the region began to lose rainfall and dry-up, those people migrated towards the Nile River settling in the Aswan area between Elephantine Island and Abu Simbel. The authors argue these black people were the predecessors of the ancient Egyptian pharaohs. A similar concept is indicated in Toby Wilkinson's **Genesis of the Pharaohs** (2003) which holds much that we have come to recognize in pharaonic practice was very early evident in the Easter Desert of Upper Egypt and this appeared "at least 1000 years before Winkler's Mesopotamians!"

**Black History Extravaganza - Photo -** Abu Simbel Temple of Rameses II. The key that locks and unlocks the great doors of this magnificent work of architectural wonder built in Nubia.

The current work seeks to high-light some of the subject-matter that engaged the pursuits of the master teacher, Dr. Yosef Antonio Alfredo Ben-Jochannan; who, for many years of his lengthy life insisted we examine his body of work and especially his "Trilogy" **Africa:**

# FREDERICK MONDERSON

**Mother of Western civilization**; **African Origins of the Major Western Religions**; and **Black Man of the Nile,** later, **Black Man of the Nile and His Family.**

**Black History Extravaganza - Photo -** Minister Clemson Brown (above) and Dr. Jack Felder were there, recognizing the wonderful work of the man and to pay respects to Dr. Ben-Jochannan while wishing him the very best for his journey as a revered ancestor.

# BLACK HISTORY EXTRAVAGANZA
# HONORING DR. BEN-JOCHANNAN

**Black History Extravaganza - Photo -** Abu Simbel Temple of Rameses II. Eight colossal Osiride statues and a decorated ceiling greet the visitor at the temple's entranceway.

# FREDERICK MONDERSON

## II. WISDOM OF THE ANCIENT EGYPTIANS

### By
### Dr. Fred Monderson

**The Wisdom of Ancient Egypt** is renown from a wide range of disciplines, expressions and practices. From religious and mortuary practices, the crafting of art and architectural masterpieces, to work executions in songs and other expressions, in guiding official and unofficial conduct through social interaction expressing love, literacy and righteous lifestyles and religious ritual and practices, the depth of the Egyptian mind has been recognized, praised and respected throughout ancient, medieval and modern times. The potent vehicle through which this philosophical, even spiritual and social achievement is sought for, even queried is first explained by Theophile Obenga in *African Philosophy: The Pharaonic Period*: 2780-330 B.C. wherein the author recognizes: "The aphorisms and moral precepts variously known as wisdom literature, instructions, maxims, teachings, etc., belong to a literary genre cultivated in ancient Egypt from the Old Kingdom (2780-2360 B.C.) to the Late period (1085-333 B.C.)." Thus, he writes (2004: 187) regarding Egyptian "Wisdom Literature" which "comprised a series of moral treatises proffering declarations on ethics, psychology, politics and social issues. Generally, wisdom literature contained the moral code of Egyptian antiquity. Some of these moral treatises had an impact on Jewish consciousness at the time of the Old Testament. The number of studies devoted to Egyptian wisdom is considerable." As such and in that age of the birth of intellectual, religious and social creativity, "In Athens, psychological analysis was born in the 5$^{th}$ Century B.C., in Egypt, it was born in the 27$^{th}$ Century B.C." Thus, along the way, in that cauldron and crucible of creative literary compositions, in essence, and principally The **Instructions of Amenemope** is considered to be "the direct source of an entire passage of the **Biblical Proverbs**." However, "what we have here," writes Obenga, "are excerpts from the **Maxims of Ptah-Hotep**. The author was the equivalent of a Prime Minister under the last but one

# BLACK HISTORY EXTRAVAGANZA HONORING DR. BEN-JOCHANNAN

king of the Fifth Dynasty, Isesi, about 2450 B.C." He then (2004: 188) explains the make-up of such a thought package described as a maxim: "An Egyptian maxim, in effect, is a veritable ritual performance. It should be so sequenced, intellectually, as to lead necessarily to knowledge, culture, moral rectitude, good conduct, and the setting of a good example. In sum, its aim is moral, ethical, methodical and artistic." This the African mind bequeathed the world, without doubt.

**Black History Extravaganza - Photo -** Seriousness and somber is the order of the day for this sister who came out to pay her respects while others line-up to enter Abyssinian Baptist Church.

**Black History extravaganza - Photo - A the Cemetery -** "We came to say a fad farewell and wish our Brother the very best.

# FREDERICK MONDERSON

**Black History Extravaganza - Photo -** Mr. Michael Hooper of **Roots Revisited** and Mr. Haskins were there to pay their respects to the indomitable Dr. Yosef Ben-Jochannan, the Harlem Icon, historian, Egyptologist, teacher and African-nationalist.


As we begin to explore these early thought processes that molded codes of conduct in man's earliest examples of consciousness we first encounter the sequenced religious doctrines, **Pyramid Texts** (Old Kingdom), **Coffin Texts** (Middle Kingdom), and later **Book of the Dead** (New Kingdom), well-known guides to expressions of wisdom, but there was much more in this genre whether relating to worship, prayer, praise and sacrifice; not to discount endeavors in the realm of science and even mathematics, art and architectural attainment as the brilliance of the African mind began to evolve. Such early and fruitful modes of thinking is testament and legendary Egyptian, African. In this regard, this and additional accomplishments in medicine and science, are demonstratively attested in libraries, educational institutions and in museums and private collections at home and abroad that still continue to enlighten and mold human behavior and thinking. Just as important and most

# BLACK HISTORY EXTRAVAGANZA HONORING DR. BEN-JOCHANNAN

profound is the sustainability of that African society's philosophical and moral precepts and the manner in which that wisdom has influenced other cultures of the ancient world, be they Mesopotamian, the Hebrews prophets, Greek and Roman thinkers as well as migrating westward to others in their religious and social ideas.

**Black History Extravaganza - Photo -** Dr. Yosef Alfredo Antonio Ben-Jochannan, packaged and ready to roll as a revered ancestor who gave much and "Brought the light of intellectual activism" and who "Took Egypt to show the way!"

**Black History Extravaganza - Photo -** Greeting Dr. Ben's Son on his loss of a father and a Champion for African people.

# FREDERICK MONDERSON

**Black History Extravaganza - Dr. Yosef A.A. Ben-Jochannan -** About to make the final transition from the profane to the sacred world of Ancestors who earned the right to be counted in the revered Black pantheon.

And so, we send him on to join that revered company of great Africans who have not simply fought the good fight, "never took the pieces of silver," but dedicated their lives to the education, edification and upliftment of African people, at home and abroad.

That renown of those Africans of the Nile River culture complex in their moral, religious and spiritual manifestations has been shown by Theophile Obenga in *African Philosophy*: *The Pharaonic Period*: 2780-330 B.C. as finding commonality throughout Africa which is what Dr. Obenga's Associate, Dr. Cheikh Anta Diop so eloquently expressed in "*The Cultural Unity of Black Africa*" by the book of the same name and which he so eruditely elaborated in *The African Origin of Civilization*: *Myth or Reality* and more purposefully profound in *Civilization or Barbarism*: *An Authentic Anthropology*. In this, that creative forcefulness of thought is grounded in the philosophic influence of Ma'at that permeated all aspects of the society. Very often this wisdom counsel was delivered in the maxim calculus that emphasized beyond the demands for righteousness, viz., truth and justice, balance in one's life; that is, the requirement and utility of reason and insistence on reflection. To wit, and expressing such clarity, Obenga (2004: 189) explains: "The maxims also advocate simplicity and humility ... do not be arrogant, do not be conceited ... about what you know ... consult ... with the illiterate man ... as with the cultivated man... no one can attain the limits of knowledge. In other words, one is never sufficiently qualified in any department of science or art. The high spiritual value of these maxims lies in their advocacy of general culture as a requisite for the happy life. In this respect, Plato was wise to propose the Egyptian educational system as a model for his young compatriots."

Much more significant, Obenga recognizes the importance and utility of Ma'at as a mechanism molding social behavior and thought. He writes: "The highest value, in these maxims, is placed on a constant quest for truth and justice. Great is justice. This is an axiom in constant use from the time of Osiris, that is to say, from the beginning of time.... Ma'at is a concept of central importance. It implies order, universal balance, cosmic regulation, justice, truth, truth-in-justice, rectitude and moral uprightness. The concept of balanced order is the permanent basis of pharaonic civilization. Balanced order brings peace, condemns crime and evil. Whoever breaks the law is punished as a matter of course." This says it all, essentially and requires particularly those in power be truthful, right and merciful in administering the requirements of their responsibilities.

As such then, and in its insistence and demands upon those who shape the society's norms, "The social order secretes benevolence and loving kindness, without stifling personal initiative and work if you cultivate a farm. Ma'at castigates slander, lying, defamation, boastfulness, and flattery. All persons, great or humble, rich or poor, deserve respect; such are the unequivocal prescriptions of Ma'at. Order is a categorical imperative. Stick to the truth: do not exaggerate. In the last analysis what prevails is justice, Ma'at."

# FREDERICK MONDERSON

**Black History Extravaganza - Photo -** The vulture goddess with wings fully-extended amongst a tomb ceiling decorated with vines of grapes.

**Black History Extravaganza - Photo -** The Cartouche of Seti I on an Abacus, above the Closed-bud Capital below the Architrave at Kurneh Temple.

# BLACK HISTORY EXTRAVAGANZA
# HONORING DR. BEN-JOCHANNAN

**Black History Extravaganza - Dr. Yosef A.A. Ben-Jochannan - The Final Farewell for a Hero's Hero** who "Talked the Talk and Walked the Talk; and Talked the Walk and Walked the Walk" in defense of African people, culture and especially their women.

The American Egyptologist James H. Breasted, on the other hand, in *The Dawn of Conscience* (1933) recognized this early development and practice of wisdom in a chartered and diametrically opposed

# FREDERICK MONDERSON

passage of time from the "First great age of the human mind" to "the earliest age of disillusionment." Fortunately, however, the human spirit, refusing to be down-trodden and perhaps because of the potency and redemptive nature of the social exhilir Ma'at - viz., demands for justice, truth, righteousness, balance, responded constructively and lifted Egyptians, Africans, and humanity from the depths of despair through practice of religious praise, worship and ritual, and in social conduct, expectation and practice. Thus, through the construct of moral precepts, wisdom literature was able to shine forth and illuminate thoughts of men paving the way in a significant manner for the colorful and intellectual pageantry of human mind shaping experiences.

Down through dynastic rule, there were, perhaps, some 10 thought processes, expressions, "books," wisdom literature, that span the philosophic gamut of Egyptian thinking molding successful social behavior. Such constructive precepts were required and even served as history lessons for students. Yet, they were not principally religious in creation and interpretation. That is, with the exception of the **Negative Confessions** which essentially was religious, mortuary and social. But first, it is important to identify the "ancient wisdom," of the "ancient wisdom" as discovered, catalogued and published at the beginning of the 20$^{th}$ Century. Among these are:

1. Petrie, Flinders. *Religion and Conscience in Ancient Egypt*. London: 1898, 110-163.

2. Myer, Isaac. *Oldest Books in the World*. New York: 1900.

3. *Wiedemann, Alfred. Popular Literature of Ancient Egypt*. London: David Nutt, 1902.

4. Breasted, James H. *Development of Religion and Thought in Ancient Egypt*. New York: Scribner's, 1912.

5. Budge, E.A. Wallis. *Egyptian Literature*. London: Kegan Paul, Trench, Trubner, 1912.

# BLACK HISTORY EXTRAVAGANZA HONORING DR. BEN-JOCHANNAN

6. Erman, Adolf. *The Literature of the Ancient Egyptians*. London: Methuen and co., Ltd., 1927, 54-85, 232-243.

7. Breasted, James Henry. *The Dawn of Conscience*. New York: Charles Scribner's Sons, 1933.

8. Hertzler, Joyce O. *The Social thought of the Ancient Civilizations*. New York: McGraw-Hill Book Company, Inc., 1936.

9. Simpson, William Kelly. *The Literature of Ancient Egypt*. Cairo: The American University in Cairo Press, 2003.

10. Obenga, Theophile. *African Philosophy: The Pharaonic Period*: 2780-330 B.C. Paris: (1990) 2004.

11. Diop, Cheikh Anta. *The Cultural Unity of Black Africa*. Chicago: Third World Press (1958) 1987.

12. Carruthers Jacob H. *Intellectual Warfare*. Chicago: Third World Press, 1999.

12. Obenga, Theophile. *Ancient Egypt and Black Africa*. Chicago; Frontline International, 1992.

13. Asante, Molefi. *Kemet, Afrocentricity and Knowledge*. Trenton, New Jersey: Africa World Press, Inc., (1990) 1992.

14. Karenga, Maulana. *Maat: The Moral Ideal in Ancient Egypt*. Los Angeles: The University of Sankore Press, (2004).

15. Van Sertima, Ivan. *Great African Thinkers:* Cheikh Anta Diop. New Brunswick: Transaction Books, (1986) 1987.

16. Van Sertima, Ivan. *Egypt: Child of Africa*. New Brunswick: Transaction Publishers, (1994) 1995.

# FREDERICK MONDERSON

17. Carruthers, Jacob H. and Leon Harris. *African World History Project*. Los Angeles, California. 1997.

18. Karenga, Maulana and Jacob Carruthers. *Kemet and the African World View*. Los Angeles: University of Sankore Press, 1986.

19. Finch, Charles S. III. *The Star of Deep Beginnings*. Decatur, Georgia: Khenti, Inc., (1998) 2007.

20. James, George G.M. *Stolen Legacy*. New York: Philosophical Library, 1954.

In that glorious and enlightening experience, a number of people, social thinkers, kings, officials and even a peasant, have left their mark permeating down through the ages and their sayings, instructions, admonitions have been so powerfully influential they are often household expressions today.

For the most part, in chronological rendering, the books, teachings or lists of precepts are:

**1. Instructions of Kagemni -**

**2. The Maxims of Ptah-Hotep -**

**3. Teaching of Dauef -**

**4. Instructions for Meri-Ka-Ra -**

**5. Instructions of King Amenemhet I -**

**6. Antef -**

**7. Teachings of Sehetipebre -**

# BLACK HISTORY EXTRAVAGANZA HONORING DR. BEN-JOCHANNAN

8.     **Teachings of Amenemhap -**

9.     **Teachings of Ani -**

10.     **Precepts of the Greek Period -**

11.     **The Negative Confessions -**

12.     **The Eloquent Peasant -**

Modern sages who have dealt with the Wisdom of Ancient Egypt were many, of many nationalities, and these thinkers have left exceptional evidence of their work. Without question they extoll the power of the ancient African, Egyptian mind, while recognizing, however, there were some imperfections therein. Still, the pro exceeded the cons. Notwithstanding, for dubious reasons, some have sought to discount and disclaim the Egyptian influence especially on the Greek and Roman mind and the impact this has had on the origin of Mediterranean civilization which served as foundation for the civilization of the West including that of America.

Naturally Jean Jacques Champollion gets credit for cracking the *Hieroglyphic Code* but his predecessors and contemporaries were actively involved in the effort and deserve their places of recognition. In early modern times there's Rossellini, Lepsius, De Rouge, Chabas and Birch who have labored to advance the study and understanding of the Wisdom of the Ancient Egyptians often labeled Egyptology, though such thoughts and ideas have had profound influence in all the genres of knowledge. Garner Wilkinson deserves mention. Of course, while Lepsius is there, Auguste Mariette gets recognition for creating a repository in which to house the enormous amounts of artifacts and wisdom that was being unearthed from the bowels of "Mother Africa during much of the $19^{th}$ Century"

# FREDERICK MONDERSON

Flinders Petrie, the Englishman, and Gaston Maspero, the Frenchman, both knighted by the British Crown, were perhaps the most active revealing, collecting and presenting evidence of the Wisdom of the Ancient Egyptians. Petrie's bibliography has been numbered in excess of 1200 and Maspero, busy as an administrator and translator still had time to produce 150 volumes. Another Frenchman of *Isis* magazine fame, George Sarton, accumulated a bibliography eclipsing Petrie and approaching 1500 pieces. The other great Egyptologists were just as busy, but F. Llewellyn Griffith gets special mention for he edited the **Annual Reports of the Egypt Exploration Fund**, providing a comprehensive description of archaeological work being conducted throughout the land for nearly three decades from approximately 1890 to 1920.

Samuel Birch, Chabas, Goodwin, Naville and a number of others translated papyri and wall inscriptions which were then published in a 12-volume series entitled *Records of Egypt and Assyria*. Each volume, divided in two comprised Part One, Egypt; Part Two, Assyria. Just as in Ancient Egypt competing schools of art and thought, in the North and the South, in the various nomes, there were competing schools in Europe. The "Berlin School," the "French School," the "British School," particularly through efforts such as that of Amelia Edwards who founded The **Egypt Exploration Society** and its arm the **Egypt Exploration Fund**; Flinders Petrie in the **British School in Egypt**; the **Graeco-Roman Branch**, who chronicled the unfolding work and published an enormous compendium indicated elsewhere in this volume under the section on **The Archaeology of Egypt**. Much of this was recorded in the *Journal of Egyptian Archaeology*, Flinders Petrie's *Ancient Egypt* and contemporary *American Journal of Archaeology* complimented with untold numbers of newspaper and magazine articles and Journals from institutions as the Metropolitan Museum of Art, Boston Museum of Fine Arts, that of Cleveland, Philadelphia, and untold academic institutions and publishing houses. Grenfell and Hunt did enormous work hunting, chronicling and publishing papyri which essentially provided a great deal of the evidence of the "Greek miracle." Interestingly, however, George Sarton considers, "The

# BLACK HISTORY EXTRAVAGANZA HONORING DR. BEN-JOCHANNAN

Greek miracle an Egyptian do-over." Later in this work there will be a quote from a papyrus in the British Museum, No. 10,477 which is an indication of the volume of papyri here and elsewhere in England and across Europe and America, purposely secreted in Museum Basements.

In Germany, it was Adolf Erman and Kurt Sethe. Elsewhere, among the British thinkers, whether G. Elliott Smith working through Manchester University, or Garstang at Liverpool, even T. Eric Peet, Aylward Blackman and others all helped to highlight the potency of Egyptian wisdom. However, despite these modern minds' tremendous contribution to understanding the Egyptian cultural bonanza, we recognize "mistakes" in their interpretation. However, some modern critical scholars view these "mistakes" as "purposeful."

In America, operating out of the University of Chicago, the "Chicago School," James Henry Breasted emerged as the premier Egyptologist who published a *History of Egypt* (1905); *Ancient Records of Egypt* (5 Volumes, 1905-07); gave lectures on the *Development of Religion and Thought in Ancient Egypt* (1912); *Ancient Times* (1916); *The Conquest of Civilization* (1926); and *The Dawn of Conscience* (1933). His efforts became the yardstick by which Americans viewed the interpretation of the newly revealed Wisdom of the Ancient Egyptians. That "Chicago School" also gets credit for the efforts of J.A. Wilson *The Culture of Ancient Egypt* and Keith C. Seele *When Egypt Ruled the East* as well as "other lights" as Lanny Bell. Meanwhile, across America points of "Egyptian light" manifested in schools and museum displays such as in Boston, New York, Brooklyn, Detroit, Philadelphia, Cleveland, and elsewhere all extolling the creative wisdom of Ancient Egypt. Whether in Hasting's *Encyclopedia of Religion and Ethics*, *The Dictionary of the Bible*, early editions of *Encyclopedia Britannica*, *Isis*, Journals of Academic Institutions as Harvard, Yale, etc., and untold newspaper and magazines who essentially "made their names" publishing Egyptian data as **Archaeology** revealed the ancient secrets and its wisdom. Sadly, whether in Europe or America confusion, distortion and omission was the order of the day; people were fed misleading interpretations and thus falsity, while Egypt was portrayed and heralded as not in Africa but in the "Middle East." Foremost, as Dr. Carruthers explained, "Hegel took Africans out of Egypt and Egypt out of Africa." Herman Junker (**Journal of Egyptian Archaeology** 1921) got "good mileage" in emphasizing "The first appearance of Negroes in History." Essentially, then, as we have come to recognize the projection has been on a false foundation for the existential data did and still contradicts the symbolic representation whether in schools of education, the publishing establishment or in museum displays. Nonetheless, in a bold challenge, within the environment of that intellectual store-house, the University of Chicago, the courageous Dr. Ben Carruthers stood up and challenged the behemoth that propagated the institution's interpretation of the evidence again keeping in mind, Dr. Leonard James has long insisted, "The existential data contradicts the symbolic representation." As a result, Dr. James, as a master of the classroom, taught and encouraged his students to develop intellectual autonomy to constructively decode the academic and otherwise environment in presentation of this subject matter, all in search of and to expose falsity and allow truth to manifest.

As such, Dr. James Breasted and his European contemporaries were involved in the outstanding work of revealing to the world the Wisdom of Ancient Africa. This was insightfully explained by Dr. John Henrik Clarke indicating its creative expression first in the Ethiopian rehearsal stage then in the Egyptian platform amazing both Ancient and modern worlds. The only problem perhaps, and the reason Dr. Carruthers emerged and stood up is because like the new Disney movie, **Tarzan**, there were "no Africans in it." This is reminiscence of the **Berlin Conference** in which European nations convened a Congress in 1884-85 without inviting or telling the Africans they had **Partitioned Africa on Paper**. The next stage of this reality was **Implementation of Partition on Land**, convincing the Africans, Europeans now owned their ancestral lands. It is inconceivable that aliens can come and claim earth or as depicted in that movie in which Russians invaded America and young Americans fought valiantly in defense "of their land."

# BLACK HISTORY EXTRAVAGANZA HONORING DR. BEN-JOCHANNAN

Well, in a more legitimate expression, the Africans resisted the invaders, occupiers and ultimately conquerors; and though they fought valiantly, they fell. Thus, it is up to the generations moving forward to arm themselves intellectually and redeem the African legacy while defending Egypt as African and Black. Intellectual autonomy is a prime tool in this effort.

In reaction to the Berlin Congress actions, all across Africa the continent was aflame in resistance. Thus, we see in Central Africa where earlier Queen Nzinga resisted the Portuguese; in West Africa proper, the Africans resisted the British West African Frontier Force comprising African recruits commanded by white officers. Still, African nationalist patriotism flourished. Whether it was under Samori Toure or others resisting the French Mitrelleuse; or Yaa Asantewaa rallying the Ghanaian combatants to resist British takeover to make sure Africans did not go quietly. In South Africa, Shaka the Zulu was a military force to reckon with and Moshesh proved a master of diplomacy when he outfoxed the Boers by placing his land under a British Protectorate. In East Africa, Tippu Tib was molding his slave empire and did not prove an easy prey. In Ethiopia, **Menelik II** defeated the Italians at the **Battle of Adowa** foiling Italian imperialist machinations over this ancient state. However, in South-West Africa, Herrero resistance and their extermination exposed the barbarity of German suppression methods, ultimately not uncharacteristic of other colonial efforts elsewhere in Africa, a mirror image of Prescott's description of the **Conquest of Peru** and the Incas.

Again, and more particularly, Adu Boahen in *Topics in West African History* (London: Longman, 1975: 133) adds even more an understanding of the African response especially in West Africa: "During and after the Conference the European powers sent out more envoys and soldiers who, by persuasion or force or bribery, got African rulers to sign agreements, in which they ceded away, in some cases innocently, their territories. Most of these rulers later realized the full significance of these agreements and rose up in rebellion. But such rebellions were crushed and the rulers were either killed or exiled. Others, like Lat-Dior, Samori Toure, Ba Bemba and Behanzin put up resistance right from the beginning but they failed to maintain their independence. Lat-Dior of Cayor resisted the French till he was killed in 1885. Samori Toure defended his huge empire stretching from Boure to northern Ghana from 1891 until 1898 when he was captured and deported to Gabon where he died in 1900. Ba Bemba of Sikasso also bravely stoop up against the French and in 1894 he killed himself when he found the odds too heavy against him 'preferant le suicide au deshonneur.' Behanzin, the King of Dahomey, opposed the French from 1892 to 1894 when he was arrested and imprisoned and then deported to Martinique and then to Algeria where he died in 1906. Similarly, it took the British a substantial part of the first decade of this century to suppress the resistance in Bornu and the Fulani emirates of Northern Nigeria."

However, while justification was offered for "rescuing the Africans," modern efforts of Dr. "Let's Skip" Gates revealed contrary to popular and misguided views, intellectual activities were encouraged and flourished in the Western Sudan at the Universities of Timbuctoo, Sankore and Djenne where manuscripts were being produced in the principal fields of knowledge. Consistent with the Wisdom of the Ancient Egyptians, if not somewhat scaled back there is continuity in the Nile River state intellectual creativity given evidence exists of migrations from that region to the western part of the continent. Nevertheless, much evidence was hidden and so preserved for posterity to recover and learn from. There is, however, evidence that as the changing nature of activities changed, particular the geopolitical realities from the headwaters of the Nile to the Mediterranean, populations of Ancient Egyptians, caught in the throes and dynamics of historical evolution, migrated westward across the Sudan bringing that intellectual capability so enshrined in the Wisdom of the Ancient Egyptians. According to Anthony Browder, the Africans of the Nile valley perceived the ancient civilization would fall and encouraged some "six streams of migrations" across the Sudan to the west. They probably envisioned the Western Sudan would also fall and either hid that knowledge or imbedded that wisdom in the DNA of the African who would ultimately be transported and enslaved within the New World. However, possessing the physical, psychological, spiritual and

# BLACK HISTORY EXTRAVAGANZA HONORING DR. BEN-JOCHANNAN

intellectual tenacity, resolve and capabilities of physiological wisdom, the Africans in America amidst the enormous social, education and political challenges visited upon they, still preserved initiating intellectual survival strategies not simply for their own survival living the reality of ancestral wisdom that also benefitted whatever society they were part of. However, as the modern events described were unfolding, a new form of intellectual conquest was taking shape, this was "intellectual imperialism," conquest of the mind, particularly in search for the Wisdom of Egypt. In this, we must never discount but seek to comprehend the significance and strategy of colonialists in conducting surveys of all facets of African natural resources to more effectively exploit such for Europe's benefit.

Just as old-style imperialism emphasized acquisition and "holding" real estate and other property, now it was about artifacts and wisdom literature of elsewhere in Africa, but more particularly in Egypt. From the time of Napoleon's invasion of Egypt and through the efforts of Champollion and Rosellini, places such as Turin's museum acquisition efforts, not forgetting Belzoni and Consuls of various powers as Henry Salt, a fire had been lit in the minds and hearts of Europeans to possess "things Egyptian," that is, whether artifact or literature. Still, and not discounting the enormous accumulation of artifacts, the hundreds of thousands of papyri; one source quoted several hundred thousand papyri scattered across Europe in museums and educational institution, enrichening the European intellectual landscape, making the wisdom of ancient Egypt thus, "a culture in captivity."

As arrogance, whether military, political or intellectual reigned supreme across the global landscape; in Egypt especially, a "few voices were crying in the desert," warning and issuing challenges to destruction, acquisition, misrepresentation, distortion and omissions. In one example or as Dr. Leonard James taught his students principles of historical evolution grounded in critical comparative historical analyses with components into the affective and effective areas of learning such teachings were designed to acquire intellectual autonomy to recognize, remain critical and reinforce the idea that

# FREDERICK MONDERSON

"The existential data contradicts the symbolic representation" as first pointed out by Count Volney in his *Ruins of Empire* in 1793.

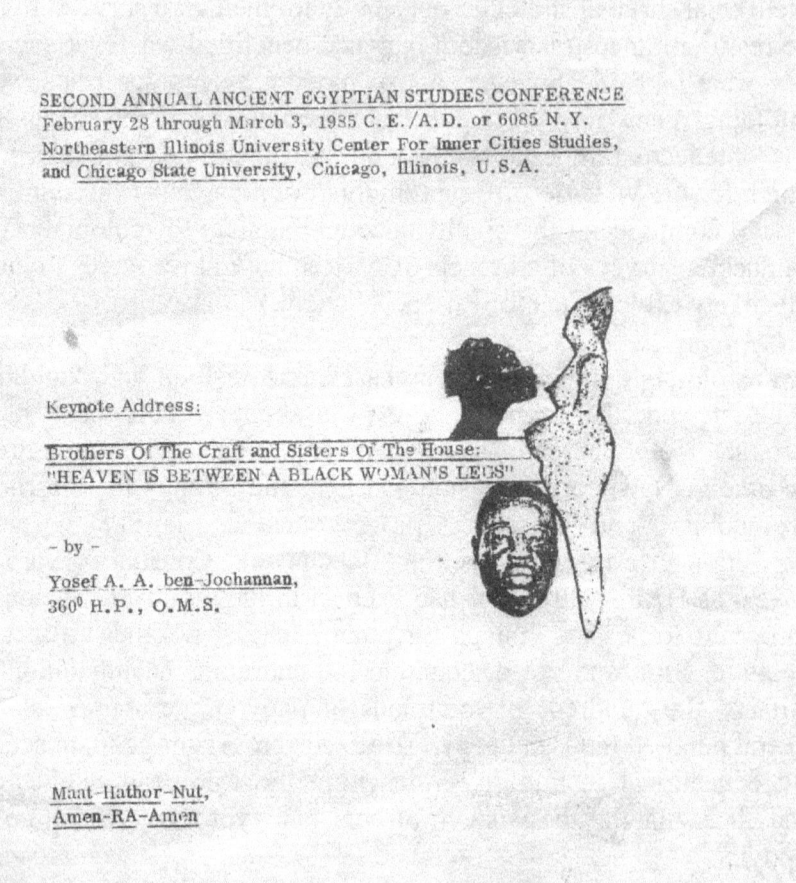

**Black History Extravaganza** - Dr. Ben's Book - **"Brothers of the Craft, Sisters of the House: Heaven is Between a Black Woman's Legs."**

# BLACK HISTORY EXTRAVAGANZA HONORING DR. BEN-JOCHANNAN

Meanwhile, as greed and avariciousness predominated, destruction and acquisition or seizure being the order of the day, Lepsius shipped 18,000 pieces of artifacts to Berlin and Reisner, through Maspero's generous blessings unloaded some 400 boxes for the University of California. De Morgan as Cairo Museum Antiquities Curator gave away untold numbers of artifacts to museums in Europe and America, seeking contributions in return as *quid pro quo*. Now, and in addition, multiply the volume shipped or carried home by the thousands of scholars, adventurers, plunderers, tourists, and this provides a glimpse into what Brian Fagan in his book called *The Rape of the Nile*. Following Volney's *Ruins of Empire* in 1793, in 1836 Sir Godfrey Higgins published *Anacalypsis* in 2 volumes. However, by the end of the 19th Century Gerald Massey authored *A Book of the Beginnings*, *Natural Genesis* and *Ancient Egypt: The Light of the World*, all in two volumes. His disciples Albert Churchward and Raymond Dart issued their efforts decrying falsity, distortion and omission in the historical record and challenged the propensity of "naked," "enlightened" and "intellectual imperialism."

Meanwhile discoveries were being made on a wide scale beginning with the 1881 "Deir el Bahari Cache," of 18th and 19th Dynasty pharaohs, queens and nobles; the 1898 Amenhotep II tomb discovery of other kings by Loret; even the 1898 discovery of the tomb of Mentuhotep II, the Middle Kingdom monarch who built his magnificent Deir El Bahari masterpiece which served as transitional Old Kingdom to New Kingdom religious and mortuary building practice. Though his tomb was discovered in 1898 and cleared by Edouard Naville in 1903-1905, after this scholar's magnificent effort of clearing Hatshepsut's classic gem of architecture a decade previous 1893-1896; even after Howard Carter's discovery of Tutankhamon's tomb in 1922, it was not until 1959 that W. Stevenson Smith in *The Art and Architecture of Ancient Egypt* would exclaim Mentuhotep II had "black flesh" and the implications this meant for the argument of ethnicity of the ancient Egyptians as well as the decades of heralded false information masquerading as true or correct history. Perhaps through their "European colored glasses" this was not observed, certainly not stated for half a century by the Breasteds, et al.

# FREDERICK MONDERSON

However, in bold and true African intellectual assertion, Dr. Carter G. Woodson insisted we must recognize *The Miseducation of the Negro*, and a companion volume *The Education of the Negro* while also producing *The African Background Outlined* as well as co-authoring with Charles H. Wesley, *The Negro in Our History*. Echoing such intellectual efforts, prominent thinkers of the earlier age included Martin Delaney, Henry Highland Garnett, Bishop Adjai Crowther, and especially Edward Wilmot Blyden, "the eloquent spokesman of an expatriate's Black nationalism," emerged as champions of a prostrate Africa and its sons and daughters. Blyden, as Lewis H. Gann and Peter Duignan in *Africa and the World* (San Francisco: Chandler Publishing company, 1972: 478) opined: "Perhaps the most prominent of them all was Edward W. Blyden, a West Indian born at St. Thomas in 1832. Blyden tried to study in the United States, but racial prejudice prevented him from gaining admission to an appropriate institution. In 1851 he emigrated to Liberia, where he made his name as a scholar and statesman and where he served periodically as tutor to Joseph Jenkins Roberts, one of the most distinguished of Liberian presidents. Blyden believed that each race, including the black race, had its own cultural contribution to make to the advancement of humanity. He spoke, perhaps for the first time, of the 'African personality,' which he believed to be endowed with a unique form of spirituality, a special proclivity for cooperation and for sympathetic communion with nature. Africans, in Blyden's view, had a more pronounced sense of the numinous than Europeans. The great religions of the world had all originated in Africa, he claimed. The ancient Egyptians and Ethiopians had been of the black race. Africans should therefore look with pride upon their golden age, develop their own racial genius, and avoid miscegenation or contamination by alien thought."

Highlighting this view, W.E.B. DuBois' *The Negro* (1905), *Black Folks Then and Now* (1903); and *The World and Africa* (1946); Drusilla Dungee *The Wonderful Ethiopians* (1926); and John Huggins and John Jackson *Introduction to African Civilizations* (1936); J.A. Rogers *Sex and Race* (3 Volumes) *World's Great Men of Color* (2 Volumes); again, John Jackson *Introduction to African Civilization* (1970); John H. Clarke and Yosef Ben-Jochannan *New Directions in*

# BLACK HISTORY EXTRAVAGANZA HONORING DR. BEN-JOCHANNAN

*African History*; and Yosef Ben-Jochannan's **Trilogy** of *Africa: Mother of Western Civilization* (1970), *African Origins of the "Major Western" Religions* (1971) and *Black Man of the Nile*, later *Black Man of the Nile and His Family* (972); Ben Carruthers' *Intellectual Warfare, Mdr Ntr: Divine Spee*ch, *Essays in Ancient Egyptian Studies*; Molefi K. Asante's *Kemet, Afrocentricity and Knowledge* and *Ancient Egyptian Philosophers*; Carruthers and Maulana Karenga's *Kemet and the African Worldview*; and Karenga's *Ma'at* are all deep-thinking African-American responses to the distorted image of Egypt's portrayal while setting the record straight. Naturally the publishing establishments' reaction to their work was swift and severe but to no avail for "the die had been cast." Coupled with Cheikh Anta Diop's *The African Origin of Civilization: Myth or Reality, The Cultural Unity of Black Africa*, and *Civilization or Barbarism: An Authentic Anthropology* as well as the work of his associate Theophile Obenga in *Egypt and Black Africa* and *African Philosophy: The Pharaonic Period* - 2780-330 B.C. the challenge was met. However, and nonetheless, while these seminal works represent substantial and credible responses and critiques of the established record, good in some ways but bad in others, especially from the ethnological perspective given misrepresentation in false presentation, no attempts were made by European or Americas scholars to correct the misstatements falsity that still stands in contrast today.

Nevertheless, and adding to the great volume of intellectual focus, Ivan Van-Sertima issued *They Came Before Columbus*, then contributed four significant monologues, *Nile Valley Civilizations, Egypt Revisited, Egypt Child of Africa* and *Great African Thinkers: Cheikh Anta Diop* to which his associate Runoko Rashidi recently released *The Van Sertima Papers: Uncovering the African Past* to which, for good measure we can add Fred Monderson's *Intrigue Through Time, Where Are the Kamite Kings, Egypt Essays on Ancient Kemet, Research Essays on Ancient Egypt, Grassroots View of Ancient Egypt, Celebrating Dr. Ben-Jochannan* and *Black History Extravaganza: Honoring Dr. Ben Jochannan* and *Let's Liberate the Temple, Black History Everyday* - *Part One* and *Part Two* and *Into*

# FREDERICK MONDERSON

*the Egyptian Mind.* From these disparate yet converging avenues of intellectual focus we recognize, examine and praise the multi-faceted dynamics of the Wisdom of Ancient Egypt and the virtuous and defiantly courageous defense and correction of that legacy. As such, then, we allow Donald Redford to bring it home in shining more light on that wisdom we speak so wonderfully well of.

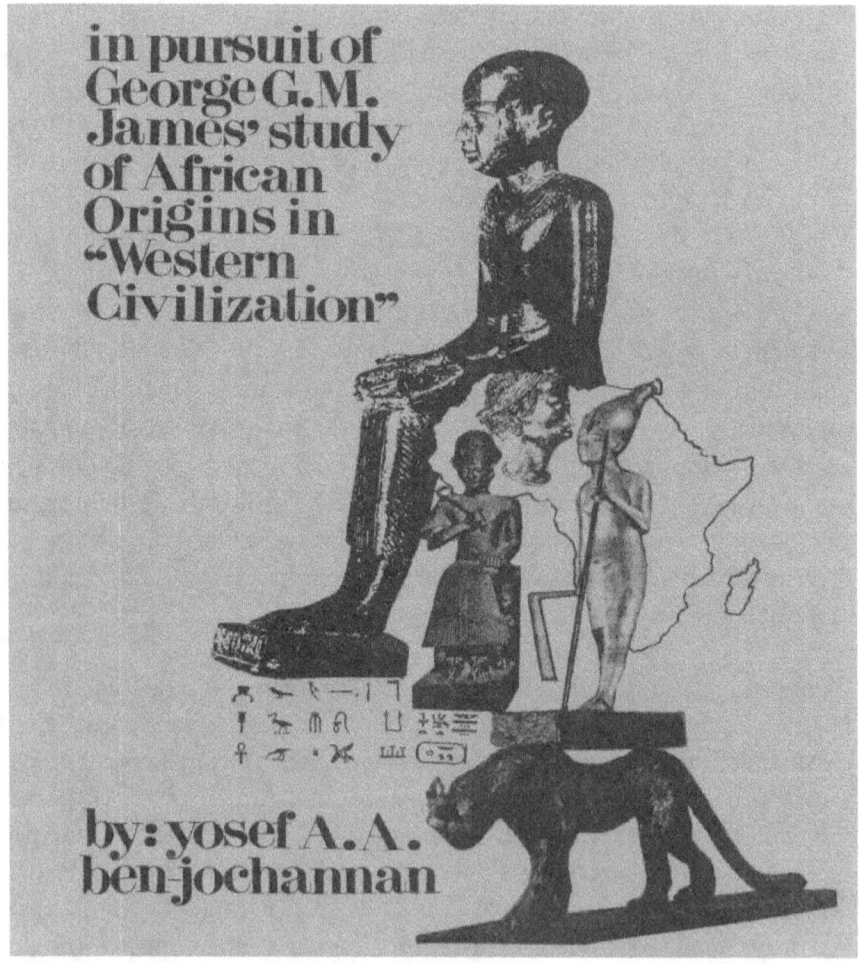

**Black History Extravaganza** - Dr. Ben's Book - **In Pursuit of George G.M. James' Study of African Origins of "Western Civilization."**

# BLACK HISTORY EXTRAVAGANZA HONORING DR. BEN-JOCHANNAN

THE ALKEBU-LANIANS OF TA-MERRY'S
"MYSTERIES SYSTEM," and the RITUAL-
IZATION OF THE LATE BRO. KWESIE
ADEBISI, O.M.S./7⁰▲L⚲

-by-
Yosef A.A. ben-Jochannan, O.M.S./360⁰▲⏋☥

Professor of History, Africana Studies and Research Center, Cornell University, Ithaca, New York
Professor of History, Pan-African Studies Department, Temple University, Philadelphia, Pennsylvania
Associate Professor of History, Malcolm-King College Harlem Extension, Harlem, New York City, New York [of Marymount College Manhattan, Mount Saint Vincent College, and Fordham University, New York]

*From Frederick Henderson by Yosef ben-Jochannan: July 31, 1997 C.E.*

## Black History Extravaganza - Dr. Ben's Book - In Pursuit of George G.M. James' Study of African Origins of "Western Civilization" - Overleaf of the Cover Page.

In this, Donald Redford eloquently states in outline, focusing on "Egyptian Religion: The Literature" (MacMillan Publishing Company, 1987: 54-65), *The Encyclopedia of Religion* Vol 5, (New York: Macmillan Publishing company, 1987, contending *inter alia*,

# FREDERICK MONDERSON

"The Temple Texts furnish descriptions of the deities, their mythic significance, daily rites, and festivals and to some extent, the interaction between the human and divine worlds." and more fully (1987: 54-65), he states: "The literature" is enumerated as follows:

1. **Pyramid Texts - Old Kingdom**

2. **Coffin Texts -Middle Kingdom**

3. **Book of Going Forth by Day - Book of the Dead - Per-em-Hru - New Kingdom**

4. **Underworld Literature - Religious nature and afterlife.**

    a. Am Duat - What is in the Underworld
    b. Book of Gates - Portals to the Underworld
    c. Book of Caverns - Afterlife drama
    d. Book of Traversing Eternity - How the gods travel

5. **Communications between the living and the Dead**

6. **Mythology - About the gods and their interaction with humanity**

7. **Cosmogonies - Creation stories**

    a. The primeval ocean and the creator-god or creative element that appears within

# BLACK HISTORY EXTRAVAGANZA HONORING DR. BEN-JOCHANNAN

    b.    The separation of the earth from sky, both personified in a sexual union

    c.    Creation by means of a skilled craft e.g. The ceramic expertise of Khnum; the Plastic modeling of Ptah, or the Weaving of Neith

    d.    The conflict between the hero-gods and monsters, out of whose carcass the world is created

8. Myths of kingship and fertility - How the monarchy came into being

9. Speculative Literature -

10. Dialogues and Harpers' Songs -

11. Discourses -

12. Magical Texts -

13. Wisdom Literature -

14. Temple Libraries -

15. Beatifications -

16. Hymns -

17. Mythological Compendiums -

# FREDERICK MONDERSON

18. Chronicles and Narratives -

19. King lists and Offering lists -

20. Annals of the Gods -

21. Directories and Prescriptions -

22. Omen Texts and related genres -

23. Oracle Texts -

24. Medical Texts -

25. Administrative Texts -

26. Temple Inscriptions -

27. Stelae -

28. Biographies -

29. Autobiographies -

30. Hymns, prayers and testimonials -

Additionally, Theophile Obenga, Dr. Diop's associate, as indicated above in *African Philosophy*: *The Pharaonic Period* 2780-330 B.C., provides remarkable insights into the Wisdom of the Ancient Egyptians. In erudite comparison with classical wisdom scholarship, that of Plato and Aristotle, Obenga states, "The aim of learning is the

# BLACK HISTORY EXTRAVAGANZA HONORING DR. BEN-JOCHANNAN

acquisition of wisdom." More purposely focused, Obenga (2004: 264-65) writes regarding Greek choices for edification: "The Egyptian model being the best, it is the one that ought to be adopted for the physical, moral and intellectual education of Athenian youth. In sum, the reference is consistently to Egypt, not to Babylon or Assyria, when the issue is the *education* of Athenian youth, the ancient *history* of the Greeks themselves, *wisdom* (philosophy), the *arts* and *sciences* (arithmetic, geometry, astronomy), writing, games, (draughts), *music*, or *dance*. "

This, then is the legacy and we're prepared to fight to maintain Egypt is African, a Black Civilization as Dr. Cheikh Anta Diop and so many others have demonstrated, admonishing "we must live and die on the battlefield of African historical reconstruction to correct the record by exposing distortion and including omissions." That is, given the "Existential data contradicts the symbolic representation."

**Black History Extravaganza - Photo -** The freedom and virtuousness of having one's own craft and sailing along the "Heavenly Nile" in the "Afterlife."

# FREDERICK MONDERSON

## III. Dr. YOSEF A. A. BEN-JOCHANNAN A TRIBUTE
## By
## Dr. Fred Monderson

It is with great sorrow that I announce the death of my mentor, friend and world renowned African historian, Egyptologist and humanitarian **DR. YOSEF ANTONIO ALFREDO BEN-JOCHANNAN**. At this time, **AFRICAN PEOPLE HAVE LOST A CHAMPION OF GREAT MAGNITUDE**, wisdom and intellectual fortitude. **LET US WISH HIM A WONDERFUL RECEPTION INTO THE PANTHEON OF GREAT AFRICAN ANCESTORS** who have never compromised in quest of the best for African people.

Among his many accomplishments, Dr. Ben has placed the Black Woman on the **HIGHEST PEDESTAL** to be admired and respected in the hope she will continue to do what no Black man can ever do!

**DR. BEN HAS** been a **LIGHT** and he has shown us the **LIGHT**!

**LET US ALSO HOPE PEOPLE, YOUNG AND OLD, WILL CONTINUE TO READ HIS BOOKS AND FOREVER DRINK FROM THE FOUNT OF HIS ENLIGHTENMENT EFFORTS** as Tour Guide, archaeologist and nationalist spokesman whose 97 years on earth have been a tremendously wonderful and enlightening experience. He possessed a vision that looked far into the future. His efforts **HAVE KNOWN NO LIMITS** in quest for the very best for **AFRICAN PEOPLE**! Again, his books should be introduced into the schools to let young people understand the man and forces at work!

# BLACK HISTORY EXTRAVAGANZA HONORING DR. BEN-JOCHANNAN

## GOD BLESS DR. BEN-JOCHANNAN AND MAY HIS EFFORTS AND MEMORY CONTINUE TO BE AN INSPIRATION AND GUIDE TO US ALL!

Dr. Ben was an extraordinary man of many talents, but principally a man who held the African woman in the highest esteem. He taught us in the beginning was the African woman! Creation came out of the African woman! As the obelisk is a small pyramid on a tall base, this is the pedestal upon which Dr. ben-Jochannan placed the African woman. He honored the Black Woman who is the source of the Black Family! He taught us the Black Woman is a Goddess! He also led the light to the Nile Valley. He "took Egypt to challenge and destroy white supremacy!" It's like Marcus Garvey said, "the cubs are running free out there," and thanks to Dr. Ben, intellectual cubs are challenging the distortions, omissions and putting Africa in its proper place in world civilization history given its accomplishments in Nubia and Egypt, Nile Valley cultures that point to inner, Central and Southern Africa as well-springs of intellectualism, that gave so much to the world.

The Twentieth Century has been blessed with great African and African-American writers and historians. These include Dr. W.E.B. DuBois, Dr. Carter G. Woodson, Dr. Kwame Nkrumah, Dr. Ivan Van Sertima, J.A. Rogers, Cheikh Anta Diop and **Dr. Leonard James, Emeritus Professor of New York City Technical College of the City University of New York**, among others. This enormous collection of brainpower equally extends into the Twenty-First Century. However, none of these giants singularly surpass the literary production, commitment, tirelessness, and sincere dedication of Dr. Yosef Alfredo Antonio ben-Jochannan. Outspoken visionary, iconic symbol and above his time; controversial and not afraid to take an iconoclastic and individual if a somewhat idiosyncratic point of view; Dr. Ben was always prepared to defend his position, irrespective. His friends and students, affectionately call this father, teacher, historian, friend and Egyptologist, "Doc Ben."

**Black History Extravaganza - Photo -** Entrance view of Rameses II's Abu Simbel temple highlighting the eight-colossal Osiride Statue in its Hypostyle Hall, the ceiling decoration and looking beyond.

# BLACK HISTORY EXTRAVAGANZA HONORING DR. BEN-JOCHANNAN

In fact, back there in the early 1970s when even "Black folks" did not readily accept "Dr. Ben," ever wonder how he got his name? It was a young man named "Barney" and myself, Fred Monderson, who first started calling him not "Dr. Ben" but "Ben Jo" and the name stuck and finally when a fellow student Curtis Dunmoodie picked it up and said we must be more respectful, we began calling him "Dr. Ben" in defiance of those "feather bedders" who said "Dr. Ben has no PhD!"

**Black History Extravaganza - Photo -** Amon as a Black god sits enthroned before two Goddesses (Hathor in two moods) and behind him another whose foot is shown. This set of images was located at Medinet Habu in the rear of the temple but has now vanished and cannot be seen by visitors.

# FREDERICK MONDERSON

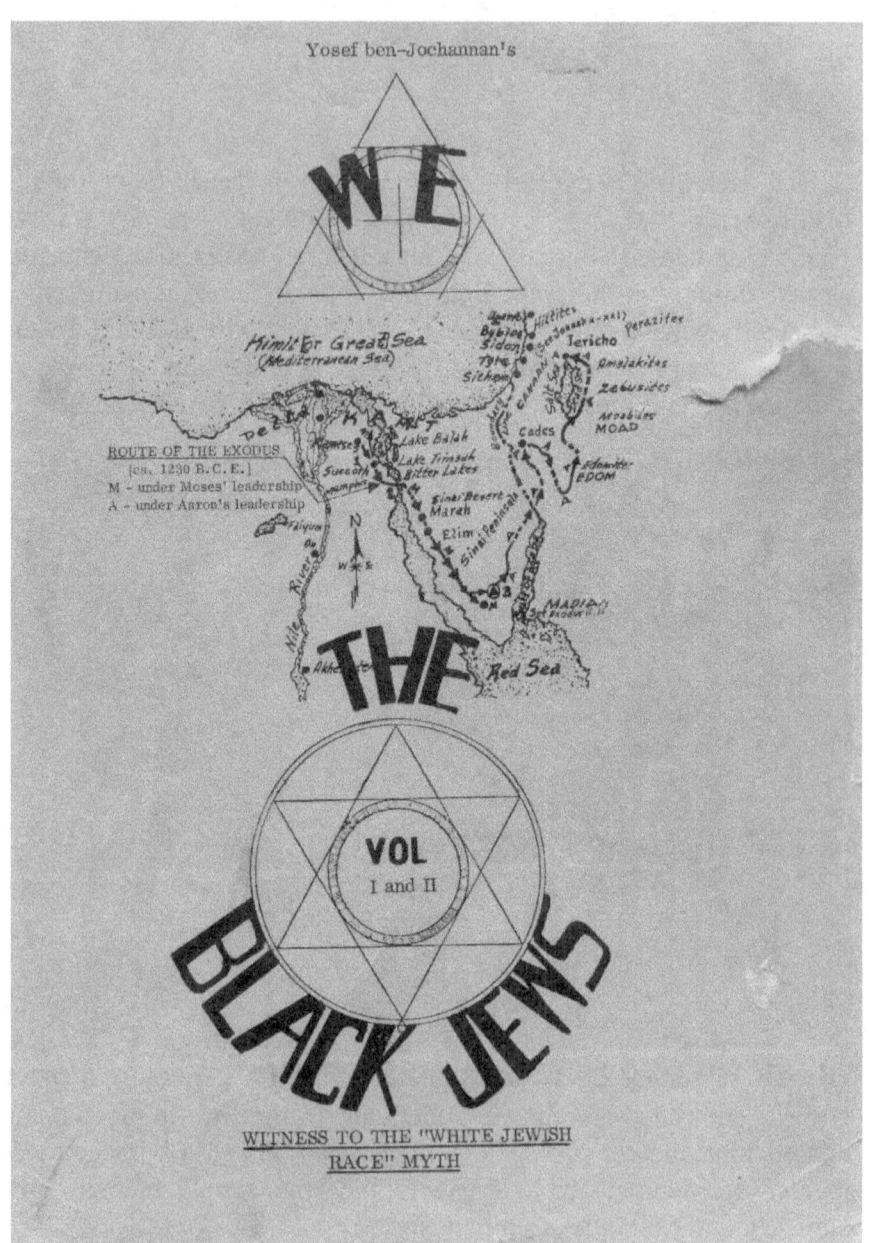

**Black History Extravaganza** - Dr. Ben's Book - **We the Black Jews.**

# BLACK HISTORY EXTRAVAGANZA
# HONORING DR. BEN-JOCHANNAN

VOLUME - I

by
## Yosef Ben-Jochannan

Adjunct Professor of History, Africana
Studies and Research Center, Cornell
University, Ithaca, New York
Visiting Professor of History, Malcolm-
King College - Harlem Extension,
New York City, New York

**Black History Extravaganza** - Dr. Ben's Book - **We the Black Jews - Overleaf of the Title Page.**

# FREDERICK MONDERSON

Ever cried for Dr. Ben? This odious statement once made me cry at New York City (Community) Technical College. I hurriedly took the **A-Train** to 125$^{th}$ Street to their second-floor office on Lennox Avenue across from the **Choc-Full-O-Nuts** Coffee Shop in Harlem, before Prof. George Simmonds calmed me down, showing me Dr. Ben's Doctorate in Anthropology on the wall. That is what some of the "false prophets" still do today in academia to him and others! And so, you ask them to match their literary production with their in-clandestine vituperativeness and they cannot! Period!

Here was a serious scholar, Dr. ben-Jochannan, who spent a lifetime researching, writing, and defending the integrity and intellectual capabilities of African people worldwide. Dr. Ben pioneered in indigenous ancient African terminology. Imagine a European-American scholar discovered the bones of a fossilized African woman in Ethiopia and named her "Lucy" after an Englishman's song "Lucy with Diamonds," then playing on the radio in camp. Dr. Ben said "No! Her name is *Denk Nesh* not Lucy!"

In 1989, Doc Ben celebrated fifty years of visiting ancient Kemet, Ta-Merry (Egypt) and the Nile Valley cultures. This prolonged involvement has under-girded the basis of his researches, speeches, writings and educational tours. Equally, he began and for some time maintained archaeological digs on the Island of Elephantine and elsewhere. Alas, these have been discontinued.

**Black History Extravaganza – Tomb of Nakht** - The Nobleman fowling.

# BLACK HISTORY EXTRAVAGANZA
# HONORING DR. BEN-JOCHANNAN

**Black History Extravaganza** - Dr. Ben's Book - Dr. Ben and Co-Author Professor George Simmonds wrote this extraordinary book, **The Black Man's North and East Africa** to counter the prevailing view Egyptians were Caucasian in control of North and East Africa.

# FREDERICK MONDERSON

This writer was happy to be a part of that epoch-making tour that marked Doc Ben's Fiftieth Anniversary visiting the ancient African "holy-land" and the next year for the First Nubian Festival. More importantly, I met "Doc Ben" in early 1972. This was right after the publication of his seminal "Trilogy" works, *Africa: Mother of Western Civilization* (1970), *African Origins of the Major Western Religions* (1971), and *Black Man of the Nile* (1972), later *Black Man of the Nile and his Family*. The style of his writings, copious nature of referents employed to defend things African, and his Afrocentric pioneering approach made "Doc. Ben," a very well-respected scholar and elder, and in his later years a sought after speaking attraction, a man who "tells it like it is!"

**Black History Extravaganza - Photo -** The Gods at Medinet Habu, that can't now be seen because they have vanished.

# BLACK HISTORY EXTRAVAGANZA HONORING DR. BEN-JOCHANNAN

**Black History Extravaganza - Photo -** Papyrus rendition of Tutankhamon's death mask.

Dr. ben-Jochannan (he asked for a small "B" meaning "Son of Jochannan") has compiled an impressive thirty-odd publication that I

# FREDERICK MONDERSON

am intimately familiar with, having bought most in first edition which the author subsequently autographed. He helped set the stage for a whole new approach in interpreting Africa's contributions to civilization and its legacy. He lit the fire of intellectual and cultural consciousness in Africans worldwide. The Diasporian style of dress with an Afrocentric flavor is also credited to him. Establishing connections between Africans in America, the Caribbean, Africa, Asia and Europe are all attributed to Dr. ben-Jochannan, a man of vision, a seer, and intellectual giant. Many of his books challenged the distortions of Europeans in writing, publishing and disseminating knowledge about the arts, sciences, religion, etc., of the ancient people today called Egyptians. Dr. Ben has rightly included omissions and corrected distortions systematically implanted and perpetrated by racist Western, European and American historiography that has falsified the historical past with a prejudiced interpretation against African people. Many of his books challenged the distortions of Europeans in writing, publishing and disseminating knowledge about the arts, sciences, religion, etc., regarding origins in ancient Africa as represented in modern interpretation. Dr. Ben dared to expose the hypocrisy of western scholarship. He attacked the foundational pillars upon which this false legacy rests. Naturally, he paid a price!

Very early he also expressed the view some scholars are confused because they were taught from a wrong premise. In his own right, and as a result of his teachings, he had no choice but to produce, publish and distribute his works without the aid of major publishing firms. He was thus a pioneer in self-publishing, launching **Alkebu-Lan Publishing Company** and appealing and winning the support of many upcoming nationalists as "they purchased his books in first edition form!"

Initiating a new approach to history, the end result was an exposition and critical analysis of dynamic forces of Europe and Africa in struggle to claim heritage of the ancient and modern historical record. Dr. Ben addressed professionals, laymen, clergy, students and educators. He stressed vitality, resilience and creative expressions that shaped the modern African personality and worldview. Such an approach found ready ears among a people yearning for enlightening

# BLACK HISTORY EXTRAVAGANZA HONORING DR. BEN-JOCHANNAN

factual information about their illustrious African past in effort to free their minds from the oppression of slavery and colonization. These young and old minds were enthused by the positive nature and potency of their cultural African heritage as "Ben" outlined it. He also took great pains to explain that there were lusterless pages in Africa's past but these must be remembered but discarded. Nevertheless, his concern fueled their emerging aspirations. This outlook brought Dr. Ben the adulation and respect of a grateful people, he for long deserved. They understood and welcomed his contributions among the litany of great African-American literary artists.

**Black History Extravaganza - Photo -** Ceramic wall decoration depicting the Horus Hawk, some have labeled a falcon.

# FREDERICK MONDERSON

Dr. Ben's writings, lectures and educational tours over the years have stressed two essential themes. The first is that the "emergence of civilization, viz., science, religion, government, architecture, agriculture, philosophy, and the arts, began in Africa." The mouth of these utterances became the conduit of today's Egypt and the Nile Valley. In his approach, Dr. Ben has shown how the structural foundations of western civilization developed from discoveries and scientific applications in this ancient African land. Lastly, he took great pains to show the writing and teaching of modern history has been distorted to elevate Europe and denigrate Africa, which is clearly wrong and must be rectified. This fundamental view helped establish the need for African historical reconstruction and interpretation particularly as we navigate this new century and millennium.

The second of Dr. Ben's themes has been that "Africans worldwide should be proud of their ancestors' accomplishments. The arts and sciences that today govern the world are Africa's legacy. African-Americans should show great pride and dignity in their history and heritage." They must respect themselves and carry themselves with dignity and pride. Those who know can and should teach the young how to identify with Africa. In so doing, they must form study groups and visit Africa. Yet, they must also be aware of the machinations of cultural imperialism and cultural genocide constantly at work. Further the young must immerse themselves in an African-centric perspective and research, write and teach others in turn. They must study languages such as French, German, Swahili, Greek, Latin, Coptic, Arabic and *Medu Netcher* or Hieroglyphics. They must become conversant with The Archaeology of Egypt and how anthropology shaped its interpretation to write its history. They must struggle to correct the recent distorted history of Africa's past. In this way, future leaders would help to better the lot of humanity and save the world from its impending moral, spiritual and scientific destruction. To accomplish these objectives, the good doctor has supplied a reservoir of information from his life's researches in the arsenal of published works he has created. Of course, these works must be read, ingested and digested and returned to time and again. This is important for as Dr. John Henrik Clarke once said, "People buy but never read Dr. Ben's books." Herein then is the dilemma.

# BLACK HISTORY EXTRAVAGANZA HONORING DR. BEN-JOCHANNAN

The author's major thesis of his *African Origins of the Major "Western Religions"* is that African religious practices were denigrated and called "fetishism" and "paganism." In fact, these early thought processes he showed are the fundamental bases of Judaism, Christianity and Islam. He argued that these ideas were first developed and nurtured in Central Africa among indigenous peoples and then migrated and extended throughout the Nile Valley. Echoing Cheikh Anta Diop's *Cultural Unity of Black Africa*, Theophile Obenga in *African Philosophy: The Pharaonic Period*: 2780-330 B.C. equates similar thoughts and practices, religious and scientific, among many peoples and cultures spread across Central and Southern Africa. The foundations and connections of these ideas are not to be found in Asiatic places of origin of "White Egyptians." After all, Mosso in *Foundations of Mediterranean Civilization* noted, "Asiatics did not penetrate the Nile Valley nor the Aegean region." Conversely, they found greatest fruition in Kemet (Egypt) and were preserved by its civilization advances and the nature of its geography. After decades of oral recording and practice, the early knowledge was first written down in such selections as the "Book of Gates," "Book of Knowing Ra," etc. These were part of the earlier "Pyramid Texts" (Old Kingdom); then "Coffin Texts" (Middle Kingdom); and the later Book of the Dead or Book of Going Forth By Day (New Kingdom); and the "Mysteries of Sais" (Egypt). The fortunes of geography enabled Africa's second cultural daughter, Kemet, to rise to greater prominence than did the eldest, Ethiopia, Dr. Ben explained! He stressed and still maintain to this day, despite all the "new evidence," that civilization began to the south of Egypt! However, despite modern falsification of history and the insistent propagation of such falsity, his thesis is as credible as ever.

# FREDERICK MONDERSON

**Black History Extravaganza - Photo -** Garden entranceway to Rameses II's Abu Simbel Temple.

**Black History Extravaganza - Photo -** Rameses, wearing the Khnum Crown of Horns with feathers and uraei with sun-disks, presents a plant to Khnum, god of the Cataract with Bastet at his rear.

# BLACK HISTORY EXTRAVAGANZA HONORING DR. BEN-JOCHANNAN

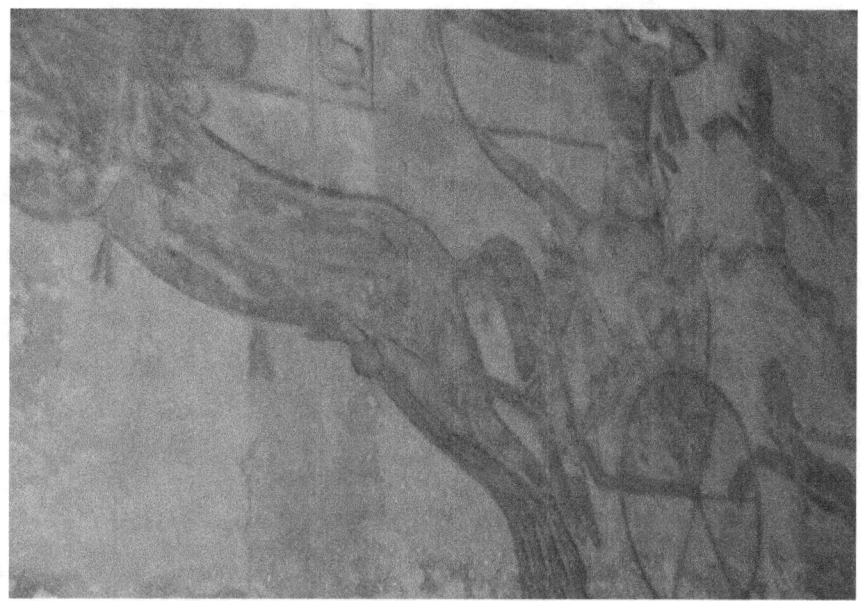

**Black History Extravaganza - Photo -** Rameses, in his chariot, fires his arrows at enemies at the **Battle of Kadesh**.

Another of Dr. Ben's seminal works is *Africa: Mother of Western Civilization*. Its major thesis holds that the "fundamental laws, principles, philosophies, ideas, arts and crafts that educated the west, are indigenous to Africa through the Nile Valley cultural experience." For critical teachers who face this dilemma he has some advice. As such, he wrote: "The only credentials necessary in the experience of African history, otherwise mis-nomered 'the Black Experience' and 'Black Studies' are the documented proofs and the sources from whence they are taken."

For this reason, *Africa: Mother of Western Civilization* is an enormous compendium of facts, sources, illustrations, and analyses that challenge laymen and scholars alike. It suggests all educators and lay persons alike become involved in reclaiming the stolen heritage of Africa. This **magnum opus** opens new vistas for historical investigation and provides a wide array of references relating to the significance of Africa in world civilization.

*Black Man of the Nile and His Family* marks the third in the "trilogy of Dr. Ben's seminal works." This particular source represents the maturity of his thoughts and presentations for it focuses on the role Black men and women have played in bequeathing science, religion, arts, metaphysics, agricultural method, boat building and Nile River navigation to the world through Africa's conduit in Egypt and Nubia. It also contains a number of objectives the author seeks to accomplish.

The first of these objectives is, "an attempt to create in young African, African-American (Black person), and all other African people, a sense of belonging in the great African heritage." It is, writes Dr. Ben "specifically directed to those who have criminally demasculinized, denuded, and otherwise denigrated the Africans of their **CULTURAL**, **ECONOMIC**, **POLITICAL**, **SCIENTIFIC**, **SPIRITUAL**, and all other forms of their heritage and human decency." To this we should add the intellectual heritage as represented in Egypt; that is, through "acquisition methods," and teaching, writing and representation of the artifactual evidence.

It also presents: "**AFRICAN ORIGINS OF EUROPEAN CIVILIZATION**" in a manner whereby, "scholars can find interesting use for it in their research; as much as the layman can for processing information."

Dr. Ben views his role as gadfly presenting, "pertinent information needed in the African peoples' **RE-IDENTIFICATION** with their great ancestral heritage." Lastly, he continued, the "major desired accomplishment this volume seeks to achieve, is to provide anthropological evidence in the ancient heritage of the Africans" and their contributions all over the world.

*Abu Simbel to Ghizeh*: *A Guide Book and Manual* is in itself another useful piece of writing. But, there are other books.

# BLACK HISTORY EXTRAVAGANZA HONORING DR. BEN-JOCHANNAN

In the acquisition of knowledge, Sir Francis Bacon (1561-1626) noted: "Some books are to be tasted, others to be swallowed, and some few to be chewed and digested." This much can be said of the trilogy of Dr. ben-Jochannan's works, *Black Man of the Nile and his Family*, *Africa: Mother of Western Civilization* and *The African Origins of the Major Western Religions*. The others are equally interesting! Everyone must buy and read these books and pass them on to others particularly their sons and daughters and nephews and nieces.

Finally, as a student of his, and based on observations and analytic critique, this writer would like to add a 15-point summation of how we can view Dr. Yosef Alfredo Antonio ben-Jochannan's contribution as an unselfish and fearless elucidation of the historical record systematically distorted to elevate Europe and denigrate Africa while wrecking psycho-social debasement of the African spirit and persona, in especially America and globally.

Without question, whether through omission, distortion and even false presentation, the urban youth across America have most seriously been victimized in the systematic alienated educational process they have been subjected to. As such, the potent cultural lifeline Dr. Yosef Alfredo Antonio ben-Jochannan has provided is today critical in rescuing these young people adrift in the academic and intellectual cosmos of these modern times going forward. The prescription therefore is as follows:

1. We must praise and show thankfulness for the man who, for more than half a century challenged the behemoth of western intellectual oppression of Africa and her offspring while enlightening many to the wonders of a creative African cultural heritage.

# FREDERICK MONDERSON

**Black History Extravaganza - Photo -** At Rameses II's Abu Simbel Temple, the king holds Egypt's enemies by the hair and pummels them before Amon-Ra in "blackface." Ma'at sits on a standard behind the king.

**Black History Extravaganza - Tomb of Nakht -** While the Master sits, workers are busy with their functions.

# BLACK HISTORY EXTRAVAGANZA HONORING DR. BEN-JOCHANNAN

**Black History Extravaganza - Photo -** At Abu Simbel, Rameses wearing the "Double" Red and White Crown, kneels before an enthroned Thoth, god of wisdom and also a moon god. Both the king and the god are shown on an equal plane.

2. We must commend Dr. ben-Jochannan for the humanitarian work he did among the Nubians in Egypt and Sudan, viz., Aswan, Daboud, Wadi Halfa, Dongola Province and Fashoda.

3. We must recognize his call to action to combat the cultural genocide in the African-American studies curriculum predating the Afrocentric insistence on multi-culturalism.

# FREDERICK MONDERSON

**Black History Extravaganza - Papyrus -** Colorful papyrus showing the king riding in his chariot and firing his arrow, while the Vulture Goddess flies above his head and holds the Shen Ring.

4. We should continue to emulate his style of critical analysis of contemporary developments, whether it was historical omissions in Alex Haley's *Roots*; misrepresentation in King Tut's exhibition that has taken place several times in America; taking to task T. Eric Peet's "The Problem with Akhenaton;" Criticism of Father Placide Temple's *Bantu Philosophy*; challenge to another writer's description that Rameses II had "badly abscessed teeth," and so forth. We must emphasize "New World tobacco" found in the intestines of the king's mummy and its implications.

5. We can appreciate his identifying "They all look Alike, All," thus linking African peoples across the globe who were victims of religious bigotry, racial hatred and cultural aggression.

6. His early clarification of the differences between the **Black Nationalist and the Black Marxist** was very timely and inspiring and still is.

# BLACK HISTORY EXTRAVAGANZA HONORING DR. BEN-JOCHANNAN

7. First to outline the *Chronology of the Bible*, he challenged the *Black Clergy Without a Black Theology* and offered *A Black Bible for Black Spiritual and Religious Consciousness*.

8. We must acknowledge as a human, he may have made some mistakes, miniscule, as they were outweighed by the foundational reservoir of ethical, intellectual and cultural **Ma'at** he Dr. Ben implanted in the consciousness of African people worldwide.

9. His insistence that all African-Americans visit the Nile Valley to imbibe in the cultural heritage and grow from the intellectual exposure, but more particularly their dress code and mannerism among the people must not be construed as the "arrogance of Ugly Americans" was and is still timely and insightful.

10. His outspoken nature, love for Marcus Garvey and his *Philosophy and Opinions*, praise of Black Goddesses, critique of Academics who are "fifth columns" made him anathema to people with ill-intentions, Black and White, toward African people.

11. Dr. ben-Jochannan had little respect for people in high positions who never promoted the aspirations of their Black subordinates. He pointed to many in academic, business enterprise and even the military who never advanced the positions of their fellow Africans as did other cultural and ethnic groups in similar situations.

12. A staunch **Pan-Africanist**, he aspired to see accomplished sustained and measurable economic, political and educational empowerment for people of African heritage worldwide.

13. He said, "I took Egypt to show our people the proper way" and to challenge its misrepresentation, racism and religious bigotry inherent in teachings related to this ancient African culture.

14. He insisted we not just read books and do research on Ancient Egypt in Africa, but also form study groups that debate and discuss

# FREDERICK MONDERSON

these important issues raised by him as well as personally critique status quo's positions. He also insisted we must visit Egypt and observe and let the monuments teach.

15. He asked us to standardize our learning and take responsibility for our own history. He stated: "Until African (Black) people are willing, and do write their own experience, past, and present, we will continue being slaves, mentally, physically, and spiritually to Caucasian and Semitic racism and religious bigotry." This latter we must never allow to happen, for as Dr. John Henrik Clarke has admonished, "African people must write their own history" because the "People who preached racism colonized history" and as a result, "When Europe colonized the world, it colonized the world's history." Therefore, we must recognize that Dr. Yosef Alfredo Antonio ben-Jochannan has made a major contribution to African intellectual growth and consciousness. He created a cosmological vision over time that allowed us to see the light. His work has been seminal! In fact, **he was our light**! He taught us how to persevere to persevere! He asked that we establish and maintain a standard for our behavior, and "Don't fear, don't fear defeat, don't fear death!"

**Black History Extravaganza - Photo -** Ramesseum, Mortuary Temple of Rameses II from a distance on the bus.

# BLACK HISTORY EXTRAVAGANZA HONORING DR. BEN-JOCHANNAN

**Black History Extravaganza - Photo -** At Abu Simbel Temple of Rameses II, the king kneels and presents two ointment jars to an enthroned Ra-Horakhty.

# FREDERICK MONDERSON

**Black History Extravaganza - Photo -** At Abu Simbel, in a rather rare pose, the king kneels on the same plane with Horus as Ra-Horakhty, this time both his hands are empty and raised in adoration.

## IV. DR. BEN-JOCHANNAN LETTER ENDORSING DR. FREDERICK MONDERSON

Dr. Yosef A.A. ben-Jochannan
Lennox Terrace
40 West 135$^{th}$ Street
New York, New York 10030
June 5, 2010

Subject:    Permission to conduct tributes, seminars, "calls for papers," in my name!

Greetings to All!

# BLACK HISTORY EXTRAVAGANZA HONORING DR. BEN-JOCHANNAN

Dr. Frederick Monderson has been a student of mine for nearly 4 decades and has travelled to Egypt with me on several occasions. On one such occasion, he demonstrated a particular excellence that has remained indelibly imbedded in my memory. In addition, he possesses practically all my books in first edition; many of which I affectionately autographed.

Dr. Monderson has consistently demonstrated the highest standards of academic scholarship, proficiency in research techniques, is a prolific writer and staunchly defends Egypt as African. For nearly two decades he has written extensively on ancient Egypt, African history and local events, in New York's black press, and this deserves the highest praise. His work as a researcher and Egyptological scholar deserves recognition in the excellent tradition in which he was taught. I commend his commitment to the education of African people!

Mr. Monderson has written extensively in praise of me as an elder, Egyptologist, historian and scholar. He has held seminars in tribute to my efforts to educate African people and this is commendable. As a result, I give Dr. Frederick Monderson permission to continue sponsoring academic tributes, calls for papers and any intellectual pursuit in my name that reflects the highest standards demonstrated in interest of African people.

As such, I am confident, any tribute, calls for papers, sponsored tours of Egypt conducted in my name will reflect the high standards he has consistently demonstrated and will be a credit to the African people we both love and serve diligently.

Again, I endorse the work of Dr. Frederick Monderson that reflects the highest standards of academic excellence and feel confident he will continue to be a credit to my name and the African people he serves. Thank you. My love and respect to all!

---

Dr. Yosef Antonio Alfredo ben-Jochannan
Harlem, New York ▪ June 5, 2010

# FREDERICK MONDERSON

**Black History Extravaganza - Photo -** Rameses kneels and presents a plant and water pitcher to Horus enthroned as Ra-Horakhty.

**Black History Extravaganza - Photo -** Rameses kneels and presents a baboon to enthroned Ptah, god of the artisans.

# BLACK HISTORY EXTRAVAGANZA HONORING DR. BEN-JOCHANNAN
## V. DR. BEN-JOCHANNAN'S LETTER RECOGNIZING DR. FREDERICK MONDERSON

Dr. Yosef A. A. ben-Jochannan
Lennox Terrace
40 West 135th Street
New York, New York
November 15, 2010

Greetings

Today I recognize Dr. Frederick Monderson as an outstanding scholar, researcher and writer of Egyptological studies and expresses confidence in his ability to defend Egypt as African!

As our people move forward, the history and significance of Egyptian - Nile Valley - civilization remains crucial to Black-African intellectual development and consciousness. To sustain this effort requires the best researchers and writers to continue the tradition of excellence established by many including myself and Dr. John H. Clarke of Hunter College of the City University of New York.

Dr. Monderson is a product of that "Hunter School." As a student of mine who has travelled to Egypt with me on several occasions and possesses all my books, he has admirably answered the age-old question I posed decades ago: "Now that you have come to Egypt and seen what you have seen, what are you going to do with this knowledge?" As an African historian and Egyptologist, Dr. Monderson has responded admirably by writing hundreds of articles and dozens of books on this vital field of interest.

I thankfully praise his writings on my behalf, welcome his **Memorial Day Tribute** to my work and endorse his efforts as a

# FREDERICK MONDERSON

**Tour Guide to Egypt**. Encouraging him to choose one of fifty countries in Africa to specialize in and he Monderson choosing Egypt, I'm pleased with his development as an outstanding Egyptological researcher and writer.

As such, I recognize the valuable role he has, can and will play in educating our people about the wonderful resource of Egyptian history, culture, science and spirituality.

Therefore, I unequivocally give my blessings to Dr. Frederick Monderson's work in Egyptian studies and feel confident he will continue to educate and enlighten many, particularly the young, about the glorious African past in the Nile Valley.

_____

Dr. Yosef A.A. ben-Jochannan
Harlem Resident, historian, lecturer, writer and
Egyptological Master Teacher.

**Black History Extravaganza - Photo -** Rameses kneels and presents two ointment jars to Horus n Double Crown.

# BLACK HISTORY EXTRAVAGANZA HONORING DR. BEN-JOCHANNAN

**Black History Extravaganza - Photo -** Rameses kneels to present a platter of goodies to enthroned Horus in Double Crown as Ra-Horakhty.

## VI. THE AWESOME EGYPTIAN TEMPLE
## By
## Dr. Fred Monderson

Before there was the church or cathedral, synagogue or mosque, there was the Egyptian temple. It originated in the beginning and set the standard by which subsequent religious structures would later express their religiosity. Ancient Egyptian evidence indicates, the temple came into being when the god manifested his divine omniscience to the "servants of the god" and instructed them on how to construct and maintain his abode on earth. From that first encounter, the temple evolved from the simplest form and materials to the more complex and durable, long-lasting structure it came to represent. As such, the Egyptian temple has been one of the most fascinating creations emanating from the mind of man especially because it was guided by instruction and inspiration from the divine. To explain this, Stephen

# FREDERICK MONDERSON

Snape (1996: 8) has written: "The form of the Egyptian temple is influenced by many concerns: it is a space for specialized cult activities, but its architectural form and decoration are also vital in conveying aspects of accepted belief to the spectator. This accepted belief can include what we might term political propaganda, ideas about how the cosmos is ordered and specific myths connected with that particular temple. Form and decoration link each individual temple with others in terms of a general background in belief, while having its own particular concerns. No two temples are identical, yet none is completely unique." It's been postulated that Herbert Spencer rightly laid it down, "the first architects were priests" inspired by divine provenience on how to build the house in which the god would reside on earth. In that undertaking, constructive architectural construction for deity presence preceded that of monarchy and even though the kings built these structures, they built for the gods, their father, before they built for themselves; first worship temples for the gods, then mortuary temples for the kings. Thus, over time, in order to showcase the goodness and beneficence of God, the temple evolved from being constructed of the simplest material to more durable stone befitting the almighty. In the ongoing and evolving temple, not only did the materials change or improve but the siting, sophistication and decoration of the temple this endeavor became even more elaborate particularly reflective of the wealth of the state or respective monarch as patron who built to glorify the father and equally to demonstrate the power and prestige of the "Servants of the God" whose organization was entitled the Priesthood. To this end, the temple liturgy and ritual developed a series of complex practices ranging, after conception and construction, from the "Consecration of the Temple;" through "The Opening of the Mouth Ceremony;" "The Liturgy of the House of the Morning;" "Bringing the Foot;" and all were part of "Episodes in the Temple Liturgy."

# BLACK HISTORY EXTRAVAGANZA
# HONORING DR. BEN-JOCHANNAN

**Black History Extravaganza - Ceramic Art -** Water and the Hand.

The Egyptian temple, therefore, as house of the god was a manifestation of cosmic realization that appealed to the religiosity of human consciousness. Snape (1969: 9) sees this as a "paradox" to which he says: "On one hand the gods and goddesses of Egypt could embody the elements and great forces of nature, such as the sun, the sky, the earth or the Nile, or they could be deities with control over fundamental aspects of human experience, like Osiris, god of the dead. On the other hand, these deities were also regarded as behaving in a very human way and with the same needs. They are often found in family groups and they looked to their devotees for the same range of domestic service as a potentate, and in definite fixed places, the house, the palace or the temple."

# FREDERICK MONDERSON

The king was considered the "Son of God" and himself a god on earth, but when he died he received full god status at the place where the gods are born. Thus, in this life and the next he received the same god treatment of washing for purification of his body and spirit. This is explained much further by Harold H. Nelson in "The Egyptian Temple: The Theban Temples of the Empire Period" published in *Biblical Archaeologist*, Vol. 7, No. 3 (September 1944: 51) who wrote: "The ruler was himself a god, the son of the deity who dwelt in the temple. The relationship of them was one of mutual advantage, that of a father and his eldest son." Yet, the posture he assumed in the temple, in the same way was more from a stance of equality though the wording of the temple service speaks of the king lying prostrate himself before the god.

Still, even though the king was considered a spiritual and social intermediary between the god and the common man, as Nelson (1944: 52) argues, "The king might be the one who approached the god in his holy sanctuary, but the ordinary man could still address his prayers even to the mighty king of gods. In fact, one of the epithets of Amon is 'he who hears petitions and prayers.'"

To understand this further and as an example, we look to a wall in the rear passage of Kom Ombo temple, to see a set of "ears" there for petitioners to make their requests of the gods. The priests, as oracles who manipulate the god's image in procession oftentimes give answers to those petitions. Nonetheless, Nelson (1944: 52) explained this action of the petitioner in the following statement: "One imagines that the farther down the social scale he stood, the less assurance did the petitioner feel that his prayer would be heard. Possibly for some such reason there was a tendency to appeal to the god nearer to hand and so some people worshipped "household gods" in domestic shrines. While, as we have seen, the official religion held that the god was one, though with diverse names and dwellings, the common people apparently developed the conception of a distinct individuality attached to the local form of the god who dwelt in their own locality. Such a tendency among the ignorant is not unknown in Christianity, where the Virgin of one district will find here champions against the claims of a rival Madonna in a neighboring town. In the letters of late

# BLACK HISTORY EXTRAVAGANZA HONORING DR. BEN-JOCHANNAN

times we find the writer calling down upon his correspondent the blessings of Amon-Re, king of gods, of Mut, of Khonsu, and of all the gods of Thebes, of Re-Harakhte when he shines and when he sets, of Amon, United-with-Eternity, of Amon of Jame, of Amon of the throne of the Two Lands, of Amon Userhet, etc., as though these latter were separate divinities of Mut, Khonsu and Harakhte. Undoubtedly the ordinary citizen felt nearer to the form of Amon who was connected with his local shrine than he did to the more remote and august deity who lived in grandeur in his imposing fane at Karnak, a conception which would undoubtedly be encouraged by the local priesthoods to enhance their own prestige and, perhaps, emoluments."

**Black History Extravaganza - Photo -** At Abu Simbel temple, Duality of the king is expressed here where (left) in Blue Crown Rameses appears before Amon in plumes; and (right) before enthroned Ra-Horakhty with Thoth to his rear.

In respect to this human/divine interacting experience, Byron E. Shafer in *Temples of Ancient Egypt* (1998: 2) has provided an interesting explanation of cosmological forces at work when he says: "Temples and rituals were loci for the creative interplay of sacred space and sacred time. Sacred space is 'a place of clarification (a focusing lens) where men and gods are held to be transparent to one another' and 'a point of communication,' the 'paradoxical point of passage from one mode of being to another.' In sacred space, one is oriented to the cosmos and immersed in primordial order; there one experiences truth and renews life. Over time, such space appears unchanged and unchanging, 'stable enough to endure without growing old or losing any of its parts.'"

Even further, Shafer (1998: 2) continued: "What has been said of sacred place can, for the most part, be said of sacred time as well. It is a moment, or season, or cycle of such clarification and communication, orientation and immersion, experience and renewal. Time, however, is not so stable a dimension of order as space. Egyptians experienced time as a spiral of patterned repetitions, a coil of countless rebirths. The purest moment of sacred time was the first, the moment of creation, when the existent and its order emerged from the nonexistent and its aspect of disorder. Subsequently, time, as a component of order, proved vulnerable to chaos. So, for example, the intervals between sunrise and sunset came to change from day to day and season to season, and the beginning of each new 365-day year came to rotate slowly backward relative to the seasons and the helical rising of the star Sirius. Because of order's ongoing vulnerability to chaos, Egyptians needed to conceive of creation not as a single past event but as a series of 'first times,' of sacred regenerative moments recurring regularly within the sacred space of temples through the media of rituals and architecture." Thus, according to Egyptian beliefs, because evil and demonic persons and forces existed and were active, to combat such required priests be kept busy protecting their sacred space in unending ritual and prayer so the god's safety can be assured and he maintain harmony or Ma'at in the universe.

The first and most significant act in protecting the sacred space is its actual washing and fumigation with incense. These two important acts were first applied to begin the purification of the temple. A particularly important part of this act was the washing of the altar upon which so much of the ritual was conducted. Equally too, washing was an important feature in the daily lustration of the Sun-god and also of the king before he entered to preside in the temple ritual. The dead,

# BLACK HISTORY EXTRAVAGANZA HONORING DR. BEN-JOCHANNAN

whether king or commoner, was also washed to be considered pure in order to dwell in the abode of the gods which was a place of great purity, and so all those who dwelt there must be pure. Nevertheless, the temple had to first be built whereby the king and the goddess Seshat with the queen impersonating the divinity "stretched the cord" or lay-out the parameters and boundaries of the new structure with its added decoration. After this work is finished, the temple had to be consecrated before being handed over to the resident divinity and this entire process, to the untrained eye or ear, may seem a mystery.

**Black History Extravaganza - Photo -** Anubis sits enthroned behind Nephthys as the Gods were enthroned at Rameses III's Medinet Habu Mortuary Temple.

# FREDERICK MONDERSON

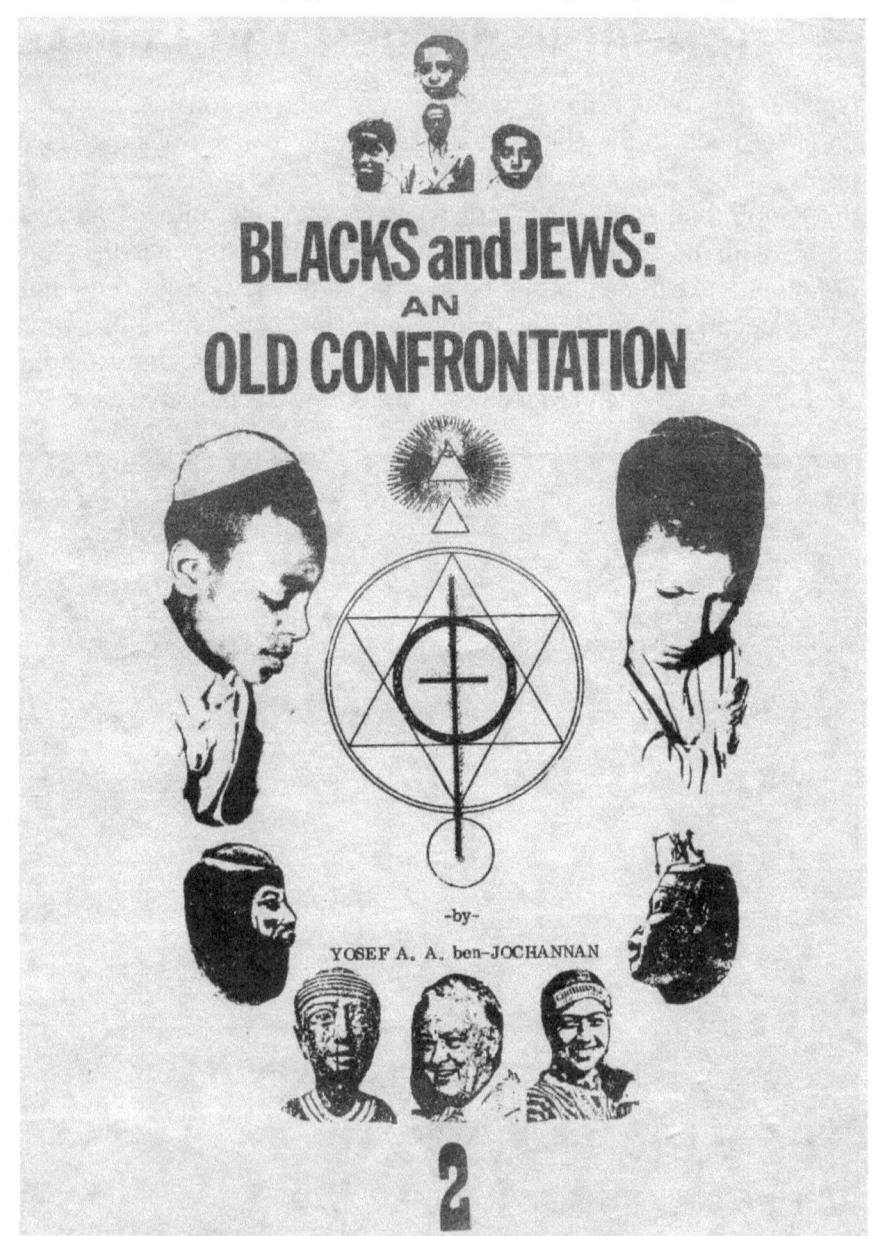

**Black History Extravaganza** - Dr. Ben's Book - **Blacks and Jews: An Old Confrontation.**

Abu Simbel's Great Temple was dedicated to 4 gods, Ra-Harakhte, Amon-Ra, Ptah and Rameses II as a deified god while still alive. Some

# BLACK HISTORY EXTRAVAGANZA
# HONORING DR. BEN-JOCHANNAN

temples were dedicated to a single god while a few were dedicated to several.

Abu Simbel's Lesser Temple - for his wife Nefertari was dedicated to Hathor and Ptah.

Abydos temple of Osiris was dedicated to 7 gods - Osiris, Isis and Horus; Ra-Harakhte, Amon-Ra, and Ptah; and Seti I, deified.

Kom Ombo was dedicated to 2 gods, the Elder Horus and Sobek the Crocodile god.

Deir el Bahari, dedicated to Amon-Ra, also had sanctuaries to Ra-Harakhte, Hathor and Anubis, while Sokar and the Queen's father Thutmose I was also worshipped within. The Temple of Isis at Philae, while dedicated to the Goddess also housed sanctuaries to Arsnuphis, Imhotep and Mendulese, in addition to a chapel dedicated to Hathor.

**Black History Extravaganza - Tomb of Nakht -** Ladies in attendance at entertainment.

# FREDERICK MONDERSON

**Black History Extravaganza - Photo -** Enthroned Ra-Horakhty offers life to a hawk or falcon all before cartouches of Rameses topped by Sun-Disks and a Uraeus holding an ankh and beneath a disk.

In their spiritual and metaphysical dynamics, symbolism and symbolic logic were significant parts of all aspects of Egyptian religious practices and in the consecration, this also applied. As the ritual unfolded in the process of consecration, not simply the first time when the temple was completely finished before being handed over to the resident god, means were undertaken, as a survival at the Temple of Horus at Edfu, so this ritual was structured to continuously recur. The intent of the liturgy was to make every image, statue, inscription, food, drink, hymn, litany, in fact, the entire temple, come to life, all part of the Opening of the Mouth Ceremony! And so, the magical formula, now written on the walls of Edfu and Philae temples, possess inherent qualities that made the said process automatic and recurring. That is, in the "Opening of the Mouth Ceremony" whether that of king

# BLACK HISTORY EXTRAVAGANZA HONORING DR. BEN-JOCHANNAN

or commoner, statues of the deceased, images engraved on stela or in the tomb, all are given the ability of voice, sight, touch, to eat, move around and come alive as in the earthly experience. Thus, this "Opening of the Mouth" is in many respects similar to the "Consecration" in that the entire temple with its constituent parts, viz., altar, statues, wall decoration with images and ritual, stairways, halls, unguents, food and drink, sacrificial implements and animals and flowers, holy water and incense for fumigation, are all "Open" and come to life. In regards the temple, extreme precaution is taken in preparation for the god to appear and remain safe and comfortable thereby able to receive praise and offer deserved rewards.

Thus, after the temple's construction, before it was handed over to its owner, it naturally had to be purified in the ceremony of "Consecration." Let me point out, in the earlier temples the ritual was generally contained on papyrus or even on tomb walls or sometimes an official may remark on his stela outside his tomb, his participation in a particular ceremony. However, by the time of the Greeks and Romans, temple designs radically changed and each room or hall therein had its walls illustrated with the ritual performed in that part of the temple. Thus, we now have preserved in stone some sacred rituals of the most ancient times. Two good examples of this are Edfu Temple of God Horus the Falcon and Philae Temple of Goddess Isis.

So, in "The Consecration of an Egyptian Temple According to the Use of Edfu" Aylward M. Blackman and H.W. Fairman in *The Journal of Egyptian Archaeology*, vol. 32 (December 1946: 85) write: "As is well known, the Opening of the Mouth was regularly performed on behalf of the statues of divine and human beings, statuettes used for magical purposes, and even on behalf of the heart-scarab, to imbue them with life and identify them with the beings or creatures they represented. Our two texts ... indicate that the Rite of Consecration of a temple employed the sequence and character of the ceremonies composing the rite suggesting that first of all it was performed on behalf of the cultus-statues and that then the 'Mouth of the Temple' itself was opened. The idea evidently was that not only the cultus-statues were enabled to become alive and active through the due performance of this rite, but the figures in the wall-reliefs also and the entire edifice with all its appurtenances." Thus, the entire structure became alive after the ceremony. At the end of such a ceremony, the entire structure with its occupants and accoutrements "went back to sleep" until awaken the next time for a recurrence of the rite.

Again, the use of Edfu Temple is simply because it has survived intact, contains a great deal of temple ritual that reach back to the most ancient times and provides a useful sample of ancient liturgical practices. As indicated, that symbolic magic was a hallmark in temple worship, wherein Blackman (1946: 87) points to the decorative strategy concerning the consecration. He writes, "Now the current Egyptian belief that the same magic power resided in the text inscribed on their temple - and tomb-walls as in the similarly situated relief, it was naturally desired to make our two texts as magically efficacious as possible and so ensure that the ceremonies they embody should continue to be performed, either as one combined rite, or as two single rites celebrated simultaneously. Thus, it was felt, the mysterious life originally imparted to the whole temple and its occupants by the Rite of Consecration would be perpetually renewed, that is as long as the two texts remained intact. Nevertheless, it must also be borne in mind that the actual performance of such ceremonies and the recitation of the accompanying formulae were naturally regarded as more efficacious than sculptured representations and mere written words."

H.W. Fairman in "Worship and Festival in an Egyptian Temple" in *The Bulletin of the John Rylands Library*, Manchester, Vol 57 (1954-55: 165) indicates: "The texts in these late temples include long descriptions of the temple room by room, each room, hall, or part of the building being named and its purpose, decoration and dimensions recorded. Each room and hall usually contains additional texts that repeat its name and give fuller information concerning its use. Similarly, each door is named and bears texts that state when and for what purpose it was used. Another long series of texts records the festivals celebrated in the temple throughout the year, indicates the date and duration of each, and sometimes outlines the ceremonies performed. An independent series of longer texts describes in greater detail some of the more important festivals." Even further, Fairman

# BLACK HISTORY EXTRAVAGANZA HONORING DR. BEN-JOCHANNAN

(1954: 165-166) explains: "This rich treasure of inscriptional material, illustrated as it often is by well-preserved reliefs, enables us to describe the function of every part of the temple from the smallest chapel to the largest hall, from the gargoyle and water-spouts to the pylons and obelisks. It is possible to reconstruct the furnishing and equipment of certain rooms, to tell when, how and where the offerings were prepared, to indicate the precise doors through which they were introduced into the temple, to trace the order of the ritual and the route of the great processions, and even to know what happened to the offerings after the services and festivals were ended. Moreover, there is evidence that in general the texts are based on sound ancient tradition, that in vocabulary and context they often go back to the early days of Egyptian civilization, and that, if used with due care and discretion, they provide us with a unique and exceedingly rich source-book of Egyptian religious practice."

**Black History Extravaganza - Papyrus -** Anubis sits atop a palanquin exhibiting that "1000-yeard stare."

# FREDERICK MONDERSON

As such, then, "The temple of Edfu thus affords us our best opportunity of studying a complete Egyptian temple and its various religious activities that took place within it day by day throughout the year."

**Black History Extravaganza - Photo -** Abu Simbel Temple of Rameses II. Somewhat defaced, the king kneels to present two ointment jars to an enthroned divinity.

Naturally there would be some slight variation among the different temples, as for example, what transpired between Karnak and Abydos, but essentially the main features, viz., what happens when the pharaoh visited and the ritual activities he engaged in remained essentially the same. That is how he is received, perhaps at the water's edge, how he is ushered through, possibly, the "Avenue of Sphinxes," as he entered through the Pylon into the Great Court, Hypostyle Hall for the procession and the approach to the "Holy of Holies." However, though the temple may differ somewhat in physical structure, their locations, names, functions performed in each space the liturgy and ritual were essentially the same. Now, once into the Hypostyle Hall,

# BLACK HISTORY EXTRAVAGANZA HONORING DR. BEN-JOCHANNAN

at Karnak the space before the "Holy of Holies" is called the Wadjit. Once there, we know of who follows him into the vicinity of the divinity, how he breaks the seal of the door, what greeting is offered at the door, how the room is fumigated with incense, what transpires within and finally how he "Brings the Foot." That is, how he removes footprints from the enclosure with his broom before he again closes the door and seals it until the next visit.

Then again, we must understand that the temple has to be rejuvenated as on the "first occasion" and on a daily basis. That is to say, the temple and its constituent parts and divine personnel in statues, wall depictions, etc., must be invoked to come alive time and again and once the entire structure comes alive then such parts of the ritual as cleansing, purification, etc. can then commence. In essence, since the god had to be visited, invoked, cleansed, fed and bejeweled, three times per day, the temple, certainly the inner reaches had to be cleansed three times per day.

The actual performance of the ceremony dictates, Blackman (1946: 90) writes: "After the chanting of a hymn of praise to Re, the gods were summoned to their repast and then the image of the goddess Ma'at was presented to the sun-god, as the words clearly imply. The presentation of Ma'at immediately after the gods are 'summoned' is by no means inappropriate, for Ma'at was regarded both as a substitute for food and drink and as the organ whereby they were transmitted to the belly and the breath of life was inhaled. The presentation of Ma'at and the offering of food and drink are accordingly closely associated in the *Bw-th-imn* version of the Opening of the Mouth." The washing of the altar as a necessity becomes apparent because of the ceremony entitled, "Setting the meal in order upon the altar" in which bread, meat and beer are served here and elsewhere. The purification of the priest is also an important part of any ceremony. "Part of the purification of a priest, before entering upon his course of service in the temple to which he was attached, was his drinking of natron for a certain number of days. The purification undergone by the Pharaoh in the House of the Morning, or temple vestry, before he officiated in the temple liturgy, included the chewing of natron for the cleansing of his mouth, this substance being spat out when sufficiently chewed. Lastly, we are informed that the wailing women who bemoaned Osiris had to purify themselves four times before they could stand within the door of the Broad Hall, and they also washed their mouths, chewed natron, and purified themselves with incense, in order that they and the lamentations with which they beautified the dead god might be pure."

However, when the above and central ceremonial repast was over, "the officiating priests visited each hall and chapel separately, censing and asperging them, and, it may well be, making mimetic gestures with their ceremonial adzes and other implements. It was presumably by many of these performances that not only the temple as a whole, but all its individual parts and furnishings became alive. The divinities could now become immanent at will in their figures appearing in the reliefs, while the inanimate objects depicted therein became the actual equivalents of what they represented - food, vessels, floral offerings, and the like."

The next significant undertaking was the "Opening of the Mouth Ceremony" that was applied to the gods, the king, and the deceased and as just mentioned, in the temple example and its entire accruements. That is to say, "The Rite of Opening the Mouth in Ancient Egypt and Babylonia" as Blackman in the *Journal of Egyptian Archaeology*, Vol. 10, No. 1 (April 1924: 470) explained, serves an important comparison: "The ancient Egyptian rite of Opening the Mouth, practiced on mummies, statues, and figures used for magical purposes," whereupon, using the Babylonian example, before he "started upon the actual consecration of the statue, the priest had to see that certain objects and commodities were ready to hand. These consisted of various kinds of stones, blocks of gold, silver, and copper, unguents enumerated as 'best oil,' 'finest oil,' and 'cedar oil,' and lastly butter and honey. Our text does not tell us to what use the stones, metals and oil were put. However, this seems probable that with the last mentioned the priest anointed the statue. The honey and butter were mingled with the date-wine and employed as a drink-offering, and they were also used, so another tablet informs us, for the washing of the statue's foot. The first act of consecration was to bind

# BLACK HISTORY EXTRAVAGANZA HONORING DR. BEN-JOCHANNAN

strands of red, white, and bluish wool about the statue's neck. The priest then shut the door of the room or building in which this part of the rite was taking place, and, while so doing he recited a formula. He next fumigated the statue with incense, offered it a lighted torch, the Egyptians used a candle, and sprinkled it with holy water. After that he swept the floor and sprinkled it also with holy water. Once more the priest burnt incense, placing cedar - and cypress - wood on the censor, poured out a libation of sesame-wine, and scattered meal on the holy-water bowl, - each action being performed to the accompaniment of a thrice-repeated formula."

Again, another text informs, the "formulae were employed to consecrate plants, woods, and similar substances, used in these washing and opening of the mouth rituals. In fact, all lustration material was so consecrated. He points out, too, that the burning of incense, the presentation of meal-offerings, animal sacrifices, the pouring out of libations, and the use of butter and honey, 'belong to the ceremony of invoking the aid of the great lustration deities, and of the deity whose image was being consecrated."

**Black History Extravaganza - Photo - At Abu Simbel Temple,** the King kneels to present a plant (left) and two ointment jars (right).

# FREDERICK MONDERSON

However, while there are some similarities between the Babylonian and Egyptian rites, indicating there was a similar original source from which both were taken, Blackman (1924: 59) does argue, "One thing seems certain is that the Egyptians did not get the rite from the Babylonians. It is essentially Egyptian as we know it and, as already stated, is closely linked with all the main Egyptian religious rites. It should here be pointed out the rite of 'Opening the Mouth' of an Egyptian statue was also supposed to be celebrated at dawn." He then asked the pointed question, "It will have been observed that the Babylonian rite was likewise celebrated in the small hours of the morning, terminating just after dawn. The question I would like to put to Asyriologists is: Was there any reason why the Babylonian ceremony should take place at that time? If not, then it is just possible that the Babylonians borrowed the rite from Egypt, and adapted it thoroughly in course of time to Babylonian ideas and mythology, meaningless incidents like the night to dawn celebration of the rite surviving. Finally, were the colored wools of significance in Babylonian ritual, or are they survivals from, or misunderstandings of, the Egyptian colored cloths?"

Now, while the Pharaoh is considered not simply the Son of God on earth but also the chief priest, he could not be in every temple, every day, for every ritual service and so he deputized priests in various temples to fulfill this function. However, just as the priest had to be purified before he could officiate at any temple ceremony; the king also had to be purified before he entered the temple. In "The House of the Morning," Aylward Blackman in the *Journal of Egyptian Archaeology*, Vol. 5, No. 3 (July 1918: 148) explained how this was achieved: "Pharaoh had to undergo purification before officiating in a temple. Inscriptions in the temples of Edfu and Philae, and two passages in the famous Piankhi Stele inform us that the purification took place in a special chamber called pr-dwet." This ceremony is described in two text passages as follows: "His majesty proceeded to the House of [Ptah], his purification was performed in the pr-dwet, there were performed for him all the ceremonies that are performed for a king. (Then he entered the temple.), (He) came in procession to the House of Re and entered the temple with loud acclaim, the chief lector praising the god and repelling those hostile to the king. The

# BLACK HISTORY EXTRAVAGANZA HONORING DR. BEN-JOCHANNAN

(Rite of the) pr-dwet was performed, the sbd-vestment was fastened on, and he (the king) was thus purified with incense and cool water."

This purification of the king is done by a "Unique Friend," a person of the highest rank. These numbered among the sons of the king, the Vizier who was sort of "Prime Minister," or the "Royal House-Superintendent of the Lord of the Palace," the "Inspector of the Great House" or even the "Controller of the Palace." Naturally only those individuals of this class enjoyed this privilege to serve the king. There are others such as "Keeper of the Crown," "Superintendent of all the adornment of the king," "Director of the Wig-makers of the King," "Superintendent of the king's linen," and "Superintendent of the Pharaoh's bath-room" and "Superintendent of the (royal head dress)" as well as the "Superintendent of the chamber of the ims-scepter." In this regard, Blackman (1918: 152) writes: "The fact that the office of Supervisor of the pr-dwet is combined with the care of the king's diadem, wigs, ornaments, apparel, and the superintendence of his bath-room, indicates that pr-dwet has the same meaning here as in the inscriptions referred to at the beginning of the article, namely that of Toilet-chamber, - in other worlds, the *pr-dwet* of this Old Kingdom title was the apartment or group of apartments in his palace wherein the Pharaoh was assisted at his daily toilet by specially privileged courtiers."

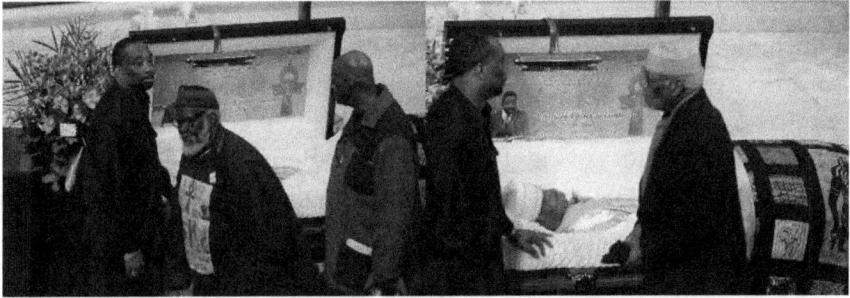

**Black History extravaganza - Photo** - Dr. Ben's son, Kwame stands strong as Dr. Jack Felder visits (left); and again, Kwame stands form as Herb Boyd also offers condolences at the revered Dr. Ben rests majestically, after a well-lived life in defense of African people.

# FREDERICK MONDERSON

**Black History Extravaganza - Ceramic Art -** The Great Goose, a manifestation of Amon, in flight.

One thing should be pointed out, while the king was a divinity and son of a divinity there was still some difference between the two. Here too, an example is given by Blackman of the significance of portrait statues in the following (1918: 161) note: "It might have been expected that when the use of a portrait-statue was introduced into the funerary cult, the rite, as in the case of divinities, would have been performed in its presence and that the lustral water would have been sprinkled on it. But it must be borne in mind that there was this difference between the cult of divinities and the cult of dead kings; if the cultus-statue of a divinity were to have been destroyed or to have perished with age it would have been replaced, for the worship of a divinity was for the benefit of the community; the maintenance of the

# BLACK HISTORY EXTRAVAGANZA HONORING DR. BEN-JOCHANNAN

cult of dead kings, however, was in most cases for their own benefit only, and their successors could hardly, therefore, be expected to renew their statues if any mishap befell them, hence the only safe course was to wall them up."

In the ceremony of "The King of Egypt Grace Before Meat" as described by A.M. Blackman in *the Journal of Egyptian Archaeology*, Vol. 31 (December 1945: 72) in which "the title of the offering-formula, 'Presenting pieces of flesh,' which that formula itself identifies with 'pieces of flesh' of the hawk's foes, asserting that they have been cut up in his presence.... Then that meal must be regarded as a sacramental rite the object of which was not merely the satisfying of the Pharaoh's hunger, but, as was the ultimate object of so many religious ceremonies, the ensuring of the safety and well-being of his person and of the death and elimination of his enemies. In this particular case, their death as enacted in the preparations for the meal, i.e., in the slaughtering and dismembering of cattle and poultry, their final destruction in the eating of the joints and other meat-portions served up for the royal repast, which, thus, it might well be supposed, assumed the character of a triumphal banquet. What favors this interpretation is the fact that it fully explains why the King's 'Grace' includes an invocation addressed to Sekhmet, for one of the chief functions of this goddess was to protect the King from his enemies and to destroy them. That she should be invited, therefore, to be present and play her part at the enacting and celebration of their destruction appears particularly appropriate."

All this notwithstanding, while there is a religious, theosophical or spiritual aspect to the temple, this survivability equally depended on an economic incentive that supported the sustainability of the sacred space. It's like the church needing funds to continue its work. Early theorists have postulated the view, priests were the earliest architects, in their other worldly connection with the divine who instructed them psychically as to the dimensions and spatial arrangement of the principal features of the sacred space. However, temples were generally gifts of monarchs who actually built them. Having done so, they next created economic endowments to sustain their creation as an obligation to their father, being sons of the god in the divine lineage with its attendant obligations, responsibilities and benefits. Yet, having been endowed with the structure and "seed money," the caretakers of the temple sought to economically increase their largess by initiating a number of strategies such as the manufacture of crafts and creation of building and decorative skills that beautified their residence but also became trade commodities. Agricultural produce was grown to feed residents and surplus food exported in trade. Gardens produced flowers that were an essential part of the daily ritual of lustration of the god. Temple land holding were rented for rental income. Nonetheless, as Nelson maintains a "considerable burden" of taxation was placed on the peasant class who, for the most part, bore it cheerfully. Thus, this involved an untold number of individuals working in harmony depending on the size of the temple and the prominence of the god relative to the age in which he was worshipped.

In addition, the temples became schools that trained members of the government bureaucracy, produced medical and dental professionals, catered to mortuary needs of high and low and became literary help-centers for the majority of the population who were illiterate and needed documents such as letters, contracts, wills, etc. Again, and particularly more important, as the god and priests conspired to instill an imperialist mentality in vigorous warrior pharaohs, who went forth to conquer, significant portions of their captured spoils were donated to the temple as endowments for the deity who had brought good fortune to these kings. The most significant example of this relationship is that of Thutmose III and Amon who engineered his claim to the throne and was splendidly rewarded with booty from his imperial conquests.

# BLACK HISTORY EXTRAVAGANZA HONORING DR. BEN-JOCHANNAN

**Black History Extravaganza - Photo -** At Abu Simbel Temple, the hand of Rameses extends above a **"Table of Offerings"** to Amon as Min with Mut at his rear.

# FREDERICK MONDERSON

**Black History Extravaganza** - Dr. Ben's Book **- The Black man's or the "negro's" bicentennial year of ??? from 1619-20 to 1976 C.C.: Black Mental Illness and the Bicentennial - Volume I**

# BLACK HISTORY EXTRAVAGANZA
# HONORING DR. BEN-JOCHANNAN

the Black Man's,
or the "negro's"
bicentennial year
of ??? from
1619 - 20 to 1976 C.E.

BLACK MENTAL ILLNESS AND THE BICENTENNIAL
Volume I

A Socio-political and Anthropological
Student's and Researcher's Edition

by...
Yosef ben-Jochannan

Vstg. Prof. of History, Africana Studies and
Research Center, Cornell University, Ithaca,
New York

Adjct. Prof. of History, Shaw University,
Raleigh, North Carolina

Adjct. Assoc. Prof. of History, Malcolm-King
College, Harlem, New York City, New York

Alkebu-lan Books Associates
[a subsidiary of Alkebu-lan Foundation, Inc.]
209 West 125th Street, New York, New York

*From Yosef A. A. ben-Jochannan*
*to Federick Monderson, July 27, 1977.*

Copyright © by Yosef ben-Jochannan, New York City, New York, 1976 C.E./A.D. All rights reserved. No part of this book may be reproduced in any form whatsoever without the expressed written consent of the author or his representatives. Front cover design by the author and protected under this copyright [see other page for details of the collage, etc.]

**Black History Extravaganza** - Dr. Ben's Book - **The Black man's or the "negro's" bicentennial year of ??? from 1619-20 to 1976 C.C.: Black Mental Illness and the Bicentennial - Volume I - Overleaf of the Cover Page.**

# FREDERICK MONDERSON

This increased wealth enabled the god's domain to be significantly beautified and expanded, so much so, the Middle Kingdom and New Kingdom capital temple at Karnak, home of the Empire God Amun (Amen, Amon), experienced 2000 years of "vegetative growth" as untold numbers of pharaohs vied with each other to reward the good fortune the god granted them.  In all this, the priests having formed their confederated body called the Priesthood came to wield significant power and influence in their own right, becoming "king makers" and "king breakers."

However, while the strong kings manipulated the priests through endowments, buildings and the threat of their military prowess, their weak counterparts stood in awe of the priests because, though they claimed to be gods on earth, the priests as true god intermediaries knew these kings' weaknesses. They themselves, however, were unsure how much the priests knew or how much power and influence they could wield with the god.  It's like the older priests knew where all the skeletons were! Notwithstanding, and though the nation declined in its material and military power, its religious beliefs and spirituality remained a potent force even though conquerors came, destroyed much and even tried to inculcate and emulate what Egyptians had been doing for three thousand years of pharaonic rule. Notwithstanding, thousands of years later, this spirituality is still evident when one visits the temple.  That is, providing one's mind and body is in the right place to recognize this spiritual phenomenon.

The architecture created in the sacred space is a fascinating subject that challenges the imagination, excites the intellect and titillates the art appreciation *sensitivities* regarding the august house of the god. The well-known Dr. Yosef ben-Jochannan has always emphasized studying to understand the principal architectural features of the temple. In so doing, he instructed his students to visit the Hypostyle Hall at Karnak five or six times so as to comprehend what the magnificent hall stands for, as a "forest at creation." Equally to complement this admonition and directive, Mann in his work *Sacred Architecture* (1993: 14) has supplied a very penetrating view in describing several ways in which the symbolic or the spiritual is

# BLACK HISTORY EXTRAVAGANZA HONORING DR. BEN-JOCHANNAN

expressed through sacred architecture manifesting in sacred space. These are: "First, sacred architecture reflects the structure of the cosmos. Before there were buildings, humanity worshipped the stars and planets, the four elements, the earth, and its animals and plants, as gods. In our progression from caves to modern buildings, the symbolism of this early integration with the cosmos has been central, and still activates the deepest essence within us, the core of our psyche. Initially, sacred monuments were associated with a particular god, goddess, or the natural or supernatural powers they represented. They were aligned by or with the stars or planets in the sky, which represented the god or goddess. They were also geographically oriented and located in places significant to the gods. Some monuments were used by priests or priestesses as observatories to measure the movements of the planets or heavenly bodies they worshipped, while others were sited in accordance with planetary motions. Most megalithic monuments echoed some or all of these functions in their siting, design and function."

"Second, sacred monuments were organized using primary geometric shapes and proportions, described by number symbolism. Mathematical mysticism or sacred geometry is a profound part of sacred architecture, and it's often mentioned in relation to the Egyptians and Pythagoreans. Pythagoras created a humanistic philosophy which utilized mathematical harmony and proportion as primary tools in daily life, including art, architecture, music, morality and history. He believed that the order inherent in numbers, a number symbolism, creates specific effects on the observer, both psychologically and spiritually. The discovery of the innate meaning of numbers is therefore a primary creative legacy of sacred architecture. The exploration of the numbers and proportions of the sacred brings a higher understanding to architecture."

# FREDERICK MONDERSON

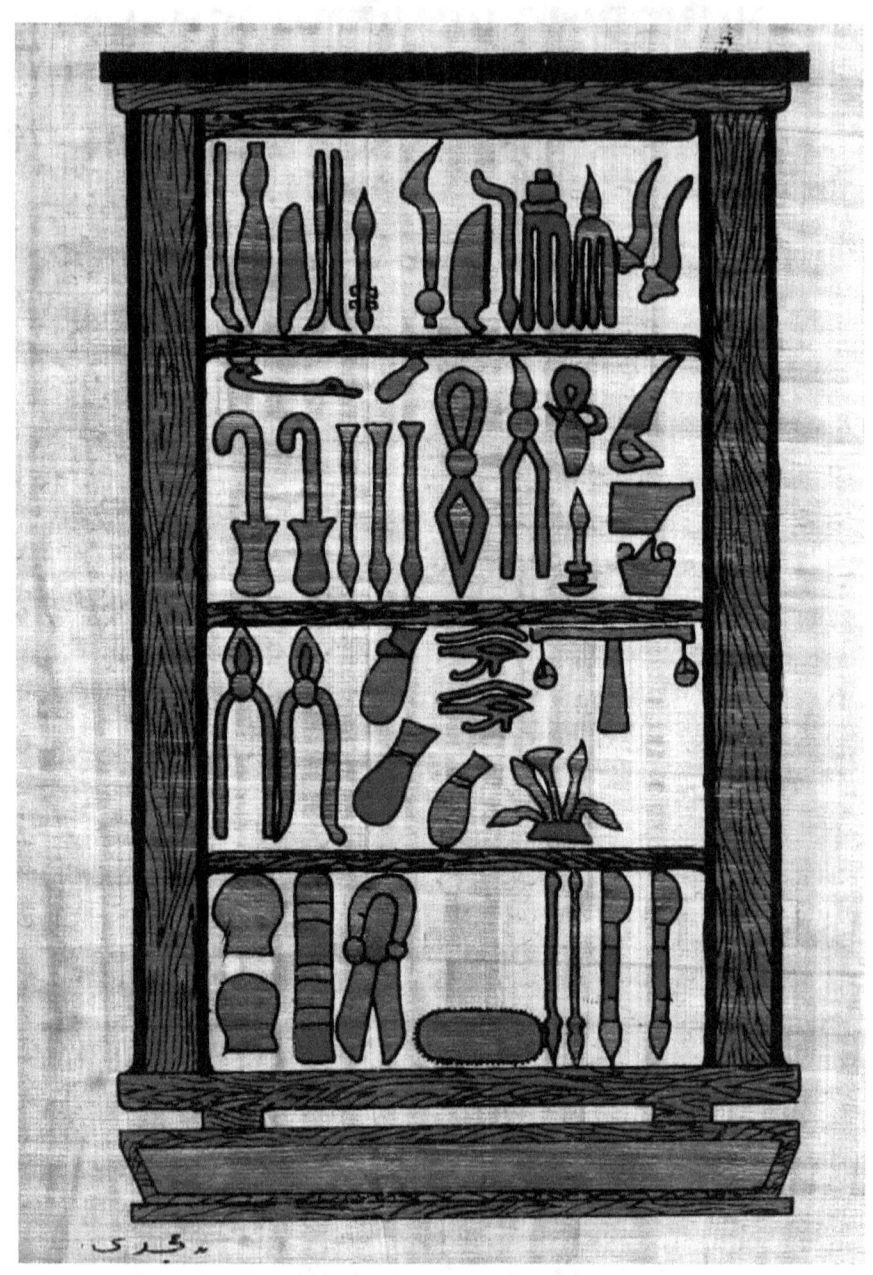

**Black History Extravaganza - Papyrus -** A sort of "cabinet case" exhibiting various instruments and symbols.

# BLACK HISTORY EXTRAVAGANZA HONORING DR. BEN-JOCHANNAN

"Third, the sacred lives in buildings or monuments in which the structure and decoration follow clear and basic patterns derived from the ancient conception of the four elements, earth, water, air, and fire, the forms of nature and from living energies and the geometries derived from them. Proportion systems amplifying natural rhythms and patterns bring a natural and organic energy and spirituality to sacred architecture - the building contains an elemental as well as a human quality evoking the spiritual."

As a result, Mann (1993: 106-07) concludes: "The creation of sacred buildings echoes the creation of the universe, and both seek to follow similar mathematical laws. Therefore, the Golden Section (phi) is found to govern the growth of plants and animals, and is also the primary proportion found in sacred buildings and monuments. In their use of numbers as a symbolic language, the Egyptians predate and influence Pythagoras and Plato. The Egyptians communicated symbolic astrological and astronomical concepts beyond the actual form of the buildings. Similarly, their hieroglyphic language used symbols instead of mere signs. A sign has a limited meaning, while a symbol evokes correspondences and widens understanding. The Egyptians used their mythology to further understanding because it was more than simple history. Their gods came from the stars, beginning wisdom, understanding and power. Their myths were cosmic myths, describing planetary movements, and brought the mathematic reality of the stars to humanity."

Interesting, however, throughout the duration of my association with Dr. Ben-Jochannan, as student, at his home exhibiting his library or on his many trips to Egypt, he has always emphasized architecture and particularly temple architecture as most reflective as totality of the Nile Valley cultural experience. Without question, his favorite has been Karnak Temple. Whether it has been because of his association with the venerated Brother Abdul, a "Master of Karnak," Professor George Simmonds, another "Master of Karnak" or the fact of the temple's size, duration in construction or the multi-faceted features of its wholeness, Dr. Ben greatly emphasized the significant resident deity, Amon or Amon-Ra, his family and the sister or twin home in

# FREDERICK MONDERSON

Luxor Temple. Within Karnak itself, his favorite location has been the Hypostyle Hall built and decorated by Rameses I, Seti I, and Rameses II. He also made us aware there were principally two types of temples, worship or god temples and king or mortuary temples. Karnak and Luxor are New Kingdom worship temples. Dendera, Philae and Edfu are also worship temples built during the Graeco-Roman period. Deir el Bahari, temple of Hatshepsut; the Ramesseum of Rameses II and Medinet Habu of Rameses III, are New Kingdom mortuary temples. That is, temples built to worship the king in life and in death. Not much has survived of late or (Greco) Graeco-Roman mortuary temples. Within the two types of temples there were two types of sanctuaries, open and closed. The open sanctuary is generally associated with the Sun-god which allowed his rays to penetrate into the sanctuary altar upon rising and setting. The closed sanctuary was associated with a particular god whose mysteriousness manifested in the darkened environment. Since the god or his emblem resided therein, that is, the sanctuary was called "heaven" and when the pharaoh or high priest visited the sacred spot he was said to "open the doors of heaven." However, this feature is not to exclude since Amon was worshipped at Karnak (and open Sanctuary), and at Luxor, a closed sanctuary.

In addition, there were two forms of temples, free standing and rock-cut. Karnak, Luxor, Ramesseum and Medinet Habu were free standing temples. So too were Dendera, Philae and Edfu.

Let me elaborate further by using a local analogy to clarify the difference between the free standing and rock cut temples. I will use our own domestic architecture to clarify my position. Some houses are built to stand alone. These are called detached. So, for example, we have range houses, sometimes four structures attached such as numbers 1, 2, 3, 4. Numbers 1 and 4 are called semi-detached. That is, 1 has 2 on one side and 4 has 3 on one side, the other side is "vacant" or blank. On the other hand, while 2 has 1 and 3 on both its sides and 3 has 2 and 4 on its sides. These are called attached. Now the free-standing temples may have associated temples nearby but not attached. The rock-cut temples are different; they represent the second form of temple. That is, generally they are dug into a mountainside.

# BLACK HISTORY EXTRAVAGANZA HONORING DR. BEN-JOCHANNAN

In their siting of temples geographical features play an important part. Free standing temples are generally constructed on a hill. Rock cut temples are dug into a mountain and there is a belief the mountain is part of the divine sacred realm. In his article "Temples" in *The Oxford Encyclopedia of Ancient Egypt* Vol. 3, edited by Donald B. Redford (Oxford University Press, 2001: 363-379) Rolf Gundlach (2001: 370) explained how this aspect of the natural architectural feature factors in temple design. He states as an example: "Thus the towering rock behind the mortuary temple of Mentuhotep II in Deir el-Bahari should be viewed as part of the temple itself, because not only is the tomb of the king deeply thrust into the rock, but the cultic image chamber is also designed as a niche built into the rock. The same holds true for the Amun temple in Gebel Barkal [Ethiopia], behind which rises a high promontory that can be interpreted as a statue of Amun on account of its natural shape. The mountain itself, called "pure (= holy) mountain," the bowels of which are reckoned to be in the otherworld, is the seat of sacred powers. This can be seen clearly in the main valley of the Wadi Hammamat, the southern wall of which is seen as the 'palace' of the local god Min (time of Mentuhotep II). The goddess of the dead, Hathor, in Western Thebes is depicted stepping out of her house, the rock wall mentioned above."

Equally, the nearby "semi-detached" temple of Hatshepsut fits into this category somewhat. I say semi-detached from Mentuhotep's temple though it was actually alongside. However, Thutmose III of the 18$^{th}$ Dynasty came and built his temple, a small one between the two larger structures, Mentuhotep's 11$^{th}$ Dynasty and his sister or aunt Hatshepsut's 18$^{th}$ Dynasty structure, making three temples in the same location with the mountain as a backdrop. Yet, only Thutmose III's temple could be considered attached, having temples on both sides, while the others would be semi-detached, having only one temple on one side. Now, while Mentuhotep's tomb is principally in the mountain, Hatshepsut's is somewhat similar though some features stretch from the Valley Temple to the rock face and the Sanctuary is dug into the mountain. Equally, Hatshepsut's tomb is in the Valley of the Kings which required a circuitous voyage around the mountain to reach the place of internment. To solve this "problem" the queen designed and began to construct a tunnel beneath the mountain to link her temple and tomb in order to be taken directly to internment after the funeral ceremony. Unfortunately, the soil was soft and could not sustain such a project and the plan was abandoned. However, and conversely, Rameses II's 19$^{th}$ Dynasty worship temple at Abu Simbel and the adjoining temple of his wife Nefertari are both dug entirely in the mountain. The king's temple was dedicated to 4 gods, Ra-Harakhte the sun-god; Amon-Ra, combination of Amon and Ra, the New Kingdom god; Ptah, god of artisans, people who make things and he constructed the heavens; and Rameses II, the king, himself deified as a god. His wife's temple was dedicated to Hathor though Ptah and Horus are represented within.

An interesting feature of this temple, somewhat like the open temple, in which the sun god's rays bathed the altar upon which his image was placed; was that on the morning of the king's birthday October 22 and again February 22; when the sun rose, its rays penetrated into the deep recesses of the temple to bathe the king's statue as it stood beside the other three gods. From right to left sat Rameses II, Ra-Harakhte, Amon-Ra and Ptah. The sun, however, only bathe three gods; it never touched Ptah sitting next to Amon-Ra. However, with the construction of the Aswan High Dam, this temple in Nubia and several, some 20 other temples, were in danger of being submerged. **UNESCO** appealed to nations that had experience in Nile Valley archaeology to come and hurriedly dig and try to save some of these that would be lost forever in the newly created Lake Nasser. So, the temple was photographed, cut up into many pieces and raised to a higher location that duplicated the original site. However, despite modern technological advances they were never able to have the sun bathe the king again on his birthday.

Two things are to be considered in this region of Africa, particularly about moving temples. The Temple of Philae dedicated to Goddess Isis and the Temple of Kalabsha dedicated to God Mendulese were both moved because of the dams at Aswan. The "Low Dam" built in 1902 and the "High Dam" especially built in the 1960s displaced

# BLACK HISTORY EXTRAVAGANZA
# HONORING DR. BEN-JOCHANNAN

many Nubians. The Nubians call them the "Damn Dam" because they displaced thousands in villages and submerged their culture. Philae was moved to nearby Agilka Island specially rearranged to duplicate its original location and remove it from being submerged when the river rose. Kalabsha was photographed and cut up into 16,000 pieces then relocated and set up nearby again out of the river's way.

**Black History Extravaganza** - Dr. Ben's Book - **Influence of Great Myths on Contemporary Life, or The Need for Black History in Mental Health: Black Mental Illness and the Bicentennial - Volume II**

# FREDERICK MONDERSON

Influence Of Great Myths
On Contemporary Life,
or
The Need For Black History
In Mental Health[1]

BLACK MENTAL ILLNESS AND THE BICENTENNIAL
Volume II

A Socio-political and
Anthropological Student's
and Researcher's Edition

by...
Yosef ben-Jochannan

Vstg. Prof. of History, Africana Studies and
Research Center, Cornell University, Ithaca,
New York

Adjct. Prof. of History, Shaw University,
Raleigh, North Carolina

Adjct. Assoc. Prof. of History, Malcolm-King
College, Harlem, New York City, New York

Top: Africans [BLACKS]
of Carthage "Sign Of Tanit"
ca. 300 ♦ B.C.E. Bot.:Nile
Valley "Ankh" 4100 B.C.E.

Alkebu-lan Books Associates
[a subsidiary of Alkebu-lan Foundation, Inc.]
205 West 125th Street, New York, New York

*From Yosef A. ben-Jochannan
to Frederick Monderson. July
24, 1997.*

---
1. Based on a "PAPER" of like name [see pages 1 – 6] and
"EXTEMPORANEOUS LECTURE", with "QUESTION AND
ANSWER PERIOD", presented to the State of New York, Department of Mental Hygiene's "MINORITY SUMMER MEDICAL and ADMINISTRATIVE SEMINAR", at New York School of Psychiatry, Wards Island, New York City, N.Y. [Dunlap Bldg.], July 28, 1975 – Audrey P. Harvey: Convenor/Coordinator/etc.

**Black History Extravaganza -** Dr. Ben's Book **- The Black man's or the "negro's" bicentennial year of ??? from 1619-20 to 1976 C.C.: Black Mental Illness and the Bicentennial - Volume II - Overleaf of the Cover Page.**

# BLACK HISTORY EXTRAVAGANZA HONORING DR. BEN-JOCHANNAN

In the salvage work conducted by various nations, the University of Chicago team led by Keith Seele discovered and deposited in the basement of the University Museum, what turned out to be evidence published in *The New York Times* entitled, "The world's earliest monarchy or kingship discovered at Qustol, Nubia." Recovered was an image showing the king on a throne and wearing a White Crown, as well as a palace façade, an incense burner, ships, etc. We see this symbolism some 200-years later in Egypt, seeming to indicate this is where it originated.

Now, there is a reason the temple is significant for besides being the home of the Nome or national god, it was also the nucleus and barometer of the nation's economic, philosophic, religious, spiritual and moral well-being. Just as the mind of Egypt understood the philosophical concept of the laws of opposites, religiosity and spirituality, these ancient Africans believed there were good and bad spirits or forces operating in nature and affecting man's existence. The function of the good forces as represented by the god and his disciples led by the pharaoh was to maintain harmony in nature and thus the well-being of the society. That is, such being contingent upon the king and subordinates behaving in a certain manner in respect to their cosmological and earthly obligations.

**Black History Extravaganza - Tomb of Nakht** - Black and white etching of the Nobleman in various attitudes.

# FREDERICK MONDERSON

**Black History Extravaganza - Photo -** An example of one of the eight standing colossal statues of the king wearing the Double Crown at Rameses II Abu Simbel Temple.

# BLACK HISTORY EXTRAVAGANZA HONORING DR. BEN-JOCHANNAN

Among those obligations were the practices of righteousness, washing for cleanliness and purity. Strange that while these three attributes were applied to the gods, they were also applied and expected of kings and deceased persons. The king as the Son of God, himself a god on earth though not possessing the full attributes of "godship" until dead and ascended into the heavenly realm; having had to manifest righteousness, truth and justice; and such was also expected of his subordinates. In this responsibility, he was expected to demonstrate purity and especially when he presided in the temple ritual he was required to be purified through baptism. This cleansing or washing for purity purposes as applied to the gods and king must also be applied to the deceased, for in order to ascend and to dwell in the divine realm, everyone must be purified.

Blackman, in quoting Kurt Sethe, explained: "A striking feature of Egyptian religious texts is the way in which the so-called Pyramid Texts states he is frequently represented as undergoing purification by washing in the Field or Pool of Earu or in the Field of Life. According to the Piankhi Stele, l. 101f., the Sun-god was wont to wash his face in the Cool Pool, the Stream of Nun, which seems to have been situated somewhere between Heliopolis and Kher-Eha. The purification which the texts describe was apparently a daily matutional one, preceding the god's appearance above the Eastern horizon. Two passages in the Pyramid Texts indicate that Horus and Thoth acted in the capacity of the Sun-god's bath-attendants, rubbing his back and feet at the conclusion of his ablutions. Another passage represents the goddess Kebhowet as emptying four pitchers of water over him. The same collection of texts informs us that after his ablutions Nut, the Sky-goddess, grasped the arm of the Sun-god, who, with the assistance of Shu, was thus drawn up into heaven."

# FREDERICK MONDERSON

**Black History Extravaganza - Ceramic Art -** Fancy ankh surrounded by twisted Flax or thread.

In the texts, Pyramid 710a and Aylward Blackman in "Sacramental Ideas and Usage" in *Proceedings of the Society of Biblical Archaeology* (March 13, 1918: 58) states: "The purity attributed to the Sun-god also characterizes the denizens of his celestial kingdom and the things connected with them and himself. For example: the abodes of the Sun-god are pure, those who voyage in the boat of Turn-Face, the celestial ferryman, the lotus flower which the Sun-god holds to his nose, the deceased Pharaoh's throne in heaven and his seat in the Sun-god's ship, neither of which he can occupy unless he is pure." The quality of "Life," generally rendered "good fortune," "protection," "stability," "health," and "happiness," is, in many special degree properties of the Sun-god. "Given life like Re," is a constantly

# BLACK HISTORY EXTRAVAGANZA
# HONORING DR. BEN-JOCHANNAN

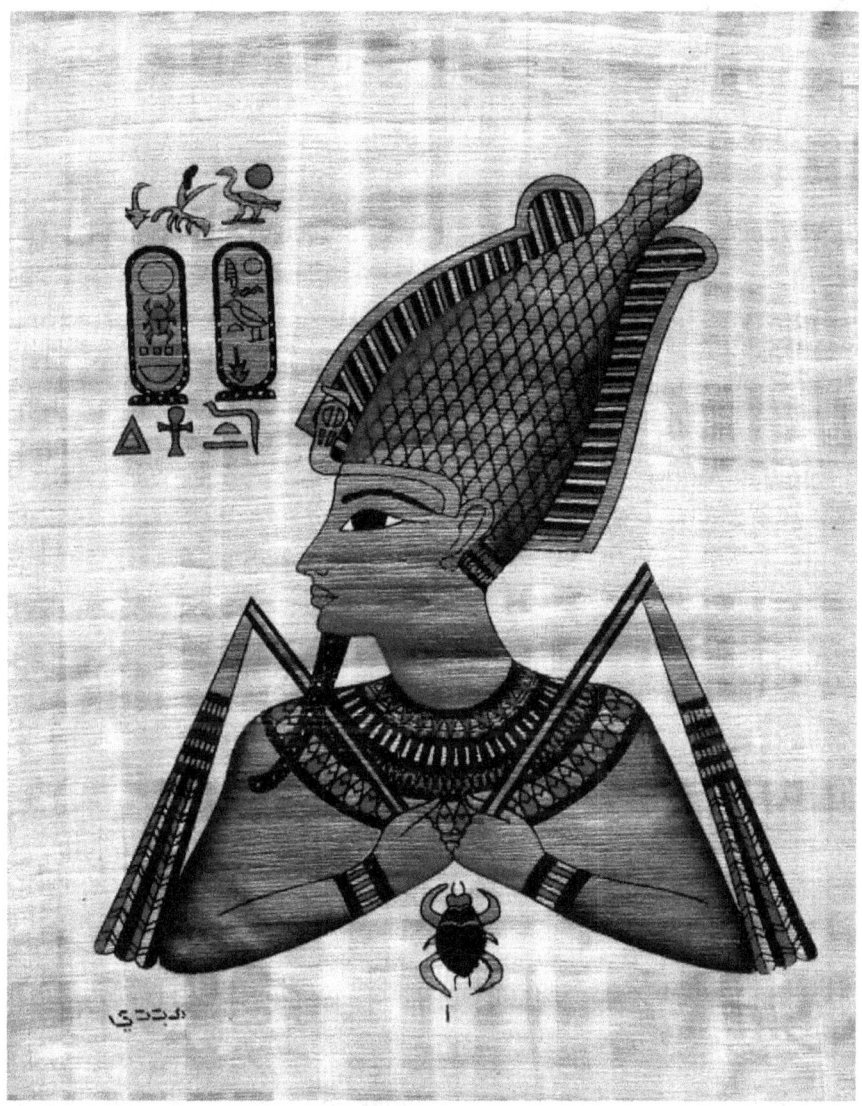

**Black History Extravaganza - Papyrus -** Osiris holding two whips or flails. Notice the God's beard is curved, while images of the king show him with a straight beard.

recurring Pharaonic attribute, and the following phrase, or an abbreviated version thereof, occurs behind the figure of the Egyptian sovereign in almost every relief in which he appears, "All protection, life, stability, good fortune, all health, all happiness, behind him like Ra, every day."

The Sun-god is generally characterized by his love of righteousness and his hatred of wrong doing. Blackman says, "A man had to be able to 'offer right to the great god, the lord of heaven,' 'in order that it might be well' with him 'in the great god's presence.' The Sun-god was believed actually to have created righteousness, and he was said to live (i.e. feed) on it, just as the Nile-god Hapi was said to live on fish." Thus, in a hymn to the Sun-god we find: - "I have come unto thee, lord of gods, Atum-Re-Harakhte, that I may present unto thee righteousness, for I know that thou livest thereon."

So, the uncontrolled actions of the bad spirits or forces were to wreak havoc and create disequilibrium in the state. As such then, constant worship and ritualizing of the good forces kept their opposites in check and the society prevailed and prospered in a harmonious manner. Thus, the temple served to maintain the perpetual flame of the nation's ethical and moral well-being, its philosophical compass and its requisite social equilibrium.

However, beside this religio-spiritual reality, the temple also served an economic function, in preserving its own financial survival. It served an administrative function not simply in managing their own affairs, economic and social; but also, that of the state or the king. They also engaged in training members of the state bureaucracy. They were the engineers of building and artistic decoration of their constructions; were *Avante Garde* as school of art decorating structures and crafting statues to represent man and god. They were medical institutions that taught medicine and also treated sick persons. They conducted embalming and other funerary practices; officiated at feasts, festivals and participated in processions; managed the nation's and the monarch's treasury and store-houses as well as their own property and treasury. They collected taxes and disbursed payments. Theirs were also a perpetual pursuit of astronomy, other sciences and every form of knowledge. These divine powerbrokers even goaded warrior pharaohs into imperialist ventures. Important, as the pharaoh's

# BLACK HISTORY EXTRAVAGANZA HONORING DR. BEN-JOCHANNAN

deputized representatives they served as middlemen between the god and men and could invoke divine presence. Thus, these people, the priests and their organization became powerful and such power threatened the normal function of the state.

**Black History Extravaganza** - Dr. Ben's Book - **Abu Simbel to Ghizeh: A Guide Book and Manual.**

# FREDERICK MONDERSON

*Respect and admiration to brother Monderson from Yosy Ben-Jochannan, Old Cataract Hotel, Aswan, Upper Egypt, Northeast Africa, Aug 1996*

# ABU SIMBEL TO GHIZEH

**Black History Extravaganza** - Dr. Ben's Book - **Abu Simbel to Ghizeh - Overleaf of the Cover Page.**

As was to be expected, not every temple and its god shared in the full or equal panoply of responsibilities and requisite rewards or benefits resulting from the functions outlined above. Depending on the period in question, whether Old, Middle or New Kingdom, at Heliopolis, Memphis or Thebes, the monarch lavished endowments, built or repaired structures and celebrated festivals at his favorite or more prominent divinity. At Heliopolis Ra was worshipped; at Memphis, it was Ptah; and at Thebes, the principal deity was Amon (Amun, Amen) along with his Triad and Ennead. However, while the fortunes of

# BLACK HISTORY EXTRAVAGANZA HONORING DR. BEN-JOCHANNAN

these gods rose and fell, Osiris as God of the Dead, housed at Abydos, remained consistent for most of dynastic duration. Nevertheless, while Memphite religious architecture of the Old Kingdom was creative and original, it did not last as long as the New Kingdom architecture particularly that originating at Thebes. It did, however, bequeath to the Middle Kingdom's its traditional features and techniques which in turn influenced that of the New Kingdom where, building upon the foundations of that earlier period, the later period was able to further innovate new ideas in its religious architecture. For example, in the Old Kingdom the god or worship temple was in close proximity to the king's mortuary temple with a subsidiary god temple nearby. Now, by the time of the New Kingdom, the god or worship temple was separated from the king or mortuary temple. Also, by the time of the imperial New Kingdom and the enormous wealth pouring into temple coffers, the worship temple became more elaborate and was generally situated on the east bank while the mortuary temple of the king was built on the west bank. Perhaps this is because "the God was born in the east and died in the west." Naturally, none of this was really "written in stone" for the worship Temple of Hathor at Medina is on the west bank and texts seem to indicate the Hypostyle Hall in Karnak, a worship temple, was indeed a mortuary temple of King Seti I.

**Black History Extravaganza - Photo -** A fallen colossal head of Rameses II at his Mortuary Temple, The Ramesseum.

## VII. FREDERICK MONDERSON
## WHO WERE THE ANCIENT EGYPTIANS?
### By
### Dr. Fred Monderson

## Introduction

Dr. Ben-Jochannan spent much of his teaching life lecturing, writing, pointing out, sponsoring trips to the "Holy Land," even arguing and proving the Africans of Egypt were much more than they are given credit for by scholars and others dominating the field of Egyptian studies. As one writer recently put it, "I know Europe kidnapped Egypt!" We must never forget, the New York radio personality Gary Byrd often admonished, "The information you don't have could kill you!" Now, in this technological age, the technical information you don't have is just as potent! This meant one has to be *Encyclopedic* in acquiring and assessing data of a historical relevance relating to the subject. This conceptual approach appropriately applies to understanding 'Who were, in fact, the Ancient Egyptians?' This means the search must be unending and widespread. Dr. Diop has argued not only have Western and American writers, omitted and distorted much about ancient Egypt but they have made it tremendously confusing, even in concert with unwitting natives and destroyed much. So much so, they have shattered and scattered the truth across a wide expanse of intellectual geography. As such, to this end, the proposition is well stated by Herbert J. Foster in "The Ethnicity of the Ancient Egyptians," published in the *Journal of Black Studies* Vol. 5 # 2 (December 1974: 175) which explains: "A persistent historical misconception has been that Black people have developed no important civilizations, nor have they made any significant contributions to world culture."

Dr. John Henrik Clarke, writing in *Freedomways*, Vol. 14, No. 4, and (1974: 345) in a Review quotes Cheikh Anta Diop in *The African Origin of Civilization: Myth or Reality* who noted: "Western historians for the last five hundred years wrote or rewrote history

# BLACK HISTORY EXTRAVAGANZA HONORING DR. BEN-JOCHANNAN

glorifying the people of European extraction and distorted the history of the rest of the world." This means the assiduous researcher must ferret out facts strewn in myriad bits of a jigsaw puzzle dynamic that must be challenged by unrelenting work of African historiographic reconstruction.

In the movie **Men of Honor**, the young diver was not unlike scholars' attempting to disentangle the twisted pretzel of ancient Egyptian interpretation. When, given parts to assemble underwater, while colleagues were given theirs in a bag; the hero's was thrown into the murky water. He had to find the parts on the ocean floor then assemble them. In similar fashion, the assiduous researcher seeking to rectify the ethnography of ancient Egypt must search far and wide but with persistence can still ferret out constructive existential gems often contradicting symbolic representations in order to make his case for an African and Black Ancient Egypt! However, the obstacles are formidable considering "top notch" European scholars; white historians have made quick reputations as authorities on African history and culture. Equally, in that racially malicious onslaught they expended much energy denigrating Africans and denying their role in Egypt, but in the process, have exposed a less than human mindset. Foster (1974: 175-176) exposed the bigotry, ignorance and falsity of a few whose influence has been far-reaching in helping to establish "The Conspiracy Against Ancient Egypt!"

# FREDERICK MONDERSON

**Black History Extravaganza** - Dr. Ben's Book - **Understanding the African Philosophic Concept behind the "Diagram of the Law of Opposites."**

# BLACK HISTORY EXTRAVAGANZA HONORING DR. BEN-JOCHANNAN

In this he states, "Hugh Trevor-Roper (1965: 1), Regis Professor of History at Oxford University, wrote: 'Undergraduates, seduced as always, by the changing breath of journalistic fashion, demand that they should be taught the history of black Africa. Perhaps in the future there would be some African history to teach. But at present there is none, or very little: there is only the history of Europeans in Africa. The rest is darkness.... Men existed even in dark countries and dark centuries, but to study their history would be to amuse ourselves with the unrewarding gyrations of barbarous tribes in picturesque but irrelevant corners of the globe." Even further, Foster writes: "Comments of European colonial administrators in Africa also reflected this misconception of the African past. Basil Davidson (1959: ix) has noted that in 1958 Sir Arthur Kirby, commissioner of British East Africa in London, told the Torquay Branch of the Overseas League that 'in the last sixty years... East Africa has developed from a completely primitive country, in many ways more backward than the 'Stone Age.' The former British Governor of Kenya, Phillip Mitchell (1968: 3), declared: 'The forty-two years I have spent in Africa ... cover a large part of the history of sub-Saharan Africa, for it can hardly be said to extend much further back than about 1870." That is 63 years after the British were forced to outlaw the Slave Trade and 36 years after outlawing Slavery in the British Empire, while holding the freedman in a "kind of Juneteenth" for another four years of apprenticeship after, these "civilized Englishmen" had grown "fat and flourishing" while perpetuating one of the more savage and barbaric acts dubbed "crimes against humanity." They then turned back and further effectuated colonialism's "direct rule" as an imperialist ploy to hold territory and employ Englishmen as they conducted all manner of surveys, mineralogical, botanical, cultural, artistic, so as to be able to export natural resources to feed industries in their home country! What Roper, Kirby and Mitchell should be ashamed of is English civilized barbarism and unlawful seizure of "culture in captivity" artifacts now adorning private and public collections in their land! Nevertheless, Foster (1974: 176) sums it all up in the following: "The real issue in this debate is not merely a matter of whether the ancient Egyptians were white or black, but that African blacks were well assimilated into

# FREDERICK MONDERSON

Egyptian society, and as such played a significant role in the development of this great cradle of Western civilization."

Notwithstanding all that has been said, in *Dawn of Conscience* (1933) James Henry Breasted, while examining the Pyramid Texts dismissed the anteriority and influence of Mesopotamia and Babylonia, origins of the Caucasians, over Egypt as "not warranting a response!" This is consistent with Diop's contention that "Egypt was a distinct African nation and was not historically or culturally a part of Asia or Europe. An even more alarming revelation deals with the 17$^{th}$ Dynasty. Most of what is said of this dynasty is that Sekenenra Tao died of an axe-blow to the head; the family waged the War of Liberation against the Hyksos; and the sons Kamose and Ahmose expelled the Hyksos and founded the 18$^{th}$ Dynasty and New Kingdom. This means, the 17$^{th}$ and 18$^{th}$ Dynasties are actually a continuation fused in one family rule. Practically nowhere is it stated as Flinders Petrie has, seemingly as an afterthought "Given away the goods" in "Egyptian Religion" published in *Encyclopedia of Religion and Ethics*, vol. 1, p. 247, "The XVIIth dynasty from Nubia, holding Thebes as its capitol," Thus, these irreconcilable facts challenge the contention of Emery, Derry, certainly Petrie himself, and especially John David Wortham that "The ancient Egyptians were Caucasians!"

Nevertheless, the challenge to most books on Western Civilization which begin with a chapter on Ancient Egypt that previously began with a chapter on Greece and Rome seem to express the unmistakable view the ancient Egyptian were Caucasians. The iconoclastic approach is necessary therefore because this falsity conflicts with the revelations made by critical, scholars on Egypt. Misguided books and writers ignore the constructive new analyses of the African world's methodology depicting the falsity of such an assumption most people are fed. Thus, in the search for the truth about the ancient Egyptians we must not simply look especially to modern documented and written history but also to the fields of archaeology, anthropology and art as well as a number of other specializations such as mathematics, science, medicine, philosophy, religion, hematology, biometrics, and more to truly and fully understand the culture and issues. Equally, we

# BLACK HISTORY EXTRAVAGANZA HONORING DR. BEN-JOCHANNAN

must insistently adhere to Dr. Yosef ben-Jochannan's admonition, "When doing research on ancient Egypt get the oldest materials you can find and work from there." Nonetheless and importantly, anyone who still believes the ancient Egyptians were Caucasian is either a moron, mis-educated or perniciously supports the notion of "white supremacy," which is in itself a fallacy. Prof. Diop admonished, "We must live and die on the battlefield of African historiographic reconstruction consciousness!" This means, whether you're in the front-line trenches or on the periphery of the struggle, you must have all the available information. You must know who is saying what about the culture of ancient Africa, the Nile Valley and Egypt and Ethiopia. Equally, one must be more fully apprised of what the historical record reveals about the ancient Egyptians. That is to say, how do we reconcile the existential data that conflicts with the symbolic representation?

Further, in that disparate reservoir of knowledge, an important work entitled, *The Predynastic Origin of Egyptian Hieroglyphs: Evidence for the Development of Rudimentary Forms of Hieroglyphs in Upper Egypt in the Fourth Millennium, B.C.*, William S. Arnett (University Press of America, 1982) is wide-ranging in critique of the literature and states, yet offers half a loaf in the statement: "In reference to Dr. Diop's theories, this writer would like to say that he agrees with the latter's refutation of the efforts to define the 'Dynastic Race' as being 'white,' but finds his efforts to prove that the ancient Egyptians were black 'unconvincing.'" Nevertheless, and in as much as Mr. Arnett has done a credible job assessing some of the literature regarding the origins of the ancient Egyptians, he certainly got it wrong regarding Dr. Diop's position! In fairness, he did not challenge Wortham's statement in *Genesis of British Egyptology* statement that the Egyptians were "Caucasians!" Still, while this falsity has attracted many disciples, it has yet been proven to be just that! Falsity! Consider Diop in "Origin of the Ancient Egyptians" in Van Sertima's *Egypt Revisited* (1991: 14) who clearly contends: "In the tomb of King Ka (first dynasty) at Abydos Petrie found a plaque showing an Indo-European captive in chains with his hands behind his back. Elliott Smith considers that the individual represented is a Semite. The dynastic epoch has also yielded the documents illustrative in Pls. 1.9 and 1.14 showing Indo-European and Semitic prisoners. In contrast, the typically Negroid features of the Pharaohs (Narmer, first dynasty the actual founder of the Pharaonic line; Zoser, third dynasty, by whose time all the technological elements of Egyptian civilization were already in evidence; Cheops, the builder of the first Great Pyramid, a Cameroon type; Mentuhotep, founder of the eleventh dynasty, very black; Sesostris I; Queen Ahmosis-Nefertari, and Amenophis I show that all classes of Egyptian society belonged to the black race." Again, for purposes of clarity, if this writer quotes or use a name such as Amenophis it is simply this is the Greek version of the name and it is how Flinders Petrie especially helped ingrain such uses as part of the conspiracy to misrepresent. Dr. Ben-Jochannan was the first among African-American scholars, to insist on and began using the indigenous names. Amenophis should be Amenhotep and Tuthmosis should be Thutmose. Nevertheless, and in the broader dimension of history Dr. Diop established a niche, Prof. John Henrik Clarke (1974: 341) argued, that, "history cannot be restricted by the limits of ethnic groups, nation, or culture. Roman history is Greek as well as Roman, and both the Greek and Roman histories are Egyptian because the entire Mediterranean was civilized Egyptian; and Egypt in turn borrowed from other parts of Africa especially Ethiopia."

**Black History Extravaganza - Photo -** At Abu Simbel, Rameses II kneels to present two ointment vases and behind him his cartouche enclosed by Uraei, all three wearing sun disks.

# BLACK HISTORY EXTRAVAGANZA HONORING DR. BEN-JOCHANNAN

**Black History Extravaganza - Papyrus -** Replica of the death mask of King Tutankhamon.

# FREDERICK MONDERSON

Even further, Dr. Clarke (1974: 341) states: "Africa came into the Mediterranean world mainly through Greece, which had been under African influence. The first Greek invasion was peaceful and scholarly. This invasion brought in Herodotus. Egypt had lost its independence over a century before his visit. This was the beginning of the period of foreign domination over Egypt that would last, in different forms, for two thousand years."

Nevertheless, and principally, in iconoclastic refutation of Indo-European claims, Diop laid it down in his *African Origins of Civilization: Myth or Reality*, that "though the branches" of his "tree could use some pruning, the roots and trunk is fundamentally strong." That is, while African Origins, an original Doctoral Thesis may have had some flaws, Diop's maturity was proven in the 1974 Cairo Conference when he and Theophile Obenga outdistanced the pedestrian competition in his classic presentation of the "Origin of the Ancient Egyptians" in "The Peopling of the Nile Valley" that formed the basis of **UNESCO's** final report affirming the "fundamental blackness of ancient Egypt."

The "great researcher" Dann*y Kaye* in his monumental and groundbreaking work *The King's New Clothes* eloquently articulated and identified that the king was not wearing anything as he paraded before the people. He was embarrassingly naked! Equally, Baron de Montesquieu, author of the *Spirit of the Laws*, has argued that man should 'act as if your actions,' and in this case, writings, 'can become a universal law.' Now, when we examine some early writings on Egypt that fall within what by today's standards we can easily call pseudo-scientific writings; in view of historical revelations, such work certainly emerges as questionable and pejorative at best. At worst, it appears somewhat dishonest, vindictive and mean-spirited, some say racist! As part of the great conspiracy regarding distortion and omission, Prof. John H. Clarke, in his "Introduction" to Anthony Browder's *Nile Valley Contributions to Civilization* (1992: 9) puts it best in the statement: "Except for Egypt, African people have been programmed out of the respectable commentary of history. Europeans have claimed the non-African creation of Egypt in order to downgrade the position of African people in world history. They have laid the

# BLACK HISTORY EXTRAVAGANZA HONORING DR. BEN-JOCHANNAN

foundation of what they called Western civilization on a structure that the Western mind did not create. In doing so, they have used no logic!" Let us also remember, Prof. John Clarke equally pointed out, "The people who preached racism colonized history," and that "When Europe colonized the world, it also colonized the world's knowledge!"

Let us first not forget, modern interpretation of the culture of ancient Egypt/Kemet in contemporary times has been essentially oriented as Europeans ascended the Nile from North to South as opposed to the flow of the river and culture it created emanating from South to North and therein lies the conundrum; some say misinterpretation, some say racist, view of ancient Egypt and its relationship with Africa or should we say, Africa's relationship with Egypt, "Ethiopia's eldest daughter." As an example, we know the Tigris-Euphrates Rivers flowed from North to South. The comparative view would be to argue civilization ascended the river by an invading force that created the culture. This is the type of argument being presented in the European conception of culture ascending the Nile River. This is also why Diop argued Eduardo Naville "got it wrong" in that "his right side was to the west rather than the east banks of the Nile." Additionally, Naville is not the only one whose interpretation has been termed wrong, viz., Maspero, Petrie, Erman, etc. There is no question these individuals made great contributions to the field but none has ever recanted any statement they made. At least Diop said, his tree "could use some pruning!"

Pardon this quotation but it says essentially what needs be said. In the article "King: Egyptian" George Foucart in *Encyclopedia of Religion and Ethics*, Vol. 7, (1914: 712-13) states: "This figuration of the king as heir of the crown of the north and crown of the south is of purely sacerdotal origin, and not historical, resting upon an astrological conception of the division of the world and its forces. It was regarded as figuring a state of things which had actually existed in Egypt, and it has given rise to the idea that at the period anterior to history there had really been two kingdoms in Egypt, one of the north and one of

# FREDERICK MONDERSON

the south, and that they were united under Menes I. Most scholars seem to have adopted that view, unconsciously investigated, perhaps, by the opinion of the first Egyptologists, who were more or less influenced themselves by some fugitive connections with Biblical history. Things took place probably in a less simple manner, and the collection of kingdoms or of pre-historic principalities of which Egypt was formed must rather have passed through phases similar to those of the formation of the modern kingdom of the 'King of Kings' of Ethiopia."

Conversely, because of its relation to the Nile, at its headwaters, the ancients believed the Ethiopians influenced Egypt. Prof Clarke quotes Gaston Maspero (1846-1916) who wrote: "By the almost unanimous testimony of the ancient historians, they [the Egyptians] belong to an African race which first settled in Ethiopia on the Middle Nile: following the course of the river, they gradually reached the sea." Equally significant, in ancient times all Black Africans were thought to be Ethiopians. However, like "split infinitives" Africans have been so segmented through academic differentiation designed to pinpoint and exacerbate differences; yet, a Greek or Italian, even Syrians and Nordics are all considered Caucasians, Europeans, viz., "white people." However, as the Afrocentrist Molefi Asante rightly pointed out, "There are no white people in Europe, only English, British, Scots, Germans, Spanish, French, Italians, Swiss, etc." It is only in America there are "white people."

The existential record demonstrates Ethiopians have claimed they colonized Egypt, since the peoples of the Nile were the same, being only shades of difference in color. This is a substantially plausible argument. Culturally, many modern scholars not only "read the ancients" but also saw and referred to the resemblance or "Negro mold" of Egyptian statues and depicted such in their works. Khamit Indus Kush in his book, *The Missing Pages of "His-Story"* (1993: 42) quotes several writers regarding the connection between Egypt and Ethiopia. First, Basil Davidson in "The Ancient World and Africa, Who's Roots?" (*Race and Class*, XXIX, Autumn 1987, No. 2, p. 2) wrote: "The ancient Egyptians were black (in any variant you may prefer) - or, as I myself think, it more useful to say, were African, is a

# BLACK HISTORY EXTRAVAGANZA HONORING DR. BEN-JOCHANNAN

belief which has been denied in Europe since about 1830," not generally before. It is a denial, in short, that belongs to the rise of modern European imperialism, and has to be explained in terms of the 'new racism' specifically and even frantically, an anti-black racism, which went together with and was constantly nourished by that imperialism in train of an anti-black movement that got traction throughout medieval and early modern times. I say, 'new racism' because it followed and expanded that older racism coming into view and full realization which spread around Europe and gave birth to the Atlantic slave trade that reached its high point of 'take off' in about 1630." That is to say, the 'old racism' was part of an unconscionable 'naked imperialism of slave trade and slavery.' Subsequent 'enlightened imperialism' was justification for exploitation of material and intellectual resources resulting as part of an effort to stamp out the slave trade and spread Christianity in Africa; while the 'new racism' supported the methodology of administration and operational exploitation resulting in "intellectual imperialism."

However, as Kush has argued, despite the emerging and solidifying falsity, very early the American-Egyptologist George Gliddon in *Ancient Egypt: The New World* (1843: 59) reinforced the view: "The advocates of the African origin of the Egyptians cling to the superior antiquity of the pyramids of Meroe as a proof of the origin of civilization in Ethiopia, and its consequent descent into Egypt." Again, according to Kush, despite the "New Aryan model," Professor Rossellini, "accepts and continues the doctrine, of the descent of civilization from Ethiopia and the African origin of the Egyptians." Prof. Naumann equally believed: "We will first deal with the Ethiopians, as they are the nearest neighbors of the Egyptians, and further because it is historically affirmed that the latter originally migrated from Ethiopia. Indeed, the music of the Ethiopians offers strong internal evidence in support of the assertion." In *Prehistoric Nations* (New York: 1898, p. 276) John D. Baldwin wrote: "Diodorus Siculus adds to his statement that the laws, customs, religious observances, and letters of the ancient Egyptians closely resemble

# FREDERICK MONDERSON

those of the Ethiopians, 'the colony still observing the customs of their ancestors.'"

Such works lend further credence to the profound intellect of Prof. John Clarke (1974: 342) who wrote: "If Egypt is a dilemma in Western historiography, it is a created dilemma. The Western historians, in most cases, have rested the foundation of what is called 'Western civilization' on the false assumption or claim, that the ancient Egyptians were white people. To do this they had to ignore great masterpieces of Egyptian history written by other white historians who did not support this point of view, such as Gerald Massey's great Classic, *Ancient Egypt: The Light of the World* (1907) and his other works *A Book of the Beginnings* and *Natural Genesis*. These three are in two-volume sets. Other neglected works by white historians are *Politics, Intercourse and Trade of the Carthaginians, Ethiopians, Egyptians* by A.H.L. Heeren (1883) and *Ruins of Empire* by Count Volney (1787).

And on and on! Still, this is interesting because the existential record of the Egyptians had no recollection or record of their "ancestors" the "Caucasian migrants from Asia!" We cannot forget, Mosso in *Foundations of Mediterranean Civilization* explained: "The Asiatics never penetrated the Nile Valley nor the Aegean area."

**Black Extravaganza - Photo -** Ceramic vases of King Tutankhamon in the Cairo Museum.

# BLACK HISTORY EXTRAVAGANZA
# HONORING DR. BEN-JOCHANNAN

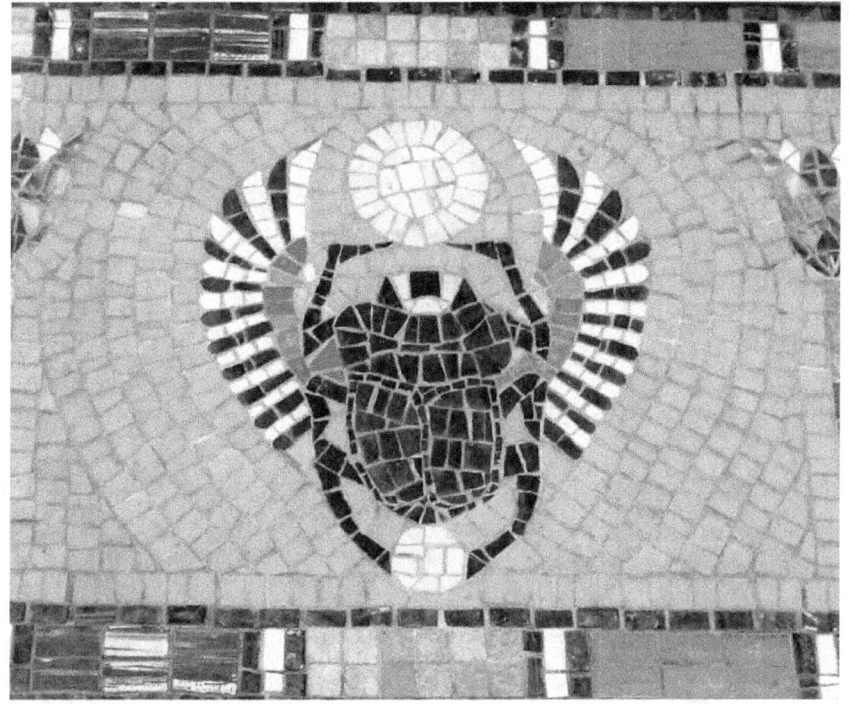

**Black History Extravaganza - Ceramic Art -** Khepre doing his job of pushing the ball of dung.

Now, in aftermath of the decision to build the Aswan High Dam, **UNESCO** appealed to nations with a history of excavation in Egypt to rescue evidence of Nubian monuments, especially temples and tombs that would be lost with the creation of Lake Nasser. Much of this is précis in the *Abu Simbel and The Nubian Monuments*: *Egypt Pocket Guide* by Alberto Siliotti, published by The American University in Cairo Press, 2000.

Significantly, from this effort, the work of Keith Seele, the leader of the American archaeological expedition, a great find was made. Bruce Williams, a graduate student, "mining the basement storage" of the University of Chicago discovered, from the remains of Qustul of the Kingdom of Ta-Seti, in Nubia, what *The New York Times* reported, "Evidence of the Earliest Monarch found in Nubia," evidence of

# FREDERICK MONDERSON

Pharaonic regalia, viz., white crown, 3 sailing boats, enthroned king, scepter and flail, incense burner, palace facade, etc., c. two hundred years before such appear in Egypt. This "field for mining" is not unique. Given that among others, on his return from Egyptian excavation, George Reisner offloaded hundreds of boxes at the University of California. Now, multiply this by the hundreds who excavated, collected and "carried home" and this can give one an inkling of the enormous Egyptian "artifacts in captivity" worldwide. Nevertheless, and underscoring this discovery, Dr. John H. Clarke previously had reminded, the Tasians, Badarians, the people from Merimde and Badari, all prehistoric Egyptians, were Negroes! In fact, he said, the Egyptian civilization, like a play, was "rehearsed in Ethiopia before it made its debut on the stage in Egypt."

We know of Bauval and Brophy *Black Genesis* regarding the people of Nabta Playa in the Western desert, Black Africans, who were "Predecessors of the Pharaohs;" and Toby Wilkinson's *Genesis of the Pharaohs* of the Eastern Desert whose Petroglyphs were "1000 years before Winkler's Mesopotamians." Despite what is called the "Delta cover-up theory," particularly if we accept Randall McIver's theory of "Two peoples, white and black, living side by side; whites in the north and blacks in the south;" we are confronted with the fact the south always predominated in all things, cultural, kingship, religion, etc. Seeking to argue that "the beginning of hieroglyphs" is of southern origin, Arnett indicates, "their origin antedates the coming of the Dynastic Egyptians into the Delta and lies in Upper Egypt (the south) and not in the Delta." Equally, in Diop's refutation of Moret's "Delta claims," he too argued while evidence of cultural origins and sites of historic monuments are located in the south and none in the Delta, Arnett again reinforces this view (1982: 1) in the statement: "The majority of Predynastic sites in Egypt are located either in Middle or Upper Egypt and are grouped in a line from north to south, and confined to a 160-mile stretch of the Nile Valley. These are: Deir Tasa, Badari, Naga-ed-Der, El Mahasna, Abydos, El Amrah, Diospolis Parva, Deir-el-Ballas, Coptos, Naqada, and Hierakonpolis. With the exception of the first two and the last-mentioned sites, all these are within an even more confined sixty-mile stretch of the Valley." Even further, in his *The Predynastic Origin of Egyptian*

# BLACK HISTORY EXTRAVAGANZA HONORING DR. BEN-JOCHANNAN

*Hieroglyphs* (1982: 3) Arnett also writes, "The fact does remain, however, that Southern (or Upper) Egypt is the primary location of the Late Predynastic Egyptian cultures, there being as many as eleven sites in the region.... the origins of the so-called 'Dynastic Race' are to be found within the region of Southern Egypt .... In fact, the evidence gathered from the excavations of these eleven Upper Egyptian sites and of Gerzeh and Tarkhan in Lower Egypt, specifically in the matter of primitive hieroglyphs, indicate considerable continuity between the Predynastic cultures of Upper Egypt and the civilization practiced by the Egyptians beginning in the Protodynastic period (after 3000 B.C.)."

The register was one of the earliest and greatest inventions the Egyptians made to express their art. It represented the escape for disorder to order in its representation. In W. Stephenson Smith's *Art and Architecture of Ancient Egypt*, he stated: "Art appears in the Nile Valley as early as the seventh millennium B.C. The earliest productions are the rock-drawings executed on the cliffs bordering the Nile in Upper Egypt and Nubia. The most ancient of these consist principally of geometric designs such as concentric circles or half-circles and net-patterns, or abstract figurations the exact meaning of which is obscure. Representational themes appear later. There are many hundreds of drawings of animals pursued by the earliest hunters and of weapons and traps. Although the publication of these drawings is quite complete, their chronology is still problematic. Drawings of cattle and boats can be definitely associated with the developed Neolithic cultures of Upper Egypt and Nubia, and with the Egyptian Predynastic, Nubian C-Group and later historic cultures."

# FREDERICK MONDERSON

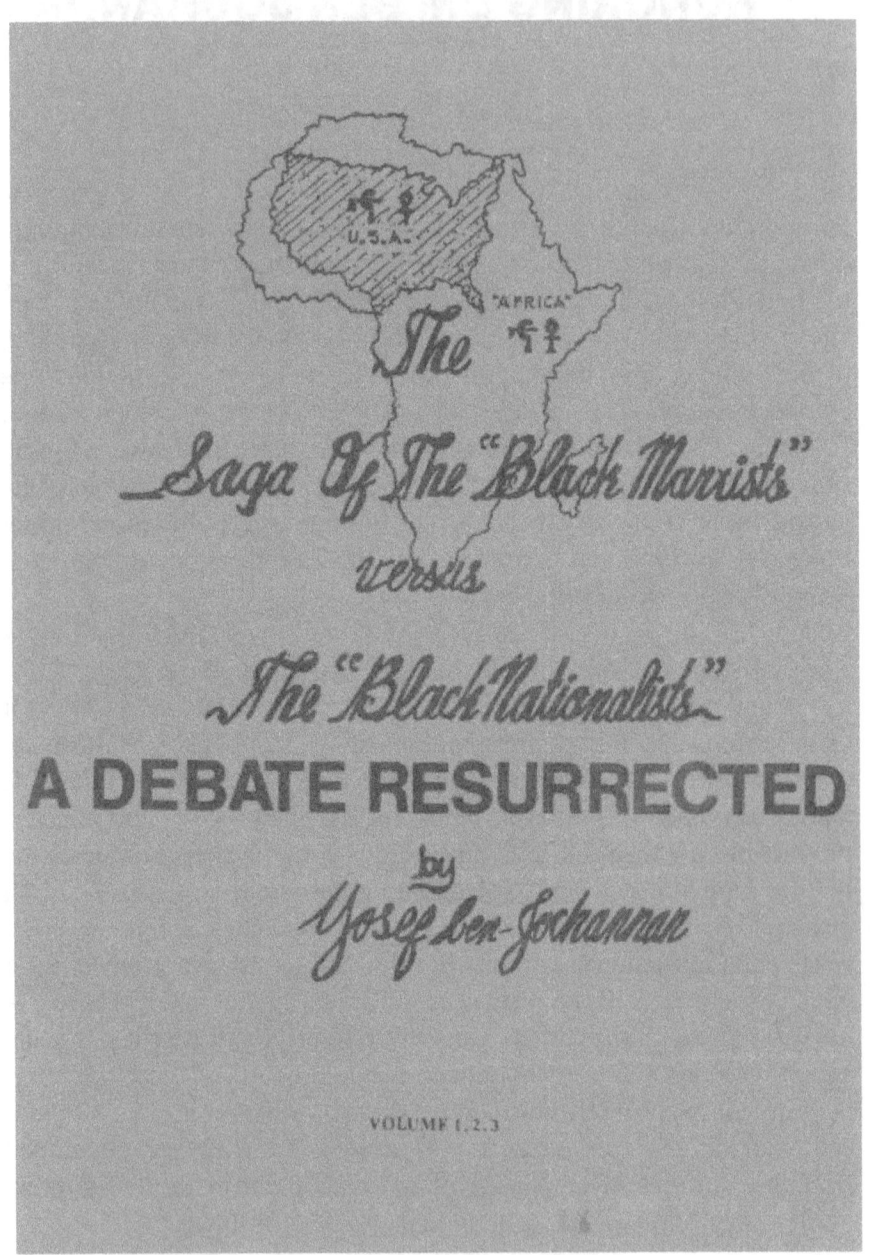

Black History Extravaganza - Dr. Ben's Book - **The Saga of the "Black Marxists" versus the "Black Nationalists" - A DEBATE RESURRECTED.**

# BLACK HISTORY EXTRAVAGANZA HONORING DR. BEN-JOCHANNAN

"MAN [African/Black; never "Negro/Colored/Integrated/Amalgamated/etc.] KNOW YOUR SELF!"[0]

Volume/Book I, II, III

THE SAGA OF THE "BLACK MARXISTS"
versus
THE "BLACK NATIONALISTS":
A Debate Resurrected

by:

Yosef A. A. ben-Jochannan

Adjunct Professor of History, Africana Studies
 and Research Center, Cornell University,
 Ithaca, New York
Adjunct Associate Professor of History, Malcolm-
 King College Extension of Marymount
 College of Manhattan, Mount Saint Vincent
 College and Fordham University

*Respect and Love to Bro Murchison from Yosef ben-Jochannan. 2/24/93*

---

[0] From the teachings by indigenous Africans [Black People] of the Nile Valley and Great Lakes region "Mysteries System" centered in the Grand Lodge of Luxor, and its Subordinate Lodges established by said Africans in Asia and Europe as conquerors, "civilizers", teachers and "diviners", etc. [see Y. ben-Jochannan's "Our Black Seminarians and Black Clergy Without A Black Theology; and Chapter VIII of "Black Man Of The Nile And His Family"; etc.

**Black History Extravaganza - Dr. Ben's Book - The Saga of the "Black Marxists" versus the "Black Nationalists" A DEBATE RESURRECTED - Overleaf of the Title Page.**

# FREDERICK MONDERSON

To reinforce all that has been said, we can argue drawing or art is the earliest form of writing and the illustrations Toby Wilkinson discovered in the high ridges of the Eastern Desert of Upper Egypt *Genesis of the Pharaohs* (2003) that we see as later Egyptian motifs, can be argued in support of Arnett's emerging hieroglyphs. Naturally, all this flies in the face of Winkler's "Mesopotamians" argument.

Significantly, the reason for the great hunger for Egypt is best explained in a quote from W.J. Perry in *The Growth of Civilization*, Penguin Books (1924) (1937: 48-49) where he quotes G. Elliot Smith in *The Ancient Egyptians* who stated: "The Egyptians did a great deal more than merely invent agriculture and devise the earliest statecraft and religion. Not only did they devise the methods of working wood and stone and the art of architecture, they seem also to have been the inventors of linen and of the craft of weaving, of the use of gold and copper, and the making of metal tools and implements. They were the first people to measure the year and to devise a calendar, and later on to substitute for the rough calculation based upon the date the observation of the sun's movements. They also invented shipbuilding and constructed the first sea-going ships. In a thousand and one of the details of our common civilization the originality of Egyptian civilization is revealed. The art of shaving, the use of wigs, the wearing of hats, the invention of the kilt and of the sandal and subsequently of a variety of other articles of dress, many of our musical instruments, chairs and beds, cushions, jewelry and jewel-cases, lamps - these are merely a few of the items picked at random out of our ancient heritage from the Nile valley."

Interestingly, however, when he uses the term "our" he means Europeans, not all of humanity or Africans. This, then, is what is at stake and must be corrected in unrelenting challenge!

# BLACK HISTORY EXTRAVAGANZA
# HONORING DR. BEN-JOCHANNAN

**Black History Extravaganza - Photo -** In simplest form, at Abu Simbel Temple, Rameses offers an object before an enthroned deity wearing the Double Crown.

In the reality of the "Slave Trade and Slavery," the western world could not admit at the back of their civilizations of Greece and Rome, were the creations of the people they were enslaving. In fact, this is what Count Volney affirmed in his *Ruins of Empires*, p. 16.

Notwithstanding, commenting further on the significance of ancient Egyptian contribution to civilization, Margaret Murray in *The Splendor that Was Egypt*, New York: Hawthorn Books, Inc., (1949) (1969: xvi) wrote the following, reinforcing the view previously expressed and attributed to G. Elliot Smith: "For every student of our modern civilization Egypt is the great storehouse from which to obtain information, for within the narrow limits of that country are preserved the origins of most (perhaps all) of our knowledge. In Egypt are found the first beginnings of material culture - building, agriculture, horticulture, clothing (even cooking as an art); the beginnings of the sciences - physics, astronomy, medicine, engineering; the beginning of the imponderables - law, government, and religion. In every aspect of life Egypt has influenced Europe, and though the centuries may have modified the custom or idea, the origin is clearly visible. Centuries before Ptolemy Philadelphus founded his great temple of the Muses at Alexandria, Egypt was to the Greek the embodiment of all wisdom and knowledge. In their generous enthusiasm, the Greeks continually recorded that opinion; and by their writings they passed on to later generations that wisdom of the Egyptians which they had learnt orally from the learned men of the Nile Valley." Arnett's denial nevertheless, and contrary to Murray's mentioning "the Greeks," Diop names these people and enumerates their views!

Further, in her explanation, Murray (1969: xvii) confessed: "Egypt was the supreme power in the Mediterranean area during the whole of the Bronze Age and a great part of the Iron Age; and as our present culture is directly due to the Mediterranean civilization of the Bronze Age, it follows that it has its roots in ancient Egypt. It is to Egypt that we owe our division of time; the twelve months and three hundred and sixty-five days of the year; the twelve hours of the day and the twelve hours of the night are due to the work of the Egyptian astronomers. The earliest clocks, the clepsydra, were the invention of Egyptian physicists. The earliest known intelligible writing is the Egyptian, so also are the earliest recorded historical events. It is due to the passion of the Egyptians for making records that so much has been preserved of their history and their literature, of their religious beliefs and their religious ritual. This passion for writing made them invent the first actual writing materials - pens, ink, paper - materials which could be packed in a small compass, were light to carry, and easy to use."

Thus, it is reasonable to argue, "this passion for writing" evolved from the simplest art, through the emergence of hieroglyphs and thus the invention of the tools to express the ideas and concepts generated therefrom.

However, and having scored a home-run, Murray (1969: xvii) continued highlighting Egyptian contributions even more, by contrasting this earliest culture with subsequent civilizations in the human drama and pointing out how Egyptian accomplishments have left them in the distance. She wrote: "The splendor of Egypt was not a mere mushroom growth lasting but a few hundred years. Where Greece and Rome can count their supremacy by the century, Egypt

# BLACK HISTORY EXTRAVAGANZA HONORING DR. BEN-JOCHANNAN

counts hers by the millennium, and the remains of that splendor can even now eclipse the remains of any other country in the world. According to the Greeks there were **SEVEN WONDERS OF THE WORLD**; these were the Pyramids of Egypt; the Hanging Gardens of Babylon; the statue of Zeus at Olympia; the Temple of Diana at Ephesus; the Tomb of Mausoleum; the Colossus of Rhodes; and the Lighthouse of Alexandria. Of all these great and splendid works, what remains to the present day? Babylon and its gardens are a heap of rubble, as ruined as a bombed city; the statue of Zeus was destroyed long ago; the Temple of Diana is utterly demolished, leaving only a few foundations; fragments of the Mausoleum are preserved in museums where they are a source of interest to experts only; the Colossus of Rhodes survives only in legend, so completely has it disappeared; the Lighthouse of Alexandria has perished almost without a trace.

Of the **Seven Wonders, the Pyramids of Egypt alone remain almost intact**, they still tower above the desert sands, dominating the scene, defying the destroying hand of Time and the still more destructive hand of Man. They line the western shore of the Nile for more than a hundred miles, and are the most stupendous and impressive as they are the most ancient of all the great buildings of the world." It is interesting, all of these wonders built by Caucasians in Europe have disappeared but the most significant one built in Africa, Egypt, has survived and is yet claimed by Caucasians. Equally too, the one surviving, has no counterpart from whence the Caucasians came. There is no prototype in Asiatic lands. This means they not only had no knowledge of the pyramids, yet they came to Egypt to build them. Thus, "the superior mentality" argument is nothing but arrogance on the part of the European man! More important, not only are there numerous pyramids in Nubia as well (South of Aswan), human made and naturally formed over thousands of years, but Dr. Ben-Jochannan spoke of "silt pyramids" predating the man-made ones. Let us also further recognize Hatshepsut's mortuary temple at Deir el Bahari, today considered an architectural and artistic masterpiece even after surviving the ravages of time and also the

# FREDERICK MONDERSON

hands of man, was never given the designation "Ancient Wonder," yet it has survived all but the one such glorious monument.

Nonetheless, and even more penetrating, Lester Brooks in *Great Civilizations of Ancient Africa* (1971: 28) confirms: "From the cemeteries dating back before 3200 B.C., anthropologists have identified remains they label 'Eurobond' (indicating those of Cro-Magnon types), "Negroid" and some Asian types, with the 'Europoids' predominating in the north and the 'Negroids' predominating in the south. As one expert puts it, 'the races were fused on the banks of the Nile well before Pharaonic civilization came into being. These people were black by the operating definition of skin color as well as by the general physical characteristics they had then.'" Even more, Brooks (1971: 28-29) continued: "The Greeks were surprised twenty-five hundred years ago to discover that the Egyptians were the darkest-skinned peoples of the so-called Near East. Typically, they were - and are today - not homogeneous. Their skin color ranges from red-black to yellow. Their hair is black and wavy, curly or wooly; their eyes are bright and black; their bodies are lean and muscular, generally tending to tallness. Egyptian noses usually are large and straight, but frequently aquiline; their jaws generally tend to thrust forward with fleshy lips, often curled back. We can say without the slightest hesitation that the ancient Egyptians would have been considered Negroes by American standards, and until the passage of the **Civil Rights Act of 1964** not one of the Egyptian Pharaohs could have bought a cup of coffee in a white drug store in the southern states of the U.S.A."

**Black History Extravaganza - Photo** - More of the wonderful audience, those in **Kente Cloth** (left); and those who just came to say, "Thank you, Dr. Ben-Jochannan."

# BLACK HISTORY EXTRAVAGANZA HONORING DR. BEN-JOCHANNAN

"

**Black History Extravaganza - Papyrus -** Tutankhamon as a Sphinx between the Pyramids with a Black Cartouche (Shennu) on the side.

Still, and again, contrary to Arnett's contention of not sufficient evidence for his position; in his "Argument for A Negro Origin" in *African Origin of Civilization: Myth or Reality,* Cheikh Anta Diop (1974: 134-155) utilizes "Totemism," "Circumcision," "Kingship," "Cosmogony," "Social Organization," "Matriarchy," "Kingship of the Meroitic Sudan and Egypt," "Cradles of Civilization Located in the Heart of Negro Lands," and "Languages," as evidence for his position. On the other hand, the postulated position for an Asiatic Caucasian origin is that "for some unknown reason," these people left their homes and brought "a superior mental attitude" that essentially reinvented Narmer's wheel is nothing but white supremacy arrogance! Diop's "two-cradle" theory for "ice" and "sun" environments and their influences, and patriarchy as opposed to matriarchy, viz., Europeans in the North and Africans in the South, were equally very convincing.  Using as an example, cultural influences including costume and dress, Brooks (1971: 29) also sheds even more light on this situation: "What African elements can be discovered in the extremely sophisticated civilization of Egypt?  Among others, the complicated religious beliefs wherein tribalism, animism and taboos had extraordinary force - with special rites for the major activities such as planting, harvesting, fishing, hunting and war, in addition to the *rites du passage* - birth, marriage, death." Even further he points out: "We think of African witch doctors with fantastic, colorful costumes. Look again at a formal portrait of a Pharaoh. Note that, he wears an enormous headdress. From his 'double crown' sprout the head of a vulture and the 'fire-spitting' flamed head of a female hooded cobra, supposedly capable of consuming rebels in flames. The pharaoh was the son of the falcon-god, and was considered a falcon himself, endowed with magical powers and an all-seeing eye. From his waist hangs an animal tail; on his shaven chin, he wears a false beard, which is, itself, considered a god. In his hand, he carries a scepter with the head of the god Seth atop it - recognizable in the curious curved snout, long, straight ears and almond-shaped eyes."

Adding even more to this fanfare, Brooks demonstrates further: "In processions, banners are carried before the king. These banners bear the symbols of the many powerful brother gods who have blessed him and whose aid is his to command." Of course, pharaohs also wore arm bands, a necklace, rings, a girdle or apron with Uraeus, sandals and carried a dagger, a flail, and either a mace or bow and arrows, with which to slay his enemies, who as a god and superhuman on the battlefield could slay "'hundreds of enemies at a stroke all by himself.' 'His eyes scrutinize the depths of every being.' Nothing is impossible for him: 'Everything which he ordains comes about.'"

# BLACK HISTORY EXTRAVAGANZA
# HONORING DR. BEN-JOCHANNAN

**Black History Extravaganza - Photo -** At Abu Simbel, Rameses kneels to present two ointment jars to the enthroned Ra-Horakhty falcon.

In this respect then, the answer to the question of "Who were the ancient Egyptians?" should not have done so, but still has baffled, confused, has contradicted and often been obfuscated by modern scholars, viz., historians, journalists, archaeologists, anthropologists, columnists, lecturers, teachers, debaters, and every other form of commentator particularly those who use the film and video medium, create displays as in Museums, as well as persons involved in book, journal, magazine and newspaper printing, dissemination and distribution of the distorted information relative to Egypt. All this has left many scholars, students and average citizens in a state of confusion. In fact, these end up engrained in the fallacy or as U.S. Congressman James Clyburn terms it, "Defending a Myth!" Quite frankly, these latter may have been misinformed intentionally or even unintentionally because of the falsity fed by the previous generations upon whose "facts" they have come to rely. Truthfully, and upon close examination, generation after generation of scholars and lay people, have been misinformed regarding the origin of the ancient Egyptians. Let us not consider the role of Hollywood. Much of this and more, some have argued, has been intentional and when it has not been so, it has been due to ignorance. Some of it is traceable to Wilhelm Hegel and other German scholars, who held, for much of the 19th Century that 'Africa was outside the realm of history,' and by extension the Egyptians were an Asiatic people in the "Middle East" being part of the "Fertile Crescent."

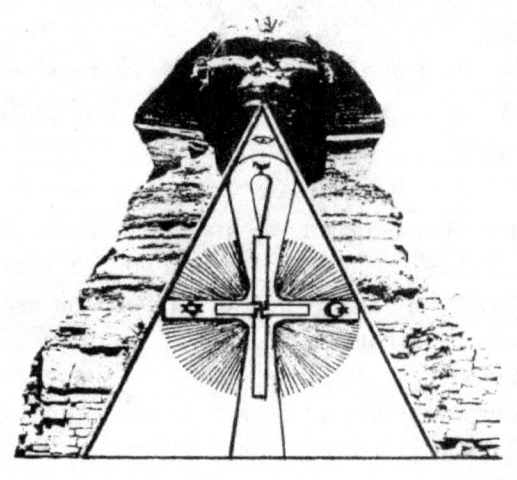

**OUR BLACK SEMINARIANS and BLACK CLERGY without A BLACK THEOLOGY**

—by—
Yosef A.A. ben-Jochannan

**Black History Extravaganza** - Dr. Ben's Book - **Our BLACK SEMINARIANS and BLACK CLERGY without a BLACK THEOLOGY.**

# BLACK HISTORY EXTRAVAGANZA HONORING DR. BEN-JOCHANNAN

OUR "BLACK SEMINARIANS" and "BLACK CLERGY" WITHOUT A "BLACK THEOLOGY": The Tragedy Of Black People/Africans In Religion Today

by:
Yosef A. A. ben-Jochannan

Adjunct Professor of History, Africana Studies and Research Center, Cornell University, Ithaca, N.Y.

Adjunct Associate Professor of History, Malcolm-King College Harlem Extension of Marymount Manhattan College, Mount Saint Vincent College, and Fordham University, N.Y.C., N.Y.

*Respect and love to bro Marchison from Yoy Ben-Jochannan 4/24/93*

Alkebu-lan Books and Education Materials Association [Affiliate of Alkebu-lan Foundation, Inc.], 209 West, 125th Street, Suite 218, New York, N.Y. 10027

**Black History Extravaganza - Dr. Ben's Book - Our BLACK SEMINARIANS and BLACK CLERGY without a BLACK THEOLOGY - Overleaf of the Title Page.**

# FREDERICK MONDERSON

The notion of the "Fertile Crescent" is a good example of distortion. We have been led to believe the "Fertile Crescent" curves from Mesopotamia to Egypt in a downward spiral. Marcus Garvey, on the other hand, reminded, instead, the "Fertile Crescent curved outward and up from the Nile." Egypt has always been the breadbasket of the ancient world and Middle East. After all, even Biblical lore speaks of Asiatics, migrating to Egypt to purchase corn. "Corn in Egypt" has always been a prodigious shibboleth.

However, and further, as Dr. Jacob Carruthers in *Intellectual Warfare* and *Mdn Ntr: Divine Speech* has explained, "Hegel took Africans out of Egypt and then Egypt out of Africa;" the same mindset belongs to C.G. Seligman, who, in *Races of Africa* (1930) wrote: "The civilizations of Africa are the civilizations of the Hamites." Davidson clarifies, "These are Caucasian, i.e., they belong to the same branch of mankind as almost all Europeans." This position has been buttressed by others subscribing to this same false and perverted view as that of Carl Meinhof, a German, who in 1912 wrote, "Hamitic peoples subjugated and governed dark pigmented Negroes," and in the 1920s, Reginald Copeland also wrote, as if parroting Hegel, "Africa proper had no history. The heart of Africa was scarcely beating." Equally, the Oxford Don, Hugh Trevor Roper expressed the view, "There is no history of Africa, only a history of Europeans in Africa." Thus, in the European nationalist, imperialist, colonial climate of the 19$^{th}$ and early 20$^{th}$ Century mentality, coupled with emergence of the "Penny Press" in the age of rapid publication of archaeological discovery, such efforts ossified the misrepresentation and false notion of who were the ancient Egyptians while equally glorifying Europeans and denigrating non-Europeans. But objectively speaking, revelations of the existential evidence demolish the falsity for as "old ideas die hard" avaricious Europeans want to take credit for initiating all forms of knowledge! The contention regarding such a position posed, as Molefi Asante has held, "There is a problem when you occupy all the space and no one else gets any!"

Still more significant, it is understandable the position of "white supremacy" was enunciated during the greatest humiliation,

# BLACK HISTORY EXTRAVAGANZA HONORING DR. BEN-JOCHANNAN

degradation and inhumanity practiced against Africans, that was so repulsive at the height of the slave trade and slavery it gave birth to the abolition movement to outlaw the slave trade. In aftermath and as the American, French and Haitian revolutions happened and in the stream of history, Napoleon's invasion of Egypt and consequently the discovery of the Rosetta stone occurred. Millennia prior to that most people believed the Egyptians were Africans and Black! However, in unfolding world history and after the discovery of the Rosetta stone in 1798, Champollion, DeSacy, and Young actively sought to decipher the hieroglyphic script, which the ancient Egyptians had named *Medu Netcher*. Of these great intellects, Champollion was the most successful getting the greatest credit for deciphering the hieroglyphs in 1822. This linguistic break-through concomitantly gave birth to the discipline of Egyptology and in result an effervescence of societies was founded fueling an antiquarian movement to not simply study antiquity but to collect and "acquire things Egyptian." Diop pointed out the young genius' elder brother Champollion-Figeac falsified the meticulous antiquarian pioneer's intent and exclamations based on his studious observations. Equally, others such as Herodotus whose observations about the ancient Egyptians, have conveniently been ignored. Interestingly, those parts of Herodotus that fits the European narrative have been accepted and those that challenge such have been rejected. For example, Wortham accepts Herodotus' description of the types of mummification and Petrie also accepts Herodotus placement of "Colchians in the Caucasus." All the while, there is a prevailing belief; the ruling Egyptian elite was white who ruled over a black underclass. Important, either these "fake" rulers never came out of their palaces; never looked down their windows; or even came into the streets because Herodotus never saw them. As Dr. Diop states, "The Greek writer Herodotus may be mistaken when he reports on the customs of a people. But we must grant that he was at least capable of recognizing the skin color of the inhabitants of countries he visited. His descriptions of the Egyptians were the descriptions of a Black people." Nevertheless, following Champollion's revelations of how the Egyptians classed the races, viz., Egyptians, Africans, Asiatics, Europeans (whites) and his work, particularly after the publication of the French Masterpiece *Description of Egypt*, an acquisition mentality

# FREDERICK MONDERSON

developed in Europe resulting in a mad dash for antiquities collection in what Brian Fagan later dubbed "**The Rape of the Nile**" in his book of the same name!

**Black History Extravaganza - Photo -** At Abu Simbel Temple of Rameses II, Thoth sits enthroned before a table with vases.

As such then, when it comes to the truth about the ancient Egyptians there is an unbridgeable chasm, because whitest people, Europeans, and now that the Chinese, Japanese, Koreans, Indians, are coming to Egypt, these are all led to accept the symbolic view, albeit false view that the ancient Egyptians were white. On the other hand, most Blacks with any sense of historical understanding believe the ancient Egyptians were Black! Interesting, in the heart of even present-day Egypt, whether in restaurants, hotels or bazaars, locally made statues of Egyptians are mostly colored black!

Nevertheless, a lot of ink has been spilt on the color of these early Africans of Egypt. This is particularly so of the "red color" of the Egyptians. At the Cairo Conference, Dr. Diop took to task Prof. Vercoutter's claim the Egyptians were "black-skinned white men!"

# BLACK HISTORY EXTRAVAGANZA HONORING DR. BEN-JOCHANNAN

However still, while we have heard of "white, white men," "red, white men," and "black, white men," one thing is certain, unmistakably the ancient Egyptians were never white! Importantly, at the Ancient Nubia Conference in Philadelphia some years ago, David O'Connor, a Curator at the Philadelphia Museum expressed to this author, "The Egyptians were not white!" That is not to say others have not also done so! The point is, if this "mainstream white scholar" could say the "Egyptians were not white," why has Wortham and equally others as well contradicted this position as an issue that should have been put to rest long ago; but it is not! Let us not forget, if there were any, even painted evidence of white Egyptians, it would have been magnified many times. However, while the ancient Egyptians were painted red, they were also painted black; and even Osiris was painted green but Egyptians were never painted white! In fact, green, blue and brown are variants of black! The *Journal of Egyptian Archaeology*, in the 1930s, described the God Amon as "so black he was blue" and evidence of this is particularly evident in the apartments south of the *Akh Menu* festival temple of Thutmose III at Karnak Temple. We know, to the Egyptians, green, blue and brown are variants of Black. However, it is understandable the "Red color of the Egyptians," the "Races of Red Men inhabiting North Africa," has led to much confusion.

The question of color is an interesting one. While Bauval and Brophy in *Black Genesis* mention the people of Nabta Playa in the desert of southern Upper Egypt, "Precursors to the Pharaohs" as Black Africans, Toby Wilkinson in *Genesis of the Pharaohs* deals principally with the culture and Petroglyphs of the people of the Eastern Desert, but never mention their color. On the other hand, Wallis Budge in *Egypt* (1925) provides tremendous evidence that reinforces the indigenous argument: "The prehistoric native of Egypt both in the Old and New Stone Ages, was African and there is every reason for saying that the earliest settlers came from the South."

Budge (1925) further states: "There are many things in the manners and customs of the historic Egyptians that suggest that the original home of their prehistoric ancestors was in a country in the neighborhood of Uganda and Punt." Now, if we triangulate Punt, Uganda and "Foothills of the Mountains of the Moon" we are in Central Africa, the realm of the Gods, not Asia or the Caucasus. Again, we must remember, all we have about the Caucasians, is "for some unknown reason," and "a superior mental impetus," nothing else! This is nothing but pure speculation and racist arrogance.

Nonetheless, from the time of the Stone Age, man has had a penchant for **red** as his favorite color and this led us to believe the Egyptian, followed in this vein, and painting of him in the color red, is simply to demonstrate love for this color. Gay Robbins in *The Art of Egypt* has pointed out, the Egyptian believed red and even gold had a solar connection and as a people who believed they were divinely chosen they used red to depict themselves. Dr. Ben-Jochannan often said, the Egyptians painted themselves "red because they were dead;" while Brugsch-Bey explained they were painted red to be illuminated in the dark passage of the underworld. They, however, also used black to depict themselves, (Thutmose I, Aahmes-Nefertari, Tutankhamon, among survivals) though they never used white for such a depiction! Cheikh Anta Diop said the Egyptians painted themselves red to distinguish themselves from other Africans since they considered themselves "special." Henry L'Hote in "Tassili Frescoes;" Mary Leakey on "East African Stone Age Art" paintings speak of the "predominant red" used by these early or ancient painters. In October 2011, *The New York Times* published the discovery of a "paint factory" in South Africa dated to 107,000 years ago with existential evidence of mixed "red paint" and brush found in a container. It also indicated this process of paint mixing "pushed complex African thinking far back in time!" Important, the "South Africans" were "manufacturing" the "predominant red" which would be so important in early painting. There have been claims of early paint use but this distinct and irrefutable fact and its early dating settles the issue!

Contributing to and continuing the confusion, in September 2005, a young female guide in the Cairo Museum, in referring to the intact statue of Mentuhotep II found in his Middle Kingdom temple at Deir el Bahari, told this writer: "He was painted black for the funeral

# BLACK HISTORY EXTRAVAGANZA HONORING DR. BEN-JOCHANNAN

ceremony because he was dead." Obviously, she did not know, and is being taught to falsely propagate such by saying 'My Professor told me this at the American University in Cairo!' What they did not tell her, not that the mummy did have a black substance administered as a protective coating; more important that the brown or black skin was often visible underneath. Interesting, though found in 1898 in his temple and excavated in 1903-04, untold commentators wrote and spoke on Egypt without elaborating on his color, even downplaying Mentuhotep II, until in 1958, he was described by E. Stephenson Smith in *The Art and Architecture of Ancient Egypt* as having "black flesh!" The female guide even told this researcher she never saw Osiris, God of the Dead, painted black! So, I searched him out in the Museum and found numerous examples of papyrus and wood, not just of Osiris but other kings and gods as well. We must also remember; these wooden models particularly are what have survived the destructive elements of time and man! However, just as the two wooden statues in Tutankhamon's burial chamber, located in the position in which they were found, and were painted black to represent him, this was a standard practice with such statues placed in similar proximity to the burial chamber. After all, how could the ancient Egyptian expect to spend eternity as depicted as "purely painted black for the funerary ceremony which was not his original color? Many tombs in the Valley of the Kings; thoroughly excavated and catalogued, record fragments of painted black wood presumably used in similar internment placement. Notwithstanding, with time the black paint peels from the wood leaving only traces that is sometimes further "doctored in museum basements!"

# FREDERICK MONDERSON

**Black History Extravaganza - Photo -** Abu Simbel Temple of Rameses II. At the base of one of the seated colossal statues at the temple's entrance, the Nile gods are uniting the land beneath the cartouche of Rameses.

We are told, from the earliest time, the Egyptian believed this life was a temporary sojourn but the afterlife was for eternity. So, he structured and provisioned his tomb to enjoy all the comforts he enjoyed in this life to do so in the next. Why then would he have his features changed to appear differently in the next life? So therefore, the spurious straw-man symbolic arguments are contradictory and fall apart easily. Unfortunately, the female guide did not know, never had it explained; bitumen, the black stuff, was painted over the mummy but still its brown skin was noticeably beneath, as G. Elliott Smith has unwittingly exposed. However, even Jon Manchip White pedaled the confusing "painted black for the funerary ceremony" distraction as reality manifesting the same false symbolic representation. Let's not forget, James Henry Breasted began his *Ancient Times* in 1916 writing of "thin brown skinned men." However, he never discussed Mentuhotep II. Malcolm X said, "**They know how to put it**."

# BLACK HISTORY EXTRAVAGANZA HONORING DR. BEN-JOCHANNAN

The skillful use of "brown instead of black" is one way of "**putting it**."

On the second floor in the Cairo Museum a number of wooden statues are represented, Number J 95,655 Osiris in White Crown is painted green. However, in JE 36,465 Osiris is painted black; JE, 95,645 Osiris is black; J, 26,228 Osiris is black; J, 35,669 Osiris is black; papyrus B 24 Osiris is black. This is a lengthy papyrus depicting a winged snake with 4 feet; as 4 goddesses ride 4 uraei with double heads. Then 7 goddesses ride a lengthy snake crossing a river while 6 goddesses pull the snake's tongue as it stands behind a line of 6 goddesses and 6 gods led by Khepre towards the deceased with his back towards Nephthys and Isis standing behind enthroned black Osiris who greets the deceased who in turn offers a plant.

In Room 12 is housed funerary furnishing from royal tombs.

Statue No. 2374 - made of wood, Osiris is painted black.

Statue No. 2372 - made of wood, Osiris is painted black.

In this room, Case GL contains 9 large Afro wigs. These were discovered in the "Deir el Bahari Cache" in 1881 along with the discovered Eighteenth and Nineteenth dynasty pharaohs.

Wooden statues Numbers 3827, 3836, 3834, 3832, 3824, are all painted black. The wooden duck No. 3838 and a wooden panther No. 3840 and wooden panther No. 3842 are all painted black. In front and outside Room 12 large wooden statues 3834a and 3834b are painted black.

In room No. 22, 9 wooden statues, painted black, are placed above Case J.

4 wooden statues are above Case I
4 wooden statues above Case O
4 wooden statues above Case P

# FREDERICK MONDERSON

7 wooden statues above Case R
7 wooden statues above Case T

These are all painted black! Still, who knows what lies in the basement? We must remember the place cards for much in the Museum were done by Gaston Maspero. He, incidentally as Curator of Antiquities, in the 19$^{th}$ Century, described Prince Mahepra as "Negroid but not Negro!" He probably did not even use capitals! However, contemporary with such a description, the biographers of the musical genius Beethoven described him as "black," "swarthy," "Negroid," "Negro," etc. Thus, this writer asks, "you to do the math!"

**Black History Extravaganza - Papyrus -** The Circumcision operation being performed while at the right an individual steadies the subject.

Conversely, Dr. Yosef ben-Jochannan said the Egyptians were painted "red" because they were dead. Even further, that the Henna plant is

# BLACK HISTORY EXTRAVAGANZA HONORING DR. BEN-JOCHANNAN

used to paint, particularly young Nubian brides, red as part of a cultural ceremony. Now, in the Tomb of Vizier Rekhmara, the numerous individuals are all painted red, though some are shown making a black figure. All this notwithstanding, there are pictorial "survivals" of Egyptians and gods painted black, viz., Amon, Min, Thutmose I, Tutankhamon, Ahmose-Nefertari, wife and sister of Ahmose and their brother Kamose whose mother Ahotep and her father Sekenenra-Tao must have been black to have produced their "coal black Ethiopian" daughter. Let's face it, in *Red Land, Black Land*, red represented barrenness of the desert; and blackness represented fertility of the cultivable land. Now, as we know, the Red Land represents 96 percent of the nation's land area and the Black Land represents 4 percent, that is cultivable. Thus, when the gods say to Pharaoh, "I give you the black land," is he giving him only 4 percent of the country and not the other 96 percent? Obenga says it is the "land of the Black people" and that the determinative is about people. Osiris was black, so he represented resurrection and eternal life! In fact, Osiris was called "the Great Black!" Again, Theophile Obenga has reminded all, Kemet or the "black land" referred to the people not the land itself!

This was also the view of Gerald Massey who wrote the term Black referred to the people not the land!

Rameses II's wife Nefertari was Nubian. Yet she is painted red in her tomb in the Valley of the Queens. In December 2005, someone called this writer to look at a program on the *History Channel* entitled *Black Pharaohs* about the 25$^{th}$ Dynasty kings who were Nubian and "given as Black." In a fleeting glance, the camera showed an image of Tanutemon, one of these Black pharaohs and lo and behold, this ruler was painted red in the tomb! The *National Geographic Magazine* expose in "Black Pharaohs" could do nothing but paint these kings their natural color not much different from their Egyptian brethren! Let us not also forget, images in the tomb of the nobles at Aswan also show these southernmost Egyptians, where Nubia interacts significantly with Egypt and who were essentially black, also painted red. In tomb representations of Nubians, Ethiopians "bringing tribute" they are shown as "black," and "red" or "brown." However, at the Nubian Conference on October 1-4, 2012, the Black Nubian 25th Dynasty individuals are also shown painted red. What does all this mean? It means the Egyptians were African and not European or Asiatic, black not white and Egypt was and is still located in Africa not the Middle East or Asia. Now what is the evidence for all of this? Much has been provided above relative to the existential evidence which contradicts the symbolic representation.

**Black History Extravaganza - Photo -** At Abu Simbel Temple of Rameses II, in an image on the side of a seated colossal, beside the king's cartouche or Shennu, rests just below partial image of the Nile gods uniting the land.

Thus, this section will focus on a chronological approach showing how principally eyewitnesses portrayed the ancient Africans of the Nile Valley, Egypt; first, and as interest intensified in modern times, how Egypt was viewed by some particularly in the 19th and 20th Centuries of our era. One thing is certain, as European writers, historians and antiquarians first encountered Egypt following Napoleon's discovery and decipherment of the Rosetta stone by the

# BLACK HISTORY EXTRAVAGANZA HONORING DR. BEN-JOCHANNAN

Savant Champollion, in the emergent imperialism accelerated by the lucrative exploitation of the slave trade and slavery, many "colored" their reports to appease an emerging reading public in Europe. With time, and when given the opportunity, African scholars did significant research unearthing the distortions, omissions, and misrepresentations and revealed what they had found, that the existential evidence contradicts the symbolic representation. However, despite profound scholarship by these Blacks, European writers and their American counterparts of questionable integrity have found it difficult to accept the revealed facts or have refused to deal with the issue, side-stepping it. To wit, African research has been attacked in the most vituperative manner, minutely scrutinized and dismissed in the most unprofessional methods as if such effort was grounded in malice. The unmistaken fact is; these revealed truths shatter the pillars that support the myth of a white Egypt. In response, even those Europeans who bucked the trend and wrote otherwise of the distortion, were themselves ostracized and their works equally subject to the most insidious criticism and marginalized.

For example, much confusion has been created as European scholars, not finding any evidence of "White Egyptians" have emphasized "Red Egyptians" as being "Red Egyptian White men." Even Vercoutter remarked essentially, they were "white men in black skin!" Let's look at an example and pose a question before we begin. While discussing the Sanctuary area of the Temple of Karnak where the god Amon-Ra dwelt William J. Murnane in *The Penguin Guide to Ancient Egypt* (1983: 231) wrote: "The walls are covered with scenes illustrating the episodes of the offering rite with Amun appearing in his usual anthropomorphic guise and also in the ithyphallic form he shares with Min, the god of fertility." Further, another writer Michael Haag in the Cadogan series, *Cairo, Luxor, Aswan* (2000: 212) adds: "On the north side of the sanctuary, where there was much rebuilding a wall erected by Hatshepsut was found concealed behind a later wall of Thutmosis III, thus preserving the original freshness of the coloring. The wall has now been removed to a nearby room, and shows Amon, his flesh painted red and with one foot in front of the other, and also Amon in the guise of the ithyphallic Min, a harvest god, often amalgamated

# FREDERICK MONDERSON

with Amon, his flesh painted black." Let us remember, while Amon is here represented with "his flesh painted red," in the back room at Medinet Habu, he is shown enthroned and his skin is painted black. He is also painted blue here and at Karnak beside the *Akh Menu*!

**Black History Extravaganza** - Dr. Ben's Book - **Tutankhamun's African roots haley, et. al, overlooked.**

# BLACK HISTORY EXTRAVAGANZA
# HONORING DR. BEN-JOCHANNAN

**Black History Extravaganza** - Dr. Ben's Book - **Tutankhamun's African roots haley, et. al, overlooked** - Overleaf of the Title Page.

# FREDERICK MONDERSON

An interesting note is interjected here. What could have been done previously is now prohibited. While there has been some relaxation in the Cairo Museum, taking of photographers in tombs, in the Valley of the Kings, Seti's Temple at Abydos and so on, is now prohibited. Looking for the "gods" enthroned in the backroom at Medinet Habu, one will not find it these days. However, suffice to say, the said images are represented in Frederick Monderson's *Medinet Habu: Mortuary Temple of Rameses III*.

Now the serious first question is: "Why would white red men be worshipping black Gods or painting their gods black?" Certainly, the God is not dead and so painted for the funeral ceremony! Thutmose III's *Amon-Min* in the Luxor Museum is black and not dead! Amon-Min in Rameses II's Abu Simbel Temple depicts the god in "blackface." Also, why would Central Africa be considered "God's Land?" Equally too, another question is, "Why did Murnane not refer to the color of Amon, as Min, being black?" Elsewhere, in the *Journal of Egyptian Archaeology* Amon has been described as "so black, he was blue!" Many writers have a tendency to skillfully dance around the question of the race of the Egyptians, particularly when evidence indicates they were black! It's all part of the conspiracy against ancient Egypt that falsely portrays these ancient Africans. Much further, when evidence surfaces depicting Egyptians "painted black" the logical explanation given is they were painted black because either they were dead or for the death ceremony. Yet still, while Diop extolled the cultural accomplishments, of the first dynasties in the Old Kingdom and affirmed their blackness, and while Arnett agrees that Diop disproves the "whiteness of Egypt," he Arnett discounts claims that they were black, saying the archaeological evidence cannot prove the blackness of the ruling elite. Of course, the same "lack of evidence" was used to prove the whiteness of Egypt more than a century ago in the falsity of a white ruling class of kings and nobles ruling over a black mass who do all the work! However, no evidence exists to show Egyptians as white except as foreigners, even though the assumption and propagated falsity is that they were white! Again, a very good reason the white writer affirmed to this researcher "The Egyptians were not white" is simply because today men of reasonable intellect know the falsity of a "white Egypt" is just that, falsity.

# BLACK HISTORY EXTRAVAGANZA HONORING DR. BEN-JOCHANNAN

**Black History Extravaganza - Ceramic Art** - The "Great Goose of Amon" in picturesque color.

**Now, let us begin!**

**II.    Classical Writers** - In assessing the classical writers' contributions, Diop wrote: "To the Greek and Latin writers contemporary with the ancient Egyptians, the latter's physical classification posed no problems. The Egyptians were Negroes, thick-lipped, kinky-haired and long-legged; the unanimity of the authors' evidence on a physical fact as salient as a people's race will be difficult to minimize or Pass over."

**a.    Homer** - Most scholarship seems to date Homer to about 800 B.C. However, this may be incorrect, even though we know he is "credited" with writing the *Iliad* and the *Odyssey*. Several things need

# FREDERICK MONDERSON

to be looked at in relation to dating of Homer and even questioning his originality. First, we are told that Abu Simbel temple of Rameses II has the earliest examples of Greek writing and this writing is dated to the 7th Century B.C. Now, if Homer wrote the *Odyssey* and *Iliad* then it cannot be 800 B.C., as previously thought. Second, Cheikh Anta Diop notes, if Homer visited Egypt it had to be in the 8th Century during the time of the Twenty-Fifth Ethiopian Dynasty and much of his descriptions may be representative of later events in Egypt. Interestingly, Murray's *Handbook for Egypt* (1888) informs: "In the Ramesseum, North face of the South-East Wall of the 2nd area is a scene of combat that very much resembles what Homer tells us of his *Odyssey*." Nicely put, but there is a word for this. Plagiarism!

**Black History Extravaganza - Photo -** Another Cartouche or Shennu of Rameses II, User-Ma'at-Ra.

**b.    Herodotus 480-425 B.C. -** Herodotus visited Egypt around 450 B.C. and wrote his *Histories* devoting Book II *Euterpe* to Egypt. Diop (1989) argued in "Origins of the Ancient Egyptians" in *Egypt Revisited*, edited by Ivan Van Sertima, and quotes the "father of history" in regard to the *Origins of the Colchians*: "It is in fact manifest that the Colchidians are Egyptians by race ... several

# BLACK HISTORY EXTRAVAGANZA HONORING DR. BEN-JOCHANNAN

Egyptians told me that in their opinion the Colchidians were descended from soldiers of Sesostris. I had conjectured as much to myself from two pointers, firstly because they have black skins and kinky hair (to tell the truth this proves nothing for other peoples have them too) and secondly and more reliably for the reason that alone among mankind the Egyptians and Ethiopians have practiced circumcision since time immemorial." Herodotus says further, the Egyptians have "thick lips, broad noses and are burnt of skin," meaning they are black. Practically everything else Herodotus wrote about was accepted by moderns as observed fact other than that the Egyptians had "wooly hair, thick lips, broad noses and were burnt of skin." Much of what he heard or theorized could be considered conjecture, but his observations cannot be disputed. Naturally, he never said black as compared to what or whom!

**c.     Aristotle 384-322 B.C.** - Aristotle in his work *Physiognomy* made a somewhat controversial statement regarding the ancient Egyptians. He says: "Those who are too black are cowards, like for instance, the Egyptians and Ethiopians. But those who are excessively white are also cowards, as we can see from the example of women the complexion of courage is between the two." He was seeking to affirm that the middle ground, perhaps a "Mediterranean Race," type was the ideal. Now, while his science of cowards was wrong, for we know as proven by the many wars Africans in particular have fought; however, his description of the Egyptians and Ethiopians is essentially correct. This is one incidence in which this great philosopher and scientist was both wrong and right on the same issue.

# FREDERICK MONDERSON

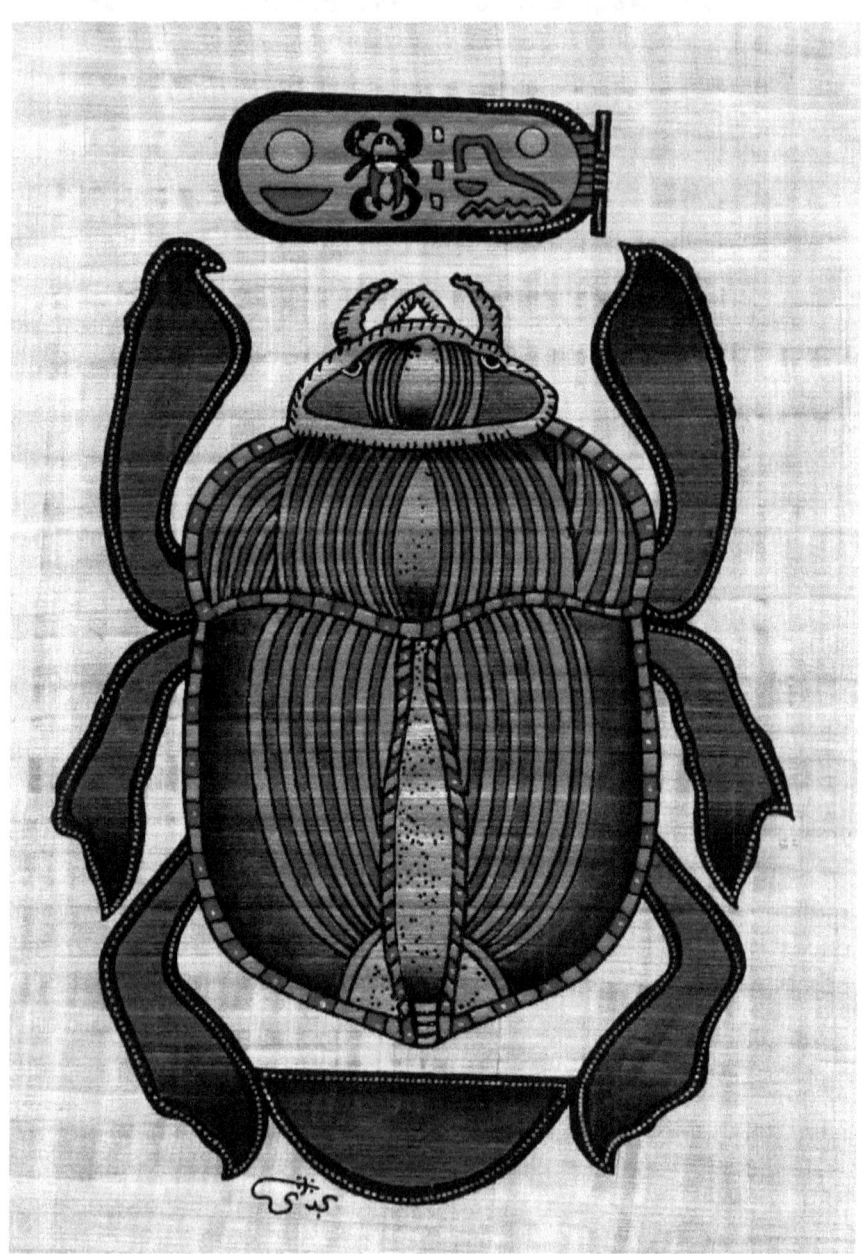

**Black History Extravaganza - Papyrus -** Khepre, in brown color, pushes the cartouche while standing on Heb.

# BLACK HISTORY EXTRAVAGANZA HONORING DR. BEN-JOCHANNAN

**d.    Lucian** - the Greek writer 125-190 A.D. speaks to Lycinus, "The boy is not only black; he has thick lips and his legs are too thin …."

**e.    Apollodorus** - first Century Greek philosopher said, "Aegyptus conquered the country of the black-footed ones and called it Egypt after himself."

**f.    Aeschylus** - Greek tragedian in *The Supplicants* describes the Aegyptaids in their vessels: "I can see the crew with their black skins and white tunics."

**g.    Diodorus Siculus** - of Sicily 63-14 B.C. - Diodorus held to the view that Ethiopians colonized Egypt. Diop says, according to Diodorus: "The Ethiopians say that the Egyptians are one of their colonies, which was led into Egypt by Osiris. They claim that at the beginning of the world Egypt was simply a sea but that the Nile, carrying down vast quantities of loam from Ethiopia in its flood waters, finally filled it in and made it part of the continent. They add that the Egyptians have received from them, as from authors and their ancestors, the greater part of their laws." Inadvertently Diodorus tells us the origin of Osiris as being Central African, a view affirmed by a Papyrus of a Nineteenth Dynasty nobleman!

**h.    Diogenes Laertes** - says of **Zeno**, founder of the Stoic School 333-261 B.C. that he was "tall and black" and "people called him an Egyptian vine-shoot."

# FREDERICK MONDERSON

**Black History Extravaganza - Photo -** Colorful view of Philae Temple against the blue sky and blue water (above) and a close-up of the Mammisi and Great Pylon.

**i.** **Ammianus Marcellinus -** the Latin historian of 33-100 A.D. notes the "men of Egypt are mostly brown or black with a skinny

# BLACK HISTORY EXTRAVAGANZA HONORING DR. BEN-JOCHANNAN

and desiccated look." He says further that the Colchians were "an ancient race of Egyptian origin." The mummy of the *Gentleman's Magazine* article of 1820 and the mummy of Rameses II were also brown! Several examples in Elliot Smith's *The Royal Mummies* (*Imprimerie De L'Institut Francais*, 1905), when the skin can be observed underneath the thick, black protective bitumen, the skin is always brown or black! That is when he chooses to refer to it!

**j.     Count Volney** - one of the Savants who followed Napoleon to Egypt at the end of the 18$^{th}$ Century, made the following statement regarding the ancient Egyptians from observations of the Copts. According to Diop, (1989) Volney wrote: "All of them are puffy-faced, heavy-eyed and thick-lipped, in a word, real mulatto faces. I was tempted to attribute this to the climate until, on visiting the Sphinx; the look of it gave me the clue to the enigma. Beholding that head characteristically Negro in all its features, I recalled the well-known passage of Herodotus, which reads: 'For my part I consider the Colchoi are a colony of the Egyptians because, like them, they are black-skinned and kinky-haired.' In other words, the ancient Egyptians were true Negroes of the same stock as all the autochthonous peoples of Africa and from that datum one sees how their race, after centuries of mixing with the blood of Romans and Greeks, must have lost the full blackness of its original color but retained the impress of its original mold. It is even possible to apply this observation very widely and posit in principle that physiognomy is a kind of record usable in many cases for disputing or elucidating the evidence of history on the origins of the peoples ...."

Even further, Volney noted: "By reverting to Egypt, its contributions to history afford many subjects for philosophic reflection. What a subject for mediation is the present-day barbarity and ignorance of the Copts who were considered, born of the alliance of the deep genius of the Egyptians and the brilliance of the Greeks, that this race of blacks who nowadays are slaves and the objects of our scorn is the very one to which we owe our arts, our sciences and even the use of spoken word; and finally recollect that it is in the midst of the peoples claiming to be the greatest friends of liberty and humanity that the most barbarous of enslavements has been sanctioned and the question raised whether black men have brains of the same quality as those of white men."

**k.    Baron Vivant Denon** - also a member of Napoleon's expedition published his *Travels in Upper and Lower Egypt* (1803) and is credited with drawing an image of the Sphinx and reported Napoleon's artillery shot off the nose. The Frenchman Gaston Maspero shielding Napoleon, later attributed this dastard deed to the Mamelukes who ruled Egypt and were destroyed by Mohammed Ali around 1800 A.D. Nevertheless, Denon did describe the Egyptians as Negroid, "having broad and flat noses, very short, a large flattened nose ... and thick lips."

**Black History Extravaganza - At the Cemetery -** Mourners stand in salutation and awe at the loss of Dr. Ben and collectively wish him a successful Transition to take his place among the Pantheon of "good and righteous Africans."

# BLACK HISTORY EXTRAVAGANZA
# HONORING DR. BEN-JOCHANNAN

**Black History Extravaganza - Photo -** Majestic art and architecture against a blue sky. How wonderful.

# FREDERICK MONDERSON

## III.　　To the Mid-19th Century

In a chapter entitled "Modern Falsification of History" Cheikh Anta Diop's in *African Origin of Civilization: Myth or Reality* discusses Domeny de Rienzi's contention that: "It is true that back in the distant past, the dark red Hindu and Egyptian race dominated culturally the yellow and black races, and even our own white race then inhabiting western Asia. At that time, our race was rather savage and sometimes tattooed, as I have seen it depicted on the tomb of Sesostris I in the valley of Biban-el-Moluk at Thebes, the city of the gods."

This is interesting, for if we believe the Egyptians were white and migrated to Africa leaving no evidence of the prototype of Egyptian culture in their place of origin in Western Asia, how did Thebes in Upper Egypt become the "city of their gods." Equally, any claim of a western Asian origin of the Egyptians ties them to the white race. Yet, the Egyptians have no recollection or record of an Asiatic past! However, let us not forget, Nubia and Central Africa was considered "God's land." Again, we are also faced with the absolutely absurd conclusion that whites from western Asia considered Africa as their "God's land!"

We should be aware, every people who migrated from one place to the next, retained some reference to their ancestral home. Contrary to popular western prognostication, the Egyptians never associated Mesopotamia, Babylonia or Southwest Asia with their origins. In fact, the record seems to indicate only one surviving native reference to origins and this was made by a 19th Dynasty nobleman who stated: "We came from the foothills of the Mountains of the Moon where the God Hapi dwells." This area is the plains of the East African mountain range. Inadvertently, he too like Diodorus also identified the place of the origin of Osiris also called Hapi, equally a god of the Nile. As John David Wortham submitted one modern 1825 mummy dissection to prove the ancient Egyptians were Caucasian how then would we regard the ancient Egyptian and the Roman Diodorus' contentions as to the origin of Osiris (Hapi) and the Egyptians? We must consider

# BLACK HISTORY EXTRAVAGANZA HONORING DR. BEN-JOCHANNAN

the latter more credible than the former based on observation rather than reconstruction.

**Black History Extravaganza** - Dr. Ben's Book - **The African Called Rameses ("The Great") II and the African Origin of "Western Civilization."**

# FREDERICK MONDERSON

"ETHIOPIA, LAND OF OUR FOREFATHERS,
LAND WHERE THE GODS LOVE TO BE."
(Beginning of UNIA's National Anthem)

"THE COLCHIANS, ETHIOPIANS, AND
EGYPTIANS HAVE THICK LIPS, BROAD
NOSES, WOOLLY HAIR, AND THEY ARE
BURNT OF SKIN."
(Herodotus, Euterpe, Book II, 450 B.C.E.)

Professor:
Yosef A. A. ben-Jochannan, 360° O.E.S.

*With sincerest respect and love to Bro. Monderson from Yosef Ben-Jochannan, Sheikh, Egypt, N.E.A., Sept. 1/90*

"I KNOW SHE WAS EGYPTIAN, SHE LOOKED
LIKE THE BLACK BIRD OF DODONNA."
(Herodotus, Euterpe, 450 B.C.E.)

"OUT OF AFRICA COMES SOMETHING
THAT'S NEW." (Ciba Symposia)

SERAKH-ANKH

**Black History Extravaganza** - Dr. Ben's Book - **The African Called Rameses ("The Great") II and the African Origin of "Western Civilization"** - Overleaf of the Title Page.

**a.    Jean Jacques Champollion - the Younger** - set to work and was successful in deciphering the hieroglyphic script, as

# BLACK HISTORY EXTRAVAGANZA
# HONORING DR. BEN-JOCHANNAN

we know, in 1822. Within ten years he was dead from overwork. However, his extensive work did unleash an interest in antiquarian studies. Diop quotes Champollion from a letter to his older brother Champollion-Figeac, who twisted the genius' words, thus helping to bring about the falsification of Egyptian history and the continued removal of Africans from this important part of African history. Champollion mentioned four groups of people starting with the Egyptians shown with a dark red color. "There can be no uncertainty about the racial identity of the man who comes next: he belongs to the black race, designated under the general term *Nahasi*. The third represent a very different aspect; his skin color borders on yellow or tan; he has a strongly aquiline nose, thick, black pointed beard, and wears a short garment of varied colors; these are called *Namou*. Finally, the last one is what we call flesh-colored, a white skin of the most delicate shade, a nose straight or slightly arched, blue eyes, blond or reddish beard, tall [in] stature and very slender, clad in a hairy ox-skin, a veritable savage tattooed on various parts of his body; he is called *Tamhou*." He wrote elsewhere: "We find there Egyptians and Africans represented in the same way." Let me also point out, the origin of the term Negro to describe Africans is 16$^{th}$ Century A.D. and any use of the word in reference to ancient Egypt is modern, false and tainted in racism as indicated by Richard B. Moore in *The Name Negro: Its Origin and Evil Use* (UB and US Communications Systems, Inc., 1960).

Even more striking, Diop argues in comparison with many West African blacks whom he names and finally states: "If the Egyptians were white, then all these fore-mentioned Negro peoples and so many others in Africa are also whites. Thus, we reach the absurd conclusion that blacks are basically whites." Even further, he writes: "On these numerous bas-reliefs, we see that, under the Eighteenth Dynasty, all the specimens of the white race were placed behind the blacks; in particular, the 'blond beast' of Gobineau and the Nazis, a tattooed savage, dressed in animal skin, instead of being at the start of all civilization, was still essentially untouched by it and occupied the last echelon of humanity."

# FREDERICK MONDERSON

**Black History Extravaganza - Photo -** Dromos to the Temple of Isis on Philae Island. To the left, 32 columns of the Western Colonnade and to the right, 17 columns of the Eastern Colonnade, fronting the temples of Harendotus, Imhotep and Mendulese. The First Pylon stands majestically beckoning come visit.

**Black History Extravaganza - Photo -** Columns of the Eastern Colonnade fronting the three chapels of Harendotus, Imhotep and Mendulese.

# BLACK HISTORY EXTRAVAGANZA HONORING DR. BEN-JOCHANNAN

**b.** **Karl Lepsius** - Diop states further Karl Lepsius offered a "Canon of proportion" in his *Discoveries in Egypt, Ethiopia and the Peninsula of Sinai in the Years* 1842-1848 (London: 1852) that denotes: "The proportions of the perfect Egyptian body; it has short arms and is Negroid or Negritian. From the anthropological point of view, the Egyptian comes after the Polynesians, Samoyeds, Europeans, and is immediately followed by African Negroes and Tasmanians. Besides, there is a scientific tendency to find in Africa, after excluding foreign influences, from the Mediterranean to the Cape, from the Atlantic to the Indian Ocean, nothing but Negroes or Negroids of various colors. The ancient Egyptians were Negroes, but Negroes to the last degree."

**c.** **Garner Wilkinson** - An English nobleman, spent several years in Egypt, particularly Thebes, during mid-19th Century. He did extensive research and produced significant works on the Egyptian culture that is still consulted by experts in the field.

# IV. To 1900

**a.** **Auguste Mariette** - Was of an age when great interest in Egypt very early attracted many scholars, adventurers and antiquities hunters and collectors from different countries, in the aftermath of Napoleon's discovery of the Rosetta stone and Champollion's decipherment of the language. However, his vision seemed different from most of his age principally bent of antiquities acquisition. Ruffle (1977: 8-9) best puts the man and his time in perspective. "With funds from King Friedrich Wilhelm IV of Prussia, Richard Lepsius made a great survey of the monuments (published in a mammoth twelve-volume work) and collected many objects, which formed the basis of the great Berlin collection. The increasing scholarly interest highlighted the need for orderly and controlled excavation. Auguste Mariette, who was sent by the Louvre to collect antiquities in Egypt,

# FREDERICK MONDERSON

realized this. With the support of the Khedive he founded the Egyptian Museum and Antiquities Service and became its first director, often pushing through his scientific policies in the teeth of opposition from other European Egyptologists."

**Black History Extravaganza - Photo -** The Western Colonnade with its 32 columns on the Dromos to the Temple of Isis on Philae, now Agilka Island.

"Mariette's concern was matched by the painstaking methodology preached by William Matthew Flinders Petrie, grandson of the explorer of Australia and the first person to hold a chair in Egyptology [in England] - University College, London. This chair had been founded by Amelia Edwards whose un-intentional Nile cruise - she had gone there when a sketching holiday in France was rained off - had filled her with an enthusiasm for Egypt that led her to found not only Petrie's chair but also the Egypt Exploration Fund. Other learned societies were also formed - notably the *Deutsche Orient Gesellschaft* in 1888 and the *Mission Archaeologique Francaise* in 1880, later the *Institut Francais d'Archaeologie Orientale*."

# BLACK HISTORY EXTRAVAGANZA HONORING DR. BEN-JOCHANNAN

**b.**     **Brugsch-Bey** - Karl Heinrich Brugsch-Bey in his *Egypt Under the Pharaohs* (London: John Murray, 1902: 2-3) has argued: "Suffice it to say, however, that, according to ethnology, the Egyptians appear to form a third branch of the Caucasian race, the family called Cushite; and this much may be regarded as certain, that in the earliest ages of humanity, far beyond all historical remembrance, the Egyptians, for reasons unknown to us, left the soil of their early home, took their way towards the setting sun, and finally crossed that bridge of nations the Isthmus of Suez, to find a new fatherland on the banks of the Nile." For argument sake, immigrants to Australia and to America knew of the land, had fellow citizens there and so migrated to settle bringing and retaining their cultural traits. However, Brugsch-Bey's "Caucasians" probably didn't know of Egypt and thus can't say they had citizens there which would mean they probably did more than one migration. Time and time again, the Egyptians were described as "boat people." The earliest boats we see images of were in the Upper Nile! Imagine "a boat people" crossing the desert but Africans who live on the river are not given due consideration. Nevertheless, many of these individuals such as Brugsch-Bey generally argue on speculation and offer no facts to support their contentions because none exists.

**Black History Extravaganza - At the Cemetery -** Sisters stood tall.

# FREDERICK MONDERSON

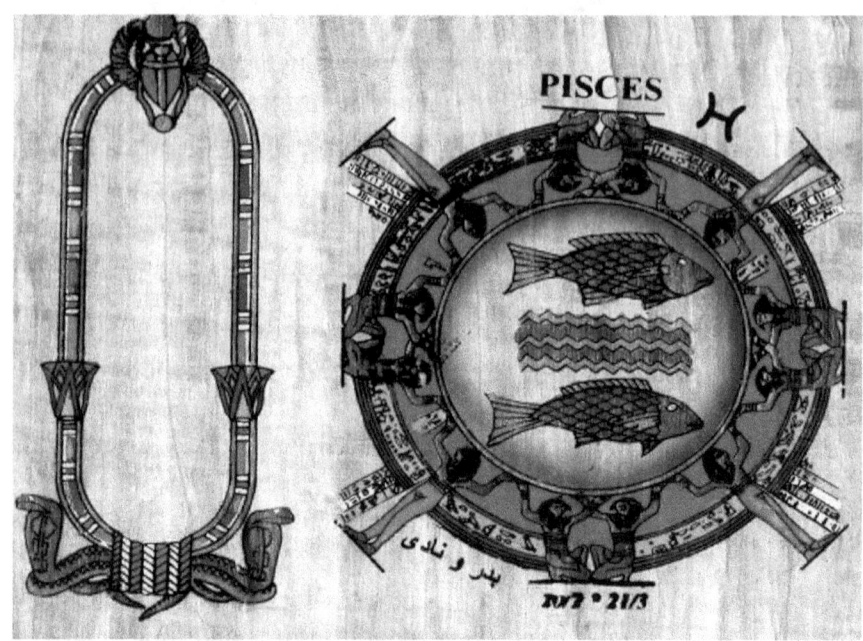

**Black History Extravaganza - Papyrus** - A Blank Cartouche and the Astrological sign for Pisces.

**c. Adolf Erman** - German scholar extraordinaire. It's been argued Erman was probably the only modern who understood exactly what the Egyptians meant in their language. Nevertheless, Charles Finch writing "Black Roots of Egypt's Glory" in *Great Black Leaders: Ancient and Modern* (1988: 140-141) edited by Ivan Van Sertima, has stated: "As the 19th Century wore on, German scholars began applying their meticulous methods of research to the study of ancient Egyptian language. Finding many similarities in words and syntax between Egyptian and the Semitic languages, the Germans unhesitatingly proclaimed Egyptian to belong to this group. As a result, their leading Egyptologists Eber, Erman and Brugsch - concluded that the impetus for Egyptian civilization itself came from a western Asiatic or Semitic source. Like others, they saw in the human figures on the Egyptian monuments - many colored a reddish - brown - evidence of a non-African 'Mediterranean race.' Anthropologically speaking, no such race ever existed, but that did not trouble them overmuch and the term has remained in vogue to this day." Obviously, there was somewhat of a turn-around because

# BLACK HISTORY EXTRAVAGANZA HONORING DR. BEN-JOCHANNAN

**Black History Extravaganza - Photo -** At her temple, Isis as Hathor sports a Vulture headdress atop a mortar with horns and sun-disk crowned by Isis' throne name. Her accentuated breast is an art feature of Graeco-Roman times.

Erman later wrote in *Life in Ancient Egypt* (New York: Macmillan, 1894: 32) confirming: "The inhabitants of Libya, Egypt and Ethiopia have probably belonged to the same race since prehistoric times. In physical structure, they are still Africans." Otherwise, he implied, they were all white! Let me also add, Brugsch is different to Brugsch-Bey!

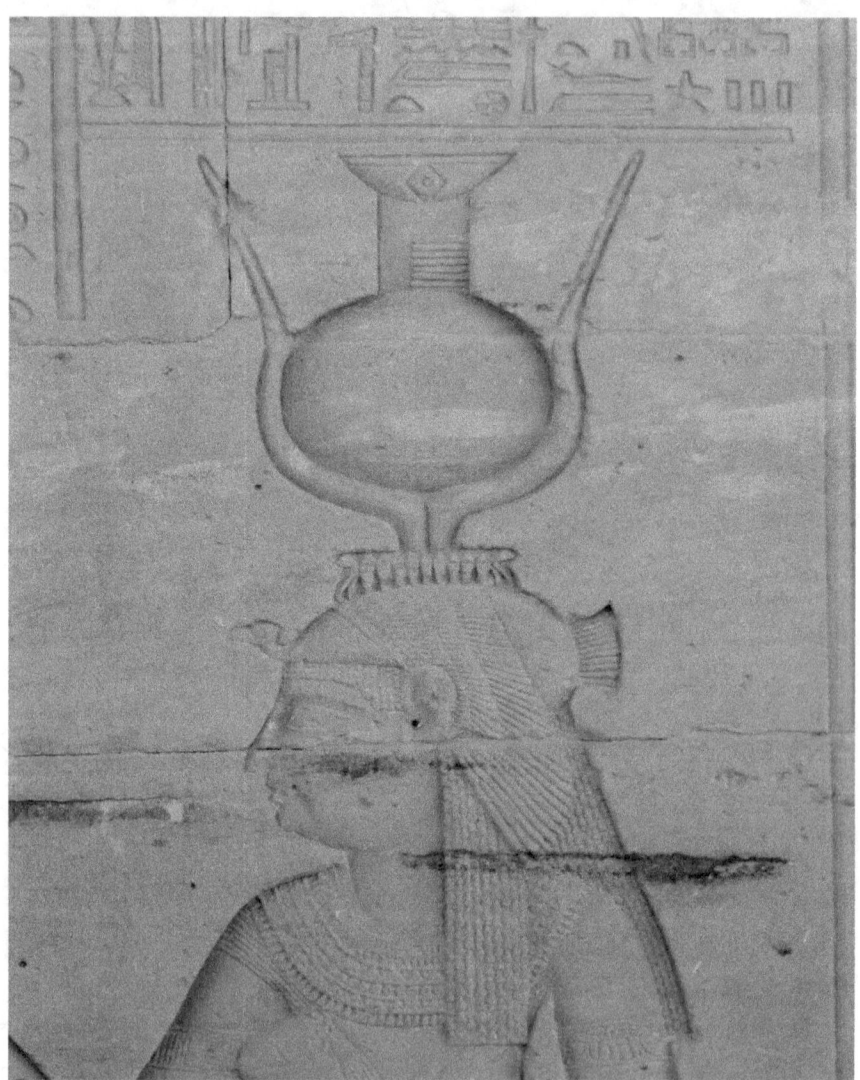

**Black History Extravaganza - Photo -** At Isis's Philae Temple, Nephthys as Hathor sports a Vulture headdress atop a mortar with horns and sun-disk crowned by her Heb name. Her accentuated breast is an art feature of Graeco-Roman times.

# BLACK HISTORY EXTRAVAGANZA HONORING DR. BEN-JOCHANNAN

**d.  Gaston Maspero** - French Egyptian expert who discovered the Pyramid Texts has written extensively on the history and culture of Egypt while Director of Antiquities in Egypt. He held this post twice. However, his take is that the ancient Egyptians were of European origin, crossed over to North Africa and entered Egypt from the west. What a pity! Henry L'Hote in "Tassili Frescoes" identified Negroes in the Sahara between 7500 and 6000 B.C. Why could these blacks not be able to enter the Nile Valley from the Sahara but whites could cross over to North Africa from Europe, generally living on the shores of North Africa in the Libya environs and then follow essentially the same route into the Valley? If they did enter the valley at all, it would probably be from the Libya area and so into "Lower Egypt." Suppose the Africans never got to the Mediterranean Sea shores, then their entry would be more southward. As such, there is a difference in that Maspero's whites probably entered into the north. They would, therefore, have to contend with the Nabta Playa Blacks who entered into, and controlled Upper Egypt. That is, from the southern frontier to Memphis, considered all of Upper Egypt.

**e.  William Matthew Flinders Petrie** (1853-1942) - The "Father of modern archaeology," did extensive research in Egypt and was one of the most prolific writers of his day, influencing a great many people with his still, now considered, racist views. Stuart Tyson Smith's "Race" in Donald B. Redford's Edited *The Oxford Encyclopedia of Ancient Egypt* Vol. 3, (2001: 111) has written: "The origins of the modern conception of race derive from the work of nineteenth-century anthropologists like L.H. Morgan and E.B. Taylor, who developed 'scientific' unilinear evolutionary theoretical models for the development of human beings from 'Savagery' to 'Civilization.' Racial groups were ranked by evolutionary categories, linked to intellectual capacities, based on elaborate cranial measurements; supposedly, this provided causal links between phenotype (observable) traits, mental capacities, and

# FREDERICK MONDERSON

socio-political dominance. This model not coincidentally reinforced the existing European-American domination of third-world peoples with the claim of scientifically 'objective' methodologies based on race and evolution." Even further Smith continued: "The unilinear evolutionary model did influence some early Egyptologists. W. M. Flinders Petrie used it to develop his notion of the 'Dynastic Race,' to explain the rapid development of Egyptian civilization. In part, this was based on prevailing models of culture change that emphasized migration as an explanation for cultural change, but, ultimately, racist notions drove the model. *The implication was that Egypt had a 'white' or 'brown' ruling class dominating a native 'black' African underclass who supplied the labor to build Egypt's great monuments.* [Author's italics.] The Egyptological community as a whole never enthusiastically accepted Petrie's model, although the idea persisted through a few enthusiasts." James Henry Breasted echoed the sentiments of most contemporary Egyptologists in seeing the Egyptians as indigenous, but as a brown rather than black race, related to other northeastern Africans. It is interesting to note that the Egyptians became 'White' for a classroom textbook [*Ancient Times*], presumably reflecting the racism of the day. The last serious argument in support of the Dynastic Race theory appeared in Walter Emery's *Archaic Egypt* (New York, 1961)."

**Black History Extravaganza- At the Cemetery** - Prof. James Smalls contemplates his thought as the Kher-Heb priest.

# BLACK HISTORY EXTRAVAGANZA
# HONORING DR. BEN-JOCHANNAN

**Black History Extravaganza - Photo -** Wearing the Osiris Crown of Horns, uraei with sun disks and white crowns anchored by sun disks, the king presents a sphinx to the god whose scepter and hand is shown.

# FREDERICK MONDERSON

**Black History Extravaganza - Photo -** In the little Chapel of Hathor at Isis's Temple at Philae, engaged screen-walls are illustrated while the Pylon and wall of Isis' temple proper stands in rear.

**f.     Ernest Alfred Wallis Budge -** Wallis Budge was Keeper of Egyptian and Assyrian Antiquities at the British Museum and a prolific writer who wrote about *The Gods of the Egyptians, The Mummy, Egyptian Magic,* an *Egyptian Hieroglyphic Dictionary,* and a whole lot more.  Regarding Budge, Finch (1988) states; though, "Unusual for an Egyptologist, he had conducted extensive research among the peoples of the Sudan and Ethiopia - encountering cultural practices, religious ideas and languages which showed clear and identifiable linkages to ancient Egypt.  It became clear to Budge that everything about ancient Egypt could be understood only by reference to Africa; there was nothing fundamentally Asiatic about Egyptian culture.  In 1920, in his massive and erudite *'Egyptian Hieroglyphic Dictionary,'* Budge, reversing a 100-year trend and his own earlier opinion, classified Egyptian as an African rather than a Semitic language."

# BLACK HISTORY EXTRAVAGANZA HONORING DR. BEN-JOCHANNAN

**Black History Extravaganza - Ceramic Art -** An early form of the ankh in decorated style.

# FREDERICK MONDERSON

Then again, we know the Egyptian religious writing is the oldest in the world. By the First Dynasty, the *Book of the Dead* was a compilation of much earlier works, which meant Egyptian writing certainly took some time to develop into that state. How come the people from Asia or wherever they came from never invented Hieroglyphics in their point of origin, nor probably had any writing until they came to the Nile Valley? Even when they did, their "ancestors" wrote on stone. Imagine a student carrying a bag full of stone tablets! The answer debunks Brugsch-Bey. Certainly Diop, Arnett and even Winkler show the development of rudimentary forms of Hieroglyphs in the Upper Nile region dating perhaps as early as 6000 B.C. However, while Diop and Arnett see them as indigenous; Winkler holds to Mesopotamian origins while those of the Eastern Desert of Upper Egypt are seen by Toby Wilkinson as "a thousand years before Winkler's Mesopotamians!"

**g.     Canon George Rawlinson -** In *The Story of the Nations*: *Egypt* (1893: 23-24) Rawlinson debunks the Asiatic notion in the statement: "It is generally answered that they came from Asia; but this is not much more than a conjecture. The physical type of the Egyptians is different from that of any known Asiatic nation. The Egyptians had no traditions that at all connected them with Asia. Their language, indeed, in historic times was partially Semitic, and allied to the Hebrew, the Phoenician, and the Aramaic; but the relationship was remote, and may be partly accounted for by later intercourse, without involving original derivation. The fundamental character of the Egyptian in respect of physical type, language, and tone of thought, is Nigritic. The Egyptians were not Negroes, but they bore a resemblance to the Negro, which is indisputable. Their type differs from the Caucasian in exactly those respects which when exaggerated produce the Negro. They were darker, had thicker lips, lower foreheads, larger heads, more advancing jaws, a flatter foot, and a more attenuated frame. It is quite conceivable that the Negro type was produced by a gradual degeneration from that which we find in Egypt. It is even conceivable that the Egyptian type was produced by gradual advance and amelioration from that of the Negro."

# BLACK HISTORY EXTRAVAGANZA HONORING DR. BEN-JOCHANNAN

**Black History Extravaganza - Photo -** The Kiosk of Trajan at Isis Temple on Philae now Agilka island.

**Black History Extravaganza - Photo -** The Second Eastern Colonnade between the Two Pylons at Isis' Temple.

# FREDERICK MONDERSON

**h.   M. le Vicomte J. de Rouge -** is mentioned in an article in *American Journal of Archaeology*, Vol. 1 (1897: 393-95) where he raises the question of "The Origin of the Egyptian Race" and attempted to "prove the theory of the Asiatic derivation." Emphasizing statues found belonging to the third, fifth and sixth dynasties, he stated: "The types of the faces do not belong to the later Egyptian style, but possess elements of the more refined Semitic organization; and this fact is used by the writer as a proof of the importation of a fully developed civilization into Egypt." Essentially, the article argued there are three theories as to the origin of the Egyptian race: (1) that the entry of the population into Egypt was made by way of Asia, passing through the Isthmus of Suez; (2) that Egypt became occupied by a colony which came in part from Asia, but passed through Ethiopia; (3) that the majority of the Egyptian population had its origin in Africa and passed into Egypt by the west and southwest." This last is a more recent theory which has been in a measure accepted by M. Maspero, and is supported by a large number of students of natural history and of ethnology, while the theory of the Asiatic origin is based on linguistic comparisons and a study of the monuments, especially the primitive monuments of Babylonia."

He says further: "The Egyptians seem not to have preserved any tradition or indication, or even memory, of their foreign origin, for they consider themselves as autochthones, and regard their country as the cradle of the human race." In addition, he argues: "The most ancient monuments discovered up to this time appear to belong to the third dynasty, such as the recently discovered bas-relief of King Sozir; that of Prince Ra-Hotpu and of Princess Nofrit, etc. The statues of the two last mentioned royal personages show that the art of sculpture was already in an advanced stage of development, and the types of the faces, with their aquiline noses and thin lips, recall the Semitic race rather than the Egyptian. The great Sphinx of Ghizeh, which is perhaps the most ancient relic of Egyptian art, is also anterior to the fourth dynasty." He never says anything more regarding the "Negro features" of the Sphinx. Of course, Dr. ben-Jochannan, the master-teacher, extolled the Egyptian nobleman who specifically stated: "We came from the headwaters of the Nile, at the foothills of the mountains

# BLACK HISTORY EXTRAVAGANZA HONORING DR. BEN-JOCHANNAN

of the moon where the God Hapi dwells." This area is in the East African region of Mounts Ruwenzori, Kenya and Kilimanjaro near Uganda and Kenya. Importantly also, it places the origin of Osiris in Central Africa!

**Black History Extravaganza - Photo -** The majesty of Egyptian architecture as demonstrated at the Kiosk of Trajan and reflected against a blue sky overhead.

**Black History Extravaganza - Photo -** While the "Musicians" "make merry" (left); Dr. Rosalind Jeffries joins another beauty at the Podium.

# FREDERICK MONDERSON

**Black History Extravaganza - Photo -** That majesty of Egyptian architecture is accentuated in this Capital on the Kiosk of Trajan in which each member differs from the other.

**i.     Eduardo Naville -** a Swiss Archaeologist, he cleared the two Deir el Bahari temples. The *American Journal of Archaeology* XVIII (1913: 202) reported Eduardo Naville presented a paper on "The African Origin of Egyptian Civilization" published in *R. Arch* XXII (1913, pp. 47-65) that stated essentially: "The rise of Egyptian civilization after the Neolithic period was due to conquest by an African people from the South, called Anou. The people who caused the changes when the Thinite period ends and the Memphite period begins may have been Asiatic but they brought in no important new elements, - they merely gave a new impulse to the existing civilization." This means these Asiatics comprised the third and fourth dynasties ruling at Memphis and all they brought were their "pretty white selves." However, Petrie mentioned the founder of the third dynasty was Ethiopian from observing his features in the Sinai. Notwithstanding, from their images, Snefru of the third and Khufu, Khafre (Khafra) and Menkaure, builders of the fourth dynasty Ghizeh Pyramids, were, by operating definitions, black or Negro!

# BLACK HISTORY EXTRAVAGANZA
# HONORING DR. BEN-JOCHANNAN

**Black History Extravaganza** - Dr. Ben's Book - **The Black Man's Religion - Volume II.**

# FREDERICK MONDERSON

**j.** On the subject of race, **G. Elliot Smith** in *The Ancient Egyptians and Their Influence Upon the Civilization of Europe* (London and New York: Harper and Brothers, 1911: 32-39) provided proof of the rather in-depth search for the correct formula. As such, he states: "Even such eminent scholars as de Rouge, Heinrich Brugsch, and Ebers, among many others, claimed that Egypt derived her language as well as much of her culture and knowledge of the arts from Asia; and Hommel and others went much further, and claimed that the whole Egyptian civilization was Babylonian in origin ...."

Even further, Smith continued: "De Morgan and his collaborators claim that the Ancient Egyptian language and mode of writing, the importation into Egypt of the knowledge of metals, and of such crafts as brick-making and tomb-construction, and even the fauna and flora of the country in ancient times, all point to Babylonia as the place where the roots of Egyptian civilization should be sought." More so, however, "But, under Dr. Reisner's critical analysis of the foundations upon which these speculations were supposed to have been based, practically the whole of the elaborate edifice has tumbled to the ground. As Eduard Meyer has said, 'the suggestion that a culture, or even its chief elements, can be derived from another people is unthinkable and historically false: but influences must have been at work, and the Egyptians and Babylonians must have given and taken.'"

**Black History Extravaganza - Photo -** Professor Carr of Howard University (left); and Minister Hafeez of the Nation of Islam, Mosque Number Seven, both praise and thank Dr. Ben-Jochannan for an outstanding life and work.

# BLACK HISTORY EXTRAVAGANZA
# HONORING DR. BEN-JOCHANNAN

**Black History Extravaganza - Photo -** Again, that majestic architecture of the Egyptians is here highlighted in another of those different capitals, particularly as it is emphasized against a blue sky. Notice the Abacus supporting the architrave bridging the gap overhead.

Even more, Smith wrote: "Dr. Reisner has proved the indigenous origin of Egyptian civilization in the Nile Valley, and has revealed the complete absence of any evidence to show, or even to suggest, that the language, mode of writing, the knowledge of copper, or the distinctive arts and crafts were imported."

"Schweinfurt argued that the 'invaders' of Egypt - the stereotyped phrase used by so many writers, tacitly assuming as a fact the idea of an immigration into Egypt - came from Southern Arabia (Subarea or Hadramut), across the Straits of Bab el-Mandeb, thence through

Abyssinia and the eastern Desert into Nubia, from which they spread along the banks of the Nile into Egypt ...." In essence, these people passed through Nubia heading down-river. One has to wonder whether Nubians were standing on the river banks and cheered them on! On the other hand, "Lortet and Gaillard, the most recent writers to discuss the fauna of Ancient Egypt, protest against the conclusions of Duerst that certain of the domestic animals of Ancient Egypt were brought from Asia; and they tell us that the animals known to have lived in Egypt at the time of the Ancient Empire were all African, that is, local in origin ...."

Referring to previous statements, such as preceding his book by almost a century, "Blumenbach began the serious study of the physical characters of the Ancient Egyptians. Since then a considerable number of scholars have contributed to the discussion of the significance of the anatomical evidence - in America, Nott, Gliddon, and Meigs might be mentioned as pioneers; in France, Perrier, Pruner, Broca, Quatrefages, Hamy, Fouquet, Zabarowski, Cantre, Lortet, and Verneau have made contributions of varying importance; in German-speaking countries, Carus, Czermak, Virchow, Hartmenn, Emile Schmidt, Stahr, and Oetteking may be mentioned; in England, Bernard Davis, Huxley, Owen, Petrie, Garson, Randall-MacIver, Thomson, Macalister, Karl Pearson and his school of biometricans, Myers and Keith represent some of the outstanding names of those who have written about the craniology of the Egyptians; and last, but by no means least, Italy has added the important and highly suggestive writings of Sergi, Biasutti, and Giuffrida-Ruggeri."

G. Elliot Smith, the anatomist from the University of Manchester examined the royal mummies and is the author of the "Diffusionist theory" that Egyptian culture spread far and wide influencing many people with its contributions to human civilization development. His book, *The Ancient Egyptians and Their Influence upon the Civilization of Europe* is a classic. However, some guides have commented on his bitterness, for, after having examined the

# BLACK HISTORY EXTRAVAGANZA
# HONORING DR. BEN-JOCHANNAN

mummies, he was ushered from the room, paid, but without his notes. This may have led to some enmity towards the ancient Egyptians.

**Black history Extravaganza - Papyrus -** The Ankh in magnificent splendor.

# FREDERICK MONDERSON

## V.     To 1950

**a.     Randall MacIver** - Mr. Randall-MacIver did a study in 1905 and came to the conclusion that there were two peoples living in Egypt, side by side, Africans and Europeans. His position has been; whites were in occupation in the north and blacks in the south. There was much discussion about this but it forces us to wonder how the critics in Europe, England especially, could come to agreement on this so later disputed fact.

**b.     Arthur Weigall** - Young and impetuous, he was an Englishman who first studied with Petrie at Abydos. He wrote a book, among others, entitled *Flights into Antiquity* in which he entitled a chapter, "Exploits of a Nigger King," dealing with the XXVth Dynasty. The title of this chapter signals his contempt for Africans and thus he would not have seen Egypt as African and black. As Inspector of Upper Egypt, he wrote *The Antiquities of Upper Egypt* and cooperated with Alan Gardiner in doing work on Tombs at Thebes, He is the writer who claimed Rameses II was Syrian. Which begs the question, 'Why would Rameses, in the **Battle of Kadesh**, call on an African god, Amon, saying his ancestors had worshipped the god from time immemorial, and sought his help at that crucial and challenging time.' Imagine a Syrian, Asiatic, calling upon an African god while doing battle in Asia! Further, imagine this same Syrian calling upon and even worshipping an African god whose alter ego, Min, was black! We also know Amon was black. This also questions the contention that Osiris was black because of his role as god of the dead. Fact is the straw men arguments easily fall apart!

# BLACK HISTORY EXTRAVAGANZA
# HONORING DR. BEN-JOCHANNAN

**Black History Extravaganza - Photo -** Another of the magnificent capitals in the Kiosk of Hadrian at Philae.

**c.   James Henry Breasted -** pioneering American Egyptologist - Charles S. Finch III again in "The Black Roots of Egypt's Glory" quotes James Henry Breasted who wrote pejoratively: "Unfitted by ages of tropical life for any effective intrusion among the White Race, the Negro and Negroid people remained without any influence on the development of civilization."

It is amazing that people of Breasted's hue could write about such significant historical issues with such profound racial venom. Breasted's *History of Egypt, Ancient Records of Egypt, Ancient Times, The Conquest of Civilization, The Development of Religion and Thought in Ancient Egypt* and *Dawn of Conscience* are classic "primary sources of the primary sources" of ancient Egypt. The thought of a German American writing about a people of ancient Africa and could entertain the above quote raises a whole series of questions about intent and influence. We need never forget, Goethe believed, "wherever Germans went, they corrupted whatever culture they found!"

# FREDERICK MONDERSON

You mean to tell me, while writing his *Ancient Records Egypt* in 1905, by the time his *Ancient Times* was published in 1916 where he described the Egyptians as "brown men," he did not know Mentuhotep II had "black flesh" even though his statue was discovered in 1898. Perhaps also, the gold of Tutankhamon blinded Breasted to the young king's black skin. In his *Ancient Times* published in 1916, Breasted described the ancient Egyptians as "Brown-skinned men of slender build, with dark hair ...." However, when he re-issued the work in 1935, he only dealt with "the great white race." Some have argued, because Rockefeller gave monies to fund his Oriental Studies Program, this turn-around was the "quid pro quo." Again, nowhere does Breasted refer to Mentuhotep's "black flesh."

Nevertheless, it is well-known that the resurrection and reclamation of ancient Egypt occurred in the 19th Century and early part of the 20th Century. However, in the period before "The Rape of the Nile," was published, consistent cries were made about destruction of the ancient culture, both by natives and European plunderers, seeking treasure and collectibles. Often reports would be made that natives were destroying sites whether for purposes of fuel or in order to secure and sell antiquities to anyone who would buy them. Generally, Europeans who wanted to draw attention to the problem and help to preserve the ancient record made these reports. However, very seldom did the finger get pointed to or identify European plunderers and all that is said is that this or that antique was damaged. Who knows what was destroyed purposely or by "accident?" Certainly, "strongman Egyptologist" Belzoni did his share of destruction in 1818-1819 and beyond!

# BLACK HISTORY EXTRAVAGANZA HONORING DR. BEN-JOCHANNAN

AFRICA'S NILE VALLEY, PEOPLE, CULTURE AND HISTORY: A Major Problem For The A.D.L.'s Hit Squad

Yosef A. A. ben-Jochannan
N.Y. 6094/H.C.4600/C.E. 1994

**Black History Extravaganza** -Dr. Ben's Book **- Africa's Nile Valley, People, Culture and History: A Major Problem for the A.D.L's Hit Squad.**

# FREDERICK MONDERSON

Still, one has to entertain a credible question, with today's hindsight, which is, 'How accurate is the work of people like Breasted?' or, 'Has there been any distortion, omission or exclusion in their work?' In the reconstruction of the role of Blacks in ancient Egypt, evidence has to be gleaned from fragments and from the honest reports of men of good will, simply because much of racially or ethnically relevant material has been destroyed in the trampled-over state. However, as more and more research focuses on these fragments they emerge larger than originally thought, for "truth crushed to the earth shall rise." In this, the work of racist and pseudo-scientific writers and historians are highlighted and the smoke and mirrors they constructed around the historical truth are now being blown away; and the true and marked naked prejudice of their writings and thinking that have misinformed for so long, are finally being blown away. And there they stand, "naked, without clothes" in a world of political and historical correctness.

**Black History Extravaganza - At the Cemetery -** Measuring the space to make sure everything fits perfectly!

# BLACK HISTORY EXTRAVAGANZA
# HONORING DR. BEN-JOCHANNAN

**Black History Extravaganza - Photo -** What a magnificent image of capital, abacus and double sun-disk with outstretched wing and uraei on the overhead architrave.

# FREDERICK MONDERSON

**Black History Extravaganza - Photo -** Another magnificent image of capital and abacus below overhead architrave under a blue sky.

# BLACK HISTORY EXTRAVAGANZA HONORING DR. BEN-JOCHANNAN

**d.     T. Eric Pet** - Another Oxford scholar, Editor of the *Journal of Egyptian Archaeology* and part of the Egypt Exploration Fund staff. He was critical of Akhnaton in an article entitled "The Problem with Akhnaton." While doing important work in the reclamation of Egypt, he too had and helped foster the same false conception that the Egyptians were white! Nevertheless, as his Bibliography indicates, he did extensive work and so his influence was widespread.

**e.     Foster** (1974: 178) - mentions the "Monogenesis" and "polygenesis" theories dating to the 18$^{th}$ Century that helped lay the basis for the 19$^{th}$ Century's "Hamitic Hypothesis" which reinforced the view, 'Any evidence of civilization found in Africa were brought there by a people of white morphology!' This racist but now refuted "Hamitic Hypothesis" reinforcing the view Hamites were Caucasians was given great credence by C.G. Seligman's (1930) *Races of Africa* as stated in Foster: "Apart from relatively late Semitic influences… the civilizations of Africa are the civilizations of the Hamites, its history the record of these peoples and of their interaction with the two other African stocks, the Negro and the Bushman, whether this influence was exerted by highly civilized Egyptians or by such wider pastoralists as are represented at the present day by the Beja and Somali. The incoming Hamites were pastoral 'Europeans' - arriving wave after wave-better armed as well as quicker witted than the dark agricultural Negroes."

While Foster goes on to elucidate the contributions of Huntingford (1966) and; Sonia Cole (1963); we need be reminded of Robert July's *A History of the African People* (1970) and *Precolonial Africa: An Economic and Social History* (1975); Robin Hallett's *Africa to 1875* (1970) Oliver and Fage *History of West Africa* (1962) he pointed put much of their writings, by today's research revelations, would be labeled "Distortions." George Peter Murdock in *Africa: Its Peoples and Their Culture History* (1959: 101) continued essentially adhering to Seligman's dogma of falsity: "Around 5000, B.C., when the Negroes of the Upper Niger were apparently making their first experiments with the cultivation of plants, the inhabitants of the lower

# FREDERICK MONDERSON

Nile were taking a parallel step. Sebilian, a Mesolithic hunting and gathering culture, was being replaced by Neolithic cultures, variously called Merimdean, Fayum, Tasian, and Badarian, borne by people indistinguishable in physical type from the later Dynastic Egyptians. From adjacent Southwest Asia, where agriculture and animal domestication had already been practiced for perhaps 2000 years, they borrowed the means and techniques of food production and freed themselves from their earlier dependence upon food gathering. Radiocarbon dating shows that they had made this advance by 4500 B.C." He goes on to further extol the view: "We must, however, examine those aspects of culture which this volume attempts to cover for other parts of Africa, so that we may be able later to assess the influence of ancient Egyptian civilization elsewhere in the continent. This impact is to be sought first of all, of course, in the cultures of the peoples who bordered Pharaonic Egypt. These were four in number: The Berbers, who inhabited the Mediterranean coast and adjacent desert oases immediately to the west; the Beja, who occupied the arid region lying between the Nile Valley and the Red Sea to the southeast; the Nubians, who dwelt around the Nile to the south beyond Wadi Halfa; and, across a stretch of uninhabitable desert to the southwest, the Teda of Fezzan and Tibesti. The last two were Negro peoples with completely alien languages. The Berbers, however, were Caucasoid, like the Egyptians, and the three peoples spoke languages of different sub-families of the same Hamitic stock, namely Berber, Cushitic, and Egyptian. Traces of borrowing from Pharaonic civilization discovered in the cultures of these neighboring groups may then be pursued into other areas as far as the evidence leads."

# BLACK HISTORY EXTRAVAGANZA
# HONORING DR. BEN-JOCHANNAN

**Black history Extravaganza - Photo -** Another magnificent view of the elevated columns of Trajan's Kiosk at Isis Temple on Philae.

# FREDERICK MONDERSON

**Black History Extravaganza - Photo -** Oh, my goodness. Magnificent!

This all goes to show, the layers and layers of efforts to reinforce the European, Caucasian, Egyptian type. But, despite his mistaken view

# BLACK HISTORY EXTRAVAGANZA
# HONORING DR. BEN-JOCHANNAN

of Diop, William Arnett did prove one unmistaken fact: "Diop did prove the Egyptians were not Caucasians!" Even, David O'Connor echoes the same view, "The Egyptians were not white!"

## VI. The Black Challenge to 2000

a. **W.E.B. DuBois** - An exceptional scholar, he began *The Negro* (Oxford University Press (1915) (1970: 140) by affirming Negro blood ran in the veins of the Egyptians, but held they were mulatto! He wrote: "With mulatto Egypt Black Africa was always in close touch, so much so that to some all evidence of Negro uplift seems Egyptian in origin." While he also wrote, *Black Folks Then and Now* (1903), he continued this in *The World and Africa* but **could not fully defend the argument of a black Egypt**! Yet, in *The World and Africa* (1946) (1971: 91-92) he does quote Palgrave who says: "As to faces, the peculiarities of the Negro countenance are well known in caricature; but a truer pattern may be seen by those who wish to study it any day among the statues of the Egyptian rooms in the British Museum: that large gentle eyes, the full but not over protruding lips, the rounded contour, and the good-natured, easy sensuous expression. This is the genuine African model; one not often to be met with in European or American thoroughfares, where the plastic African too readily acquires the careful look and even the irregularity of the features that surrounded him; but which is common enough in the villages and fields where he dwells after his own fashion among his own people; most common of all in the tranquil seclusion and congenial climate of Surinam plantation. There you may find also, a type neither Asiatic nor European, but distinctly African; with much of the independence and vigor in the male physiognomy and something that approaches, if it does not quite reach, beauty in the female. Rameses and his queen were cast in no other mold." Such a claim flies in the face of those museum displays that misrepresents in catering to please European and American visitors.

# FREDERICK MONDERSON

**b.     Carter G. Woodson** - The "father of Black History" who detailed *The African Background Outlined* and in *The Mis-Education of the Negro* (Trenton, New Jersey: Africa World Press, 1993: 154), and *The Education of the Negro*, he was a writer for Marcus Garvey's newspaper, *The Negro World*. Woodson wrote: "We should not underrate the achievements of Mesopotamia, Greece and Rome; but we should give equally to the integral African kingdoms, the Songhai (Songhay) empire, and Ethiopia, which through Egypt decidedly influenced the civilization of the Mediterranean world."

**c.     J.E. Harris** - (Editor) of *Pillars in Ethiopian History* (Howard University Press) (1981: 6-7) has discussed the work of William Leo Hansberry, who, at Howard University began teaching about "Negro Civilizations of Ancient Africa" and developed the following courses:

**1.    NEGRO PEOPLES IN THE CULTURES ANDCIVILIZATIONS OF PREHISTORIC AND PROTOHISTORIC TIMES.** This was a survey course based on the latest archaeological and anthropological findings concerning the Paleolithic and Neolithic cultures of Africa, the pre-dynastic civilization of Ancient Egypt, and relations to the proto-historic and early historic civilizations of the eastern Mediterranean, and western and southern Asia.

**2.    THE ANCIENT CIVILIZATIONS OF ETHIOPIA.** This course was a survey from about 4000 B.C., covering the general areas encompassed by the present-day countries of Sudan and Ethiopia. Hansberry relied on Egyptian, Hebrew, and Greek sources as well as archaeological and anthropological data from several expeditions, including Harvard-Boston Expedition at Kerma, Napata, and Meroe.

# BLACK HISTORY EXTRAVAGANZA HONORING DR. BEN-JOCHANNAN

**3. THE CIVILIZATIONS OF WEST AFRICA IN MEDIEVAL AND EARLY MODERN TIMES.** This course surveyed the political and cultural development of Ghana, Mali, Songhay and Yorubaland as portrayed in Arab chronicles, and the archaeological and anthropological evidence in English, French and German investigations.

**d.     Prof. John H. Clarke** in John G. Jackson's *Introduction to African Civilization* (1970: 12) says "the 19th Century German scholar Arnold Herman Heeren" in discussing trade between the Carthaginians, Ethiopians and Egyptians, "gave more support to the concept of the southern African origin of Egyptian civilization."

**Black History Extravaganza - Photo -** Again, the majesty of Egyptian architecture as depicted in these raised columns in the Kiosk of Trajan at Isis temple at Philae, now Agilka Island.

**e. Yosef A.A. ben-Jochannan** wrote extensively and very early began carrying people to Egypt to experience the monuments and he meticulously pointed out disparities in reporting by Western and American writers. He made a special effort to point out, in the Cairo Museum the role Gaston Maspero played in shaping the interpretation of ancient Egypt by creating the "Place Cards" of the cases. He particularly pointed to Maspero's determination that Mahepra, a prince, was "Negroid but not Negro." This was tremendously important because Mahepra was of that 19th Dynasty age in which it was pointed out specifically the place of "Origin of the Egyptians" and from whence the God Hapi (Osiris) came.

**Black History Extravaganza - Papyrus** - Turning grapes into wine.

**f.** **J.A. Rogers** in *Sex and Race* Vol. I (1967: 42), echoing sentiments similar to Diop's contention that "The true Negro is nothing more than a cigar-store concoction," says essentially Herman Junker, who had written about "The First Appearance of the Negroes in History" *Journal of Egyptian Archaeology* (1921) was mistaken in looking for Negro traits in the graves of 5000 to 3600 B.C. "The Ethiopians, or Nubians, who were described by Herodotus, Diodorus Siculus, Ammianus and others as black and woolly-haired, were Hamites, he declares." Rogers continued: "It is no wonder he did not find any of that type, however, because the kind of Negro created by

# BLACK HISTORY EXTRAVAGANZA HONORING DR. BEN-JOCHANNAN

the right-wing ethnologists is a rarity. It is no more characteristic of the race than the ape-like creature of the bogs that was once used to represent the Irish was true of all Irishmen." We must remember Winwood Reade wrote: "The typical Negro is a rare variety even among Negroes." Frobinus says also, "Open an illustrated geography and compare 'The Type of the African Negro,' the bluish-black fellow of the protuberant lips, the flattened nose, the stupid expression, and the short curly hair with the tall, bronze figures from Dark Africa with which we have of late become familiar, their almost fine-cut features, slightly arched nose, long hair …. In other respects, too, the genuine African of the interior bears no resemblance to the accepted Negro type.'"

**Black History Extravaganza - Photo -** From within the Kiosk, looking skyward against a blue sky, three columns with their capitals.

# FREDERICK MONDERSON

**Black History Extravaganza - Photo -** From within the Kiosk, looking skyward against a blue sky, three columns with their capitals.


Even further, Joel A. Rogers mentions: "Livingstone said that the Negro face as he saw it reminded him more of that on the monuments of ancient Assyria than that of the popular white fancy." Sir Harry Johnston, foremost authority on the African Negro noted: "The Hamite, that Negroid stock which was the main stock of the ancient Egyptians, is best represented at the present day by the Somali, Galla, and the blood of Abyssinia and Nubia. Sergi compares pictorially the features of Rameses with that of Mtesa, noted Negro king of Uganda, and shows the marked resemblance. Sir M.W. Flinders Petrie, famed Egyptologist, says that the Pharaohs of the X dynasty were of the Galla type, and the Gallas are clearly what are known in our day as Negroes. He tells further of seeing one day on a train a man whose features were 'the exact living type' of a statue of ancient Libya, and discovered that the man was an American mulatto."

# BLACK HISTORY EXTRAVAGANZA HONORING DR. BEN-JOCHANNAN

**g.    Ivan Van Sertima** - in his "Race and Origins of the Egyptians" in *Egypt Revisited* has argued: "The African claim to Egyptian civilization rests upon a vast body of evidence. Some are cultural (ritual practices of the ancient Egyptian can be traced to the African - his totemism, circumcision, form of the divine kingship is distinct from that of the Asian); some are linguistic (Diop demonstrated convincingly at the **UNESCO** debate in 1974 that the Egyptians belonged beyond question to the family of African languages); some indicate a shared techno-complex (the forerunners of mummification and pyramid-building are found south of Egypt in pre-dynastic times).    Most important, however, are the physical evidences. The Greeks saw the Egyptians and described the typical Egyptian circa 500 B.C. as dark-skinned with wooly hair. Studies in ancient Egyptian crania by Falkenburger tried to prove that only one-third of the Egyptians were of the classical Negroid type and that most of them were Euro-African or, to use the term invented by Sergi "the brown Mediterranean race" classification. Chatterjee and Kumar in a 1965 study ... analyzed crania from pre-dynastic Egypt and compared them with skulls of the Old Kingdom as well as the much later Middle Kingdom ($12^{th}$ and $13^{th}$ Dynasties) and found that all these skulls in respect to 'long head, broad face, low orbit and broad nasal aperture have the same characteristic features of the Negroid type.'"

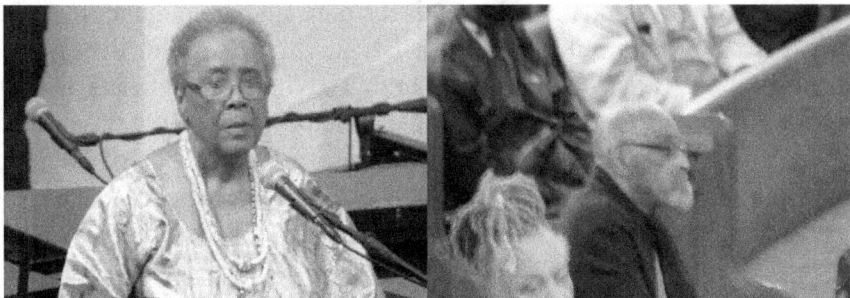

**Black History Extravaganza - Photo -** Sister Camille Yarbrough (left); and Brother Jeff Garrison (right), educators in their own right, were there to make sure everything went all right for the Master Teacher.

# FREDERICK MONDERSON

**Black History Extravaganza - Ceramic Art -** The powerful "Eye of Horus" carries a message.

Further, in *Egypt: Child of Africa* (1998: 20) Ivan Van Sertima wrote: "There was probably no civilization in the world, be it African, European, or Asian, that was entirely pure and homogeneous. The great Roman historian Pliny, who first saw the Briton in the second century A.D., describes some of them as having complexions as dark as the Ethiopian. Claudia, reporting the victory of the Roman general, Theodosius, over the English, mentions a good number of 'nimble blackamoors' among them. The Chinese themselves recorded that there were men of black skin among the rulers of the Shang dynasty (1766-1100 B.C.). They actually speak of them as *Na-Khi* (*Na* in Chinese means black and *Khi* means man). Schliemann and Evans, who excavated Minoan Crete, also tell us of the black skins of many of these Cretans who entered Greece in great numbers at an early time. Yet nobody would dare to pose questions such as: Were the ancient

# BLACK HISTORY EXTRAVAGANZA HONORING DR. BEN-JOCHANNAN

Chinese Black or yellow? Were the ancient Greeks or the ancient Britons White or Mixed? No. No. No. No. No."

**Black History Extravaganza - Photo -** Egyptian architecture accentuated against a blue sky is a site to behold.

**Black History Extravaganza - Photo -** Egyptian architecture accentuated against a blue sky is a site to behold.

# FREDERICK MONDERSON

**II.    So Here We Are!** - We must affirm, articulate, teach, preach and fight to defend ancient Egypt as **African and Negro or Black.** This is essentially what our intellectual ancestors, researchers, historians, lecturers, writers, publishers and activists, who, after their many years, sometimes more than thirty years of research have discovered, as being omitted and distorted regarding the history of the Ancient Egyptians and that important culture of the Nile Valley.

## VIII.    CONCLUSIONS

As more and more evidence is unearthed and equally more Afrocentric scholarship unmasks untruths, distortions and omissions through vigorous analytic examination, the effort of African historiographic reconstruction will not only correct the historical record but also expose perhaps the ignorance but especially the prejudice and vindictiveness involved in earlier writers' works. Some years ago, while a student at Oxford University this writer met a **Black Englishman** who, in discussion, told me, 'In any debate between a **Black Historian and a White Historian**, the black will always hold his own. All he has to do is to show what White men have been doing all around the world and with any sense of conscience the White man has to back-pedal.' Hence, despite efforts to 'hold back the dawn,' unmistakable truths are changing the minds of some while others 'prefer not to discuss such.' They simply skirt around the issues, and with today's knowledge and vision, are ashamed that their mentors, teacher and predecessors had been wrong and prejudiced in reporting the history of Black men and women who began humanity along the civilization pageantry of art, architecture, agriculture, medicine, science, agriculture, astronomy, knowledge, history, period! It is reassuring to show that despite Breasted's venom, Black men and women have given and continue to give knowledge and enlightenment to all who seek the truth but more important, "the existential data contradicts the symbolic representation."

# BLACK HISTORY EXTRAVAGANZA
# HONORING DR. BEN-JOCHANNAN

**Black History Extravaganza - Photo -** Two Nubian gentlemen from the Aswan area.

**Black History Extravaganza - Photo -** Another look at the Kiosk of Trajan oat the Temple of Isis.

## IX. REFERENCES

Brooks, Lester. *Great Civilizations of Ancient Africa.* New York: Four Winds Press, 1971.

Browder, Anthony. *Nile Valley Contributions to Civilization.* Washington, D.C.: The Institute of Karmic Guidance, 1992.

Clegg, Legrand H.H. "Black Rulers of the Golden Age" in *Nile Valley Civilizations.* Edited by Ivan Van Sertima, (1985) (1986: 39-68).

Diop, Cheikh Anta. *The African Origin of Civilization: Myth or Reality.* New York: Lawrence Hill and Company, (1967) 1974.

_____. "Origin of the Ancient Egyptians" in *Egypt Revisited.* (Edited by Ivan Van Sertima) New Brunswick, New Jersey: Transaction Publishers, (1989: 9-37).

DuBois, W.E.B. *The Negro.* New York: Oxford University Press, (1915) 1973.

_____. *Black Folks Then and Now.*

_____. *The World and Africa.* New York: International Publishers, (1946) 1971.

Erman, Adolf. *Life in Ancient Egypt.* New York: Macmillan, 1894.

Finch, Charles S. "Black Roots of Egypt's Glory." *Great Black Leaders: Ancient and Modern.* Edited by Ivan Van Sertima. Transaction Books, (1988: 139-143).

Harris, J.E. *Pillars in Ethiopian History.* Washington, D.C.: Howard University Press, 1981.

Jackson, John G. *Introduction to African Civilizations.* Secaucus, New Jersey: Citadel Press, 1970.

Kush, Khamit Indus. *The Missing Pages of "His-Story."* Laurelton, New York: D and J Books, 1993.

Murray, Margaret A. *The Splendor That Was Egypt.* New York: Hawthorn Books, Inc., (1949) 1969.

Perry, W.J. *The Growth of Civilization.* Hammondsworth, England: Penguin Books, (1924) 1937.

Rawlinson, George. *The Story of the Nations: Egypt.* London: T. Fisher Unwin, 1893.

Rogers, J.A. *Sex and Race.* New York: Helga M. Rogers, 1967.

# BLACK HISTORY EXTRAVAGANZA HONORING DR. BEN-JOCHANNAN

Van Sertima, Ivan. "Race and Origin of the Egyptians" in *Egypt Revisited*. Edited by Ivan Van Sertima. New Brunswick, New Jersey: Transaction Publishers, (1989: 3-8).
_____. "African Origin of the Ancient Egyptian Civilization" in *Egypt: Child of Africa*. Edited by Ivan Van Sertima. New Brunswick, New Jersey: Transaction Publishers, (1994) 1995.
Woodson, Carter G. *The Mis-Education of the Negro*. Trenton, New Jersey: Africa World Press, (1990) 1993.

**Black History Extravaganza - Papyrus -** Tutankhamon and his Queen between two black cartouches - Shennu - with vultures soaring overhead holding ankh and Shen rings.

# FREDERICK MONDERSON

**Black History Extravaganza - Photo -** Another view of the Kiosk of Trajan while departing from the Nile.

**Black History Extravaganza - Photo -** View of an Image of the rocks in the Nile at Isis' Temple at Philae, now Agilka Island.

# BLACK HISTORY EXTRAVAGANZA
# HONORING DR. BEN-JOCHANNAN

**Black History Extravaganza - Photo -** The Temple of Isis sparkles between the Nile River's waters and the Blue Sky overhead.

**Black History Extravaganza - Photo -** Another view of the Eastern Colonnade with its 17 columns at Isis Temple.

# FREDERICK MONDERSON

**Black History Extravaganza - Photo -** Left and Right Feet of the fallen colossal statue of Rameses II at his Mortuary Temple, the Ramesseum.

# BLACK HISTORY EXTRAVAGANZA HONORING DR. BEN-JOCHANNAN

## VIII. THE ARCHAEOLOGY OF EGYPT
### By
### Dr. Fred Monderson

The **Archaeology of Ancient Egypt** is a fascinating subject that first stumbled then systematically reclaimed the rich Nile River cultural heritage from the misty past in which it lay buried in the debris of soil and time. As an emerging science, we can generally date Egyptian archaeology to the beginning of the 19th Century when Napoleon arrived and his savants after traversing the land in systematic study produced their *Description of Egypt* or *The Monuments of Egypt* based on linguistic and visual study of the language and monuments. By the end of the 19th Century archaeology had been placed on a more scientific footing and the mist was significantly cleared by then. The 20th Century saw the maturing of the discipline. Nevertheless, in all of this, as the Mighty Sparrow said in one of his songs: "Hurried birds make crooked nests" and so the *Story of Egypt* was not correctly told because of the multitude of issues interplaying among global powers! During the age of colonization, from 1880 onwards as archaeologists began to reclaim ancient Egypt, with all the shenanigans going on, the work of the British archaeologists particularly emphasized rapid publication of discoveries to feed the rapidly expanding "penny press" and a public hungry for antiquarian knowledge to bolster "white supremacy" as Europe manifested its might globally.

# FREDERICK MONDERSON

**Black History Extravaganza - Line Drawing -** Ehnasya: Temple **-** Scenes from Tomb **-** V Dynasty, Boundary Stone.

# BLACK HISTORY EXTRAVAGANZA HONORING DR. BEN-JOCHANNAN

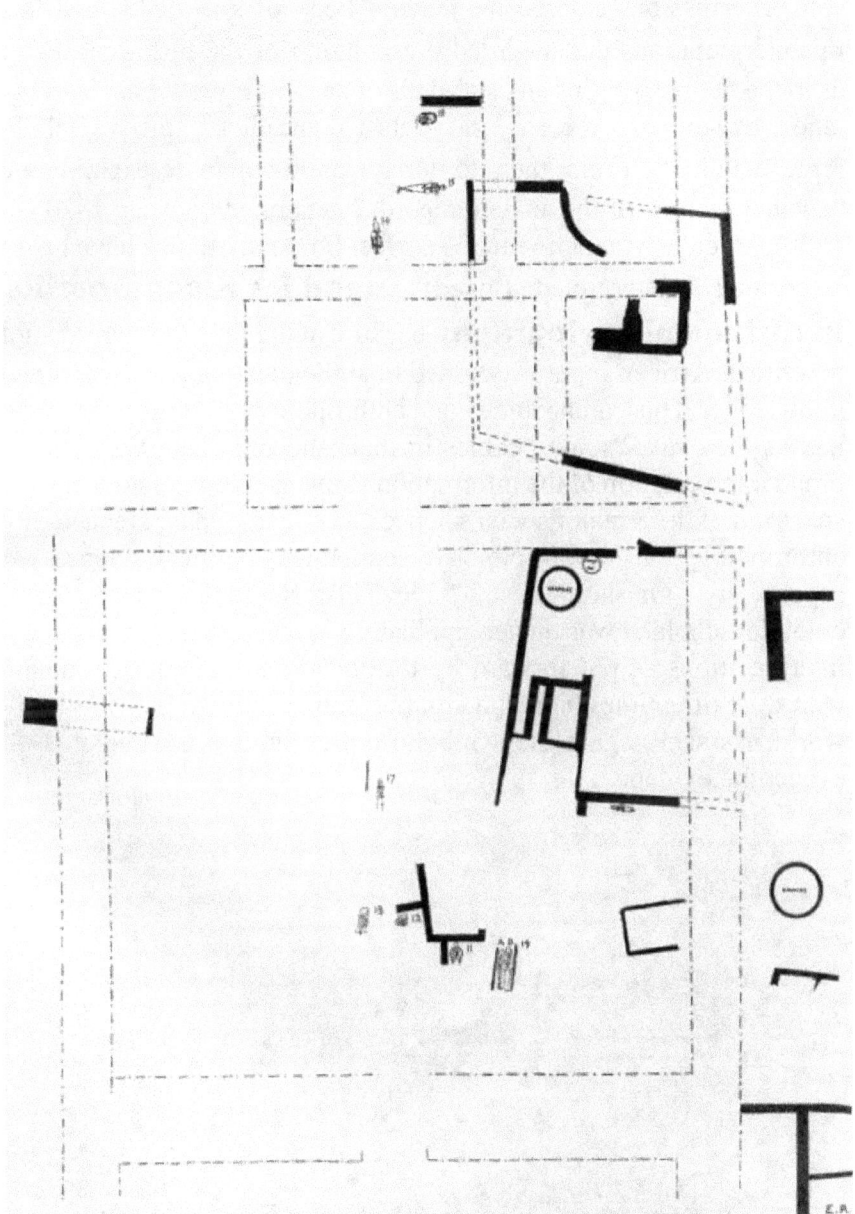

**Black History Extravaganza - Line Drawing -** Ehnasya: Building and Graves under temple, XI Dynasty.

# FREDERICK MONDERSON

As such, much was said but equally many errors and distortions as well as omissions entered the general body of knowledge and thus misinterpretations under-girded presentation of the historical record as to the people, origins and survivals of ancient Egypt. That is to say, "the existential record or data contradicts the symbolic representation." From then to today, as scholars re-examine the "ancient records of the ancient records" generated between 1870 and 1930 particularly, much remains correct but many things have had to be correctly reinterpreted. Hence the **need for reconstruction in African historiography** because at the time of interpretation no critical African input was added to authenticate the corpus of new knowledge. Thus, archaeology and anthropology, its sister discipline, had as they say, "some pebbles in their shoes." There was never a broad interpretation of the information using as its cornerstone the full spectrum of the 8 major social sciences, viz., geography, archaeology, anthropology, history, sociology, economics, political science and psychology. Or should I say critical historiographic analysis from credible scholars was never applied to question the findings and interpretations as put forward by European and American scholars, who were oftentimes biased in arguing from a Eurocentric view of the world. As such, again the symbolic representation contradicted the existential evidence.

**Black History Extravaganza - Photo -** Winged Sun-Disk with uraei on a cornice.

# BLACK HISTORY EXTRAVAGANZA HONORING DR. BEN-JOCHANNAN

**Black History Extravaganza - Photo -** Presenting a platter of delectable to one's partner.

Notwithstanding, Egyptian archaeology has helped define and establish parameters of Egyptology by its comprehensive excavation of viable sites and monuments throughout the land. On the one hand, the definition of Egyptology includes an understanding of the history, geography and language of ancient Egypt! On the other, the study of **Classical African Civilization** is much different because not only does it include examination and analysis of the entire Nile Valley's various forms of knowledge, it is not done from a European epicenter and perspective, it not only studies this culture but vigorously reclaims its heritage by pointing out distortions and seeking to include omissions. This African centered study of ancient Africa is not simply committed to comprehensive African historiographic reconstruction placing Africans as subjects not objects of this phenomenal historic dynamic by infusing the philosophic social exhilir of Ma'at, righteousness with its components or truth and justice to uplift the African mind from the European dead level to an inordinate level of consciousness enabling him to help bring good into

# FREDERICK MONDERSON

the world. However, in this cultural awakening, Dr. Ben-Jochannan not simply researched and wrote books, he taught his students, carried them to Egypt, pointed out discrepancies, distortions, omissions, defacements, in exposing them to the wonders of the monuments. He even explained the message and meanings of such monuments to more fully assess the challenges and contradictions posed by modern archaeology and archaeologists. However, while a great many African and African-American scholars viz., Edward Wilmot Blyden, Martin Delaney, W.E.B. DuBois, Marcus Garvey, Duse Mohammed, Drusilla Dunjee, Carter G. Woodson, John Higgins, John G. Jackson, J.A. Rogers, George G.M. James, Chancellor Williams, Ivan Van Sertima, Prof. Scobie, Asa Hilliard, Benjamin Carruthers, Maulana Karenga, George Simmonds, Molefi Asante, Cheikh Anta Diop, Theophile Obenga, Leonard Jeffries, Leonard James, even Walter Rodney among others, have incessantly extolled the blackness of ancient Egypt and the Nile Valley; the "warrior scholars" John Henrik Clarke, Yosef A. A. ben-Jochannan and James Smalls, among others, most adamantly had much to say about the people, culture and history of North-East Africa. They also emphasized why the young must become involved in this study.

**Black History Extravaganza - Photo -** Picturesque view of the top part of the magnificent Kiosk of Trajan at the Temple of Isis.

# BLACK HISTORY EXTRAVAGANZA HONORING DR. BEN-JOCHANNAN

**Black History Extravaganza - Photo -** Dressed in Lion-Skin and backed by another while holding a magic wand and incenser, this priest demonstrates before a seated official.

Dr. "Ben" as he was affectionately called, spent some sixty years challenging the distorted presentation of Egyptian history including significant omissions while setting the record straight as he brought the light and educated thousands, some say millions, pointing out the intellectual crimes committed against Africa and its sons and daughters. Nevertheless, in this widespread examination, excavation or Archaeology, the now empowered and enquiring African minds have delved into not just temples and tombs, but cemeteries, and private dwellings and fortified buildings. They have begun mining museum collections all along seeking truth. As such, and moving beyond Roman and Greek periods, structures where towns have remained intact as at Kuft, Kom Ombo, El Ayandiyeh, and even on the outskirts of Karnak at Thebes, these have been revealed to date to the Middle and New Kingdoms. Surviving towns and private dwellings date from the Twelfth Dynasty at Kahun and equally at Abydos where remains go back to the earliest times. The town of Tell

# FREDERICK MONDERSON

el-Amarna, still standing, allowed archaeologists to reconstruct that important city of the religious revolution though this location suffered tremendously in the reaction having posed a challenge to Amon's supremacy.

**Black History Extravaganza** - Dr. Ben's Book - **The Black Man's Religion - Volume III.**

# BLACK HISTORY EXTRAVAGANZA HONORING DR. BEN-JOCHANNAN

At Tell el Maskhuta, the twin towns of Pithom and Rameses established connection with biblical times and events. The two fortresses at Abydos date to the beginnings of Egyptian history. Work of excavation was conducted on the ramparts of El Kab, Kom el Ahmar, el Hibeh, Kuban (opposite Dakkeh), of Heliopolis, and of Thebes where structures were still standing during the early development of the science of Archaeology.

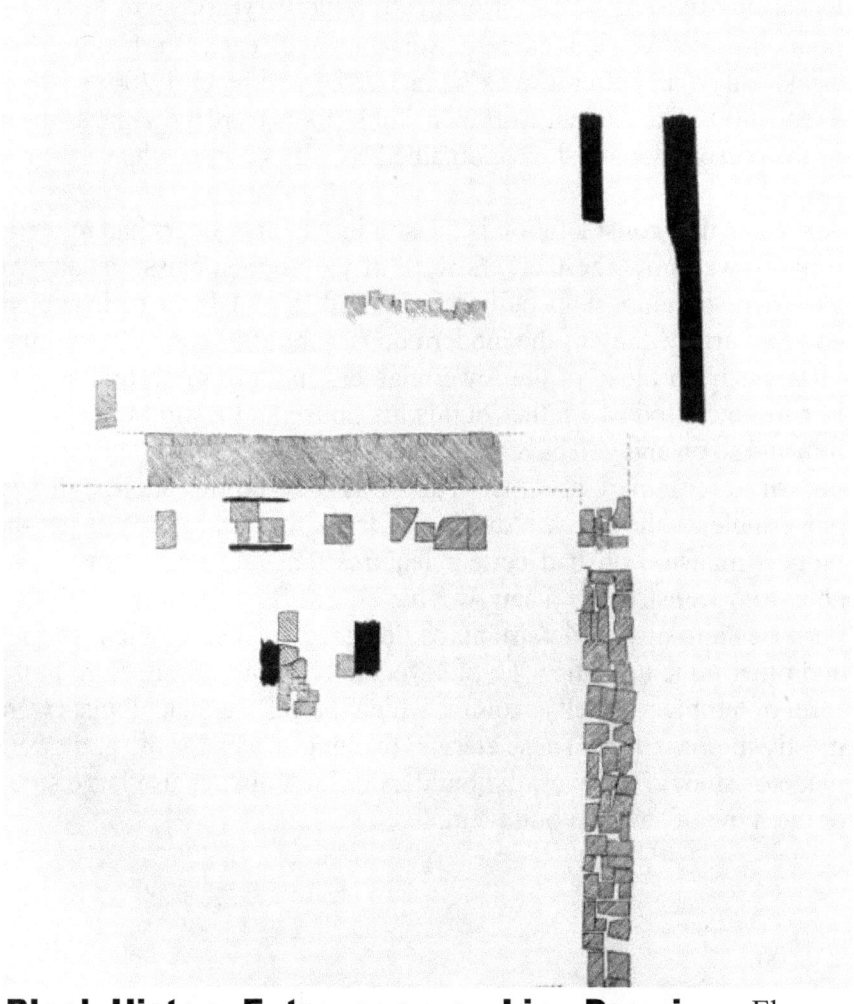

**Black History Extravaganza - Line Drawing -** Ehnasya - Temple of the XII Dynasty.

# FREDERICK MONDERSON

Archaeology therefore revealed the earliest dwellings made of wattle and daub. Later, materials consisting of mud mixed with sand and chopped straw, were molded into oblong bricks then dried in the sun. Regarding mastery of the brick-making industry, Maspero (1914: 4) pointed out: "A good modern workman will easily turn out 1,000 bricks a day, and after a week's practice he will reach 1,200, 1,500 or even 1,800. The ancient workman whose tools were the same as those of the present day must have obtained equally good results."

An interesting consideration is the soil in which builders had to work. Equally we know the workers were of the poorest class. Today we call them fellahin, who built homes no different from their ancient counterparts. Many of the modern houses, built of concrete are quite different from those of the lower classes, and, are in several stories. For instance, today a father builds his house and a son builds above him and so on and you have the modern multistoried buildings, though not of a commercial type. This was not so in ancient times. Nevertheless, the private dwellings from the simplest huts to the biggest mansion all had certain features that archaeology has been able to reconstruct. Then we have fortresses built for military purposes and also civic structures designed for Government service and other civic activities. To this we add religious architecture in the form of temples as well as tombs, which the early archaeologists were mostly interested in. These eternal dwelling places for the gods were made of stone. However, the builders did not always use large stone or one type of stone to build temples.

# BLACK HISTORY EXTRAVAGANZA HONORING DR. BEN-JOCHANNAN

**Black History Extravaganza - Photo -** Site Ticket for Luxor Temple, now at 60-Egyptian Pounds.

**Black History Extravaganza - Photo -** Paying homage to the Horus falcon.

# FREDERICK MONDERSON

In these temple constructions, Maspero (1914: 53) described the type of materials they used: "The size varied greatly according to the purpose for which they were intended. Architraves, drums of columns, lintels, and doorjambs were sometimes of very considerable dimensions. The largest architraves known, those above the central aisle of the hypostyle hall at Karnak, average 30 feet in length. Each one represents a solid block of 40 cubic yards and weighs about 65 tons. Generally, however, the blocks are not larger than those in ordinary use among us. They vary from 3 to 4 feet in height, from 3 to 8 feet in length, and from 18 inches to 6 feet in breadth."

**Black History Extravaganza - Photo -** Decorated Umbel Capital beneath Architrave at the Ramesseum, Mortuary Temple of Rameses II.

# BLACK HISTORY EXTRAVAGANZA HONORING DR. BEN-JOCHANNAN

**Black History Extravaganza - Papyrus -** Image of Tutankhamon holding Uas scepter and whip or flail.

# FREDERICK MONDERSON

Seldom was a temple built of one single type of stone. In fact, variety was sometimes the rule. To this, explaining, Maspero (1914: 53) say further: "Some temples were built throughout in one kind of stone, but more frequently materials of various kinds and quality are associated, although in unequal proportions. Thus, the main buildings of the temple of Abydos are of very fine limestone, while in the temple of Seti I the columns, architraves, jambs, and lintels, all those parts where limestone might not be sufficiently strong, are in sandstone, granite, and alabaster. Similar combinations are to be seen in the temples of Karnak, Luxor, Tanis, Deir el Bahari, Ghizeh, and Memphis. At the Ramesseum, at Karnak, and in the Nubian temples, where all these materials are combined, the columns rest on a solid foundation of crude brick. The stones were dressed more or less carefully according to the position they were to occupy."

## POEM TO RA - THE SUN GOD

O Ra, King of the Gods, you enjoyed a prominence matched by few divinities. Founded as a site of religious and intellectual worship by the Black African Anu, you emerged at Heliopolis, and once absorbed, you extended your significance throughout dynastic times. Father of the Gods whose souls are exalted in the hidden place, your symbols are the Disk of the Sun, encircled by the serpent Khut, as well as Ankh, with scepter and tail from your waist. Self-begotten and Self-born creative vigor, Power of Powers with two uraei, you are a doubly hidden and secret god. Lord of Eternity, Sovereign of the Gods, you exist forever, Lord of Souls. You possess **14 Kas or life forces**, as strength, might, prosperity, food, veneration, eternity, radiance, glory, fame, magic, authority, sight, and hearing and perception, Lord of Heliopolis, Supreme Power.

# BLACK HISTORY EXTRAVAGANZA HONORING DR. BEN-JOCHANNAN

**Black History Extravaganza - Photo -** Kom Ombo. Double Temple of Haroeris, the Elder Horus and Sobek, the Crocodile God. This temple possesses a Double Aisle, Double Sanctuary and double Priesthood.

Sekhem, begetter of his gods, from Heliopolis, your priests influenced political developments in the Old Kingdom when Pyramid builders incorporated your name into theirs, becoming Son of the Sun, hence the title Son of Ra. These kings built sun temples with names as 'Favorite Place of Ra' and 'Satisfaction of Ra' all in Praise of you Lord of Rays. Self-Created, King of Heaven, Great Duration of Life, Lord who advances, you are the Soul that do good to the body. Governor of his Eye, Lord of Generation, invisible and secret, you are

# FREDERICK MONDERSON

Governor of the Tuat, Double Obelisk God, Lord of the Eastern Bend, and Supporter of the Heavens who dwells in Darkness. Born as the all-surrounding universe, you send forth the plants in their season, Eternal Essence.

**Black History Extravaganza - Photo -** Acknowledging in adoration the power of Two Anubi, God of the Dead.

**Black History Extravaganza - Photo -** "Get the Drummer on!"

# BLACK HISTORY EXTRAVAGANZA HONORING DR. BEN-JOCHANNAN

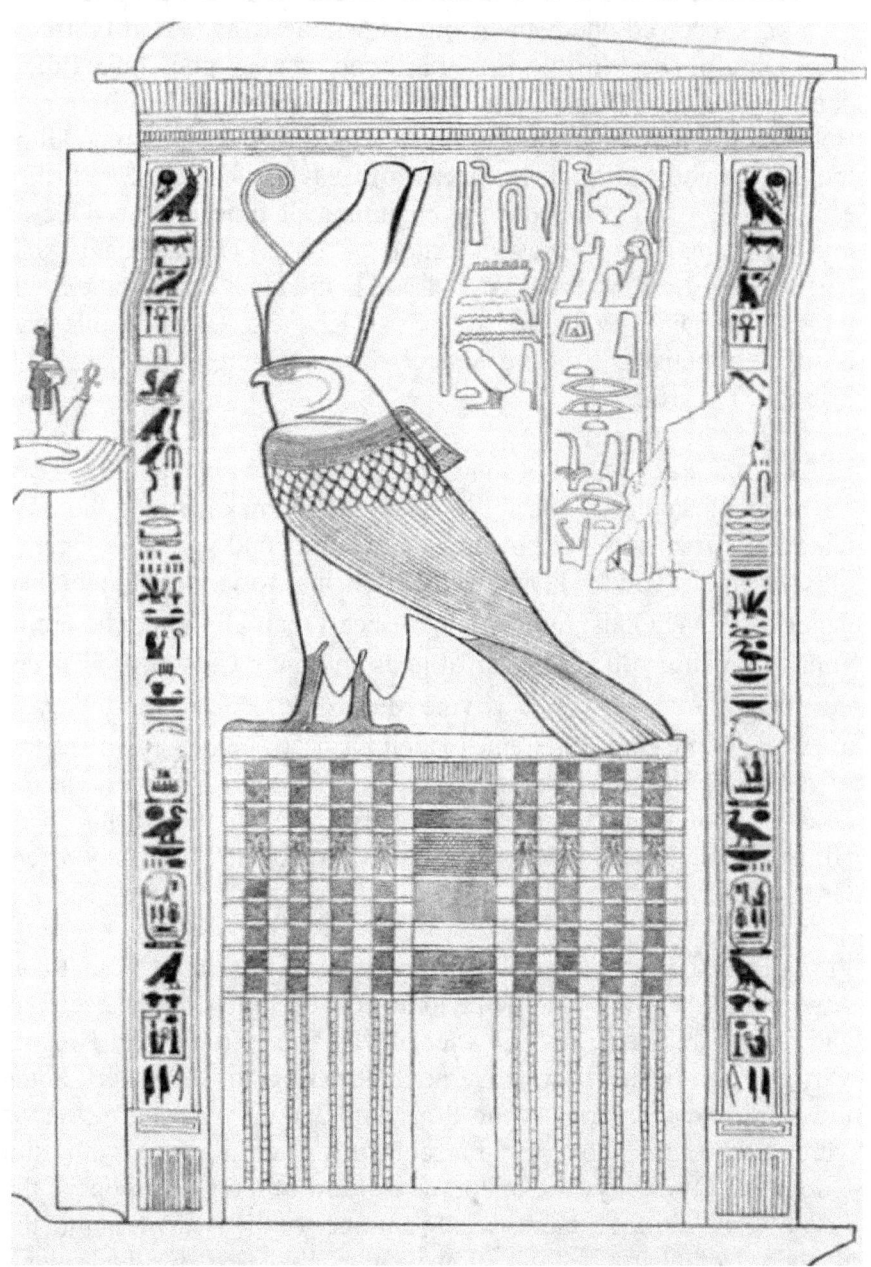

**Black History Extravaganza - Line Drawing -** Offering one's name to a falcon wearing the Double Red and White Crown.

# FREDERICK MONDERSON

Maker of the Gods, Governor of your circle, Aged One of Forms, Memphis received endowments in the Middle Kingdom in Praise of thee, King of the World. The Priesthood of local gods linked their deity to the Sun God's name Ra, Mighty in Majesty, Vivifier of Bodies. The Theban triumph merged Amon with Ra assuming all of the ancient god's attributes as Maker of Heaven where you are firmly established. God One from the beginning of time, Mighty One of myriad forms and aspects, Creator of Laws Unchangeable and Unalterable, Lord of Truth your shrine is hidden. You are the Soul, which give names to his limbs, Body of Khepera, God of Souls who is in the Obelisk. You are Master of the Spheres who cause the Principles to arise.

Chief of the Earth, Lord of the Gods, Judge of Words, and the glory of Ra manifested in Amon at the Temple of Karnak. During the New Kingdom, Thebes gloried in the imperial age, and you were Opener of Roads in the Hidden Place, who confers his crown on Pharaoh. The Ruler of all the Gods, more-strong of heart than all those who are in your following, you are maker of gods and men, Creator of Heaven, Earth and the Underworld. Divine Man-Child, Heir of Eternity, you are Chief of the Gods, Supreme in their Districts, being Crowned King of the Gods, Ram, Mightiest of Created Things. You Provide the Breath out of your Throat for the Nostrils of Mankind, Fashioner of Himself, and Tonen who produces his members, Supremely Great One.

Provider of the Sovereign Chiefs, Governor of the Holy Circle, Re as Amon brought victory and fame to those who followed his teachings and praised his name, as Crowner of Pharaoh. Proclaimed King of Earth, Prince of the Tuat, Governor of the Regions of Aukert, Souls in their Circles ascribe your Praises. Beautiful Being, Rays of Turquoise Light, you are Personification of Right, Truth and Goodness, O Mighty One of Journeys, Lord of the Gods, light of the lock of hair. Your Emblems secure entrance of the Dead Man into the Kingdom of Osiris. Chief of the Great Cycle of the Gods, your principles have become your manifestation. Chief of the Powers inhabiting the holy sphere, you raise your soul, hide your body, shine and see your mysteries.

# BLACK HISTORY EXTRAVAGANZA HONORING DR. BEN-JOCHANNAN

Creator of Hidden Things, Lord of Heaven, Lord of Earth, for untold ages men praise the Exalted of Souls. The Maker of Eternity, Ra you sail a Boat of Millions of Years. In all your glory, you emerge in a Morning Boat **Matet**, becoming strong at Midday. The day's work done, and weak, you ride the Evening Boat **Semktet**. Confronting your mortal enemy Apep, fishes **Abtu and Ant** swim before the Boat of Ra as its defenders at the ready. United in Numbers, Destroyer of Darkness, Night, Wickedness and Evil, on the dawn of a new day, there are Acclamations of your Rising in the Horizon of Heaven, Only One. Soul that speaks, rests, creates the developed hidden intellects, you shine in your sphere and hide what it contains, moving luminary.

Ra, Lord of Truth, Lord of the Horizon, Horus of the East, Lord of Fetters of your enemy, protector of hidden spirits, you conquer the fiends of the underworld. Souls of the East follow and Souls of the West praise you, while you get Support of the Circle of Amenta. God of Life, King of Right and Truth, you are the World Soul that rested on his High Place. The Soul who moves onward, Opener of the roads in the Hidden Place, One Alone with many hands, Ra, you are the Great God who lifted up his two eyes. You address your eye and speak to your head, the spirit that walks, that destroys its enemies, that sends pain to the rebels, you impart the breath of life to the souls that are in their place, Brilliant One who shines in the Waters of the Inundation.

Hidden Face, Glorious Creator of Eternity, you make beings come into existence in your creations in the Tuat. You rise like unto Gold, Great Light Shining in the Heavens illuminating darkness. Oldest One, Great One, you are Self-begotten, Self-created and Self-produced, the Soul Who Departs at his Appointed Time. You existed forever and would exist for Eternity, Illuminer of Light into his Circle. Source of Life and Light, Glorious by reason of thy Splendors, you are Joy of Heart within your Splendor. Mighty One of Victories, Ra, how wonderful was your manifestation among early Africans, initiating laudable moral, spiritual and intellectual standards of

# FREDERICK MONDERSON

creative genius, Mighty one whose body is so large it hides its shape, Double Luminary.

**Black History Extravaganza - Ceramic Art -** The Great Goose, again in colorful splendor.

Generator of Bodies, True Creative Power of Divine attributes, Sender of Light into his Circle, Ra you rise in the Horizon, and are Beautiful. So too, Rat, Mistress of the Gods, your female counterpart, Lady of Heaven, Mistress of Heliopolis. Hathor and Isis are also your companions. Mightier than the Gods, Glorious Being, Lord of Love, Double Sphinx god, you are Ruler of Everlastingness. God of Motion, God of Light, Lord of Might, you send destruction, fire into the place of destruction and destroy your enemies, Light that is in the Infernal Regions. Protector of hidden spirits, the Souls that Mourns, the God that Cries, you are the Soul One who avenges his children and who calls his gods to life when he arrives in the hidden sphere.

# BLACK HISTORY EXTRAVAGANZA HONORING DR. BEN-JOCHANNAN

**Black History Extravaganza - Photo -** Giving praise to the Guardians of the two lands as transited by the Sun-god.

Aged one of the Pupil of the Utchait, Ra, Lord of the hidden circles, creative force who gathers together all seed, you are manifold in your holy house. Great One, who rules what is in him, you send forth the stars and make the night light, in the sphere of hidden essences. Master of the Light, Only One who names the earth by his intelligence, the vessel of heaven, Powerful, Ra in his disk with Brilliant Rays, Lord of Wisdom your precepts are wise. Lord of Mercy, at whose coming men live, you make strong your double with Divine Food. Creator of Hidden Things and Generator of Bodies, Enlightener of the Earth, Lord of the Gods who lights the bodies on the horizon, Africans need your continued illumination and Blessings now more than ever.

# FREDERICK MONDERSON

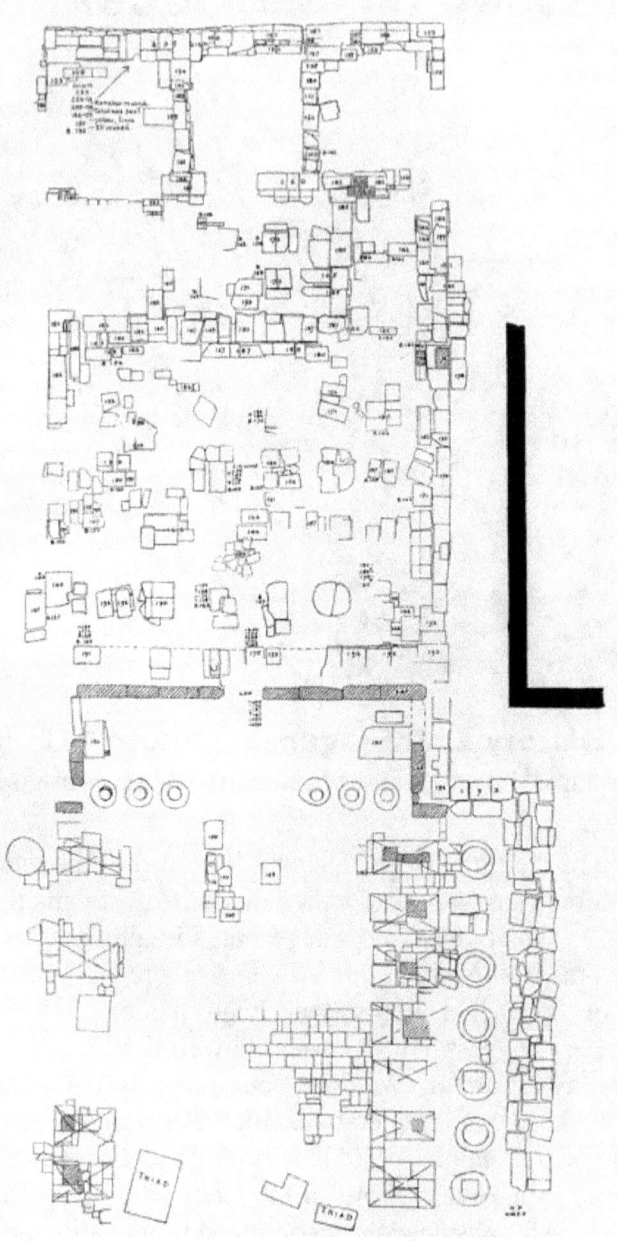

**Black History Extravaganza - Line Drawing -** Ehnasya
- Temples of XVIII and XIX Dynasty

# BLACK HISTORY EXTRAVAGANZA HONORING DR. BEN-JOCHANNAN
# ARCHAEOLOGY

Archaeology has taught us a great deal about ancient Egypt. It has enabled us to delve deep into the prehistoric period, into the Paleolithic period as far back, perhaps more than 300,000 years ago. Scholars have defined the Paleolithic or Old Stone Age as divided into the Lower, Middle and Upper. The Mesolithic represented the Middle Stone Age while the Neolithic period is considered the New Stone Age. This is also the time when farming and settlement began. Homo Habilis, "true man," made tools to a set and regular pattern and thus overcame his environment in a process dating back and evolved through more than a million years. We find evidence of this in Ethiopia and East Africa.

Paleolithic sites in Egypt were found at Merimdeh, Fayum, and Kharga Oasis where hand-axes have been unearthed. Such axes were also found at Thebes dating back hundreds of thousands of years! Where were the Mesopotamians? Where were the Mesopotamians when these Africans were beginning these craft skills? Kom Ombo is also a Paleolithic site. These hand-axes and choppers gave way to man learning to use bone-tools. During this period, he used such materials as tools made of flint, antler, and ivory. Lance heads and knives were made of all these materials. As tools became more sophisticated he began to become more enlightened, we see the emergence of early burial practices and family dynamics and relationships. By the end of the Paleolithic period he began using the bow and arrow, with arrowheads made of various materials and he also began to carve animals. At this time, there is also a big change in the history of man. He enters the Neolithic period and moves from being a nomadic hunter and gatherer to a sedentary producer of food. In the Paleolithic period, he hunted and gathered his food, with meats consisting of some 90 percent and 10 percent agri-vegetation. That is leaves, roots, fruits, shoots, whatever he found growing. Sometimes even grass. He was a **scavenger on nature**! With the change in food production he began to grow crops, domesticated animals, he became sedentary. Now, in a change, his diet consisted of some 10 percent meats and 90 percent agri-produce. He began to cooperate with nature. He started building early containers for grain and invented sickles and started winnowing his grain. With this came the emergence of division of labor and specialization of craft. We credit women with beginning agriculture for they accidentally disposed of seeds that grew and so food production began! The "oasis theory" of domestication of animals describes how man came to overcome these creatures. That is, he set up camp near the oasis and as the animals came to drink and feed he soon became familiar to them, fed them and so tamed them.

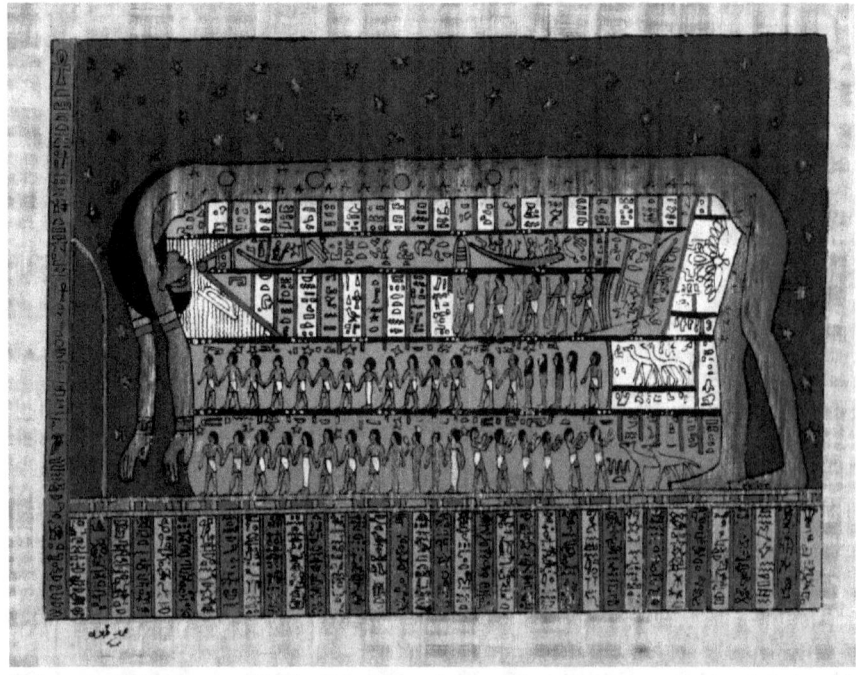

**Black History Extravaganza - Papyrus -** Colorful drama in the Heavens as Nuit spreads her body across the starry sky.

All these things we learn from archaeology while paleo-archaeology acquaints us with the much older fossilization of early human and animal bone deposits. There were three prehistoric or pre-dynastic cultures that emerged in Neolithic Egypt. These were the Badarian,

# BLACK HISTORY EXTRAVAGANZA HONORING DR. BEN-JOCHANNAN

Amratian and Gerzean or Naqada I and Naqada II. The last is called the proto-dynastic period.

An interesting contradiction is posed in viewing the chronology of Egypt, that is when we do establish the **first fixed date in history** or when did the people of Egypt invent the calendar or began their long path to the establishment of dynastic Egypt. Bauval and Brophy in *Black Genesis* credits the people of Nabta Playa with inventing the first calendar!

**Black History Extravaganza - Photo -** Kom Ombo. Double Temple of Haroeis (**The Elder Horu**s) and Sobek (**The Crocodile God**). Atop the Double Aisles is a Double Cornice with Double Sun-Disk and Uraeus. Notice twin Cobra Frieze (left and right) beyond the third level of columns. Notice the varied capitals.

# FREDERICK MONDERSON

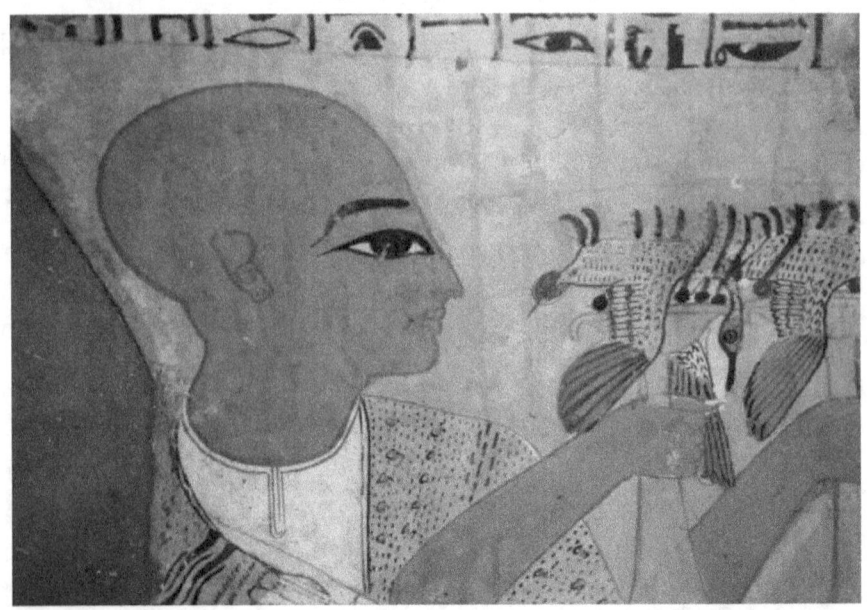

**Black History Extravaganza - Photo -** Presentation of Wild Geese offerings.

The Badarian is named after the site of Badari in Upper Egypt where Flinders Petrie began dating by pottery sequence. At Badari were discovered ivory figurines showing some sort of religious significance. These early Africans created and used cosmetic palettes and jewelry was made of shells, and turquoise. There was much traveling and trading via the Nile River as the principal transportation highway. Pottery was burnished or burnt. The second sequence is the Amratian found at Merimdeh and Amrah that is generally characterized by beehive huts. A shrine of the local god was found and people seen hunting. A woman sits at a loom and there is a figurine of a dancing lady. The "Bird Lady" figurine in the Brooklyn Museum comes from this site. There were male ivory amulets and a woman in a barrel. The mother goddess figurine is also transitional to the Gerzean or Naqada period.

# BLACK HISTORY EXTRAVAGANZA HONORING DR. BEN-JOCHANNAN

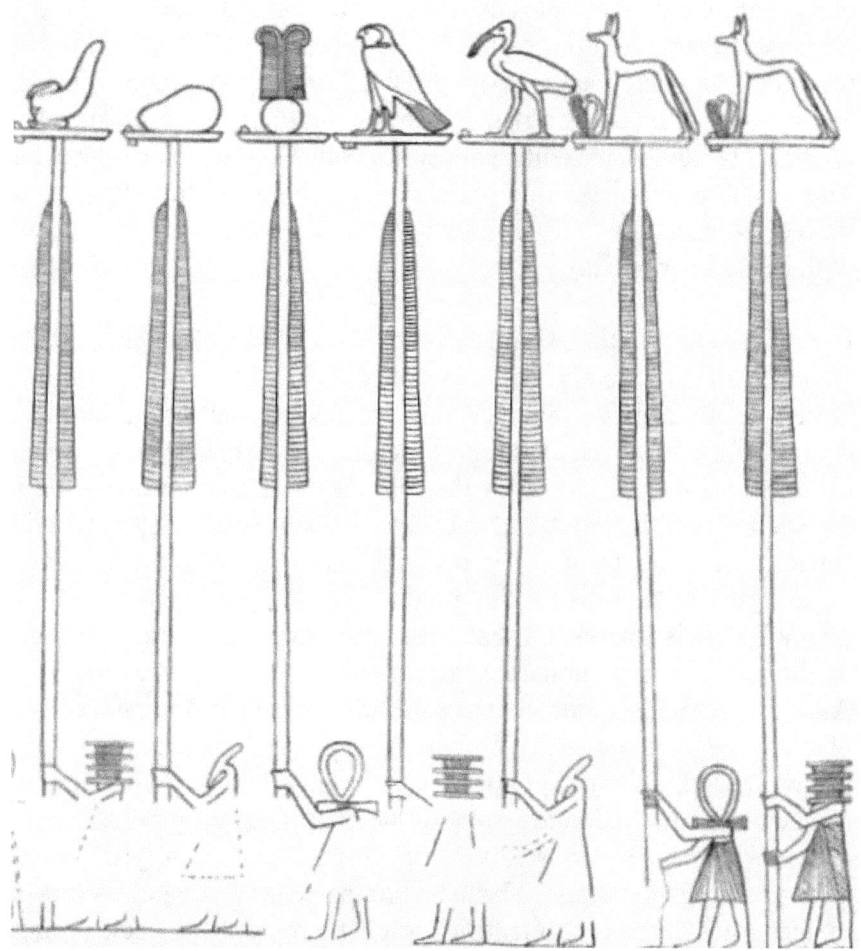

**Black History Extravaganza - Line Drawing -** Standards on display.

During the Gerzean or Naqada I and II periods we find white incised pottery decorated with a ripple pattern. Here we see the first incised pottery with people and animals, as well as a double shaped pottery. The black topped pottery; burnishing and various designs now emerge. The Naqada site is in Upper Egypt. Petrie also did his sequence dating at Naqada. A tomb from nearby Gebelein shows

# FREDERICK MONDERSON

early representation of boats ushering in the Amratian period. We also have the first clear figures on pottery. A piece of linen fabric from Gebelein is the earliest ever found. There are hippopotamus figurines and a man fishing using a net. Pottery is found *in situ* or on site. The Gerzean pottery represents variety in pottery, stone and alabaster. There is great sophistication in the pottery. Some pottery changed to votive representation. Rock carvings show use of bow and arrows with kilts as garments.

In regards the "Mother Goddess" idea, Brophy and Bauval in *Black Genesis* (2011) have argued the people of Nabta Playa of the Western Desert seems to have invented this practice as well as pastoralism, studies of the heavens, creation of a clock, etc. As their environment changed due to desiccation by the sun, they migrated east to settle in the vicinity of the First Cataract and Aswan area. Bringing their science and other forms of knowledge, the two authors proclaimed these Nabta Playa folks the precursors or "predecessors of the pharaohs." It is interesting that Bruce Williams discovered evidence of the world's first monarchy at Qustol, between Abu Simbel and Aswan. The evidence of the Qustol find shows an enthroned king or pharaoh wearing the white crown, sailing boats, an incense burner, palace façade, animals, possibly cows, etc., some 200 years before such emerges in the iconography of the pharaohs. Toby Wilkinson in *Genesis of the Pharaohs* (2003) discovered boat prototypes of the gods and kings in parade. These he compared with the more colorful images later seen. He identified such Petroglyphs as being made "1000-years before Winkler's Mesopotamians." Now, in the Origin Argument, are we to believe migrating Asiatics left their lands and came to the Nile to carve boats on the high plateaus and the Africans who live on the Nile are alien to such creations. This brings us to Dr. John Clarke's position, "Europe's Caucasian claims to Egypt is not based on logic."

# BLACK HISTORY EXTRAVAGANZA HONORING DR. BEN-JOCHANNAN

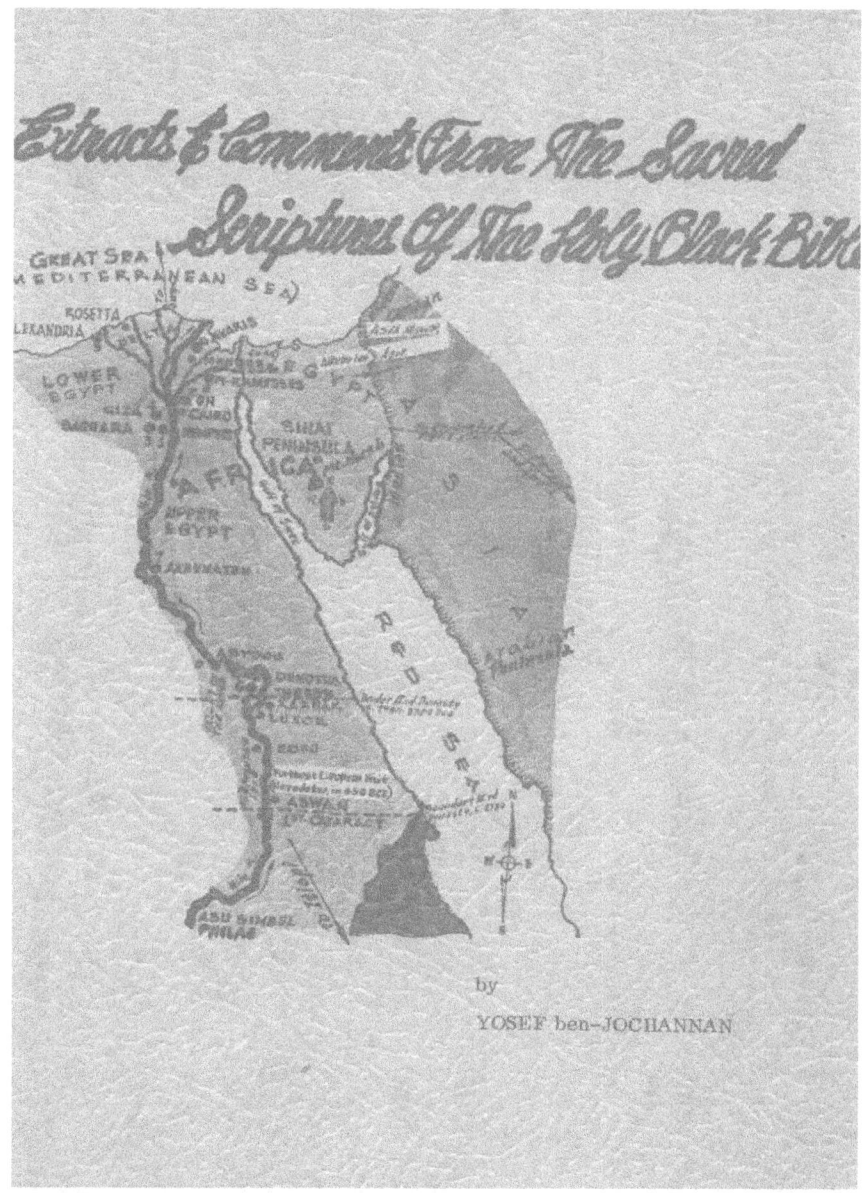

**Black History Extravaganza** - Dr. Ben's Book - **Extracts and Comments from Sacred Scriptures of the Holy Black Bible.**

# FREDERICK MONDERSON

As such, one of the arguments of the question then becomes, what is the connection between Qustol and Nabta Playa? It's all good, for these are African people in the purest sense.

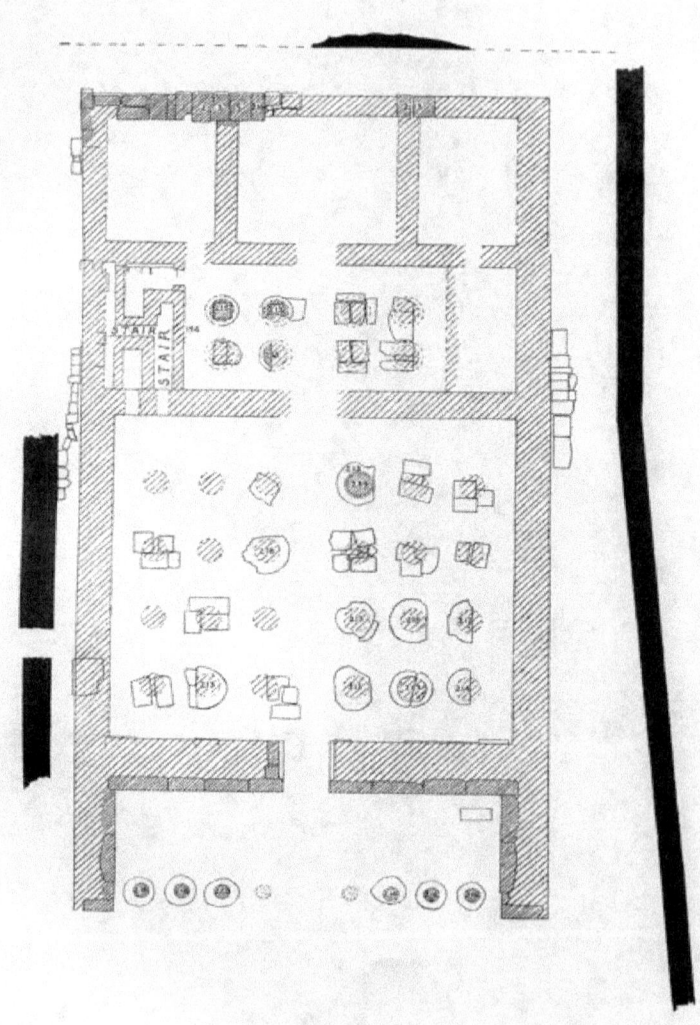

**Black History Extravaganza - Line Drawing -** Ehnasya - Temple of XXIII-XXX Dynasty.

# BLACK HISTORY EXTRAVAGANZA HONORING DR. BEN-JOCHANNAN

In the proto-historical or pre-1$^{st}$ Dynasty period we now enter into an "Age of Slate Palettes" that begin to serve as "historical documents." However, we now also enter the "Age of Contradiction!"

## Jean Capart - Primitive art in Egypt

The *Dog Palette* in the Louvre Museum shows mythical animals. By the end of the Naqada period there is much fighting for domination and the economic bounty of the Nile Valley. Narmer's conquest led to the formation of the dynastic period. There are many battle scenes. The palettes close this period. They are thus considered "historical documents" for they show much pictographic representation of contemporary events and are considered to show the beginning of hieroglyphic writings. We must also consider in the north-south dynamic dichotomy, most, if not all of these developments are taking place in Upper Egypt and the eastern and western deserts of Upper Egypt. The scorpion king is a proto-dynastic figure. He is also shown as Horus and in other animal guises. The Dynastic period begins at 3150 or sometimes 3050 B.C., depending on the particular scholarly focus, with Narmer or Menes conquering the North and uniting the land. That is, if one accepts the "Short Chronology" or the "Long Chronology" that may be 2000 years longer. Hierakonpolis and Abydos thus supply much evidence of this early period. Art in registers appear. The magnificently sculptured **Gebel Arrack** knife that comes from Hierakonpolis has naval battle scenes. Despite the attempts to link it with Mesopotamia, Diop things it is clearly African. The painted tomb at Hierakonpolis at 3100 B.C. (**Short Chronology**) provides much evidence of the proto-dynastic period. Abydos is thought to be the burial site of Osiris. King Scorpion is seen on a Macehead from Hierakonpolis. He is seen opening a new canal with scenes of defeated enemies. He is also depicted wearing a White Crown.

# FREDERICK MONDERSON

**Black History Extravaganza** - Temple Site Drawing - Ticket of Aswan's Prince's Temple, though picturing Philae, still the price is 40-Egyptian Pounds.

The insightfulness of Dr. Ben led us to understand the "Myth of the North" is a European concoction! That is, while significant early kings are seen wearing the "White Crown" the earliest example of both the Red and White Crowns are found in the Eastern Desert of Upper Egypt as part of the petroglyphs of these Africans, that Toby Wilkinson dates "1000 years before Winkler's Mesopotamians" in his book *Genesis of the Pharaohs*.

The **Narmer Palette** depicts or represents the unification of Egypt and the establishment of organization. At this period, the First Dynasty begins. There is some confusion as to the difference between Narmer, Menes and Aha. The **Narmer Macehead** shows the king under a canopy purportedly marrying a queen from the north. To some this was a strategic marriage for he chose a wife from his defeated enemies in the North. However, new evidence and interpretations seems to point to her being from the South. This is

# BLACK HISTORY EXTRAVAGANZA HONORING DR. BEN-JOCHANNAN

another example of the existential proving the symbolic a contradiction. Others think the whole scene represents the earliest representation of the Heb Sed Festival of rejuvenation and succession to the throne. Thus, Narmer united the Red Crown with the White Crown and formed the Red and White Double Crown. That is, the White Crown resting or sitting on the Red Crown. The name of the Red Crown of Lower Egypt is **Deshret**; that of Upper Egypt, the White Crown is **Hedjet**. The name of the Double Crown of a United Egypt is **Pschent**.

**Black History Extravaganza - Photo -** Giving praise where due. No wonder the Egyptians ascribed mythical powers to such an animal.

We know that by the new Kingdom Amon's **alter ego** was the God Min, a Black God. However, it needs be pointed out, as Wilkinson has shown, the first represented image of a god in history is that of Min, his emblem and creative organ shown most prominent in the pictographs of the Eastern desert. Notwithstanding, Albert Churchward in *Signs and Symbols of Primordial Man* has argued the earliest image of God was Bes, the Pygmy! Still, they are both African deities.

Again, it was the discipline of archaeology that lets us reconstruct these cultural developments from a time when there was no writing or substantial monuments. We know that the sun and Nile are the two constants of Egypt. They shaped the culture in numerous ways. That is, whether its economics, religion, art and architecture, science, medicine, river transportation, even its astronomy and time measurement, river and sun "made Egypt!"

**Black History Extravaganza - Photo -** Kom Ombo. Double Temple of Haroeis (The Elder Horus) and Sobek (The Crocodile God). Remains of the Peristyle Colonnade of the Left Court. Notice the Cobra Frieze to the top right.

# BLACK HISTORY EXTRAVAGANZA HONORING DR. BEN-JOCHANNAN

**Black History Extravaganza - Photo -** Another view of the entire Court with its Peristyle Columns and the front and cornice of the temple to the left.

Because of its historical, religious and architectural ruins, unlike most other areas, Thebes has attracted a most impressive array of archaeologists and other scholars. Their excavations in temples and tombs, repairing, strengthening, and restoring structures, cataloguing of antiquities and publications of their work, has helped to supply data to make this aspect of ancient history as complete as possible. Much like the Old Kingdom Mastabas, New Kingdom tombs supplied abundant cultural evidence in artistic representation of religious beliefs, industrial and craft activity and social practice. Agricultural exercises, entertainment, war, civil administration and titulary, all interacted in the dynamics of this city of awe, beauty, spiritualism and majestic mystique. Kamil (1984: 141-42) explained how the architects of Thebes' heyday decorated their mortuary structures. "Their tombs are hewn out of solid rock and inscribed with sacred texts from the *Book of the Dead* (developed from the *Coffin Texts* of the Middle Kingdom which were appropriated and revised selections of the *Pyramid Texts* of the Old Kingdom). The smallest tomb is that of

# FREDERICK MONDERSON

Tutankhamon, which was found intact and contained, the priceless treasures with which the world is now familiar. The largest belongs to Seti I. It is 100 yards in length and contains fine sculptured wall paintings in perfect preservation."

The temples and tombs of Egypt were very early of greatest importance to archaeologists. When these were laid bare the experts turned to cemeteries where the hot sand preserved many aspects of the ordinary lives and some remains of natural mummification was evident. All this notwithstanding, in 1895, Robert Cust wrote an article entitled "Protest against the Unnecessary uprooting of Ancient Civilizations in Asia and Africa." The behaviors mentioned highlighted the negative side of archaeology and other nefarious practices in Egypt especially during the 19th Century.

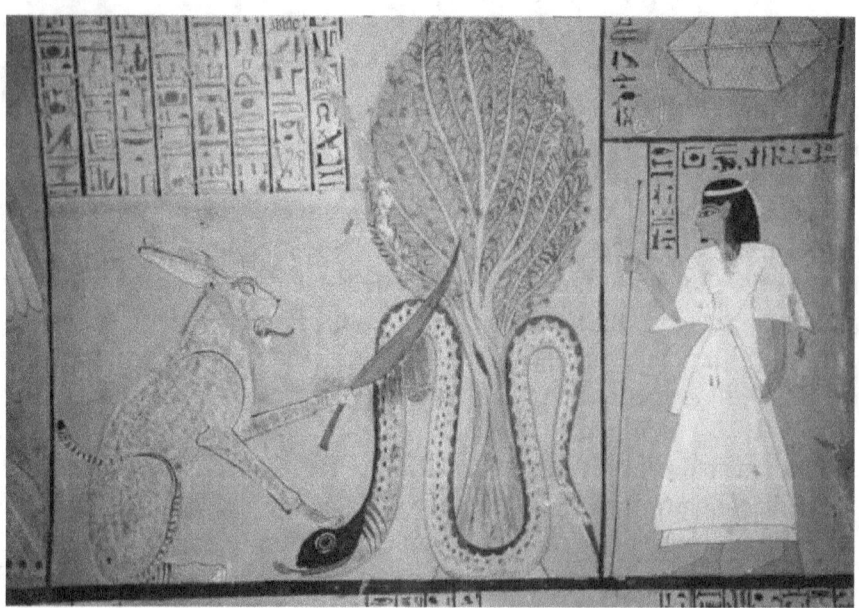

**Black History Extravaganza - Photo -** The "Great Cat" slays the "Great Snake" beside the sycamore tree as the deceased looks on at the drama.

# BLACK HISTORY EXTRAVAGANZA HONORING DR. BEN-JOCHANNAN

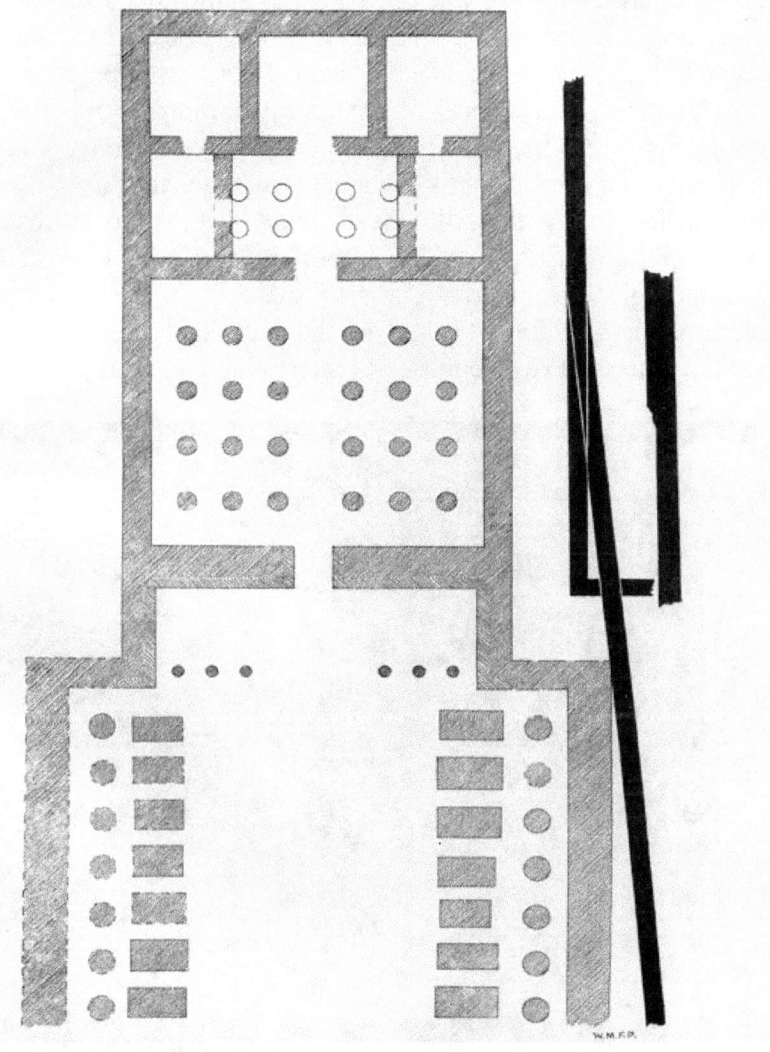

**Black History Extravaganza - Line Drawing -** Ehnasya - Temple of Various Dates, XII-XXX Dynasty.

The Archaeology of Ancient Egypt is thus an interesting subject that lets us see how knowledge of the early African culture unfolded and helped to shape modern perceptions and understanding of a civilization that has been so influential in building, domestic implements, science, medicine and so much more. A whole cadre of

# FREDERICK MONDERSON

European scholars was involved in the reclamation, reconstruction and reinterpretation of ancient Egyptian culture and history. There were no Africans involved in this age of systematic excavation and study to provide constructive criticism. These developments followed the slave trade and slavery and the heyday of rampant imperialism and colonialism in Africa when the continent lay prostrate. Thus, there was none of that special criticism that challenged the "European view" of ancient Egypt! All their good works notwithstanding! Anthropology also played an important part as a twin adjunct to archaeological reconstruction. As such, then, the following is a chronological listing of some of the important events and change agents of the last two centuries of interest in ancient Egypt!

**Black History Extravaganza - Ceramic Art -** Three pitchers reminiscent of the "four pitchers of water the Tree Goddess" poured over the deceased on way to the Hall of Judgment.

## 1. Pre-Napoleonic Interest

# BLACK HISTORY EXTRAVAGANZA HONORING DR. BEN-JOCHANNAN

2. From Napoleon to Champollion

3. Champollion to Mariette

4. Mariette to Petrie

5. Egypt Exploration Fund

6. British School in Egypt

7. Archaeological Survey of Egypt

8. Archaeological Survey of Nubia

9. Events to World War I

10. Anthropological Implications

11. King Tut and Beyond

12. The Black Challenge

13. Where do we go from here?

# FREDERICK MONDERSON

**Black History Extravaganza - Photos -** Two Brothers (top left and Right); Dr. Calvin Butts (Middle) at the Podium at Abyssinian Baptist Church; and members of the Audience as "Eyewitnesses" and Testimonials to a life in service to African people globally.

# BLACK HISTORY EXTRAVAGANZA HONORING DR. BEN-JOCHANNAN

**Black History Extravaganza - Photo -** As the family gathers, "mom and pop" sits and to be presented by servants.

**1. Pre-Napoleonic Interest -** Before Napoleon's invasion of Egypt, Europe was mostly ignorant of the intricacies of the ancient culture, but from readily visible facial features of such monuments as the Sphinx and statues, even accepting Herodotus' description, they accepted **Egypt as a Black Civilization**! Counts Denon and Volney extolled the African inventive spirit, nature and blackness of Egypt at the end of the Eighteenth Century. Denon painted the Sphinx and Volney, in his *Ruins of Empire* (1798) wrote: "The fundamental laws that today govern the universe were developed along the banks of the Nile by a people of sable skin we now hold in slavery!"

# FREDERICK MONDERSON

**Black History Extravaganza - Papyrus -** Horus wearing the Double Crown introduces the king holding scepter and whip to enthroned Osiris in the white crown with feathers.

# BLACK HISTORY EXTRAVAGANZA HONORING DR. BEN-JOCHANNAN

Fact is, if one person can see and understand some fact that is established, then others except those with an insidious agenda, must come to recognize such.

**2. From Napoleon to Champollion** - Following the discovery of the Rosetta stone in 1799, in addition to the emerging interest in antiquities, Imperial Europe slowly began to pay interest in Egypt and artifacts and so the race to decipher was on, involving a great many scholars. Significantly, the great interest in antiquarian artifacts led to what Brian Fagan depicted in his book of the same name entitled **The Rape of the Nile**. That is to say, as much of Africa lay prostrate, colonized, especially Egypt, antiquities collection became a free for all. When the British defeated French forces at the "Battle of the Nile," which was actually fought in the Mediterranean, the artifacts collected by the vanquished, especially the Rosetta stone, was demanded by the victor. Fortunately, the friezes and writings on the ancient culture somehow made its way to France and were published in the Description!

**Champollion (1790-1832)** - *Description of Egypt* - A brilliant linguist who spoke many languages including Coptic, he deciphered hieroglyphics in 1822. Within ten years in 1832 he was dead from overwork, trying to decipher as many documents as he could find; yet, eh created a Dictionary and laid the foundation for the new discipline. Together with the Italian Rosellini they helped produce *The Description of Egypt* and this magnificent piece of work opened the floodwaters of interest in the ancient culture and the hastened development of antiquarian societies.

**Henry Salt (1780-1827)** - A British Consul and friend of Mohammed Ali in Egypt, he amassed an enormous collection of antiquities and sold it to his friend Sir Joseph Banks at the British Museum that became the basis of their collection. He subsidized the work of several people including Belzoni, Captain Caviglia, and Genovese ship owner, Drovetti, William John Bankes and others. He

# FREDERICK MONDERSON

returned to Egypt and amassed a second collection of greater size without showing any respect for the land he and cohorts were plundering.

**Rosellini the Italian** - Did early excavation in Egypt around the time of Champollion. He helped produce the *Description of Egypt* with Champollion. Much of his acquisitions ended up in the Turin Museum. It is interesting that, when the "Deir el Bahari cache" was discovered in 1881 under Assistantship Herr Brugsch during Sir Gaston Maspero tenure heading the Antiquities Department, it was said only then was the Cairo Museum, at that time named Bulak, considered on par with the Turin Museum.

**Black History Extravaganza - Photo -** Kom Ombo. Double Temple of Haroeis (The Elder Horus) and Sobek (The Crocodile God). Peristyle Colonnade of right side of the Court. Again, notice the Cobra Frieze at top left.

# BLACK HISTORY EXTRAVAGANZA HONORING DR. BEN-JOCHANNAN

**Black History Extravaganza - Photo -** Close-up of side view of the columns. Notice the columns, three rows by four rows, and that each capital is different.

**Giovanni Belzoni** (1778-1823) - A circus entertainer who was one of the earliest "raiders of the Egyptian Ark." He did some small-scale digging and clearance of tombs but he also looted many tombs and acquired more than one collection of antiquities. He was dubbed "The strongman Egyptologist" and was typical of those involved in the "Rape of the Nile" and even destruction of artifacts. However, he was given credit for discovering Seti's tomb and clearance of Abu Simbel temple. In fact, Fred Gladstone Bratton in *A History of Egyptian Archaeology* (New York: Thomas Y. Crowell Company, 1968: 63) says of the monumental effort of Belzoni as he traversed the land seeking collectibles: "The removal of the Ramses head was followed in turn by an investigation of the tomb of Rameses III, and exploration of the Valley of the Kings, and an inspection of the temples of Esneh, Edfu, and Kom Ombo. At Aswan, he saw the lovely temples of Philae before they were drowned by the dam. Here also he saw the Philae obelisk which figured so significantly in the decipherment of the hieroglyph. Philae had been the terminus for practically all previous Egyptian explorers. Belzoni, accompanied by his wife, now undertook the dangerous voyage beyond the First Cataract, and after many days of hazardous sailing arrived at Abu Simbel." Even further, in Conclusion, Bratton (1968: 66-67) continued: "The accomplishments of this improbable, astonishing genius - the removal of the Rameses Head, the clearing and exploration of the Rameses temple at Abu Simbel, the discovery and exploration of the tomb of Seti I, and his entrance into the Chephren Pyramid were incredible, considering the period and the lack of modern tools and knowledge. He was motivated, like most nineteenth century explorer-archaeologists, by the fanatical desire to find treasure and sell them to collectors. His methods were at times destructive, caring, as he did, more for the intrinsic value of an object than for its archaeological importance. Granted that these criticisms have much truth in them, the fact remains that his investigations prepared the way for the later and more scientific work on Egyptology. It is only in our time that the Great Belzoni has been given proper recognition for his pioneer work as an Egyptologist."

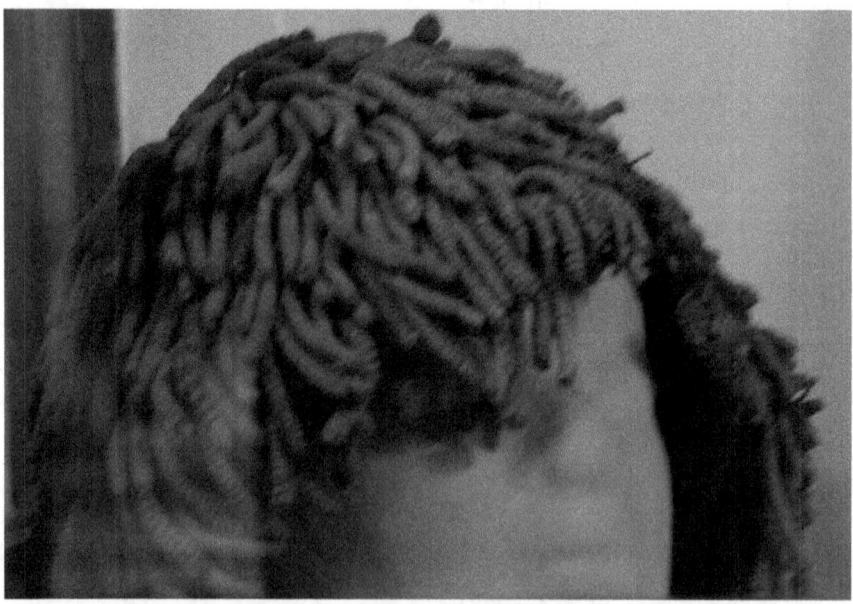

**Black history Extravaganza - Photo -** Wigs discovered in graves and now in the Cairo Museum of Egyptian antiquities.

# BLACK HISTORY EXTRAVAGANZA HONORING DR. BEN-JOCHANNAN

**Black History Extravaganza** - Dr. Ben's Book - **THEY ALL LOOK ALIKE! ALL?!** - Volume III and IV.

# FREDERICK MONDERSON

Sudanese Woman Weaving    PNG's Ex-P.M. M. Samore

A-G Ex-Student Member At Abu-Simbel

Volume III and IV

"THEY ALL LOOK ALIKE!; ALL OF THEM"?

From Papua New Guinea To Egypt
With ben-Jochannan

by:

Yosef A. A. ["Doc"] ben-Jochannan/360⁰

Adjunct Professor of History, Africana Studies and Research Center, Cornell University, Ithaca, N.Y.

Adjunct Associate Professor of History, Malcolm-King College Extension [Marymount Manhattan College, Mt. Saint Vincent College and Fordham University], New York City, N.Y.

Professor of History, Pan-African Studies, Temple University, Philadelphia, Pa.

PNG's Blacks With Woolly Blonde Hair
And Black Hair People

U.S.A. Woman In PNG

PNG's P.M. A. Chan

A-G Ex-Students Members In Desert At Ghizeh

**Black History Extravaganza** - Dr. Ben's Book - **THEY ALL LOOK ALIKE! ALL?! - Volume II and IV – Overleaf of the Title Page.**

# BLACK HISTORY EXTRAVAGANZA HONORING DR. BEN-JOCHANNAN

**3.  Champollion to Mariette** - In the early part of the century, a significant contradiction arose, for while scholars were assiduously engaged in decipherment activities others were involved in rampant seizure of artifacts, particularly those above ground.

**Black History Extravaganza - Photo -** Ehnasya - Image of Rameses II, Usr-Ma'at-Ra. The lips speak volumes.

# FREDERICK MONDERSON

**Black History Extravaganza - Line Drawing -** Ehnasya - Temple: Scenes from Tomb, V Dynasty, Boundary Stone.

This was an age when antiquities hunters ran amok up and down the Nile looking for collector's items, dismantling picturesque images,

# BLACK HISTORY EXTRAVAGANZA HONORING DR. BEN-JOCHANNAN

removing sarcophaguses, there being no regulation regarding collection and exportation of artifacts or thievery and illegal removal from the country. They also destroyed much of the historical remains. Who really knows what evidence of the "Blackness of Egypt" was destroyed in this rampage?

**David Roberts** - Scottish Artist (1786-1864) - He traveled to Egypt and drew many beautiful and colorful pictures of the monuments that encouraged interest in the antiquities. His art showed the monuments, as they lay buried in the sand but they also served to depict potential antiquities treasure troves ripe for the picking.

**Karl Lepsius 1840s** - Richard Karl Lepsius was a lecturer in Philology and comparative linguistics at the University of Berlin. Sent to conduct an expedition in Egypt, Bratton (1968: 74-75) says it "virtually marks the end of the wasteful and destructive period of amateur archaeology and the beginning of a transition to modern Egyptology." His *Denkmaler* in 24-volumes was a masterful compendium of plans, colorful illustrations, that helped preserve many features now lost owing to recent ravages of time and man. "The expedition made an auspicious start with the excavation of the remains of thirty previously unknown pyramids and 130 mastabas from the Old Kingdom. ... Lepsius proposed a theory that the size of a pyramid was determined by the length of the owner's reign. This has been called the accretion theory and, while it is true that certain pyramids such as Zoser's underwent changes and were enlarged during the king's lifetime, the idea does not necessarily hold true.... In 1844 the expedition surveyed the entire Valley of the Kings and excavated at Tell el-Amarna, the Fayum, Thebes, Silsileh, Philae, Abu Simbel, and other Nubian sites. Lepsius' work in making copies of reliefs, cartouches, and his translation of tomb and temple inscriptions resulted in his twelve-volume Monuments of Egypt and Ethiopia (1849-59). The subject of dating was given its first great impetus by Lepsius' publication of *Egyptian Chronology* (1849) and his *Book of Egyptian Kings* (1850). Lepsius himself sent home some fifteen thousand objects to Berlin, including three tombs from Memphis, and obelisk, and a pillar from the tomb of Seti I at Abydos.... Lepsius rationalized his own policy by the statement that only by rescuing the antiquities and sending them to a European museum could they be preserved from destruction."

**4. Mariette to Petrie** - After Champollion and Belzoni, Bratton (1968: 71) writes: The period of early exploration comes to an end with the work of Hippolito Rosellini, Garner Wilkinson, Joseph Bonomi, and James Burton, who represent a somewhat more advanced state of systematic study in view of the fact that they operated with at least a partial knowledge of the hieroglyphs." Significantly, from Mariette to Petrie, these men moved the discipline from the mist of disorder to order and established scientific foundations in approach to retrieving the ancient culture. Petrie spent some 50 years in archaeology and produced an impressive bibliography of his endeavors, while making important discoveries tremendously aiding understanding of the history of ancient Egypt and setting standards for archaeological excavation.

**Sir Gardner Wilkinson** - *The Manners and Customs of the Ancient Egyptians* - An English scholar who did extensive recording of texts, illustrations and monuments presenting masterful pieces that today are standards of works of study. His work remains a standard text of reference for temple, tombs and things cultural; some have still not been published; and he has preserved images now lost through avarice and greed. He was awarded an English Knighthood for his intellectual contribution to the body of knowledge.

**W.M.F. Petrie** (1952-1942) "Father of Modern Archaeology." He worked in Egypt actively from 1881-1925, and could boast of "50 years in archaeology." He was probably the most prolific writer of his age, setting Egypt and archaeology on a scientific footing and was appointed as "Egyptological Chair" at University College of London. He did **sequence dating at Naqada** and identified several sequences of pottery which became a standard for dating remains. Besides his many site reports, Petrie established his "Sequence of Prehistoric Remains," "On the Sources of the

# BLACK HISTORY EXTRAVAGANZA HONORING DR. BEN-JOCHANNAN

Alphabet," "The Use of Diagrams," and discovered "An early Dynastic Cemetery in Egypt." He also conducted "Excavations at Memphis and Hawara in 1911." He did extensive archaeological excavation at Abydos and found first dynasty kings there. He spent much time at Thebes, producing among his many works, *Six Temples at Thebes* (1896).

**Black History Extravaganza - Photo -** While the "Boat of the God Ra-Horakhty" sails above between two mummies, the Nobleman and his wife are shown in several scenes in his tomb.

Jean Capart, in *Egyptian Art: Introductory Studies* (New York: Frederick A. Stokes Company, 1923: 45-46), comments on Petrie's archaeological work in which "tombs of a special type" were unearthed. He states: "These tombs took the form of a more or less regular trench dug in the desert in which the body was laid in a position different from anything previously known to Egyptian funeral archaeology. Beside the corpse were arrayed an abundance of objects which conformed to no known type. There was some hesitation in assigning these burials to any definite period of Egyptian history until it was recognized, when further documents came to light, that they could be designated as the very earliest tombs of the inhabitants of the Nile Valley."

# FREDERICK MONDERSON

Capart (45-46) goes on to say: "Let us now examine a few types. In one, the body, in a contracted attitude, with the knees drawn up to the chest and the hands bent over the face, was wrapped in matting and laid in a cavity more or less oval in shape. In another, the trench is rectangular, the body is lying in the usual manner on its left side in the attitude just described, and all round it is vases of various types intended to contain funereal food. Sometimes the body, the flesh having previously been removed, is placed in a coffin of burnt clay, in which likewise are found the various objects which made up the funerary gear. The pottery coffin, or chest, sometimes fills only a part of the trench; in such cases the gear is arranged partly within the chest and partly outside it. The trench, which in other cases reaches considerable size, is divided into a number of compartments, the greatest being in the funereal chamber proper, the others forming a kind of repository for the burial objects and for offerings."

"The determination of the epoch of which these tombs are assignable being generally admitted it remained to attempt a classification of them in chronological succession. Professor Petrie, in his memoir on Diospolis, was able thanks to the abundance of material he found and to the minute care with which excavation was conducted, to draw up a chronological basis for these primitive tombs. He distinguished a certain number of trenches, marked by the numbers 30 to 80, which he called 'Sequence Dates.' (The numbers below 30 were reserved for the discovery of burials still more ancient.) The general development of the civilization revealed by this study showed that two periods could be distinguished. This resulted mainly from the analysis of the pottery, which was, as we have seen, particularly abundant, and provided a whole series of distinct varieties. The first period is characterized by pottery with a red ground, whilst the second is chiefly marked by pottery with a light ground."

Those listed above all represent a paltry sum of more than 12 pages of bibliographic reference of Matthew William Flinders Petrie's body of work, a man who revealed a great deal of ancient Egypt to the world.

# BLACK HISTORY EXTRAVAGANZA HONORING DR. BEN-JOCHANNAN

## 5. Egypt Exploration Fund 1879 - 1900
-

This was an archaeological society in London, founded by Amelia Edwards and Prof. Lane Poole. They encouraged English and American interest in Egypt, raised money and sponsored digs throughout the land from which artifactual gifts were given to those who made donations. They helped produce and had printed a great many works on different sites, but they all seemed to be devoid of ethnic reference to the blackness of Egypt, as if it was intentional. Whenever such a reference was discovered it was quickly hushed-up or not made much of. Nevertheless, the regularly conducted exhibitions to display evidence of artifacts unearthed from the various digs. However, given they exercised "Pick of the Crop" and were rewarded with some rare and beautiful pieces that were exhibited, these never made it back to Egypt and were left to comprise parts of significant museum collections.

**Black History Extravaganza - Papyrus -** Osiris, painted as a Black God, sits enthroned before a deceased lady with Khepre in expanded wings and a huge snake sits behind his throne, in the Cairo Museum.

# FREDERICK MONDERSON

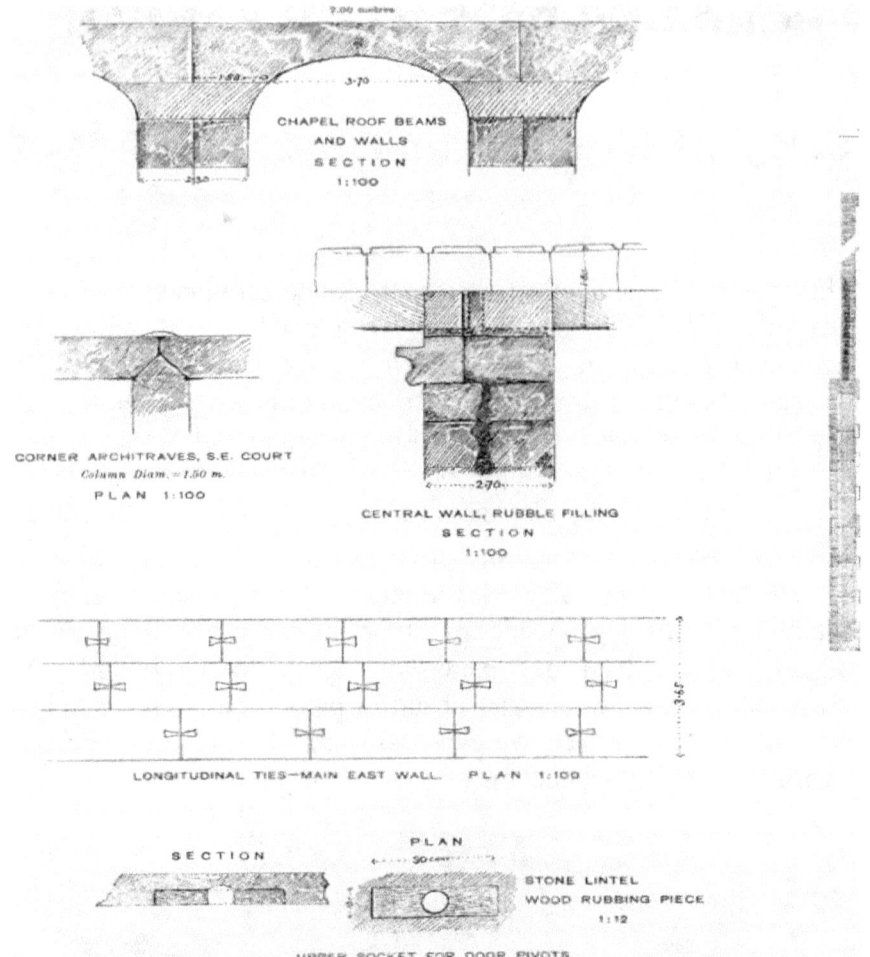

**Black History Extravaganza - Line Drawing -** Chapel roof drawings.

# 6. British School of Archaeology in Egypt and the Egyptian Research Account - These institutions were adjuncts to the **Egypt Exploration Fund** with the intent of exploration and publication. The **British School of Archaeology in Egypt** and the **Egyptian Research Account** produced many works on

# BLACK HISTORY EXTRAVAGANZA HONORING DR. BEN-JOCHANNAN

excavation of various sites. Their body of work included among others *Naqada and Ballas, The Ramesseum, El Kab, Hierakonpolis I and II, El Arabah, Mahasna, Temple of the Kings, The Osireion, Saqqara Mastabas I, Hyksos and Israelite Cities, Gizeh and Rifeh, Athribis and Memphis I, Qurneh and the Palace of Apries* (*Memphis II*). Young African-American scholars and associates must know of the existence of these important sources. Then there are *Meydum and Memphis III, Historical Studies, The Labyrinth and Gerzeh, Portfolio of Hawara Portraits, Tarkhan and Memphis V, Heliopolis I and Kafr Ammar, Riqqeh and Memphis VI, Tarkhan II, Lahun I, The Treasure and Harageh.* We must also include *Scarabs and Cylinders, Tools and Weapons, Prehistoric Egypt, Lahun II, The Pyramid, Sedment I, Sedment II, The Gospel of St. John, Coptic MS., Tomb of the Courtiers and Oxyrchynchus, Buttons and Design Scarabs, Ancient Weights and Measures, Glass Stamps and Weights, Gurob, Objects of Daily Use, Gerar, Qua and Badari I, Badarian Civilization, Bahrein and Hemamieh, Beth-Pelet I, Corpus of Palestinian Pottery, Qua and Badari III, Antaeopolis* (*Qua*), *Beth-Pelet II, Ancient Gaza I, Ancient Gaza II, Ancient Gaza III* and *Ancient Gaza IV*.

**Black History Extravaganza - Photo** - Kom Ombo. Double Temple of Haroeis (The Elder Horus) and Sobek (The Crocodile God). A Baboon presented to Hathor and platter to Sobek.

# FREDERICK MONDERSON

**Black History Extravaganza - Photo -** The solemn mood at the Cemetery to "Lay the Great Man Down."

## 7. Archaeological Survey of Egypt -

Another British vehicle for archaeological excavation, mapping and publication of books and reports relative to Egyptian studies, was produced under the auspices of the **Egypt Exploration Fund**. Their publications, edited by F. LL. Griffith include *Beni Hasan I, Beni Hasan II, El Bersheh I, El Bersheh II, Beni Hasan III, Hieroglyphics from the Collections of the Egypt Exploration Fund, Beni Hasan IV, The Mastaba of Ptahhotep and Akhethetep at Saqqareh, The Rock Tombs of Sheikh Said, the Rock Tombs of Deir el Gebrawi I, The Rock Tombs of Deir el Gebrawi II, The Rock Tombs of El Amarna I, The Rock Tombs of el Amarna II, The Rock Tombs of El Amarna III, The Rock Tombs of El Amarna IV, The Rock Tombs of El Amarna V, The Rock Tombs of El Amarna VI, The Island of Meroe, Meroitic Inscriptions, Five Theban Tombs, The Rock Tombs of Meir I, The Rock Tombs of Meir II, and The Rock Tombs of Meir III.*

# BLACK HISTORY EXTRAVAGANZA HONORING DR. BEN-JOCHANNAN

**Black History Extravaganza - Ceramic Art** - Girdle, Ankh and Heb.

Another organ of the Fund included the **Graeco-Roman Branch** dealing with papyrus published: *The Oxyrchynchus Papyri I, The Oxyrchynchus Papyri II, The Oxyrchynchus Papyri III, The Oxyrchynchus Papyri IV, The Oxyrchynchus Papyri V, The Oxyrchynchus Papyri VI, The Oxyrchynchus Papyri VII, The Oxyrchynchus Papyri VIII, The Oxyrchynchus Papyri IX, The Oxyrchynchus Papyri X, and The Oxyrchynchus Papyri XI*. There were also yearly summaries of *Archaeological Reports* Edited by F. Ll. Griffith, The *Year's Bibliographies* of Published Works, as well as the *Sayings of Jesus and Fragment of a Lost Gospel, Fragment of an Uncanonical Gospel* by B.P. Grenfell and A.S. Hunt and *The Theban Tomb Series Vol. I* by Nina de G. Davies and Alan H. Gardiner. Flinders Petrie founded the Journal *Ancient Egypt* in 1914, which aided in publication of his and other scholars' works on Egypt.

# FREDERICK MONDERSON

**The Egypt Exploration Fund** also launched **Journal of Egyptian Archaeology** in 1914. As all this unfolded, every conceivable reading vehicle, whether newspapers, magazines, journals, etc., published reports of archaeological findings making Europe, America and the Western world very knowledgeable about ancient Egypt and ingraining the unchallenged interpretations as they saw fit. Interesting enough, many of the false interpretations published in newspapers, magazines, journals, reports became solidified in the minds of the readership public and thus today new approaches to historical study have begun to reveal how racism influenced reporting.

**Black History Extravaganza - Papyrus -** Laying a Table of Offerings before the Ennead in the Cairo Museum.

# BLACK HISTORY EXTRAVAGANZA HONORING DR. BEN-JOCHANNAN

**Black History Extravaganza - Line Drawing -** Gurob - Steles.

# FREDERICK MONDERSON

**Black History Extravaganza - Line Drawing** - Gurob - Steles and Shabti Jar, XVIII-XIX Dynasty.

## 8. Archaeological Survey of Nubia -

With Egypt practically exhausted, scholars now turned to excavate Nubia to determine to what extent she had an impact on Egypt. At least two such reports were produced. Harvard, among several American Universities, also did archaeological excavations in Nubia.

# BLACK HISTORY EXTRAVAGANZA HONORING DR. BEN-JOCHANNAN

Much, much later such findings as the Discoveries at Qustol would shed more light on the impact Nubia truly had on Egypt.

**9. Events to World War I** - The two decades from 1895 to 1915 saw enormous advances in the recovery of Egypt, the interpretation of the materials found and a deluge of publication that framed the issue in the minds of Europeans and Americans regarding the origins and peopling of ancient Egypt. We must keep in mind, as early as 1800 of the current era, the German scholar Hegel, perhaps in conspiracy with others began the **systematic removal of Egypt from Africa claiming Africa had no history**! With that "pronouncement from the mantle of white supremacy's absolute wisdom" by a prominent European scholar, the Black role in Egypt began to be diminished and all manner of studies began to be made and projected, many based on faulty data and interpretation. A good source to read that points out the contradictions in European scholarship, seriously unchallenged by European scholars, is Cheikh Anta Diop's *African Origin of Civilization: Myth or Reality*. In this, he outlines all the pros and cons of the arguments. This masterful work needs to be given the serious consideration it truly deserves for it unmasks the deceit in Egyptological studies masterminded by racist scholarship in Europe and America. Strange, even Egyptian scholarship has bought into the falsify and the American University in Cairo and its Press is not challenging the falsity. In fact, they help to propagate the "Myth of a Caucasian Egypt."

It is interesting how writers of the Nineteenth and Twentieth Century write without even mentioning Africans in Egypt. Imagine giving migrating Asiatics from the Caucasus region credit for settling in Egypt yet ignoring Africans who initially migrated to people the world. As the people supposedly migrated across the Nile Valley the record falsely claim Africans seem to stand idly by. The size of the migrating force is another question that needs re-evaluation. Equally too, all comparative references are made to European cultural examples and African cultural norms are conspicuously absent.

# FREDERICK MONDERSON

Important, we need to question the images when told European artists are painting reproductions of images in tombs. So "the Ethiopians were Black!" Looking at the painted image of Queen Amenardis, sister of Piankhi, founder of the 25th Dynasty as depicted in **Great Ones of Ancient Egypt** one sees quite the opposite! Yet, we are asked to accept this!

We must remember, Mosso in The Foundations of Mediterranean Civilization pointed out, The Caucasians never penetrated the Nile Valley nor the Aegean region."

As such, the foundation of modern artistic representation is questionable. It is very similar to A.E.P. Weigall's *Flights into Antiquity* that published a white photo of the Queen of Sheba and entitled one of his chapters "Exploits of a Nigger King," while the American Tabloid *News of the World* similarly showed the Queen of Sheba as a white woman!

**Black History Extravaganza - Photo -** Kom Ombo. Double Temple of Haroeis (The Elder Horus) and Sobek (The Crocodile God). On columns, presenting the "Eye of Horus" to Shu (left); and two ointment jars to Horus in Double Crown (right).

## 10. Anthropological Implications -

Anthropology came to the aid of Archaeology and these twin disciplines, to coin a phrase, "skewed the issue" in their determination of whom possibly the ancient Egyptians were. What is interesting is

# BLACK HISTORY EXTRAVAGANZA HONORING DR. BEN-JOCHANNAN

with the deluge of printed books, journals, magazines and newspapers, even the movies, the Mummy Series, Queen Cleopatra and most important, Ten Commandments. It's often wondered how did so many people become so hoodwinked into such great falsehood. To quote Congressman James Clyburn, they were inculcated in **"Defense of a Myth**!" How could those great minds who studied Egypt and examined all the evidence, seem to get it so wrong? Then, again, all this unfolded in an age of colonialism, imperialism, European domination of the world and an avalanching march towards war and even self-destruction. After all, after slave trade and slavery came colonialism and the masters could not reconcile that the slaves were capable of such intellectual achievements so far back in time before they themselves had become civilized.

This is an aspect of historical evolution. Keep in mind, the mighty Greeks of antiquity, by the end of the 19$^{th}$ Century, were scoring lower on tests than African-Americans who had been out of slavery less than three decades.

A great deal of discoveries came under discussion at a multitude of venues. One such place of interest was the *British Association for the Advancement of Science*. One of their principals was the anatomist G. Elliot Smith from Manchester University who worked out of Cairo, Egypt and examined the mummies of several pharaohs. Some have argued that he was bitter because after he had done his anatomical post mortem examinations of the pharaohs he was rushed from the room after washing his hands and paid, while many of his notes were confiscated. Still, he wrote about Egyptian "diffusionism" and made the **Opening Statement** of the "Discussion On the Influence of Egyptian Civilization on the World's Cultures" which W.J. Perry reported on. Smith was **Chair of the Committee and did the Report** on the "Physical Characters of the Ancient Egyptians" released in 1912. Regarding the "Physical Remains," he provided a **final report** in 1914. The **British Association for the Advancement of Science** met annually, had papers presented and discussed the implications of the papers presented. Yet, one has

# FREDERICK MONDERSON

to wonder how could these honest meetings, discussions, debates, etc., disregard the Black element in Egypt, that was later proved to be there even as the ancient writers recognized and archaeology also revealed a great, quantity of associated facts about ancient Egypt such materials as tools and weapons, gems and precious metals, building stones, and other resources. In *Introduction to Egyptian Archaeology* (2$^{nd}$ Edition, Cairo general Organization for Government Printing Office, 1961: 139-146) R. Engelbach writes, in this regard, telling that "mason's tools, during the whole of the dynastic period, consisted of chisels, mallets, balls and mauls of diorite for rough dressing the hard rocks, some form of blunt pointed pick, saws ... plumb-line rules, squares, the cord-and-reel, and tubular drills." Still, ethnologically many reports were presented as objective scholarship that generated significant discussions on the papers presented. Equally, a number of disciplines adjunct to archaeology were also initiated to fine-tune analysis of the numberless discoveries being made. It's like Prof. Diop said, the African scholar must be multidisciplinary and as Dr. Leonard James taught this writer, the interdisciplinary methodology, I have a better understanding of the events and documents especially of the period of 1870-1930, which I have studied intently. To complement archaeology and anthropology, anthropometry, measurement of the skulls, biometrics, and a whole lot more came into service to analyze and compartmentalize, wrongfully to distort and omit the role of Blacks in Egypt. Young African-American and African-Caribbean students need to be grounded in these problem-solving skills.

**Black History Extravaganza – Photos** - Rev. Calvin Butts of Abyssinia Baptist.

# BLACK HISTORY EXTRAVAGANZA HONORING DR. BEN-JOCHANNAN

**Black History Extravaganza - Line Drawing -** Gurob - Stele - Presentation of feathers of Ma'at to Amon as Min.

Monderson's **Where are the Kamite Kings** is a history of Egypt packed with extremely important annotated information needed for a true understanding of the issues and as preparatory for a more systematic analysis of the unfolding of the knowledge of ancient Egypt. This author's "Who Were the Ancient Egyptians?" also gives a comprehensive reclamation of the relevant data for an encyclopedic base of this knowledge.

**Black History Extravaganza - Papyrus -** Ra-Horakhty and Queen Hathor sit enthroned before a blank cartouche or Shennu.

## 11. King Tut and Beyond - The discovery of King Tutankhamon's tomb by Howard Carter in 1922 proved a conundrum for European scholars. Here we have the boy king, with his two painted Black statues guarding his tomb that says volumes. Since the press and public were at the tomb when it was opened people of questionable intent could not destroy these figures and so many incriminating pieces have been preserved.

We must remember Dr. Zahi Hawass, of the **Supreme Antiquities Council in Egypt** has reminded all, "Tutankhamon is the only king we know of with real certainty." This is because he was found in his sarcophagus in a sealed tomb. Though we recognize all the others, they still have to be re-categorized

# BLACK HISTORY EXTRAVAGANZA
# HONORING DR. BEN-JOCHANNAN

because they were not so lucky! Recently, however, Queen Hatshepsut's mummy has been identified through archaeological and scientific sleuthing by matching an unidentified mummy's missing tooth with one found in the Queen's jewel box. Nevertheless, a strange twist has developed in interpreting the meaning of these Black statues of Tutankhamon that were replicas of the boy king placed just outside his burial chamber.

**Black History Extravaganza - Photo -** On a panel at Esneh Temple, Thoth (left) and Horus (right) baptize the king with streams of ankh and scepter.

# FREDERICK MONDERSON

Some scholars tell us the statues were painted black for the internment ceremony. How interesting! Therefore, where are all the other statues for the numerous embalmed bodies found that should have been painted black for the internment ceremonies? Curiously, right there on the wall beside the statues in the Hall of Tutankhamon, two plaques contradict the claim of blackness for the internment ceremony. Actually, there are three plaques. They seem made of bronze and copper. One shows the black base of the surface with the boy king and writing shining through as copper. Another depicts the boy king as a bronze sphinx trampling his enemies. A third shows the boy king, again, painted bronze and trampling other Africans painted black. Are we to believe these vanquished are painted black for the internment ceremony or that their blackness is similar to the black statues of the boy king. The various works that deal with the Valley of the Kings mention broken wooden fragments found lying about. The question is, whether these are portions of replicas similar to Tutankhamon's statues.

**Black History Extravaganza - Photo -** Husband and wife tilling the field of their plot in the next life.

# BLACK HISTORY EXTRAVAGANZA HONORING DR. BEN-JOCHANNAN

**Black History Extravaganza - Line Drawing -** Abydos - Temple of the Kings. Shrine of Osiris.

If such is the case, a number of question and propositions are posed.

# FREDERICK MONDERSON

1.      If the statues were painted black for the internment ceremony; making black so important, then there would be no "Red" or "White" images of Egyptians in "Heaven!"

2.      Of all tombs in existence, why is only one, an intact one at that, shown with such statues?

3.      Why is black shown to describe other Africans who were not part of the internment ceremony?

4.      We were told one of the wives of Mentuhotep II, Kemsit was painted black but not the others or her servants? Does this mean she was the only one who may have participated in an internment ceremony? However, while she is painted black and described as Negro, her husband also painted black but not Negro and only done so for the internment ceremony!

5.      Why is it only wooden statues are painted black?

6.      What are we to make of the many small, wooden statues of gods, kings and animals painted black in the Cairo Museum in out of the way places far from visitors who rush to see and are only satisfied with Tutankhamon's treasure?

7.      How is it Mentuhotep's statue in the Cairo Museum, discovered in 1898, his temple actually cleared in 1903-05 and removed to the Cairo Museum, where it rests to this day, yet it took until 1959 before W. Stephenson Smith in *Art and Architecture in Ancient Egypt* described it as having "black flesh?" Did Petrie, Erman, Ranke, Breasted, Griffith, Davies, etc., not notice such or could not make a similar deduction and statement? Can the American University in Cairo Press publish a piece that truly and factually addresses this travesty?

8.      By extension, how is it Keith Seele could overlook the important Qustol discovery and secreted such in the University of Chicago's Museum basement without any announcement and it was up to Bruce Williams, a graduate student, mining such "packages of

# BLACK HISTORY EXTRAVAGANZA HONORING DR. BEN-JOCHANNAN

artifacts" to discover and inform all of "The World's Earliest Monarchy" discovered at Qustol in Nubia?

**Black History Extravaganza - Photo -** Gurob - Presenting to Pharaoh on a Stele, but notice the King's lips.

# FREDERICK MONDERSON

9.      Why did sponsors of the 1976 "King Tut" tour of the United States choose the alabaster bust as its symbol and not the two black statues that depict the boy king in a statelier manner? After all, he is decked out in royal attire of crown and other regalia. Then again, after the vociferous protest, why did they come back 30 years later with a brown image of the King? Are we to believe, in another 30 years, the next American "Tut Exhibit" will feature one or both statues?

**Black History Extravaganza - Photo -** Lenora and Grandmother were there to see this "**Son of Africa**," **Dr. Yosef A.A. Ben-Jochannan**, "**put away nicely**."

10.     We know, contrary to most popular belief, the Egyptians were not white, so why are protestation so vociferous when the question of the Blackness of Egypt is raised and articulated and such is not mention in "definitive books" by European and American writers" who imply they were white. As such, why is it no one questions the spoken and in some cases unspoken assumption that the ancient Egyptians were white?

To recap! Another interesting comparison is shown in a room just to the left of the Hall of Tutankhamon. Several cases contain small black

# BLACK HISTORY EXTRAVAGANZA HONORING DR. BEN-JOCHANNAN

wooden statues of kings. One of Amenhotep sits next to a black wooden statue of a leopard. Are we to believe the leopard is painted black for the internment ceremony? Such a case is away from the beaten path. Nevertheless, its only archaeological sleuthing of unintentionally undeclared remains of black Egypt that challenges the false house of cards regarding the role of Blacks in Egypt.

12. **We in America must remember**, when the Middle Kingdom temple of Mentuhotep II was discovered, a statue of the king wearing the Heb Sed Festival dress and the Red Crown of Lower Egypt was unearthed, and placed in the Cairo Museum. Despite volumes written about Egypt right after, no one made any commentary about its race! It was until 1959; 56 years later, that W. Stephenson Smith of Boston in his *Art and Architecture of Ancient Egypt* said Mentuhotep had "black flesh." This revelation, nearly half a century later, was ground-breaking and gives some indication of the misinformation that even the white public is subjected to.

**Black History Extravaganza - Photo -** That couple, again working the fields in the **Afterlife**.

# FREDERICK MONDERSON

Pardon this digression! In September 2005, a young female Egyptian guide in the Cairo Museum told this writer: "Mentuhotep was painted Black because he was dead. This is what my teacher told me!" Imagine, in this day and age this is being taught in Egyptian schools and fed to visitors by tour guides particularly by Western instructors. From as far back as Petrie's earliest "Min statues" discovered at Koptos and now housed in the Ashmolean Museum in Oxford, to those in a not much visited room in the Cairo Museum, wooden statues, whether kings or gods, were all painted Black! The absurd question is, were these statues also painted black for the funerary ceremony? All other statues simply reflected the nature of the materials they were made of. Therefore, this is one of the principal ways the Egyptians referred to their skin color. Consider the regular designation, "Red Land, Black Land" scholars use this dichotomy to describe the fertile land next to the desert encompassing the country of Egypt as well and particularly the very fertile Delta region. However, whenever the gods bequeath Egypt to the king it's always said "I give you the black land" never the red land! However, since Egypt does encompass both red and black lands, does it mean the gods only give the "land of the Black people" to the king? That is, only the black half and not the red half as part of the country? This is a thought that should really be given serious consideration. In addition, whereas red represents barrenness of the desert, death, and black represents fertility, life, resurrection, we must consider the red in tombs as reference to dead people.

13.  **The Black Challenge** - As they say, "Truth crushed to earth shall rise." Blacks began to become involved in Egyptian studies and to do the critical research that enlightened their people, so long oppressed and kept ignorant in America. As early as the 19th Century with Martin Delaney and Caribbean interest in Egypt, begun with Edward Wilmot Blyden and then fueled by the nationalism of Marcus Garvey, Blacks began to seek after their cultural history.

# BLACK HISTORY EXTRAVAGANZA HONORING DR. BEN-JOCHANNAN

**Black History Extravaganza - Ceramic Art** - The Ram of Amon in horns.

**W.E.B. DuBois** - Following his 1896 Harvard Ph. D. *Suppression of the Slave Trade to America* 1638-1880 thesis, DuBois wrote *Black Folks then and Now* (1903); *The Negro* (1915); and *The World and Africa* (1947); Drusilla Dunjee *The Beautiful Ethiopians* (1926); Carter G. Woodson *The Mis-Education of the Negro* (1932); *Education of the Negro* (1933); and *The African Background Outlined* (1934); J.A. Rogers - *World's Great Men of Color* and *Sex and Race* I (3 volumes); Cheikh Anta Diop *African Origin of Civilization: Myth or Reality, Civilization of Barbarism: An Authentic Anthropology, Cultural Unity of Black Africa,* and *Pre-Colonial Black Africa*; Theophile Obenga, Diop's associate *Egypt and Black Africa* and *African Philosophy: The Pharaonic Period* 2780-330 B.C.; Yosef A. A. ben-Jochannan *Black Man of the Nile and his Family* (1972); *Africa: Mother of Western Civilization* (1970); *African Origins of the "Major Western Religions* (1971);" and *From Abu Simbel to Ghizeh* (1989); Ivan Van Sertima *Nile Valley Civilizations*; *Egypt: Child of*

# FREDERICK MONDERSON

*Africa*; *Egypt: Revisited*; *Great African Thinkers: Cheikh Anta Diop*; Maulana Karenga, Jacob Carruthers, Tony Browder, Molefi Asante, Wade Nobles, Leonard James, etc., all produced credible works that exposed the hypocrisy of European scholarship, vis-à-vis, Egypt, together with their American co-conspirators who are just as guilty. We must always remember what **Prof. John H. Clarke**, at Hunter College of the City University of New York, "The Hunter School" of which I am a graduate twice over, often reminded: "The People who preached racism colonized history" and "When Europe colonized the world it colonized the world's knowledge!"

**Black History Extravaganza - Photo -** Winged Sun-Disk with uraei.

# BLACK HISTORY EXTRAVAGANZA HONORING DR. BEN-JOCHANNAN

**Black History Extravaganza - Photo -** The family members, grieving, yet sitting strong and **Nobly** at the end of a terrific and consciously **Noble** journey of one of Africa's beloved sons.

14. **Where do we go from here? -** We must teach the young, when the time is right, visit Egypt, read voraciously, study various languages as German and French where huge bodies of evidence are contained and also study hieroglyphics, form study groups and continue to teach young and elderly Africans while advocating, **Egypt is African and Black**. Equally as important, we must remember Dr. Ben-Jochannan's admonition, "When doing research on ancient Egypt, get the oldest materials you could find!" Some of it is not as twisted and sanitized as the projected and propagated modern embed misconceptions.

# FREDERICK MONDERSON

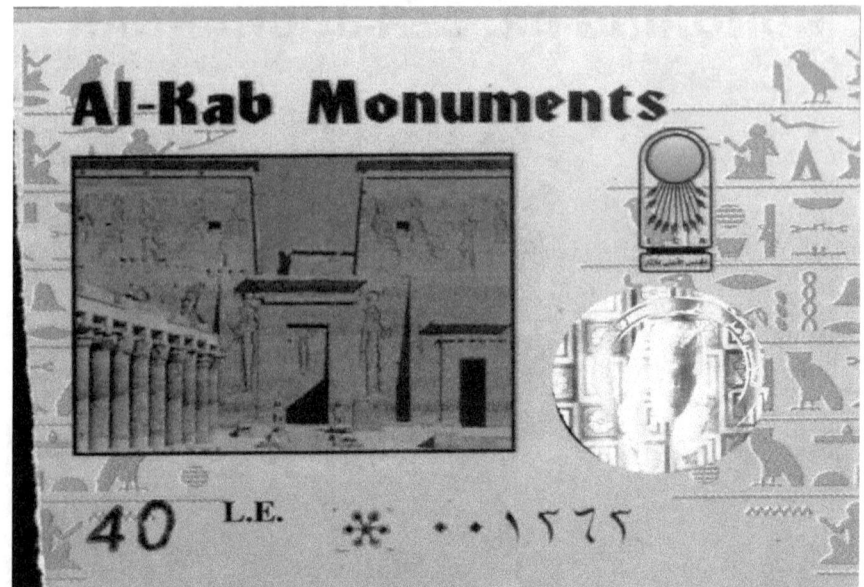

**Black History Extravaganza - Temple Site Tickets -** Again, using Philae façade for El-Kab Monuments, still the price is 40-Egyptian Pounds.

**Black History Extravaganza - Cairo Museum -** Ushabti figures of King Tutankhamon wearing various crowns.

# BLACK HISTORY EXTRAVAGANZA
# HONORING DR. BEN-JOCHANNAN

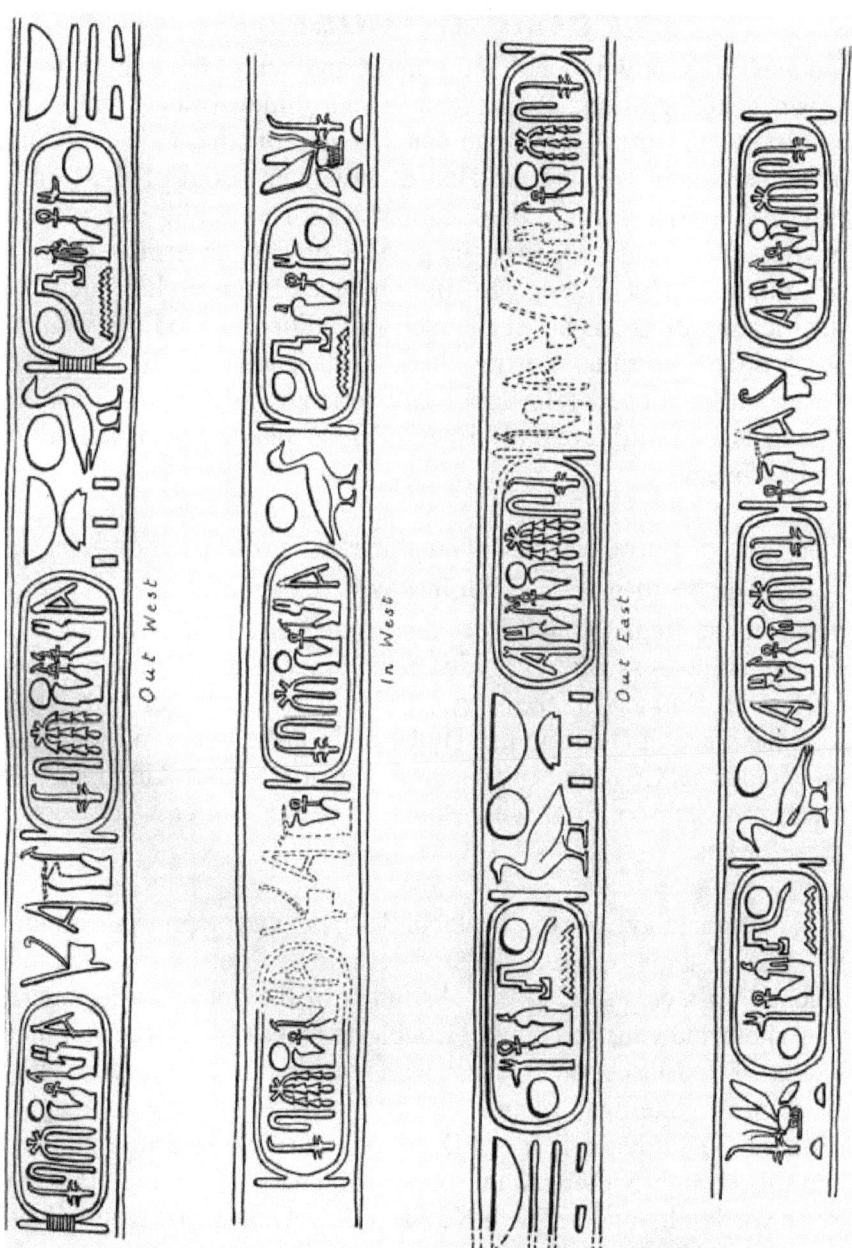

**Black History Extravaganza - Line Drawing -** Gurob - Temple, Granite Architraves.

# FREDERICK MONDERSON

## Poem to Thoth

Divine Thoth, how revered is thy name and being, three times great, Trismegistus, majesty. Rising with Ra in primeval times and Prime Minister of Horus, you are Intelligence of the Gods. Chief administrator in the African Hall of Judgment, Lord of the Books, Prince of Laws, you are the Heart of Ra. The infallibility of your instrumentation and integrity you give the process, determine the faith of millions who enter. In like manner, you orchestrated the justification of Osiris at the Council in Heliopolis. God of Wisdom, these souls' spiritual destiny held in balance in your Ma'atian Psychostasia, Lord of Heliopolis, Patron Divinity of the Learned. Thoth, as ibis, you were on Narmer's Palette together with Hathor, the Lady of Heaven.

You Lord of Hermopolis, who combines with four pairs of gods, are Self-created, Self-produced. Shrines were constructed at Hermopolis, place of the 'high ground,' at Abydos and elsewhere. Strength of Gods, you possess Life, Stability, Sovereignty and Dominion, Moon in Heaven, Bull among the Stars, Leader of the Gods, Lordly Ibis you took the place of Horus in the Titulary of Khufu, Letter Writer of the Nine Gods, as Governor of Mankind, you are Lord of Kindliness. In the Horus/Seth conflict, with words of power you created a cow's head for Isis.

When Osiris fell victim to the plot of Seth, Isis and Nephthys lamented the loss of their beloved. This protestation of sorrow and anguish reached Ra's ears in Heaven. As father of the gods, Ra dispatched you Thoth and your companion Anubis, to make Osiris True of Voice. O One of Red Jasper and Quartz, with Anubis you became emissaries of comfort, intelligence and security providing Isis with magical formulas. Your Knowledge of Divine speech gave confidence to Isis, and this brought victory to her quest. Thus, Thoth, strong deliverer, Scribe of Truth, together with Nephthys and Anubis, you bear witness to the revivification of Osiris, Lord of Goodliness.

# BLACK HISTORY EXTRAVAGANZA HONORING DR. BEN-JOCHANNAN

**Black History Extravaganza - Photo -** Oh yes, even in the **Afterlife**, the trees bear fruit.

When Horus staked his claim in the Imperial Court of the Divinities, Master of Laws you defended him. Lordly Ibis, your legal mind vindicated his right to mount the Throne of Egypt.

Unquestionably your departed companion Osiris lauded your legalism on his behalf. Victorious Horus, his mother Isis and aunt Nephthys were equally pleased with your actions, Scribe of the Gods, who sails in his divine boat, and stands among the Lords of Truth, Vicar of Ra. Your attributes are impressive, Lord of Divine Words. You gained mastery over your own heart and opened your mouth to bestow life, embracer of heaven. As Divine Patron of writing, the arts, astronomy, and science your origination heralded these gifts of Africa to the world. Back in ages when Black men and women were founts of creativity and wisdom, your intellect Thoth and the Quintessence of Ma'at, your counterpart, were great African moral and intellectual contributions to humanity's progress.

# FREDERICK MONDERSON

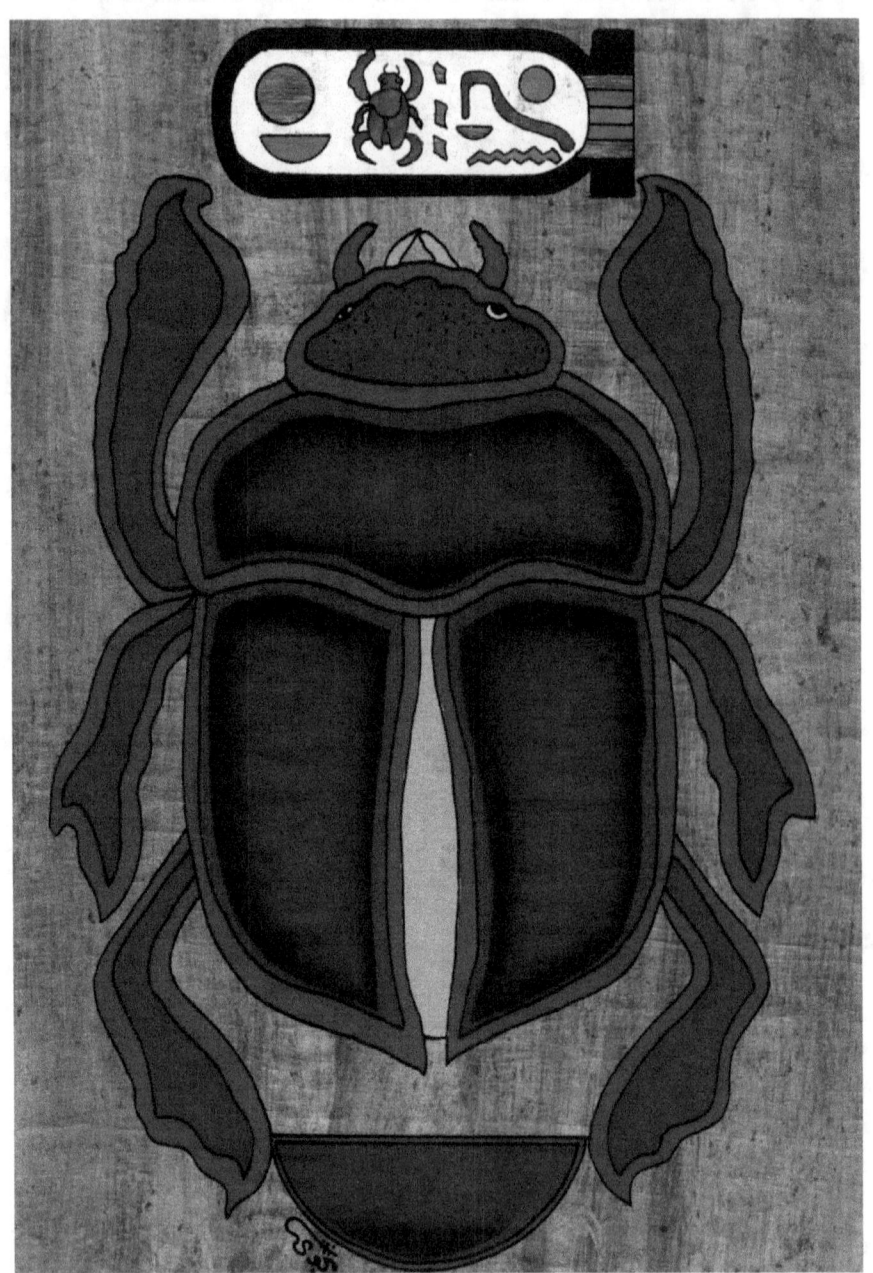

**Black History Extravaganza - Papyrus -** This time, in Blue, Khepre pushes the Cartouche.

# BLACK HISTORY EXTRAVAGANZA HONORING DR. BEN-JOCHANNAN

Thoth, as an African divinity of brilliance and integrity, you are Master of Physical and Moral Law. Your knowledge and power calculated the heavens and the earth, keeping them in equilibrium. Moon God, symbol of the Equinoxes, your compatriots, the Gods, respect your judgment without question. For in that august weighing of the hearts of men in the Great Balance, 0 Lord of Divine Words Your findings determine instant death or Life and Eternal Existence, because you speak truth and are the embodiment of Justice. Lord of Khnumu, you record in writing deeds and actions of Gods, kings and men, so continue to Open Your Eye to Give Life.

Thoth, you symbolize the grace and majesty of the Ibis, and clear-sightedness of the baboon. Your scales of Balance represent order in every situation, God of Equilibrium, Lord of Ma'at. You transcribe and interpret the thoughts and aspirations of eternal African spirits who breathe life into creation, 0 Lord of Heaven, Great Deliverer and Creator of Everlastingness, you illuminate the Earth with your Beauty. Great Dom Palm sixty cubits in height, Sweet Well for one that thirst in the Wilderness, you give prosperity and advancement to mankind who worship you, Patron Divinity of the Learned, who stood in place of Ra.

How interesting these Black immortals have destined the talents and intellect of the God Thoth. Lord of Knowledge and understanding who Possess Power Greater than Osiris and Ra, empower us to cultivate the development of arts, sciences, intellectual growth, and ethical and moral advancement. This way we can save humanity, within the philosophical construct of the fatherhood of god and the brotherhood of man.

# FREDERICK MONDERSON

**Black History Extravaganza - Line Drawing -** The Bark of Osiris at Abydos.

**Black History Extravaganza - Photo -** The whole family is out-there bringing some offering for the festival.

# BLACK HISTORY EXTRAVAGANZA
# HONORING DR. BEN-JOCHANNAN

**Black History Extravaganza - Photo -** Interesting the "Prince of the City" whose image is always high up in esoteric places is also often the victim of defacement. Notice the ankh and Uas standards with hands on the bottom row.

**Black History Extravaganza - Photo -** Kwesi Ashra and Greg Hardy, long standing friends, students and associates of Dr. Ben-Jochannan were at the "Cemetery to Lay the Great Man down!"

# FREDERICK MONDERSON
# IX. THE ART OF ANCIENT EGYPT
## By
## Dr. Fred Monderson
## Introduction: Art of Ancient Egypt I

The Art of Ancient Egypt is one of its most beautiful and enduring accomplishments visible in that nation and equally adorns museums and private collections worldwide. Egyptian Art can be observed in its technology, burial methods, tomb decorations, buildings and its methods and building techniques, sculptures, paintings, reliefs, pottery, hieroglyphs, stelae, in the art of mummification, quarrying and even river transportation of stone and other materials, while its most distinctive features are "its effective use of lines and its decorative values." Even in its geography art played an important part because in the mythology, the land first emerged from the flood of the inundation. While much ink has been spilt trying to argue foreign, South West Asia, importation of art forms, Denison Ross rightly points out, "The art of Egypt was purely local in origin." That being so, many of its buildings were based on lines and vertical and horizontal orientation.

The XVIIIth Dynasty temple of Hatshepsut at Deir el Bahari is a perfectly good example of such lines and vertical and horizontal orientation readily apparent as the visitor ventures into the inner features. Nonetheless, and even more important, the location of pyramids, temples and tombs were chosen based on such an erection or building being sited next to some geographical feature. Reinforcing this view, E. Denison Ross in *Egyptian Art Through the Ages* (1931: 1) has argued, "When ancient Egypt first began to occupy the attention of the West, the linguist and the historian were the interpreters of her civilization, and the aesthetic value of her monuments was hardly recognized. Hieroglyphs were deciphered and read, but our classical and modern prejudices hindered us from appreciating an art so essentially unfamiliar. It took the artistic world long to rid itself of the obsession of Hellenic formulae, and to approach the masterpieces of the Pharaohs with an open and impartial mind." Yet still, with all we

# BLACK HISTORY EXTRAVAGANZA HONORING DR. BEN-JOCHANNAN

know, Egypt is even more coveted for the books on Western foundations now begin with a chapter on Egypt.

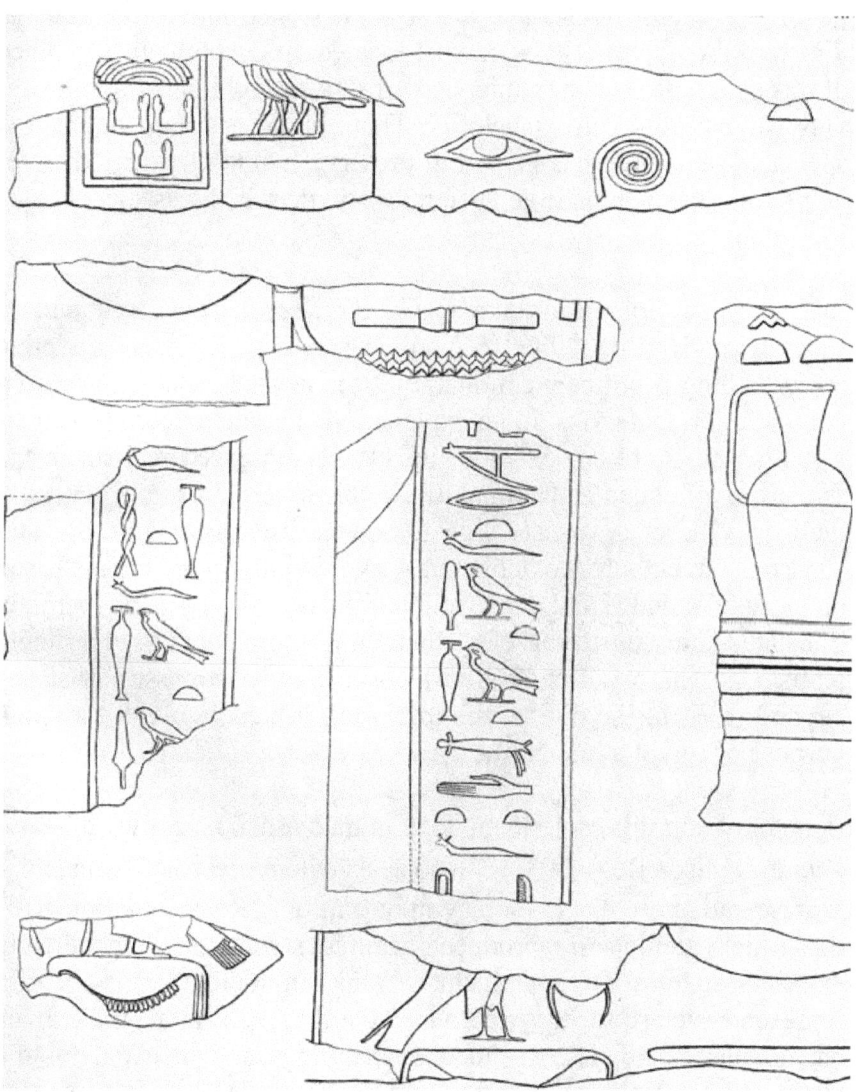

**Black History Extravaganza - Line Drawing -** Ehnasya - Temple Fragments of Senusert III and Amenemhat III, Middle Kingdom.

# FREDERICK MONDERSON

Neverthele4ss, the role of geography as influencing architecture as well as history is unmistaken. This is unquestionably so, given the pyramids were constructed on a flat plain, while temples were built near the river and by the New Kingdom tombs were hidden in valleys of kings, queens, nobles and artisans. It is also interesting that the tombs of the nobles at Aswan were located on the high cliffs. Choice of this spot with its panoramic view of Aswan highlights the splendid view of nature's canvas below. This choice is art in a timeless spectacle the desert has helped to preserve, while the adjacent river helps color the manmade and natural work of art below is sheer genius in its conception.

In this respect, John Boardman in *The World of Ancient Art* (London: Thames and Hudson, 2006: 156) projects a view: "'Official' Egyptian art is nothing if not conventional, but it is never boring: an apparent contradiction that looks for an explanation. Throughout the history of Egyptian art there are examples of closely observed realism in the rendering of human and animal life, yet the overall result is generally realistic. These are artists able to render life as well as did any Classical Greek but who deliberately avoided it. Their idiom is based on close knowledge and observation of the real but it was deliberately translated into something else, something more timeless than mere realism.... The result is an art which brilliantly expresses what lies beyond realism, the divine, the immortal, in keeping with the main purpose of Egypt's major arts."

In is foray into this esoteric mode of human artistic creativity, T. Eric Peet in Denison Ross (1931: 6) also deals with representative and non-representative art. That is to say in definition, "Representation art is that which attempts to reproduce or imitate something which already exists in nature or manufacture. Thus, modeling sculpture are representative art, for they reproduce the figures of men and animals and inanimate objects. So, too, are paintings and incising, for the craftsman must paint or incise something otherwise he is not an artist. On the other hand, the arts of the architect, the potter, the stone-vase maker and the jeweler are non-representative. All these create things which are not necessarily copies of anything which exists. When, however, the artist proceeds to add statues or reliefs to a building, or

# BLACK HISTORY EXTRAVAGANZA HONORING DR. BEN-JOCHANNAN

paint scenes on a vase, or gives to his bracelet, the form of a bird or animal he passes over into the realm of representative art. Thus, the two types of art, representative and non-representative, may easily, and often do, cross each other's boundaries. Nevertheless, this does not take away from the usefulness of the division for practical purposes."

**Black History Extravaganza - Photo -** Well, there's that couple again tending their field in the **Afterlife**.

This dynamic sense of form and proportion developed as early as the Predynastic Period and improved with the passage of time reflecting spiritual aesthetics manifested in religious expression guided by practices of Ma'atian ethics. In attempting to create an understanding of such a creative force that molded this peculiar Egyptian human being we look, in part, to H. Frankfort's commentary "On Egyptian Art," *Journal of Egyptian Archaeology* Vol. 18 (1932: 33) where he insists: "Schafer has lately stated what he believes to be the only scientific attitude towards Egyptian art: namely that one should try to penetrate as deeply as possible into all the manifestations of spiritual

# FREDERICK MONDERSON

life of the Ancient Egyptians which have come down to us, to rouse in oneself what might be called Egyptian thought and feeling, and then to approach Egyptian art and interpret it. The classical scholars, however, have taken as their starting point the general and essential character of all art, that it is a creation of form, which can only be understood by an appreciation of its formal qualities. Everything which is not form becomes, from this point of view, of entirely secondary importance: 'We may know a great deal about a thing as it really exists - its history, composition, market value, its cause and its effects - all that is as good as not there for the aesthetic attitude. It is all incidental; not present in the aesthetic object.'"

Even further, he goes on to say, "This attitude is obviously legitimate, not only within the framework of a history of art, but also from the point of view of Egyptology. We cannot understand the ancient Egyptian to the full if we refuse to consider him as subject to aesthetic feeling, while continuing to interpret him as a religious or ethical being; we cannot understand him, or his culture, without treating his art as art, as an object of aesthetic contemplation. That this contemplation must result in the forming of distinct and intelligible conceptions in order to obtain scientific significance at all, is obvious."

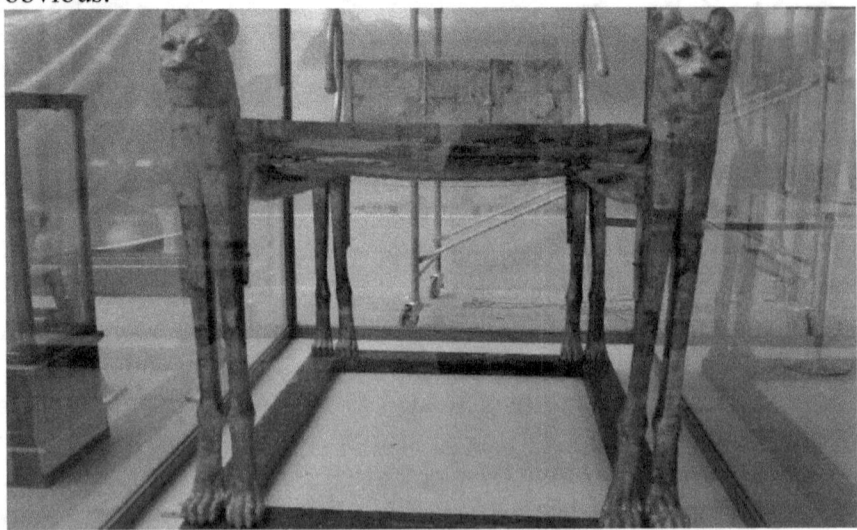

**Black History Extravaganza - Cairo Museum -** An early version of a bed or lounging chair of King Tutankhamon.

# BLACK HISTORY EXTRAVAGANZA HONORING DR. BEN-JOCHANNAN

**Black History Extravaganza - Ceramic Art** - Feather and Uraeus with Disk, what a feature.

Equally too, in his **Introduction**, Irmgard Woldering in *The Art of Egypt: In Time of the Pharaohs* (Baden-Baden, Germany, 1963: 11) makes such understandings even clearer: "For a long time Egyptian art remained misunderstood by Europeans, since they proceeded from false premises. To those brought up in the Greek school, the Egyptian treatment of form inevitably seemed rigid and primitive. It was thought to possess the clumsiness appropriate to an early stage of development, when men had not yet succeeded in representing in an organic and lively manner the world they saw about them. Only in the 19$^{th}$ Century, when excavations were begun and an abundance of works reached European museums, did it become clear how inadequate this traditional aesthetic approach was in attempting to appreciate the genius of Egyptian art. The relationship between the viewer and the work of art is no doubt always determined by aesthetic considerations, but it must not be forgotten that the image obtained in this way is bound to be a subjective one. In order to assess Egyptian art objectively, it is necessary to know something of Egyptian history in pharaonic times, of Egyptian religion, and of the Egyptian way of life."

**Black History Extravaganza - Photo -** Pharaoh in Double Crown incenses Ra-Horakhty at Kom Ombo Temple.

Nevertheless, "Egyptian art is not all stone architecture and sculpture." So, writes John Boardman (2006: 157) in explaining: "The richness of finds in tombs and the conditions of burial have told us more about the arts applied to furniture and dress, to materials that generally perish, than have finds elsewhere, except perhaps where the

# BLACK HISTORY EXTRAVAGANZA HONORING DR. BEN-JOCHANNAN

conditions are as wet as, in Egypt, they are dry. The jewelry is exquisite and colorful. For seals they at first used cylinders with simple patterns, like those of Mesopotamia, but came to prefer stamp seals carved or molded in the form of the sacred scarab beetle and these, like the Chinese seals, carried inscriptions, usually royal names or mottoes rather than figure subjects. The form became the standard for amulets and seals through much of the Mediterranean world, for Phoenicians, Greeks and Etruscans." In an equally interesting comment particularly as it relates to the question of 'Who were the Ancient Egyptians" and from whence they came. Keeping in mind that Breasted dismissed Mesopotamian and Babylonian anteriority over Egypt as not requiring a credible response, Boardman explained: "In early days Egyptian civilization had not developed without knowledge of Mesopotamia, and there are points of contact in the pre-Dynastic arts. Some Egyptian kings came to have extra-territorial ambitions and even challenged Assyria. The result, in the arts, was generally to ensure that it was Egyptian styles and subjects that were well diffused through the Levant and Anatolia, while there was very little return traffic in kind. But the Egyptian styles that traveled were pretty rather than profound: slim-winged discs, a variety of gods, demons and headdresses, scarabs, some jewelry techniques."

Within this dynamic, we notice the Egyptian artist used symbolism in the writing, the decoration, painting and sculpture to emphasize meanings not easily comprehended. In the artistic development, all the facets of the civilization were thus aided by the craft of the artist who represented every conceivable feature of the culture, building, decoration, writing, statues, stelae, etc. From his perspective, Cyril Aldred (1980: 15) in *Egyptian Art* makes the artistic connection between language and culture when he speaks to: "The use of symbolic forms in Egyptian art is intimately associated with a characteristic Egyptian culture, the employment of hieroglyphics in a system of writing which has no exact counterpart in other civilizations."

# FREDERICK MONDERSON

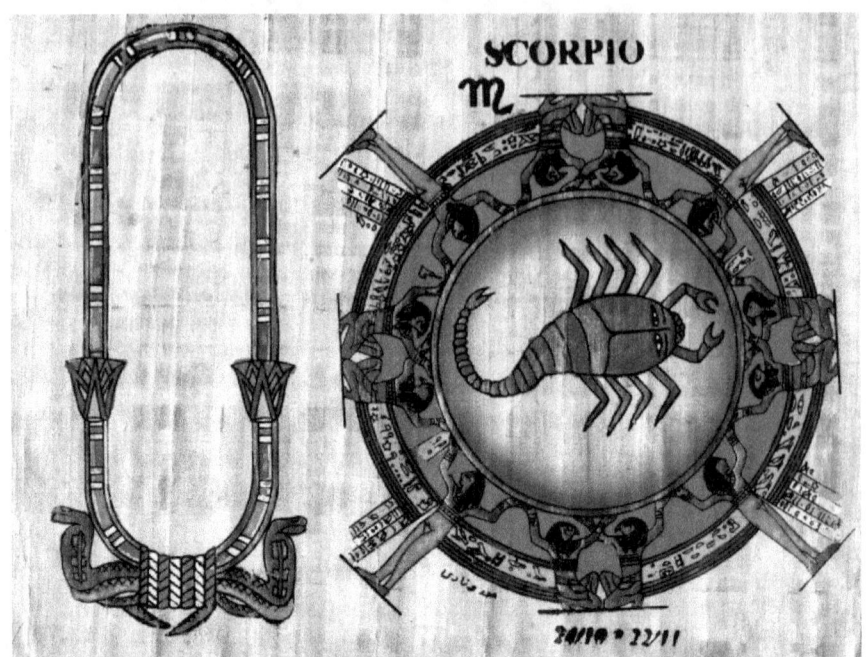

**Black History Extravaganza - Papyrus -** An empty cartouche beside the horoscope symbol for Scorpio.

Interestingly, their artists' use of color has led to much speculation regarding particularly the skin color of the Egyptians. Historical and archaeological evidence supports the view by the Old Kingdom they were using the colors red, blue, black, and green, and yellow imposed on a white background. Long before the prehistoric Badarian, Amratian and Gerzean or Naqada I and II culture sequence, painting of the flora, fauna, hunting, etc., the "predominant red" generally characterized ancient man's use of color in Africa as well as the Nile Valley as he sought to overcome and represent his environment particularly using red as an esoteric, divine color, same as gold. However, through the Old, Middle and New Kingdoms and the Late and Graeco-Roman Periods, regional art schools developed that either continued older traditions or innovated techniques that spawned competition and even more creative productions emphasizing the two characteristics of line and decoration that reached back into the Predynastic period. Nevertheless, throughout his long history the Egyptian relished in tradition and the unchanging golden accomplishments embodied in the social and religious creative

# BLACK HISTORY EXTRAVAGANZA HONORING DR. BEN-JOCHANNAN

reverence the past held. In *Ancient Egypt: Anatomy of a Civilization* (1989, 1993: 26) Barry J. Kemp explained this phenomenon in the following manner: "Departures from the picture of the ideal past were few, and (the Hyksos Period excepted) confined to individuals. More typically the past was the fount of authority and authenticity. A characteristic image is provided by King Neferhotep of the 13$^{th}$ Dynasty (c. 1750 B.C.), piously visiting 'the house of writings,' examining the 'ancient writings of (the creator-god) Atum' in order to discover the correct form for a new statue of Osiris, laid down by the gods themselves at the beginning of time. With a similar reverence for ancient forms Egyptian artists retained the original shapes of hieroglyphs with scarcely any modification for 3000 years. The general continuity of style in art and architecture owes itself to the careful reproduction of codified styles created in the Early Dynastic Period and Old Kingdom. But there was an element of self-deception in this. Significant changes of ideals and forms did occur, and these must reflect intellectual development, something directly apparent from written sources also."

**Black History Extravaganza - Cairo Museum** - A Multi-colored Bracelet.

# FREDERICK MONDERSON

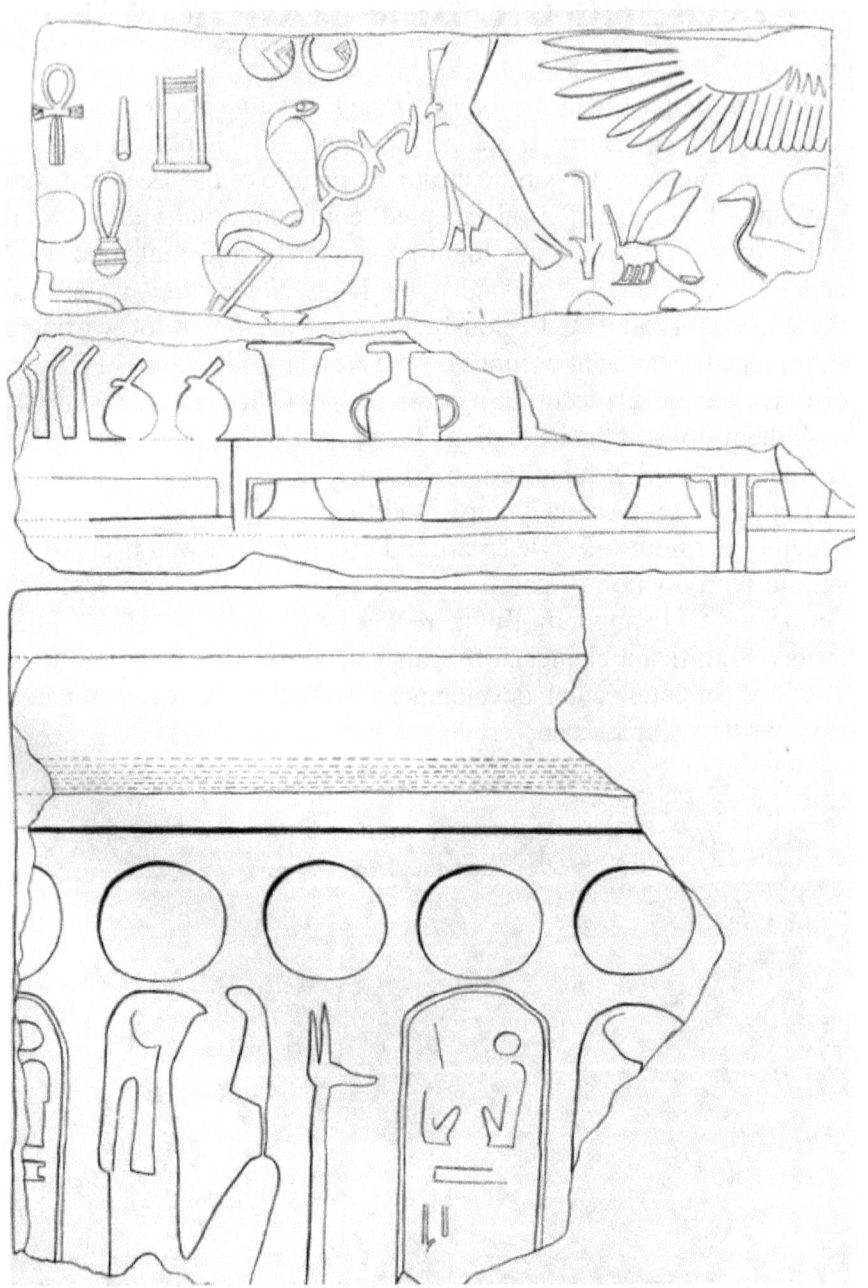

**Black History Extravaganza - Line Drawing -** Ehnasya - Pieces of XII Dynasty and Ramessu II Cornice.

# BLACK HISTORY EXTRAVAGANZA HONORING DR. BEN-JOCHANNAN

Even further, he continued: "The whole modern scholarly apparatus of art history in Egyptology is based upon the premise that style did change from period to period. Thus, the brooding, careworn images of kings in Middle Kingdom statuary conveyed a very different message from the idealized youthful images of the Old Kingdom. King Neferhotep's new statue of Osiris would have been recognizably a product of craftsmanship of its time. Indeed, the 'writings' that the king examined can have specified the nature of ancient image in only general terms, such as the precious materials of which it was composed. The Egyptians could not have put into words a description of the style of a statue. The same was true of architecture. The New Kingdom saw a major reappraisal of temple architecture in which, at least as it relates to the royal mortuary cult, we must recognize significant shifts in meaning. Change did occur, but on the whole tastefully and reverently through retention of the basic vocabulary of traditional forms, sometimes reinforced by appeals to the past."

Notwithstanding, throughout, particularly during the dynastic period, Kings in order to beautify their palaces and in temples and tombs were major patrons of the arts. However, while some noble families equally played a role, much of this art is represented in their tombs as the only surviving examples of private endeavors. In praising their gods in various religious expressions, temples played a role in fostering growth, development and expansion of this tangible method of cultural creativity.

**Black history extravaganza - Photo -** The Crowd outside trying to get the last photo of the coffin in the hearse (left); and Sister Camille Yarbrough in a somber mood within Abyssinia Baptist Church on day of the Viewing.

# FREDERICK MONDERSON

**Black History Extravaganza - Photo -** At a banquet with the family in attendance, a Priest in Lion-Skin pours a libation.

**Black History Extravaganza - Line Drawing -** Tell er Retabeh - (Rameses II) - Left half of Temple front.

# BLACK HISTORY EXTRAVAGANZA HONORING DR. BEN-JOCHANNAN

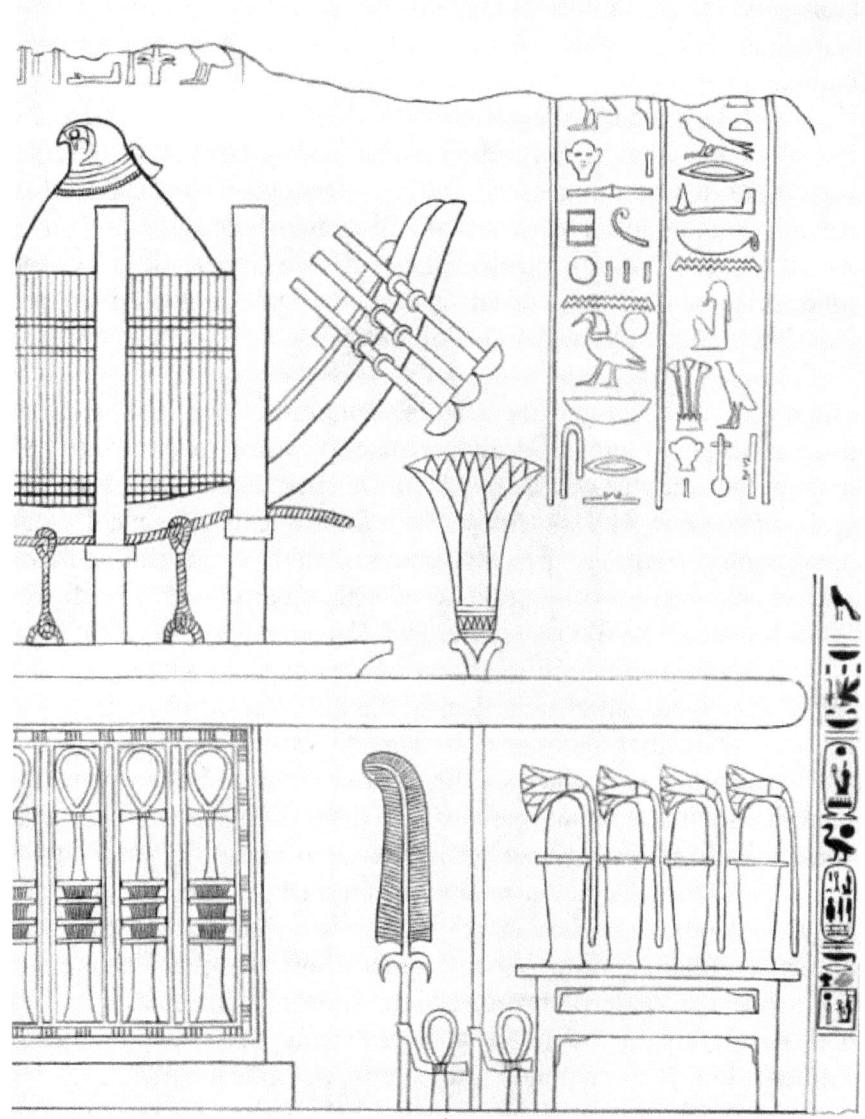

**Black History Extravaganza - Line Drawing** - Abydos - Temple of the Kings. Barque of the Mummied Hawk

Extensive archaeological excavation has revealed evidence beginning in Predynastic graves, as well as monumental structures as the Step-

# FREDERICK MONDERSON

Pyramid, and large mastabas at Sakkara; the group of Great Pyramids at Ghizeh; the Old and Middle Kingdom tombs of the Nobles on the high cliffs at Aswan; the Middle Kingdom Tombs at Beni Hasan; the Middle Kingdom Temple of Mentuhotep II at Deir el Bahari; the New Kingdom worship and mortuary temples at Thebes; the venerated Valley of the Kings, Valley of the Queens, Valley of the Nobles, and Valley of the Artisans with their tremendously colorful tombs; the very Late Period temples at Edfu, Kom Ombo, Esneh, Philae, Kalabsha; and equally Abu Simbel, all demonstrate Egyptian Art of the highest and enduring quality. Many artifacts from these places and time periods can be viewed in private and public collections worldwide titillating the delights of art lovers.

The enduring beauty of the statues, sculptures, paintings, papyrus decorations, buildings, sarcophaguses, wall decorations and inscriptions, the *Pyramid Texts*, *Coffin Texts*, and the decorated *Book of Coming Forth by Day* (*Book of the Dead*), as well as picturesque hieroglyphic writing are all unmistakably wonderful cultural attainments expressed in art. The writing is particularly significant, for as Richard H. Wilkinson in *Reading Egyptian Art* (1996: 10) notes: "All Egyptian hieroglyphic writing is made up of pictures, yet it is seldom realized that a great deal of Egyptian art is in turn heavily influenced by, and many occasions made up of hieroglyphic words and written signs." Much of this writing is an imitation of nature themes of plants, animals, humans, and the landscape, domestic, civic and military as well as personal objects from every aspect of the society. Other Pharaonic paraphernalia such as crowns, scepters, sandals, rings, bracelets, anklets, girdles, necklaces, armbands, amulets, collars, pectorals, and other more familiar features of jewelry, etc., now decorate museums and attest to the enduring quality and beauty of Egyptian art and the crafts that so significantly influences the modern mind. And, to think, despite the pernicious and misguided beliefs and interpretations, Black African men and women did all this even though they and their descendants do not get the full credit for their accomplishments. An interesting aside here is the manner in which this art form influenced western art and ultimately the history of art.

# BLACK HISTORY EXTRAVAGANZA HONORING DR. BEN-JOCHANNAN

**Black History Extravaganza - Photo -** Horus as Ra-Horakhty (left); Shu (center); and Bastet (right), on a wall at Kom Ombo Temple.

Modern writers have supplied the most accurately descriptive explanation of the role Egyptian art has played in influencing Greece and western civilization in their art, architecture, sculpture, painting and other forms of artistic cultural expressions and attainments. Indus Khamit Kush in *The Missing Pages of "His-Story"* (1993: 34) indicated: "The celebrated Frenchman Jean-Francois Champollion makes it plain and clear: 'Ancient Egypt taught the arts to Greece, this last gave to them the most sublime development, but without Egypt, Greece would probably never become the classic land of the fine arts.

# FREDERICK MONDERSON

I trace these lines almost in the face of bas reliefs which the Egyptians executed, with most exquisite fineness of workmanship, seven hundred years before the Christian era:' and what had the Greeks done?'"

**Black History Extravaganza - Photo -** Here's a young man with a "Message."

Kush notes further that John R. Harris (Ed) in The *Legacy of Egypt* (1971: 79) also wrote: "In fact, it is difficult to imagine where it would

# BLACK HISTORY EXTRAVAGANZA HONORING DR. BEN-JOCHANNAN

have been more natural for the Greeks to turn for artistic guidance and inspiration, as well as technical instruction, than to Egypt...where their philosophers and statesmen had traveled and become acquainted with an age-old culture which had struck them with awe and admiration, and where they had encountered a fully developed artistic tradition which was not only the oldest in the world, but unsurpassed in artistic perfection and technical skill." Kush (1993: 39) further continued: "R.W. Haskins gives a clear illustration of the Egyptian influence on Greek art when he cites a letter written by that world renown genius, Jean-Francois Champollion: 'I repeat, once more, Egyptian art owed, only to itself all that it has produced of the great, the pure, and the beautiful and without intending disrespect to those savants who make it part of the religion firmly to believe in the spontaneous generation of the art in Greece, it is evident to me, as it must be to all of the Egyptian monuments existing in Europe that the arts commenced in Greece by a servile imitation of the arts of Egypt, (which were much more advanced than is vulgarly supposed,) at that epoch when the first Egyptian colonies were in contact with the savage inhabitants of Attica, or of the Peloponnesus.'" (*The Arts, Sciences and Civilizations Anterior to Greece and Rome*. A. W. Wilgus, Buffalo, 1844, p. 20).

Commenting much further on this Egyptian influence in the Mediterranean and on Greece in particular, Kush (1993: 41) wrote: "That George R. Gliddon, author of *Ancient Egypt*, depicts the Egyptians with great admiration: "The 'Veil of Isis'...was lifted by Champollion le Jejune: and the glories of Pharaonic epochs - the deeds of the noblest, the most learned, pious ... and civilized race of ancient days - whose monarchy has exceeded by 1000 years the duration of any of our modern nations - whose works surpass in magnitude, in boldness of conception, accuracy of execution, and splendor of achievement that mightiest labors of any other people ... have, through Champollion's labors ... become familiar to all ...." (*The New World*, Nos. 68-69, Park Benjamin, Ed., J. Winchester, Publish, New York, April, 1843, p. 2).

# FREDERICK MONDERSON

**Black History Extravaganza - Photo -** Couples and their young in picturesque splendor.

# ART AS PROPAGANDA

Stepping out of the mist of prehistory, the most significant artistic achievement the Egyptian achieved was the register. The register introduced artistic order from disorder in its representation. All of a sudden, using the register, different themes could be included separately in the same picture. This was therefore, one of the most revolutionary developments in the history of art. Aside from pottery and personal effects accompanying the dead as "goods of the grave," some of the earliest and most celebrated forms of Egyptian art are on slate palettes. The most famous of these is the **Narmer Palette** and to this we may add the **Gebel Arak** knife handle. On the **Narmer Palette**, evident is abler draughtsmanship and more power of invention," and in this we recognize that "artistic advance is more pronounced in the incised designs on ivory which belong to this early or Thinite Period of art." More important politically, the king is

# BLACK HISTORY EXTRAVAGANZA HONORING DR. BEN-JOCHANNAN

shown wearing the White Crown of Upper Egypt and the Red Crown of Lower Egypt on the obverse and reverse side of the document. Scholars reason that this pharaoh is responsible for uniting the two lands and choosing to fuse the red and white Double Crown as symbol of unity. The significance of this artifact is the propaganda role it played in establishing conventions in art and political and social customs that would dominate Dynastic Egypt for three millennia.

Modern writers have supplied the most accurately descriptive explanation of the role Egyptian art has played in influencing Greece and western civilization in their art, architecture, sculpture, painting and other forms of artistic cultural expressions and attainments. Indus Khamit Kush in *The Missing Pages of "His-Story"* (1993: 34) indicated: "The celebrated Frenchman Jean-Francois Champollion makes it plain and clear: 'Ancient Egypt taught the arts to Greece, this last gave to them the most sublime development, but without Egypt, Greece would probably never become the classic land of the fine arts. I trace these lines almost in the face of bas reliefs which the Egyptians executed, with most exquisite fineness of workmanship, seven hundred years before the Christian era:' and what had the Greeks done?'"

Modern writers have supplied the most accurately descriptive explanation of the role Egyptian art has played in influencing Greece and western civilization in their art, architecture, sculpture, painting and other forms of artistic cultural expressions and attainments. Indus Khamit Kush in *The Missing Pages of "His-Story"* (1993: 34) indicated: "The celebrated Frenchman Jean-Francois Champollion makes it plain and clear: 'Ancient Egypt taught the arts to Greece, this last gave to them the most sublime development, but without Egypt, Greece would probably never become the classic land of the fine arts. I trace these lines almost in the face of bas reliefs which the Egyptians executed, with most exquisite fineness of workmanship, seven hundred years before the Christian era:' and what had the Greeks done?'"

# FREDERICK MONDERSON

**Black History Extravaganza - Line Drawing** - Tell Er Retabeh - (Rameses II) - Various Sculptures.

The **Narmer Palette** shows the king as monumental in scale to his subjects. It introduced the horizontal register as an art form. This innovation became the dividing line between pre-dynastic and dynastic art. Other early portrayals of the pharaoh, whether in agricultural ceremonials, ritual worship, smiting Egypt's enemies or dancing before the Gods, were symbolic as well as equally serving propaganda purposes.

In "Early Dynastic Art and Archaeology" in *Antiquarian Quarterly*, I (1925-26: 7), we read, as the author decries Pre-dynastic as, "On the mechanical side there is evidence of much skill: artistically there is little to boast of." We read further, "Directly we come to the Dynastic Period the change is marked. Alike in the industrial and higher arts advance is seen to be rapid and whether we regard the excellent artistry of the wood and ivory furniture, the delicate craftsmanship of the gold jewelry, the naturalistic carving of animals in amethyst,

# BLACK HISTORY EXTRAVAGANZA HONORING DR. BEN-JOCHANNAN

crystal, steatite, and other stones, the larger sculptures in limestone, schist or granite, the painted tombs and temple pylons - all alike justify to a civilization which is masterful, impressive and essentially artistic."

Thus, innovations of these beginnings set the stage for the later order, stability and unchanging reality of Egyptian Art. Together with the canon, or set of rules, for representing the human figure, art changed yet remained traditional and timeless. Classical art, certainly dating to the Old Kingdom, remained the ideal well past the New Kingdom and into the Late Period. The influence of the Greeks after Alexander's conquest in 332 B.C. brought new innovations that still looked to the past for inspiration. In this respect, Boardman (2006) notes: "When foreigners, first the Persians, then Alexander the Great's Macedonians and Greeks, did take up residence, the effect on the arts was slight but perceptible, with a few engaging attempts to reconcile the Classical with the Egyptian in later years and when Egypt fell more and more within the ambit of Roman ambitions. Classicism was long confined to the Mediterranean seaboard - notably the new city of Alexandria. A Cleopatra could be shown either as a Classical princess or in the traditional Egyptian style, depending on whether the context was Greek or native Egyptian, and in Egyptian areas the buildings commissioned by Romans were in Egyptian style. There were many hybrid products, not least the magic gems that combined Egyptian with Classical Roman. Yet the essence of Egyptian style survived for as long as did the religion (rather than the rulers) which it served. Only when the temples were closed by imperial degree did the Egyptian style also expire and give place to a doll-like version of the traditional Classical, for a Christian, Coptic population."

# FREDERICK MONDERSON

**Black History Extravaganza - Photo -** Offering a platter and two jars to Horus in Double Crown with Hathor at his rear.

# HOW EGYPTIANS REPRESENTED THE HUMAN BODY AT DIFFERENT TMES

The Egyptians used a **Canon of Proportion** to represent the human body. This changed slightly from period to period. In the Old Kingdom or Pyramid Age, 2680-2240 B.C., they used 13 divisions for the height of a man. These included, according to Flinders Petrie, "2 for the head, 1 to the armpit, 4 to the fork, 2 to the knee, 4 to the ground." For the position of the figure during much of the Dynastic

# BLACK HISTORY EXTRAVAGANZA HONORING DR. BEN-JOCHANNAN

Period (3000-30 B.C.), they insisted as a rule that "a vertical line must pass the edge of the wig, or center of the head, the middle of the waist, equidistant between the knees and between the heels."

**Black History Extravaganza - Papyrus -** Ra Horakhty and Hathor sit enthroned between two blank cartouches.

The New Kingdom began at the expulsion of the Hyksos, Asiatic nomads, who overran Egypt and ruled for a century. The wealth, glamour and opulence of the New Empire, mainly as a result of conquered plunder and tribute, built its art upon the earlier developments of the Old and Middle Kingdoms forms of style. Even more significant, however, other innovations were made such as involving the representation of birds, animals, fishes, plants, and even the human figure in motion. It's been said, the earliest form of the moving figure dates to the Old Kingdom showing a gazelle being chased. We know Mertisen the artist, who flourished during the Middle Kingdom time of Mentuhotep II, boasted he could portray people in motion. Aldred (1980: 18) quoting Dr. Fisher, lecturer at

# FREDERICK MONDERSON

the New York Metropolitan Museum of Art, remarked on placement of features of the body: "Egyptian statues normally put the left foot or arm forward when a limb has to be advanced. 'They nurse or hold children with the left arm, or carry burdens on the left side. Similarly, lions and sphinxes normally show the tail on the right side, corresponding to the rightward orientation of the hieroglyphic image of a lion.' Of course, there are exceptions to this rule, such as statues worked as pairs in some balanced arrangement; but the influence of drawing in two dimensions may be seen on the left side to be represented, whereas on the right side both legs are shown, corresponding to the rightward orientation of such figures in relief or in painting."

**Black History Extravaganza - Photo -** Majesty and sorrowful, yet seriousness in the stride; and Don't forget, "**Ole Red, Black and Green**" was also there to salute its Champion, Dr. Yosef Alfredo Antonio Ben-Jochannan.

# BLACK HISTORY EXTRAVAGANZA HONORING DR. BEN-JOCHANNAN

**Black History Extravaganza - Photo -** A collection of persons who came out to be there for Dr. Ben-Jochannan on his big day, "Going Home" to be among the Great African stalwarts who have fought for the liberation of African people worldwide.

# FREDERICK MONDERSON
# THE CANON OF PROPORTION

The Canon of Proportion for the human body changed. The height of a standing figure was divided into 19 units. In *Wisdom of the Ancient Egyptians* (1938) Flinders Petrie gives his own canon of proportion for the human figure. "The head down to the top of the shoulders is 3 units, divided at the top of the forehead and base of the nose. From the shoulders, 4 units to the waist, then 6 to the knees, and thence 6 to the ground." There was some difference for seated figures in the second canon. These seated figures were "15 squares high. Thus assigning 19-15 = 4 units to the thighbone. The seat is 5 units over the ground."

**Black History Extravaganza - Photo -** People who came out to see Dr. Ben off to the Great Ancestral Pantheon of Heroes.

# BLACK HISTORY EXTRAVAGANZA HONORING DR. BEN-JOCHANNAN

As the civilization entered its decline by the later dynasties, the 26$^{th}$ that is, they adopted a third canon. Here the figure became "22 1/2 or 22 1/3 units high; of this increase 1/3 unit is in the head, 2 units in trunk and 1 unit in the lower leg."

**Black History Extravaganza - Line Drawing -** Abydos. - Temple of the Kings - Barque of Osiris at its rear.

# FREDERICK MONDERSON

While these Africans had Canons of Proportions for the human figure, these were mainly for standing or seated figures. There were many examples of figures in motion. The long row of wrestlers at Beni Hasan in the XII Dynasty and the dancers, acrobats and workers in action in the XVIII Dynasty, are good examples of depicting people in motion. These representations all show how readily the "instantaneous positions were grouped and reproduced."

**Black History Extravaganza - Photo -** What a gift, a glorious girdle for Hathor backed by another goddess n white crown.

# BLACK HISTORY EXTRAVAGANZA HONORING DR. BEN-JOCHANNAN

**Black History Extravaganza - Photo -** A Nobleman and his wife pay homage to the gods, seated.

# MEN OF ART AS DEFINED BY LIFE

The life of the artist was pleasing yet austere. They made funerary art that was timeless yet was designed to never be seen by the human eye. Many craftsmen working side-by-side specialized in various crafts, but generally speaking and on the negative side, they were exposed to intense heat and smelt terribly and their hands were calloused. Yet still they enjoyed a sense of accomplishment. In this aside, the strict division of labor aided the creation of those beautiful works of art we came to realize and appreciate that also defied time. Ostraka or broken pottery shred were used as surfaces for sketch pieces and artists sometimes "doodled" leaving illustrated caricatures in addition to their assigned tasks.

There were guilds controlled from the palace or by wealthy nobles as well as the priesthood in temples. In these guilds, "one specialist made the designs, another worked in plaster, and other specialized in stone cutting in relief sculpture, in carving statues, in finishing and polishing them, in decorating temple walls, and so on. The jeweler's art also had specialist categories: workers, who washed the gold, did enamel work, and there was even a category of bead stringer. In theory at least, no work was executed entirely by a single artist." Sadly, perhaps and however, no craftsman signed his work.

## OFFICIAL PORTRAIT OF KINGS AND BUREAUCRATS

The ruling class comprised the Gods, pharaoh, high dignitaries and the priesthood. Their formal poses were shown in painting, sunk or raised relief and statuary. They were generally shown striding or seated. In their representation, artists were bound to observe the rules of canon when portraying this upper crust of society and this formalism did not change until Akhenaton led the Amarna revolution that gave more emphasis to naturalistic representations.

In the oldest examples, the pharaoh especially was depicted in an official portrait. Generally shown with all kingly, physical and material accoutrements, any defects or shortcomings he had were concealed by his elaborate costume. "He was a god, a living Horus, and as a divinity his body had always to be represented as timelessly youthful." Again, by Amarna times, human imperfections or wrinkles were shown to represent the complete individual.

The administrative bureaucracy was the second class of artistic models. Because of their closeness with the local people the artist did not adhere strictly to the conventions that bound the first more formal portraits. These latter presented "only the most obvious facial characteristics." Whereas, the governors or mayors, were clearly shown according to Kazimierz Michalowski, *Art of Ancient Egypt* (New York: H.N. Abrams, 1968: 87) with "sagging flesh, prominent bellies, and thick legs, but in a dignified posture carrying a staff."

# BLACK HISTORY EXTRAVAGANZA HONORING DR. BEN-JOCHANNAN

Artistically, the main difference between the way the top two classes, the nobility and the administrative bureaucracy were represented was in the modeling of the body. "The conventions of timeless youth were obligatory for the first group, whereas dignitaries were shown more realistically." Even more, Michalowski (1968: 188) wrote: "The third group of the society comprised a vast array of workers, whether skilled or not, even those involved in farming." In the Mastaba tombs of the IV and V Dynasties innovations representing social themes allowed the artist to introduce, according to Michalowski (1968: 188) any number of "reliefs of laborers, harvesters, herdsmen, and artisans at work in warehouses, fields, pastures, and workshops. Also shown were fishermen and boat builders, musicians and dancers."

In representing this group, the scribe was free to deviate from the established canon and represent subjects more as they were. As a result of this freedom of artistic expression, Michalowski (1968: 189) believes "realistic scenes of common people possess great expressive power."

**Black History Extravaganza - Photo -** Our Nobleman stands before a closed window-shutter.

# FREDERICK MONDERSON

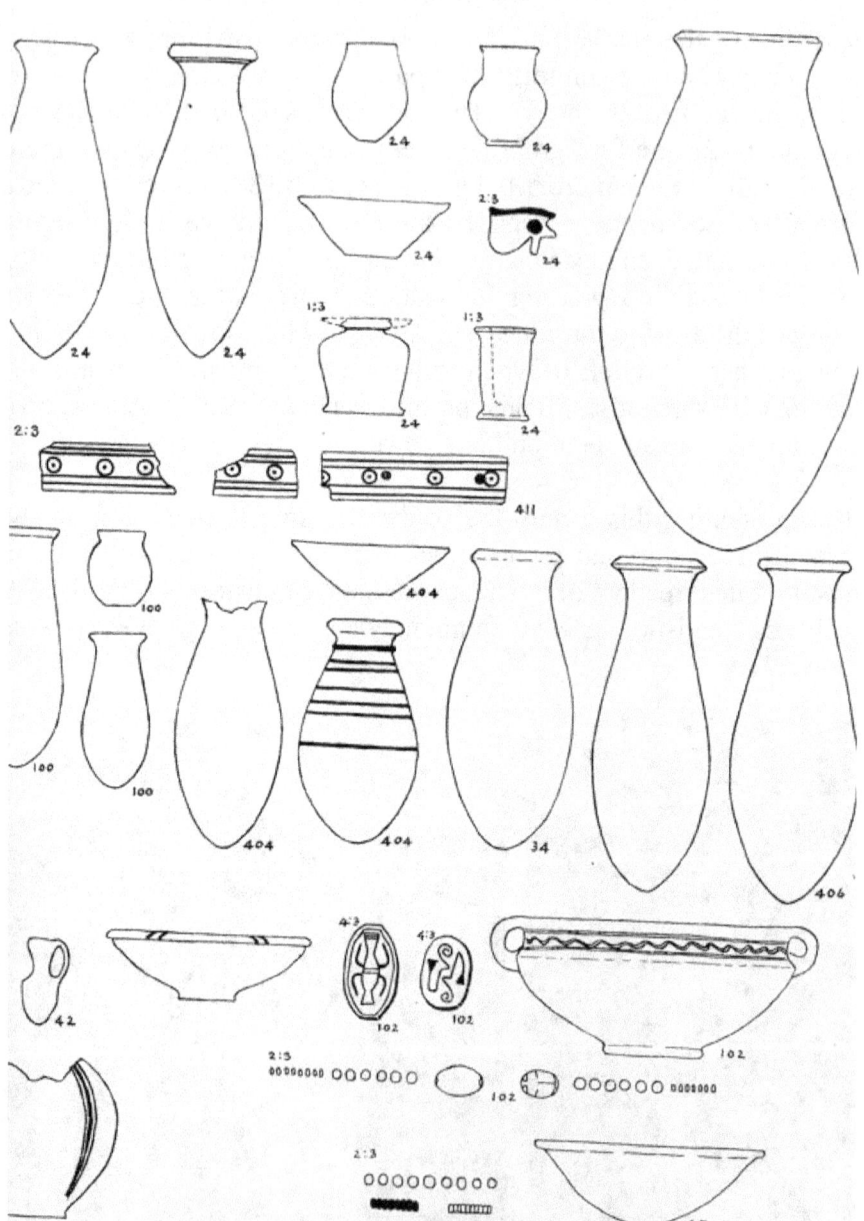

**Black History Extravaganza - Line Drawing -**
Yehudiyeh Pottery - Thutmose III Age.

The admonition,

# BLACK HISTORY EXTRAVAGANZA HONORING DR. BEN-JOCHANNAN

## "BE A SCRIBE" - "BE A SCRIBE" - THE IDEAL PROFESSION

Scribes were generally shown either in the standing or seated position. The wooden relief figure of the famous third dynasty royal scribe Hesire is now in the Cairo Museum. It stands 44-7/8 inches and was found at Saqqara. He is shown holding his working tools and the **SEKHEM** rod, emblem of executive officials. The diagram of canon for this Old Kingdom masterpiece in realistic art held "18 rows of squares," as follows: "From top of forehead to base of neck, 2 rows; from neck to knees, 10 rows: from knees to soles of feet, 6 rows. An additional row for the hair above the forehead was not included in the total of 18 rows."

The other posture of scribe was the seated position. The finest known statue of a scribe comes from the V Dynasty and is housed in the Louvre, Paris. He is called the "seated scribe." Here the subject is shown: "Wearing a loin cloth, he is seated with legs crossed, an open roll of papyrus on his knees, and a reed pen in his right hand. It is made of painted limestone and stands 20 7/8 inches." At a much later time the scribe was represented in a more obscure way simply as a block statue, with face and writings on the block.

## HOW REALISM DEFINED EGYPTIAN ART

The question is always asked whether there was realism in Egyptian art. If the term realism is defined in broad concepts denoting as Michalowski (1968: 190) explained, "the effort to represent a given phenomenon in its most typical form, and the fact recorded by the artist has thus a general significance that every viewer can grasp. In this sense, Egyptian art was certainly realistic."

# FREDERICK MONDERSON

**Black History Extravaganza - Photo -** These massive and decorated columns with their different capitals are to be found at Kom Ombo Temple of the Elder Horus and Sobek the Crocodile God.

In essence, and broadening the scope of treatment and representation, Egyptian painting and sculpture of the Old Kingdom can be summed as follows, according to Michalowski in his *Art of Ancient Egypt* (1968: 190-191):

1) The canon was a unique historical phenomenon and has a peculiar indigenous character.

2) It was the result of a lengthy process of observation and experimentation, which culminated in, an art based on the most typical

# BLACK HISTORY EXTRAVAGANZA HONORING DR. BEN-JOCHANNAN

forms of nature; as such, the canon was formulated in terms of certain constant proportions.

3) The aim of the canon was to record phenomenon in the most legible and understandable manner, to reflect reality in both its visual and its social aspects.

4) The canon performed an important function in the ideological superstructure, serving the ruling class by perpetuating the conviction that the existing social function was by glorifying the gods and the Pharaohs.

5) The canon was essential to the maintenance of artistic quality and standards of workmanship.

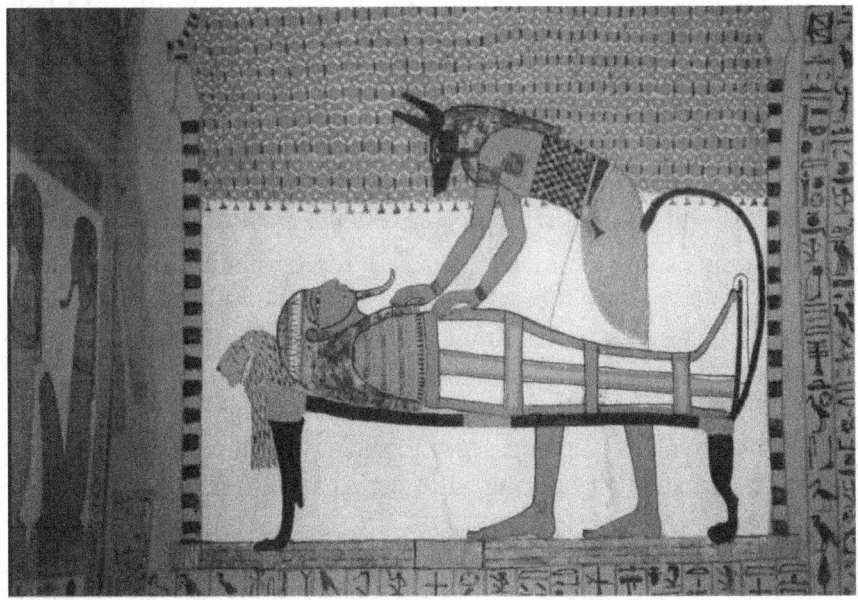

**Black History Extravaganza - Photo -** Anubis, god of the dead, administers to the mummy.

## The Art of Ancient Egypt II

# FREDERICK MONDERSON

On more firm terrain, in Egypt, like elsewhere in Africa, very early man-made tools and began to philosophize, paint and plan for the next day's hunt. Drawing animals, he hoped to hunt the next day, set him on the path to later develop beautiful and realistic human and animal portraiture as well as other forms of art as painting, sculpture, jewel making, and building boats and architectural structures, all dating to the earliest times. However, there is no question, in this early state and for its duration, art served as a social utility and not as "art for art's sake." Still, in this respect and dating these early beginnings, W. Stephenson Smith in *The Art and Architecture of Ancient Egypt* (1989: 25-26) explains: "Art appears in the Nile Valley as early as the seventh millennium B.C. The earliest productions are the rock-drawings executed on the cliffs bordering the Nile in Upper Egypt and Nubia. The most ancient of these consist principally of geometric designs such as concentric circles or half-circles and net-patterns, or abstract figurations the exact meaning of which is obscure. Representational themes appear later. There are many hundreds of drawings of the animals pursued by the earliest hunters and of weapons and traps.... Drawings of cattle and boats can be definitely associated with the developed Neolithic cultures of Upper Egypt and Nubia, and with the Egyptian Predynastic, Nubian C-Group, and later historic cultures."

Hans A. Winkler in *Rock Drawings of Southern Upper Egypt I* (1938: 18) mentions some of the early artistic representation in this part of the Nile Valley. Thus, the art of Egypt and the Nile Valley represented by gods, men and women, animals, and ancient cultural creations is very old! "The following animals are represented: gazelle, stag, ibex, antelope, cattle, hare, lion, crocodile, fish; dog, horse. There are men with bow and arrow, with lasso, with staff, with flower, man smelling lotus-flower, man in adoring attitude, Pharaoh on throne, Pharaoh with mace; women; sailing-vessels; Min, Mentu, Taurt, Anubis, Horus the falcon, uraeus." Clearly many of these animals and gods would be incorporated into the hieroglyphic corpus somewhat analogous to William Arnett's view expressed in *The Predynastic Origin of Egyptian Hieroglyphs: Evidence for the Development of Rudimentary Forms of Hieroglyphs in Upper Egypt in the Fourth Millennium B.C.* as published by the University Press of America, 1982. However, a clarification needs to be made for Winkler assigns

# BLACK HISTORY EXTRAVAGANZA HONORING DR. BEN-JOCHANNAN

these earliest examples of art to Mesopotamians. On the other hand, Toby Wilkinson in *Genesis of the Pharaohs* (2003) gives a date, "1000 years before Winkler's Mesopotamians."

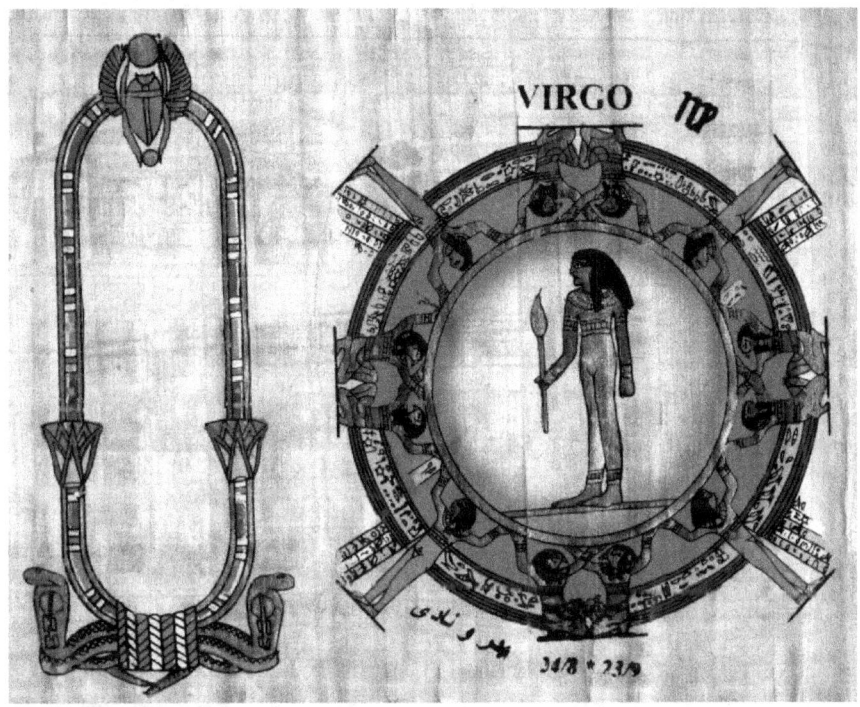

**Black History Extravaganza - Papyrus -** A Blank Cartouche binding the Khepre beetle (top) with double uraei (bottom) and Astrological sign of Virgo to the right.

In the beginning, much of the Art of Egypt in the Predynastic period can best be viewed extracted from the contents of graves of the Badarian, Amratian and Gerzean or Naqada I and II culture sequence. In "Burial Customs and Beliefs in the Afterlife" in (*Journal of Egyptian Archaeology*, December 1956: 86) Margaret Murray gives four (1) Badarian; (2) Amratian; (3) Gerzean; (4) Semanian periods of cultural evolution; though declaring the last only a small culture area. On the other hand, regarding burial customs, Guy Brunton's "The Badarian Predynastic Period," in Richard Engelbach's *Introduction to Egyptian Archaeology with special reference to the Egyptian*

# FREDERICK MONDERSON

*Museum, Cairo*, and (2nd Edition. Cairo: Government printing Office, 1961: 19) mentions pottery as their important feature comprising deep or shallow bowls, often flat-bottomed and covered with fine ripples. Even more, T. Eric Peet in "The Art of the Predynastic Period" in *Journal of Egyptian Archaeology*, Vol. 2 No. 2, (April, 1915: 84) emphasizes "use of line and its decorative value." Still, Brunton explained: "The Badarian people made linen in small pieces, but their usual clothing was finely tanned leather, sometimes stitched into garments. Their ornaments were ivory bracelets, strings of shells obtained from the shores of the Red Sea, and beads made from colored pebbles. It is probable that their blue-glazed stone beads were not made by the Badarians, but were acquired by trade, since a metal tool had apparently pierced them, and copper colored the glaze. Metal was very scarce in the Badarian Period, and copper beads were worn as precious jewelry. Nose and ear-studs were also found, together with slates, of characteristic form, on which the green eye-paint was ground."

**Black History Extravaganza - Photo -** How exhilarating it must feel, to be out there paddling one's boat in the Afterlife.

# BLACK HISTORY EXTRAVAGANZA
# HONORING DR. BEN-JOCHANNAN

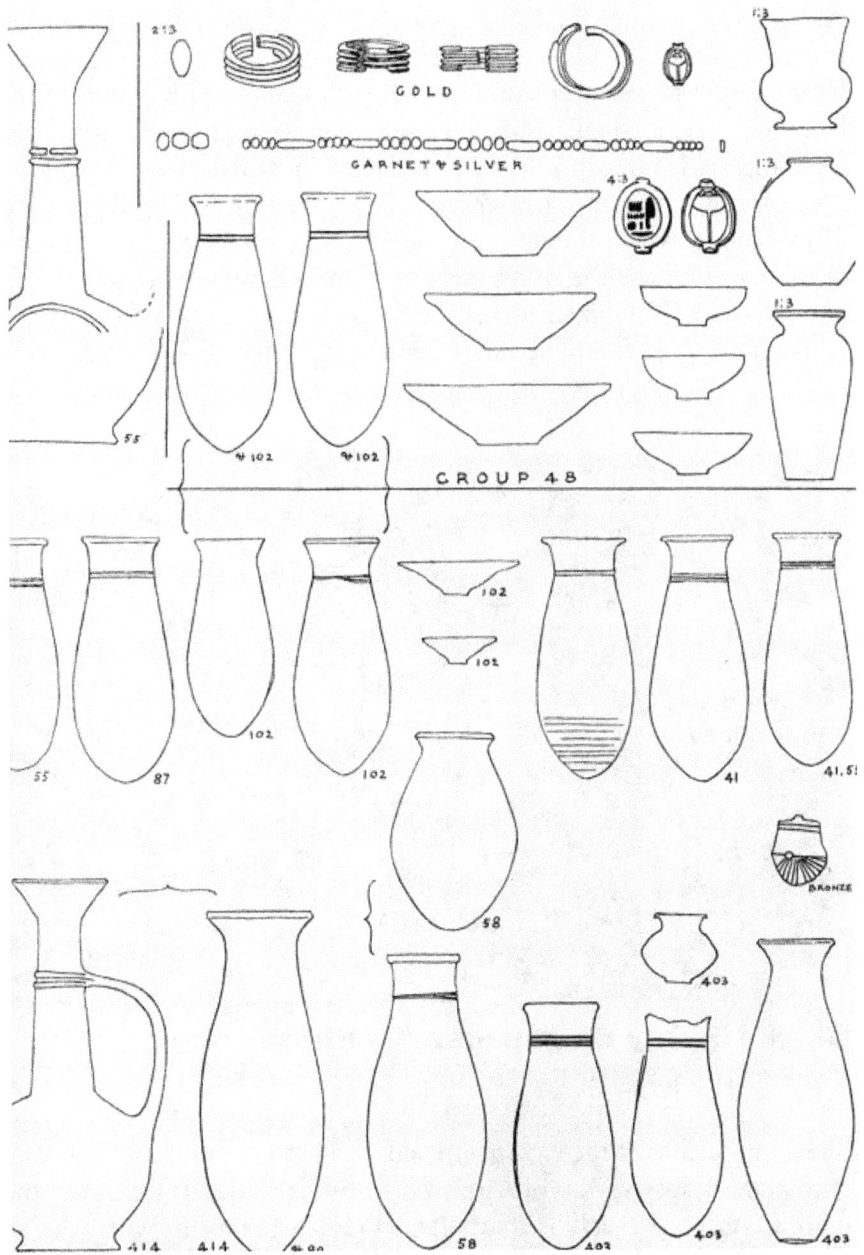

**Black History Extravaganza - Line Drawing -**
Yehudiyeh Pottery, etc. - Amenhotep II's Age.

# FREDERICK MONDERSON

J. Yoyote's "Egyptian Art" in *Praeger Encyclopedia of Art*, Vol. 2 New York: Praeger Publishers (1971:596) reinforces this view: "From the 4$^{th}$ millennium and throughout the Tasian (still Neolithic), Badarian, and Nagadian (Copper Age) periods, the population of Upper Egypt increased its output and improved its skill in all the arts. Huts of wood, reed, and mud were erected for divinities, as monumental in conception and as complex in structure as some of the royal or ritual buildings of Africa or Oceania. Flint tools were used to fashion bone, ivory, and horn into combs, pins, statuettes, and amulets decorated with outline of animals or human figures reduced to their barest essentials. Glazed soapstone beads from this prehistoric period give a hint of the future achievements of Egyptian faience-makers."

**Black History Extravaganza - Photo** - Black and White - Two lions on-guard as Ra the Sun-God traverses the two lands.

Speaking further of the expansion and development of these technical crafts and industry, Yoyote goes on to further explain: "Among the more luxurious vessels is the polished red earthenware with whitish patterns that is typical of the Amratian subdivision of the Nagadian period; the later Gerzean culture is characterized by purplish decorations on mushroom-colored pottery. These surfaces present a

# BLACK HISTORY EXTRAVAGANZA HONORING DR. BEN-JOCHANNAN

miniature painted world, sometimes abstract in design (spirals and waves) and sometimes figurative (boats, dancers of both sexes, and birds). There are even complete scenes, such as a hunting party setting out (shown on the bottom of a bowl), a hippopotamus hunt, a sailing event, and a troupe of dancers. The latter scene, painted on a linen shroud, is the oldest "canvas in the history of the world." However, as he further emphasized, it was not in the workings of such industries as ceramics "but in the making of beads, carving of palettes, and especially in the shaping of vases that one sees a promise of the Egyptian sculptors' future mastery over the hardest rocks. The times had almost come when the Predynastic Age would produce craftsmen who, with prodigious patience, were to hammer out of marble, diorite, and breccia a plentiful supply of thin-walled, capacious vessels of simple dignified form. These were polished with abrasives and their interiors hollowed out by means of a drill (which became one of the symbols to express the words 'art,' 'artist,' and 'artisan' in the hieroglyphic script." Thus, in "The Art of the Predynastic Period" T. Eric Peet in *Journal of Egyptian Archaeology* (1915: 91) would give three motives for decorative objects among these early people. These are: "for purely artistic motives; a useful purpose; and magical or religious reasons."

**Black History Extravaganza - Photo -** More of the Throngs who came to pay their respects to Dr. Ben-Jochannan.

# FREDERICK MONDERSON

**Black History Extravaganza - Photo -** Out "walking the lion" at Kom Ombo Temple of Elder Horus and Sobek the Crocodile.

**Black History Extravaganza - Photo -** Lion in painted, colorful form.

# BLACK HISTORY EXTRAVAGANZA HONORING DR. BEN-JOCHANNAN

Given that mortuary material provided the main evidence of this early culture we begin to see the dawning of the metal age with copper being found in the graves. In these funerary internments were found items the deceased deemed to be useful in the next life the culture was beginning to believe in. In addition to food, the contents of which were contained in pottery vessels, personal items including weapons and tools, knife handles, combs, and jewelry represents the earliest forms of the art. Nevertheless, other evidence exists for as Smith (1989: 26) continued: "The sculptured objects which were deposited in the ancient shrine of the southern capital at Hierakonpolis commemorate the victories of the south over the north in the struggle which finally resulted in the subjugation of the Delta which had been ruled from Buto. If we remember that there is no interviewing stage between this transitional period and Gerzean, we can continue to call it Late Predynastic or Protodynastic, which is a somewhat better term than Dynasty O, which has also been applied to it." Again, Yoyote adds, in this formative period: "Burial pits were lined with bricks, and then paved and covered with planks of wood. Fortresses and palaces were surrounded by high ramparts with redans. Ivories were decorated with grand processions of animals or other lively subjects. Large palettes of schist were covered with delicate and skillfully composed reliefs, sometimes accompanied by a commentary in hieroglyphs. On monuments of the scorpion King (one of the last Predynastic rulers) and Narmer (the first king of the $1^{st}$ Dynasty) the true characteristics of the Pharaonic style - its conventions, its figures arranged in straight lines at different levels, its iconographic themes - can be detected under appearances that is still somewhat crude."

# FREDERICK MONDERSON

**Black History Extravaganza - Temple Site Ticket -** Esna Temple, now at 30-Egyptian Pounds.

**Black History Extravaganza - Temple Site Ticket -** Tomb of Al-Mo'alla, Esna, at 20 Egyptian Pounds.

# BLACK HISTORY EXTRAVAGANZA HONORING DR. BEN-JOCHANNAN

The statues of Min painted black, found at Koptos and now in the Ashmolean Museum, Oxford, are from this period. Gold, silver, copper, tin and other precious stones were also early forms of adornment. Equally, we see the emergence of various craftsmen who in turn were supervised by masters of the crafts. However, while these specialists may certainly have existed in the Predynastic times, by the start of the dynasties their work began to take on remarkable form. In this regard, Peet (1915: 89) continued: "The discovery of the statue of Khasekhem at Hierakonpolis showed us what the royal sculptor could accomplish in the IInd Dynasty, and the stela of the Serpent King took us back to the Ist, while a series of Predynastic discoveries still continues to furnish us with works of art of an even earlier date." Nonetheless, by the time of the Old, Middle and New Kingdoms when records were being kept more accurately, there is ample evidence of their existence.

Unquestionably, religion and its adherents, the priesthood, played a key role in the development of Egyptian art. As such, there was a profound mysticism, magic, symbolism and esoteric nature attached to art that shaped the perception of and method of Egyptian Art. Magic was especially important as expressed by Cyril Aldred (1980: 11-12) who discusses the character of Egyptian Art. He states: "Egypt, like all the other nations of antiquity, was profoundly influenced by magic, by a belief in the existence of all-pervading, invisible and superhuman forces that had to be propitiated if their aid was to be secured, or neutralized if their enmity was to be avoided. Only continuous worship of these mysterious powers could keep the universe in equilibrium favorable to the survival of man and his institutions. It was the constant affirmation of the pharaoh, the divine king who presided over the destiny of Egypt and its people that he had restored the harmony (*Ma'at*) of an ideal world as it had been established at the First Time, but which could easily be jangled out of tune by human neglect or wrongdoing."

# FREDERICK MONDERSON

**Black History Extravaganza - Ceramic Art -** The great bird in colorful splendor.

Again, Aldred (1980: 11-12) goes on to make the connection depicting the priests of Ptah, representing the creative process and the emergence of art as a discipline and ultimately an industry of great significance. Accordingly: "This creativeness was not divorced from the creative process by which the Egyptian universe had come into being and was daily maintained. In historic times, the great productive power was the god Ptah of Memphis, the 'Creator' who in his more active and seminal form was depicted as a ram-headed craftsman, fashioning mankind upon his potter's wheel. In a song current in the New Kingdom, he is described as 'making this with his two hands as balm to his heart.' According to the peculiar belief of the ancient Egyptian, Ptah was also the primordial mound of earth that rose from the waters of elemental Chaos and on which all life began, just after the annual inundation of the Nile, a narrow spit of land first emerged from the flood, soon to be covered with vegetation and busy

# BLACK HISTORY EXTRAVAGANZA HONORING DR. BEN-JOCHANNAN

with animal life. Besides the flora and fauna of nature, Ptah, the New Risen Earth, contained within himself all the products from which many under his inspiration could also create things: clay, stone, metals and minerals. It is not surprising, therefore that the High Priest of Ptah should bear the title of Greatest of Craftsmen, and was originally responsible for the design and execution of all Egyptian works of art. Even in later times, when other gods shared the creative power of the demiurge, craftsmen in far-off Thebes, the city of Amun, the god of light and air, still worshipped Ptah in their local shrine and acted as his priests in their leisure hours."

**Black History Extravaganza - Photo -** They were all Eyewitnesses to an extraordinary event, the Passing of a Great Soul who stressed African redemption and upliftment in the greatest of the Pan-African tradition, **Dr. Yosef Ben-Jochannan**, nationalist extraordinaire, and whose legacy will never be forgotten.

# FREDERICK MONDERSON

**Black History Extravaganza - Line Drawing -**
Yehudiyeh - Column of Merenptah. Dyad of Rameses II.

# BLACK HISTORY EXTRAVAGANZA HONORING DR. BEN-JOCHANNAN

Concerning ownership of these wonderful creations, as previously stated, the artist never signed his name to his work, for this was considered blasphemy because of the association of art with religion and the hereafter. In *Art in Egypt*, Gaston Maspero (1912: 299) asked the question why the artist did not sign his work. "We should like, indeed, to know what they were called, what was their native city or their condition in life, who had been their first teachers, and by what efforts those geniuses who made the plans of Der-el-Bahari or the Hypostyle Hall, raised the Pyramid of Chephren, and carved the Seated Scribe in the Louvre, and Thothmes III and the Amenardis at Cairo, the Seti I and the goddesses of Abydos, outstripped the crown of their competitors. The choice that fell on them to undertake these great tasks prove sufficiently that they did not pass unnoticed among their immediate circle, and that they enjoyed in their day the reputation of being the most skillful and most gifted in their craft. Fame was not lacking in them, at least in their lifetime, and among those who surrounded them, but when their generation had passed away, the admiration of the new races was poured out on the Pharaohs or the rich men who had employed them; the memory of the bold craftsmen who dared to design and execute the Speos of Abu Simbel was not handed down with his work as was that of Ictinus with the Parthenon. It was thus that, ignorant of the ambition of immortality by fame, the action of which is so powerful among the moderns, the Egyptian masters were for the most part content to observe conscientiously, as they would have done in any ordinary calling, the rules which the teachings of their predecessors had assured them were necessary to the well-being of souls, human and divine. When by chance any were born whose inventive minds rebelled against the half technical, half religious education of the workshop, their efforts towards progress or reform had no serious results."

# FREDERICK MONDERSON

**Black History Extravaganza - Photo -** Go among the banquet goes, pour their drinks and offer them flowers to smell, as the young sit under chairs.

Even further, Maspero (1912: 300) continued: "By refusing details, Egypt gave her art that character of uniformity which strikes us. The personal temperament of the individual is revealed only by almost imperceptible shades of handling, and the majority of visitors carries away with them from museums and ruins the sense of a collective impersonality, slightly varied here and there according to time and place by the greater or lesser degree of skill in the executant. They do not understand what an amount of natural talent and acquired science the unknown authors of great temples and fine sculpture expended, to make themselves more than mere skillful craftsmen."

# BLACK HISTORY EXTRAVAGANZA HONORING DR. BEN-JOCHANNAN

**Black History Extravaganza - Photo -** How majestic this view of one half of the front of Kom Ombo Temple looks. Two panels of Uraei, and the varied capitals of the columns against a blue sky is without question, heavenly and architecturally divinely inspired.

Still, while they never signed their work, Alix Wilkinson in *Ancient Egyptian Jewelry*, (Methuen and Company, 1975: 1) nevertheless points to names given some of these ancient craftsmen. "Jewelers were called *neshedi* and *nubi* (the gold man) and *hemu nub* (gold-craftsman). A number of goldsmiths can be identified from tombs, statues and inscribed amulets. Those most likely to have been the actual craftsmen have the simple title Gold worker; others are called Chief of the Gold workers of the Estate of Amun." Still more exalted persons, who certainly never touched a blowpipe, but who were responsible for the organization of industry, were those whose titles included that of Overseer of the Treasury of Gold and Silver, Overseer of the Gold Land of Amun, Weigher of Amun. Their duties would have been to see that the materials needed for making the treasures for the temples and for the king were available and that the work was carried out as required. Neferronpet, who was Chief of the Makers of Thin Gold, a goldbeater, had his **Book of the Dead** decorated with gold leaf." Thus, whether the work was monumental or miniscule, intricate of elaborate, the artists continued to produce masterpieces intended for none but the dead to see.

Next, Wilkinson (1975: 3) mentions the method of the work of transferring raw materials into works of art. He states: "Among the processes most frequently illustrated are the preliminaries, weighing, giving out the metal and melting the gold in a crucible over a charcoal fire; then pouring out the molten metal, beating it into sheets and bars with a rounded stone, and polishing it. Gilding is first illustrated in the Old Kingdom tomb of Ibi at Deir el-Gebrawi. Scenes of drilling and polishing beds occur in the Old and New Kingdoms, but the making up of a collar, as distinct from simply holding it up for inspection, is illustrated only in the New Kingdom. In the Old Kingdom, an old man is shown making the thread for stringing beads. Glazing may be illustrated in the Old Kingdom tomb of Re-hem at Deir el-Gebrawi, where a collar dripping with the liquid is lifted out of a pot." In addition, Wilkinson (1975: 6-7) names the tools and materials utilized by the craftsmen to ply their crafts. He states: "Among the tools which are illustrated are reed pipes, tongs, rounded stones for hammering the metal, stone anvils resting on wooden blocks, crucibles and long rods for lifting them. Molds used for casting large objects like bronze doors appear in illustrations, but not molds for small objects. Several of the smaller molds have however survived, both for casting and for stamping. Casting was usually by the 'lost wax' process, but some small objects were cast solid. The 'lost wax' or *Cire Perdue* method of casting involved making a model of wax. An outer covering of damp clay was pressed around the model and allowed to dry. When the mold had hardened the wax was melted out and the molten metal poured in to the space it had left."

# BLACK HISTORY EXTRAVAGANZA HONORING DR. BEN-JOCHANNAN

**Black History Extravaganza - Papyrus -** A Blank Cartouche stands beside the Astrological sign for Aquarius.

Clearly there were other types of tools. "The carpenters had saws, but the jewelers did all their piercing and cutting with chisels. The beadmakers used bow-drills and these must also have been available to the goldsmiths. Pointed tools survive which may have been used either for repousse work or for burnishing, and there are measures for gold dust from Naqada dating from the XVIIIth Dynasty, and hammers in Berlin made of serpentine which date from the first century A.D."

In addition to the crafts and tools, we add: "The materials used by the ancient craftsmen were gold and silver, carnelian, lapis lazuli, feldspar, jasper, amethyst, button-pearl, turquoise, amber, agate, onyx and glass imitating colored stones."

Sommers Clarke and R. Engelbach in *Ancient Egyptian Construction and Architecture* (1990: 200) quote A. Lucas, a chemical engineer,

# FREDERICK MONDERSON

who wrote about Egyptian metals and materials. According to Lucas: "Most of the Egyptian pigments were naturally-occurring mineral substances, simply powdered.

**Black History Extravaganza - Photo -** Individuals sit under an enormous image of a falcon.

# BLACK HISTORY EXTRAVAGANZA HONORING DR. BEN-JOCHANNAN

'The white was generally carbonate lime, but sometimes sulphate of lime.

'The black was carbon, being sometimes soot and sometimes a coarse material, probably powdered charcoal.

'The grey was a mixture of black and white.

'The red was red ochre, either natural or made by calcining yellow ochre. In Roman times, however, red lead was also employed as well as pink made from madder.

'The browns were all natural ochres.

'The yellow was of two kinds, either natural or made by calcining yellow ochre and the other, which, however, was not used until about the XVIIIth dynasty, was sulphide of arsenic (orpiment), and as this latter does not occur in Egypt, the supply must have been imported.

'The principal blue was an artificial frit, consisting of a crystalline copper-lime-silicate made from malachite, limestone, and powered quartz pebbles, possibly with the aid of natron-though this latter was not necessary. This is known as early as the XIth Dynasty. Another and earlier blue was powdered azurite, a naturally occurring basic carbonate of copper, which was used before the artificial frit was discovered. Still another blue, the occasional use of which has been reported, was a cobalt compound.

**Black History Extravaganza - Photo -** The Line was long outside Abyssinia Baptist Church as people sought to get a last glimpse of Dr. Ben-Jochannan. This was a sort of necessary Pilgrimage to view one who has given so much throughout his life.

# FREDERICK MONDERSON

**Black History Extravaganza - Photo -** Colorful winged disk with uraei atop a decorated architrave.

'The green used was of two kinds; that employed at first being powdered malachite-a copper ore found in Egypt-and at a later date a green frit, analogous to the blue frit already mentioned.
'The medium with which the colors were put on was water and not oil, with size, gum, or white of egg. It has not yet been definitely established which of the three was used.
'The Egyptian painting was in reality a distemper.'"

# BLACK HISTORY EXTRAVAGANZA
# HONORING DR. BEN-JOCHANNAN

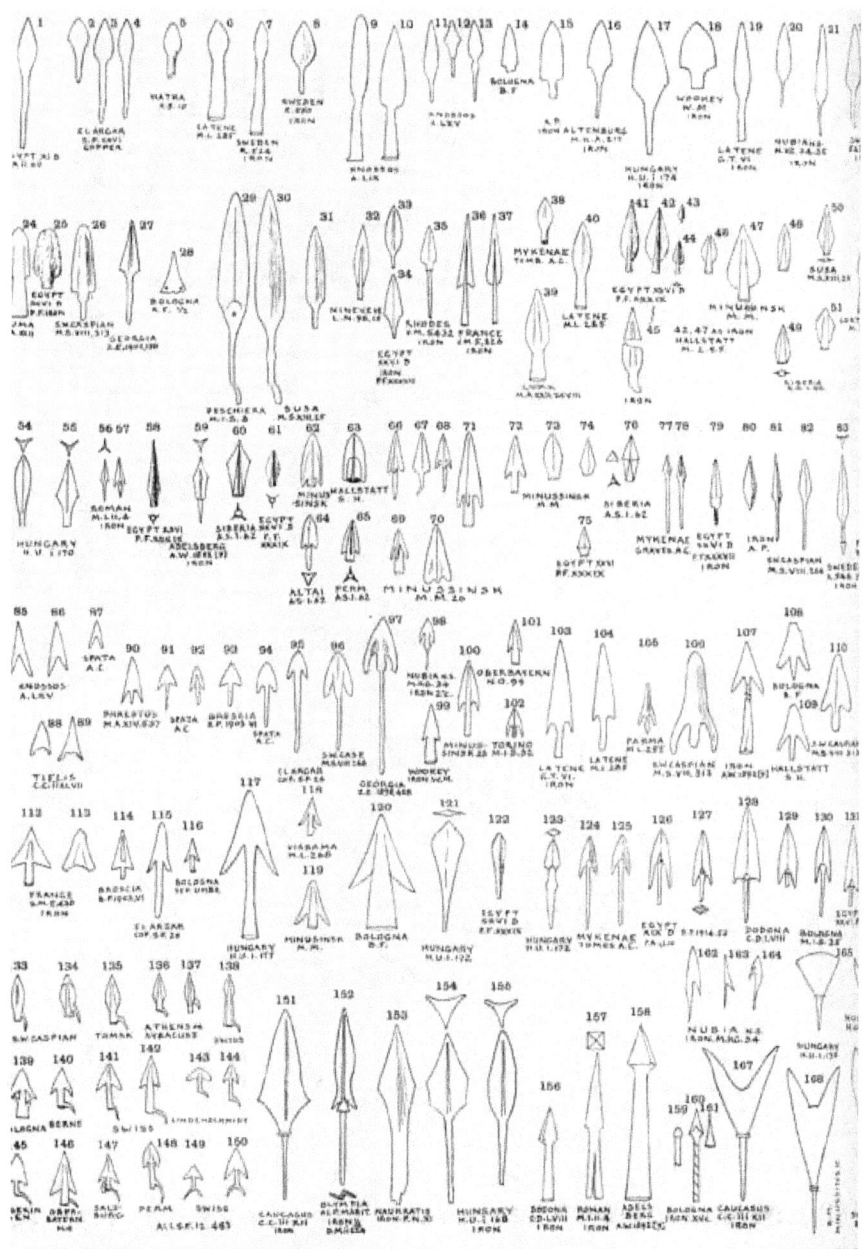

**Black History Extravaganza - Line Drawing -** Tools and Weapons - Arrow and Dart - Bronze.

# FREDERICK MONDERSON

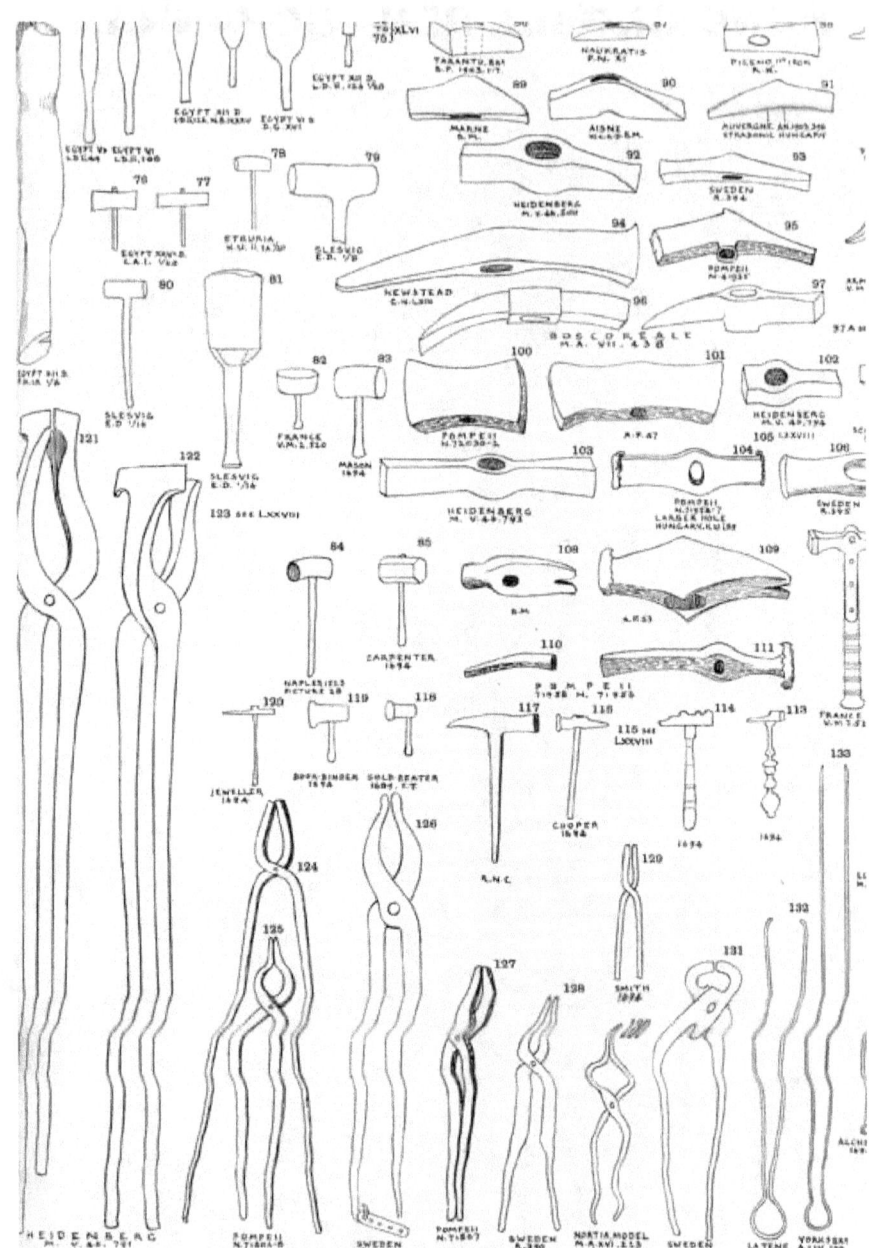

**Black History Extravaganza - Line Drawing -** Tools and Weapons **-** Mallet **-** Hammer and Tongs.

# BLACK HISTORY EXTRAVAGANZA
# HONORING DR. BEN-JOCHANNAN

**Black History Extravaganza - Photo -** Paying homage to the Gods who sit and observe.

Next to jewelry, one of the earliest forms of Egyptian art is the slate palette used for grinding cosmetics. However, they serve an even

# FREDERICK MONDERSON

more historical purpose because they are illustrated pictographic documents recounting early and important events. The **Bull Palette**, the **Libya Palette**, the **Narmer Palette** and the **Narmer Macehead**, are all early and enduring fine works of arts. In this regard, Peet in Dennison Ross (1931: 8) mentions: "The great slate palettes, probably ceremonial embellishment of the simple palettes used for grinding eye-paint, form a series which enables us to watch the development of the art of sculpture in relief. In the earliest, or at any rate the crudest, that of the huntsmen, the human figure is very roughly treated, though the artist is more at home with animals. In the great animal palette, we see early signs of that adroitness in adapting a subject to the space at his disposal which was throughout one of the Egyptian decorative artist's chief merits; and the two giraffes feeding off a palm tree on the London and Oxford palette well illustrate another of his gifts, namely a wonderful feeling for what is known as 'line.' In technical excellence, however, all these are surpassed by the great Narmer palette; here we see clever composition, a keen sense of decorative effect, and delicate rendering of detail; there is even some attempt at modelling the almost flat surfaces and at indicating the muscles. At the same time, we must not exaggerate the qualities of this work of art; it has stiffness, an awkwardness and a lack of life which make it rank far behind the best work of the Old Kingdom."

**Black History Extravaganza - Cairo Museum** - An ancient bracelet.

# BLACK HISTORY EXTRAVAGANZA HONORING DR. BEN-JOCHANNAN

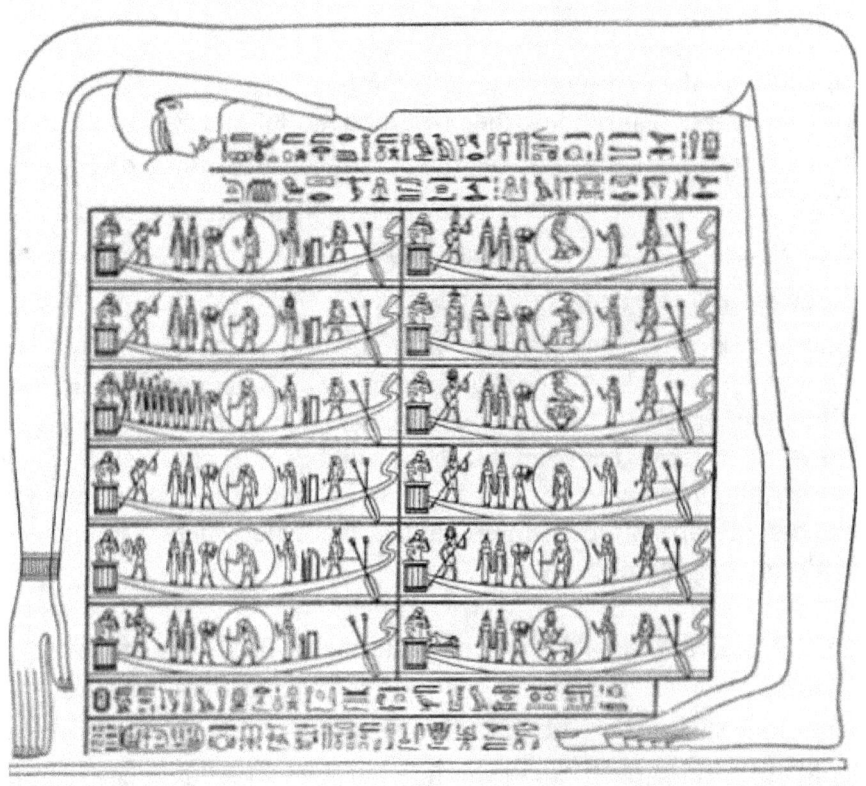

**Black History Extravaganza - Line Drawing -** The 12-hour period of the day is depicted in Nuit spanning the heavens.

The funerary evidence, principally from Abydos and Sakkara show an increase in the goods of the grave and the emerging architecture of king's tombs.

Significantly, by the Third Dynasty, when Imhotep erected the Step-Pyramid at Sakkara, on the outskirts of Memphis, new innovations were made in architecture and art. The "Colonnade," the "Enclosure Wall," "Open Court," "Heb Sed Pavilion" and "Court," "Dummy Buildings," emphasis on the lotus and papyrus emblems of the Upper and Lower Kingdoms and other facets of kingly paraphernalia became highlighted. Glazed blue wall tiles within the Step-Pyramid of Zoser, and illustrations of the Heb Sed race within the Great Court are interesting examples of early artistic accomplishments to represent the king in action.

In addition, the enormous Mastaba tombs of the nobles began to be richly decorated, providing the great motivation for artists to ply their skills. At Sakkara, the tomb of Hesi-Re to the North; tomb of Ti to the West; tombs of Idut, Nebet Khnum-Hotep, Niankh-Khnum, Nefer and Nefer Hent Ptah and Iruka-Ptah to the South; tombs of Mereruka, Kagemni, Thetu and Nefer-Sheshem-Re, Ankh-Mahor and Nefer Sheshem-Ptah to the East, are all magnificent funerary decorated canvases upon which Egyptian art reached its pinnacle in the old Kingdom. The five pyramids with texts, dubbed the *Pyramid Texts*, are those of Unas, Teti, Pepi I, Merenra and Pepi II, have helped carry the writing to its highest developments and set in stone the religious beliefs of this earliest empire along the Nile where art reached enduring heights.

In this regard, G. Baldwin Brown (1915-16: 220) lends interesting insights into Mastaba tombs that complement the pyramids. Using a line from Shakespeare of "The cloud-capped towers" he writes: "The epithet 'cloud-capped' applies properly to the mountain peak, and to transfer it to the structure of mortal hands is an immense exaltation. Still more so is the effect of the collocation: 'The solemn temples, the great globe itself,' as if the human monument were comparable with the solid mass of the earth. These lines might have been written under the shadow of the Great Pyramid or of the Sphinx, for Nature has indeed lent to these incomparable works her own majesty, while on the other side human reason has permeated them in every part, and by its complete mastery of them has stamped them with the impress of style."

That is to say, "The square mile of desert rock and sand that is the site of the so-called cemetery of Ghizeh, opposite Cairo, is for the student of the monumental the most sacred ground in the world. There is a great deal more of interest upon it than the Great Pyramid, or than the three great Pyramids which bulk so largely in the eyes of the visitor to

# BLACK HISTORY EXTRAVAGANZA HONORING DR. BEN-JOCHANNAN

Cairo. The cemetery has to be studied as a whole, and upon the relations of the various structures it enshrines not a little new light has been recently shed. Each of the three royal tombs has its own adjuncts of structural and of religious interest, and, besides the royal mausolea, grouped round and in relation to these are innumerable sepulchers of the nobles in the form of what is known as the Mastaba tomb. The arrangements of the upper world are here reproduced, and just in the capital of the Empire there would be a royal quarter with quarters of the Court retainers disposed about it, so in the cemetery the king lies in his tomb encompassed with the graves of all his company. These mastabas tombs, moreover, are arranged in regular streets, crossing each other at right angles and oriented north and south, east and west, in the same directions as the Pyramids. The whole cemetery may in this way be regarded as the oldest example of town-planning in the world, for the Orthodox Oriental rectangular scheme is entirely in evidence."

**Black History Extravaganza - Photo -** In the "Boat of the Gods," stand Thoth, Ra-Horakhty and their company.

# FREDERICK MONDERSON

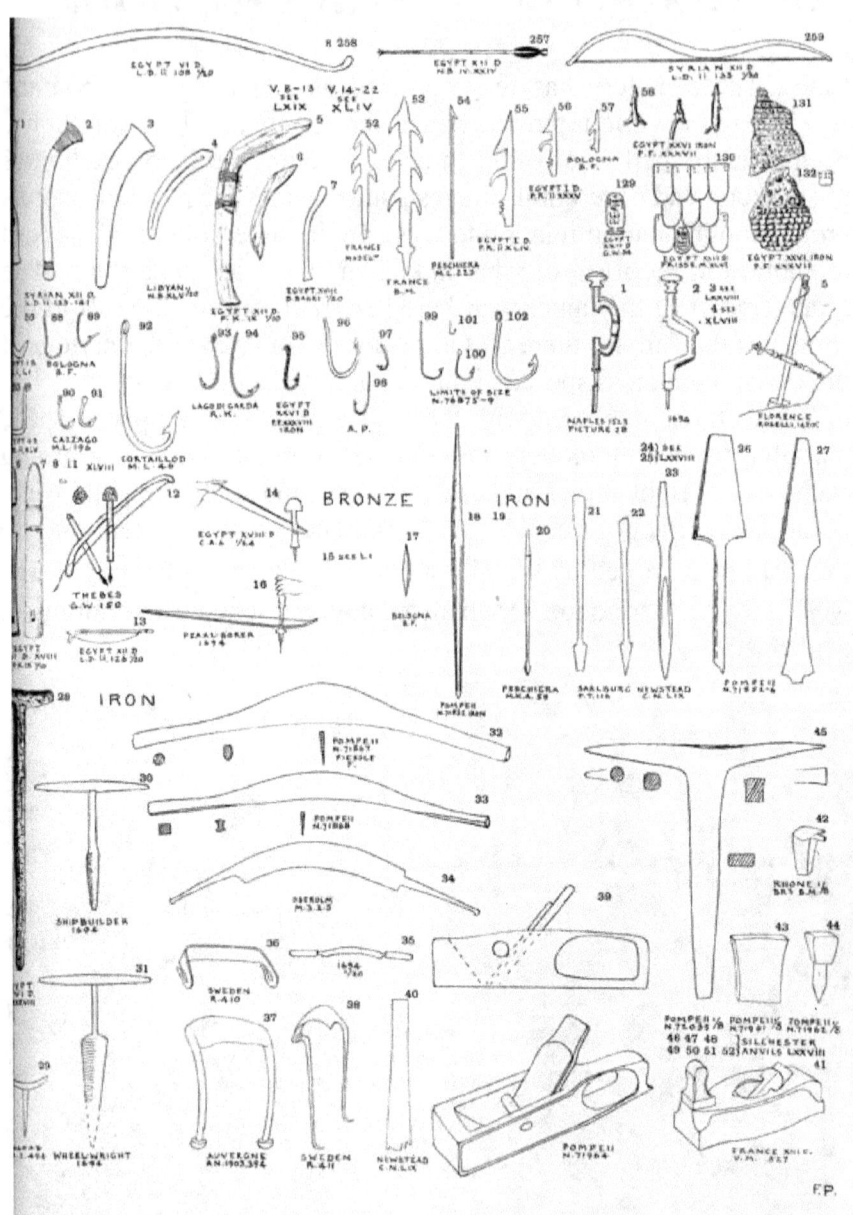

**Black History Extravaganza - Line Drawing -** Tools and Weapons - Bow and Arroe; Throw-Stick; Harpoon; Armor; Fish-Hook; Boring, planning.

# BLACK HISTORY EXTRAVAGANZA
# HONORING DR. BEN-JOCHANNAN

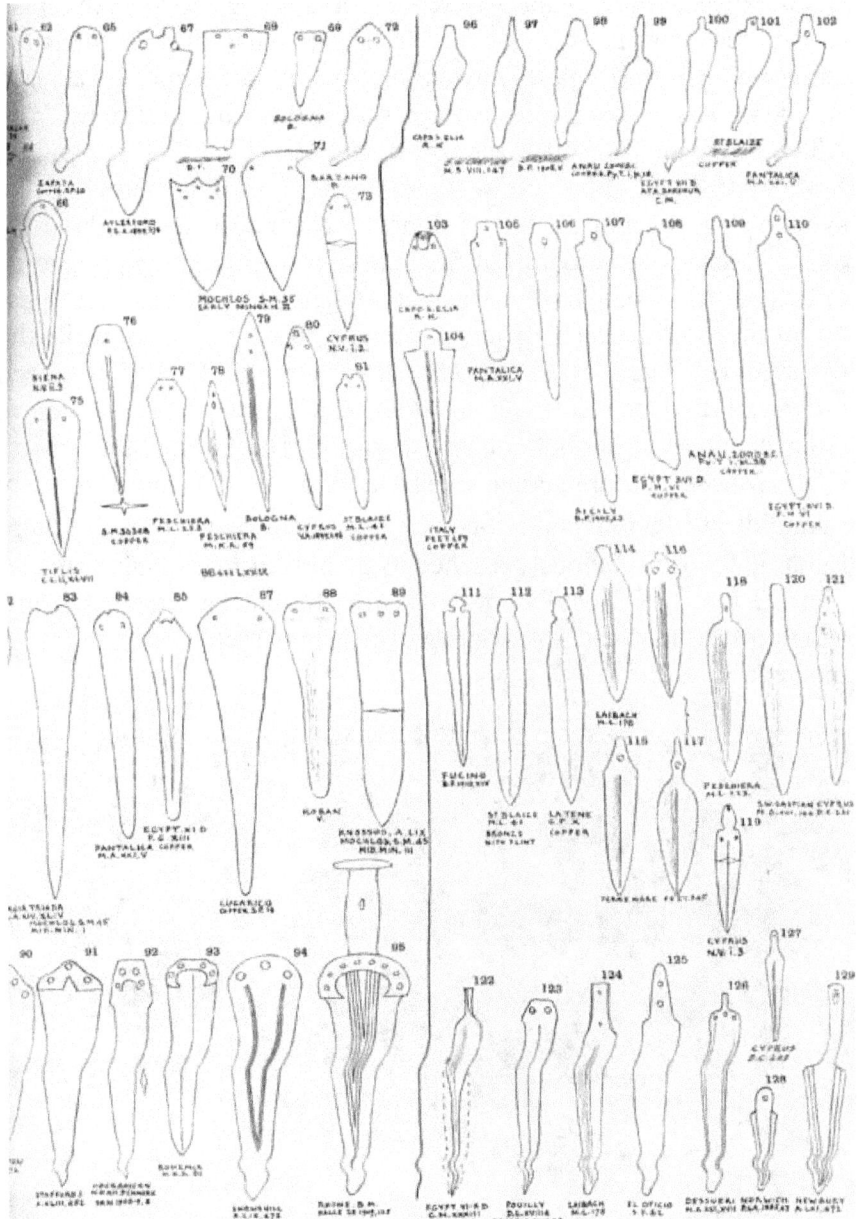

**Black History Extravaganza - Line Drawing -** Daggers, Without Tang. With Tang: Copper and Bronze.

# FREDERICK MONDERSON

He goes on to say, "The mastabas are of great constructive significance, for they appear to reproduce in a regular form the heap of sand fenced round with a wall of mud brick that formed the visible memorial over the earliest known tombs of a monumental character at Abydos. On the other side, we can see in them the prototype from which the pyramid itself was destined to be evolved. The pyramid at first sight looks like a direct copy in crystalline form of the symmetrical cairn or mound of stones or earth heaped over the body of the departed chieftain, but the shape has not been arrived at as directly as this would imply. There is the clearest evidence that it grew out of the mastabas. The latter, it is true, is oblong in plan, while the pyramid is square. It so happens, however, that there have been preserved two earlier pyramids than the fourth dynasty ones at Ghizeh, and these are both oblong in ground plan, while they possess other Mastaba characteristics. These two are the third dynasty pyramids at Meidum and at Saqqara, the latter the well-known Step-Pyramid that has obviously reached its present form through a process of accretion. The Great Pyramid of King Chufu is the first that is on a square plan, and that was systematically constructed through-out in this regular form."

**Black History Extravaganza - Photo -** One of two Sanctuary Altars at Kom Ombo Double Temple of the Elder Horus and Sobek, the Crocodile God.

# BLACK HISTORY EXTRAVAGANZA HONORING DR. BEN-JOCHANNAN

While the 6-story Mastaba Step-Pyramid carried architecture to the new frontier of building innovation, the true pyramid at Ghizeh set in stone the more perfect alignment and permanent work of art that today still defies the ravages of time. Strange, the Pyramids of Ghizeh were not illustrated nor painted, though the name of Khufu was singularly found in his great pyramid.

"At the revival of art at the beginning of the 12$^{th}$ Dynasty, sculptors seem to have taken for their models the best works of the 5$^{th}$ Dynasty, and the bas-relief - of which, alas too few remain - vie with them in vigor of conception and delicacy of execution. The draughtsmanship in many of the mural paintings is superb. Firmness of line is combined with great freedom of handling; while in the portrait statues the realism is free from any touch of vulgarity or the commonplace virtue of mere literalness. The artist of the 12$^{th}$ Dynasty knew, indeed, exactly what was to be done, and he did it with a joyous abandon in which there is no trace of self-consciousness. Looking at the drawing of a cat watching for prey, so sympathetically copied by Mr. Howard Carter, or Champollion's drawing of peasants tending goats (both reproduced in Maspero's *Art in Egypt*, and say if any modern paintings, tied by similar conditions of labor or the same limitation of materials, could have gotten a more vivid presentment of the subject or a truer rendering of essential features."

Nevertheless, G. Baldwin Brown, in discussing "The Monumental Art of Egypt" in *Journal of the Royal Institute of British Architects* XXIII, third Series, (191516: 217) states essentially "Monumental" is a term generally misused. However, "The truth is that the term implies an emphasis on certain special qualities the impression of which is made predominant, whereas buildings such as those first mentioned exhibit a perfect balance of qualities, which forbids our singling out any one or any more set of these for particular mention."

# FREDERICK MONDERSON

**Black History Extravaganza - Photo -** Two respectable gentlemen with the deepest connections to Dr. Ben pay their respects at the Cemetery's final farewell.

Even further, "The special qualities here referred to are, of course, those of magnitude and mass, though not of mere bulk. For a structure to appear monumental it must be handled with a studied reference to the particular effect desired, and must possess that consistency of treatment which results in the impression of style. Sometimes it will be that the one essential quality of vastness is brought out through an austere rejection of architectural graces, at other times the elements that make for greatness will be deliberately exaggerated, and in contrast other equally valuable aesthetic qualities consciously depreciated or even sacrificed. The Romans achieved monumental quality in their great engineering structures through the austerity of treatment just spoken of. These were primarily things of utility, and make no direct pretense to aesthetic quality, yet they are at the same time productions of art and are really the best things that the Romans have left us."

# BLACK HISTORY EXTRAVAGANZA HONORING DR. BEN-JOCHANNAN

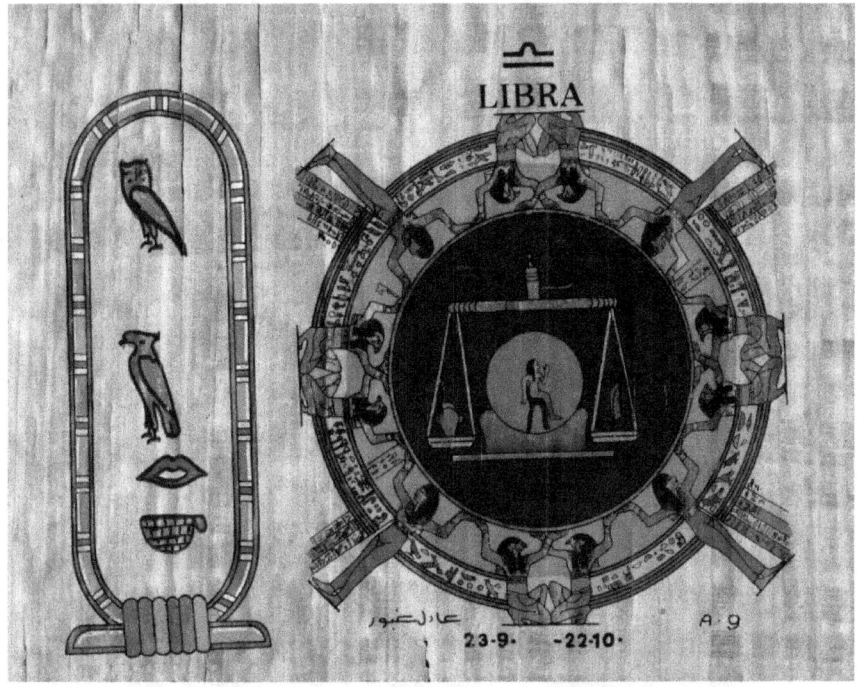

**Black History Extravaganza - Papyrus -** This time a decorated Cartouche with the Astrological sign of Libra.

The Middle Kingdom, as a period of transition in many respects, from the Old to the New Kingdom, not only brought new life and vitality to the new age of reorganization, consolidation and expansion, but it encouraged writing, art, trade, science, etc. That is, while the eleventh dynasty essentially consolidated, the twelfth dynasty experimented and produced masterpieces in the new areas of art and architecture, in both worship and mortuary experimentation, especially in statuary. In fact, Yoyote mentions, "Increasing numbers of stelae and statuettes of private persons are seen in the temples. This popularization of the arts is at the same time closely associated with a new spirit in the liturgy of the dead.... [including] the custom of placing statuettes of the dead in the actual vault (not only, as hitherto, in the chapel), and the use of anthropoid coffins in which the properties of statues and mummy were combined, and the employment of ushabtiu."

# FREDERICK MONDERSON

The Intefs and Mentuhoteps created and bequeathed to the Usertesens or Sesostrises and Amenemhats political stability and extensive commercial considerations. The twelfth dynasty built on the tranquility and was able to carry artistic creativity to great heights. This Middle Kingdom artistic experimentation was sometimes difficult to define because of its "crossroads" nature in bridging time.

**Black History Extravaganza - Photo -** The **RAS** were there to show some love and so **Red, Black and Green!**

# BLACK HISTORY EXTRAVAGANZA HONORING DR. BEN-JOCHANNAN

**Black History Extravaganza - Photo -** The gods on display, one resting, Ra Horakhty; and another being carried on the back of a cow, an emblem of Hathor.

Nevertheless, we begin to discern in its cultural syncretism and explosion, says Yoyote, "the naturalism of the tomb paintings, which are sometimes full of animation, may be contrasted with the formalism of votive statuary; the forceful muscularity of royal colossi with the broad masses of Osiride images, those remote stone

# FREDERICK MONDERSON

mummies representing the resurrected Pharaoh who were identified with Osiris; and the formalized and abstract modeling of attenuated bronzes with the lifelike immediacy of animal statuettes made by artists specializing in this genre. Similarly, although Sesostris III is portrayed with inhuman stiffness in his official statues, he is revealed in other portraits as having a careworn countenance pitiable in its human frailty. Taking into consideration the general climate of the period, it is difficult to sum up the complex style of the $12^{th}$ Dynasty more adequately than by calling it an Egyptian interpretation of humanism."

There is evidence linking the Middle Kingdom with the Seventeenth Dynasty. Flinders Petrie, in this regard wrote, "The XVIIth Dynasty, coming from Nubia held Thebes as its capital...." Even more, we know the Seventeenth Dynasts upon expulsion of the Hyksos found the Eighteenth Dynasty. As such, artistic styles may have been interrupted by the War of Independence, but upon cessation of hostilities pursuit of art creativity resumed. Nevertheless, and still, A.E.K. in "Theban Art of the XVIIth Dynasty" could confess in seeing contradiction, for: "Those who attended the MacGregor Sale in 1922 will not have forgotten the obsidian head of Amenemhat III a gloriously fragment which beat all records in Egyptian prices soaring to the astonishing figure of ten thousand pounds. The head conveys a striking impression of sedate and noble calm in its blending lines and contours, and the greatness of the work makes itself increasingly felt every time one studies it. The impression of pensive dreaminess conveyed in the work is extraordinary, and when one considers that the material is obsidian, a species of volcanic glass, our sense of the greatness of the achievement is achieved. Though hardly more than half the size of life the head has all the bigness of feelings of the head of a colossal."

# BLACK HISTORY EXTRAVAGANZA HONORING DR. BEN-JOCHANNAN

**Black History Extravaganza - Photo -** The "Eyes of Horus" peer out from the side of a wooden coffin.

Continuing his description, (1915-16: 58) he wrote: "The massive grey granite head of Amenemhat III, now in the British Museum (No. 774) is another work of singular power. Its simple planes have the mobile suggestiveness of great Greek work, and imparts a dignity to the features which is highly impressive: while the seated statue of the same king in the Cairo Museum is almost equally good, a superb figure, expressing aloofness and disdain, and every in each a king. The names have sometimes been removed from statues of this period, and others of a much later date substituted. Meneptah II (19$^{th}$ Dynasty) (Merenptah), supposed to be the pharaoh of the Exodus and Osorkon II, of the 22$^{nd}$ Dynasty, were arch-offenders in this way."

All this notwithstanding, the temple of Mentuhotep II at Deir el Bahari cannot go unnoticed in any discussion of the period for, not only was it in existence some five hundred years later but it inspired and influenced Senmut's construction of his queen's and, linking adjacent masterpiece. Bridging the distance from the river's valley temple, the long sphinx-lined walkway, pylon, colonnade and pillar alternation, ramp to ascend to the higher levels of terrace and courts as well as the

# FREDERICK MONDERSON

Sanctuary dug into the mountain linking this world with the next was nothing short of brilliance twice over.

The Art of Egypt in the New Kingdom became more prolific and extensive. E.A.K. writes in "Egyptian Art of the Second Theban Age" in *Antiquarian Quarterly* II, (1926-27: 84), explaining that "...whether in architecture, sculpture or painting, there is abundant material on which to base a study of the art of the Second Theban Age. The normal, highly conventional art so faithfully persisted in under all the pharaohs till the time of Akhenaten, may be studied in any of the great museums and in combining it with masterpieces of the twelfth dynasty, we may notice a tendency - not always too accentuated to surrender strength to sweetness, and breadth to treatment of elaboration of detail."

**Black History Extravaganza - Ceramic Art -** A Blank Cartouche with white insides.

With the supremacy of Amon and with imperial wealth flowing into his coffers, art blossomed and bloomed. Regional schools competed extensively, particularly with the Theban School, to produce the timelessness reflected in the paintings, statues, architecture, obelisks, etc. Decoration in Mortuary and Worship temples; in the Valley of the

# BLACK HISTORY EXTRAVAGANZA HONORING DR. BEN-JOCHANNAN

Kings, Queens, Nobles and Artisans art depicted every aspect of the social, religious and afterlife experience of the Egyptian. In the worship and mortuary temples, there were statues to complement the colonnades, porches, ramps, doors, altars, walls, halls, shrines, and obelisks. The halls were decorated with praises to the gods as well as the king on the inside and military and other exploits of the king on the outside. While the Sanctuary was often dark and sometimes undecorated on the inside, the outside, in the Hypostyle Hall as at Karnak, to some extent at Luxor, were decorated with episodes of the ritual.

**Black History Extravaganza - Photo -** Another of the Altars of the Double Sanctuary at the Double Temple of the Elder Horus and Sobek the Crocodile God.

# FREDERICK MONDERSON

**Black History Extravaganza - Photo -** An extremely interesting double image of the deceased in his tomb paying respects to Ptah (left) and Osiris (right).

Three political periods generally distinguish the New Kingdom, with each leaving its imprint on the art of the time and influencing future creativity. This experimentation and later explosion, fueled by imperial expansion following expulsion of the Hyksos included the reigns of the Tuthmosids, the Amarna Revolution and successes of the Ramessides, spanning the 18$^{th}$ through the 20$^{th}$ Dynasties. Though temples were considered great architectural achievements, tombs also were accorded great artistic license and those of nobles and artisans were done with such distinction, they are a major tourist attraction today. Yoyote (1971: 611) says of such structures, especially: "The graves of Theban nobles were simple chapels hollowed out of the hillside and surmounted by a small pointed pyramid. Although the majority of these have disappeared, they are known to us from drawings of the period. The design of these private hypogea is usually quite elementary. In itself, therefore the funerary architecture of the New Kingdom has little to claim our admiration, however remarkable we may find the geometric balance of the tomb of Rekhmara (vizier of Thutmose III) or however impressed we may be by the richly decorated columns that support the chapel of Ramose (vizier of Amenhotep III). If experts and amateurs alike make their way to Qurneh, Dra Abu al Nega, Guret, Murai, and Deir el Medina, it is to look at the paintings and reliefs that enliven the chapels and vaults."

# BLACK HISTORY EXTRAVAGANZA HONORING DR. BEN-JOCHANNAN

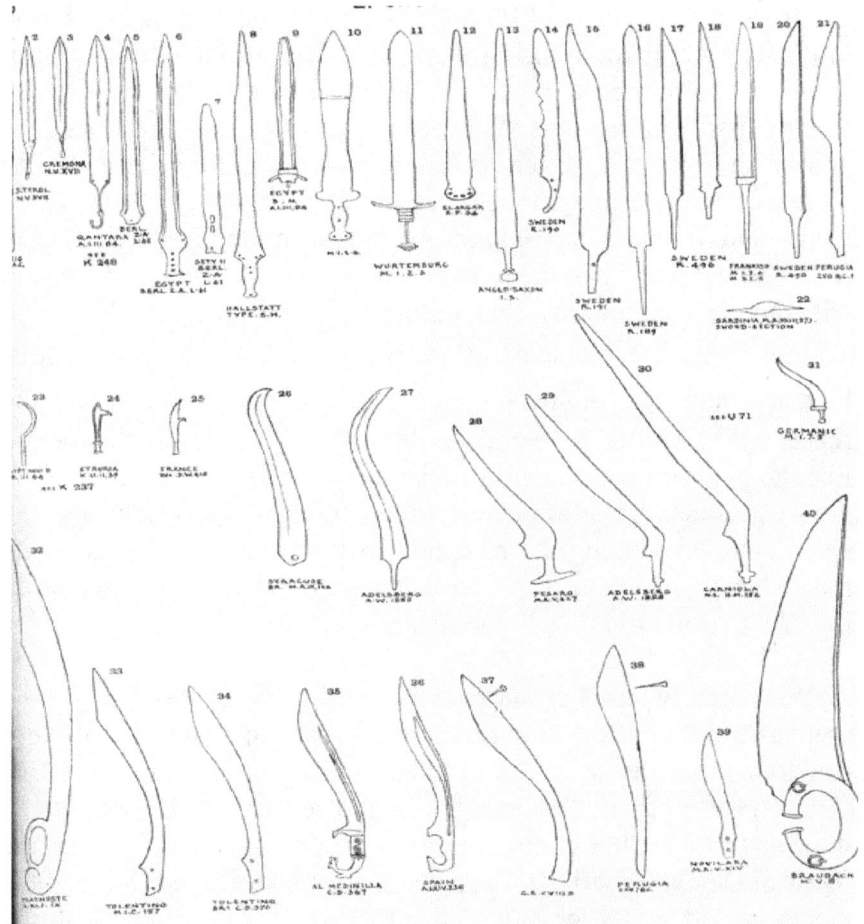

**Black History Extravaganza - Line Drawing -** Tools and Weapons - Swords.

Commenting further (1971: 611) on the first of the three period of artistic splendor characteristic of the New Kingdom, that of the 18th Dynasty, Yoyote goes into more detail: "The 18th Dynasty witnessed a marvelous florescence in the two techniques used in mural decoration - relief and painting - with magnificent scenes in the temples and intimate scenes in the tombs telling anew the story of daily life in Egypt. In the temples, one finds not only the eternal ritual of pictures of oblations, but also spectacular scenes of annual ceremonies and certain national festivals. At Deir el Bahari, for instance, one can imagine oneself to be participating in a sort of regatta held on the feast of Hathor, goddess of joy, or in an expedition of the Egyptian fleet to the distant land of Punt on the Red Sea coast. In the private tombs, a larger part is played by specifically religious themes than was customary in earlier times, and paintings begin to appear showing the owners of tombs praying before the gods. By contrast, certain sacred acts such as the traditional offering to the dead, the communal meal that reunites the family at the time of the 'great feast of the valley,' and the funeral ceremonies themselves are treated with an easy familiarity that mitigates the severity of the ritual. Moreover, all the incidents of everyday life - the arts and crafts, industry, and agriculture - reappear as in former times, and the repertoire of scenes is augmented because dignitaries of this period liked to place on record their official missions as well as some of the purely personal episodes in their careers. In this imperialistic age, the ceremony surrounding the reception of the tributary peoples was a theme much in vogue and one that gave artists a valid excuse to introduce exotic motifs into their paintings."

At this point, two sets of masterpieces of the $18^{th}$ Dynasty art can be emphasized that attest to excellent craftsmanship. The first of these was found in a shrine at Deir el Bahari built by Amenhotep I, A.E.K (1926: 84) explained: "It was in the latter place that Naville discovered the wonderful Hathor group, which has now passed into history as the 'Cow of Deir el Bahari.' It was found almost intact in the shrine of the Goddess, and was at once acclaimed as equal if not superior to the greatest animal sculpture in the world. The two figures of Pharaoh which form part of the group (They are both later than Amenhotep I), may be disregarded. It is in the cow that the artist has eclipsed himself as an interpreter of animal form. With all her dignity, the cow is no conventional beast but a most life-like creature 'of rare color' as Maspero graphically says, 'of perfect purity of form, intelligent expression, graceful and an excellent milker to boot.' (*New Light on Ancient Egypt*, p. 272). Egypt has nothing to show like it in animal sculpture, and not even the Greeks have done anything quite so good. Both cow and shrine are now in the Museum at Cairo."

# BLACK HISTORY EXTRAVAGANZA HONORING DR. BEN-JOCHANNAN

The second set of a masterpiece of the 18$^{th}$ Dynasty can be grouped, as A.E.K. (1926: 84-85) has done in the following: "The greater quality of the period is nobly expressed in such masterpieces of sculpture as the exquisite Mond statue in the Cairo Museum and the statue of Sennefer and his wife in the same historic treasure-house. The atlas head of Thutmose I, also in Cairo, is in its own way, an extraordinary production too, though the head is beautifully finished, the simple treatment has a certain Phaedian greatness about it. The reliefs in the famous temple at Der-el-Bahari at Thebes forms good examples of sculptured excellence in another class. The commercial exploits of Queen Hatshepsut form the subject of these wonderful reliefs. They are executed with a precision and withal bigness of feeling which leave nothing to be desired; while the vivid pictures of the historic expedition to Punt constitute an invaluable and circumstantial commentary on the great enterprise."

At the Temples of Luxor and Karnak, and many other structures associated with Rameses II, the treaty with the Hittites ending the "Battle of Kadesh" is often depicted on the pylon or other external walls. Rameses' "Girdle Wall" at Karnak is replete with wonderful illustrations of the king presenting to and praising the gods. The Temple of Mut of the Theban Triad, had hundreds of sculptured statues of the lion-goddess Sekhmet placed there by Amenhotep III. Further, at Luxor, on the west and east walls of the Processional Colonnade, the events surrounding the "Opet Festival" are depicted. Across the river at Deir el Bahari, statues of the Queen as well as depictions of the "Expedition to Punt," recounting the Queen's Divine, some say Virgin, Birth, the Chapels of Anubis, the Upper Court, all have powerful examples of Egyptian art. The "Kiosk of Seti II" in the Great Court at Karnak and the "Kiosk of Hatshepsut" in the Court of the "Ramessean Front" at Luxor Temple usurped by Thutmose II and repaired by Rameses II were both dedicated to the Theban Triad of Amun, Mut and Khonsu. Both are inundated with the most beautiful sunk reliefs. The Temple of Abu Simbel has beautiful bas-relief paintings as also the Temple of Seti I at Abydos decorated by both Seti and Rameses II. Many agree the best such surviving art in the entire valley is to be found at Abydos Temple of Seti I of the

# FREDERICK MONDERSON

19th Dynasty. This Temple of Seti I, instead of being dedicated to the Theban Triad of Amon, Mut and Khonsu, or even Osiris, Isis and Horus, is in fact dedicated to seven deities including Osiris, Isis and Horus of the Osirian group; Ra-Harakhte, Ptah and Amon, the great gods of the Empire; and Seti I, deified; and it also boasts the most beautiful illustrations. The Kiosk at Abydos Temple Seti dedicated to Osiris with its beautifully illustrated and preserved colorful painting is dedicated to Osiris, Isis and he Seti I. The Ramesseum and the Temple of Medinet Habu mortuary structures of Rameses II and Rameses III respectively, carried the art of massive building, pictographic decoration, and hieroglyphic representation to the highest heights and show Egyptian art in its finest features. Still, some critics find fault with the work of these last two, Rameses II and Rameses III.

**Black History Extravaganza - Photo -** The Deceased stands with empty hands in adoration before Ptah.

# BLACK HISTORY EXTRAVAGANZA HONORING DR. BEN-JOCHANNAN

However, there was more to the art than architectural representation, and as such the decorative features of painting deserve mention. Von Reben (1902: 42) provides some insights into sculpture, painting, and other aspects of Egyptian "fine arts." First, he tells us in adding color to this great age of art during the New Kingdom, patience was an indispensable asset. "A great majority of the Egyptian works of sculpture were cut with marvelous patience in the hardest materials, in variously colored granite, diorite, syenite, and basalt. Limestone and alabaster were rarely employed for colossal or life-size statues, but were used more frequently for works of smaller dimensions; these were also burned in clay with a surface of blue or green glazing, or were cut in more valuable stones, such as agate, jasper, carnelian, and lapis lazuli. Enameled clay idols were manufactured in great numbers; modern museums contain hundreds of these figures of perfectly similar form. The so-called scarabaeus is very common-beetle shaped bodies of clay, or of the above-named stones-with incised figures of hieroglyphics upon their lower surface. Such amulets were perforated and worn as beads, and were placed loosely in the coffins with the mummies."

**Black History Extravaganza - Photo -** Just an orderly group waiting their turn to enter Abyssinian Baptist to be part of history paying tribute to a Great African intellect and nationalist.

# FREDERICK MONDERSON

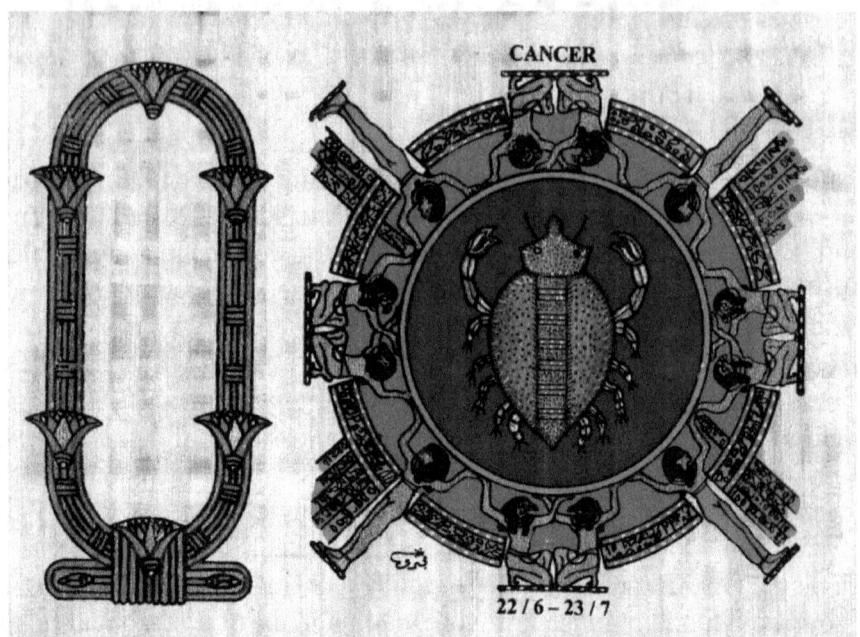

**Black History Extravaganza - Papyrus -** Another Blank Cartouche sits beside the Astrological sign for Cancer.

Again, Von Reben (1902: 44-45) continued: "Representation of profane scenes are more varied and are exceedingly interesting; the technicalities of Egyptian art are shown by the cutting of a monolithic palm-column, the polishing of a granite chapel, the painting of walls, the writing of hieroglyphics upon tablets and papyrus, the carving and painting of sphinxes and statues, the making of bricks and walling of brick masonry, the interior of houses, even the plans of dwellings and gardens. Besides numerous tools and the products of manufacturing trades, there may be recognized upon these paintings weavers, rope-makers, the preparers of paper and of linen cloth, ship-builders, carpenters with hand-saw and auger, and the cutters of bows and lances, who employ adzes quite similar to those still in use. Commerce on land and sea is represented by wares, unpacked or in bales, by scales, various kinds of wagons and trading vessels, etc., all shown in the clearest manner possible. Ploughs, sowing and harvesting, the gathering of figs and grapes, the pressing of oil and wine, illustrate the condition of agriculture; while the especial ability

# BLACK HISTORY EXTRAVAGANZA HONORING DR. BEN-JOCHANNAN

of the Egyptian for animal representations is exercised in the hunting scenes of lions, tigers, buffaloes, jackals, and gazelles; by the snarling of birds and fishes in nets, as well as by the admirably characterized figures of apes, porcupines, etc. There are also historical paintings, great battle scenes, the storming of cities, and the triumph of the returning victors, who bring with them booty and prisoners, the nationality of whom is often readily distinguishable by peculiarities of physiognomy and costume. The Egyptian kings appear in superhuman size, either fighting from splendid war-chariots, or striding forward to sacrifice their kneeling enemies, a dozen of whom, seized at once by the hair are decapitated at a blow."

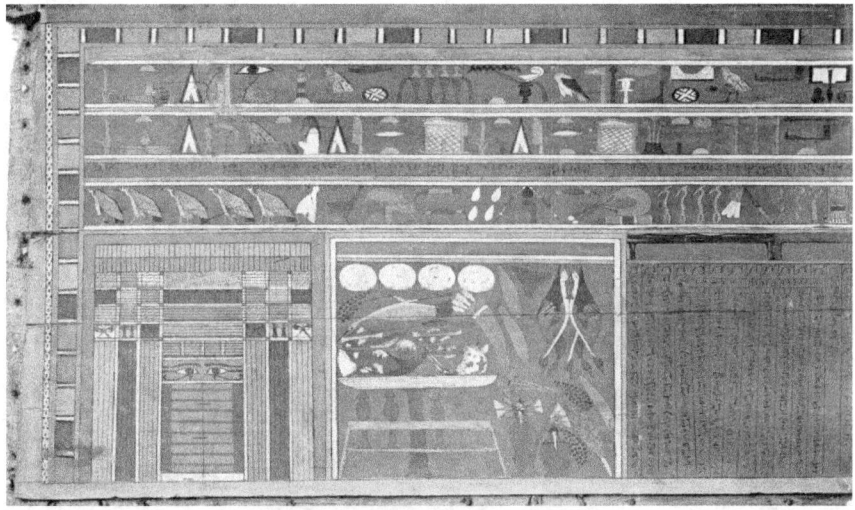

**Black History Extravaganza - Photo -** Interesting how various scenes are simultaneously depicted, the use of the register and the "Table of Offerings."

Even further, Von Reben (1902: 47) summarized his views: "The painting of Egypt existed unchanged for a period of more than two thousand years, with a stability unequalled in the other civilizations of the world. It was perhaps not quite so extensively employed in the ancient kingdom as in later times: paintings can be dated as far back as the third dynasty (3338-3124, according to Lepsius), but they were restricted to interior decoration. The walls of the pyramids were

# FREDERICK MONDERSON

unadorned by color. After the practice of art had been greatly limited by the invasion of the Hyksos (from the thirteenth to the seventeenth dynasty, 2136-1591 B.C.), it arose with new vigor at the advent of the modern kingdom, especially during the eighteenth and nineteenth dynasties, when the architecture which flourished from Thebes offered a wide field for painted decorations. From that time, the walls lost their bareness, and richly colored ornaments were employed over the exterior, enlivening the dead and heavy character of Egyptian building and somewhat supplying the deficiency of its exterior development."

**Black History Extravaganza - Photo -** Working out the details for the viewing of Dr. Ben-Jochannan's final time among us.

# BLACK HISTORY EXTRAVAGANZA HONORING DR. BEN-JOCHANNAN

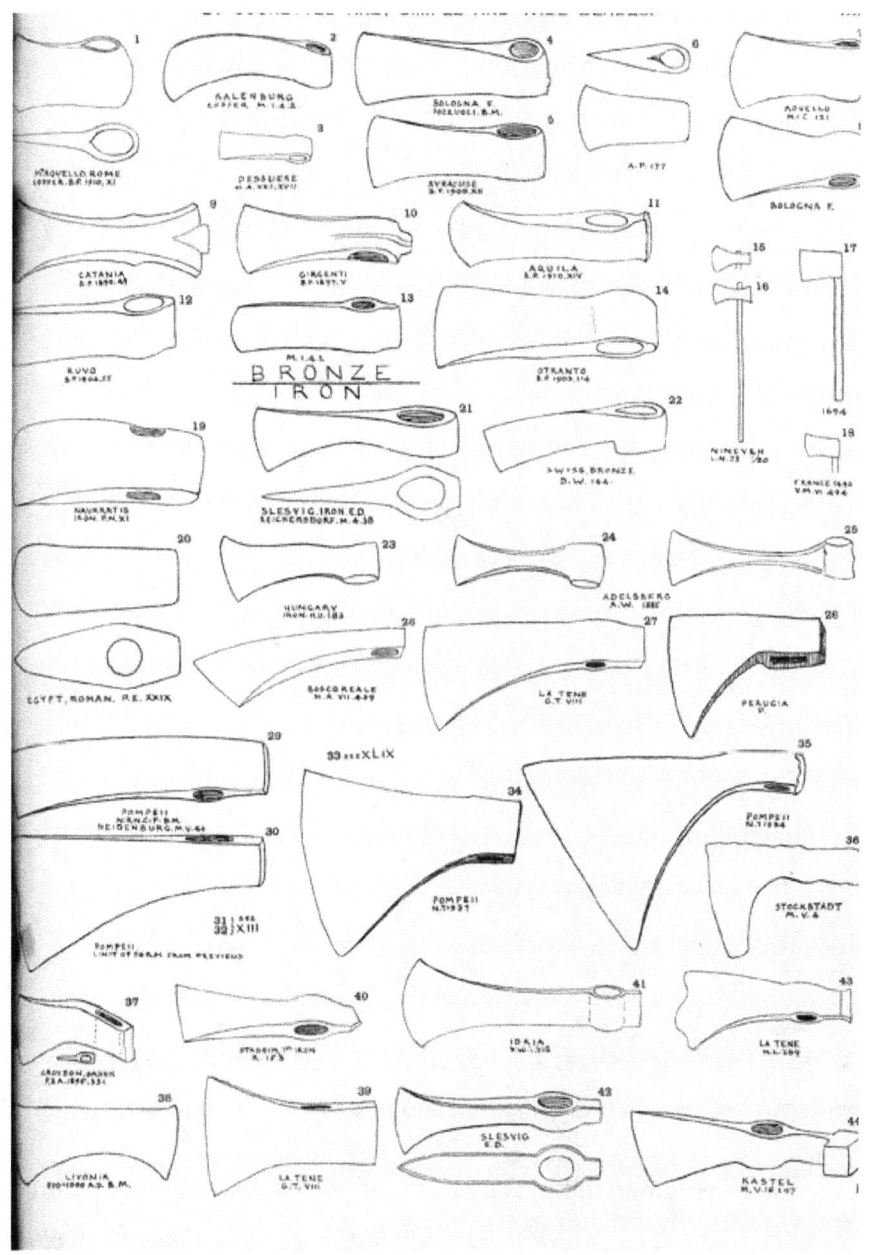

**Black History Extravaganza - Line Drawing -** Tools and Weapons - Socketed Axe. Simple and Wide Blades.

# FREDERICK MONDERSON

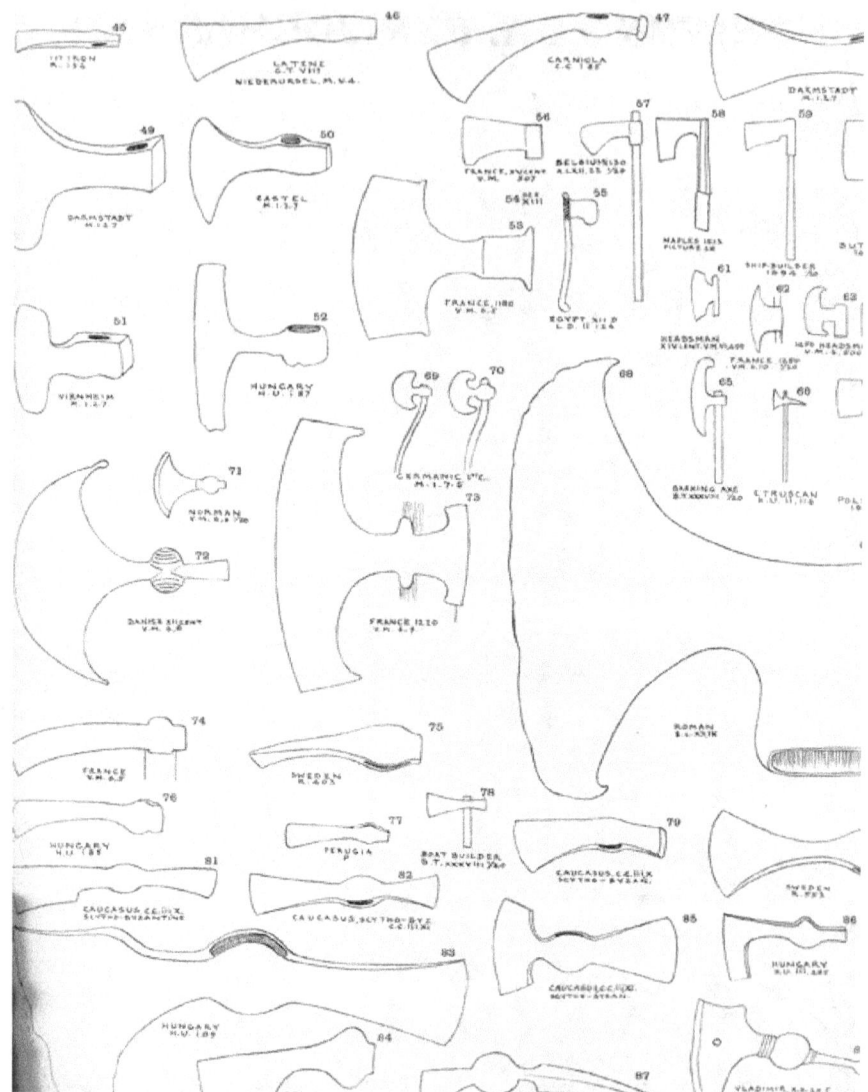

**Black History Extravaganza - Line Drawing -** Tools and Weapons - Socketed Axe. Deepened and Round Sockets.

The Graeco-Roman temples of Isis at Philae, Kalabsha, Kom Ombo, Edfu and Esneh contain more painting, reliefs and sculpture than all surviving earlier Egyptian temple combined. The Temple of Horus at Edfu has done an excellent job of preservation of the ritual feature adorned in artistic splendor. The good thing about this is that they help to record, save and transmit much of the earlier beliefs and

# BLACK HISTORY EXTRAVAGANZA HONORING DR. BEN-JOCHANNAN

practices. By this time, native Egyptian art had entered a decline but there were infusions and innovations made by the conquerors who changed the nature of Egyptian art. Some commentators have argued that the Greeks and Roman brought much needed change and infusion. However, one thing is certain, the early Africans of Egypt created lasting and picturesque art that was original in its conception and their displays in museums worldwide attest to the beauty and timelessness of their creations.

**Black History Extravaganza - Photo -** Seriousness of expression undergirding intensity of devotion to the "Search for Knowledge" as Dr. Ben taught these "Young cubs" who came to say fare-thee-well, father, teacher, friend, Great African nationalist.

## REFERENCES

Aldred, Cyril. *Egyptian Art: In the Days of the Pharaohs 3100-320 B.C.* New York: Oxford University Press, 1980.

Brunton, Guy in "The Badarian Predynastic Period" in Engelbach, Richard. *Introduction to Egyptian Archaeology with special reference to the Egyptian Museum, Cairo.* $2^{nd}$ Edition. Cairo: Government Printing Office, 1961.

# FREDERICK MONDERSON

Clarke, Somers and R. Engelbach. *Ancient Egyptian Construction and Architecture*. New York: Dover Publications, Inc., (1930) 1995.
Kush, Khamit Indus. *The Missing Pages of "His-Story."* 1993.
Maspero, Gaston. *Art in Egypt*.
Peet, T. Eric. "The Art of the Predynastic Period." *Journal of Egyptian Archaeology* 2 (1915: 88-94).
Smith, W. Stephenson. *The Art and Architecture of Ancient Egypt*. New York: Penguin Books, (1958) 1981.
Von Reben, Dr. Franz. *History of Ancient Art*. New York: Harper and Brothers Publishers, 1902.
Wilkinson, Alix. *Ancient Egyptian Jewelry*. New York: Methuen and Co., (1971) 1975.
Wilkinson, Richard H. *Reading Egyptian Art*. London: Thames and Hudson, (1992) 1996.

**Black History Extravaganza - Photo -** They came to be part of history and to pay respects to one who so deserved the recognition that comes from a selfless life in devotion to the upliftment of a people, their history, culture and religion.

# BLACK HISTORY EXTRAVAGANZA HONORING DR. BEN-JOCHANNAN

**Black History Extravaganza - Photo -** On a back-wall at Kom Ombo Temple, monumental inscriptions stand next to a gigantic figure. Notice the several crocodiles (10) in the middle row on top.

## PTAH

Ptah, Great Architect of the Universe, you were among the earliest African Gods. At Unification of Kemet, Narmer founded the White Wall at Memphis, as his capital in *Aneb-Hetch*, the first Nome of the Lower Kingdom. Lord of the White Wall, the King built a temple, *Hat-Ke Ptah* at *Khut-Taui*, Horizon of the Two Lands and established worship of your triad Ptah-Sakhet-Nefertum, later worshipped at Thebes. While the fortunes of other gods rose and fell, yours as Patron

# FREDERICK MONDERSON

of Artists, Artisans and Artificers remained not paramount, but consistent, and your festival was celebrated on March 21, Lord of Truth, Great Chief of the Axe.

Lord of the Hidden Throne, whose hidden form is unknown, Powerful One, at Memphis, your High Priest, Great One, Commander of Workmen, was the Chief Artist of the Court. From here, the Great Chief of Artists played a prominent role in state politics, as you Ptah established Ma'at throughout the Two Lands. Father of Fathers, Power of Powers, you are the Master Architect and Designer of Everything which exist in the World and was employed in the Construction of the Heavens and the Earth, Great of Handicrafts.

Ptah, Disk of Heaven, you illuminate the Two Lands with the Fire of your Two Eyes. The Theban triad dominated the Middle and New Kingdoms and you, Great Chief of the Hammer resided in the palace of their abode, with a temple at Karnak. Father of the Gods, the emblem of your Majesty is a close-fitting garment, and from an opening in front project your two hands with Scepter, Ankh, and Tet representing power, life, stability. The *Menat*, symbol of pleasure and happiness hangs from the back of your neck.

Lord of Thebes, Fire God, while little evidence of Middle Kingdom temples remain, yet the 18th Dynasty embellished your Sanctuary at Karnak and Memphis, the City of Walls. Ramesside kings were your most ardent champions, O God Who Stands upon the Ma'at Pedestal. Rameses II erected two great sandstone statues at Memphis, one over 10 feet high, in your name. God of the Beautiful Face in Thebes who

# BLACK HISTORY EXTRAVAGANZA HONORING DR. BEN-JOCHANNAN

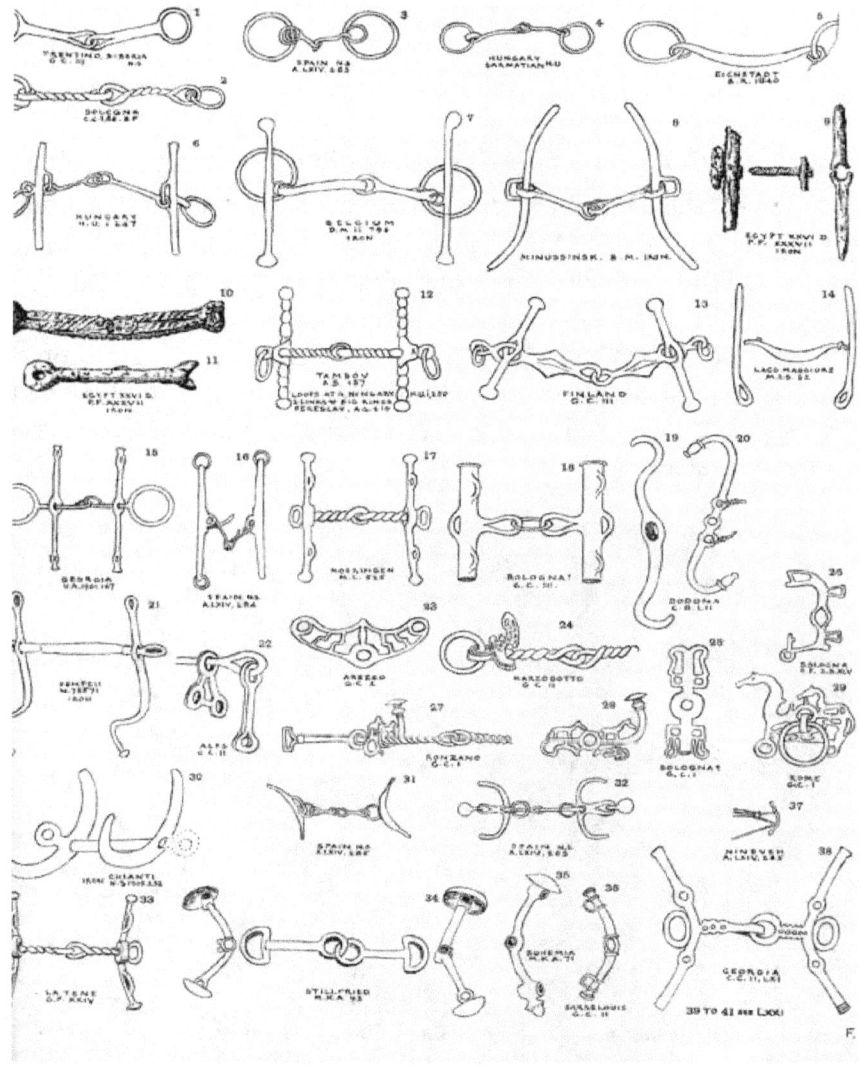

**Black History Extravaganza - Line Drawing -** Tools and Weapons - Horse Bit. Bronze.

Created his own Image, and Fashioned his own Body, you oversaw the Construction of that great city, being Chief of All Handicraftsmen and of all Workers in Metal and Stone, God of Wisdom, you understood things before Creation.

# FREDERICK MONDERSON

Very Great God who came into existence in the earliest time, you are the Blue-Collar God, Master-workman of the Universal Workshop, the Supreme Mind. Mind and Tongue of the Gods, all things proceeded from you Ptah, Lord of Ma'at, King of the Two Lands. As a form of the Sun God, Father of Beginnings, you are the Creator of the Eggs of the Sun and Moon. In this you are the Personification of the Rising Sun, Artificer in metals, smelter, caster, sculptor, great Celestial Workman and Architect, preparing the primeval elements of earth and water.

**Black History Extravaganza - Photo -** Anubis "clothed" in black, stands gazing into the distance, looking for the deceased.

# BLACK HISTORY EXTRAVAGANZA HONORING DR. BEN-JOCHANNAN

**Black History Extravaganza - Ceramic Art -** The beautiful reed in wonderful color.

Drawing God, the Father and Son, Lord of Justice, Divine Sculptor, you gave and still give forms to all things and beings on earth. Opener of the Ways, you fashion the Souls of the Dead to live in the Underworld. As Ptah-Seker, with crook, whip, scepter, crown of disk, plumes, horns and uraei with disks on their heads, the Office of your High Priest existed form the time of the Second Dynasty. Great God

# FREDERICK MONDERSON

who came into being in the beginning with two feathers of Ma'at, Lofty Plumes, you rested upon the darkness as King of Eternity, Everlastingness and Lord of Life. You bring the Nile from its source to make flourish the staff of life and to make grain come forth aged one of Nu. In same manner, you make fertile the watery mass of heaven.

Ptah-Tanen, Disk of Heaven, in peace you light up the world with your brilliant rays. Ready Plumes, of multitudinous forms, with the Sun and Moon as your eyes, you pass through eternity and everlastingness. Builder of your own limbs, maker of your own body, your upper part is heaven; the lower part is the Tuat. Maker of the Tuat with all of its arrangements, you make to come forth the water on the mountains to give life to all men and women in your name *Ari-Ankh*, Lord of Justice. Aged one traversing Eternity, Prince of Annu, you judge the dead and give them access to the Field of Peace, Field of Reeds, Field of Grasshoppers.

**Black History Extravaganza - Photo -** Great Pylon to the Mortuary Temple of Rameses II at Medinet Habu.

# BLACK HISTORY EXTRAVAGANZA HONORING DR. BEN-JOCHANNAN

**Black History Extravaganza - Photo -** One of two remaining, the Horus Hawk or Falcon in the Great Court at the Temple of Horus at Edfu.

# FREDERICK MONDERSON

Ptah, you make all land and all countries. As you mold gods, men and everything produced Great God who stretched out the heavens; you make your disk to revolve in the body of Nut as you fashion yourself without the help of any other being. Fully equipped you came forth fully equipped. The Company of Gods of your Supreme Company praises you, one with many companions.

**Black History Extravaganza - Photo -** A baboon and animals in procession stand behind an elevated Falcon who faced Horus as Ra-Horakhty.

Ptah-Seker-Asar, Triune God of Resurrection, you Dwell in a Secret Place. Lord Ta-Tchesetet, pygmy with large baldhead and thick limbs, beetle and plumes, you are the Governor of Everlastingness. Begetter of Men, Maker of their lives, Creator of all the Gods, you are the Father of the Father of the Gods. Ptah-Tanen, Babe Born Daily, Aged One on the Borders of Eternity, Lord of Life, Giver of Life at Will, you hear the prayers men make to you.

The Hapi or Apis Bull, incarnate of Ptah, emerged as the Ptolemaic Serapis in the Memphis Mausoleum or Serapeum of the Greeks, where the great Imhotep was recognized as your son. From this House of the Aged One, your temple *Aneb-Abt* in Memphis, Men-nefer, the House of the Beautiful Face, you maintain the Balance of the Two Lands.

# BLACK HISTORY EXTRAVAGANZA HONORING DR. BEN-JOCHANNAN

**Black History Extravaganza - Photo -** Minister Clemson extends a hand to console Dr. Ben's grieving son.

**Black History Extravaganza - Photo -** Dr. Ben's son, grieving sisters and Brother Jarvis.

# FREDERICK MONDERSON

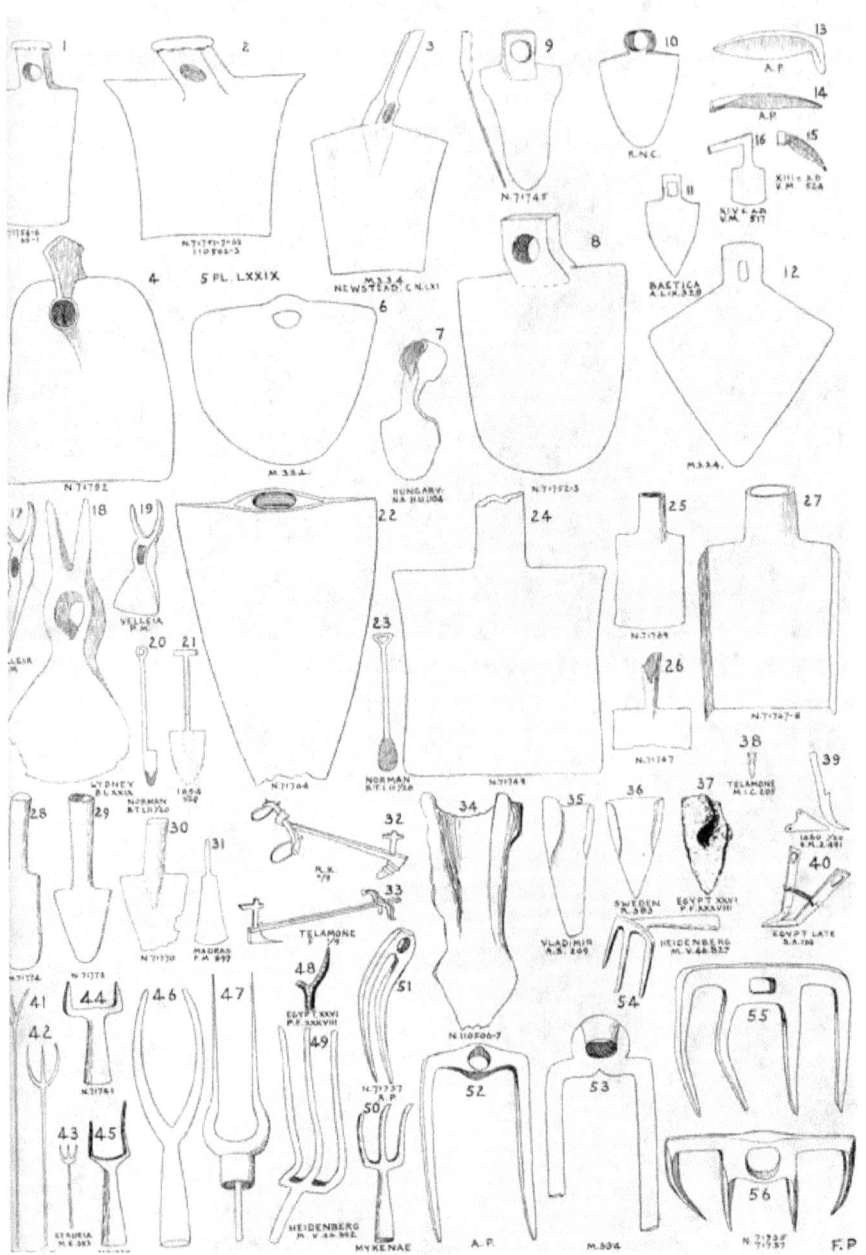

**Black History Extravaganza - Line Drawing -** Tools and Weapons - Agricultural Tools.

# BLACK HISTORY EXTRAVAGANZA
# HONORING DR. BEN-JOCHANNAN

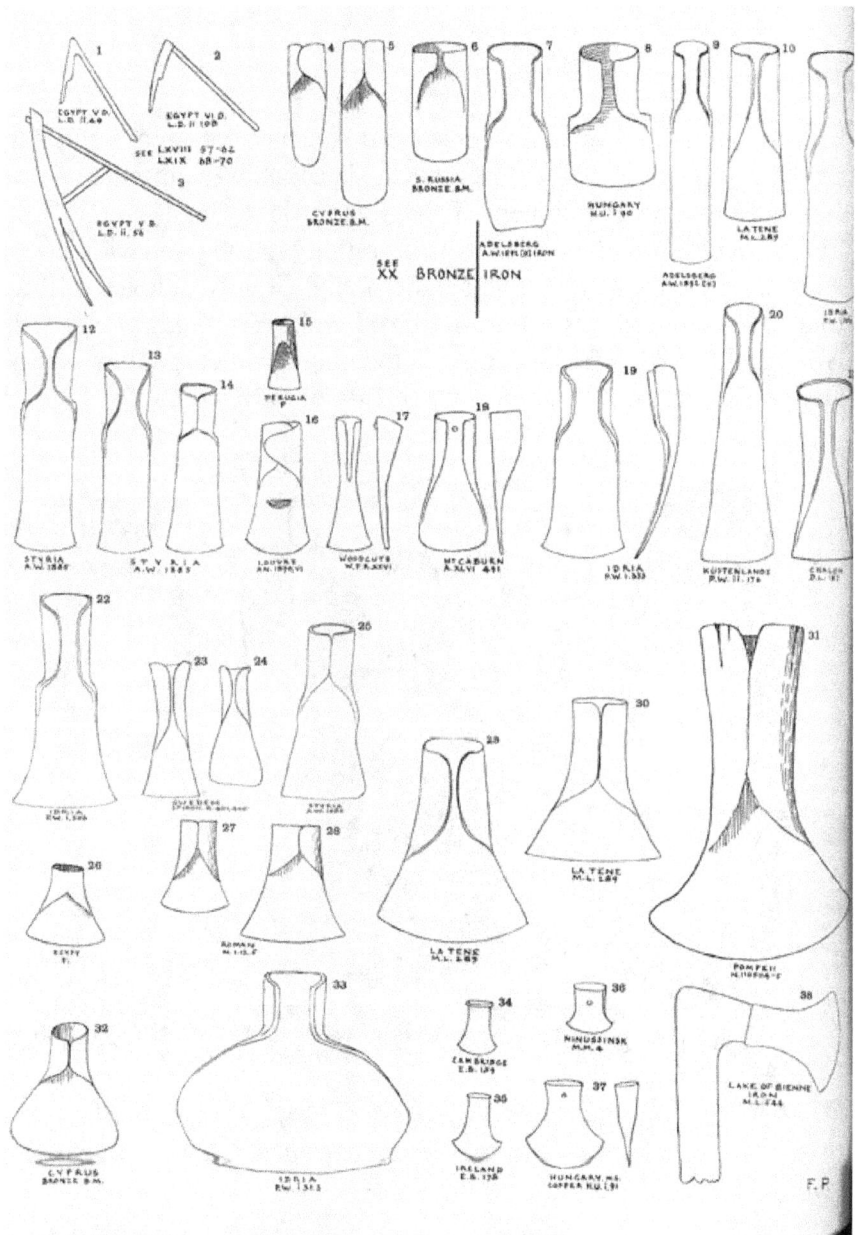

**Black History Extravaganza - Line Drawing -** Tools and Weapons - Metal Hoes.

# FREDERICK MONDERSON

In this City of White Wall, Persea and Acacia trees bloom and here reside your female counterpart Sekhet, sister and wife, mother of your son Nefertum, later Imhotep. This great African Goddess, the Great Lady, Lady of Sa, Queen of Ant, is mighty, strong and violent. O Holy One, the Lady of Flame, Mighty Lady, Greatly Beloved of Ptah, Lady of Heaven, is Mistress of the Two Lands. You Gods of Holiness, Bless and Protect African people in the many challenges they face, O Divine Artificer of Creation, Lord of Life of the Two Lands.

**Black History Extravaganza - Papyrus -** Goddess Mut offers two ointment jars to two blank cartouches topped by soaring vultures (above) and uraei (below).

# BLACK HISTORY EXTRAVAGANZA HONORING DR. BEN-JOCHANNAN

**Black History Extravaganza - Line Drawing -** An assortment of Vessels

# FREDERICK MONDERSON

**Black History Extravaganza - Photo -** Majesty and beauty in all its glory as this "Daughter" pays tribute to the Elder who Praised African Womanhood to the Max.

# BLACK HISTORY EXTRAVAGANZA HONORING DR. BEN-JOCHANNAN

## X. ARCHITECTURE OF ANCIENT EGYPT

By

Dr. Fred Monderson

The Architecture of ancient Egypt was its great glory. Beginning with the simplest materials in the pre-dynastic age, the craft of building grew from use of windbreaks, and mud and daub to erecting shelters, to unfired or sun-dried then fired bricks and finally into the more durable material, stone. Papyrus stalks lined roofs in homes. Now, while the buildings of kings or commoners were constructed of wood, bricks and other perishable material, the temples of the gods were made of stone to last forever befitting a deity who represented everlastingness. The temple was said to be 'made of fine stone to stand for eternity.' Yet, this notwithstanding, while the dwellings of kings and commoners ascribed to social conventions and practices, the temple of a god was shrouded in magical symbolism and mysteriousness. This reality not only symbolized the eternal nature of the deity, it also represented the notion of the coming into being of that divinity and the subsequent dynamic admonitions regarding its security and the ritual and liturgy upon which his existence was daily practiced and administered to in order that his function on earth would be accomplished, viz-a-viz, the Egyptian state.

This metaphysical construct can be conceptualized if, in going back to earlier times one understands, as Yoyote explained: "A pyramid may perhaps be compared with the primordial rock where the sun was born, and the tunnels in the Valley of the Kings with the passages in the netherworld where the sun regenerated itself." The temple, on the other hand, was a primordial hill from which the god emerged from the waters of chaos at creation. The hypostyle hall with its massive columns represented a "forest as at creation."

# FREDERICK MONDERSON

**Black History Extravaganza - Photo -** Goddess Hathor resting on Heb with a shrine on her head.

Notwithstanding, G. Baldwin Brown (1903: 219) compares these two forms of architecture and arrives at an interesting conclusion. This is explained as he, Brown argued, "For a building to merit the term 'monumental' something more is wanted than mere size. Loosely designed edifices of multitudinous parts may, like some of the early Renaissance palaces ... cover a vast extent of ground, but their want of consistency and style offends that aesthetic sense." Nevertheless, "The principle that size is not the criterion of the monumental applies in ancient Egypt. The tourist is there chiefly impressed by two buildings, the Great Pyramid and the Temple of Karnak, and he generally accords to each the same tribute of awe and admiration. But, aesthetically speaking, the two buildings are very different, and it is by no means necessary to place Karnak, or any New Empire structure, on the same artistic level as the older work. The latter, as we shall see perfectly fulfils the conditions of the monumental. It possesses prodigious mass treated by the constructor with the most austere self-abnegation in the refusal of ornament and details, and is the very embodiment of style. The former, the Temple of the New Empire, possesses mass only in the mechanical sense of a vast number of cubic

# BLACK HISTORY EXTRAVAGANZA HONORING DR. BEN-JOCHANNAN

yards of stonework, but there is no such treatment of the mass as to convey the impression of the monumental. It has abundant detail and a superfluity of ornament, but the various parts have not passed through the crucible of the imagination to issue thence worked into a harmonious unity."

**Black History Extravaganza - Photo -** Part of the Peristyle Court's Colonnade with its roofed Ambulatory and inner face of the Great Pylon at the rear of Horus's Temple at Edfu. Notice closely, each column's capital is in a different style.

He goes on to comment, in the same critical method, "In the famous hypostyle halls of the Egyptian temples the supports are far too crowded, so that the effect of an interior is quite lost. They are immeasurably too numerous and too bulky for the work they have to do in supporting the roof, while the form of them suggests soft and yielding rather than rigid material. We may compare them with the Doric columns of the Greeks. In both cases the original support was of plant origin, in Greece the tree-trunk, in Egypt the tall and swaying stem of the papyrus, or even at times the pulpy and succulent stalk of the water-lily; but when the Greeks transferred the plant form to stone they petrified it, so that it bears a thoroughly lithic character. The Egyptians contended themselves with preserving the shape and character of the plant stem and only copying it on an immense scale of enlargement in stone. Hence the form and the material are out of accord, and the effect of the corpulent Egyptian column is that of a gigantic and overgrown baby. The most effective part of the Egyptian temple is after all the pylon, for this, though crude enough, is in its frontal aspect a sort of crystallization of the vertical cliffs bounding the Nile valley, that form the background of every Egyptian landscape. Similarly, the obelisk is the crystallization of the upright unwrought stone or menhir. As such the pylon and obelisk come more or less into line with the pyramid and Mastaba of the Old Empire, which are crystallizations of the mound or tumulus, the most natural and most primitive funeral monument."

**Black history Extravaganza - Photo -** Karnak Men who hold the keys to the Great Temple of Amon-Ra.

# BLACK HISTORY EXTRAVAGANZA HONORING DR. BEN-JOCHANNAN

Equally too, since the temple was a fortress for the god-force dwelling within, it had to be equipped with all manner of protective, nurturing, decorative, ritualistic and service paraphernalia to lure the god and to make him feel comfortable at home, nurtured, satisfied, worshipped to provide resulting beneficence. As such then, temple architecture came to represent all that was good within the society and hence it was endowed with elaborate ritual, the buildings exhibiting lavish wealth fueled by the successes of imperial warrior pharaohs whose New Kingdom exploits bequeathed enormous riches to the society and temples.

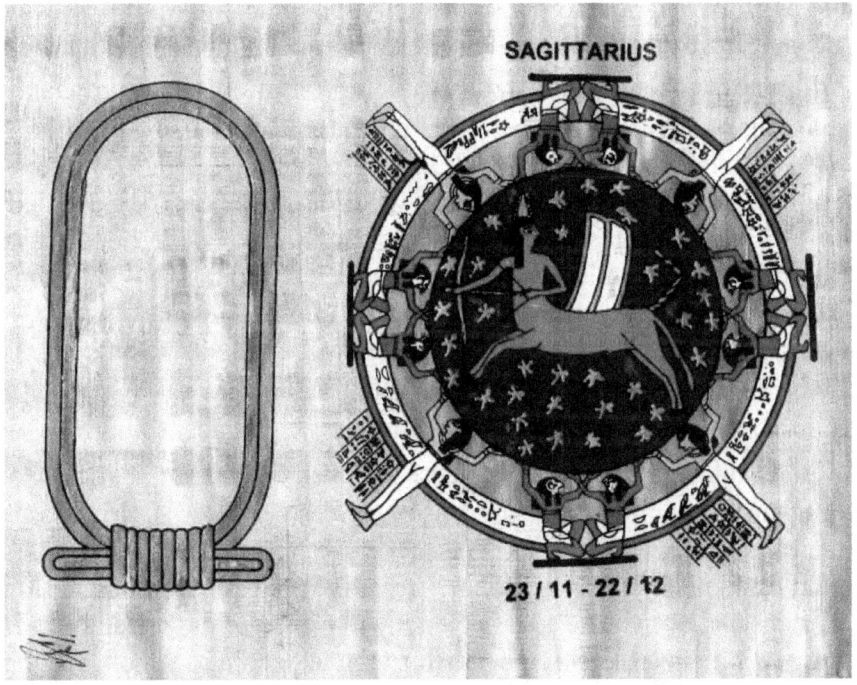

**Black History Extravaganza - Papyrus -** A Blank Cartouche with the Astrological sign for Sagittarius.

In explaining this phenomenon of how religious beliefs influenced architectural developed intermixed with mortuary practice, one example is provided by James Henry Breasted in *The Dawn of Conscience*, (New York: Charles Scribner's Sons, 1934: 57) offered in this respect, wherein the "Pyramid tomb was a solar symbol of the highest sacredness rising above the mortal remains of the king to greet the sun who's offspring the pharaoh was." These accomplishments rested upon Old Kingdom foundations, philosophical and practical, evolved from architectural experimental and representation dating back to the earliest times of philosophic and theological emergence as man's artistic and architectural consciousness formed and became crystallized finally in stone.

Therefore, while the culture created and could boast of domestic, civil, religious and mortuary, even military structures, architecture thus came to embody not simply the quarried stone for the building endowed by pharaoh to house the deity, but much more. It possessed a magical, mystical, esoterically metaphysical significance that was brilliant in its conception and execution. In its multi-faceted dynamic religious and philosophic belief, temple architecture came to embody one or more outstanding and artistic features as an Avenue of Sphinxes, gates, pylons, propylon, with flagstaves and flags, an axis or two, enclosure walls, forecourts and inner courts, doorways, portals, stelae, walls, doors, colonnades, columns, stone drums, capitals, architraves, pavements, floors, shrines, statues, kiosks, a sacred lake, obelisks, decorations, gardens, trees, halls, chambers, the "Holy of Holies" or Sanctuary, altars, Sacred Lakes, gardens, Nilometers, sphinxes, standards, libation vases, incense-burners, as well as animals, viz., - cattle, geese, chickens, pigs, horses, donkeys, lions and the implements used by the priests, stewards, priestesses, their kitchens, vine cellars, crypts, bakers, confectioners, store houses, gold and other precious stones, treasury, a library, craftsmanship, gardens and even more as reflected in the wealth of the priesthood. To this we may add industrial crafts for temple decoration and trade that encouraged flourishing and competing schools of arts and crafts that produced jewelry and other statuary masterpieces. Land holding was an important part of temple wealth. Most temples were considered a "House of Life" that doubled as schools, practiced medicine and served as "Service Centers" for persons in need of literary documents as letters, wills, and other correspondence.

# BLACK HISTORY EXTRAVAGANZA HONORING DR. BEN-JOCHANNAN

**Black History Extravaganza - Photo -** The Pronaos of Horus Temple at Edfu with one surviving hawk at the forefront. There, at the Court's edge, screened column provide entrance to the Hypostyle Hall. Again, notice, the columns have different capitals.

Thus, the architecture of Egypt was not simply symbolic but also alive, for it fed upon and fed multitudes; or should we say, it fueled social systems engaged in the protection, nurturing, worshipping, and ritualizing of the deity on a daily and repetitious basis. Ritual, magic and decoration went hand-in-hand. The "Overseer of the Works," the ritualist and master mason and decorator, all cooperated to give life to their building projects. Maspero has pointed out, at Deir el Bahari, a ceremony was performed with white sand laid out covering the intended temple space; sacrificial animals killed and the blood let to run; in addition to which tools bearing the name of the founder, perhaps in a cartouche, was placed there; offerings were made; the breaking of statues at the site of erection; that were all part of blessing and providing protection for the temple embodied in the foundation that marked the beginning of construction that represented the "guiding light" of divine seed-germ encouraged to come and bless the structure's contemplation to provide the spark of philosophic and spiritual protection. Thus, before and after completion, the builder

# FREDERICK MONDERSON

consecrated the living home of the deity. Equally, as in the decoration of tombs, magic was utilized and enabled to give life to what was represented in its spiritual, mystical and art and architectural wholesomeness.

Now, to understand the path through the social and politico-religious system just sketched we must trace the architecture of Egypt from the prehistoric beginnings through the early kingly burials at Abydos as well as the fortresses there at the beginning of the dynastic period; the Memphis "white wall;" seek to understand the emergence and significance of the dynamic Step-Pyramid of Zoser; follow the evolution of Snefru's "bent" and "red" pyramids, and the next stage in the "true pyramid" at Ghizeh, necessitating the expanded "pyramid complex" concept concurrent with the sun temples of the fifth dynasty; linked by the Middle Kingdom temple at Deir el Bahari transmitting to arrive at New Kingdom struggles and in imitating the early art forms and finally Graeco-Roman architecture trailblazing that still sought to and looked back in imitative fashion and thus helped preserve much of the earliest ides embodied in these structures. Some scholars have argued the pyramid originated in Nubia in the form of silt and more anciently "natural wind shaped pyramids." Several of these latter can be seen at Abu Simbel and along the road to and therefrom. Nonetheless, it was argued, "There are more pyramids in Nubia than in Egypt itself."

# BLACK HISTORY EXTRAVAGANZA HONORING DR. BEN-JOCHANNAN

**Black History Extravaganza - Photo -** Security Chief (red shirt) Handaka and a Friend in the Open-Air Museum at Karnak Temple of Amon-Ra.

By the New Kingdom, principally three types of temples were in use, the god or worship temple such as at Karnak and Luxor; the mortuary temple or "Mansion of Millions of Years," as that of Hatshepsut's at Deir el Bahari, the Ramesseum and Medinet Habu of Rameses II and Rameses III respectively. The west bank, "land of the dead," an architectural reservoir, was decorated with mortuary temples of practically all the New Kingdom pharaohs. Unfortunately, the principal surviving temples today's tourists visit, Deir el Bahari, Ramesseum of Rameses II, Medinet Habu of Rameses III, Seti I's temple at Gurneh, and even the temple of Merenptah, that is now closed, are interesting ones that have withstood the ravages of time and man. In addition, there was the processional temple, such as the Middle Kingdom "White Chapel" of Sesostris I, reassembled and now in the Karnak Open Air Museum; there also is to be found Hatshepsut's "Red Chapel," both were profusely decorated representing masterpieces of art and architecture constructed by individual pharaohs. There were others such as kiosks, chapels, speos,

# FREDERICK MONDERSON

grottos, etc. This processional temple or Kiosk, was designed as a resting place to house the god, manifest in his statue, when he left his main sanctuary generally in procession as part of some festival celebration. Surviving Kiosks to the Theban Triad as in the Great Court at Karnak and in the "Ramessean Front" at Luxor Temple are other forms of processional temples for worship of the deity outdoors and away from the sanctuary. However, the Kiosk at Abydos, dedicated to Isis, Horus and Seti I are within the temple and near the Sanctuary in the Osirian complex at Abydos as opposed to others in the "open air." Note the Karnak and Luxor Kiosks are outdoor and dedicated to the Theban Triad of Amon, Mut and Khonsu. On the other hand, the Abydos Kiosk is dedicated to Osiris, Isis and Seti I, the king deified!

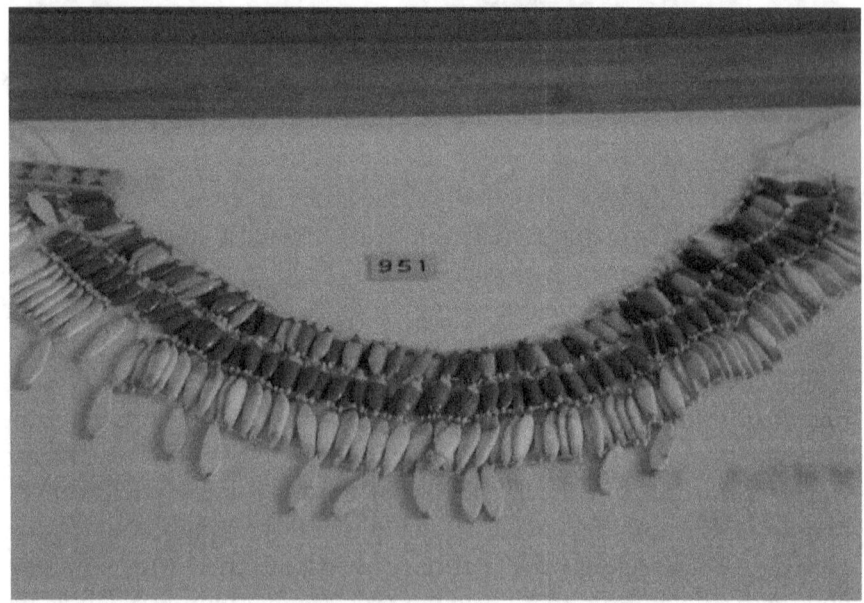

**Black History Extravaganza - Cairo Museum** - Multi-colored precious stone Necklace.

# BLACK HISTORY EXTRAVAGANZA HONORING DR. BEN-JOCHANNAN

**Black History Extravaganza - Photo -** Jewelry in the form of rings and bracelets.

# FREDERICK MONDERSON

Recognizing the timelessness of this great science, architecture in ancient Egypt has thus been of several forms. However, while the society created domestic, civic, military, and religious and mortuary forms, this paper will focus primarily on religious, mortuary and tomb architecture. In "The Sources and Growth of Architecture in Egypt," *Journal of the Institute of British Architects* (Vol. III, Third Series, 1901: 340) W.M. Flinders Petrie, in his article proposed to show the transformative use of "new material to shape the evolution of building." He states: "The use of wrought materials, and the form which result from such; then the use of wrought wood; of stone, rough and lastly, the development of the pillars." In this he further elaborates: "The unwrought materials, which were everywhere at hand in Egypt, were palm-ribs, papyrus, reeds, maize stalks, and mud, together with palm-fiber roughly twisted. At the present day a native sets-up a row of maize stalks for a fence, binding them by weaving some stalks in and out in opposite directions along the upper part. Needing a closer lien for shelter, he places the stalks touching, and lashes on some cross stalks by means of palm string. This stage is seen in an enclosure in a scene on the great mace head of Narmer (4800 B.C.). To keep out the wind this wall of stalks is plastered with mud, and so a hut is formed." Even more, "A striking sight of the beginnings may be seen any day in a nomad settlement on the desert edge. Side by side stand (1) a black goat-hair Arab tent, long and low, open always on the leeward side; (2) a tent fenced along part of the open side with a row of maize stalks; (3) a tent fenced all round with maize; (4) a tent in a maize fence mud-plastered; (5) a dwarf wall of brick round the fence; (6) a high brick enclosure with a tent inside to roof it, the tent ropes stretching out through the wall; lastly, a roof is put on the wall, and the tent has disappeared."

# BLACK HISTORY EXTRAVAGANZA HONORING DR. BEN-JOCHANNAN

**Black History Extravaganza - Photo -** Wearing the Double Crown himself, a defaced image of Pharaoh presents crowns, Red (left) and White (right).

Thus, from the earliest period, architects began using the simplest materials such as leaves and branches for windbreaks; they added Nile mud, using leaves to create a strengthened mud and daub to build the earliest structures. Then they graduated to brick, un-burnt and burnt types. Later, as quarrying and river transportation methods developed and advanced, they began using stone transported from great distances to place of erection. The first stone use has been dated to the tomb of King Den of the First Dynasty and King Khasekhemwy of the Second Dynasty. This material, nonetheless, came into very general use by the Third and Fourth Dynasties.

# FREDERICK MONDERSON

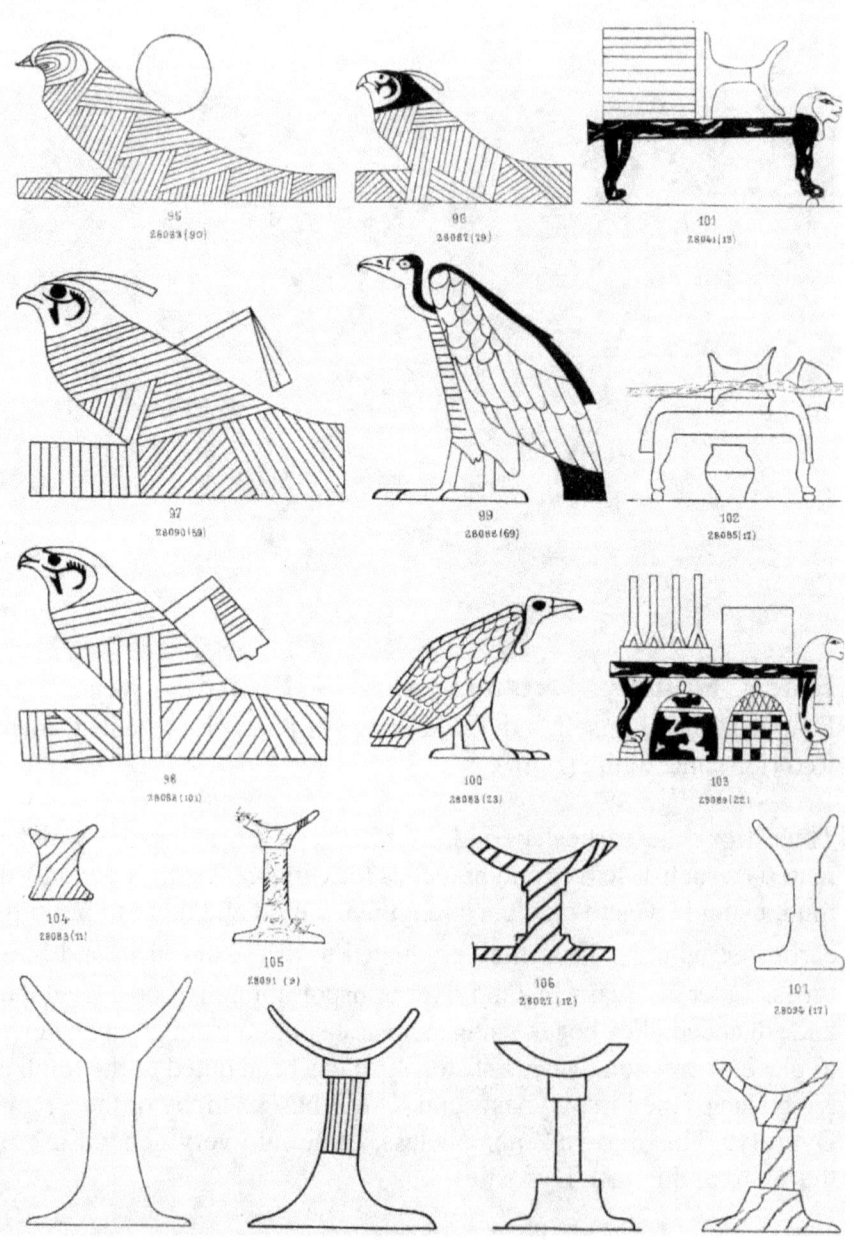

**Black History Extravaganza - Line Drawing -** Vultures, hawks and head-rests.

# BLACK HISTORY EXTRAVAGANZA HONORING DR. BEN-JOCHANNAN

Now for the types of structures they erected, like all builders, the Egyptian was concerned with the location of his building and how it blended with the environment. In every age, as the nature of building construction changed in its evolution, different challenges faced the architect. The massive pyramid required a different foundation, special orientation than a New Kingdom temple or tomb. Nonetheless, whatever the type of building, the design was harmonized with the landscape. For the pyramids, the expansive area as in a desert surrounding was cleared to the bare rock and the dimensions set out before building commenced.

**Black History Extravaganza - Photo -** Oh, to be backed by a pretty Lady as one faces the future.

But there were other issues regarding these constructions. Henri Stirlin's edited *Architecture of the World: Egypt* (ND: 131) has indicated: "The Egyptian builders considered the problems of organization of work, economy and speedy construction to be of greater importance than questions of mechanics and technical progress, the use of tough materials or more effective tools, or a quest for a more lasting, lighter form of structure." However, while such problems were refined through the ages and with continued practice, no significant changes in construction techniques were made until the XXVth Ethiopian and XXVIth Saite Dynasties and the later Graeco-Roman Periods. These changes included "arch vaults, and improved methods of pre-planning foundations and stone-work." Equally, foundations varied according to size of building, wall or even obelisk and according to soil they were erected upon. Sterling (137) again comments: "The general principle was to dig a trench a little wider than the wall to be supported and to line the bottom of it with a thin covering of sand which was stopped from running away by little side walls made of brick. The real foundations were laid in these trenches: stones for the main walls, bricks for the less weighty features. The empty spaces were afterwards filled up with sand." To give an example, to construct walls at Medinet Habu 34 ½ feet wide and 60 feet high, they dug 10 feet deep in the clay's soil. Equally too, at Karnak some foundations as the $8^{th}$ Pylon, built on clay, were 10 feet deep. On the other hand, at Deir el Bahari in the firmer soil beside the mountain, some walls had a foundation of 20 inches.

Still, they never misused materials. Even more, Sterling (137) demonstrates: "The actual foundations were often composed of seemingly inadequate materials: small stones, sometimes set edgeways below a first course of large blocks placed lengthways or various elements taken from earlier ruined monuments. Huge squared blocks and drums or half drums of columns were set side by side, caving between them empty spaces unfilled by mortar. This motley collection of masonry frequently shifted ground causing fractures in the lower courses." Significantly, however: "From the twenty-fifth dynasty onwards, and especially during the Ptolemaic period, greater care was taken with regard to foundations: the great temples of later periods were built on proper platforms formed of several layers - up to nine or ten - of well-dressed slabs."

In addition, transportation of stone from distant quarries took place primarily during the Inundation period when the river was high and thus, water made the stone more manageable and these sites more easily accessible. Flat bottom boats were generally used. Deir el Bahari temple has a surviving illustration showing two obelisks being

# BLACK HISTORY EXTRAVAGANZA HONORING DR. BEN-JOCHANNAN

transported on these boats drawn by smaller tugs. Lighting also played an important part in their buildings and the **Clerestory** window became an important feature in the New Kingdom temples at Karnak, the Ramesseum and Medinet Habu. The *Akh Menu* Festival Temple of Thutmose III at Karnak seems to have the earliest form of the clerestory idea. The Processional Colonnade with the nave higher than the flanking areas allowed light into the Hypostyle Hall's temple space. Equally too, roofing and ceilings varied according to temple. Some temples had windows generally a part of the Clerestory on the elevated Processional Colonnade, while others did not. Of course, mathematics was an essential part of their construction methods and techniques. Egyptian geometry as applied to architecture was key. They used primarily the simplest materials, which perished early, the palaces of kings were made of simple materials, primarily clay and mud-brick. However, the temples of the gods and burial places of the kings were reinforced with stone. Civil projects, to the extent that they were in pivotal places such as gateways, wharves for landing craft, public buildings, etc., all utilized stone.

Military fortifications were built to garrison forces stationed particularly in foreign lands. Nevertheless, some of the oldest such ruins are found at Abydos and date to the beginning of dynastic times. Here too, in this city, some of the earliest tombs were built for pharaohs of the First and Second Dynasties. Petrie discovered "Ten Temples at Abydos" dating back to the beginning of dynastic rule. These earliest and budding architecture experiments certainly reflected high quality craftsmanship whose efforts withstood time and the elements and left evidence of their existence and techniques of building.

# FREDERICK MONDERSON

**Black History Extravaganza - Papyrus -** Painted image of the Sphinx with Ghizeh's three pyramids in the Background.

Religious architecture included pyramids, mastabas, temples and later rock-cut tombs. There were god or worship temples, mortuary temples, kiosks or processional temples as well as chapels. Alexander M. Badawy in the article "Egypt" in *Dictionary of Art* (Edited by Bernard S. Myers) (London, 1969: 329) in discussing the cult temple, states the god or cult temple and the king or mortuary temple were the most important religious structures. Of the two, the god or worship temple was still more important. He writes: "The temple is the 'castle of the god' who was embodied in the small cult statue of gilded wood set within a naos (shrine). The representative temple as exemplified by those built by Rameses II and Rameses III at Karnak is laid out symmetrically along a longitudinal axis. Its tripartite plan (the three transverse parts) consist of (1) a pylon (monumental two-towered gateway); (2) a courtyard, usually having columned porticoes on one or more sides; (3) a hypostyle columned hall with a central nave, bordered by tall columns and flanked by two lower aisles; and (4) at the rear a Sanctuary with a naos and several subsidiary chambers. The levels of the floors of the various parts are higher towards the rear

# BLACK HISTORY EXTRAVAGANZA HONORING DR. BEN-JOCHANNAN

while their ceilings become correspondingly lower. This gradual reduction in the height of the apartments, combined with a reduction in the lighting, tends to impress the worshipper with the hallowed mystery of the Sanctuary." Even further, Badawy (1969: 329) continued: "All the walls and columns are usually of stone, carved and painted with scenes and hieroglyphs related to the ritual performed in the various rooms. The layout conforms to the system of harmonic design that controls the growth of the structure by accretion whereby the later courtyards and pylons added in front are larger than the earlier ones according to set proportions."

**Black History Extravaganza - Ceramic Art -** The Great bird, emblem of Amon (Amon-Ra) in Flight.

More mortuary than religious, were tombs to house the bodies of kings, queens, nobles and artisans. It gained the name "eternal house" because, according to belief, the deceased hoped to spend eternity in this structure. That is, after the Judgment before Osiris, ruler of the Underworld. As early as Predynastic times, poor people were generally buried in sand-pits where the dry soil accomplished natural mummification quickly and easily and this phenomenon helped reinforce the concept of immortality and led to the development of the practice of mummification as a practical aspiration of the dead. However, during the Old Kingdom the pyramid combined mortuary and religious structures. The Mastaba tomb became more mortuary and social as its decoration depicted the owner's status and sometimes daily activities. Some of these were very elaborate with large rooms with lots of decorative scenes providing great usefulness to scholars helping to provide descriptions of the social and cultural landscape. As an important architectural construction, Mentuhotep II's temple and pyramid at Deir el Bahari is the best example of surviving Middle Kingdom temple architecture that provided transitional building techniques and decorations from the Old to the New Kingdom. This structure comprised a pyramid on a raised platform reached by ramps and a Peristyle Court and Hypostyle Hall with many pillars and columns as well as burial spaces dug into the mountain.

**Black History Extravaganza - Photo -** Pectoral of Rameses II depicting vulture Goddess Nekhbet and Cobra Goddess Wadjit, the "Two Ladies" title of the King, mounted by a hawk or falcon with outstretched wings, holding Shen rings in both talons.

# BLACK HISTORY EXTRAVAGANZA HONORING DR. BEN-JOCHANNAN

In "The Beginning of the Egyptian Style of Architecture" Professor Sir Martin Conway in *Journal of the Royal Institute of British Architects* Vol. X, Third Series, London: 1903: 373) explained essentially, the Egyptian style of architecture "appears to have arisen about the time of the Fourth Dynasty, and to have rapidly developed during the Fifth. The elements of which it was composed, or from which it was derived, existed earlier, but not till the Fourth Dynasty were they definitely compounded into an architectural style applicable, and thenceforth continually applied, to buildings in stone."

There is "evidence that the palaces and doubtless most other buildings of the early dynastic period were built of crude brick, and that the architecture of that time was an architecture of mud and reeds, not of stone, still less of wood. The characteristic feature of exteriors was the rectangular niche - niches within niches. The supports were bundles of reeds, or clustered bundles, plastered over with mud and modelled above, for capital, into the likeness of buds or flowers. It would be easy to construct imaginary restorations of such buildings, but they would not carry us further that our bare statements carry us."

**Black History Extravaganza - Photo -** Standing behind the king, this queen wears a necklace and holds a sistrum with the head of Hathor.

Even further, Sir Conway continued: "Thus far we have obtained no information whatever as to the origin of Egyptian stone-architecture.

# FREDERICK MONDERSON

Of the beginnings of stone building Professor Petrie has already told us the important facts. He has actually revealed a granite pavement in a chamber of the tomb of the First Dynasty king, Den, but so far was that from being an architectural feature that it was actually covered over by a layer of mud-bricks. He has further brought to light the first known chamber built of stone, which is that of King Khasekhemui, of the Second Dynasty.... All this, however, is mere building, not architecture. The same statement is true of the Step-Pyramid of Sakkara, which dates from the Third Dynasty. That is built of stone, but if it ever possessed any architectural features no trace of them has survived. It contained indeed a chamber covered with glazed tiles, a decoration no doubt adopted from contemporary crude-brick buildings, which, like similar buildings in Chaldea, would naturally be so decorated by people who knew the art of glazing; but such flat wall decoration, without division of areas of any special adaptation to the chamber, is no more an architectural feature than so much wall-paper would be. The decoration can, of course, be made an architectural feature - as it was in Persia - but the tile decoration of the third pyramid chamber is not in any sense architectural. The lesson of the Meydum pyramid and its adjacent chapel is the same. The masonry is better; the pyramid approaches without actually reaching the developed type, but it is in no sense a work of architecture."

**Black History Extravaganza - Cairo Museum -** Tutankhamon's Canopic Jars of alabaster.

# BLACK HISTORY EXTRAVAGANZA HONORING DR. BEN-JOCHANNAN

**Black History Extravaganza - Photo -** At a funeral with a wailing woman and other professional mourners, priests carry the image of Anubis, god of the dead.

In the evolution of mortuary architecture, internment changed from the Old Kingdom pyramids and mastabas for kings and queens to tombs for high officials and nobles so that by the New Kingdom, for security reasons, Thutmose I chose to move from the burial on the plains to begin hidden burials in the Valley of the Kings at Thebes. By the middle of the $20^{th}$ Century of our era, a total of some 65 tombs had been found hidden in this select burial place. Today that number has increased and the number of Noble tombs discovered have also increased. "The dig continues." However, on the principle of the kings' internment, there was a separate burial place for other important individuals such as the Valley of the Queens, Valley of the Nobles, even Valley of the Artisans. Archaeology has revealed a great deal of the nation's cultural history is preserved in the painting of these tombs, though much has been desecrated and destroyed. The last is most important, for, though the artisans built for kings, queens and nobles, they used the same techniques and decoration practices to embellish their final resting places. More important, however; imperial military adventure and the allure of captured wealth not only

# FREDERICK MONDERSON

attracted many to the call but the reward was great and much of the riches went into temple and tomb construction and decoration.

Every part, feature, utility or location of a type of architecture had its own peculiarity, whether the foundation, floor, ceiling, walls, description of the ritual, decoration, quarrying, transportation, each had its own character. However, some have argued, as the society progressed from the Old on through the Middle and New Kingdom, as the society got wealthier, temple size increased. Thus, as temple size increased, so Pylon size also increased outward from the "Holy of Holies" while in the reversed conception and configuration, particularly for temples oriented east to west, path of the Sun-God, pylon apertures decreased allowing less light to shine backwards as the sun sank beyond the Western mountains at day's end. At this juncture the Sun enters the realm of the afterlife where ultimately it enters the kingdom of Osiris. Flower gardens and vines for grapes as well as other plant forms were cultivated in some temples or just beyond their walls enhancing the beauty of the architectural layout while these gardens produced flowers to supply the daily temple ritual. There were other gardens that provided the victuals of consumption for the priestly class and workers assigned to the temple.

**Black History Extravaganza - Photo -** While the Queen stands behind him holding a Sistrum, symbol of Hathor, Pharaoh presents Crowns, Red (left) and White (right) to Horus in Double Crown as Ra-Horakhty.

# BLACK HISTORY EXTRAVAGANZA HONORING DR. BEN-JOCHANNAN

Now let us briefly sketch the history or evolution of building practice from the earliest times. Let us begin with Memphis.

**1. Memphis - The White Wall -** At unification, Narmer or Menes diverted the Nile River near Memphis, and created a plain of dry land where he founded his administrative and capital city. He built around it an Enclosure Wall, then painted it and hence the title "white wall." This was the first significant civic construction in ancient Egypt. However, it is interesting, Professor Sir Martin Conway in "The Beginning of Egyptian Style of Architecture" in *Journal of the Royal Institute of British Architects*, (November 1902-October 1903) Vol X, Third Series, does not consider this an "architectural construction." In fact, he says regarding the topic, "That style appears to have arisen about the time of the Fourth Dynasty, and to have rapidly developed during the Fifth. The elements from which it was composed or from which it was derived, existed earlier but not till the Fourth Dynasty were they definitely compounded into the architectural style applicable, and thenceforth continually applied, to building in stone." Nevertheless, in this new capital, Narmer built a temple and established the worship of the God Ptah. While this "white wall" structure has generally disappeared, it noticeably remains in literature and mythology.

In these architectural beginnings, Badawy (1969: 329) notes: "The embryo of the cult temple can be recognized in the tripartite plan of the archaic shrine of Khentiamentiu at Abydos. The strictly symmetrical plan of the cult temple is projected at right angles to the river bank. Its walls and columns are covered with religious scenes in low relief, stuccoed and painted to offer visual instruction to the illiterate masses. Cult temples grew by accretion, attained extensive proportions at Thebes. Most of the structures were built on top of earlier remains or on hallowed ground."

# FREDERICK MONDERSON

**2.  Step-Pyramid of Zoser -** By constructing the Step-Pyramid for the Third Dynasty King Zoser at Sakkara, Imhotep stands large at the beginning of Egyptian building/architectural history, and for that matter in world architectural construction history.  This structure was the first significant building utilizing stone as well as containing a number of new features including the colonnade, standing and engaged columns, the Enclosure Wall, false entrances, cobra friezes, glazed tiles, multi-story construction, great court, "dummy buildings," a temple for worship, buildings symbolic of his role as King of Upper and Lower Egypt, and a court for running the Heb Sed race; etc.  Much of this, still stands 4,600 years later which says something about this earliest form of construction/building techniques as well as its builder. Certainly along the way, some of these decorative features earn the designation of architecture for this building practice. Imhotep was more than an architect; he is considered the world's first multi-genius.  He was an astronomer, mathematician, priest, medical doctor, administrator as Grand Vizier and poet. He has been credited with the saying of the ages: "Eat, drink and be merry, for tomorrow you die." His tomb, thought to be in the Sakkara area, has never been found.  For his medical prowess, he was later deified as a god of medicine and praised by the Greeks in their "Hippocratic Oath," as the personage Aesculapius.  This Step-Pyramid, of which there were several represented the earliest multi-tiered structure in history and while other large buildings have disappeared these buildings remain; some revealed others are still buried.

**Black History extravaganza - Photo -** Part of the audience who came to be with Dr. Ben during the Viewing.

# BLACK HISTORY EXTRAVAGANZA HONORING DR. BEN-JOCHANNAN

**Black History Extravaganza - Papyrus -** Another Blank Cartouche beside an Astrological sign of Gemini.

**3.     Snefru's Bent-Pyramid -** Snefru, the last king of the Third Dynasty or first king of the Fourth Dynasty built two pyramids and experimented with the "true pyramid." The two pyramids are the "Red Pyramid" and the "Bent Pyramid." The "Bent Pyramid" "collapsed," or so it is thought, but it set the stage for his son Khufu in the Fourth Dynasty to accomplish the "true pyramid at Ghizeh." Rather than ending the Third Dynasty, Snefru also gets credit for beginning the Fourth Dynasty, though in fact the Third and Fourth Dynasties should be fused. It needs be pointed out and reiterated; the idea of the pyramids probably finds its prototype in the natural pyramids carved in the sand-blown highlands of which some are seen at or on way to Abu Simbel temple in the south of Egypt. There are also pyramids in Nubia that are as numerous as those in Egypt.

# FREDERICK MONDERSON

**Black History Extravaganza - Photo -** Horus as Ra-Horakhty wearing the Double Crown stands within a shrine and enclosed by ("Two Ladies), a hawk wearing sun-disk and vulture wearing the Osiris Crown and holding a whip.

4. **The True Pyramid at Ghizeh -** The "True Pyramid" is the highlight of the "Pyramid Age" of the Old Kingdom. Built to harness the unemployed population at inundation time, as a final resting place for the pharaoh and to awe his contemporaries, it is a masterpiece of architectural accomplishment, building technique of great exactness and administrative organization and manpower utilized in its construction. Having withstood time, it continues to awe, inspire and amaze attesting to the ingenuity of ancient African architectural creativity so early in time. Some have argued it still radiates philosophic, mystical, spiritual, theosophical, epistemological and metaphysical power. It is truly an amazing work of architectural construction. The author of *A Search in Secret Egypt*, Dr. Paul Brunton, a mystic, spent the night in the Great Pyramid and reported on the spirit and manifestations of ancient Egyptians still resident in the monument who admonished him to live life as if to "bring good into the world" as Maulana Karenga, creator of Kwanza, has himself admonished!

# BLACK HISTORY EXTRAVAGANZA HONORING DR. BEN-JOCHANNAN

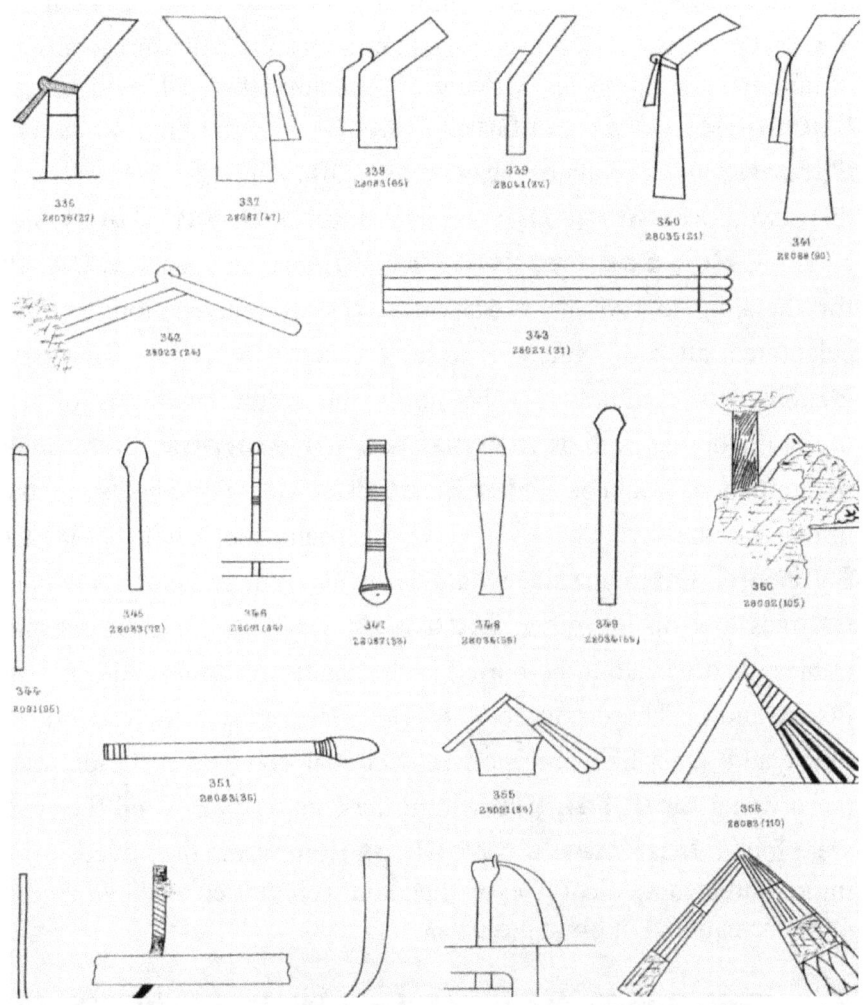

**Black History Extravaganza - Line Drawing -** Whips, scepters and other pharaonic iconography and paraphernalia.

**5.     The Pyramid Complex -** When we see the Pyramids, say of Ghizeh, in pictures or from a distance, the only things visible are "three triangles against the horizon" and the inner workings and juxtapositioning of the architectural layout is seldom considered. The

Pyramid was housed in a complex, a sort of "mortuary village." As such, the **Pyramid Complex** consists of an **Enclosure Wall** surrounding the entire complex, with an entrance often camouflaged; a **Causeway** or walkway into the structure; and a **Valley Temple** where the deceased is first introduced into the surroundings of his final resting place. Moving further along this path evident is a **Sacrificial Altar** and **Sun Temple** with the king's massive **Pyramid** in the center of the complex. Off to the right or thereabout there would be **Magazines** for storage, a **Great Court** and equally a **Heb-Sed Festival Pavilion** and an open area **Court** for the king to run the **Heb-Sed** race of rejuvenation, at first celebrated after 30 years of rule. There would be "**Dummy Buildings**" symbolizing the north and south kingdoms of his unified nation as well as **magazines for storage**. Before the pyramid there would be **Solar Boat Pits** with buried boats to ferry him across the sky. There were five pits found near Khufu's **Great Pyramid**. Off to one side would be smaller pyramids for his female relatives and on the other, **Mastaba Tombs** for officials and nobles, who wished to be buried in the shadow of their god-kings in his pyramid. These courtiers' **Mastaba** tombs were laid out in block and street-like precision in sectional cemeteries. Oftentimes there was a **God Temple** within the complex. Beyond the wall were found **workmen's dwellings** from where they lived, were injured, treated medically, even died and were buried as they labored on those national or civic projects.

**6.     The Sun Temples of the Fifth Dynasty** - The Sun Temples of the Fifth Dynasty sought to emphasize and incorporate a temple to the god as well as one to the king. They generally had an outdoor altar where ceremonies and ritual worship of the Sun God took place in the blazing sun. Many innovative and associated features characterized this form of building layout.

# BLACK HISTORY EXTRAVAGANZA HONORING DR. BEN-JOCHANNAN

7.   **Middle Kingdom** - Mentuhotep II's Middle Kingdom temple at Deir el Bahari, the most complete and oldest surviving temple at Thebes, represented a transitional form from Old Kingdom to New Kingdom building practice. It encompassed all the elements of a **pyramid** on a **raised platform with ramp**, **colonnades**, a **Peristyle Court** of pillars and **Hypostyle Hall** with columns, and shrines or **Sanctuary** up against the face of the mountain. There were also tombs for burial of princesses discovered here though no one knows what happened to the king's body. A valley temple lay at the river's edge and this led to the temple. Along this pathway lay a tree-lined **Avenue of Sphinxes**. In the temple, a statue of the king was found wearing the **Heb Sed Festival** gear, the Red Crown of the North and his skin painted black; or as W. Stephenson Smith in *The Art and Architecture of Ancient Egypt* (1959) has indicated, Mentuhotep had "black flesh!" Presumably, given the king was found wearing the Heb Sed Festival gear with the Red Crown, there would have been a corresponding statue of him wearing the White Crown.

**Black History Extravaganza - Photo -** Rev. Daughtry among the Clergy in attendance for Dr. Ben-Jochannan at Abyssinian Baptist Church in Harlem.

# FREDERICK MONDERSON

**Black History Extravaganza - Photo -** Middle Kingdom Pectoral of a cartouche enclosed by two hawks wearing the Double Crown backed by uraei holding ankhs.

The assumption is that there was also a similar statue of him wearing the white crown and in the same attitude as the other, given the dual nature of the king as monarch of Upper and Lower Egypt. Some have written there were actually six statues. It would certainly be something if the other statues were found with Mentuhotep wearing the White Crown and painted reveal the color of that statue! This would certainly put to rest the notion of the "Red Egyptian." This falsity was, however, unlikely since he was Black!

**8.   New Kingdom -** The New Kingdom broke with the past and made a separate temple to worship the god and one for the dead king, called his "Mansion of Millions of Years." They also separated the location of their siting. The burial place was also now separated from the temple. While not absolutely so, worship temples were located on the east bank, "land of the living" and mortuary temples on the west bank, "land of the dead." One scholar believed Seti I

# BLACK HISTORY EXTRAVAGANZA HONORING DR. BEN-JOCHANNAN

conceived of the **Hypostyle Hall at Karnak** as a **Mortuary Temple** in a **Worship Temple**. Then there was a later period worship temple to Hathor on the west bank near Deir el Medina. Of course there was a third temple called **Processional**, in which the god rested when traveling away from his main sanctuary. Karnak and Luxor, the Temple of Mut and that of the War god Montu, were typical worship temples of the New Kingdom and situated on the east bank of the Nile, "land of the living," at Thebes. Practically every New Kingdom monarch built a mortuary temple to his deified self. The west bank at Thebes, therefore, was host to many such structures or "Mansions of Millions of Years." Not many have survived the ravages of time and man. The principal ones visited today are at Deir el Bahari, Ramesseum and Medinet Habu. The temple of Seti I at Gurneh has also survived, been repaired and is now open to visitors.

**Black History Extravaganza - Photo -** Image of an individual wearing the fanciful version of the Osiris Crown.

The Mortuary Temple of Seti I at Abydos dedicated to Osiris, the god of the dead, is only one of many built here at the home of the judge of the underworld. While the ritual drama of the African Judgment took

# FREDERICK MONDERSON

place in the Hall of the Double Maati at Heliopolis, here at Abydos the ritual of the death and resurrection of the god took place. Here, the God stood at the "Stairway to heaven." The main structure of this temple has survived well and has colonnades in the lower and upper Hypostyle Halls and very good colored illustrations. Some scholars have argued that Seti's temple is not simply to the God Osiris but to Seti's predecessor kings whose burial sites are not far off in the desert. This particular claim lays to rest the idea of where the kings were buried. Abydos seems to be the real site with the body while Memphis housed a cenotaph or empty tomb, though still furnished with "Goods of the Grave." It's been pointed out, Seti's Temple to Osiris faces the desert where the ancestor kings were buried and he should know more about this than moderns.

**Black History Extravaganza - Photo -** In Lion Skin and holding incenser and vessel for libation, a priest faces seated official with cone on his head, while behind him in another scene, two females sit also with cones in their heads, all before "Tables of Offerings."

Petrie found 10 successive levels of temples at Abydos dating back to the beginning of dynastic rule, where evidence of some important kings was discovered, including that of Khufu, builder of the Great

# BLACK HISTORY EXTRAVAGANZA HONORING DR. BEN-JOCHANNAN

Pyramid, who worshipped here. Perhaps there were others of perishable materials of the Prehistoric Period but none remain, only those beginning at the start of the dynastic period. Nonetheless, this temple of Seti has the best surviving illustrations in all of Egypt to this date. Though dedicated to Osiris as his principal temple with requisite inner chapels because his head was buried at Abydos. Again, and to reinforce the idea, the temple was actually a monument to the archaic kings, Dynasty One and Two, who were buried in the desert to which the central axis of the Holy Site points.

**9.    Late Period** - Architectural constructions continued into the Late Period particularly during the XXVth Ethiopian and the XXVIth Saite Dynasties. All the principal worship sites received new construction, reconstructions, repairs, endowments, embellishments, additions, etc., during this period. This attention, therefore, attests to Ethiopian and Saite concern and respect for the gods and culture. As such, building practices received new impetus especially in the XXVth Dynasty under the Ethiopians where foundations were more firmly laid out to support walls especially. The XXVIth Dynasty also experienced some of the construction techniques upgrade.

**10.    Greek and Roman Periods** - Building of Egyptian temples never finished during the Greek and Roman periods. In fact, these foreign conquerors added a significant feature of inundating the temples with inscriptions that helped retain much of the ancient ritual representing copies of even earlier times. New features also entered the illustrations in terms of how individuals were represented. At Kom Ombo we see Cleopatra's breast exposed. The Mammisi or "birth house" where the god was born was added as a new feature during Roman times. The temple of Horus at Edfu has supplied a tremendous amount of detail regarding ritual practice and decoration. Each temple had one and some had two Nilometers to measure the significant volume of the river at Inundation time.

Esna, Edfu, Kom Ombo, Dendera, Philae and Kalabsha are all surviving temples of the Greek and Roman Period built by Egyptian

# FREDERICK MONDERSON

architects along ancient specifications under foreign over-lordship. Kalabsha, however, was first built during the New Kingdom. Much of such surviving temples are built on even earlier sacred foundations taking them back to the earliest times. Certainly Edfu and Dendera are among these. Clearly there were changes in these Graeco-Roman temples with the much older ones. However, even with changes they did continue the tradition of building and ritual and worship with basically the same elements and practices.

**Black History Extravaganza - Ceramic Art -** Khepre in rather colorful composition does his job of pushing the sun as a ball.

Now let me wind down and sketch the architectural layout of the temple.

First and foremost, after conceiving and laying out the dimensions of the temple, a foundation ceremony had to be conducted to mark the conception and commencement of building of every temple. Sir

# BLACK HISTORY EXTRAVAGANZA HONORING DR. BEN-JOCHANNAN

Gaston Maspero discovered evidence of such a foundation ceremony at Deir el Bahari and another at Luxor Temple. Thus, this ceremony is a given for all major temples whether worship or mortuary. Second, every temple was given a name in its original conception. That is, not the modern name given through location or in association with the builder but given by the founder as to why he or she built it. This also applies to major projects, as for example, the reason Hatshepsut gave for erecting her obelisks at Karnak.

Thus, Karnak, Deir el Bahari, Luxor, Ramesseum, Medinet Habu, all had names and statements regarding the reason for building these temples.

**Black History Extravaganza - Photo -** Oh the beautiful Ladies, flanked by tremendously decorated yet blank cartouches with lions at their feet.

In this respect, Alexander Badawy in *A History of Egyptian Architecture: The Empire* (1968: 154-55) wrote: "The temple is usually the 'castle of god (Egyptian *hwt-netjer*), but the desert temples and the rock-cut temples are often called 'strongholds.' The mortuary temples on the western bank of Thebes or the cult temples at Soleb

(Nubia) or at Redesiya provide examples. This conception is emphasized in the text itself (Soleb) '… making for him an excellent fortress, surrounded with a great wall, whose battlements shine more than the heavens, like the great obelisks ….' The enclosure of the mortuary temple of Thutmose IV at Thebes is the 'Fortress-of-Menkheperura' and it is actually filled with captives from Kharu and Nubia. Rock temples are explicitly said to be hewn out of the cliff: Rameses II, the great specialist in rock temples, says about his small temple for his wife at Abu Simbel: '… he made (it) as his monument for the Great King's-Wife, Nefertari, beloved of Mut …, a house hewn in the mountain of Nubia, of fine, white and enduring sandstone, as an eternal work.' His father Seti I had described the work on the rock temple at Redesiya: "… that there should be made by digging in this mountain, this temple, where is Amon…."'

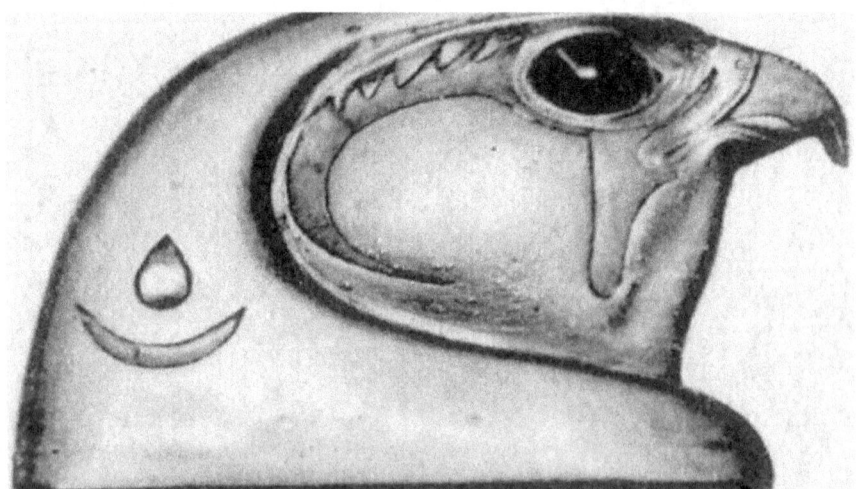

**Black History Extravaganza - Photo -** Head of Horus as a hawk, some say a Peregrine falcon.

This naming of things as in the personality of the individual was very important to the ancient Egyptian. Among the nine parts of the soul, the name was considered very important for without it the individual did not exist. In similar fashion, as Badawy states: "The temple is usually 'like heaven, beautiful, pure, glorious and excellent.' Its pylons 'reach heaven and the flagstaffs the stars of heaven.' They are 'of real cedar, wrought with Asiatic copper, their tips of electrum,

# BLACK HISTORY EXTRAVAGANZA HONORING DR. BEN-JOCHANNAN

approaching heaven.' 'Two mighty obelisks of red granite, with pyramidions of electrum, rise at the double façade of the temple.' The columns 'wrought with electrum,' usually in stone, but originally in wood. The shrines 'of sandstone, ebony or enduring granite, lined inside with electrum, or gold of the best of the hills, are placed upon a base of alabaster from Hat nub.' Doors are 'of new cedar, of the best Terraces (Lebanon), mounted in real black copper and wrought with inlaid figures in electrum or gold, representing the great name or the shadow (of the god),' 'like the luminous mountain-horizon of heaven.' The 'shadow' of the god is the representation of the deity on the copper lining of the door as if coming out of his temple. Pavements are covered with silver or gold, and offering tables are of silver, gold, bronze, or Asiatic copper. One boasts of using the 'beautiful stone of Ayan, fine white sandstone, every splendid costly stone,' or finally 'that never was done the like since the beginning.' In the description of restoration work the building is said to have been in ruin. The walls were rebuilt in stone and brick, ruined doors replaced by new ones, and wooden columns by stone ones."

**Black History Extravaganza - Photo -** Horus in a shrine under Heb while to the right, the "Prince of the City" has his face defaced, perhaps because he looks so African, Nubian, "in the Nubian or Negro mold."

# FREDERICK MONDERSON

Equally significant, when the pharaoh visited the temple there was much fanfare on the part of officials, priests, musicians, etc. The typical scene is a visit to Karnak temple, where the king's barge docked. From the Quay at the riverside the pharaoh disembarked upon arrival. In some cases, he traveled via a canal that connected the river to the temple's entrance. In others, he followed an Avenue of Sphinxes led to the First Pylon. At Karnak, for example, there were two small obelisks erected before the temple's entrance pylon, while at Luxor there were two seated statues, two regular sized obelisks and four standing statues in front of the pylon. Of the four, statues at Luxor, one standing statue remains while parts of at least two lie reassembled nearby. While the Eastern Obelisk is still in place on its pedestal, only the pedestal of the Western Obelisk remains as the shaft was given to King Louis Philippe of France in 1836. As one enters both the Luxor and Karnak temples the earliest parts are to the rear and the later parts are first encountered.

**Black History Extravaganza - Photo -** To be held by the hand of Horus is an exceptional honor.

# BLACK HISTORY EXTRAVAGANZA
# HONORING DR. BEN-JOCHANNAN

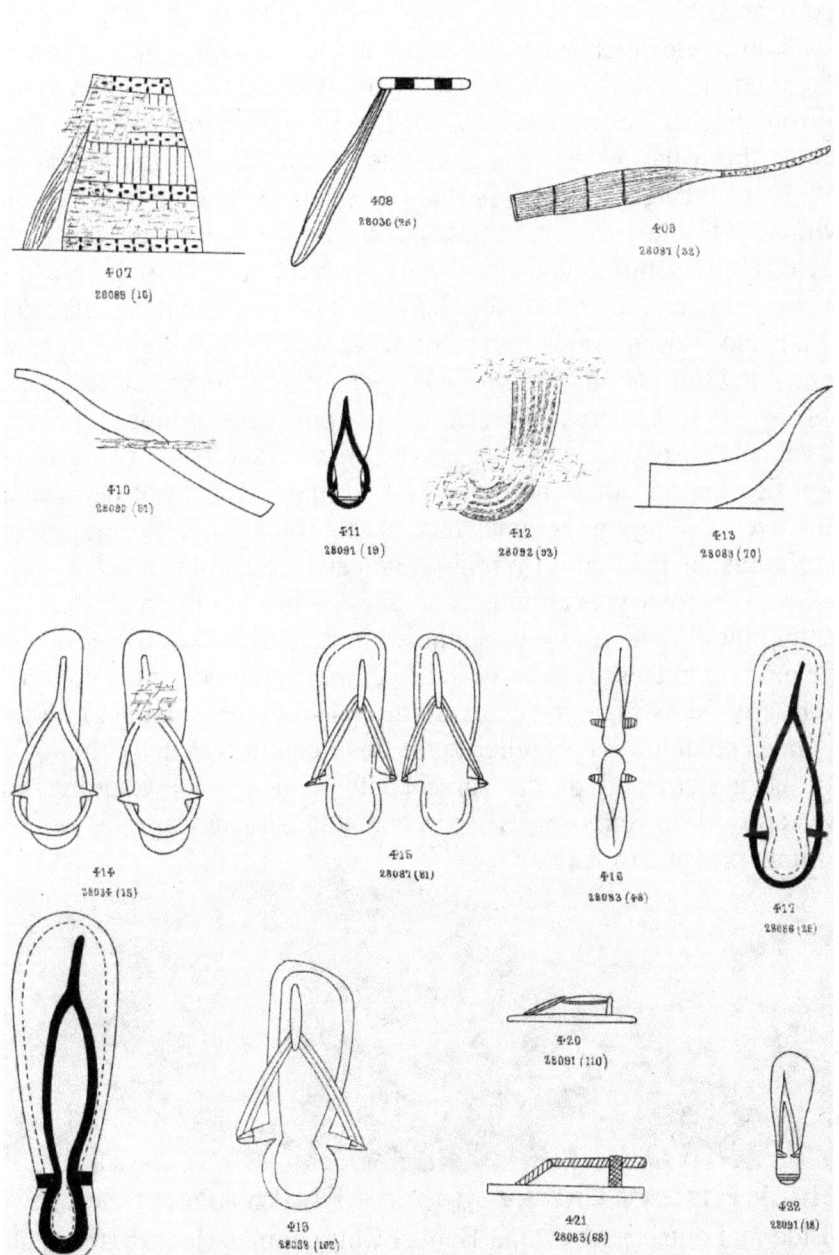

**Black History Extravaganza - Line Drawing -** Sandals.

# FREDERICK MONDERSON

At Karnak, an Avenue of Croix-sphinxes; sphinxes with rams' heads; are fronted by a miniature figure of the king between the paws; all stand on an elevated pedestal, leading to the temple's Pylon entrance. The Pylon is a massive gateway with a tower that was attached to the surrounding enclosure wall all designed to block out the temple's doings from the prying eyes and ears of outsiders. This enclosure Wall also created the fortress that protected the god and his retinue within. On the Pylon were flagstaves flying flags of the temple's divinity, the national god, the Nome and nation. Some pylons are decorated while others are not, depending on whether it was finished or not. Such decorations maybe on the broad face of the pylon as at Luxor and Edfu or on panels as at Dendera. Even though it took nearly 2000 years to construct, Karnak temple remained unfinished. Some have held, workers were called away to fight wars of national significance, and thus the pylon was unfinished and not decorated. However, resting on the inner face of the Southern half of the pylon at Karnak, a mud ramp remains indicating how the heights were scaled. The two westernmost columns of the Southern Colonnade behind the Southern row of sphinxes in the Great Court, and beside the mud ramp these remain unfinished, indicating how such columns were erected as segmented square drums and then pounded into the rounded columns to be similar to the other columns in this colonnade. At the eastern end of the same southern colonnade abutting the western wall of Rameses III's perpendicular situated temple, the last column is also unfinished.

**Black History Extravaganza - Photo -** Part of the Crowd inside and outside Abyssinia Baptist Church in Harlem, wishing Dr. Ben-Jochannan a safe and successful Transition to become one of the Revered Ancestors in the Black Pantheon of Heroes and Heroines.

# BLACK HISTORY EXTRAVAGANZA HONORING DR. BEN-JOCHANNAN

**Black History Extravaganza - Photo -** Esneh Temple of God Khnum. This photo is taken some 30 feet above at city level indicating how the land has risen through the Inundation over the centuries since the temple was built.

Beyond the Pylon is a Great Court where most noble visitors came and this was as far as they got. In such a Court, there were shrines, kiosks, an altar or two, sphinxes, statues, colonnades, and much more. At Karnak, a smaller temple of Rameses III was built in the southwest corner of the Great Court on a north-south Axis. At the northwest end of the Court there is a Kiosk to the Theban Triad, Amon, Mut and Khonsu, built by Seti II of the Nineteenth Dynasty. The remaining intact columns of Taharka, of which various numbers of ten, twelve and fourteen are given, represents this king's Kiosk in this Court. Beyond two standing statues of Rameses II, expropriated by Rameses III and others, a portico led to the Second Pylon which served as the western face of the Hypostyle Hall. Also, at Karnak, a temple that took 2000 years to build, a Processional Colonnade centered the great Hypostyle Hall conceived by Horemheb, and begun by Rameses I, built and partially decorated by Seti I and finished and decorated by Rameses II. Beyond this, another, the Third Pylon led to another Open Court. Beyond this a Fourth Pylon, actually the first such structure built at Karnak. Between the Fourth and Fifth Pylons were obelisks erected by Thutmose I. Between the Fifth and Sixth

**Black History Extravaganza - Photo -** Goddesses leads the king in Double Crown to Horus in horns, disk and feathers. Notice a miniature image of the king standing on a symbol of a united Egypt.

# BLACK HISTORY EXTRAVAGANZA HONORING DR. BEN-JOCHANNAN

Pylons, Hatshepsut erected two other obelisks. Before the smaller Sixth Pylon Thutmose III erected two pillars highlighting the emblematic papyrus and lotus symbols of the Upper and Lower Kingdoms under unification.

Thutmose III and his grand-father Thutmose I built the Sixth Pylon before the Sanctuary. With warrior pharaohs, Thutmose I and III, each placed a separate line of Osiride statues and papyrus bundle columns along this path towards the Sanctuary in an area called the Wadjit.

Unlike any other New Kingdom sanctuaries, the one at Karnak was open at the east and west ends so the sun could shine through on rising and setting. There was a Sacred Lake nearby so priests could wash themselves before officiating and the god's barge could sail here on festive occasions.

In the south-west portion of this second axis bearing a number of courts and pylons, seventh through tenth, stood the Temple of Khonsu, the third member of the Theban Triad. Its entrance Pylon was fronted by a number of recumbent lion sphinxes. An Avenue of Sphinxes led out from there. From the tenth pylon another Avenue of Sphinxes led three miles linking Karnak and Luxor temples, while still another Avenue links Karnak with the Temple of Mut his wife, the earth goddess.

**Black History Extravaganza - Photo -** Cross-section of the audience who chose to be there for Dr. Ben-Jochannan because he was there so often as a Champion of African Culture and History.

# FREDERICK MONDERSON

**Black History Extravaganza - Photo -** Husband and wife salute Ra-Horakhte and Hathor enthroned in their shrines while a "Table of Offerings" stands before the structures.

Perpendicular to the original east-west axis, four other pylons were added on a second axis linking the original temple with the god's wife Mut's temple to the south. The gods were generally shown as a family of husband, wife and son. Interestingly, on the east-west axis, the statues face the center line of the axis on the Processional Way, while on the north-south axis they face north along the path of this second axis rather than the center line of the axis on which they stand. In this national temple, called "the palaces" there were a total of some 22 temples of differing sizes to various gods and goddesses who were also worshipped at Karnak, besides the Theban Triad of Amon; Mut, his wife; and Khonsu, their son. Given that the Theban Ennead at Karnak comprised only 15 members, not every divinity had a temple there and some may have more than one or a monarch may build more than one. That is the case with Rameses III who built this miniature temple in the Great Court, the temple of Khonsu further and another in the temple of Mut. Beside Khonsu's temple, Rameses III built a temple to Osiris.

# BLACK HISTORY EXTRAVAGANZA HONORING DR. BEN-JOCHANNAN

**Black History Extravaganza - Photo -** The Great Falcon emblematic of Horus, son of Osiris and Ra-Horakhty, depending on which headdress he wears. Notice his claws.

# FREDERICK MONDERSON

East of the main Sanctuary is a Court of the Middle Kingdom with an altar and remains of pillars. Beyond this Thutmose III built his Festival Temple, the *Akh Menu*. Rameses II came by later and finished the hypostyle hall's decoration begun by his grandfather Rameses I and his father Seti I. Then he erected a "Girdle Wall" to enclose the original temple on the east-west axis running along the Sanctuary, the Middle Kingdom Court, and the *Akh Menu*. Beyond the *Akh Menu* chapel to worship Thutmose III was decorated with the "Botanical Garden." Beyond this Rameses II built the "Temple of the Open Ear." Further on, Taharka erected a second Kiosk before the Eastern Gate. Just to the north lay the treasury and further on the Temple of Ptah with the Goddess Sekhmet still *in situ*.

There are six gates or entrances to Karnak, though today as in ancient times, the most important one was on the west nearest the river, while the Eastern Gate, remains for the most part, closed.

**Black History Extravaganza - Photo -** The Gods on Duty!

# BLACK HISTORY EXTRAVAGANZA HONORING DR. BEN-JOCHANNAN

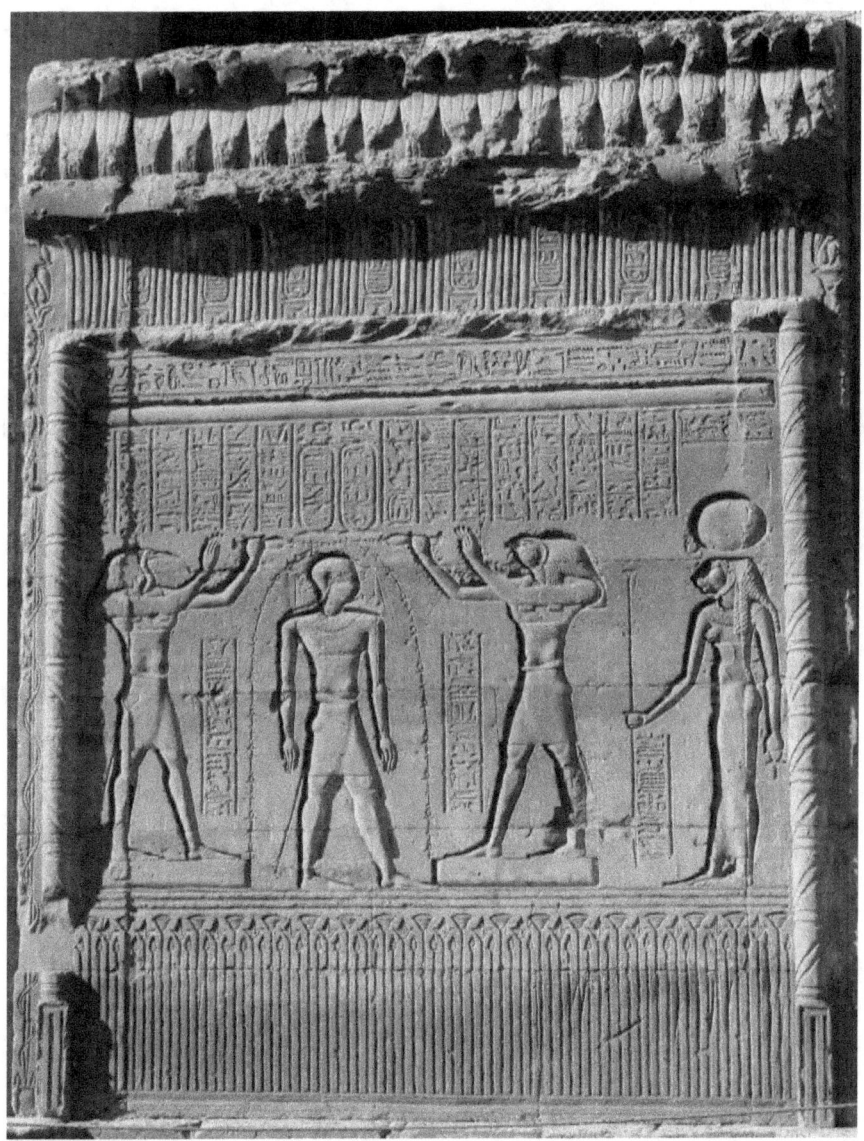

**Black History Extravaganza - Photo -** Thoth and Horus baptize the King with streams of ankhs and scepters, while Bastet looks on.

# FREDERICK MONDERSON

Columns play an important role in the religious architecture of ancient Egypt. In the colonnade represented in the Hypostyle Hall (a roofed enclosure with columns) and an open court, a Peristyle, with columns on one or more sides generally with a roofed walkway between the columns and the wall, generally called a roofed ambulatory. The columns can be decorated or plain. Beside the Sacred Lake, just nor of where Hatshepsut's broken obelisk lies, Taharka erected another of his building at Karnak. Flinders Petrie in "The Source and Growth of Architecture in Egypt" in *Journal of the Royal Institute of British Architects*, London, Vol. VIII, Third Series (1901: 349) summarizes the evolution of the Column in the following: "Columns of maize stalks bound together are commonly used in huts at present; and stalks bound and plastered with mud are the usual supports of the heavy swinging shadufs used for raising water. Hence we can understand one early form of column which shows the splaying base needful to prevent crushing, and the spread top, bound round for some way down."

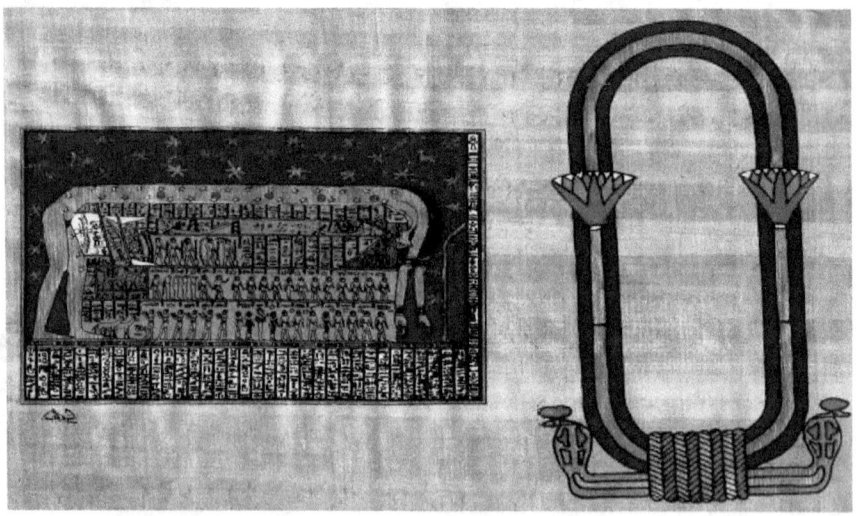

**Black History Extravaganza - Papyrus -** Goddess Nuit stretches her body across the heavens to encompass the divine drama while to the right stands a Blank Cartouche.

# BLACK HISTORY EXTRAVAGANZA HONORING DR. BEN-JOCHANNAN

"The wooden column appears as an octagon in the models found in the First Dynasty, and in the actual pieces which I have found in the Twelfth Dynasty, and the copies of such in stone at Beni Hasan."

"The fluted column is found copied in ivory in the First Dynasty tombs, and is well figured as a hieroglyph in the Fourth Dynasty."

"The most peculiar form of column is that derived from the tent-pole, as figured in the hieroglyphs. This was the origin of the strange form known as the inverted bell capital in the Eighteenth Dynasty at Karnak." These are found in Tuthmose III's *Akh Menu*, Festival Temple at Karnak, behind the Sanctuary and great Court.

**Black History Extravaganza - Photo -** A Sem Priest wearing leopard skin incenses and pours a libation on the structure carrying the mummy while wailing members of the family look in their sorrow.

"The lotus column has been discussed by M. Foucart, whose work I had the pleasure of bringing to your notice recently (*Journal of the Royal Institute of British Architects*, Vol. IV, 3$^{rd}$ series, p. 361) The

# FREDERICK MONDERSON

earliest example known is of the Fifth Dynasty (about 3600 B.C.), and shows the stems of papyrus bound together, and then decorated with lotus flowers and buds. The later examples of the Twelfth Dynasty, of the Eighteenth Dynasty, and of the Nineteenth and Twentieth Dynasties, show a series of lamentable decadence. Each age in Egypt had its special excellence. In the Eighteenth Dynasty a delicate and freely flowing ornamental treatment; in the Fifth Dynasty the finest figure sculpture; in the Fourth Dynasty the grandest constructions; and in the First Dynasty the most lavish use of hard stones for hand objects and table furniture. Diorite, porphyry, and such materials were cut in thin and beautiful forms with a familiarity which was never known in later times. But every branch of art, when once it had fully grown, decayed rapidly, and the later work in every respect cannot bear comparison with the older triumphs."

**Black History Extravaganza - Photo -** One of the Security men at the Gate of Karnak, Temple of Amon-Ra (left); and Brother Nasser, kin to Brother Abdul, brother extraordinaire.

# BLACK HISTORY EXTRAVAGANZA HONORING DR. BEN-JOCHANNAN

**Black History Extravaganza - Photo -** Woman, held in equal stature with men in this African society.

# FREDERICK MONDERSON

## XI. THE RELIGION OF ANCIENT EGYPT I
### By Dr. Fred Monderson

## I. Introduction

The Religion of Ancient Egypt is arguably the oldest on record, dating back several millennia before "Unification under Menes." This is probably before any other culture, perhaps only the Ethiopians southwards of Egypt, experienced similar early joys of sweet communion with deity. Albert Churchward dates this phenomenal experience southward along the Nile to some 300,000 years ago. This land, considered by the ancient African along the Nile as extremely sacred, became an early, perhaps the earliest, site of religious worship. The Africans of Egypt created and left a great body of religious texts, mythical narratives, hymns, rituals, and the **Pyramid Texts**, the **Coffin Texts** and the **Book of the Dead** that detail how their religious beliefs evolved over time and came to exert tremendous influence on the early consciousness of their time which essentially was the center of the crossroads of the ancient world. That is the confluence where Africa, Europe and Asia met seemed the ideal place for which the creative human mind experienced leaps and bounds in cultural excellence as divine forces molded human behavior and thought.

In this emerging relationship, Alfred Wiedemann in *The Religion of Egypt* notes, "the relationship between divinity and humanity was thought of by the inhabitants of the Nile Valley as reciprocally conditioned."

As Adolf Erman in *A Handbook of Egyptian Religion* (London: Archibald Constable and Co., Ltd., 1907: 5) indicated, sometime in this early period of consciousness: "The people had already learnt to

# BLACK HISTORY EXTRAVAGANZA HONORING DR. BEN-JOCHANNAN

carve rough figures of gods either in human or animal form and these they chose to distinguish by a variety of crowns, but as yet their imagination did not go beyond diadems formed either of handfuls of reeds, the horns of sheep or cows, or of ostrich feathers. For a scepter, their gods carried a staff such as every Bedouin cuts for himself at the present day, and their goddesses were contented with a simple reed. Their temples were mere huts with walls of plaited wicker work; the front of the roof was adorned with projecting beams. A few short posts and two high masts in front of the building were added to provide further decoration. The altar consisted of a reed mat, and for the celebration of festivals, simple bowers were erected." It is thus amazing how they built upon such an early foundation and progressed in their religious worship and religion in turn helped the society to progress.

**Black History Extravaganza - Photo -** At Esneh Temple, Khnum as a Ram with a youthful image at his rear. He offers life and duration to pharaoh in Double Crown.

In "Egyptian Religion," Hasting's *Encyclopedia of Religion and Ethics* Vol. 5, (1912: 236), Flinders Petrie explained how the land and

# FREDERICK MONDERSON

environment shaped religious belief. He wrote, under "Character of the Land," "the peculiar nature of the country reacted on the religion, as upon all other interests of man. The continuous contrast of desert and of cultivation impressed the whole Egyptian character. It produced those contrasts which seem so contradictory - a people who had the reputation of gloomy stubbornness, and who yet covered their tombs with scenes of banquets, dancing, and gaiety: a people to whom the grandeur of the tomb was one of the great objects during life. The constant presence of the dead in the cliffs and desert overlooking the scenes of their lives, or, in later times, more familiarly kept surrounding the family life in the atrium of the house, preserved a sense of continuity with the Other-world which made a far more contrasted life than we see elsewhere. As opposed other luxuriance and fatness of the rich plain, there was always visible on either hand the desert, little known, dreaded, the region of the malevolent gods, of strange monsters, of blinding, suffocating storms, of parching thirst and heat."

Even further, "Religion was thus essentially a part of politics. Fanatical fervor is the product of the political necessity of union. Small bodies, which are liable to be broken up, need a true membership, and a moral consciousness that they are in the right and their enemies are in the wrong, foul, miserable, and despicable. All this is given by a religious antipathy. The god is the rallying cry; the triumph of his followers is his triumph. Hence, the mythic victories of the gods, one over another, are the records of the victories of their worshippers; and even the marriages of the gods are in many cases the expression of the marriage of the tribes who upheld them."

**Black History Extravaganza - Photo -** Night and day!

# BLACK HISTORY EXTRAVAGANZA HONORING DR. BEN-JOCHANNAN

**Black History Extravaganza Photo -** Arrival of Queen Adelaide Sanford!

Nevertheless, and unquestionably, in as much as the Egyptians exported much of their culture, the sum total of such forms of religious expressions also influenced the manner in which other cultures evolved and participated in and enjoyed this wonderful spiritual experience. Thus, as stated previously, the nature of their environment being the Sun and Nile as two constants, enabled them to craft cosmological views that may seem strange to the modern mind but were early and "revolutionary" by the evolving contemporary standards as the world emerged from the mist of history. Again, Erman (1907: 6-7) offers the view: "Numerous are the ideas concerning the universe, and the representations by which the people attempted to express their ideas. In one of these the sky appears as an immense cow whose feet are resting on the earth. In another the sky is a woman, who supports herself with hand and feet on the earth. But the most usual representation, at least in later times, is one on where the sky is a sheet of water, on which the stars sail in boats; or again it rests on the so-called four pillars of heaven, fabulous mountains, situated at the four corners of the earth. While the sky is usually

# FREDERICK MONDERSON

regarded as being feminine, a woman, and a cow, the earth figures as a man on whose back it is that vegetation grows. Apparently the grammatical gender of the two worlds - pet, 'Sky' is feminine, to 'earth' is masculine - led to this conception.

**Black History Extravaganza - Photo -** The Great goose of Amon in majestic splendor, very colorful.

Equally too, Egyptian writing is certainly one of the oldest written forms of religious expression period. For that matter, the culture bestows on us the oldest form of writing period! Most, important, their equally oldest religious literature, discovered as it was in the pyramids remained unchanged for millennia. These enabled scholars to understand not simply Egyptian writing but also various aspects of their literature and religious "beliefs and practices" as well. After, perhaps millennia of experimentation and ultimately being codified, then housed as it was in their architecture, the "Pyramid Texts," "Coffin Texts," and even later the "Book of the Dead" these writings revealed much about their skills as religious visionaries and practitioners as well as social commentators, thinkers, and even builders whose ideas not simply challenged the society but importantly also stood the test of time as wisdom literature. Significantly, the writings discovered in the pyramids, represented a

# BLACK HISTORY EXTRAVAGANZA HONORING DR. BEN-JOCHANNAN

process of religious development that probably extended for millennia back into the past before they were codified then came to later decorate the Vth and VIth Dynasty pyramids. Thus, the evidence available for study by scholars throughout much of Egyptian history includes inscription in temples, on texts, in tombs and on monuments.

**Black History Extravaganza - Photo -** This image from Esneh Temple is interesting. It happens in a temple, evidence at left; the small figure (right) wears a leopard skin; the ankh with legs hold standards of a Ram, Isis, Falcon and Anubis figures. Below is a sun disk with feathers on a standard.

However, and particularly significant for the problems of origins, E.A. Wallis Budge in *Egyptian Religion* (1900) (1991: 18) offers an interesting caveat, while affirming: "There is no evidence whatever to guide us in formulating the theory that it was brought into Egypt by immigrants from the East." Again, Budge (1991: 18-19) continued: "All that is known is that it existed there at a period so remote that it is useless to attempt to measure by years the interval of time which has elapsed since it grew up and established itself in the minds of men, and that it is exceedingly doubtful if we shall ever have any definite knowledge on this interesting point." Even more, Budge (1991) pointed out, "But though we know nothing about the period of the origin in Egypt of the belief in the existence of an almighty God who was One, the inscriptions show us that this Being was called by a name which was something like Neter, the picture sign for which was an axe-head, made probably of stone, let into a long wooden handle." That far back in time, some scholars have argued, the Egyptians were

# FREDERICK MONDERSON

probably not very far removed from thinking as prehistoric peoples. Nevertheless, if we accept the view of science and the origins of man in Africa, this development may extend back thousands of years to underscore the emergence of religious consciousness in this part of Africa.

For argument sake, if we entertain the notion Caucasians could migrate across the desert environment from South West-Asia and find themselves in Egypt, then we can credit Africans with the capability of equally migrating from Central Africa down the Nile, given the fact they essentially lived on the river which is their home. Again, if we accept a people can cross a desert to an unknown location, it is reasonable to accept others can follow the passage of any waterway. Again, if we accept the path from South Africa to North Africa, whether through the Rift or Nile Valley we have the potential for cultural and historic migration and continuity. Now, also given *The New York Times* newspaper article of discovery of "a paint factory with red paint," dated to some 107,000 years ago that pushed "complex thinking" far into the past, beyond accepted times, we have an existential fact, with great potential for religious and other forms of knowledge, thinking and cultural creativity active in the minds of a people that is purely African, certainly isolated from the world at large and particularly "South African."

# BLACK HISTORY EXTRAVAGANZA HONORING DR. BEN-JOCHANNAN

**Black History Extravaganza - Photo -** Heavenly drama at Esneh. The blackened state is from people living in the temple and lighting fires.

Notwithstanding, bridging this gap and positing a view of earlier Egyptian religiosity, even further, Budge (1991: 23) affirmed: "As a matter of fact, we know nothing of their ideas of God before they developed sufficiently to build the monuments which we know they built, and before they possessed the religion, and civilization, and complex social systems which their writings have revealed to us ...." In this respect and in that early beginning, "the primitive god was an essential feature of the family, and the fortunes of the god varied with the fortunes of the family; the god of the city in which a man lived was regarded as the ruler of the city, and the people of that city no more thought of neglecting to provide him with what they considered to be due to his rank and position than they thought of neglecting to supply their own wants. In fact, the god of the city became the center of the social fabric of that city, and every inhabitant thereof inherited automatically certain duties, the neglect of which brought stated pains and penalties upon him." However, what we do know of the early Egyptian religion with certainty, for the most part, their earliest religious ideas are contained in their earliest writing called the "Pyramid Texts," because they were found in pyramids of the Fifth and Sixth Dynasties.

**Black History Extravaganza - Photo -** Isis (left) and Horus (right) embrace pharaoh between two Blank Cartouches.

Now, as Egyptian discoveries and scholarship unfolded, modern scholars in the 19th Century coined the name *Book of the Dead* that the ancient actually termed the *Book of Per-em-hru* or *the Book of Coming or Going Forth by Day*. As such, for convenience, the *Book of the Dead* evolved from the *Pyramid Texts* of the Old Kingdom and the *Coffin Texts* of the Middle Kingdom. In essence, these are a collection of spells that guided the soul in the afterlife and encompassed the judgment and what happened to individuals after death. In this early religious literature, the *Book of the Dead*, as Flinders Petrie (1906: 78) informs, was essentially a "Bible" of religious and spiritual and moral literary words of armament that protected the deceased on way to the Judgment, throughout that examination and dictated the nature of his existence afterwards. As

# BLACK HISTORY EXTRAVAGANZA HONORING DR. BEN-JOCHANNAN

such, he stated: "We can distinguish certain groups of chapters, an Osirian section on the kingdom of Osiris and the service of it, a theological section, a set of incantations, formulae for the restoration of the heart, for the protection of the soul from spirits and serpents in the hours of night, charms to escape from periods ordained by the gods, an account of the paradise of Osiris, a different version of the kingdom and judgment of Osiris, a Heliopolitan doctrine about the ba, and its powers of transformation entirely apart from all that is stated elsewhere, the account of the reunion of soul and body, magic formulae for entering the Osirian kingdom, another account of the judgment of Osiris, charms for the preservation of the mummy and for making efficacious amulets, together with various portions of popular beliefs." Another contemporary source in *Encyclopedia Britannica*, Vol. IX (Cambridge, England, 1910: 48) describes the Pyramid Texts as "a vast collection of incantations inscribed on the inner walls of five royal tombs of the Vth and VIth Dynasties at Sakkara, discovered and first published by Maspero. Much of these texts is of extreme antiquity; one incantation at least has been proved to belong to an age anterior to the unification of the Northern and Southern kingdoms. Later copies also exist, but possess little independent critical value. The subject-matter is funerary, *i.e.* it deals with the fate of the dead king in the next life. Some chapters describe the manner in which he passes from earth to heaven and becomes a star in the firmament, others deal with the food and drink necessary for his continued existence after death and others again with the royal prerogatives which he hopes still to enjoy; many are directed against the bites of snakes and stings of scorpions. It is possible that these incantations were recited as part of the funerary ritual, but there is no doubt that their mere presence in the tombs was supposed to be magically effective for the welfare of the dead. Originally these texts had an application to the king alone, but before the beginning of the XIIth Dynasty private individuals had begun to employ them on their own behalf. They seem to be relatively free from textual corruption, but the vocabulary still occasions much difficulty to the translator."

# FREDERICK MONDERSON

**Black History Extravaganza - Photo -** Osiris (Center), Isis (right) and Horus (left); Pectoral depicting Amon-Ra (left) and Khnum (right) enthroned.

Equally too, also mentioned (1910: 48) are the changes these religious expressions were subject to down through the ages of dynastic rule. That is: "The Book of the Dead is the somewhat inappropriate name applied to a large similar collection of texts of various dates, certain chapters of which show a tendency to become welded together into a book of fixed content and uniform order. A number of chapters contained in the later recensions are already found on the sarcophagi of the Middle Kingdom, together with a host of funereal texts not usually reckoned as belonging to the Book of the Dead; these have been published by Lepsius and Lacau. The above-mentioned nucleus, combined with other chapters of more recent origin, is found in the papyri of the XVIIIth-XXth Dynasties, and forms the so-called Theban recension, which has been edited by Naville in an important work…. In the Saite period a sort of standard edition was drawn up, consisting of 165 chapters in a fixed order and with a common title "the book of going forth by day;" this recension was published by Lepsius in 1842 from a Turin papyrus. Like the Pyramid Texts, the Book of the Dead served a funerary purpose, but its contents are far

# BLACK HISTORY EXTRAVAGANZA HONORING DR. BEN-JOCHANNAN

more heterogeneous; besides chapters enabling the dead man to assume what shape he will, or to issue triumphant from the last judgment, there are lists of gates to be passed and demons to be encountered in the nether world, formulae such as are inscribed on sepulchral figures and amulets, and even hymns to the sun-god. These Texts are for the most part excessively corrupt and despite the translations of Pierret, Renouf and Budge, much labor must yet be expended upon them before they can rank as a first-rate source."

**Black History Extravaganza - Photo -** More of that Heavenly Drama gracing the ceiling at Esneh Temple, and more of the blackened state from people living and lighting fires in the temple.

# FREDERICK MONDERSON

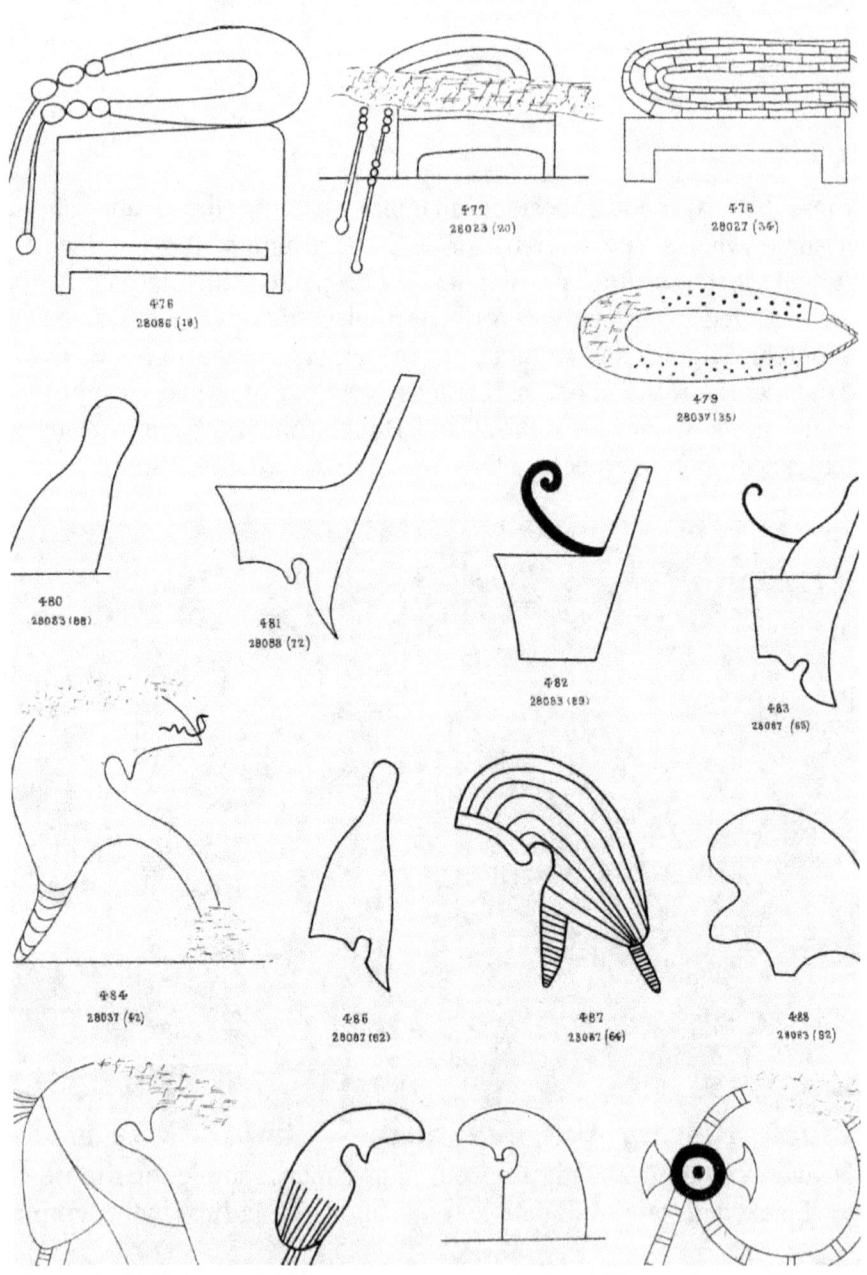

**Black History Extravaganza - Line Drawing -** Crowns and other forms of headdress, even a menat.

# BLACK HISTORY EXTRAVAGANZA HONORING DR. BEN-JOCHANNAN

These ideas, therefore, cover the widest conception of the human intellect as the Egyptians conceived of the idea that death is not the final human experience. Naturally with the passage of time and extensive research and analysis, any number of modern scholars have evaluated and commented on these religious writings.

For example, here are some modern sources:

Ben-Jochannan, Yosef. *African Origins of the Major Western Religions*. New York: Alkebu Lan Publishers, 1971.
Bonwick, James. *Egyptian Ideas and Modern Thought*. London: The African Publication Society, 1983.
Budge, Wallis. *Egyptian Religion*.
_____. *From Fetish to God in Ancient Egypt*. Oxford at the University Press, 1934.
Karenga, Maulana. *The Book of Coming Forth By Day: The Ethics of the Declarations of Innocence*. Los Angeles: University of Sankore Press, 1990.
_____. *Ma'at: The Moral Ideal in Ancient Egypt*. Los Angeles: University of Sankore Press, 2004.

Equally, in anticipation of this Afterlife drama, the social tenet of Ma'at guided the individual's action in his daily life. Such complexity of thought most certainly needed millennia to develop and the "paint factory theologians" may very well have begun that process of complex thought, religious and social.

# FREDERICK MONDERSON

**Black History Extravaganza - Photo -** The portrait.

# BLACK HISTORY EXTRAVAGANZA HONORING DR. BEN-JOCHANNAN

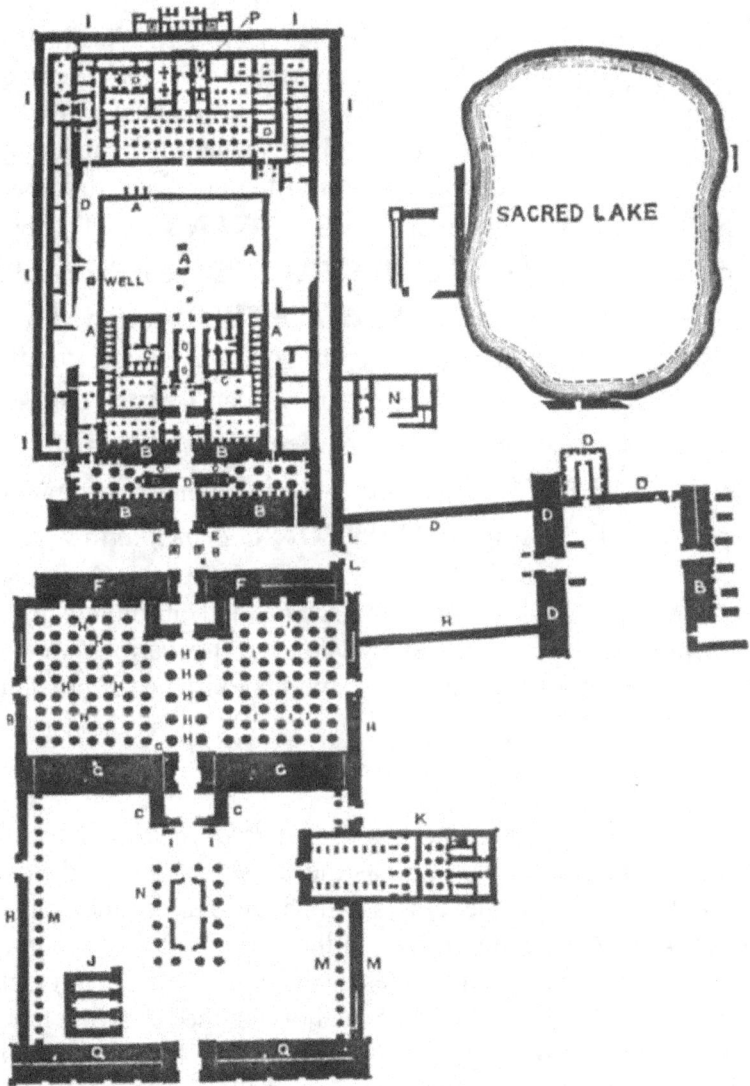

Karnak under the Ptolemies. From Mariette, *Karnak*, Pl. VII.

A. Walls standing before the time of Thothmes I.
B. Pylons built by Thothmes I.
C. Walls and obelisks of Hatshepset.
D. Walls, pylon, etc., of Thothmes III.
E. Gateway of Thothmes IV.
F. Pylon of Amenophis III.
G. Pylon of Rameses I.
H. Walls and columns of Seti I.
I. Columns, walls, and statues of Rameses II.
J. Temple of Seti II.
K. Temple of Rameses III.
L. Gateway of Rameses IX.
M. Pillars and walls of the XXIInd dynasty.
N. Pillars of Tirhakah.
O. Corridor of Philip III. of Macedon.
P. Chamber and shrine of Alexander II.
Q. Pylon built by the Ptolemies.

**Black History Extravaganza -** Plan of Karnak Temple Under the Ptolemies.

# FREDERICK MONDERSON

In his classic *From Fetish to God in Ancient Egypt*, E.A. Wallis Budge (1934: 3-4) provided a further explanation of the theological significance of the Egyptian belief system and pointed to the early notion of One God belief initiated by these ancient African along the Nile River. He wrote, "The foundation of the popular opinion about the religious beliefs of the ancient **EGYPTIANS** was laid by the great pioneer of Egyptology **E. DE ROUGE** about the middle of the last century. He stated that the **EGYPTIANS** believed in One self-existent, supreme, eternal, almighty god, who created the world and everything in it, and endowed man with an **immortal soul, which was capable of receiving punishments and rewards. DE ROUGE's** words were to all intents and purposes a paraphrase of the passage in **NEWTON'S** *Principia* in which the great scientist expressed his belief in the Unity of God who is supreme, infinite, omnipotent, omniscient, and absolutely perfect. Who is present always and everywhere! The various works of creation are the product of his ideas, and his existence is proclaimed by them."

Still, and notwithstanding, other than the *Book of the Dead*, there were, in addition, other literature as the *Book of Gates* and *Book of Am-Duat* that describe the drama which unfolds as the Sun God finishes his day's work and traverses the domain of the underworld. The Osirian *Book of Gates* describes the gates of the hours of the night the sun had to navigate to arrive on the horizon the following morn as well as the segments of the Kingdom of Osiris. The Theban *Book of Am-Duat* describes the successive hours of the night through which the boat of the sun god Ra passes and the acclimations he received in this *Litany of the Sun* in as much various monsters tried to impede his journey so as not to arise on the horizon the next day. Also included is the Sun-god's encounter with Osiris as he traverses is kingdom.

# BLACK HISTORY EXTRAVAGANZA HONORING DR. BEN-JOCHANNAN

**Black History Extravaganza - Photo -** Brother Abdul's Son, Abdul Kabibi, a merchant at Karnak Temple in the Rear.

# FREDERICK MONDERSON

**Black History Extravaganza - Photo -** At Dendera Temple of Hathor, Decorated ceilings, walls and columns tell the story of religious beliefs.

Generally speaking, the Book of Am-Duat or Book of What is in the Underworld represents the beliefs of the Theban locality held by the Priests of Amen-Ra; while the Book of Gates are those held by the Priests of Osiris. These religious writings are very old and extend to the earliest periods of Egyptian history, to a time before they were actually written. Nevertheless, we do know, by the time of the First Dynasty, a Book of the Dead was found in the temple of King Sempti. There was another found during the reign of King Menkaure of the Fourth Dynasty. Even at these early times, these books were revisions of much earlier works. Additionally, over time the "Chapters" or Book of the Dead went through many versions or Recensions. These revisions were the "Heliopolitan Recension" done by the Priests of Ra at Heliopolis in the Old Kingdom. There were also revisions made as in the "Theban Recension" of the New Kingdom, and the "Saite Recension" of the Late Period of the XXVIth Dynasty. Over the years, through the editing, revision, duplications and expansions, the "Chapters" were expanded to as many as 175 with certain chapters as number 125 being tremendously important. In fact, many were duplications but there were actually only 153 chapters.

The religious beliefs on the Theban tomb walls add to the corpus of literature of which that in the Tomb of Seti I and Thutmose III are tremendously graphic and complete. At a later period, "among the later religious books one or two deserve a special mention, such as *The Overthrowing of Apophis*, the serpent enemy of the sun-god; *The Lamentations of Isis and Nephthys* over their murdered brother Osiris; *The Book of Breathings*, a favorite book among the Theban priests. Several of these books were used in the ritual of feast days, but all have received a secondary funerary employment, and are therefore found buried with the dead in their tombs."

To these we must add the temple ritual depicted on inner walls, chief of which is that of the Temple of Seti I at Abydos that mirrors though somewhat limited that of Amon at Karnak. For the longest magic has played a role in the life and death of the Egyptian. In death, magical texts, "deal for the most part with the healing of diseases, the bites of snakes and scorpions, but incidentally cast many sidelights on the mythology and superstitious beliefs. The best known of these is the **Papyrus Harris** published by F.J. Chabas, but other papyri of a great or greater importance are to be found in Leiden, Turin and other collections. A curious book published by A. Erman contains spells to be used by mothers for the protection of their children. A papyrus in

# FREDERICK MONDERSON

London contains a calendar of lucky and unlucky days. A late class of stelae, of which the best specimens have been published by Golenischeff, consists of spells of various kinds originally intended for the use of the living, but later employed for funerary purposes."

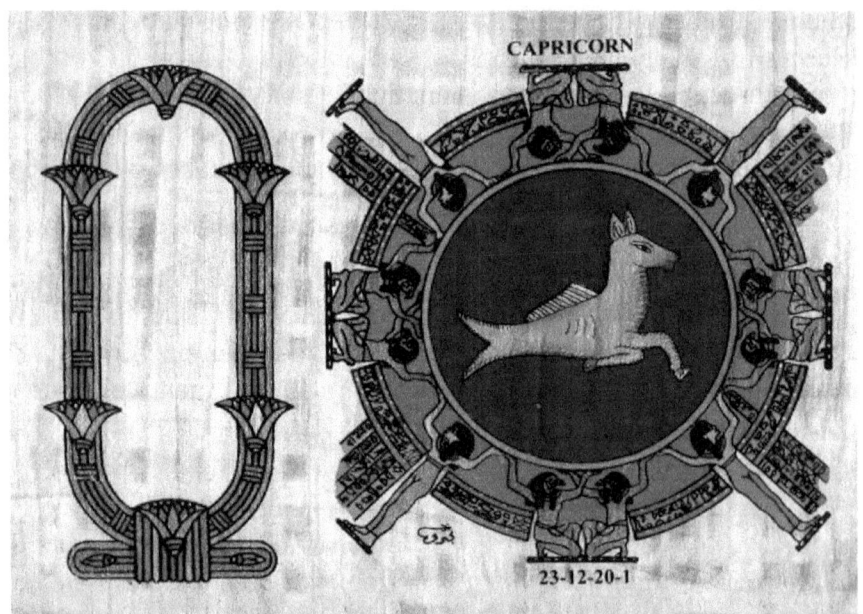

**Black History Extravaganza - Papyrus -** A Blank Cartouche sits beside the Astrological sign of Capricorn.

Stelae or gravestones serve not simply a religious purpose but also as autobiographies recounting of individuals' outstanding service as the followers of their kings on successive expeditions, military or otherwise.

# BLACK HISTORY EXTRAVAGANZA HONORING DR. BEN-JOCHANNAN

**Black History Extravaganza - Photo -** Coffin depicting the two "Eyes of Horus."

# FREDERICK MONDERSON

Complementing the above religious literature, Budge (1934: 25) adds more to our understanding of ancient Egyptian religious writings in the statement: "Among the earliest examples of religious drama may be mentioned the 'Book of Opening of the Mouth,' and the 'Book of the Liturgy of Funeral Offerings.' In the first work the ritual acts and the spells are enumerated which were believed to have the effect of enabling the deceased to breathe, think, speak, walk, etc., in spite of the fact that his body was rough bound tightly with funerary swathing. In the second work, the object of which was to maintain the life of the deceased in the Other World, the **KHERI HEB** or chief priestly magician presents to a statue of the deceased a long series of offerings of meat, drink, unguents, wearing apparel, etc. As he presents each he repeats a spell, the effect of which could be used by the deceased in the Other World. Every act in every 'mystery' had originally a special signification, or was symbolic of some well-known happening. Eventually the meanings of such actions were forgotten in many cases, but the repetition of the actions never ceased."

**Black History Extravaganza - Cairo Museum -** Decorated Sarcophaguses in the Old kingdom section of the Museum.

# BLACK HISTORY EXTRAVAGANZA HONORING DR. BEN-JOCHANNAN

**Black History Extravaganza - Photo -** More of the decorated columns and walls at Dendera Temple of Hathor.

Notwithstanding, these and so much more have shown that the religion of ancient Egypt is very unique. Even more so, than the three western religions of Judaism, Christianity and Islam which some scholars consider lay upon an Egyptian foundation, have threads linking Egyptian Religion with eastern and even New World ritual and practice. Thus, the religion of ancient Egypt is very distinct in that it is one of the earliest to emerge from the mist of antiquity at this crossroad of the ancient world. Principally it is a monotheistic religion emphasizing the unity of god that in later dynasties had elements of polytheism. It was solar or celestial and anthropomorphic and subterranean and boasted colorful representations of its principal gods, who in many respects, were manifestation of the same principle rather than the many gods the simple minded seem to discern.

Explaining some aspects of that ancient Egyptian religious belief and godhead, G.K. Osei's (1983) *African Contribution to Civilization* expresses the view: "The creator is an active force. He commands; he guides; he inspires; and he ordains man's destiny." This "Oneness," is underscored by Budge (1934: 4-5) who further offers the clarification: "There is no doubt that monotheism was a tenet of the Egyptian Faith, but it was entirely different from the monotheism of Christian peoples. When the **EGYPTIAN** called his god 'One,' or the 'One,' or the 'Only One,' he meant exactly what he said and what the Muslim means today when he says, 'There is no god but God.' And that god was the sun in the sky from which he received light and heat and the food whereon he lived. The **EGYPTIAN** in his hymns called many gods 'One,' but these gods were all forms of the Sun god, and, as I understand it, he was a monotheist pure and simple as a sun-worshipper. It avails nothing to call his monotheism 'henotheism.' A time came when Osiris was associated with Khepri, the sun at dawn, and with RA at noon-day, and with Temu as the setting sun, and the Pyramid Texts make it clear that under the VIth dynasty Osiris usurped all the attributes and powers of the 'Sun, the One lord of heaven.' There was, of course, a time when men thought that the Sun-god had no counterpart, no offspring, and no associate or equal." Thus, there was clearly a combining or syncretism of gods in this early period. However, let us also seek to understand; while the sun was considered a manifestation of God, it was actually the magical, mystical, metaphysical and esoteric essence behind the sun which was

# BLACK HISTORY EXTRAVAGANZA HONORING DR. BEN-JOCHANNAN

actually god. This was a sort of religious significant "power behind the throne" syndrome.

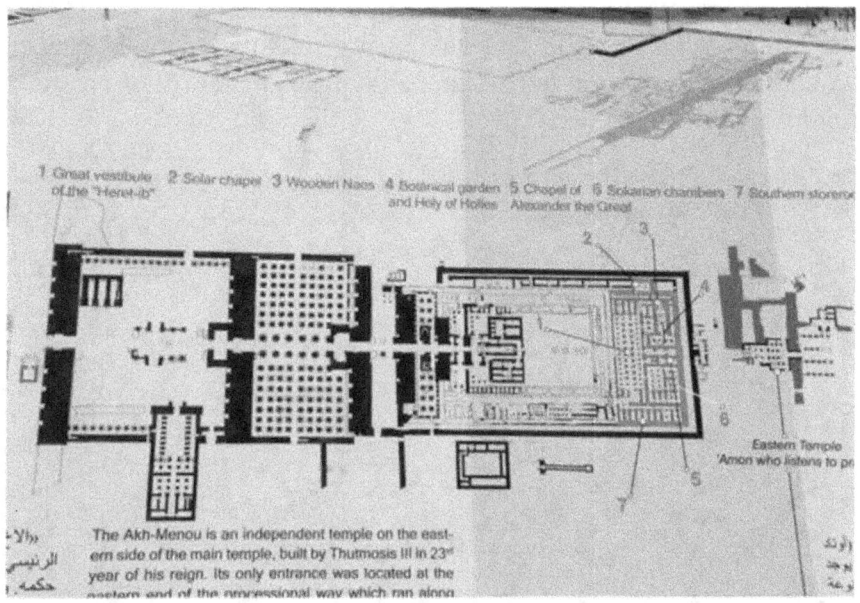

**Black History Extravaganza - Photo -** Temple of Karnak emphasizing (red) Thutmose III's "Festival Temple" the *Akh Menu*, located east of the "Holy of Holies" and the Middle Kingdom Court.

The religion of ancient Egypt is also unique because the principle of governance by divine right was enshrined in the belief of god working in the king as guardian of the state. In this respect, Frankfort (1961: 30) has disclosed: "The Egyptian state was not a man-made alternative to other forms of political organization. It was god-given, established when the world was created; and it continued to form part of the universal order. In the person of Pharaoh, a superhuman being had taken charge of the affairs of man. And this great blessing, which ensured the well-being of the nation, was not due to a fortunate accident but had been foreseen in the divine plan. The monarchy then was as old as the world, for the creator himself had assumed kingly office on the day of creation." Even further, Frankfort (1961: 30-31) continued in referring to the great god: "Pharaoh was his descendant

# FREDERICK MONDERSON

and his successor. The word 'state' was absent from the language because all the significant aspects of the state were concentrated in the king. He was the fountainhead of all authority, all power, and all wealth. The famous saying of the French king Louis XIV, *L'etat c'est moi*, was levity and presumption when it was uttered, but could have been offered by Pharaoh as a statement of fact in which his subjects concurred. It would have summed up adequately their political philosophy."

**Black History Extravaganza - Ceramic Art -** Though a crack in the wall, the "water" still runs through in this beautiful color scheme.

The religion of ancient Egypt very early established the notions of heaven and hell and the philosophical tenets and principles that applied, thereto, viz., Ma'at, reverence, deference, righteousness, truth, justice, etc., that guided the individual's ethical behavior and standards of conduct that, as such, related to the expectations of this other worldly drama and reality. The religion of ancient Egypt is again unique in that it presented the earliest comprehensive religious

# BLACK HISTORY EXTRAVAGANZA HONORING DR. BEN-JOCHANNAN

writings that have survived, unchanged and unedited until discovered in the 19th Century. In this early manifestation of the creative Egyptian, African, mind, the religion established parameters and paradigms of religious experience even expectations people would forever more aspire to. In this Ma'at was a powerful social metaphysical utility that was also a tremendous philosophical dynamo creating ethical standards to guide and shape the society. As a result, later civilizations benefited tremendously owing a great debt to this ancient Egyptian, African, cosmological creative experience.

**Black History Extravaganza - Photo -** The bases of the columns, even a seat for one of the guards in the Temple of Hathor at Dendera.

The religion of ancient Egypt with its many and essentially African characteristics boasted several principal deities worshipped at different centers throughout the nation. While Ben Carruthers in *Mdr Ntr: Divine Speech*, identified Ra manifesting at Heliopolis; Ptah at Memphis; Thoth at Hermopolis; Osiris at Abydos; and Khnum at Elephantine Island, he was quick to point out they were not five competing ideas, principles, gods, but manifestations of one, seen

# FREDERICK MONDERSON

from five different, not complementing perspectives or five view with the same lens. An established Priesthood serviced each deity, and in order to avoid conflict, they tried to synchronize their dogma. To accomplish the divine wish, the king, as the gods' representative on earth, built temples throughout the land and though favoring one god in one particular time, was also beneficent to the others throughout the nation. In the evolved practice, their architecture developed decorative features in stone enshrining the dogma and ritual as a lasting testament to their god. In their building practice, different types of temples were constructed to the god, the king and nation. Such effort gave birth to and helped in development of the decorative arts and a number of industries that fed the ubiquitous religious demands.

The religion of ancient Egypt is unique because very early it preached the dynamics of the afterlife and so became a true engine of molding social and ethical behavior and practice. The science of the funeral, tombs, mummification, the judgment, the Negative Confessions, the philosophic maxim of Ma'at, and the reward for the good life, were all themes and practices that later civilizations came to emulate. For worshipping and ritualizing the gods, a priesthood developed that practiced the ritual of the deity, managed the god's estate and catered to the religious aspirations of the living and the dead. In the relationship that developed with the gods, Egypt was encouraged to become an imperialist nation sanctioned by a divine spirit. As such, imperial pharaohs deployed their military forces, conquered far and wide, and in reward for divinely inspired success heaped untold wealth on such divinities resulting in the building of enormous structures for religious worship that again helped further the development of the arts, science, medicine, etc. which grew out of the spoils of the experiment. In the totality of this interaction, religion helped to advance science which in turn advanced civilization and thus Africa, through Egypt and the Nile Valley, can be considered **the mother of invention** aiding humanity's progress.

# BLACK HISTORY EXTRAVAGANZA HONORING DR. BEN-JOCHANNAN

**Black History Extravaganza - Photo -** The Deceased in adoration before Osiris backed by Isis then Nephthys.

The unmistakable fact of all this is that the *Pyramid Texts*, *Coffin Texts* and *Book of the Dead* are the oldest extant and unchanged religious

# FREDERICK MONDERSON

literature and monotheism is the basis of Egyptian religion. In this Egyptian, African, religious drama, while the fortunes of other gods rose and fell; the worship of Osiris and Re or Ra, remained consistent throughout. In the practice of worship and ritualizing the gods, temples became larger, more durable and decorative; the liturgy and ritual became more expansive; all this while the social and ethical rewards of Egyptian religion helped advance the cause of humanity. A bureaucracy aided religious worship, managed the god's estate, catered to the afterlife requirements of the individual souls and thru this exercise religion advanced the development of knowledge, and civilization, viz., philosophy, science, metaphysics, ethics. Art and architecture, trade and economics, and medicine and social norms and institutions, all this and more the African bequeathed to the world, while his descendants have not gotten the proper credit for this legacy in the much distorted and falsified modern conception of humanity's long march along the evolutionary path of human physical and cultural development.

**Black History Extravaganza - Photo -** Thoth and Horus baptize the King in a "Laying on of hands" moment while Amon in Ram head-dress backed presumably by Mut, looks on.

# BLACK HISTORY EXTRAVAGANZA HONORING DR. BEN-JOCHANNAN

In the enormous compendium of the *Book of the Dead*, as stated, there are more than 172 "Chapters" and some versions of "Chapters" are duplicates. Still some "Chapters" seem more important than others and "Chapter" 125 is probably the most important. This important chapter as discussed by Flinders Petrie is comprised of 4 parts, an Introduction, the Negative Confessions, Conclusion, and Psychostasia or Weighing of the Heart. The latter part, takes place in presence of 12 great gods of Egypt acting as judges, who were Ra-Harmachis, Temu, Shu, Tefnut, Seb, Nut, Isis, Nephthys, Horus, Hathor, Hu and Sa. Thoth and Anubis are also involved in weighing the heart. However, the **Papyrus of Hunefer** mentions 14 gods and the **Turin Papyrus** lists the 42 gods to whom the **Negative Confessions** were recited. Nevertheless, Osiris was the great judge and final arbiter. Himself judged and found "justified" at Heliopolis as defended by the legal eagle, Thoth; thence after, every deceased person was thus subject to the same standards of philosophical and ethical examination to succeed and attain life everlasting, to dwell for eternity among the gods.

**Black History Extravaganza - Photo -** Quite a turnout. The Lady in the middle has grey hair, so evidently, she must be the oldest.

# FREDERICK MONDERSON

Why there are 42 confessions is not certain. Some scholars such as Dr. ben-Jochannan believed they are part of a larger body of 147 or 153 Confessions. Nonetheless, 42 seems a logical number given there were said to individual gods, each of whom represented a particular Nome and given many of these ideas are prehistoric and the number of Nomes were not set until well into dynastic times, the 42 number may not be correct despite the fact, by the New Kingdom the number of nomes and number of gods in the Judgment was set. However, we do know for sure, the "eater of the dead," **Am-mitt**, was a woman, whose "Forepart is that of a crocodile, her hind part is that of a hippopotamus, and her middle is that of a lion." Why a woman we do not know! However, she stood at the judgment hoping the deceased would fail that examination process, not having lived by the tents of Ma'at, and then become her "lunch."

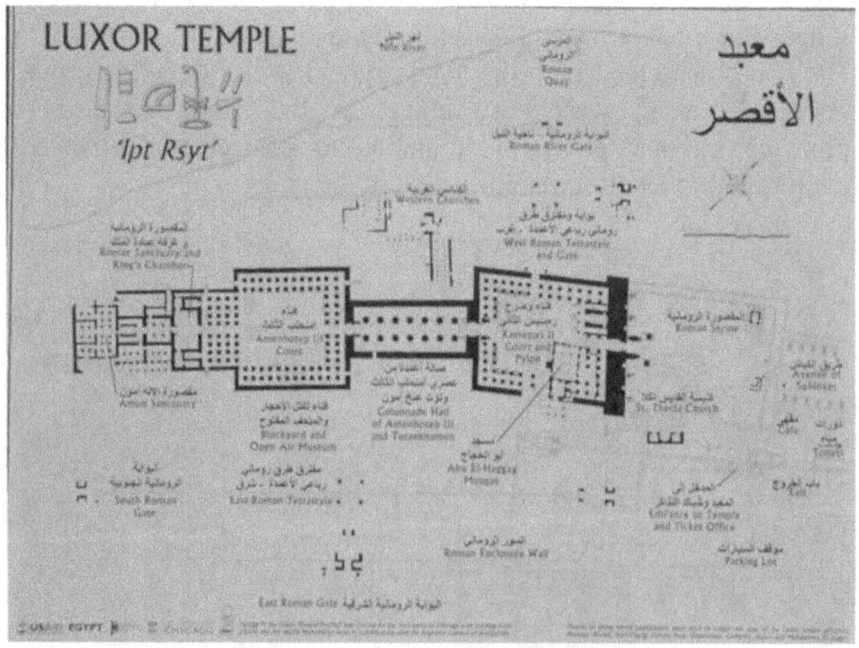

**Black History Extravaganza - Photo -** Temple of Luxor built by Amenhotep III (18th Dynasty) and expanded by Rameses III (19th Dynasty).

No one knows when the Judgment actually happens, whether immediately upon death or whether there is a waiting period or whether it's after the burial or mummification. One thing is certain, each soul is judged individually and the deceased hoped, when the **Psychostasia** unfolded, and his heart was being weighed against a feather, in the **Hall of African Judgment**, his (or her) heart would not speak negatively against him or her and this was determined by the life the individual had lived on earth. Now, after a successful Judgment he or she attained to the heavenly Elysian Fields with its components of Fields of Reeds, Field of Peace, etc. In the earthy preparation for this process, to gain eternal life, Reid (1925: 117) believed: "The Egyptian ideal was to avoid those things that are denied and to do those things that are affirmed."

However, a number of factors can be appended here. (1) More than likely the Judgment did not occur immediately after death. Georges Foucart believed there is a cavern in the Deir el Bahari vicinity into which the deceased entered on way to the Judgment. The *Book of the Dead* sketched the pathway and the "some 20 Portals or Gates" with their guards and whose names he had to identify before he was allowed to proceed beyond each. (2) Because the domain of the Judgment was a place of purity the deceased both physically and spirituality had to be declared pure. Through physical and spiritual washing or cleansing, before and after the mummification process, at the tomb, even on the way, the "Tree Goddess" poured "four pitchers" of water on him. Arriving at the place of examination, he was again washed to essentially attain that purity. The first occurred at mummification and again at burial. The second occurred when he could enter the Hall of Judgment. Then, after he was declared "justified" or "pure of voice" and allowed to enter the Kingdom of Osiris. He had to be cleansed again before he could enter the realm of the blessed where the gods dwelt, itself a place of purity.

# FREDERICK MONDERSON

**Black History Extravaganza - Papyrus -** Image of two of the seated colossal statues outside Rameses II's Abu Simbel Temple.

Symbolism, whether of logic or magic, was very much part of the Egyptian conception of cosmological, theological, metaphysical or spiritual reality, even to bring about equality in social matters. While there appeared four principal gods, Ra, Ptah, Amon and Osiris (five including Khnum); their realms, solar or celestial and subterranean, again, were oftentimes not contradictory but complimentary and fused as their theologians sought harmony and unanimity in the shared religious experience. Throughout, the belief was held that the god

# BLACK HISTORY EXTRAVAGANZA HONORING DR. BEN-JOCHANNAN

gave everything to Egypt and Egypt should give everything to the god. This view therefore pervaded every aspect of their earthly and otherworldly preparation and existence. In all of this, magic even music played an important part in the society, and magical provision for the dead in the future life became an accepted fact from the earliest times.

In "Egyptians Religion" *Encyclopedia of Religion and Ethics*, Vol. 5, Edinburgh: T. and T. Clarke (1912: 247) Flinders Petrie pointed out, "Amon is often shown in the ithyphallic form of Min. Had the princes of Thebes not risen to general dominion, probably Amon would have been as little known as many other local gods; but the rise of the XIth and XIIth dynasties brought Amon forward as a national god; and the XVIIth dynasty from Nubia, holding Thebes as its capital, entailed that Amon became the great god of the most important age of Egypt - the XVIIIth-XX dynasties." That "the 17$^{th}$ Dynasty, coming from Nubia, held Thebes as its capital..." is an interesting admission not found in most books on this subject.

**Black History Extravaganza - Photo - Nefertari's Tomb -** The deceased, Nefertari, Queen of Rameses II, stands before enthroned Thoth; while to the left, Ptah stands within his shrine.

# FREDERICK MONDERSON

"Magic apparently began in the prehistoric age. A small box was found containing three little flat carvings in slate tied together, and two carved ivory tusks, none of which had any useful work. Such ivory tusks were carved with a human head at the pointed end, and kept in pairs, one solid, one hollow. They are probably connected with the present African belief in charming a man's soul into a tusk. Many small amulets were in use - not only the figures of sacred animals, but also such as a fly, a claw, a lance-head, or a vase."

Even further, Petrie (*Encyclopedia of Religion and Ethics* 1912: 237) continued: "In the early historic age, magic appears as the basis of the popular tales: the forming of a crocodile of wax and then throwing it into the water to pursue a victim; the bringing together the head and body of a decapitated goose and restoring it to life; the turning back the waters and descending to the river bed to find a lost jewel - such are the pivots of the early tales. There appears to have always been a strong belief in the virtue of words and names, creation was attributed to the work or speech of the creator, as among the Hebrews. Even animals and objectives had names given to them, to render them effective; without a name those could hardly be in existence…. In the later magic writings and inscriptions, names - generally corrupted and mistakes - are the moving power of the spells. In the later Ramesside times a conspiracy formed upon making wax figures, and sending them into the harim, to compass the death of the king…. It seems not too much to say that an Egyptian was dominated throughout his life by the belief in the magical control exercised upon the gods, upon spirits in life and death, and upon material objects."

In the Judgment conducted in the "**Hall of Two Truths**," the deceased bare his soul in the **Negative Confession** in which he affirmed or confessed the following:

## THE NEGATIVE CONFESSIONS

1. I have not done Iniquity

# BLACK HISTORY EXTRAVAGANZA HONORING DR. BEN-JOCHANNAN

2. I have not robbed with violence
3. I have not done violence to any man
4. I have not committed theft
5. I have not slain man or woman
6. I have not made light the bushel
7. I have not acted deceitfully
8. I have not purloined the things which belong to God
9. I have not uttered falsehood
10. I have not carried away food
11. I have not uttered evil words
12. I have not attacked any man
13. I have not killed the beasts that are the property of God
14. I have not acted deceitfully
15. I have not laid waste the land which has been ploughed
16. I have never pried into matters to make mischief
17. I have not set my mouth in motion against any man
18. I have not given away to wrath concerning myself without a cause
19. I have not defiled the wife of a man
20. I have not committed any sin against purity
21. I have not struck fear into any man
22. I have not encroached upon sacred times and seasons
23. I have not been a man of anger
24. I have not made myself deaf to the words of right and truth
25. I have not stirred up strife
26. I have made no man to weep
27. I have not committed acts of impurity, neither have I laid with men
28. I have not eaten my heart
29. I have abused no man
30. I have not acted with violence
31. I have not judged hastily
32. I have not taken vengeance upon the god
33. I have not multiplied my speech over much
34. I have not acted with deceit, and I have not worked wickedness
35. I have not uttered curses on the king
36. I have not fouled water

37. I have not made haughty my voice
38. I have not cursed the god
39. I have not behaved with insolence
40. I have not sought for distinctions
41. I have not increased my wealth, except with such things as are justly mine own possessions
42. I have not thought scorn of the god who is in my city

**Black History Extravaganza - Photo - Nefertari's Tomb** - Colorful and fat cows make their way, perhaps to be sacrificed as the Queen stands to the right and left.

However, there was more to it than simply reciting the above Confessions. Adolf Erman in *A Handbook of Egyptian Religion* (London: Archibald Cox and Co., 1907: 101-102) in quoting the "Great Chapter of the Book of the Dead" or **Chapter 125** described the **Psychostasia** process as follows: "In a large hall, whose roof is ringed with flames of fire and symbols of truth, Osiris is enthroned in a chapel; before him is the symbol of Anubis, the four sons of Horus, and the *devourer of the west*, a fabulous animal who serves as protector to the god. Above, i.e., farther back in the hall sit

# BLACK HISTORY EXTRAVAGANZA HONORING DR. BEN-JOCHANNAN

the forty-two judges of the dead; below again, i.e., in front, is the great balance, in which the heart of the dead is to be weighed. The dead will be received by the goddess of truth on entering the hall [though Ma'at does not appear in the illustration]; Horus and Anubis then take his heart, and weigh it in the balance to prove whether it is lighter than truth. Thoth, the *scribe of the gods*, notes the results upon his tablet and communicates it to Osiris."

Even further, Erman (1907: 102-104) continued his explanation of this fascinating process of judgment. In this, he states: "More remarkable, however, than this representation is the speech of the dead man, when *he arrives at this hall of the two truths, when he is freed from all evil which he has done, and when he beholds the face of the god*. Thus runs his prayer: "*Praise is to thee, thou great god, thou lord of the two truths. I have come to thee, oh my lord, that I may behold thy beauty. I know thee, and know the names of the forty-two gods who are with thee in the hall of the two truths, who live on the evil doers, and who drink their blood each day of the reckoning before Wennofre.*

**Black History Extravaganza - Photo -** In Red and White Crowns, the Goddesses takes Pharaoh in Double Crown to Amon wearing horns, disk and feathers.

# FREDERICK MONDERSON

*I come to thee and bring to thee truths, and chase away wrong doing.*

*I have committed no sins against mankind… I have not done that which the gods abhor. I have made no man evil in the eyes of his superior. I have not caused to hunger. I have not caused to weep. I have done no murder. I have not commanded to murder. I have not occasioned grief to any. I have not diminished the food in the temples. I have not lessened the bread of the gods. I have not stolen the provisions of the illumined. I have not committed impurity in the pure abodes of the god of my city. I have not diminished the corn measure. I have not diminished the cubit measure. I have not falsified the field measure. I have not added to the weights of the balance. I have not falsified the tongue of the balance. I have not stolen the milk from the mouth of the child. I have not stolen the cattle from his pasture. I have not snared the birds of the gods. I have not caught the fish in their lakes. I have not hindered the water (of the inundation) in its time. I have not damned up running water … I have not injured the herds in the temple domains. I have not hindered the god in his revenues."*

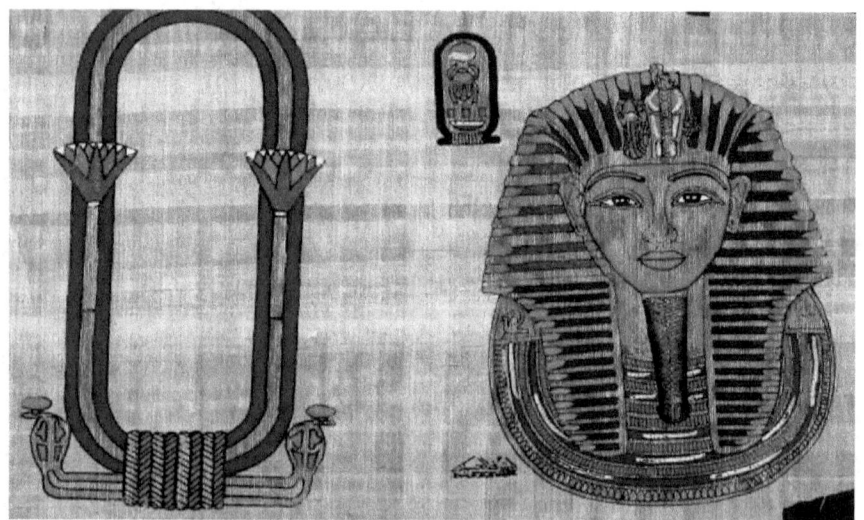

**Black History Extravaganza - Papyrus -** A Blank Cartouche rests beside the small Cartouche and Mask of Tutankhamon of the 18th Dynasty.

# BLACK HISTORY EXTRAVAGANZA HONORING DR. BEN-JOCHANNAN

Here a second Confession is made, as stated above previously, in which he must testify to his innocence. However, in this case the deceased addresses the gods individually by name. *"Oh thou, wide of stride in Heliopolis, I have committed no sin. O Clasper of flames in Kher-Ahau, I have not stolen. Oh Nose in Hermopolis, I have not defrauded. Oh Devourer of Shadows in Kerert, I have not stolen. Oh Looker backward in Rosetta, I have not murdered men. Oh double lioness in heaven, I have not diminished the measure of corn. Oh Knife-eyed in Letopolis, I have done nothing dishonest. Oh Flame in Khetkhet, I have not stolen the temple property. Oh Bone-breaker in Herakleopolis, I have not lied. Among other sins the dead man disowns before White-teeth, Devourer of blood, Devourer of entrails, Wanderer,* and other similar terrible beings, are the following:

*"I have stolen no food. I have not slain sacred animals. I have not lain in wait. I have not committed adultery. I was not deaf to words of truth. I have not caused weeping. I have not consumed my heart (with remorse). I have not calumniated. I have not uttered many words. I have not reviled the king. My voice was not loud. I have not reviled the god,* etc. Then again the dead man addresses the terrible judges: '*May ye be praised, ye gods. I know you and know your names. I shall not fall by your sword. This god in whose following ye are, reports to you nothing evil about me. You are not concerned with me, ye speak the truth concerning me before the lord of all. For I have done justly in Egypt, I have nor reviled the god, and the king in time had nothing against me.*

"*Praise to you, ye gods, ye who are in the hall of the two truths, in whose body is no lie, and who live in truth ... before Horus who dwells in his sun. Deliver me from Bebon, who lives on the entrails of the great ones, in the day of the great reckoning. Behold, I come to you, without sin, without evil... I live by truth, and feed myself with the truth of my heart. I have done that which man commandeth and that wherewith the gods are content. I have pleased the god with that which he loveth. I have given bread to the hungry, water to the thirsty, clothing to the naked, and a passage over the river to him who had no*

# FREDERICK MONDERSON

boat. I have made offerings to the god and funerary gifts to the illuminated.

*"Deliver me, protect me; Ye do not accuse me before the great god. I am one who hath a clean mouth and pure hands, one to whom those who see them cry, 'Welcome, welcome.'"*

**Black History Extravaganza - Ceramic Art -** The great falcon, hawk, in picturesque splendor.

These "Confessions" helped mold the social, moral and ethical conduct of the life of the ancient Africans, Kamites, called Egyptians of the united Upper and Lower Kingdoms, enabling them to be awarded wonderful bliss for all eternity.

However, in a deeper search for meaning as to the true nature of what the (deceased believed would happen in the Afterlife he prepared for, Erman 1907: 106-107) uses two tomb inscriptions as examples not

# BLACK HISTORY EXTRAVAGANZA HONORING DR. BEN-JOCHANNAN

simply to explore the offerings the deceased hoped to receive in the Afterlife but more important that he may walk in the sunlight after death; for the true title of the Book of the Dead was actually the Book of Coming (or Going) Forth by Day (into the Sunlight). These two inscriptions belong to Nachtmin a New Kingdom "Superintendent of the Granary" and Paheri, Prince of El Kab. Erman writes, "Nachtmin" desires for himself "splendor in heaven, power upon earth and justification in the under-world - to go in and out of my grave - that I may cool myself in its shadow - that I may daily drink water out of my pool - that my limbs may grow - that the Nile may bring me nourishment and food and all green plants in its time - that I may exercise myself upon the borders of my pool, daily without ceasing - that my soul may hover on the boughs of the trees which I planted - that I may cool myself under my sycamores - that I may eat the fruit which they give - that I may have a mouth with which I may speak like the servants of Horus - that I may mount up to heaven, and descend to earth, and not be hindered on the way that my ka may not be waylaid - that my soul may not be shut up - that I may be among the praised, in the midst of the noble ones - that I may plough my land in the Field of Earu - that I may arrive at the Field of Food, that they may come out to me with jars and loaves - with all the food of the Lord of Eternity - that I may receive my provisions from the flesh of the altar of the great god."

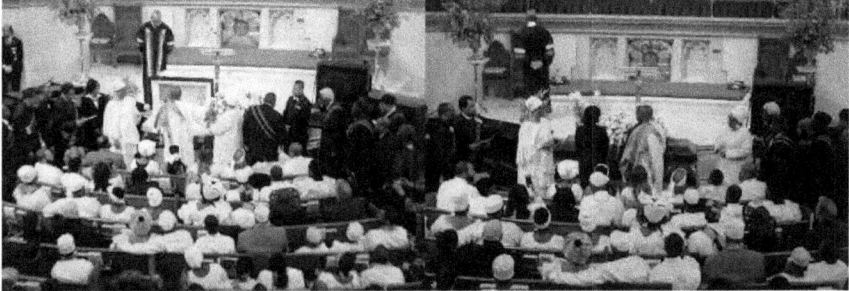

**Black History Extravaganza - Photo -** Dr. Calvin Butts observes prof James Smalls as the Kher-Heb (left); then turns to do his own private prayer (fight)

# FREDERICK MONDERSON

**Black History Extravaganza - Photo -** Thoth and Horus bathe or baptize the king with Ankhs while Bastet looks on.

Erman (1907: 106-07) then provides a wish-list Paheri's family members offered on his behalf. *"Thou goes in and out with a glad heart, and with the rewards of the Lord of the gods ... Thou becomes a living soul; thou hast power over bread, water and air. Thou changest thyself into a phoenix or a swallow, a sparrow-hawk or a heron, as thou desirest. Thou dost cross in the boat and art not hindered. Thou sailest upon the water when a flood ariseth. Thou livest anew and thy soul is not parted from thy body. Thy soul is a god together with the illuminated, and the excellent souls speak with thee. Thou art among them and (verily) receivest what is given upon earth; thou possessest water, possessest air, hast superabundance of that which thou desired. Thine eyes are given to them to see, and thine ears to hear speech, thou mouth speaketh, thy legs move, thy hands and arms bestir themselves for thee, thy flesh grows, thy veins are in health, and thou feelest thyself well in all thy limbs. Thou hast thine upright heart in thy possession, and thy earlier heart belongs to thee. Thou dost mount up to heaven, and are summoned each day to the libation table of Wennofre, thou receiveth food which has been offered to him and the gifts of the Lords of the necropolis."*

# BLACK HISTORY EXTRAVAGANZA HONORING DR. BEN-JOCHANNAN

**Black History Extravaganza - Photo -** Standing and offering praise to Osiris with Thoth, Isis and Nephthys "watching the God's back."

# FREDERICK MONDERSON

Paheri is offered additional wishes that he may exploit in the next life. *"Thou eatest bread in the presence of the god, on the great staircase of the Lord of the Ennead (of Osiris at Abydos). Thou dost exercise thyself there and art friendly with the servants of Horus (the ancient kings who reigned there). Thou dost ascend and descend and art not prevented. Admittance is not refused thee at the gate of Duat, but the folding doors of the horizon are opened to thee, and the bolts open to thee of themselves. Thou treadest the hall of the Two Truths, and the god who is in it greets thee. Thou sealest thyself within the kingdom of the dead and walkest about in 'the city of the Nile.' Thou rejoices when thou ploughest thy portion of the Field of Earu. What thou needest is produced by thy labor, and thy harvest comes to thee as corn. A rope is fixed to the boat for thee, that thou mayest sail when it pleaseth thee. Every morning thou goest out, and every evening thou returnest home. At night a lamp is lighted for thee, until the sun again shines on thy body. 'Welcome' is said to thee in this thy house of the living. Thou beholdest Re in the horizon of heaven, and gazest on Amon when he ariseth. Thou awakes beautiful by day, all evil chased away from thee. Thou dost traverse eternity with joyfulness and with the praise of the god who is in thee* (i.e. thy conscience). *Thou possessest thy heart, it doth not depart from thee. Thy food is there where it should be."*

**Black History Extravaganza - Photo -** View of the Upper Balcony who were part of the solemn, yet, happy well-wishers seeing Dr. Ben-Jochannan off to a Happy Transition to meet his Brother and Sister Heroes and Heroines of the Revered Black Pantheon.

# BLACK HISTORY EXTRAVAGANZA HONORING DR. BEN-JOCHANNAN

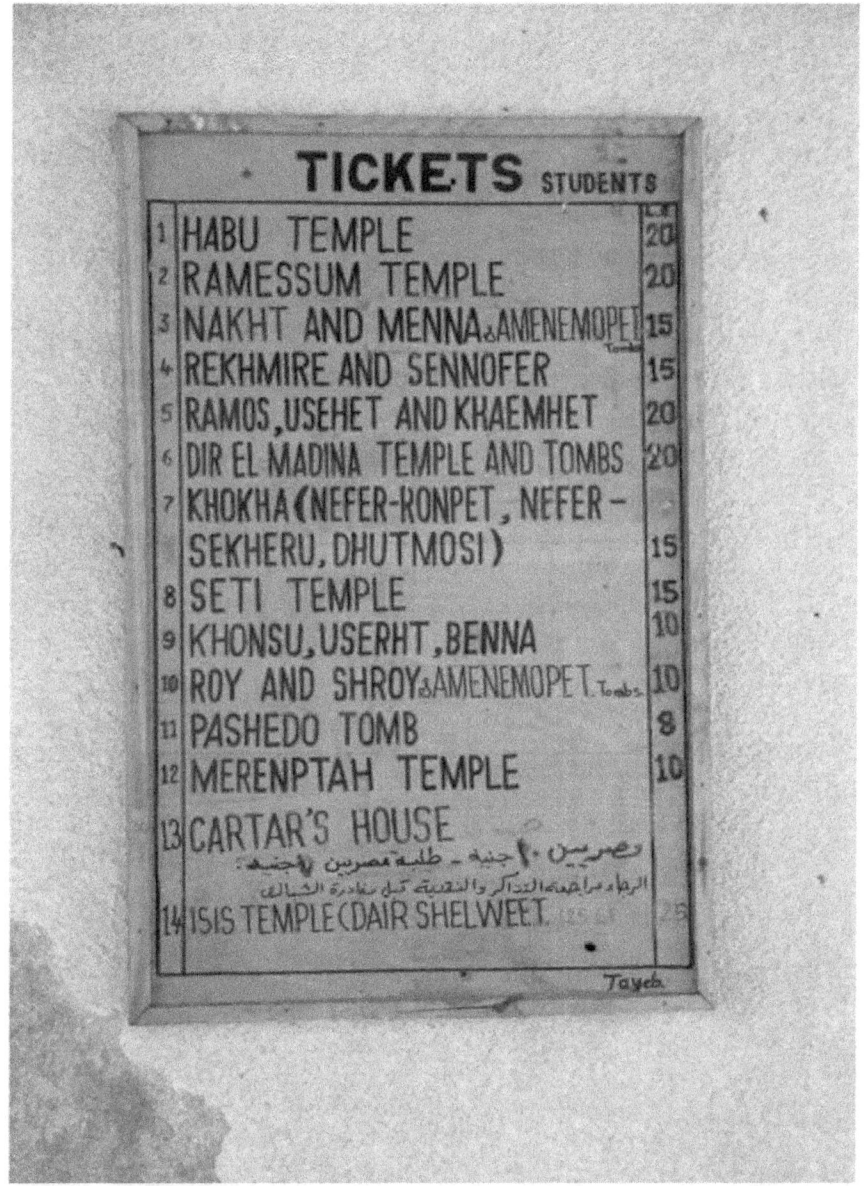

**Black History Extravaganza - Photo -** Ticket Office price board listing cost for each visit to view the different monuments and List of temples open to visitors of the West Bank.

# FREDERICK MONDERSON

```
                      OTICE
1 ALL TOMBS CLOSED AT 5 P.M.
2 TO VISIT THE TOMB OF TUT-ANKH-   N YOU MUST HAVE
  TICKETS FOR THE VALLEY OF T     NGS AND FOR KING TUT.
3 TICKETS ARE VALID FOR ONE D Y ONLY.
  YOU  UST HAVE A V. ID TICKE   O VISIT THE  MON  ENTS.
  PL ASE CHE  AND EXAMINE   IC ETS    EF RE
  LEAVING TIC' TS O ICE.
  TICK TS M    E B  GHT BY    TOU I TS    GUI ES
    HI T       F. I Y.
```

**Black History Extravaganza - Photo -** This notice needs a little work for it is somewhat battered by wear and tear; yet, the ground rules for viewing the monuments are here explained.

These "Confessions" helped mold the social, moral and ethical conduct of the life of the ancient Africans, Kamites, called Egyptians of the united Upper and Lower Kingdoms, enabling them to be awarded wonderful bliss for all eternity.

**Black History Extravaganza - Photo -** Close-up of the screened pillars of Esneh Temple.

# BLACK HISTORY EXTRAVAGANZA HONORING DR. BEN-JOCHANNAN
## II. The Antiquity of Egyptian Religion

It is difficult to establish the antiquity of ancient Egyptian religion but suffice to say that by the time of the Badarian, Amratian and Gerzean pre-dynastic culture sequence, religious expressions were already evident in the graves of these early people. Given much religious and social intangibles were of perishable materials, the only credible existential evidence available was contained in the grave. The objects included in the "goods of the grave," attest to belief in an afterlife and in a god figure. For example, warriors were buried with their weaponry, farmers their implements and craftsmen their tools so as to continue their "professions" in the next life. By the Middle Kingdom, the *Coffin Texts* proved a tremendous asset to the deceased having evolved from the *Pyramid Texts*. Beyond this, in the New Kingdom, those who could afford it had interred with them the *Book of the Dead* to help as guide in the afterlife drama. The extensive contents of the *Book of the Dead*, however, was based on an individual's ability to pay. Nevertheless, all versions had the essential parts which include the important **Chapter 125**.

Stepping out of the mist of prehistory, popular religion was generally practiced and survived in domestic worship. In the prehistoric age the larger disks carved with a coiled serpent, are pierced with a hole for suspension, showing that they were probably hung up in the house; and in the 1$^{st}$ Dynasty the usual border to the hearth was a pottery fender in the form of a serpent, doubtless copied from the serpent which they would find at dawn coiled round the fire's ashes for warmth. In the XVIIIth Dynasty there was usually a recess in the hall of the house, colored red; and in one case, where it is preserved to the top, it had a scene of adoration of the tree-goddess above it. This was, doubtless, the focus of the domestic worship, probably having different deities painted over it, according to the devotion of the master .... The domestic shrine is represented as a wooden cupboard, containing the figure of the household god, with a lamp burning before it .... Of the prayers of the gods there is evidence in the epithets of

# FREDERICK MONDERSON

Amon 'who cometh quickly to him who calls on him;' and of 'Ptah, who hears petitions,' and whose tablets have ears carved on them."

**Black History Extravaganza - Photo -** Blank Cartouche beside the Astrological sign for Gemini.

By the time of Unification at the First Dynasty, Narmer established the worship of Ptah at Memphis. On his **Slate Palette** the Goddess Hathor, whose origin Budge determined is Nubian, appears and this document lets us believe Egyptian creation stories were perhaps, at least, centuries old by this time. Given the worship of Ra at Heliopolis and he considered the highest divinity in the land, such was certainly contemporary or preceded by the religious worship of the upper kingdom. Many of the creator gods were already in existence. So having established the prehistoric origins of Ra, Ptah, Thoth, and since Narmer was a Theban, it's easy to accept Amon and his family as being in existence even though they did not come into national prominence until much later. Given these gods, certainly the followers of Horus precede Narmer; thus we can assume Osiris his father, whom the ancients believed "went north" from Nubia or Ethiopia and must have been around, though he does not become

# BLACK HISTORY EXTRAVAGANZA HONORING DR. BEN-JOCHANNAN

prominent at Abydos until around the second and third dynasties succeeding Khenti-Amenti as god of the dead. Petrie found large wooden statues of Min at Koptos that are painted black dating to this earliest period. These are now housed in the Ashmolean Museum in Oxford, England. This puts Min among the earliest company of gods. In fact, he is the earliest figure of a God shown! Toby Wilkinson in *Genesis of the Pharaohs*, depicts the image of Min as the earliest historic evidence of a god.

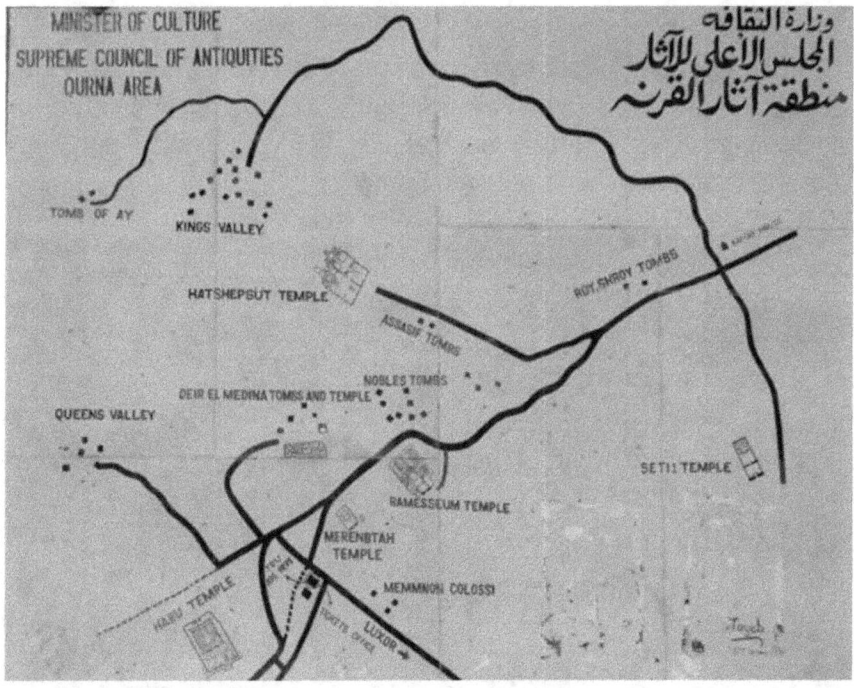

**Black History Extravaganza - Photo -** Plan of the West Bank area housing the main ancient monuments.

# FREDERICK MONDERSON

**Black History Extravaganza - Photo -** Tomb of Menna depicts the deceased and wife before enthroned Osiris. It is interesting how the faces generally seem defaced while the body essentially remains intact and this is a general practice in many places.

**Black History Extravaganza - Photo -** Keep "Getting the Drummers on!"

# BLACK HISTORY EXTRAVAGANZA HONORING DR. BEN-JOCHANNAN

**Black History Extravaganza - Photo -** Tomb of Menna - Close-up of the Nobleman and his wife. How interesting, the face is again defaced like so many others depicted in the "African or Negro mold."

# FREDERICK MONDERSON

**Black History Extravaganza - Photo -** Tomb of Menna - Close-up of Osiris. Again, the face "gets the business."

# BLACK HISTORY EXTRAVAGANZA HONORING DR. BEN-JOCHANNAN

On the other hand, Albert Churchward in *Signs and Symbols of Primordial Man* (New York: A and B Publishers Group, facing p. 154), explained who the first god anthropomorphically depicted really is: "It is the primitive human form of Horus I. Bes-Horus being the earliest type of the pygmy Ptah, the human type was not given to any before Ptah, so that the above shows that the ancient Egyptians left an indelible proof of their mythology of their descent from the first human, which was the pygmy."

That aside, we can easily say, "Essentially, two main religious systems emerged in Egypt. First, the state cults were organized, with the temples and priesthood to ensure the survival of the gods, Egypt and the King." Then there is the term we apply today called "household gods" that fits the second category of deities mentioned above. Margaret Murray in *The Temples of Egypt* says of these "household gods," that, "They were worshipped at small, domestic shrines, and had neither temple, divine cults or priesthood, but were approached by people at all levels of society for help and guidance in everyday matters."

**Black History Extravaganza - Photo -** Tomb of Menna - The Nobleman sits to inspect his responsibilities and before victuals on a sumptuous "Table of Offerings." Again, the facial defacement.

# FREDERICK MONDERSON

As religious expression expanded, rituals played an important part in the mortuary, especially in god or cult temples. Murray points to an understanding of this important feature of the religion: "In the cult temple, there were two main types of ritual. The most important ritual (known as the **Daily Temple Ritual**) was carried out three times per day for the resident god in every temple and dramatized the common-place events of everyday existence, providing food, clothing, washing and regular attendance for the god's cult-statue in his sanctuary. The second type of ritual, the festivals, varied in content from one temple to another, each being based on the mythology of the particular resident deity. These were celebrated at regular, often yearly intervals and marked special events in the god's life, such as marriage, death and resurrection. A main feature of most festivals was the procession of the god's statue outside the temple giving the crowds their only opportunity to see the deity and participate in the worship."

**Black History Extravaganza - Photo - Nefertari's Tomb -** While the Queen faces the Cows, Nephthys (left) and Isis (right) embrace Osiris as a Ram wearing horns and Sun-Disk.

# BLACK HISTORY EXTRAVAGANZA HONORING DR. BEN-JOCHANNAN

While there was a worship or cult temple of the god, there was also a mortuary temple of the king designed to worship him as a demi-god while alive and a full-fledged god after death following his Judgment, washing and purification, before taking his place in the purified abode of the great gods.

In this, royal ancestor or mortuary cult, a ritual of the daily offerings from the divine temple worship was presented to the king's dead ancestors so that they could one day welcome him into their company.

**Black History Extravaganza - Photo -** Tomb of Menna - Resources of the Nobleman's realm are in parade to be inspected.

Thus, an interesting dual reality undergirded all aspects of Egyptian life beginning within the Upper and Lower Kingdoms and the monarch ruling a unified state; the existence of worship and mortuary temples; a fruitful Black land and a barren Red land; the sun and Nile as constants; and more especially the official or government religion of the elite and the more popular or household or local religion of the masses. As such, this state of affairs remained constant throughout dynastic rule.

# FREDERICK MONDERSON

In *Ancient Egypt* (1893: 38) Rawlinson explained the dual, common and divine, nature of Egyptian Religion in the following statement: "Beside the common popular religion, the belief of the masses, there was another which prevailed among the priests and among the educated. The primary doctrine of this esoteric religion was the real essential unity of the Divine Nature. The sacred texts, known only to the priests and to the initiated, taught that there was a single Being, 'the sole producer of all things both in heaven and earth, himself not produced of any,' 'the only true living God, self-originated,' 'who exists from the beginning,' 'who has made all things, but was not himself been made.' This Being seems never to have been represented by any material, even symbolical, form. It is thought that he had no name, or, if he had, that it must have been unlawful to pronounce or write it. He was a pure spirit, perfect in every respect - all wise, almighty, and supremely good. It is of him that the Egyptian poets use such expressions as the following: 'He is not graven in marble; he is not beheld; his abode is not known; no shrine is found with painted figures of him; there is no building that can contain him;' and, again: 'Unknown is his name in heaven; he doth not manifest his forms; vain are all representations;' and yet again: 'His commencement is from the beginning; he is the God who has existed from old time; there is no God without him; no mother bore him; no father hath begotten him; he is a god-goddess, created from himself; all gods came into existence when he began.'"

# BLACK HISTORY EXTRAVAGANZA HONORING DR. BEN-JOCHANNAN

**Black History Extravaganza - Photo -** Tomb of Nakht - Close-up of the Nobleman, a New Kingdom Gardener, and his wife.

Even further, Rawlinson (1893: 38-39) continued: "The other gods, the gods of the popular mythology were understood in the esoteric religion to be either personified attributes of the Deity, or parts of the nature which he had created, considered as informed and inspired by him. Num or Kneph represented the creative mind, Phthah the creative hand, or act of creating; Maut represented matter, Ra the sun, Khons the moon, Seb the earth, Khem the generative power in nature, Nut the upper hemispheres of the heavens, Athor the lower world or under hemisphere; Thoth personified the Divine Wisdom, Ammon perhaps the Divine mysteriousness or incomprehensibility, Osiris the Divine Goodness. It is difficult in many cases to fix on the exact quality, act, or part of nature intended; but the principle admits of no doubt. No educated Egyptian conceived of the popular gods as really separate and distinct gods. All knew that there was but One God, and understood that, when worshipped was offered to Khem, or Kheph, or Maut, or Thoth, or Ammon, the One God was worshipped under some one of his forms or in some one of his aspects. He was every god, and thus all the gods' names were interchangeable, and in one and the same hymn we may find a god, say Ammon, addressed also as Ra and Khem and Tum and Horus and Khepra; or Hapi; or Osiris as Ra and Thoth; or, in fact, any god invoked as almost any other. If there be a limit, it is in respect of the evil deities, whose names are not given to the good ones."

Therefore, when the idea of God is exposed or expressed, in what form, the One God is meant!

## III. The Egyptian Holy Books have exerted a tremendous influence on the religion and social behavior and practice of man in the Nile Valley. Equally, this influence has migrated to the West and been instrumental in shaping its religious beliefs.

**a.** **The Pyramid Texts** were found in pyramids of the $5^{th}$ and $6^{th}$ Dynasties of Kings Unas, Teta (Teti), Pepi I, Merenra and Pepi II at Sakkara. R. Engelbach in *Introduction to Egyptian Archaeology with Special Reference to the Egyptian Museum, Cairo* (1961: 225) is of the view: "They are written in a far more ancient language, however, probably of the IIIrd Dynasty or even earlier, and as such are of extreme importance in the study of the ancient language. The texts are exclusively connected with the welfare of the dead king; they consist of incantations whereby his place in the sky and the other prerogatives of a dead king are assured to him, and they also incorporate the ritual which was recited in connection with the daily

# BLACK HISTORY EXTRAVAGANZA HONORING DR. BEN-JOCHANNAN

offerings made in the pyramid-temples. The discovery, quite recently, of an almost complete version of the Pyramid Texts on the walls of a tomb of a noble of the XIIth Dynasty at El-Lisht, shows that these texts were known some 500 years after the VIth Dynasty, and were, at any rate in this case, applied to a non-royal personage. During the IXth to XIth Dynasties, many excerpts from the Pyramid Texts are found written, usually in ink, inside the large coffins of that period. These are now known as the Coffin Texts."

**Black History Extravaganza - Papyrus -** Another Blank Cartouche sits beside the Astrological sign for Scorpio.

# FREDERICK MONDERSON

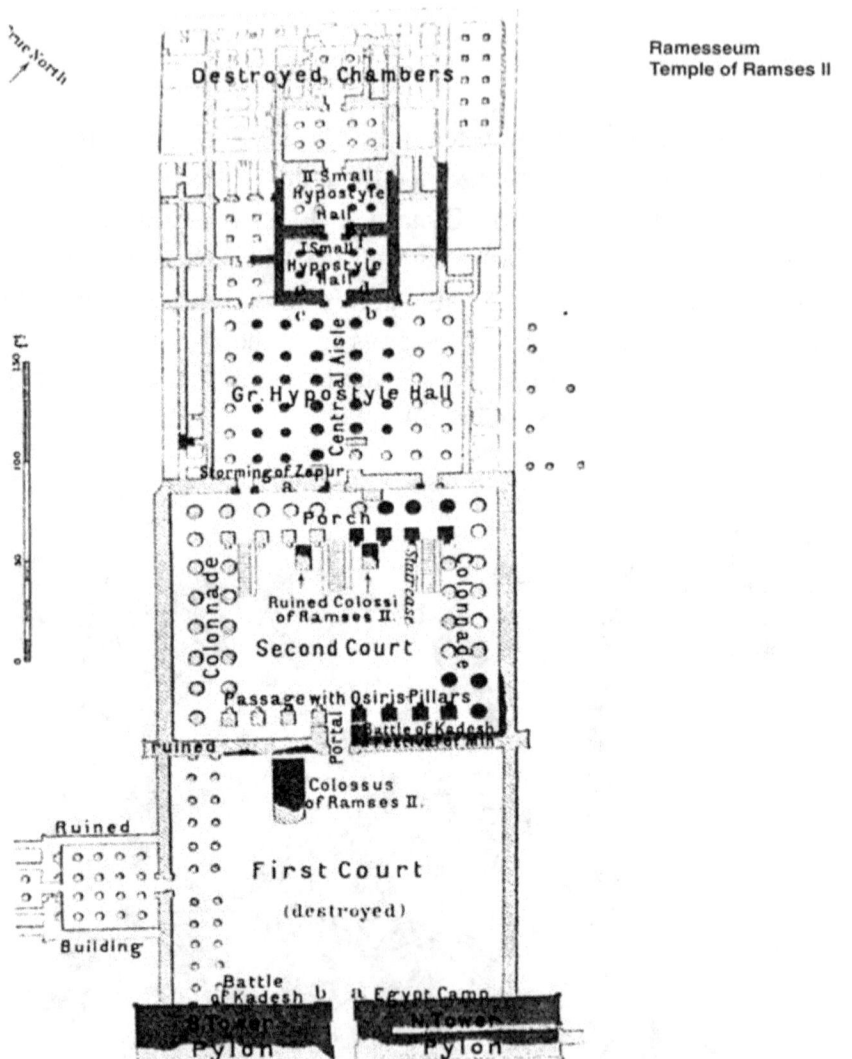

**Black History Extravaganza - Plan of a Temple -** Ramesseum, Mortuary Temple of Rameses II, often called the "Ramesseum."

# BLACK HISTORY EXTRAVAGANZA HONORING DR. BEN-JOCHANNAN

**Black History Extravaganza - Photo -** Moving the animals to the "Cattle Count."

He concluded: "A curious feature in the Pyramid Texts is that figures of fishes are never found; the religious or other reason for this is unknown." Even more important, there are no illustrations in the Pyramid Texts. Wallis Budge in *Egyptian Heaven and Hell* (1905: 3) offers the explanation: "That the Egyptians possessed artistic skill sufficient to illustrate the religious and general works which their theologians wrote or revised, under their earliest dynasties of kings of all Egypt, is evident from the plain and colored bas-reliefs which adorn the walls of their mastabas, or bench-shaped tombs, and we can only point out and wonder at the fact that the royal pyramids contain neither painted nor sculptured vignettes, especially as pictures are much needed to break the monotony of the hundreds of lines of large hieroglyphics, painted in a bluish-green color, which must have dazzled the eyes even of an Egyptian."

# FREDERICK MONDERSON

**Black History Extravaganza - Photo** - Tomb of Nakht - The Nobleman with his wife and child on his boat or skiff hunting birds in the Marshes.

**b.** **The Coffin Texts** of the Middle Kingdom were a continuation of the *Pyramid Texts* of the Old Kingdom that were now written on the insides and outsides of coffins as opposed to being written on the walls of pyramids. We are told: "The Coffin Texts contain an important collection of spells composed on behalf of non-royal personages and comprise incantations against hunger, thirst and manifold dangers of the Underworld, and incantations for enabling the deceased to assume whatever form he pleased, and incantations by virtue of which he could remain in the enjoyment of his former pastimes and partake of the society of his relatives and friends. Part of the interest of the Coffin Texts lies in the fact that they form a link between the Pyramid Text and the later 'Book of the Dead;' spells from both compilations occurring in them. The *Coffin Texts* appear to have been anciently called 'The Book of Justifying a Man in the Underworld;' when read by priests, the spells were called 'transfigurations' or 'spiritualizations.' No complete copy of the Coffin Texts has been found on papyrus, but spells from it occur on New Kingdom papyri. Mutilations of figures of animals, birds and

# BLACK HISTORY EXTRAVAGANZA HONORING DR. BEN-JOCHANNAN

serpents also occasionally occur on some versions of the Coffin Texts."

**Black History Extravaganza - Photo -** The deceased meets quite an array of gods including Osiris, Isis, Horus, Nephthys, Thoth, Anubis, and a female.

# FREDERICK MONDERSON

The *Book of the Dead's* magical spells, were to be recited by the dead man, to protect himself from injury, demons and the 'second death.' They were also to enable him to emerge from his tomb, to accompany the gods, to secure acquittal at the Judgment, and be able to enjoy the fruits of heaven or the Elysian Fields.

**c.     The Book of the Dead** - continued the religious traditions of the Old and Middle Kingdoms, only now the religious ideas were written on papyrus called books, consisting of "Chapters" of the rituals. Naturally they incorporated much of the earlier religious beliefs and importantly they were portable and could be acquired in varied forms based on a deceased person's financial abilities. Nevertheless, whatever the size, the essentials of the books worked for the deceased.

In part, for example, C.W. Goodwin (1873: 104) discusses: "The $115^{th}$ Chapter of the Turin Book of the Dead" containing "a very remarkable legend relating to the city of *An* or Heliopolis. This chapter belongs to a group of ten extending from the $107^{th}$ to the $116^{th}$ all of which have reference to the recognition by the deceased person of the Ba-u or Spirits of certain localities where he meets them. Several of these chapters contain very antique legends explanatory of the ceremonies observed in certain towns. Thus, Chap 112 professes to explain the origin of the worship of Horus in the town of Pa. Chap 113 had a legend explanatory of the commemoration of the finding of the bands of Horus in the word of Chem. The $115^{th}$ Chapter …. Contains … an account of the destruction and reproduction of the race of man in the city of Heliopolis." Continuing: "The title of the chapter is 'The Chapter of going forth to heaven, of penetrating the shrine, of knowing the spirits of Heliopolis.' The word ammahu translated 'shrine' appears to be specially applied to that part of an Egyptian temple where the sacred relics of the gods or heroes were deposited. King Piankhi is said to have visited the holy place called Zersa near Heliopolis and there to have offered oblations to Tum and his circle of gods, in the house of the circle of gods, in which is the shrine (ammahu) of the gods."

# BLACK HISTORY EXTRAVAGANZA HONORING DR. BEN-JOCHANNAN

**Black History Extravaganza - Photo -** The traditional "four pitchers," a useful tool of the "Tree Goddess," who "pours them over the head" of the Deceased on way to the Hall of Judgment.

Accordingly, the story continued: "'I was a great one in time past among the great ones.' 'I was a creature among the creatures.' 'Gods and men are all described as being created with the exception of Ra the self-produced. The meaning of this passage is that the deceased claims to have appeared as a created being in some primeval period of time, and to have played a part in a previous state of existence upon the earth.' He says: 'I appeared before One-eye.' One eye in this case may be an epithet for the Sun, the eye and light of creation. 'When the circumference of darkness was opened, I was one among you.' 'I know the spirits of An.'"

# FREDERICK MONDERSON

As the explanation goes: "The passage is one of great difficulty, although all the words of which it is composed are known. The reading Atum, of the Hays papyrus, does not help us and appears to be a mistake. 'The most glorious Atum proceeds from it, even to the limits of the things which are visible.' 'I know how the woman was made from An.' Literally, the curly haired, is the name of a curled wig worn by the priest in certain ceremonies. It is a title of Hathor, and is applied to the votaresses of Hathor. 'This took the form of a curly haired woman.' 'Then he took the form of a curly haired woman.' 'It is the curly headed of An.'"

Again, C.W. Goodwin discussed: "On the 112th Chapter of the Ritual" (Nov-Dec 1871: 144-147) and "Another Chapter of the Knowledge of the Spirits of Pa." The deceased addresses the Great Body dwelling in Zxati (16th Nome of Lower Egypt, the Mendesian) in the city of Anpu or Anu, also the bird-catcher who reigned in Pa. These personages are styled 'the elders who are without end.' 'Do you not know wherefore the town of Pa was given to Horus?'

**Black History Extravaganza - Cairo -** Anther set of illustrated stone Coffins in the Cairo Museum.

# BLACK HISTORY EXTRAVAGANZA HONORING DR. BEN-JOCHANNAN

**Black History Extravaganza - Photo -** Tomb of Nakht - The Nobleman sits to inspect people and produce of his province.

In his own situation: "'Horus says to Ra, Grant that I may see the creatures of thy eyes, see as it (thy eye) sees them.' Ra says to Horus, 'Look I pray thee, at this black hog.' Said Horus to Ra, 'Behold my eye is as though Anepu had made an incision in my eye. Then we were grieved at heart.'"

He continued: "Anpu said to the gods: 'Put him upon his bed; he will get well. It was Seth who came and took the form of a black hog. Then he fomented the wound of the eye of Horus. These words explain the cause of the accident. When Ra invited Horus to look at a black pig as one of his own creations, the evil Set came and presented himself in the form of that animal, and Horus looked upon not only a creation of Set, but Set himself. Hence the injury to his eye.' Said Horus to the gods - Who are about him - 'When Horus was in his childhood the cattle of the gods were his oxen, his goats, his pigs. They are Amesta, Hapi, Tau-ma-f, and Kabh-senu-f, whose father is Horus, whose mother is Isis.' Horus says to Ra. - 'Grant me my brother in Pa and my brother in Xen, to be within me (in my power) and to be with me, for an eternal portion.'" An important interjection and observation here is that the "black pig" is white beneath its outer covering.

## IV. The Centers of Worship

There are several other features of the religion of ancient Egypt that sets it apart from so many ancient religious beliefs. Its monotheistic nature is affirmed by Budge (1934: 44) who holds that: "There is no doubt that the **EGYPTIANS** included monotheism among their dogmas, but it is impossible to say when their theologians evolved it. Two forms of it existed, a higher and a lower. The higher is the monotheism of Ptah of Memphis, the spirit God, the Eternal Mind, who existed before everything else, and created matter by thought, and the lower is the monotheism of Ra of Heliopolis. But the African monotheism of 3800 B.C. or earlier, though not to be compared with that of modern Christian people, is a remarkable spiritual achievement." It is because it was evolved so early in time. In that process of theological evolution, Erman (1907: 6-7) explained: "Numerous are the ideas concerning the universe, and the representations by which the people attempted to express their ideas. In one of these the sky appears as an immense cow whose feet are resting on the earth. In another the sky is a woman, who supports her hands and feet on the earth. But the most usual representation, at least in later times, is one where the sky is a sheet of water, on which the stars sail in boats; or again it rests on the so-called four pillars of

# BLACK HISTORY EXTRAVAGANZA HONORING DR. BEN-JOCHANNAN

heaven, fabulous mountains, situated at the four corners of the earth. While the sky is usually regarded as being feminine, a woman, and a cow, the earth figures as a man on whose back it is that vegetation grows. Apparently the grammatical gender of the two words - pet, 'sky,' is feminine, to, 'earth,' is masculine - led to this conception."

**Black History Extravaganza - Photo -** Tomb of Nakht - The Nobleman and wife appear before Ra-Horakhty and Rat his wife, enthroned.

# FREDERICK MONDERSON

**Black History Extravaganza - Photo -** Tomb of Nakht - A "Table of Offerings" stuffed with delectable edibles.

**a.** **Ra** was worshipped at Heliopolis, a city founded by the Black African Anu, as identified by Amelineau and Diop. Ra was considered one of the oldest Egyptian gods. "Temu or Ra, the great god of

# BLACK HISTORY EXTRAVAGANZA HONORING DR. BEN-JOCHANNAN

Heliopolis, was a material being, and the source whence he came was **NUNU**, the great primeval abyss of water. Water existed before Ra and was regarded as the oldest thing in the world, and therefore the 'father of the gods.' The cult of Ra, i.e., worship of the Sun-god, was well established at Heliopolis long before the union of the North and the South by **MENES** …. The Pyramid Texts show that he had recourse to masturbation in order to produce the twins Shu and Tefnut and the peoples of the Sudan. His cult was gross and material, and the benefits which the Egyptians hoped to receive from him, were material, virility, fecundity, robust health, and abundant offspring both human and animal …. As men expected Ra to give them great material prosperity on earth, so after death, in heaven they rely upon him to provide them with divine meat and drink and apparel, and unstinted gratification of their carnal appetites. In no prayer to Ra can be found a petition by the suppliant for spiritual gifts, or any expression indicating his need of divine help, for his soul. During the great festivals when a statue of the god was carried by the priests round the town or through the country the people in crowds appeared before him, for by this act they discharged a religious obligation and, so to say, acquired merit, and they expected the god to give them in return health, strength, virility, and prosperity."

Interesting enough, when the argument is made for an Egyptian origin outside of Africa, one has to wonder why their great god Ra made the "people of Nubia" so early in his work of creation after the Gods Shu and Tefnut! Are we to believe the Europeans who migrated to Egypt very early created the people of Nubia? Or, should we also believe the Nubians were Europeans? Nevertheless, the Nubians or Black people, were created before the Egyptians. How interesting! Even more important, the people of Nubia were created before the Caucasians! Still equally important, though his residence was established at Heliopolis, just beyond the fork in the Nile, we must wonder at his connection with Nubia. Did he sail down the Nile from Nubia? Did he make man, this Nubian, these Black people in his own image? In contemplating the prototype of the Nubians, the Black people, he had to use his own image and in his likeness the Black people this means Ra was Black! It is not far-fetched to believe he was Nubian for Ra is

# FREDERICK MONDERSON

often seen coming out of Nubia. If we fast forward to the Amarna Revolution, considered a "sun worship" phenomenon, it was also considered of southern origin. That is beyond the southern border in Nubia.

**Black History Extravaganza - Photo -** Ramose Tomb - Sorrowful expressions are expressed in different attitudes.

In that process of theological evolution, Erman (1907: 6-7) explained: "Numerous are the ideas concerning the universe, and the representations by which the people attempted to express their ideas. In one of these the sky appears as an immense cow whose feet are resting on the earth. In another the sky is a woman, who supports her hands and feet on the earth. But the most usual representation, at least in later times, is one where the sky is a sheet of water, on which the stars sail in boats; or again it rests on the so-called four pillars of heaven, fabulous mountains, situated at the four corners of the earth. While the sky is usually regarded as being feminine, a woman, and a cow, the earth figures as a man on whose back it is that vegetation grows. Apparently the grammatical gender of the two words - pet, 'sky,' is feminine, to, 'earth,' is masculine - led to this conception."

# BLACK HISTORY EXTRAVAGANZA HONORING DR. BEN-JOCHANNAN

**Black History Extravaganza - Papyrus -** Colorful "Birds in a Tree" is a favorite theme of Egyptian painting.

**b.     Ptah** was worshipped at Memphis after Unification when Narmer or Menes established the beginning of the First Dynasty and Dynastic period. It is not generally discussed where Narmer, a Theban, got his idea of the ramifications involved in the origins and establishment of this worship of Ptah. He was a god of creation as well as a patron of the arts and artisans. While considered 'Father of the gods' Ptah Nunu and 'god of the great abyss of water,' he wears the solar disk and plumes. As Ptah-Tanen 'the oldest earth-god in Egypt,' he holds the crown of Seker (horns, disk and plumes) and also holds the triple scepter. However, in his most popular form as Ptah of Memphis he is shown as a mummy god, with arms emerging, from his closely-fitted garment, at his chest and holding his scepter, wearing a beard with menat hanging from the back of his neck. Erman (1907: 17) describes Ptah as, "the divine sculptor, who gave and still gives form to all things, and beings on earth. He was regarded by artists and artisans as their patron."

Forget what that fellow McKenzie says, Ptah was also a pygmy, not a dwarf, god. The pygmies originated in Central Africa, source of earliest gold and it's no wonder some of the earliest goldsmiths are pygmies. Equally, these pygmies knew how to dance the "dance of the gods" coming, as they did from "the land of the gods!"

Continuing, Budge (1934: 13-14) added: "From the text which was rescued from oblivion by **SHABAKA** we learn that **PTAH**, the Great and Mighty, had eight principal forms among which were **PTAH-NUN**, and **PTAH-TANEN**. He therefore preceded **NUN** and **TANEN** in existence and he was their creator, and he created them by an effort of his heart or mind. Thus **PTAH** was the oldest being the priests could imagine, and he was the Eternal Heart or Mind and was self-created. The male part of **PTAH** begot **TEM** or **TEMU** or **RA**, and his female portion was the mother of the Sun-god of Heliopolis. And, like Ra, Ptah was the father and mother of men, and he conceived and fashioned and made the gods. Tem was a form or figure of Ra …. Tem produced the gods Shu and Tefnut by masturbation and self-impregnation, whereas Ptah produced the gods by the motions of thoughts of his mind. Horus, the oldest Sun-god in Egypt, acted as the heart or mind of Ptah, and Thoth, the god of wisdom, as his tongue. What the heart of Ptah thought passed on to Thoth who translated it into words, which were uttered by the one great almighty mouth, from which everything which is hath come, and

# BLACK HISTORY EXTRAVAGANZA HONORING DR. BEN-JOCHANNAN

everything which is to be shall come. Though Thoth was the Word-god, his actual creative power was derived from the magical pronouncement by Ptah, who alone knew how to utter the words with the correct intonation."  However, in Amon's origins hitherto obscured though he was very probably a foundation God from the earliest time, Erman (1907: 19) writes in associating Amon with his alter ego Min: "When, therefore, a few miles south of the home of Min, we meet with another god who wears similar lofty plumes, who is frequently represented as ithyphallic, and who also resembles Min in being of purely human form with dark complexion, it is natural to regard him as another form of Min. This god is no other than Amon of Thebes, king of the gods of later Egypt. In the early times with which we are now dealing, no one could have foreseen the importance that would one day accrue to him. He was the obscure god of a small town, and even his nearest neighbors, the people of Hermonthis, worshipped another god, the hawk-headed Mont. This Mont figures as the god of war."

**Black History Extravaganza - Photo -** Ramose's unfinished tomb with bundle papyrus columns with "one band."

# FREDERICK MONDERSON

**Black History Extravaganza - Photo - Steles -** With the exception of number three (bottom left, Horus as Ra-Horakhty), Osiris is the principal divinity being worshipped or celebrated.

# BLACK HISTORY EXTRAVAGANZA HONORING DR. BEN-JOCHANNAN

c. **Amon, Amen, later Amon-Ra** or **Amen-Ra** even **Amun-Ra** rose to national prominence in the Middle and New Kingdom after the successes of his Theban adherents. He dominated the country and the ancient world for more than a good millennium until Egypt became too weak to defend itself and continue its imperialist policies under strong and determined pharaonic leadership. He was on the same level as Ptah, even possessing some of his powers. Budge (1934: 17-18), quoting Sir Alan Gardener explained the nature and attributes of Amen, Amun or Amon in the following description:

**I.** **Amen's Origin**. He was self-created and as he fashioned himself none knoweth his forms. He existed first of the Eight Gods of Khenemu (Hermopolis), [The head of this Ogdoad was Thoth.] then he completed them and became one. He became in primeval times, no other being existed, there was no god before him; there was no other god with him to declare his form; all the gods came into being after him. He had no mother by whom his name was made; he had no other who begot him, saying, 'It is even myself.' He shaped his own egg; he mingled his seed with his body to make his egg to come into being within himself. He took the form of Tanen in order to give birth to the Pautti (Companies of the?) gods.

**II.** **The Hiddenness of Amen**. His body is hidden in the Chiefs. He is hidden as Amen at the head of the gods. Amen is one; he hides himself from the gods and conceals himself from them.

**III.** **His oneness**. His Unity is absolute.

**IV.** **He was a Trinity**, i.e., he had three persons, or characters. Champollion called this the Triad, the Theban Triad of Amon, the sun god; Mut, the earth goddess his wife; and Khonsu, the moon god, his son.

# FREDERICK MONDERSON

**V.** **His Name**. His name is more helpful to a man than hundreds of thousands of helpers. The gods cannot pray to him because his name is unknown to them. The man who utters the secret name of Amen falls down and dies a violent death. His name is victory.

**VI.** **Amen as lord of time**. He makes the years, rules the months; ordains nights and days. The night is as the day to him. He the One Watcher neither slumbers nor sleeps.

**VII.** **The beneficence of Amen**. He breaks evil spells, expels sicknesses from the bodies of men. He, the Physician, heals the Eye, he destroys the Evil Eye (?), he releases men from hell, he abrogates the Destinies (or Fates) of men at his good pleasure, he hears all petitions and is present immediately he is invoked, he prolongs or shortens the lives of men at will, to the man he loves he adds to what Fate has decreed for him, and to the man who sets him in his heart he is more than millions. He was a Bull for his town, a Lion for his people, a Hawk that destroyed his attackers, and at the sound of his roaring the earth quaked."

"From what has been said above it is quite clear that there was a monotheistic element in the Egyptian Religion. The Spirit-god Ptah was One, the material god Ra was One, and Amen who was claimed by his priests to be both Spirit and Matter was One." And even Ptah, Ra and Amen were considered one in unity. Thus, if Ptah as pygmy can be considered Black; Ra as Nubian as Black; and Amun, God of the 17th and 18th Dynasties must be Black. Even more important, given that Ptah, Ra and Amon are "One in Unity" and the first two are considered Black, then Amon is also Black, especially since his alter ego Min is Black! Of course as quoted above, Erman (1907) colors Amon Black. Let us not forget, "Amon is so black, he is blue." Equally, whether green or blue, even brown, these are simply variants of black!

# BLACK HISTORY EXTRAVAGANZA HONORING DR. BEN-JOCHANNAN

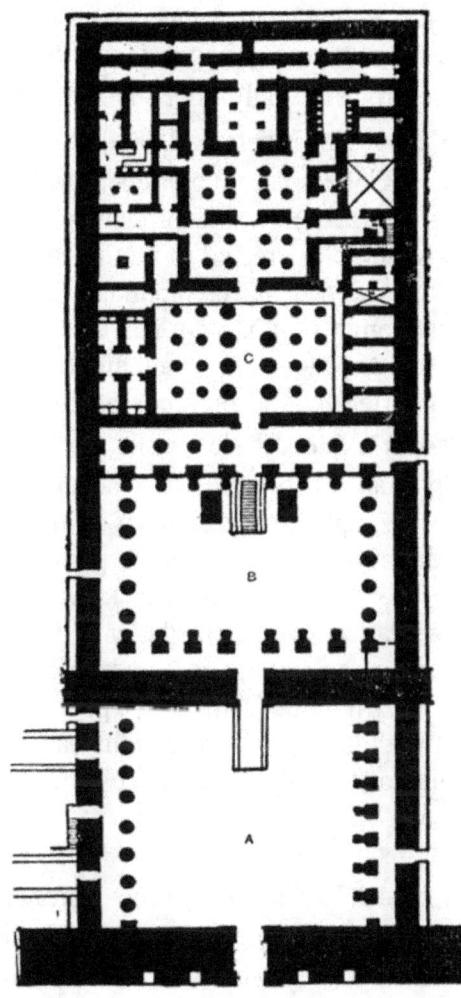

MEDINET HABU – MORTUARY TEMPLE OF RAMESES III

A. First Court
B. Second Court
C. First Hypostyle Hall
D. Second Hypostyle Hall
E. Third Hypostyle Hall
F. Sanctuary

**Black History Extravaganza - Plan of a Temple** - Medinet Habu, Mortuary Temple of Rameses III (20<sup>th</sup> Dynasty).

Thus, there is no question that the principal and more important gods were Black!

Much more important, however, is the wealth of Amon as managed by his Priesthood. Now, in terms of wealth, Amon's far exceeded all the other gods and perhaps this may very well be owing to the god's vigorous challenge executed by New Kingdom pharaohs resulting in successful military endeavors resulting in enormous booty acquired which in turn was granted the god as endowment. Much of this helped in expansive temple building construction and expansion of temple wealth under the Priesthood's control especially after the **Amarna Revolution and Restoration**. This is best explained by Erman (1907: 70) who sees the later New Kingdom as much richer. As such, he states: "So Amon-Re triumphed and how magnificent was his triumph is shown by the immense temples erected to him during the next ten years, and by the wealth of which he had command; but closer examination shows that the great convulsion had not passed without leaving traces behind. The State made peace with Amon and restored him to his rights, but it also supported the ancient gods of the great towns, Ptah of Memphis, Re-Har-akhte of Heliopolis, Osiris of Abydos, etc., far more zealously than it had previously; never had a sovereign built or rebuilt so many temples as did Ramses II; there is scarcely a temple in Egypt that did not receive proofs of is pious care, as if to counterbalance what he was doing for Amon in Karnak and Luxor. A political force was at work here. During the latter half of the New Kingdom, Lower Egypt increased greatly in importance, the royal residence was removed to a town in the Delta, and Upper Egypt once more sank into the subordinate position which naturally belonged to it. And thus in course of time the observance of the god of Thebes naturally declined."

This is further explained by Erman (1907: 70-71) who continued, quoting the Chester Beatty papyrus which states in essence: "In this second half of the New Kingdom, during the nineteenth and twentieth dynasties (about 1350-1100 B.C.) we find the Egyptian religion more magnificent and brilliant than it ever was before or after. Its gods were enthroned in those palatial temples which have no rivals in any other country or at any other period; temples that glistened with costly vessels, and where offerings and ceremonies were carried on in greatest magnificence. The property of the principal temples was immense. Under Rameses III the temple of Amon at Thebes possessed 926 square miles of land and 81,322 serfs, as well as 421,362 head of cattle. Heliopolis had 166 square miles of land, 12,963 serfs, and 45,544 head of cattle; while the respective numbers for Memphis,

# BLACK HISTORY EXTRAVAGANZA HONORING DR. BEN-JOCHANNAN

which was far behind, were nearly 11 square miles, 3,079 serfs, and 10,047 cattle. Such property and such temples naturally could not be administered in the simple fashion of earlier days, although no doubt it sill prevailed in the smaller temples. They required a complete administrative organization, where distinguished persons served as superintendents of the treasury, of the land, granaries, cattle, or peasantry, with scribes and soldiers, architects, sculptors, painters, and all classes of minor officials. The superior priests of such a temple had immense power in their hands, and the high-priest of Amon especially were men of almost royal rank."

**Black History Extravaganza - Ceramic Art -** Important Egyptian motifs resting on **Heb**.

# FREDERICK MONDERSON

**Black History Extravaganza - Papyrus -** A Gentleman and two Ladies with birds in a tree as a backdrop.

# BLACK HISTORY EXTRAVAGANZA HONORING DR. BEN-JOCHANNAN

To reinforce the view of rank and power, Erman (1907: 71) cites the experiences of a powerful individual to make his case. "The career of such a prince of the Church is described to us by one of them, Bekenkhons, a contemporary of Rameses II on his statue at Munich. He was apparently successor of another Bekenkhons, who was high-priest of Amon under Amenophis III, and had already *lived as an infant in the house of Amon*. Although from the first he was destined for the office of a priest, up to his fifteenth year he received, in common with other youths of rank, a military training as *overseer of the stables* to the king. He then entered as *we'b* into the service of Amon, and remained four years in this lowest rank of priesthood. He had then to serve twelve years as *divine father*, fifteen years as *third priest*, and twelve years as second. He was thus in his fifty-ninth year when the god made him, on account of his amazing excellence, the high-priest of Amon, an office he was destined to fill for twenty-six years, as a good father of the subordinates, who trained their successors, stretched out the hand to those in misery, who fed the poor, and acted nobly in his temple. Also he was first architect for the king for Thebes, and in this capacity adorned it with buildings and obelisks; he planted it with trees and otherwise arranged for the lordly equipment of Karnak."

**Black History Extravaganza - Photo -** The word is, "Dr. Ben was a man of integrity and unselfishness who loved Africans."

# FREDERICK MONDERSON

**Black History Extravaganza - Photo -** Stele - The Deceased stands before a **"Table of Offerings"** to address Osiris backed by Horus in Double Crown and Isis behind him.

**d.** **Osiris** was worshiped in several places throughout the land of ancient Egypt but his head was buried at Abydos and his heart was buried at Philae. As a result, these two locations became the principal centers for his worship. However, while Philae was given status it did not accord with Abydos where his principal mysteries were conducted. From the earliest times kings chose to be buried at Abydos. They built temples there as Petrie has confirmed finding 10 successive layers of temples dating back to the First Dynasty. Narmer worshipped at Abydos; so too did Khufu, builder of the Great Pyramid. In fact, the only image of Khufu, a miniature statue, was

# BLACK HISTORY EXTRAVAGANZA HONORING DR. BEN-JOCHANNAN

found in a ruined temple level at Abydos. Nobles erected stela if they could not be buried at Abydos; the dead, as indicated in illustrations, made the pilgrimage to Abydos to be near the god symbolically; and today this site boasts a surviving temple of the New Kingdom, essentially intact. This temple of Seti I at Abydos is a significant survival from the Ramesside Period and it boasts the finest surviving religious art of the entire land. His father Rameses I and his son Rameses II also built temples at Abydos.

**Black History Extravaganza - Photo -** Ramose Tomb - This Nobleman, wearing a collar and heart scarab while holding instruments of royal authority, is bathed by individuals who do not appear to be gods.

Abydos is where the mysteries of Osiris were performed as part of the re-enactment of the murder and resuscitation of the god who became judge of the dead. This sacred place became an early, perhaps the earliest, site of religious pilgrimage not simply for the living but the potential dead and the actual dead. Besides, the Abydos real estate became very valuable and those who could not purchase a plot to be buried, erected a stela, even kings did such; or, as many illustrations indicate many persons made the symbolic voyage to Abydos by river boat. One such example is the stela erected by King Rameses IV at

# FREDERICK MONDERSON

Abydos, in this "House of Life" where the learned sought knowledge of a higher science. According to Erman (1907: 80), Rameses' memorial tablet indicated he was very fond of the" house of life," the school of the learned. "He found there that *thy nature, Osiris, is more secret* than that of all gods. *Thou art the moon which is in heaven. Thou rejuvenatest thyself at thy desire, thou becomes young according to thy wish. Thou appearest in order to dispel darkness, anointed and clothed* (i.e., *in thy festival pomp), for the gods and magic come into existence to illuminate thy majesty and to bring thy enemies to the shambles ... And men reckon that they may know the month; and work addition, that they may know thy time.*"

"*Verily thou art the Nile, great upon the banks at the time of the beginning of the season; men and gods live by the moisture which comes from thee.*"

"*I have also found thy majesty as king of the under-world ... When Re rises every day and comes to the under-world, in order to survey this land and also the countries, thou sittest there also as he. Together ye shall be called Bai Demdem. The majesty of Thoth stands nigh unto you, Oh Great God, in order to execute the commands which proceed from your mouth.*"

Erman (1907: 80-81) continued further: "It will be seen that the character of god of the dead, that under which Osiris was known and venerated by every Egyptian, here takes the third place, and even then only in an unusual form. In its place the parts usually played by the moon and the Nile are attributed to Osiris. And a song which gives utterance to similar ideas, places Osiris almost on earth; it represents Osiris lying as a corpse under the earth, and, as it were, supporting it, with all that is on it; thus, his back can be regarded as the earth itself. *The earth lies upon thine arm, and its corners upon thee even unto the four pillars of heaven. Dost thou stir itself, the earth trembles, and (the Nile) comes forth from the sweat of thy hands. Thou providest the breath out of thy throat for the nostrils of mankind. Everything whereby man lives, trees and herbs, barley and wheat, is of divine origin, and comes from thee. - Are canals dug ... are houses and temples built, are monuments dragged into place, are fields laid out,*

# BLACK HISTORY EXTRAVAGANZA HONORING DR. BEN-JOCHANNAN

*are rock tombs and graves hewn out - they rest on thee, thou it is who makest them. They are upon thy back. Yet more there is of thee than can be written, there is no empty space on thy back, they all lie on thy back and (thou sayest) not: I am laden. - Thou art the father and mother of mankind, they live by thy breath, and they eat the flesh of thy body."*

e.　In addition to the above state centers of worship, Hermopolis boasted the cosmology of the Ogdoad, worship of the 8 gods with **Thoth** at its head, making 9. This notwithstanding, Thoth belonged to the Ra cycle of gods. Denise M. Doxey in *The Oxford Encyclopedia of Ancient Egypt* Vol. 3 (2001: 398-400), in explaining that Thoth was associated with science, medicine, cosmology, writing, nature and the afterlife as well as music, states: "As a moon god, Thoth regulated the season and lunar phases and counted the stars. Hence, he was associated with astronomy, mathematics and accounting. As the god of scribes and writing, Thoth, 'the lord of the sacred word,' personified divine speech. Seshat, the goddess of writing and literature, was said to be either his wife or daughter. By the Middle Kingdom, Thoth as a god of wisdom and justice was connected with Maat, the personification of rightness and world order. The Greeks viewed him as the source of all wisdom and the creator of languages."

"At Hermopolis, Thoth was worshipped as a cosmogonic deity, believed to have risen on a mound from the primeval chaos to create the Ogdoad consisting of Nun and Naunet, Heh, Heket, Kek, Keket, Amun and Amaunet, coordinated male and female couples representing various forces of nature. In solar religion, Thoth and Ma'at navigated the bark of Re." Even further, Doxey continued: "The principal cult center of Thoth was Hermopolis, ancient Egyptian Khenemu, near the modern town of el-Eshmunen. This was the site of a major New Kingdom temple, at which Amenhotep III claims to have dedicated a pair of thirty-ton quartzite baboons."

# FREDERICK MONDERSON

Thoth was considered a moon god, representative of Ra who was imaged as an Ibis-headed man. According to Erman (1907: 11) he was described as, *"the bull among the stars, the moon in* heaven as he is called in an inscription in the Berlin Collection." There Erman explained, "At the same time, he is the *scribe of the gods, and the judge in heaven*, who gave *speech and writing*, and by his arithmetic enabled the gods and men to keep account of their possessions. He is the god of all wisdom and learning, and he discovered the divine words, i.e., written characters. It is easy to see how it was that the moon god assumed this character, for he regulated time and therefore would be the representative of all reckonings and notes of events. The principal center of his worship was at Eshmunen in Middle Egypt, the town which was called Hermopolis in Greek times. Under another name, Khonsu, he who travels across the heavens, the moon was worshipped at Thebes in purely human form as a child, although this god appears to have been little known in early times outside his own abode. It is only in the New Kingdom that for a time we find representations of him appearing prominently elsewhere."

**Black History Extravaganza - Photo** - Ramose Tomb - Notice how she grasps his hand. He wears a necklace but the hair on both is not, what you would call "free-flowing Caucasian hair," but seems "cornrow type."

# BLACK HISTORY EXTRAVAGANZA HONORING DR. BEN-JOCHANNAN

As an explanation of Thoth's creative powers, Maspero (1891: 2) wrote: "The voice without speech was reputed to have the same effect as the two combined, and had been, according to certain Egyptian schools, the agent of Creation." That is: "The Supreme God who is reputed to be the God of Creation, opens his mouth, and the gods come out of it, either the gods generally, or some particular god. Once come forth, the gods each set to work on that which they were predestined to accomplish. These texts have hitherto been translated under the influence of the preconceived idea that what was here meant was a formula, and not an emission of the voice: but this is only an instinctive interpretation, and the Egyptian phrases simply state the fact of a Divine mouth opening and gods issuing from it."

**Black History Extravaganza - Photo -** While the grieving female kneels at its foot, Anubis administers to the encased Mummy with a Stela showing the deceased before enthroned Osiris and the "Two Eyes of Horus" overlooking a tomb surmounted by a pyramid in vicinity of the mountain, presumably where Hathor is generally regarded as coming out of.

He goes on to quote from a magical book in Greek that says, *inter al*, the magician addresses himself to Thoth. "'I invoke thee,' he says, 'Oh Hermes, thou who containest everything in every speech and dialect, as thou was first celebrated by the subordinate, the Sun, to whom the care of everything is entrusted.' The solar forms then salute *Thoth*, who answers them thus: 'And speaking, the god clapped his

# FREDERICK MONDERSON

hands, and burst seven times bursts of laughter. *Kha, Kha, Kha, Kha, Kha, Kha, Kha,* and when he had done laughing, seven gods were born,' one for each burst of laughter, as we see. When Hermes first laughed, light appeared, to light everything; and the Creation began to take place. He laughed six times in succession, and each burst of laughter gave birth to a fresh being and a fresh phenomenon; the earth, feeling the sound, in its turn gave utterance to a cry and bowed itself, and the waters were divided into three bodies (*masses*). Then were born Destiny, Justice, Opportunity, the Soul. The last, at its birth, first laughed, then wept, whereupon the god gave forth a breath, bent him towards the earth and produced the serpent Python, which is possessed of universal prescience. At the sight of the dragon the god was struck with stupor, and clacked his lips, whereupon an armed being appeared. The god, seeing this was again struck with stupor, as at sight of a more powerful one than himself, and, lowering his eyes towards the earth, exclaimed, *Iao!* The god who is master of everything was born of the reach of that sound."

**Black History Extravaganza - Photo** - Another Blank Cartouche beside the Astrological sign for Aries.

# BLACK HISTORY EXTRAVAGANZA HONORING DR. BEN-JOCHANNAN

## V. The Temple as Sanctuary for the Gods and Place of Worship and Ritual

**a.** The nature of the temple architecture was dictated by the geography, period, royal family or dynasty in power and shaped by the wealth they possessed in order to endow their god. The king built a temple to his god, and since the house of the god was a thing of eternity, the building was constructed in stone which had to be quarried at some distance where good stone was located. This endeavor thus gave birth to a number of enterprises and disciplines such as quarrying, boat building, river transportation and ancillary trades of building and artistic decoration. Once the stone was removed to the place of erection, the structure was further finished and beautified with elaborate artistic renderings that depicted the ritual and other facets of the pharaoh's existence, as it related to worship of his god.

**b.** Temples had names and statues, sphinxes, and obelisks generally stood before the entrance.

**c.** Pylon and Court were parts of the temple entrance that the visitor encountered as well as the pharaoh when he came to pay homage to his god. The Pylon was generally decorated on the outer face and there were openings for flagstaves that flew flags of the god, Nome and nation. Courts were decorated with a variety of features including altars, colonnades, kiosks, sphinxes, statues, other temples and sometimes a porch or portico that entranced a subsequent Pylon, even a Hypostyle Hall.

# FREDERICK MONDERSON

**Black History Extravaganza - Photo -** Userhet Tomb - While some attendants administer to cattle, others appear in adoration.

**d.** Halls and Colonnades were decorated features that carried images of the various themes and rituals of the temple and showcased the wealth of the particular god worshipped there. In some respects, this architectural feature became "the glory of Egypt." The Hypostyle Hall is where the Procession assembled and the walls depicted the ritual performed therein. It has been argued, stepping into the Hypostyle Hall, one left the confines and strictures of the mundane world to enter into the abode of divinity, and *ipso facto*, a zone of purity. Leaving, one experienced the reverse.

**e.** The Sanctuary was the place where the god rested in absolute darkness that only the pharaoh or high priest dared to enter. Naturally, because of the extensive nature of the temple ritual, the king and high priest needed assistants who carried books of the liturgy, liquid and solid offerings, clothing, food; there were musicians in attendance playing their instruments and singing, dancers, incense bearers, guards, etc. While their functions carried them in proximity to the sanctuary, they never entered into the sacred space. Interestingly

# BLACK HISTORY EXTRAVAGANZA HONORING DR. BEN-JOCHANNAN

enough, again, as one ventured deep into the temple, the floor rose and the ceiling sank so that the Sanctuary became the highest point in the structure. In the Sanctuary there was an altar upon which the lustrations of the god were performed. However, incense, as an essential part of the ritual, was never burnt on the altar, but in an incenser in some corner of this inner recess. Some sanctuaries had one, some two chambers. Some were open and others were closed.

**f.** Adjoining chambers were designed to accommodate the vestments and liquid and solid offerings of the ritual, as well as the elements of the god's toilet. Oftentimes these adjoining chambers contained a library as well as served as a bark station for the god's ark or boat. Sometimes these adjoining chambers were decorated. Some temples had halls, rooms, even chapels for subsidiary divinities worshipped in the temple. While Karnak had its principal Triad of Amon, Mut and Khonsu with their respective temples, there were altogether some 22 temples of gods in the northern, central and southern sectors of this national sanctuary, Karnak.

## VI.     The Afterlife Dynamic

**a.** The tomb was an important part of the individual's earthly existence and great effort was made to prepare and furnish it correctly since he hoped to dwell there for an eternity. In this regard, Petrie (1912: 240) writes: "The funerary branch of the religion has become better known than any other, owing to the prominence of the tombs among the other remains…. The tomb was essentially the house of the dead, where the soul would live; and the intrinsic fact which has made the Egyptian tomb so important to us is the custom of representing the ordinary course of life in sculpture and painting on the walls of the funerary chapel in order to gratify the deceased with the pleasures of life."

# FREDERICK MONDERSON

**Black History Extravaganza - Photo -** Userhet Tomb - Reading out the instructions to prepare the attendants to perform their functions.


The nature of the tomb varied with the time period referenced in the religion, the period in history and the particular individual interred there under the respective pharaoh. In Predynastic times, the deceased was buried in a hole in the desert sand where the heat of the soil rapidly created natural mummification and essentially, that was the seed germ of immortality. In the Old Kingdom, the pharaohs were buried in pyramids and before that in the earliest tombs, as at Abydos. Here at Abydos, there were real tombs and cenotaphs or dummy tombs were erected at Sakkara, burial site of the Memphis capital. His two tombs in the North and South represented the dual nature of the pharaoh as king of Upper and Lower Egypt.

Much ink has been spilled as scholars debated which tomb, at Abydos or Memphis, was the actual one and which a cenotaph or dummy tomb. Coming as he did from Thebes, Upper Egypt, Narmer may have chosen to be buried at Abydos the holy city rather than Memphis his administrative capital. His son Aha built an enormous tomb for his mother Neith-Hotep at Abydos. The consensus today is Abydos held

# BLACK HISTORY EXTRAVAGANZA HONORING DR. BEN-JOCHANNAN

the body and Memphis, an empty tomb though filled with all the amenities of an afterlife existence. Seti I's temple to Osiris at Abydos was actually oriented to face the Thinite first and second dynasty, ancestor kings buried in the nearby desert. Thus, the function and symbolism of Seti's temple; that of his father Rameses I and his son, Rameses II, including Petrie's "Ten Temples at Abydos," it can be argued for Abydos being the site of the real tomb. Thus, such purported proximity to the Archaic burials lend great credence to the bodies being at Abydos and Memphis being the cenotaphs.

These eternal resting places were provisioned with 'goods of the grave;' or as the Cairo Museum of Egyptian Antiquities labels them, 'funerary furniture.' By the time of the Old Kingdom, officials preferred to be buried near the king's pyramid, so much so that since he was assured the immortality of heaven, being in his shadow enabled them to share in his good fortune. Again, this is probably because Ra worship generally predominated in the Old Kingdom and Osiris worship at Abydos did not get the full recognition it came to at a much later time. Now, by the time of the Middle and New Kingdom, there developed what was called "democratization of the afterlife," in that now practically everyone could get to heaven, as did the king, providing the individual lived the good life as dictated by the tenets of Ma'at. Importantly, wealth and status played an important role in type of tomb and "provisioning" for eternity. We must not forget, however, the two belief systems. These were, that in one case, Ra worship: the deceased flew skywards to heaven. On the other hand, given the body was deposited in the earth, the kingdom of Osiris created the belief there were two realties of religious belief.

Whereas in the Old Kingdom Pharaohs built pyramids and nobles erected Mastaba tombs in associated cemeteries disposed in street-like patterned arrangements, they were essentially vulnerable to tomb robbers. By the Middle Kingdom a shift occurred moving from the monoliths to more subterranean tombs in the desert. Further changes occurred and for security purposes, tombs of the kings, queens, nobles and artisans of the New Kingdom were dug into the mountainside at Thebes. These were equally and tremendously decorated with scenes of this world and the next. While some tombs depicted social themes, others emphasized the afterlife and were replete with literary themes outlining the drama of the underworld. Most Middle Kingdom tombs have not been found and when this happens, these are further discovered, it would provide a bonanza of religious, artistic and societal factual data that would further refine our understanding of Egyptian belief and practices, especially in this time period.

**Black History Extravaganza - Photo -** With Khepre overhead enclosed by "Two Eyes of Horus" and Uraei, two men stand before a "Table of Offerings" before Ra-Horakhty.

# BLACK HISTORY EXTRAVAGANZA HONORING DR. BEN-JOCHANNAN

**b.** Mummification began very early in the Old Kingdom and reached a high state of perfection by the time of the New Kingdom. In fact, some scholars see mummification as beginning in Nubia before the dynasties began. In Egypt, more probably, bodies of the poor especially, buried in the hot desert sands experienced a rapid form of natural mummification; more so than the dead buried in enclosed tombs that soon disintegrated. Nevertheless, because of the religious considerations, great effort was made to mummify the body in preparation for the deceased's "return" following the pressing dynamics of the afterlife requirements. Herodotus tells us there were three types of mummification processes based on the economic status of the deceased with the wealthy being more elaborate in their choice of preparation, provision and decoration. This mummification process aided the development of science, medicine and treatment of the sick as well as dead. It also helped in creating a written record of anatomy and physiology as well as a medicinal pharmacopeia possessing great variety in medicine, mineral, botanical and animal, as well as in treatment.

**Black History Extravaganza - Photo -** Showgi Abd Rady, and friends. The fellow with the Turban is terrific.

# FREDERICK MONDERSON

**Black History Extravaganza - Photo -** Sennutem Tomb - The "Boat of Ra" sails between two baboons, images of Thoth.

**c.** The Judgment was an important part of the Egyptian's otherworldly experience and seems he prepared for it from the earliest times of his existence regarded as social and economic conscious readiness. In order to get to the Judgment, once dead, the individual had to navigate a set of challenges consisting of pylons and portals guarded by dangerous and perhaps malevolent divinities seeking to impede his entry in the Underworld as he headed to the Hall of Judgment. By having the right magical knowledge and words of power he was able to address the various guardians in order to arrive at the Hall of African Judgment unimpeded where his heart was weighed against a feather of truth, Ma'at. This was called the **Psychostasia** where sometimes as few as a dozen and as many as forty-two judges sat and observed the process. Thoth and Anubis as well as Am-mit 'searched' the deceased before finding him guilty or 'true of voice' or "Justified." Upon the latter it was announced by Thoth and the assessors or jurors affirmed his findings, then the deceased was introduced to Osiris, the Egyptian god of the dead.

# BLACK HISTORY EXTRAVAGANZA HONORING DR. BEN-JOCHANNAN

**Black History Extravaganza - Photo -** Khepre, in resplendent color, performs his function of "pushing the Dung."

**d.** Before the actual weighing of the heart against the feather of truth or Ma'at the deceased was made to make the **42 Negative Confessions** affirming that he did not commit those unacceptable behaviors. The Negative Confessions were said to the 42 assessors but some scholars, such as Dr. ben-Jochannan, believed they were part of a greater body of more than 147 such confessions. Equally there was a body of 'positive confessions' the deceased made as well indicating he had done these "good" things.

**e.** The notion of standing before your god at the end of your existence was a horrifying feeling and inherently it steered individuals to live a positive and constructive lifestyle. This quest for righteousness does not, however, lead us to believe all Egyptians lived right and truthfully espousing Justice in their relations and affairs.

# FREDERICK MONDERSON

**Black History Extravaganza - Photo -** Sennutem Tomb - The Nobleman stands, with hands raised in adoration, before the seated gods.

**Black History Extravaganza - Photo -** Sennutem Tomb - Traveling in the "Boat or Ra" with Thoth in colorful headdress on point.

# BLACK HISTORY EXTRAVAGANZA HONORING DR. BEN-JOCHANNAN

**f.**     The reward for the good life lived on earth is peace of mind in this world and eternal bliss in the next. Some people believe goodness is an outstanding moral virtue that allows the individual to live in harmony with his surroundings, people, places and even things and animals. "It makes you sleep sound at night." However, the whole notion of goodness is an essential prerequisite of being able to survive the judgment and live among the immortals in the next life to enjoy the eternal bliss of heaven, that place of spiritual and everlasting purity.

**Black History Extravaganza - Photo -** Beside a Blank Cartouche, and with "Two Eyes of Horus" overhead, a queen makes a wonderful Presentation to an enthroned king.

## VII. Worship and Ritualizing the Gods

# FREDERICK MONDERSON

**a.** The Priesthood, as a body and serving many gods, very early developed into a professional organization with a many-faceted functionality. This gained them the power of not only being protectors of the god because of their close relationship, but also having a significant impact on the society in general because of their technical, intellectual and scientific know-how. This is explained in part by Flinders Petrie in *Religious Life in Ancient Egypt* (London: Constable and Company Ltd., 1924: 41) who writes: "The priests were teachers and exponents of religious and moral duty. Every day at the sacrifice, the King had to listen to a prayer which would be a severe satire on his failings, and afterward a sermon on past history, 'that the prince might seriously consider and ponder what was most commendable in those examples. What was teaching for the king was also teaching for the subject, and the priesthood controlled education as well as being guardian of morals and character." Even further, as Diodorus says the priests "are highly reverenced and in great authority among the people, both for their piety toward the gods, and their great wisdom and learning wherein they instruct the people.... By the help of astrology, and viewing the entrails of the sacrifices, they divine and foretell future events, and out of the records in the sacred registers from things done in former times, they read present lectures for profitable use and practices."

As full-time intermediaries between the gods and king and people, their power grew immensely. Very early this organization acquired a tax-free status and came into control of much wealth because of the perennial, especially, imperial endowments they became guardians over, as they were also entrusted to propagate the memories of deceased persons. Soon kings and nobles were not only lavishing great wealth on the gods and by extension on the priesthood, especially during the New Kingdom's imperialistic age, but weak kings also became very wary and afraid of the power of this multifunctional body that could interpret the wishes of divinity. As intermediary between the divine and profane, the priests knew things and exercised an extraordinary power that made kings and commoners stand in awe and in fear.

# BLACK HISTORY EXTRAVAGANZA HONORING DR. BEN-JOCHANNAN

**Black History Extravaganza - Photo -** Is this an exchange of animals in art? Notice water bags hanging from trees in the center.

The article "Religion" in Ian Shaw and Paul Nicholson's *The British Museum Dictionary of Ancient Egypt*, (1995) (2003: 244-245) states: "Ancient Egyptian state religion was concerned with the maintenance of the divine order; this entailed ensuring that life was conducted in accordance with Maat, and preventing the encroachment of chaos. In such a system it was necessary for religion to permeate every aspect of life, so that it was embedded in society and politics, rather than being a separate category. The Egyptian view of the universe was capable of incorporating a whole series of apparently contradictory creation myths. This holistic view also led to the treatment of prayer, magic and science as realistic and comparative alternatives, as a result it made good sense to combine what might now be described as medical treatment with a certain amount of ritual and recitation of prayers, each component of the overall treatment giving the same aim; to suppress evil and maintain the harmony of the universe."

# FREDERICK MONDERSON

**Black History Extravaganza - Photo -** Sennutem Tomb - The deceased and wife receive nourishment from the "Tree Goddess."

**Black History Extravaganza - Photo -** Sennutem Tomb - The gods sit in contemplation, Osiris, Isis and others.

# BLACK HISTORY EXTRAVAGANZA HONORING DR. BEN-JOCHANNAN

The temples and their attendant priests therefore served as a perpetual means of helping to stabilize the universe. Each day they attended to the needs of the god (who was thought to manifest in the cult image), made offerings to him, and thus in their efforts kept the forces of chaos at bay. A distinction is sometimes made between, on the one hand, the important state gods (Horus or Isis) and local deities (Banebdjedet at Mendes, for example), and, on the other hand, the "popular' or 'household' deities such as Bes and Taweret."

**b.** An important function of the priesthood, beside worshipping and ritualizing the gods, was the responsibility of managing the estate of the divinity. This financial responsibility allowed the lifeblood of the priesthood to venture into and play an essential role in the society's economy; at times, with the power they were able to harness, they ventured into social and political realms. They collected taxes, owned their own land and farms, maintained ships on the Nile River that carried their merchandise of food, arts and crafts which they also manufactured for purposes of trade. There were towns given as endowments and they had to manage these so their prosperity could be multiplied. The priesthood owned untold cattle, chickens, hectares of land, ships, slaves, gardens, orchards, vessels of wine, beer, oil, and the technical sophistication to engage in all forms of trade and craft, from building, quarrying, and transportation to artistry and construction to practicing medicine and teaching science and trained the state's bureaucratic establishment and more. Thus, they built, educated others, extended the realms of science, pursued mathematics and medicine. They were engaged in engineering, farming, and essentially "managed the society," while serving their god. Their power became so immense the pharaohs, weak ones that is, kept a close eye on this religious power that also combined economic, scientific and moral power with religious acumen in addition to having the ability to interpret the will of the gods, while also having and ultimately exercising political ambitions. This latter became so acute that the priesthood was able to seize power after the collapse of the New Kingdom proclaiming one of their own pharaoh in the $22^{nd}$ Dynasty.

# FREDERICK MONDERSON

**c.** Circumstances in relationship within the society and challenges from neighbors created an imperialist outlook and pharaohs took the sword to nations abroad while they quelled resistance at home. Warrior pharaohs pursued an imperialist policy of conquest and incorporation into their very extensive and expanding empires with demands of tribute on the nations they conquered and allied with. Much of the ensuing wealth they accumulated from their exploits abroad was lavished on the gods and priesthood, enabling them to build fabulous temples with beautiful decorations, while possessing enormous quantities of gold. In pharaoh's relationship with the gods they gave him their blessing which translated into victories with attendant wealth as booty that in turn was offered as temple endowments. Naturally, persons who distinguished themselves in the king's military exploits were rewarded with distinctions of titles, gold, land and even slaves. This state of affairs continued for centuries and as the nation grew wealthier, the priesthood benefited and the god whose estate they managed became wealthier, and so this state of affairs continued. society expanded, engaged in intellectual endeavors and paved the way for humanity's continued cultural growth. When there were no young, vigorous and strong pharaohs to defend Egypt, their numerous enemies massed and were attracted to the wealth of the state and priests whose fortunes were legendary. The temples then were, for economic and practical reasons, the first targets of invading forces who looted the holy places, desecrated the sanctuaries of the gods, destroyed much and carried off significant portions of their wealth and people. They were also internal challenges that threatened the gods, the priesthood and the society, until "a savior" arose who set order back in its place.

# BLACK HISTORY EXTRAVAGANZA HONORING DR. BEN-JOCHANNAN

**Black History Extravaganza - Photo -** Sennutem Tomb - Again, the Gods seated and observing!

**d.** Religion advanced science because of its essential role in the society since the principal proponents were also the intellectual elite and this beat back the mist of ignorance. Astronomy, medicine, mathematics, government, law, education, building, quarrying, farming, arts and crafts, trade, theology, theogony, metaphysics, mummification, perhaps even warfare, sanctioned, those essential ingredients that propel society and civilization, all can be traced to the practice of religion and praise of the gods. Finally, as Dennison Ross (1931: 1) reminded in his **Introduction**, "It must not, however, be forgotten that side by side with the religious building, sculpture and paintings, there flourished in Egypt the domestic arts and that these, being secular, survived the eclipse of the Egyptian Religion. It is here that we may trace a continuity of style and technique persisting through Greco-Roman, the Coptic and the Islamic Periods." Thus, the Nile River whose effluence flowed from Central Africa manifested in a tremendous gift that served as foundation ingredient helping to enlighten and sustain Egypt and ultimately influencing the world.

# FREDERICK MONDERSON

## REFERENCES

Budge, E.A. Wallis. *The Egyptian Heaven and Hell*. New York: Dover Publications, (1905) 1996.
_____. *Egyptian Religion*. New York: Carol Publishing Group: A Citadel Press Book, (1900) 1991.
_____. *From Fetish to God in Ancient Egypt*. London: Oxford University Press, 1934.
Doxey, Denise M. "Religion." *The Oxford Encyclopedia of Ancient Egypt*. Vol. 3. London: Oxford University Press, (2001: 398-400).
Frankfort, Henri. *Ancient Egyptian Religion*. New York: Harper and Row, Publishers (1946) 1961.
Goodwin, C.W. "On the 112th Chapter of the Ritual. (November-December, 1871: 144-147).
_____. "The 115th Chapter of the Turin Book of the Dead," (1873: 104).
Maspero, Gaston. "Creation by Voice and the Ennead of Heliopolis." *9th International Congress of Orientalists*, (1-10 September, 1891: 1-10).
Murray, Margaret. *Egyptian Temples*. London: Sampson Low, Marston and Co., Ltd., 1931.
Osei, G. K. *African Contributions to Civilization*. London: African Publication Society, 1983.
Rawlinson, George. *The Story of the Nations*: *Ancient Egypt*. London: T. Fisher Unwin and New York: G.P. Putnam's Sons, 1893.
Shaw, Ian and Paul Nicholson. "Religion." *The British Museum Dictionary of Ancient Egypt*. London: The British Museum, (1995) (2003: 244-245).
Ross, E. Dennison. (Ed). *The Art of Egypt*: *Through the Ages*. London: The Studio Ltd., 1931.
Shorter, Alan W. *The Egyptian Gods*: *A Handbook*. London: Rutledge and Kegan Paul, (1937) 1981.

# BLACK HISTORY EXTRAVAGANZA HONORING DR. BEN-JOCHANNAN

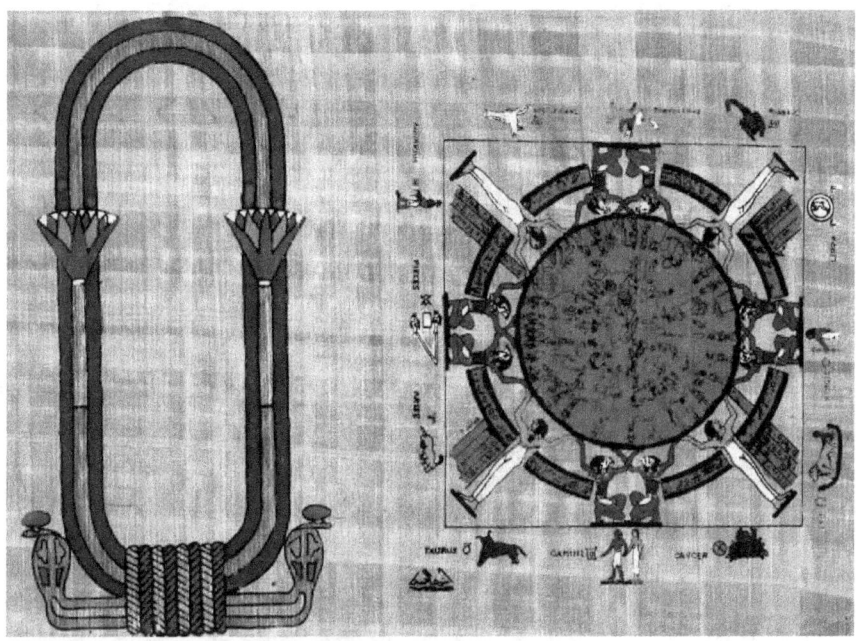

**Black History Extravaganza - Photo -** Still another Blank Cartouche beside the complete listing of the Astrological chart.

Franz Cumont, in "The Religion of Egypt." (Trans. From the French by A.M. Thielen) *The Open Court*, 24 (1910: 553-573) explained:

"At times the Egyptian ritual attributed considerable importance to purity, or, to use a more adequate term, to cleanliness. Before every ceremony the officiating priest had to submit to ablutions, sometimes to fumigations or anointing, and to abstain from certain foods and from incontinence for a certain time. Originally no moral idea was connected with this purification. It was considered a means in which the sacrifice performed by him could have the expected effect. It was similar to the diet, shower-baths and massage prescribed by physicians for physical health. The internal status of the officiating person was a matter of as much indifference to the celestial spirits as the actual worth of the deceased was to Osiris, the judge of the underworld. All that was necessary to have him open the fields of Aalu to the soul was to pronounce the liturgic formulas, and if the soul

# FREDERICK MONDERSON

declared its innocence in the prescribed terms its word was readily accepted." (565-566)

**Black History Extravaganza - Photo -** Iri Nufer Tomb - Anubis administers to the Mummy. Notice, the beard of the mummy is curved. Normally, the king's beard is straight and the beard of the god is curved. In this case, the king must have reached apotheosis or he is administering to a deceased god.

"To the Egyptians ritual had a value far superior to that we ascribe to it to-day. It had an operative strength of its own that was independent of the intentions of the officiating priest. The efficacy of prayer depended not on the inner disposition of the believer, but on the correctness of the words, gestures and intonation. Religion was not clearly differentiated from magic. If a divinity was invoked according to the correct forms, especially if one knew how to pronounce its real name, it was compelled to act in conformity to the will of its priest. The sacred words were an incantation that compelled the superior powers to obey the officiating person, no matter what purpose he had in view. With the knowledge of the liturgy men acquired an immense power over the world of spirits. Porphyry was surprised and indignant

# BLACK HISTORY EXTRAVAGANZA HONORING DR. BEN-JOCHANNAN

because the Egyptians sometimes dared to threaten the gods in their orations. In the consecrations the priest's summons compelled the gods to come and animate their statues, and thus his voice created divinities, as originally the might voice of Tot had created the world." (567)

**Black History Extravaganza - Photo -** Iri Nufer Tomb - Under the shadow of a tree, the Nobleman bends down to drink a sip of water from the Nile while a goddess kneels nearby with wings ready to be spread.

"The ritual that conferred such superhuman power developed in Egypt into a state of perfection, completeness, and splendor unknown in the Occident. It possessed a unity, a precision and a permanency that stood in striking contrast to the variety of the myths, the uncertainty of the dogmas and the arbitrariness of the interpretations. The sacred books of the Greco-Roman period are a faithful reproduction of the texts that were engraved upon the walls of the pyramids at the dawn of history, notwithstanding the centuries that passed. Even under the Caesars the ancient ceremonies dating back to the first ages of Egypt,

# FREDERICK MONDERSON

were scrupulously performed because the smallest word and the least gesture had their importance." (567-568)

The ritual and the attitude toward it found their way for the most part into the Latin temples of Isis and Serapis. This fact has long been ignored, but there can be no doubt about it. A first proof is that the clergy of those temples were organized just like those of Egypt during the period of the Ptolemies. There was a hierarchy presided over by a high priest, which consisted of prophets skilled in the sacred science, stolistes, or ornatrices, whose office it was to dress the statues of the gods, pastophores who carried the sacred temple plates in the processions, and so on, just as in Egypt. As in their native country, the priests were distinguished from common mortals by a tonsure, by a linen tunic, and by their habits as well as by their garb. They devoted themselves entirely to their ministry and had no other profession. This sacerdotal body has always remained Egyptian in character, if not in nationality, because the liturgy it had to perform remained so. In a similar manner the priests of the Baals were Syrians, because they were the ones that knew how to honor the gods of Syria." (568)

**Black History Extravaganza - Photo - Nefertari's Tomb -** While the Deceased rests in a Mummy case, the Gods stand to admire and on guard.

# BLACK HISTORY EXTRAVAGANZA HONORING DR. BEN-JOCHANNAN

"In the first place a daily service had to be held just as in the Nile valley. The Egyptian gods enjoyed a precarious immortality, for they were liable to destruction and dependent on necessities. According to a very primitive conception that always remained alive, they had to be fed, clothed and refreshed every day or else perish. From this fact arose the necessity of a liturgy that was practically the same in every district. It was practiced for thousands of years and opposed its unfaltering form to the multiplicity of legends and local beliefs."

**Black History Extravaganza - Photo** - Iri Nufer Tomb - With a Sem-Priest in Lion skin at his rear, Khepre sits enthroned holding symbols of his power, akh and scepter.

The daily liturgy was translated into Greek, perhaps into Latin also.

"The essential ceremony always was the opening (*apertio*) of the sanctuary. At dawn the statue of the divinity was uncovered and opened to the community in the naos, that had been closed and sealed during the night. Then, again as in Egypt, the priest lit the sacred fire and offered libations of water supposed to be from the deified Nile,

# FREDERICK MONDERSON

while he chanted the usual hymns to the sound of flutes. Finally, 'erect upon the threshold' - I translate literally from Porphyry - 'he awakens the god by calling to him in the Egyptian language.' As we see, the god was revived by the sacrifice and, as under the Pharaohs, awoke from his slumber at the calling of his name. As a matter of fact, the name was indissolubly connected with the personality: he who could pronounce the exact name of an individual or of a divinity was obeyed as a master by his slave. This fact made it necessary to maintain the original form of that mysterious word." (568-569)

**Black History Extravaganza - Ceramic Art -** The Great Bird in wonderful color against a golden background.

"During the entire forenoon, from the moment that a noisy acclamation had greeted the rising of the sun, the images of the gods were exposed to the silent adoration of the initiates. Egypt is the country whence contemplative devotion penetrated into Europe.

# BLACK HISTORY EXTRAVAGANZA HONORING DR. BEN-JOCHANNAN

Then, in the afternoon, a second service was held to close the sanctuary." (569)

"Death was the first mystery; it started man on the road of the other mysteries. Nowhere else was life so completely dominated by preoccupation with life after death; nowhere else was such minute and complicated care taken to secure and perpetuate another existence for the deceased. The funeral literature, of which we have found a very great number of documents, had acquired a development equaled by no other, and the architecture of no other nation can exhibit tombs comparable with the pyramids or the rock-built sepulchers of Thebes." (571-572)

"The fate of Osiris, the god who died and returned to life, became the prototype of the fate of every human being that observed the funeral rites. 'As truly as Osiris lives' says an Egyptian text, 'he also shall live; as truly as Osiris is not dead, shall he not die; as truly as Osiris is not annihilated, shall he not be annihilated." (572)

**Black History Extravaganza - Photo -** Iri Nufer Tomb - The Gods sit, paired, in majestic splendor.

# FREDERICK MONDERSON

**Black History Extravaganza - Photo -** Iri Nufer Tomb - Again, Gods sit with sun disk and stars overhead.

# BLACK HISTORY EXTRAVAGANZA HONORING DR. BEN-JOCHANNAN

G.H. Richardson, "The World's Debt to Egypt" The *Open Court* 28 (1914: 303-323).

"Sir Richard Burton speaking of Egypt said, "Egypt is the teacher of all nations."

It was the inventor of the alphabet, the cradle of letters …. and, generally speaking, the source of all human civilization.'"

Even further, that Mosso (*The Dawn of Mediterranean Civilization*) has explained, "many still believe that our civilization comes from Asia, but anthropology has decided the controversy, and we know that the Asiatic race never penetrated into Egypt, the Nile Valley, or into the isles of the Aegean. Although the origin of man is wrapped in mystery, naturalists are agreed in admitting the preponderating influence of Africa upon the population of Europe." (303)

"Our modern civilization is the outgrowth of that of the Mediterranean, and this can be traced back to the Nile valley, where, if the antiquity of the monuments is a safe guide, we find an advanced civilization many centuries before we find it in Babylon. In fact, it is in the Nile valley that we find the first civilization. When Egypt first appears in history proper we find her with a civilization practically complete - writing, administration, cults, ceremonies, a philosophical religion, and a social system. The antiquity of Egypt is almost unthinkable. 'Seven cycles of civilization take us back to the beginning, with strides for which our two cycles in Europe, the classical and the medieval, scarcely prepare us."

Nestor L'Hote, after prolonged study said: 'The farther one penetrates into antiquity towards the origins of Egyptian art, the more perfect are the productions of that art as though the genius of the people, inversely to that of others, was formed suddenly. Egyptian art we know only in its decadence.'" (303-304)

# FREDERICK MONDERSON

**Black History Extravaganza - Photo** - Iri Nufer Tomb - Two individuals stand before Ptah while the Ba-Birds flutters nearby.

"Thanks to the labors of a great number of devoted scholars, we can begin to measure the influence of Egypt upon the world's life and thought. Her arts, religion, literature, sciences, and laws are still exerting their influences. Thales the Greek astronomer was taught by the Egyptians, six centuries before Christ, to calculate eclipses; Eratosthenes was taught how to measure the circumference of the earth; Aristarchus was the first to compute the relative distances of the stars and moon, and their magnitudes, under the tutelage of Egyptian teachers; Euclid perfected mathematical knowledge of the Egyptians; Hipparchus discovered the precession of the equinoxes, made the first star catalogue and invented the planisphere; Ctesius invented the siphon; Plato and other philosophers were proud to sit at the feet of Egyptian priests. These are but a few of the names of the great who oved a debt but they are sufficient to convince us that the world owes a great debt to ancient Egypt." (304)

"The hieroglyphic system of dynastic times comes before us already perfected. Whence that originality came we have at present no definite knowledge, though Dr. Bissing maintains that it is African in origin." (304)

# BLACK HISTORY EXTRAVAGANZA HONORING DR. BEN-JOCHANNAN

"The fourth and preceding dynasties are now in the light because of the discoveries of Petrie, Amelineau, De Morgan, Naville, Reisner and others. Reisner's work has given us the key to many things which before were sealed. His work at the pyramids has opened up new fields. But the greatest work is yet to be done in the opening of the royal tombs hewn out in the quarry near the pyramid of Mycerinus, and from which Mycerinus obtained the stone for his pyramid. Reisner's work can only be briefly touched upon because of lack of space. Petrie has followed a number of others at the royal tombs at Abydos, and, in spite of the facts that so much work had been done there, he has given us much new light upon the first dynasties. The kings treated as legendary have been definitely placed in their historical succession, and to-day we can drink out of their bowls or sit on their furniture. Petrie, Naville, Quibell, De Morgan and Garstang have brought back the life and civilization of the prehistoric people. Dr. Elliot Smith and his helpers have done remarkable work in the department of ethnology, bringing to light many new facts and settling many old difficulties." (306)

**Black History Extravaganza - Photo -** Karnak Temple - The "Avenue of Sphinxes." Entrance Pylon and deep into the Temple past the Processional Colonnade.

# FREDERICK MONDERSON

"It is a peculiar theory which can see ships coming from and returning to Crete, and yet cannot see ships coming from and returning to Egypt." (307)

**Black History Extravaganza - Photo -** Karnak Temple - Processional View past Taharka's Kiosk, statues of Rameses II, Second Pylon, Processional Colonnade towards the Sanctuary area.

**Black History Extravaganza - Photo -** Kiosk of Seti II to the Theban Triad in the Great Court featuring that of Amon (Center), Mut (Left), and Khonsu (Right), while the Northern Colonnade stands further on to the right.

# BLACK HISTORY EXTRAVAGANZA HONORING DR. BEN-JOCHANNAN

## XII. THE HISTORY OF EGYPT
### By
### Dr. Fred Monderson

The History of Egypt, like so many other histories, is constantly being analyzed, re-evaluated with new propositions and positions established; wherein closer scrutiny reveal the existential data conflicts with the symbolic representation embedded principally from a Eurocentric perspective which is proving to be tremendously biased and incorrect, purposely falsified. What is significant, however, the true and definitive history of Egypt has not yet been written! This may be for a number of reasons, primarily because not sufficient information has been found. Or, more correctly, that the "found information" has not been correctly interpreted and this seems the more likely scenario because the existential data contradicts the symbolic representation. Strange! Yet, new discoveries are still being made. Much of the discoveries of the last 150 years have not been fully and accurately analyzed appropriately. The 19th and early 20th Century rush to postulate and publish has led to much mis-diagnosis. The old Adage, "Hurried birds make crooked nests," as applied to this issue has resulted, as stated in many distortions and many omissions upon which a great deal of the modern interpretation is based and biased. As such, we must constantly re-evaluate what we know. Many of the modern books are very much sanitized, gloss over and do not, among other things, address the blackness of Egypt, which was a fundamental ethnological part of its experience! Whenever Black scholars attempt to set the record straight, an increasing number of White scholars attack them with vituperativeness inclandestine that border on manifesting malice and vindictiveness. Yet, even though the tired old postulations that the ancient Egyptians were Caucasians have been challenged, discredited, and discarded, in some respects many modern writers still plant their flags in this treacherous quick-sand form of argument. Equally, while they may not vociferously proclaim

# FREDERICK MONDERSON

such, still the unspoken assumption is that the ancient Egyptians were Caucasians! What a contradiction!

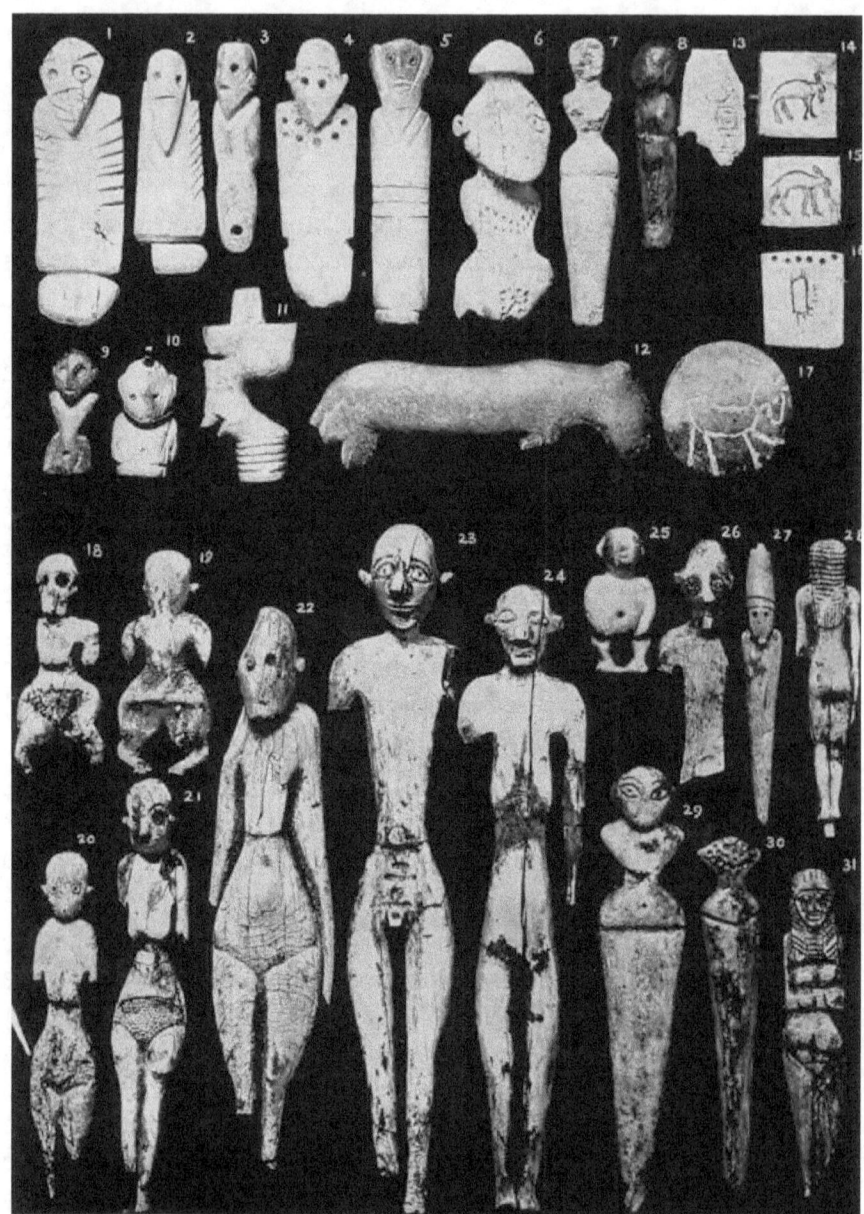

**Black History Extravaganza - Photo -** Prehistoric and early dynastic ivory evidence of man and woman.

# BLACK HISTORY EXTRAVAGANZA HONORING DR. BEN-JOCHANNAN

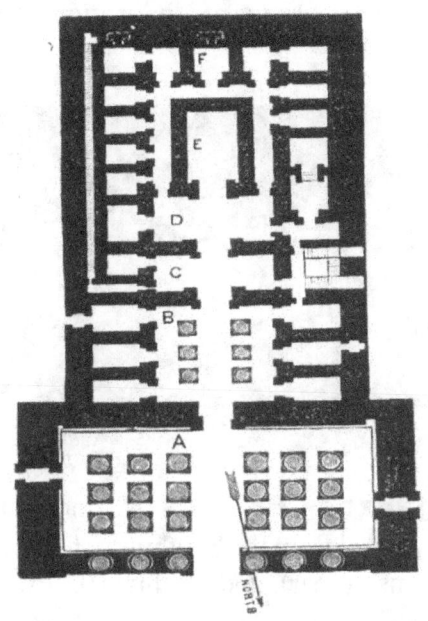

DENDERA TEMPLE OF HATHOR

A. Pronaos – First Hypostyle Hall
B. Second Hypostyle Hall – Hall of Appearances
C. First Vestibule – Hall of Offerings
D. Second Vestibule – hall of Ennead
E. Sanctuary
F. Per-Ur Chapel - Shrine of Egypt
G. Nile Room
H. Stairs to Roof
I. Laboratory
J. Harvest Rooms
K. Hathor's Wardrobe
L. Seat of Repose
M. Sacred Serpent
N. Treasury
O. Per-Neser Chapel – House of Flame
P. Per-Nu Chapel

**Black History Extravaganza - Plan of a Temple -** Temple of Dendera.

Nonetheless, in vigorous challenge, the admonition of Dr. ben-Jochannan, that when doing research on Ancient Egypt, "get the oldest materials and work from there," establishes a critical and constructive point of departure for what is at stake and what needs to be done. It must not be forgotten, Dr. Cheikh Anta Diop, a Black Senegalese Egyptologist, recognized by **UNESCO** as premier in his field, said of African scholars: "We must connect Egypt to Africa much as the west connects with Greece and Rome." Even further he insisted: "The African historian who refuses to include Egypt in African history is

# FREDERICK MONDERSON

either neurotic or an educated fool." Of course, he demolished the notion of a Caucasian Egypt affirming its blackness in his tremendously erudite book *The African Origin of Civilization: Myth or Reality?*

**Black History Extravaganza - Photo -** A "mock-up" model of the Temple of Karnak, viewed from the Southwest, featuring the Temples of the Opet and Khonsu (near), and 7$^{th}$ thru 10$^{th}$ Pylons on the North-South Axis, while the principal Amon temple lies to the left on the East-West Axis, path of the Sun God, Amon-Ra.

**Black History Extravaganza - Photo -** Columns of the Southern Colonnade fronted by Sphinxes, the last column depicts how these structures were erected (square then pounded round); and the inner, south, face of the First Pylon (right).

# BLACK HISTORY EXTRAVAGANZA HONORING DR. BEN-JOCHANNAN

It should also be pointed out, **UNESCO** sponsored a symposium in 1974, invited scholars from all over, and determined that Dr. Diop and his associate, Dr. Theophile Obenga were the most prepared of all in attendance; and equally, this institution "**Affirmed the fundamental blackness of ancient Egypt**" based on Diop's and Obenga's outstanding scholarship!

Now, having said all of that, no one knows for sure when the history of Egypt actually began. Albert Churchward acknowledges the Egyptians enjoyed religious practices over a period of 300,000 years. We know they had a Precession cycle of time period of 26,000 years with the possibility of at least 3 or possibly 4 cycles equaling 78,000, perhaps 104,000 years of stargazing. Censellus tells of a document 35,000 years old; and some have dated the Sphinx of Ghizeh at perhaps 10,000 years old. While in some respects, these dates may seem far-fetched, they nevertheless speak to a culture process and history long in evolution on the banks of the Nile in North-East Africa, the Nile Valley region. However, the framework within which the history is recounted uses either the "short" or the "long chronology." The "Short Chronology," some say for convenience sake; and contemporary with Mesopotamian South-West Asia, Caucasian state formation; begins the First Dynasty at about 3200-3100 or even 3050 B.C. Thus, the 3000 figure is a bantied about date for convenience. The "Long Chronology" on the other hand, while some scholars give 4800 B.C., by Petrie's estimation begins the First Dynasty, at c. 5700 B.C., or thereabouts. Maulana Karenga gives 6200 B.C. Therefore, it is within these time frames one must begin to consider the **History of Egypt**. Let me say the "Short Chronology" is somewhat more convenient, even though it's been argued such a short list was designed to be more contemporary with Mesopotamian civilization where the history of the West begins. The "Long Chronology" on the other hand, makes Egypt outdistance the other cultures that are purported to have had a significant influence on the Nile Valley experience. This is, despite what Dr. Chancellor Williams wrote in the **Prescript** to his book *Destruction of Black Civilization*. There the Traveler asked the Old Man: "What happened to the people of Sumer [originators of Sumerian and Mesopotamian civilization] I hear they were black?" The old man replied: "They lost their history and were forgotten." Let's not forget, Livingston said he saw more Black faces in Mesopotamia than in Egypt.

**Black History Extravaganza - Papyrus -** A Blank Cartouche beside the Astrological sign for Sagittarius.

Thus, before we begin, the sources for a history of Egypt need to be discussed so as to arrive at an understanding of these events so long ago.

Archaeology, using C-14 (carbon 14) has helped to fill gaps where records and surviving monuments fall short. Radiocarbon and thermoluminesence dating methods have also aided the science but for evaluating finds of much longer and older duration.

A number of sources have provided the basis of Egyptian chronology. These include slate palettes, mace-heads, stela or what we call burial headstones, and even labels attached to jars found in tombs of the

# BLACK HISTORY EXTRAVAGANZA HONORING DR. BEN-JOCHANNAN

earliest buried kings. The more famous of these early "documents" is the *Narmer Palette* purportedly showing the unification of the northern and southern kingdoms. Much of later pharaonic paraphernalia are evident on this palette, viz., red and white crowns, pharaoh's beard, his tunic, a sandal and sandal bearer, the serekh or palace facade, the Horus hawk, the goddess Hathor, boats, standards, a bull, etc. Then there is the *Bull Palette* showing the king as a bull battering the walls of an enemy. There is also the *Libyan Palette* and there are others. Many of these were commented on by Legge at the end of the 19th Century in the *Proceedings of the Society of Biblical Archaeology*. The *Narmer Macehead* is the next famous "document" showing the king under a canopy wearing the red crown, his queen nearby and numbers showing captives, men and animals. The number of captives of men and animals show this early in time these Africans were counting, in large numbers, in the millions.

**Black History Extravaganza - Photo -** Sign of the Ministry of Antiquities - Scientific Research Department.

# FREDERICK MONDERSON

**Black History Extravaganza - Ceramic Art -** A colorful Khepre doing his thing of "pushing the Dung."

The *Palermo Stone* is the first substantial "written document." A slab of black basalt stone, it lists the names of rulers dating from the Old Kingdom back into the Prehistoric Period when the gods ruled Egypt. Ian Shaw in *The Oxford History of Ancient Egypt* reported: "The types of event that are recorded on the *Palermo Stone* are cult ceremonies, taxation, sculpture, building and warfare - that is precisely the type of phenomena that are recorded on the proto-dynastic ivory and ebony labels from Abydos, Saqqara, and various other early historical sites." Equally, the *Palermo Stone* is also significant indicating, especially in this early period, Egyptian history was not recorded consecutively or chronologically, but marked the reign of each individual king. The *Turin Papyrus* is another significant document of early chronology but unfortunately it is a brittle, broken mass and its contents cannot be accurately read.

# BLACK HISTORY EXTRAVAGANZA HONORING DR. BEN-JOCHANNAN

**Black History Extravaganza - Photo -** Karnak Temple - The Inner Face of the First Pylon with surviving mud-ramp for scaling heights and Sphinxes before the last columns of the Southern Colonnade in the Great Court.

**Black History Extravaganza - Photo -** A Harpist at work, while to the left legs of dancing ladies.

# FREDERICK MONDERSON

**Black History Extravaganza - Photo -** With a winged Sun-Disk overhead, the deceased on this Stela stands before Horus as Ra-Horakhty, and with Osiris in Double Crown backed by Isis and Nephthys at his rear.

# BLACK HISTORY EXTRAVAGANZA HONORING DR. BEN-JOCHANNAN

There are **King Lists** of much later periods. The **Sakkara List** is Old Kingdom; the **Karnak List**, created by Thutmose III is from the 18$^{th}$ Dynasty. Now in Paris, it was stolen by Prisse de Avennes from Karnak. The **Abydos Lists**, of the 19$^{th}$ Dynasty, of which there are two, one *in situ* at the Temple of Seti I and the **Second Abydos List** from the Temple of Rameses II now residing in the British Museum. Stela are the equivalent of tombstones with an engraved biography of the owner that supplies dates and events in the person's life. They often contain a religious admonition or request that passersby read a contained inscription that magically benefits the deceased owner residing within the tomb. Tombs, particularly the Mastabas of the Nobles, dating to the Old Kingdom, are inundated with illustrations showing scenes from daily life and these help paint a broader picture of the history and culture.

**Black History Extravaganza - Photo** - Karnak Temple. View of the Court of Ramesses III (20$^{th}$ Dynasty) Temple with its Osiride Statues, the Incline and into the Pronaos and beyond. This temple is on a North-South Axis, perpendicular to the main East-West Axis.

# FREDERICK MONDERSON

**Black History Extravaganza - Photo** - Karnak Temple. Close-up view of the Court of Ramesses III (20th Dynasty) Temple with Osiride Statues of left (top), and right (bottom). Notice the incline into the inner portals.

# BLACK HISTORY EXTRAVAGANZA HONORING DR. BEN-JOCHANNAN

## The Chronology of Ancient Egypt, Etc.

|     |                          |                    |                |
|-----|--------------------------|--------------------|----------------|
| 1.  | Pre-dynastic             | 6000-3200 B.C.     |                |
|     |                          | Ben-Jochannan      | Boardman       |
| 2.  | Archaic                  | 3200-2780 -        | 3200-2780      |
|     | (Dynasties 1 and 2)      |                    |                |
| 3.  | Old Kingdom              | 2780-2270 -        | 2700-2160      |
|     | (Dynasties 3 to 6)       |                    |                |
| 4.  | First Intermediate Period| 2270-2100 -        | 2160-2134/2052 |
|     | (Dynasties 7 to 10)      |                    |                |
| 5.  | The Middle Kingdom       | 2100-1675 -        | 2134-1786      |
|     | (Dynasties 11 to 13)     |                    |                |
| 6.  | Second Intermediate Period| 1675-1600 -       | 1786-1570      |
|     | (Dynasties 14 to 17)     |                    |                |
| 7.  | New Kingdom              | 1600-1090 -        | 1570-1085      |
|     | (Dynasties 18 to 20)     |                    |                |
| 8.  | Late Period              | 1090-527 -         | 1085-663       |
|     | (Dynasties 21 to 26)     |                    |                |
| 9.  | Persian and Assyrian     |                    |                |
|     | (Dynasties 27-29)        | 526-333            |                |
| 10. | Graeco-Roman Era         | 332-640 -          | 332-385        |
|     | (Dynasties 30-31)        |                    |                |

## POEM TO AMON-RA

O mighty Amon, the Greatest of the Black African deities, ithyphallic, you were from primeval times, Lord of Gods.

Your creativity radiated over an age, father of the gods, when worshippers praised your hidden nature.

Conquering peoples and places, they brought light and civility to the world, in your immortal name, multitudinous, more numerous, not known. The vanquished contributed wealth filling your treasury and your subjects, victorious in their imperial exploits, erected mansions

# FREDERICK MONDERSON

in glory and praise of your being, Chief of the Great Ennead of the Gods, Self-Begotten, Lord of Heaven, Lord of Earth.

O Dweller in Anu, the Gods ascribe praise to you, maker of things celestial and things terrestrial, for you illuminate Egypt, President of the Apts.

**Black History Extravaganza - Photo -** Prehistoric figurine images.

# BLACK HISTORY EXTRAVAGANZA HONORING DR. BEN-JOCHANNAN

Beautiful child of Love, from relative obscurity you emerged in the Middle Kingdom and sat on your Sacred Mound of Creation.

That first time, seeking to complete the task of previous gods fallen short, you Created Brilliant Rays, Thunder in Heaven.

Black African rulers of that age imbibed in your inspiration, Lord of the Two Lands.

Mighty in Power, Lord of Awe-inspiring terror, they similarly manifested resolute courage, wisdom, intellect, and creative prowess. They therefore gained success as Warrior Pharaohs, with mighty souls, all in your name, Fashioner of the Beauty of Kings, Priests and Artisans, O Lord of the Throne of Egypt.

All the Gods are three, Amen, Ra and Ptah and none like thee. Amen is his hidden name; Ra is his face, Ptah his body.

**Black History Extravaganza - Photo -** Karnak Temple - End columns of the Northern Colonnade (left); the Taharka Column (center); statues of Rameses II (center right); and Porch to the Second Pylon with ruins of the Hypostyle Hall further on and rubble to the very right.

# FREDERICK MONDERSON

Power made by Ptah, Bull of Heliopolis, kings' architects shaped a society whose blueprint you encouraged in manifold attributes.

Lord of Scepter and Ankh, Frog, and Uraeus, Couchant Lion, your symbols include Beautiful Tiaras, Lofty Plumes, and *Ureret*, *War*, *Nemes* and *Atef* Crowns.

The prosperity you endowed your adherents generated artistic, scientific and linguistic creations, Lord of the Apts.

These first beneficiaries of your generosity toward mankind, erected temples as chapels simply to glorify your great name, Amon Lord of Thebes, Lord of the Two Lands, Lord of Might, Lord of Food, Bull of Offerings, Kamutef at the head of his Fields.

Lord of Victuals, Bull of Provisions, the gods beg their sustenance from you, Lord of Fields, banks and plots of ground.

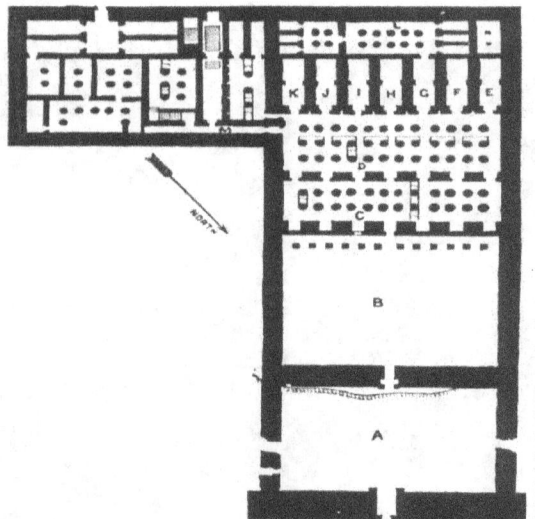

Temple of Seti I at Abydos

A. First Court – Destroyed
B. Second Court – Destroyed
C. First Hypostyle Hall
D. Second Hypostyle Hall
E. Chapel – Sanctuary of Horus
F. Chapel – Sanctuary of Isis
G. Chapel – Sanctuary of Osiris
H. Chapel – Sanctuary of Ra-Horakhty
I. Chapel – Sanctuary of Amon-Ra
J. Chapel – Sanctuary of Ptah
K. Chapel – Sanctuary of Seti I
L. Inner Sanctuary of Osiris
M. Gallery of the Abydos Tablet/List
N. Chapel of Nefertum
O. Chapel of Sokar
P. Hall of the Books
Q. hall of Sacrifice
R. Corridor of the Bull

**Black History Extravaganza - Photo -** Plan of the Temple of Seti I at Abydos.

# BLACK HISTORY EXTRAVAGANZA HONORING DR. BEN-JOCHANNAN

Lord of Truth, Father of the Gods, Maker of Men, Creator of all animals, Black African kings, men of vision, fortitude and tenacity, benefited from an earlier age of African creativity. They synthesized, experimented and with vision and bellicosity bequeathed a creative era where craftsmen, philosophers, priests and kings, were motivated to extol your name to greater heights.

Lord of Radiant Light, you Exist into Eternity as Lord of Heaven, Lord of Earth, Lord of the Gods, Lord of the High Lands and Mountains, Lord of the Joy of Heart, Mighty One of Crowns.

Your Loveliness is in the Southern Sky and Your Graciousness is in the Northern Sky.

Your name is strong; your will is heavy.

Mountains of ore cannot withstand your might, for you set in order the kingdom of eternity unto eternity.

**Black History Extravaganza - Photo - Karnak Temple -** View from the South, Taharka Column (left); Ruins of Pylon Two and the Hypostyle Hall (center); and the Obelisks of Thutmose I and Hatshepsut (left and right).

# FREDERICK MONDERSON

Lord of eternity, creator of everlastingness, you arise in the eastern horizon and set in the western horizon. Born early every day, you overthrew your enemies, steering oar, pilot who knows the water, Lord of the ship of the morning and ship of the evening, master of two stems. Beautiful form fashioned by Ptah, Ox with strong arm who loves strength; you are first in Upper Egypt, Lord of the Land of the Matoi and Prince of Punt.

Lord of Perception who speaks with authority, Lord of the Gods whose shrine is hidden, you are Lord of the Double Crown, Great Hawk who makes festive the body, fair body that makes festive the breast.

**Black History Extravaganza - Photo -** Showgi Abd Rady, Native Egyptian Guide and friends.

# BLACK HISTORY EXTRAVAGANZA HONORING DR. BEN-JOCHANNAN

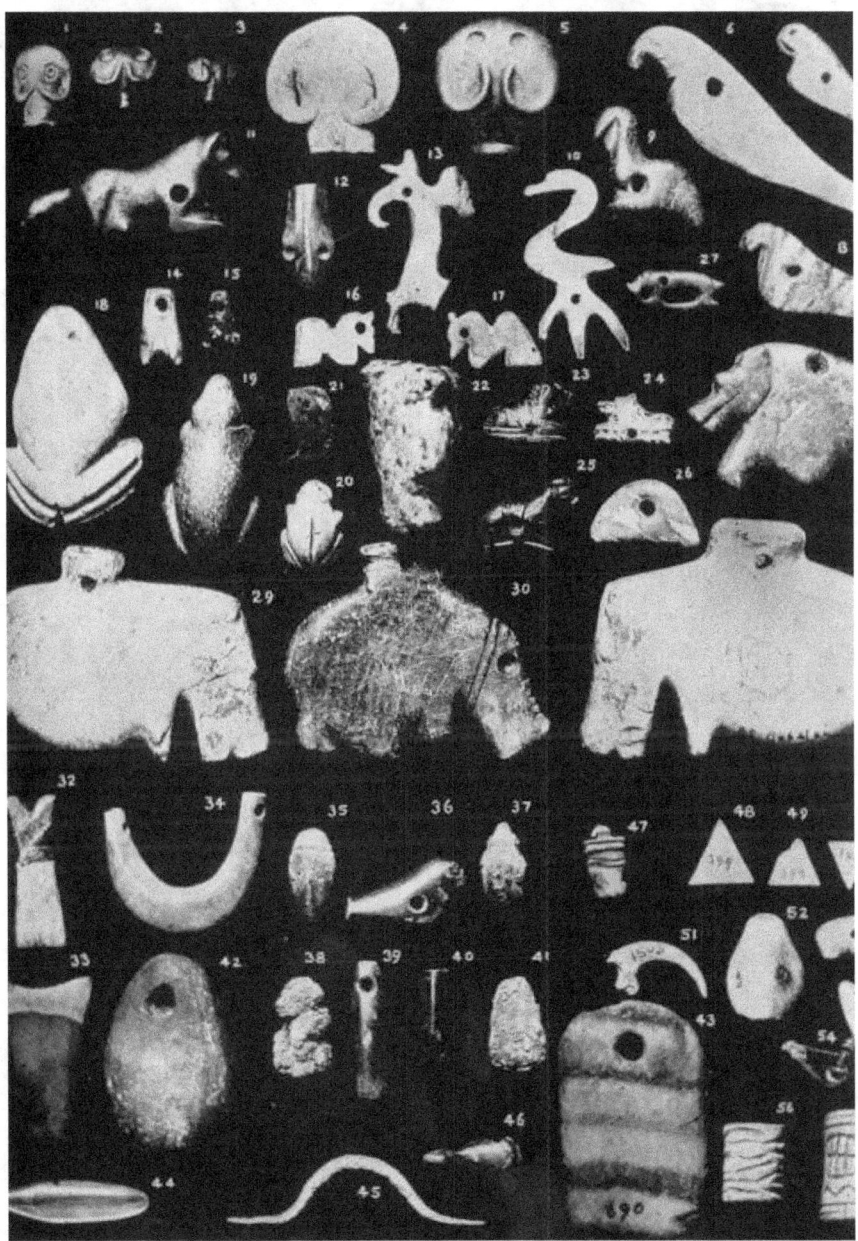

**Black History Extravaganza - Photo -** Prehistoric Amulets.

# FREDERICK MONDERSON

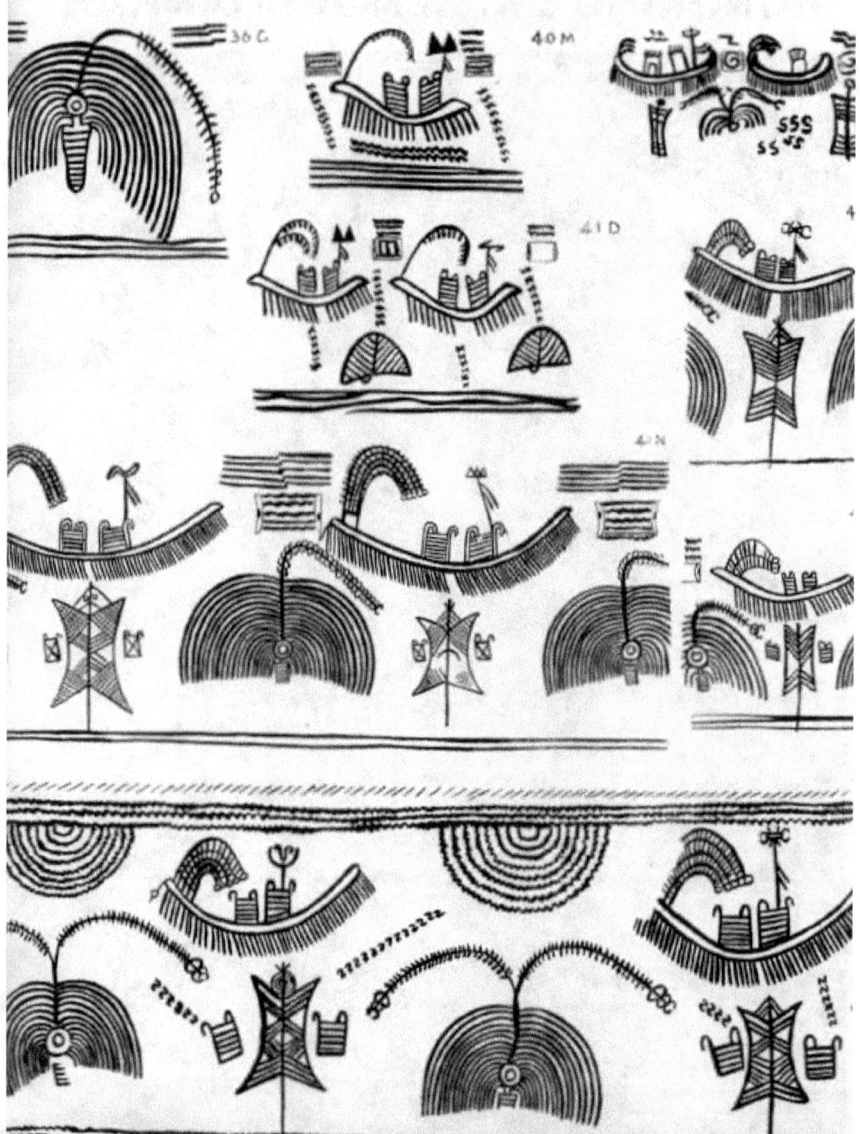

**Black History Extravaganza - Line Drawing -** Prehistoric Ship Designs.

Beneficent God, you presided over a world as King of Kings. Lord of the Thrones of the Two Lands, Bull of your Mother, New Kingdom monarchs competed trying to out-do predecessors praising

# BLACK HISTORY EXTRAVAGANZA HONORING DR. BEN-JOCHANNAN

Amon, Greater than Great of the Primordial Deities, who continues to bless his champions.
Chief of Egypt, territorial conquests, ensuing wealth, architectural constructions, and religious and philosophical sonnets, extolled the name of Amon Presider of Karnak, who dwells in the Most Select of Places, in Power and Glory, Invisible and Creative.
As Chief of all the Gods, you fashion the deities, One in his actions as with the Gods.
Stablisher of all things, Lord of things that are, you Create all Life, Lord of the *Sektet* Boat and of the *Antet* Boat.

**Black History Extravaganza - Ceramic Art -** The Falcon in colorful form.

# FREDERICK MONDERSON

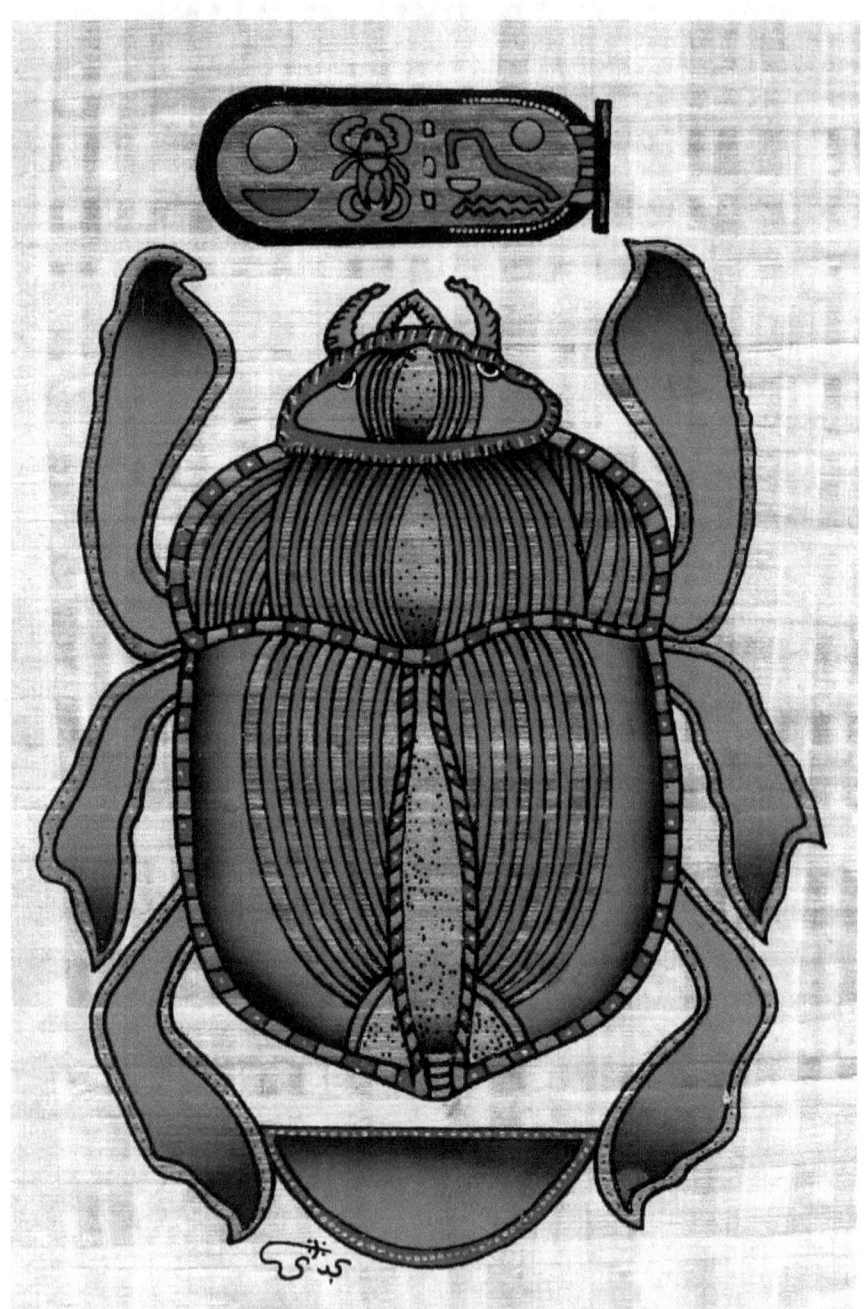

**Black History Extravaganza - Papyrus -** Khepre in Blue pushing the Cartouche or Shennu.

# BLACK HISTORY EXTRAVAGANZA HONORING DR. BEN-JOCHANNAN

**Black History Extravaganza - Photo - Karnak Temple -** Closed capital, abacus and architrave overhead of the Hypostyle Hall.

**Black History Extravaganza - Photo - Karnak Temple -** View of the Obelisk of Hatshepsut from behind the Eighth Pylon of the Queen usurped by Thutmose III, 18th Dynasty.

# FREDERICK MONDERSON

**Black History Extravaganza - Photo - Karnak Temple** - The two Obelisks of Hatshepsut (right) and that of her father Thutmose I (left).

First Born Son of the Earth, Chief of Mankind, your Sanctuary at Karnak is a splendid piece of divinely inspired architecture.
Master of the Double Crown, you receive the Ames Scepter.
Lord of the *Makes* Scepter and whip, your precinct, befits the Eternal Spirits of the Theban Triad, Amon, Mut, Khonsu, whose reigns encompassed millennia.
Priests manifested political and theological power from this sacred abode, constructed in stone while similar 'Mansions of Millions of Years' profess Amon's august name, as Source of all Light in Heaven.
Lord of Karnak, King of the South and North, Lord of Things Which Exist, Stablisher of All Creation, You Last Forever, equips all lands, fashioner of all that exists, Just One, Lord of Thebes.

# BLACK HISTORY EXTRAVAGANZA HONORING DR. BEN-JOCHANNAN

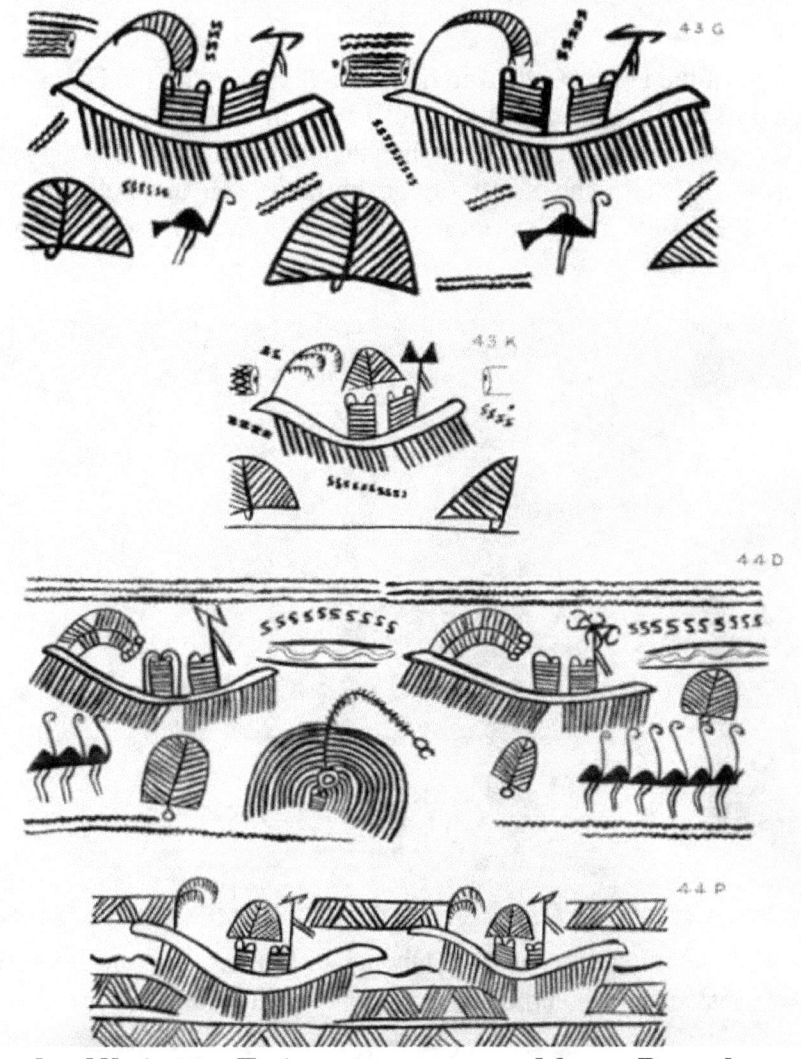

**Black History Extravaganza - Line Drawing -** Prehistoric Ship Design.


Beautiful boy whom the gods praise, maker of men and stars who illuminates the two lands, you are great of strength, Lord of Might, Chief who made the two lands, the Gods rejoice in your beauty, Amen-Ra, venerated in Karnak.

# FREDERICK MONDERSON

Lord of the Deeds Case who holds the flail, you are the Heliopolitan, first of his Ennead, who lives daily on truth.
The gods love to gaze at you when the Double Crown rests upon your brow, hawk in the midst of the horizon; you are beloved in the Southern Sky, and pleasant in the Northern Sky, possessor of praise, the Sun of Heaven.

**Black History Extravaganza - Photo - Luxor Temple**
- The one remaining (of two) Obelisk of Rameses II stands before his two seated statues and the last of four standing statues, far right.

Lord of Things that are, acting as Judge, Vizier of the Poor Who Takes No Bribes, your intellectual majesty enlightened the world in knowledge of arts and medicine.

# BLACK HISTORY EXTRAVAGANZA HONORING DR. BEN-JOCHANNAN

**Black History Extravaganza - Photo - Stelae -** On these Stelas, the Deceased stands before Osiris, Isis and Nephthys (left); and, Osiris, Horus, Isis and Nephthys (right).

**Black History Extravaganza - Photo -** Dancing Ladies, but that's Hatshepsut's Cartouche (Ma'at-Ka-Ra) to the right.

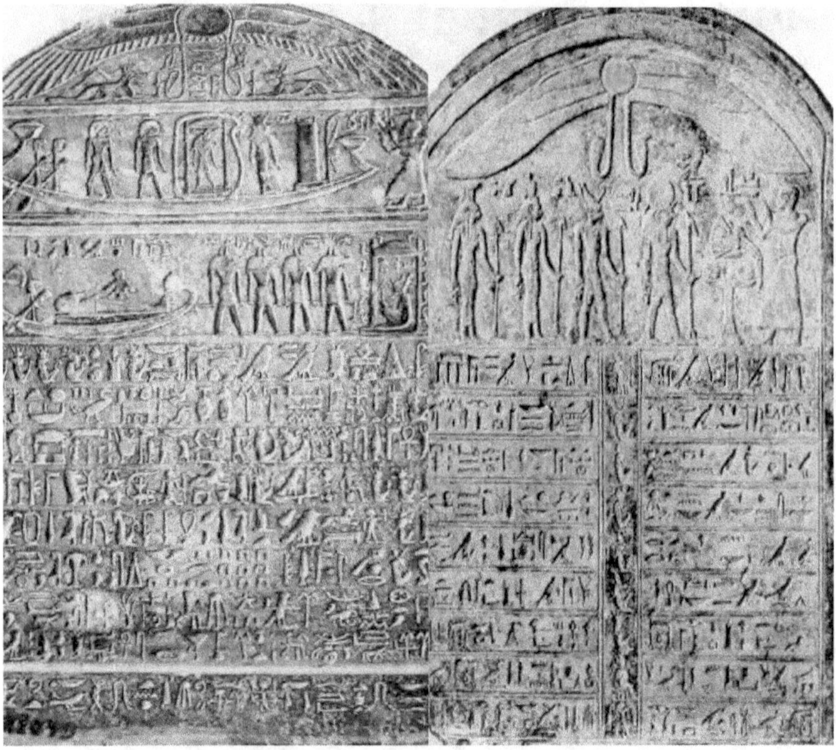

# FREDERICK MONDERSON

**Black History Extravaganza - Photo -** Stelae - The "Boat of the Gods" sails with divinity in a Shrine (above) and the Deceased as a mummy also in a boat (bottom) left; and before Horus as Ra-Horakhty, Osiris in Double Crown, Isis and Nephthys.

**Black History Extravaganza - Photo -** Dancing Ladies, men, harpist, Sistrum players and Hatshepsut's Cartouche or Shennu.

# BLACK HISTORY EXTRAVAGANZA HONORING DR. BEN-JOCHANNAN

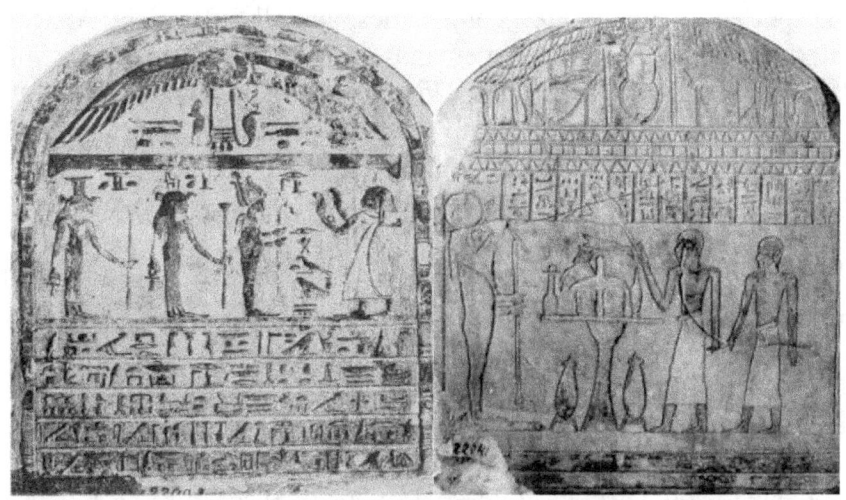

**Black History Extravaganza - Photo -** Stelae - The deceased stands before Osiris, Isis and Nephthys (left); and two individuals and a **Table of Offerings** to Horus as Ra-Horakhty.

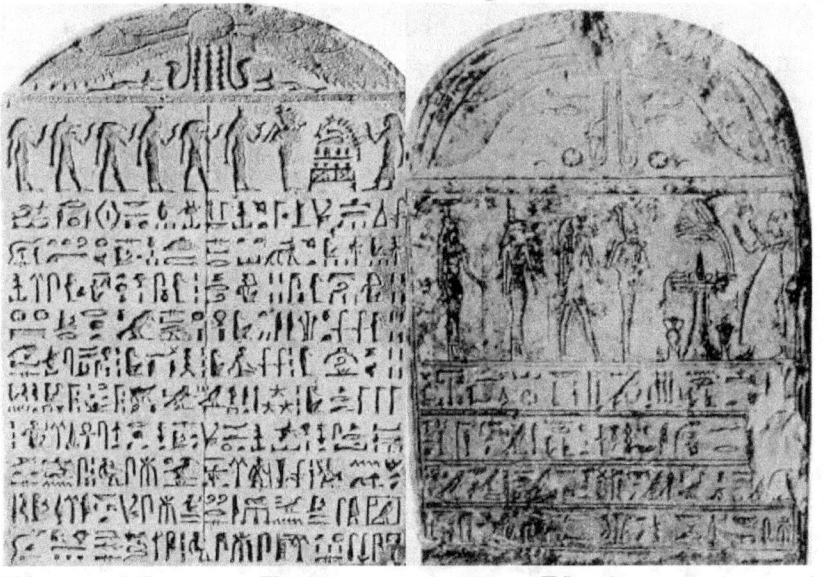

**Black History Extravaganza - Photo -** Stele -Before Osiris, Isis, Horus, Nephthys, Thoth, Anubis and another (left); and before Osiris, Horus, Isis and Nephthys (right).

# FREDERICK MONDERSON

Your inspiration pioneered astronomy, quarrying, navigation, stone-transportation, agriculture, mathematics, and all gifts of the African mind. Generations of black men and women worship and praise you mighty Amon, King of the Gods, First Born, and Resting upon Ma'at. Amenemenes, Sesostris, then Ahmose, Amenhotep, Thutmose, Hatshepsut, Seti, Rameses, Merenptah and Piankhy, Shabaka, Shabataka, Taharka, were greatest adherents, physical father of these kings, Power of the Gods.
Amen-Ra the Justified, you give your hands to those you love and assign those you hate to fire.

The Gods love to behold you and they rejoice in your beautiful acts. These divinities acclaim you the Great House and Crown you with Crowns in the House of Fire.
Homage to you, Dweller in Peace for you are Successor to Ra.
Fashioner of Kings and Queens, sole king among the gods, your collective wisdom schooled the Greeks and Romans, the newest converts.
They immersed in your wonderful cultural heritage, praising you with equal zeal and vigor.
Chief of all the Beings of the Underworld, Lord of the Nubians, Governor of Punt, King of Heaven, Amon the great African God, we beseech you, Lord of Eternity, today continue to make enlightening the Black culture of Kemet/Egypt, land of the ancestors.
Pour forth your salvation and ingenuity to inspire our people even more as they meet challenges in a new Millennium.

**Black History Extravaganza - Line Drawing -** Images of Prehistoric boats.

# BLACK HISTORY EXTRAVAGANZA HONORING DR. BEN-JOCHANNAN

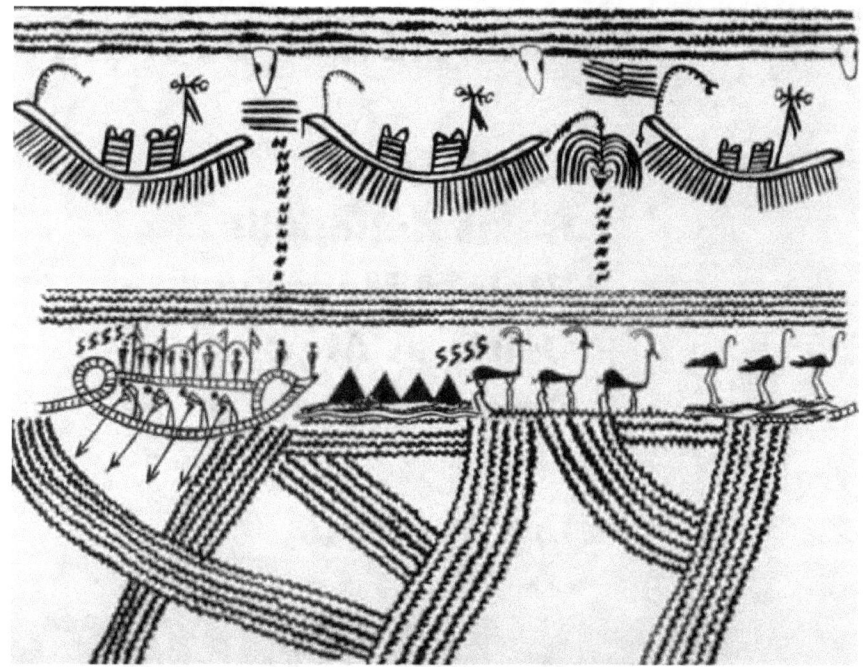

**Black History Extravaganza - Line Drawing -** More images of Prehistoric boats, with cabins (top); and individuals aboard, fisher-men, and birds and animals on land (bottom).

**Black History Extravaganza - Ceramic Art -** Ankh, etc.

# FREDERICK MONDERSON

## XIII. THE RELIGION OF EGYPT II

**1. The Principal Gods**
    Ra at Heliopolis
    Ptah at Memphis
    Osiris at Abydos
    Amon at Thebes

**2. Their belief Systems**

**Black History Extravaganza - Photo - Luxor Temple**
- View of a statue's head, the standing left or Eastern Obelisk with Baboons, two seated statues, one standing Statue and into the deep recesses of the temple.

# BLACK HISTORY EXTRAVAGANZA HONORING DR. BEN-JOCHANNAN

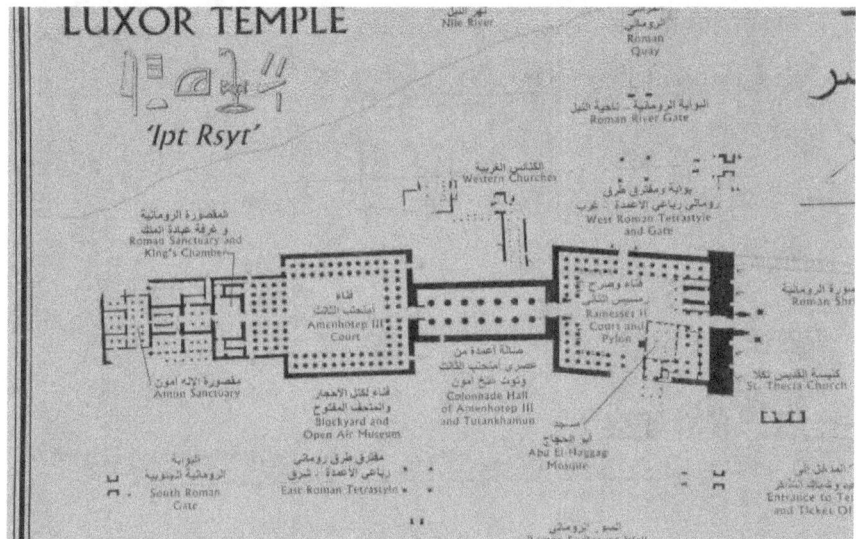

**Black History Extravaganza - Photo - Luxor Temple** - Plan of the Temple.

**Black History Extravaganza - Photo - Tomb of Iri Nufer -** "A Servant in the Place of Truth" during the Ramesside Period. The Nobleman kneels before Osiris and other gods.

# FREDERICK MONDERSON

**Black History Extravaganza - Photo - tomb of Iri Nufer -** Hathor in one of her many "moons;" and Iri-Nufer and his wife before Shu (feather) and other gods.

# BLACK HISTORY EXTRAVAGANZA HONORING DR. BEN-JOCHANNAN

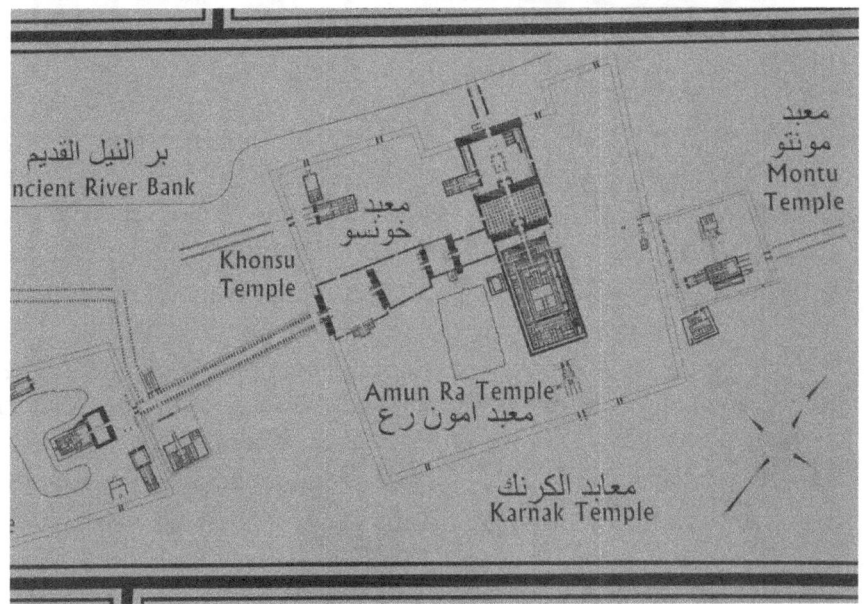

**Black History Extravaganza - Photo - Karnak Temple -** Plan of Karnak Temple in relation to others as Montu Temple, Khonsu Temple and the Temple of Mut.

## XIV. THE HISTORY OF EGYPT II
## BY
## DR. FRED MONDERSON

### Pre-Dynastic Period I: The Badarian

The dates from about 4241 B.C. to about 3100 B.C. is called the Pre-dynastic period in Ancient Egypt. Here, essentially along the Nile, principally in Upper Egypt, three cultures developed before the dynasties began. They formed the foundations on which the dynasties were able to build the lasting Egyptian civilization in Northeast Africa. These were the Badarian, oldest of the three; followed by the Amratian and Gerzean or Naqada I and Naqada Ii cultures. The first or older of these cultures was the Badarian (Ba-da-ri-an), named after a group of cemeteries around Badari on the east bank of the Nile

# FREDERICK MONDERSON

River. Much of the Badarian evidence is credited to Gertrude Caton-Thompson who worked at El-Hammamiya and Brunton at El Badari. This is not far from Aswan in Upper Egypt at the First Cataract.

The *Cambridge Ancient History* (3rd Edition) Vol. I, Part I, Edited by I.E.S. Edwards, C.J. Gadd, and N.G.L Hammond (Cambridge at the University Press, 1970: 465) states: "Tombs dating from these consecutive periods have been found in excavations at numerous sites in Upper Egypt, Badarian only in the neighborhood of El-Qaw, Naqada I only south of Asyut and in the Faiyum, and Naqada II in Lower Egypt also. The only Predynastic Egyptian site claimed to be older than all the others was found by Junker, Scharff and Menghin at Merimda Beni Salaam on the edges of the western Delta. This, it is claimed, is a 'Neolithic' culture related to that found in the Faiyum by Miss Caton-Thompson who gave it the name of 'Faiyum Neolithic.'"

Even further, (1970: 468) they write: "More of these domestic remains and also cemeteries were discovered by Brunton in later excavations at El-Mostagidde and El-Matmar, both in the El-Badari district. At El-Mustagidda, in the neighborhood of Deir Tasa, he considered that he had found a civilization, which he called 'Tasian,' even older than the Badarian. He based his identification on this culture very largely on a particular type of pottery consisting of deep bowls with a small flattish base and angular sides narrowing towards the mouth. These vessels, divided by Brunton into two classes according to their color - brown, or grey-black - seem to be cooking pots. All the other objects tentatively assigned to the Tasian culture (limestone axes, palettes of hard stones, and black incised beakers) could not be proved to be specifically Tasian by the original excavations at El-Mustagidda or the subsequent work at El-Matmar."

The Badarians were an African people who had a political system that was centralized. Their culture produced a high quality of pottery found when archaeologists dug up their graves. Archaeologists, as you know, are scientists who search for the remains of old cultures. They then try to write a history of the people based on tools, pots, or

# BLACK HISTORY EXTRAVAGANZA HONORING DR. BEN-JOCHANNAN

other remains left behind. These things tell the archaeologists about the ancient cultures.

Much of the ancient cultural remains of the Badarians were found in graves. Because very early in time these Africans believed in an "Afterlife" phenomenon, they began a process in which they structured their earthly lives in a manner to qualify for and enjoy life in the duration of eternity! Thus, they took many objects into the "Afterlife" and these were called "goods of the grave." In this, the Badarians believed they needed their tools, pots, food, cosmetics, and so on where they were going after they died and were buried. This belief would later on crystalize in the afterlife phenomenon.

The graves of the Badarians were rough circular pits about 1.5 meters across and 1 meter deep. In these graves were found cooking pots, baskets, and bone and flint tools. The body was covered with materials made from goat and gazelle skins. Their dress was made from linen or skins, sewn with bone needles. They had studs for the nose and earrings made of beads and turquoise, a semi-precious stone. The Badarians also wore stone bead necklaces and girdles. Some men wore girdle or belts of blue cylindrical beads in one case interspersed with white, arranged in many strings around their waists. Investigations proved most of the blue beads to be steatite glazed blue I imitation turquoise, though some beads of real turquoise were among them. Beads of soft stones, and only rarely of hard stones or of copper, shells, and the pink tub es of organ coral, singly or in strings, adorned necks, wrists and ankles. In three instances, small amulets were found with beads: tow represent hippopotami; the third is an exquisite little carving in bone of the head of a gazelle and was 'apparently' worn at the ankle. These amulets may have been hunting charms. Bracelets, of ivory, bone or horn, were worn on the forearm; broad narrow types have been found, all normally having a sharp ridge round the circumference. A characteristic feature was the decoration of some of these bracelets, either with a chevron pattern of inlaid blue beads, or with a succession of rounded knobs."

# FREDERICK MONDERSON

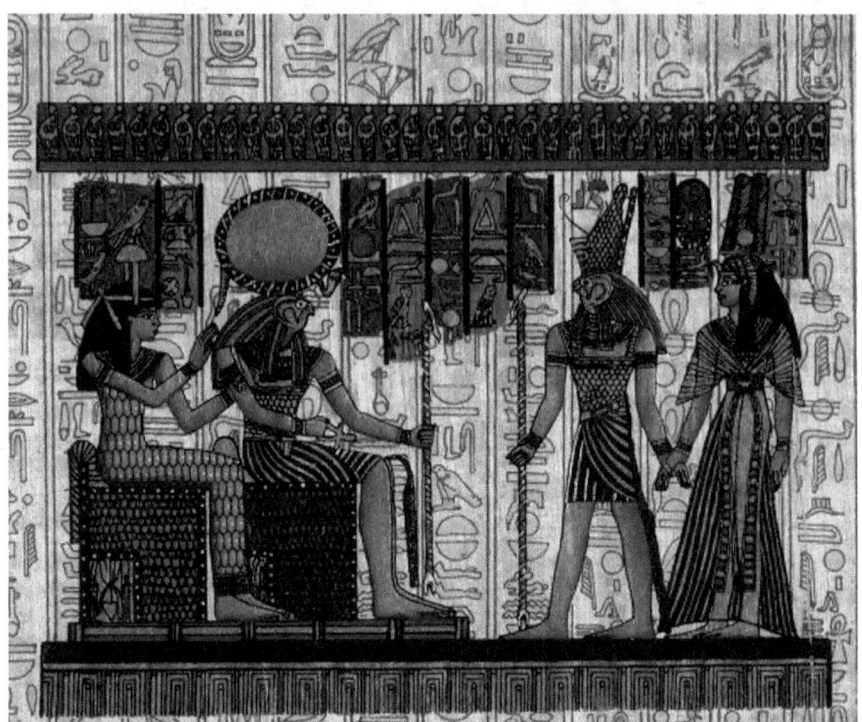

**Black History Extravaganza - Papyrus -** Horus introduces the Queen to enthroned Ra-Horakhty beside Hathor.

The Badarians had bracelets of ivory, shell, bone and horn. Evidence indicates they kept either do rog jackal, cows and sheep. Also, their combs and spoons were made of ivory and bone carved in animal or bird shapes. It is reasonable to believe they had small objects, domestic and personal, which were made of wood that perished with time. Bowls and deep cooking pots were common. They decorated their eyes and bodies with green malachite and castor oil was used for cleaning and softening the skin and much of this was created in slate palettes. Other tools included ivory or shell fishhooks and flint arrowheads. These Badarians also used vases made of ivory and stone palettes for grinding the cosmetics.

The Badarians were religious and this is evidenced by the care they took with the "goods of the grave." They made ivory statuettes of women to accompany the dead men in whose graves they were placed.

# BLACK HISTORY EXTRAVAGANZA HONORING DR. BEN-JOCHANNAN

*Cambridge* (1970: 470) also reports, "A small stud of pale green stone was found in situ in the right nostril of a man (El-Badari, grave 5359)." Their dead were buried on the side with the bodies in the pre-natal position. Also found in the graves were ivory amulets of hippopotamuses and antelopes that served as hunting charms.

Their economy was based on hunting, fishing, and agriculture and they domesticated, or tamed, animals such as dogs, jackals, goats, sheep, cattle and oxen. What is interesting, the fauna or animal life we see as miniature objects are all part of the African landscape indicating they observed nature and duplicated the creatures of their environment as most primitive people would do.

**Black History Extravaganza - Photo - Tomb of Iri Nufer -** "A servant in the place of truth,' the Nobleman and wife salute "Hathor as a Cow" before two trees with the Sun Disk of Ra-Horakhty overhead.

# FREDERICK MONDERSON

**Black History Extravaganza - Photo -** Brethren, on way to pay their respects to the Great One, Dr. Yosef A.A. Ben-Jochannan.

**Black History Extravaganza - Photo -** With Dr. Calvin Butts, pastor of Abyssinia Baptist Church in Harlem (left) and Brother James Smalls (right) at his rear, Minister Hafeez speaks his peace as members of the Audience look on to the right.

They lived in mud-brick houses and had polished black, and black-topped polished red or brown pottery. The Badarians had a high quality of pottery. "Three types of pottery were known: polished red (which means that it has a red slip which was polished or burnished

# BLACK HISTORY EXTRAVAGANZA HONORING DR. BEN-JOCHANNAN

with a pebble before baking), polished black, and red or brown polished with a black top." Their bowls had thin walls and were polished red ware, partly blackened. They decorated their pottery with a ripple pattern representing water and stained them with red ochre dye.

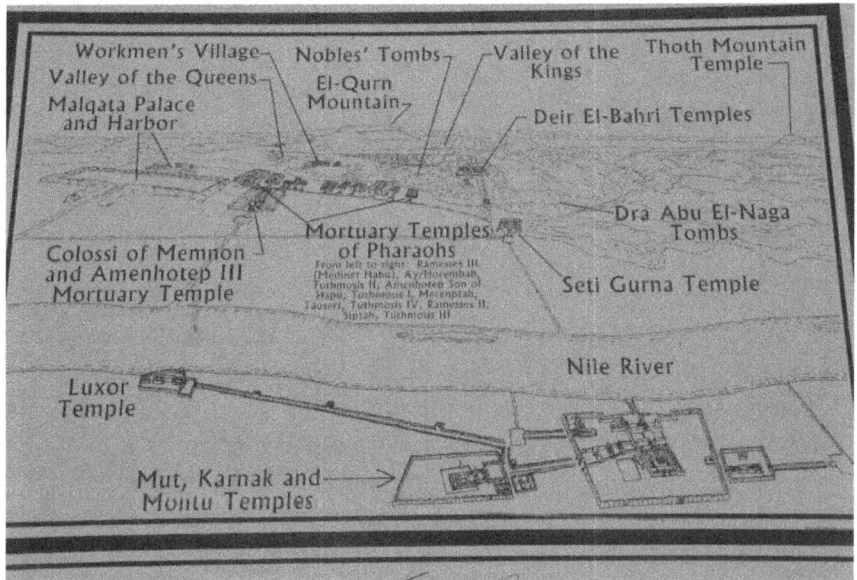

**Black History Extravaganza - Photo -** Snap-shot of Karnak and Associated temples on the East Bank and Mortuary Temples of the Pharaohs, etc., on the West Bank of the Nile River.

"The most characteristic feature is the rippled surface which decorates many of the finest pots, and is even found, though somewhat sketchily, on some of the coarse pots. This rippling was produced by combining the surface of the still soft clay with an implement having closely set teeth and then burnishing with a pebble." Even further (1970: 471) Cambridge notes: "The black top is another decorative feature of Badarian pottery, a feature that is also characteristic of some later Predynastic wares. Black-topped pottery is found in Nubia and the Sudan from very early times; it remained in fashion there long after the Egyptians had abandoned it. Until the New Kingdom it was repeatedly brought into Egypt by intruders from the south. It is likely, therefore, that the Badarians came originally from the south, for there this technique and rippling seem to have their home."

In the remains of the Badarian graves were found small-scale copper implements. Most of this metal has not survived. However, the significance of this metal use means they were beginning to step out of the Stone Age that had characterized man's existence in Africa for hundreds of thousands of years.

## Pre-Dynastic II: The Amratian or Naqada I

The next phase of the Pre-Dynastic culture of ancient Egypt is called the Amratian or Naqada I. The name comes from the sites of el-Amrah and Naqada, in Upper Egypt, Northeast Africa. The people of this period interacted with and built on the earlier cultural gains of the Badarians and this formed a continuing development in Nile Valley civilization. Again, archaeologists were able to write about the Amratians due to information taken from their graves in cemeteries. Pots were most often found. They included burnt red ware with animals, birds, plant shapes and geometric pattern decorations. Many forms or sizes of pottery were used including flasks, bowls, goblets, twin vases and tumblers.

Tools were made of stone and flint and showed the birth of a professional class of toolmakers. There were scrapers, razors, double edged blades, fish-tailed knives and lances with wood or bone handles. The cutting edge was saw-like with tiny teeth. Copper was being used for harpoons and pins. So too was gold, malachite, alabaster, basalt, ivory, bone and hard stone. Weapons were mainly made of stone and flint. The throw-stick or boomerang was in use. Ivory carving represented animals such as giraffes, birds, elephants, sheep and hippopotami. Human figures were made of ivory. Pottery figures of women had stumpy arms as handles. There were early signs of tattoo marks on the body. Women wore jewelry of shells, carnelian

# BLACK HISTORY EXTRAVAGANZA HONORING DR. BEN-JOCHANNAN

and coral around the neck. The houses of the Amratians were not different from those of the Badarians. Their huts were in Villages that were sometimes large. During this time dogs, sheep, goats, oxen and pigs had been domesticated, or tamed. There was plenty of game, fish and fowl to be caught in the river and the marshes or swamps. The cooking vessels were made of pottery and such household utensils as plates, cups, bowls, spoons, knives and other vessels were of a high quality. Much domestic utensils such as plates, spoons and knives were made of wood and have not survived. Vases were still being made of stone but they were of all sizes, shapes and very decorative. Agricultural grains were boiled for porridge and baked for bread. Grapes and barley made beverages. These early Africans of Egypt planted flax and had looms for weaving.

**Black History Extravaganza - Photo - Tomb of Iri Nufer** – "Servant in the Place of Truth," the Nobleman raises two empty arms in salutation.

# FREDERICK MONDERSON

**Black History Extravaganza - Ceramic Art -** Head of Anubis.

The dead were mainly placed in small graves with their bodies in the pre-natal position with enough space left for some "goods of the grave." Randall MacIver found evidence of "strongly curled hair" in the graves of the Amratians from the site of El-Amrah. Their dead faced south or Upper Egypt or inner Africa. Figurines of women were placed in graves. The methods of burial and things placed in graves shows the continuation of their religious beliefs. Since Egypt received little rains, it's believed the early leaders of the Amratian culture were rainmakers who were killed, as they grew older. They were probably drowned or cut-up as their powers to bring rain failed. It is also interesting that individuals with "strongly curled hair" were also found in the north or Lower Egypt!

# BLACK HISTORY EXTRAVAGANZA HONORING DR. BEN-JOCHANNAN

## BLACK HISTORY EXTRAVAGANZA HONORING DR. BEN-JOCHANNAN

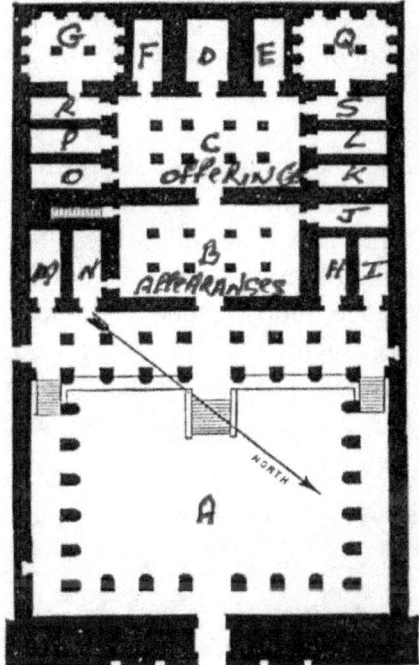

RAMESES II'S TEMPLE AT ABYDOS

A. Second Courtyard with square pillars and Osiride Figures
B. Hall of Appearances
C. Hall of Offerings
D. Chapel of Osiris Main Sanctuary
E. Chapel of Isis Sanctuary
F. Chapel of Horus Sanctuary
G. Chapel of the Ennead
H. Chapel of Rameses II
I. Chapel of the Funerary Cult
J. Chapel of Onuris
K. Chapel of Thoth
L. Chapel of Min
M. Chapel of Seti I
N. Chapel of the Ancestor Cult
O. Chapel for Robing
P. The Treasury
Q. Chapel of Osiris
R. Chapel of Onuris
S. Chapel of Onuris

**Black History Extravaganza** - Plan of the Mortuary Temple of Rameses II (19th Dynasty) at Abydos.

## Pre-Dynastic III: The Gerzean or Naqada II

The Gerzeans or Naqada II people made boats by lashing together bundles of papyrus stalks. Some boats had sails. With the development of fishing the boat-building industry grew. This new vehicle helped to develop trade as the people sought to exchange the surplus goods they had to get things they did not have. This marked

# FREDERICK MONDERSON

the beginning of commerce on the Nile that spread in Africa and elsewhere.

The Gerzean or Naqada II represents the third of the three pre-dynastic cultures that set the stage for dynastic Egypt. It is named after el-Gerza in Middle Egypt but also from the culture sequence of Naqada II from Upper Egypt. The development of the two earlier periods, the Badarian and Amratian, were continued in this final sequence.

During this period metalworking became a big industry. Copper was worked on a large scale. Gold, lead, silver, malachite, flint and ivory were also used more extensively. Stone vases were widely used. Such crafts as ivory carving and shipbuilding began to spread and develop. Egypt now finally entered the metal age, though stone continued in use well into the later periods. Copper mixed with tin made a harder metal called bronze. Most weapons were made with this tough metal. Gold was too soft for weapons. It had a mystical value and was used for religious purposes and decorative jewelry.

**Black History Extravaganza - Photo - Luxor Temple**
- View from within the Ramessean Front, Peristyle Court, Mosque of Abu Haggag (right); Kiosk of Hatshepsut dedicated to the Theban Triad of Amon, Mut and Khonsu (center); and columns of the Peristyle (left).

# BLACK HISTORY EXTRAVAGANZA HONORING DR. BEN-JOCHANNAN

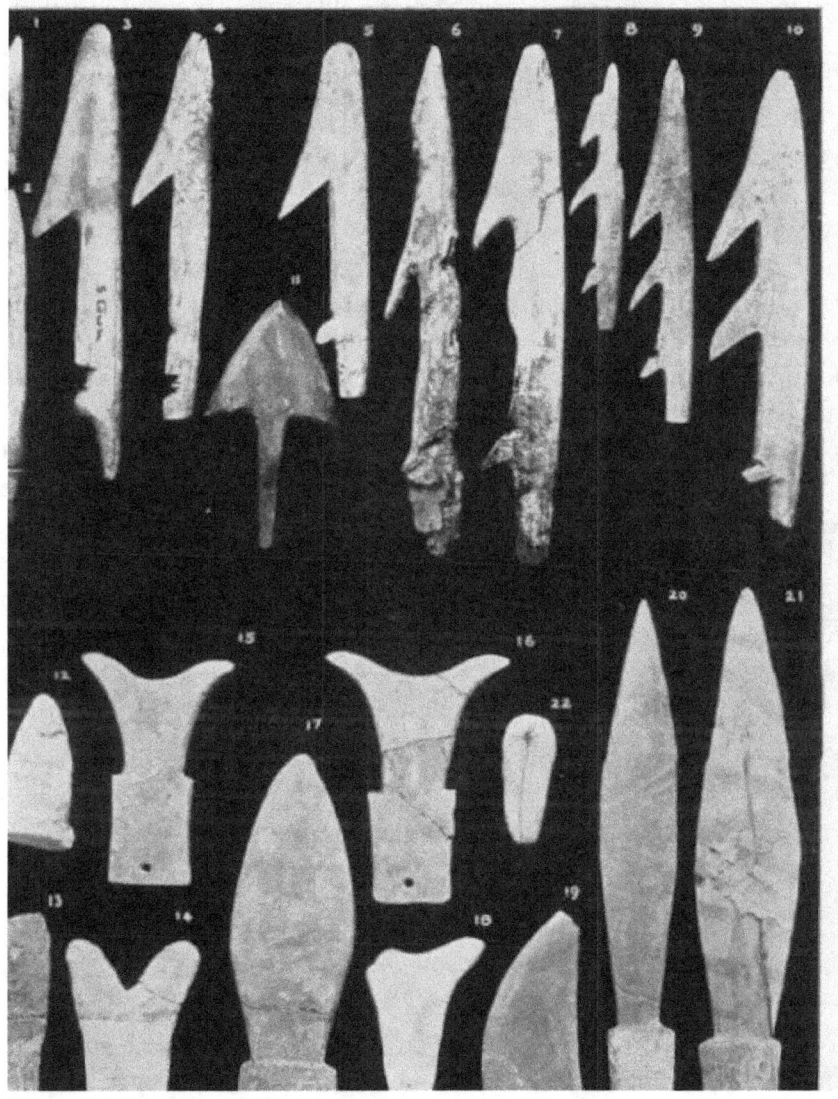

**Black History Extravaganza - Photo -** Prehistoric Bone harpoons

In the Predynastic Period craftsmen worked in gold, silver, ivory, bone, turquoise, carnelian, lapis lazuli, feldspar and jasper. They also made jewelry from amethyst, button-pearl, amber, agate, onyx, and glass. Ivory, bone, shells and beads also formed part of the jewelry worn by people. The jewelry included necklaces, girdles, bracelets, and a circlet for the head. There were anklets, finger rings and studs for the noses. Amulets of bone, ivory and colored stones were made. They represented the fertility goddess, fishes, birds, hippopotami and crocodiles. The donkey was introduced for overland trade. There were 42 nomes or small states in all of Egypt each ruled by a Nomarch, equivalent to our governor. There were 22 in Upper Egypt and 20 in Lower Egypt. It is interesting that of the 22 Nomes of Upper Egypt, the first begins at Aswan, counting northward as the river and culture headed north downstream. The number of Lower Egypt's Nomes begin at the "fork of the Delta: and extends towards the river's mouth beside the Mediterranean Sea." However, while the first set of Nome numbers were very early fixed, the higher numbers of Lower Egypt were not set until much later. In the early period, many towns built barriers to protect themselves from other towns that constantly made war over the lucrative economic resources available. This was primarily agricultural and artisan fueled by the extensive trade opportunities in the Nile Valley, and neighboring areas and the wealth generated from it.

There are a number of slate palettes and mace-heads that record the competition and wars of the time. Each state sought to gain the upper hand over its neighbors owing to the increase in trade and wealth. First the **Battlefield Palette** that shows a Libran victory over other Delta states. Then there is the **Bull Palette** showing the King as a bull goring a foreign enemy. There is also the **Libya Palette** showing cattle, asses, rams and incense trees as part of tribute for a King. Even more important is the **Narmer Palette** showing the King wearing both red and white crowns and he being credited with uniting Upper and Lower Egypt at the beginning of dynastic rule. The **Narmer Macehead** shows the King under a canopy with possibly his wife, Queen Neithhotep. It also records his capture of 120,000 men, 400,000 oxen and 1,200,000 goats. This high number is significant to show by the beginning of the First Dynasty these Nile Valley Africans were counting in the millions. Just as significant is the administration and dynamics of moving that much booty which means civilization and order, was well underway.

# BLACK HISTORY EXTRAVAGANZA HONORING DR. BEN-JOCHANNAN

**Black History Extravaganza - Papyrus -** A Blank Cartouche and the Astrological sign for Pisces.

**Black History Extravaganza - Photo - Luxor Temple.** Beside a seated statue, standing statues emerging from between columns in the south-east quadrant of the Peristyle Court of the Ramessean Front.

# FREDERICK MONDERSON

Narmer came from Thebes in the south, conquered and united Upper and Lower Egypt, though the *Cambridge Ancient History* (3$^{rd}$ Edition) Vol. I, Part II (Cambridge at the University Press, 1971) identifies the Scorpion King as "the first king of whom any historical details are known, owing to the discovery at Hierakonpolis of some fragments of a limestone mace-head decorated with scenes in relief commemorating symbolically episodes in his life." Beyond the palettes and Maceheads, a number of "historical documents" establish the basic parameters of the beginning of dynastic rule. At Narmer's "Unification" events began the First Dynasty and this marked the end of the Pre-Dynastic period. At a later period when Egypt was again divided southerners united the land during the Middle Kingdom, at the start of the New Kingdom and to begin the Twenty-Fifth Ethiopian Dynasty. Later times, in philosophic reflection, the names of Narmer of the First Dynasty, Mentuhotep II of the 11$^{th}$ Dynasty's Middle Kingdom; Kamose and Ahmose of the 18$^{th}$ Dynasty's New Kingdom, and we could add Piankhy of the 25$^{th}$ Dynasty who were all linked and recognized as uniters of that ancient African kingdom along the Nile River, now known as Egypt.

**Black History Extravaganza - Temple of Seti I at Kurneh -** Entrance with the columns on the façade.

# BLACK HISTORY EXTRAVAGANZA
# HONORING DR. BEN-JOCHANNAN

**Black History Extravaganza - Photo -** Prehistoric Amulets, etc.

## The Archaic Period

The Archaic Period comprised the first and second dynasties who built on the Predynastic foundations. They were essentially buried at Abydos, home of Osiris, god of the Dead. First and Second Dynasty kings were actually buried at Abydos and cenotaphs or "dummy tombs" were buried at Sakkara, Memphis' burial place. The double burials symbolized the king's dual nature as leader of the two, Upper and Lower Kingdoms, the Sakkara burials had all the paraphernalia of the Abydos burials except the king's body. It's been shown, Seti I's Temple to Osiris at Abydos was actually dedicated to these kings who were buried in the desert to which the festivities faced.

**Black History Extravaganza - Photo - Luxor Temple.** View of the South-East quadrant of the Court of Amenhotep III with its closed bud papyrus columns, a photographer's paradise, especially as the sun sets throwing back its shadows against the magnificent structure.

## The Old Kingdom I

The Old Kingdom lasted from about 2780-2259 B.C. It included the Third through Sixth Dynasties. This period is also called the "Pyramid Age." Those large-scale pyramid structures of stone were built at this time. The high level of technology these ancient Africans of Egypt employed enabled such structures to defy time indicating bureaucratic and organizing abilities as well as the utility of emerging medical skills to treat "on the job accidents."

# BLACK HISTORY EXTRAVAGANZA HONORING DR. BEN-JOCHANNAN

King Narmer had established the monarchy and feudal relationships at the time of unification inaugurating the First Dynasty. The priesthood justified the divine nature of the kingship. The king and his religious assistants helped define the role of nobles and Nomarchs, or rulers of the nomes, in supporting the system of pharaonic government. The priestly caste provided the bureaucratic organization and their training that administered the state apparatus.

Centralized government remained in effect until the end of the Sixth Dynasty. Social upper classes continued to grow from the time of unification in the Archaic Period. Their power increased and peaked in the Sixth Dynasty. Some scholars believe this increase in power of the nobles led directly to the end of the Old Kingdom. Position in the social order was based on birth, education and employment. Employment with the government was at central, regional and local levels. Being in the military or a high position in the religious field was also a sought-after social status position. This was especially so after the war of liberation at which time imperial ventures became an attractive undertaking with rewards for exceptional service during the New Kingdom. Great wealth was accumulated from booty and tribute. Much of this was bequeathed the emerging Priesthood for worship of the gods and as foundation for kingly and noble mortuary cults.

**Black History Extravaganza - Photo -** With Dr. Calvin Butts at the Podium (right); and Professor James Smalls in the same position (right); all that can be said, "His peers, students, supporters and admirers, gave Dr. Ben a Resounding Send-off!"

# FREDERICK MONDERSON

**Black History Extravaganza - Photo - Luxor Temple.** View in the Court's columns left (northwest) and right (northeast) and the Processional Colonnade with the Mosque of Abu Haggag and the Entrance Pylon further on.

Architecture is the most predominant feature of the Old Kingdom. It involved a search for more permanent materials used especially in constructing structures of a political nature. Their architects and craftsmen evolved from working in mud brick and wood that replaced lashed bundles of papyrus stalks, rush mat-work, palm thatch and wattle and daub mixtures. With improved building techniques, they began using stone for parts of the house subjected to hard ware as lintels, thresholds and doorposts. Soon their architects built more extensively of stone. As such, the pyramids, temples, palaces and Mastaba tombs were all built of stone. This material was sometimes quarried from far distances.

First, Imhotep built the Step-Pyramid at Sakkara, for Pharaoh Zoser. Done in the Third Dynasty, it is a six-level reducing sized Mastaba tomb with a base of 411 feet east-west by 358 feet north-south. It had a height of two hundred feet. The word Mastaba means bench in

# BLACK HISTORY EXTRAVAGANZA HONORING DR. BEN-JOCHANNAN

Arabic. Many of these tombs looked like benches to the Arab workmen who helped in the early excavation, thus the name. The very large Mastaba tombs contained hundreds of rooms underground in their substructure.

Zoser's pyramid complex had a tremendous enclosure wall of one-mile perimeter and a height of thirty-three feet. It enclosed buildings that were dwarfed by the Step-Pyramid. The stones were quarried from great distances, sometimes as far away as Aswan in Upper Egypt. Their construction showed decorated carvings of "plant forms such as papyrus stalks, pendant leaf capitals and fasciculated columns." This new architecture lent an air of fresh vitality to the buildings. The natural setting was, however, a conflict with ideas of the dead.

**Black History Extravaganza - Photo - Hatshepsut's Temple at Deir el- Bahari.** The three-levels of the temple at an age when one story was the norm. On the Upper Terrace Osiride statues of the Queen (King) that have survived.

# FREDERICK MONDERSON

**Black History Extravaganza - Photo - Hatshepsut's Temple at Deir el-Bahari**. Evidence of one of two incense trees from the Punt Expedition that were planted before the Pylon entrance to the First Court.

The success of the Step-Pyramid encouraged the architects to attempt the Bent-Pyramid at Dashur. Built c. 2600 B.C., it was also called the "Southern Pyramid" or "Snefru Gleams." It had an approximate angle slope of 54 degrees at the base of the pyramid. Rather than continue upwards to the apex there is a sudden change to an angle of 42 degrees. It was thought this change made the top collapse or it was finished in a hurry.

Pharaoh Snefru built a second pyramid. It was called the Northern Pyramid and also located at Dashur. It had a rising slope of 36 degrees instead of the earlier 53 degrees. The angle of 53 degrees became the normal angle of ascent of later pyramids. This was the first true pyramid.

The Ghizeh Plateau became the stage for the three great pyramids built by Khufu, Khafre and Menkaure. The largest pyramid has a height of 756 feet though Flinders Petrie thought the original height was 782

# BLACK HISTORY EXTRAVAGANZA HONORING DR. BEN-JOCHANNAN

feet. It is named "Khufu is one belonging to the horizon." The second largest has a height of 708 feet. It is called "Great is Khafra." The smallest of the three has a height of 306 feet. It is named "Menkaure is divine." These builders were father, son and grandson. Recall fast-forward and that the New Kingdom temples were also assigned names. Nevertheless, the achievements in the 4th Dynasty essentially characterized the Old Kingdom. Down through the ages, these structures achieved immortality for the Egyptians in the minds of man. There were also smaller pyramids nearby made for the pharaoh's female relatives. If one adds the Sphinx of Ghizeh then these monuments do characterize not only the Old Kingdom but also the permanence of Egypt. However, the "Pyramid Texts" of the 5th and 6th Dynasties are also significant accomplishments of this period.

**Black History Extravaganza - Tomb of Sennufer -** Two servants carry objects on their backs and in their hands.

# FREDERICK MONDERSON

INSCRIPTIONS ON THE LEFT HAND SIDE OF INNER WALL.

INSCRIPTIONS ON THE LINTEL AND JAMBS OF DOORWAY TO SHRINE.

**Black History Extravaganza - Photo -** El Bersheh - Tomb No. 1, Main chamber, Inscriptions on the left-hand side of inner wall and inscriptions on the Lintel and Jambs of Doorway to shrine.

# BLACK HISTORY EXTRAVAGANZA HONORING DR. BEN-JOCHANNAN

**Black History Extravaganza - Ceramic Art**. The big goose in beautiful color.

Throughout Egypt there were some 80 pyramids along the Nile River. The three at Ghizeh (Giza), however, characterized the concept of the pyramid group and the idea of the complex. In the Pyramid Complex could be found a surrounding Enclosure Wall. At the river, there was a Valley Temple. From here a Causeway or walkway, passed nearby the Sun Temple. There was a Mortuary Temple or temple of the dead and a Sacrificial Altar.

In the complex, the Main Pyramid was centrally located. In its rear was the Subsidiary or Smaller Pyramids for the Pharaoh's queen or female relatives. The dead's belongings were stored in Magazines. There was a Sphinx, Obelisk, and also a Heb Sed or Jubilee Festival Pavilion as well as a Heb Sed Court in which the King ran the Heb Sed Race of Rejuvenation. Lastly, the king had one or more Solar Boats deposited in nearby boat pit(s). In their view, this vehicle was

# FREDERICK MONDERSON

used to sail across the sky to the next world. In addition, there were Mastaba tombs for nobles and officials who served the king. These officials wished to gain immortality by being buried next to or within the shadows of their god-king. Their burials were arranged in block and street-like pattern cemeteries surrounding the Pyramid. This was the earliest form of "town planning. Such was the belief of the Cult of the god-king of the Old Kingdom.

**Black History Extravaganza - Photo - Hatshepsut's Temple at Deir el- Bahari**. From the Court of Mentuhotep II's Eleventh Dynasty Temple, the Hathor Shrine (left) and columns of the Middle and Upper Colonnades with the mountain as a backdrop.

These pyramids were not decorated, but nobles' mastabas were early canvases upon which frescoes recounting activities of daily life and hunting and fishing scenes were lavishly depicted. These individuals went to great lengths to "provision" and decorate their tombs to reinforce the idea of the awaiting leisure expected in the "Afterlife." In the $5^{th}$ Dynasty, King Unas had the Egyptian "Bible" or "Pyramid Text" inscribed on his tomb walls. In the Sixth Dynasty, similar Pyramid Texts began with the phrase "Rise up O Teti, thou shall not die." These spells were admonitions intended to help the king

# BLACK HISTORY EXTRAVAGANZA HONORING DR. BEN-JOCHANNAN

navigate and to survive the Judgment and enjoy the afterlife. Beside Unas of the Fifth Dynasty, four other kings of the Sixth Dynasty had similar work done on their pyramids.

## The Old Kingdom II

Great advances were made in diverse fields of cultural growth. The treatment of medicine expanded in the Old Kingdom lasting from the $3^{rd}$ through the $6^{th}$ Dynasties. This medical development can be traced to two reasons. First, the ancient Africans of Egypt had a profound belief in the afterlife. The burials of the poor in the hot and sandy desert led to quick preservation of the body. This led to the development of natural mummification and to the special efforts to preserve the body in the religious and philosophical belief that the deceased would return to claim and inhabit the tomb, but in a contradictory manner remain among the gods in that place of purity.

Then again, since the rock-hewn tomb was philosophically considered the dividing line or transition point between this world and the next, the belief held, the deceased remained mobile to come and go and so able to reside in the tomb. That is, after a successful Judgment and being declared "True of voice" or "Justified." The various parts of the soul, 9 in number, would then be reconstituted in the same whole person. The process of preparation to effectuate the full dynamics of the Afterlife drama was called mummification. A great deal has been written about mummies and mummification. Herodotus, c. 450 B.C. was the first of the classical commentators who wrote about mummification in Books II called *Euterpe* in his *Histories*. He mentioned the three types of mummification based on one's ability to pay. This means the priests who were the earliest "Morticians" were probably in the "for profit" business.

# FREDERICK MONDERSON

**Black History Extravaganza - Tomb of Sennufer -** The Nobleman's wife holds a sistrum with the face of "The Prince of the City."

# BLACK HISTORY EXTRAVAGANZA HONORING DR. BEN-JOCHANNAN

**Black History Extravaganza - Photo** - El Bersheh - Early form of boat with full sail and cabins on deck.

**Black History Extravaganza - Photo** - The People were there for Dr. Ben-Jochannan down to the end to wish him well before he made his transition to become a revered ancestor in our Pantheon.

# FREDERICK MONDERSON

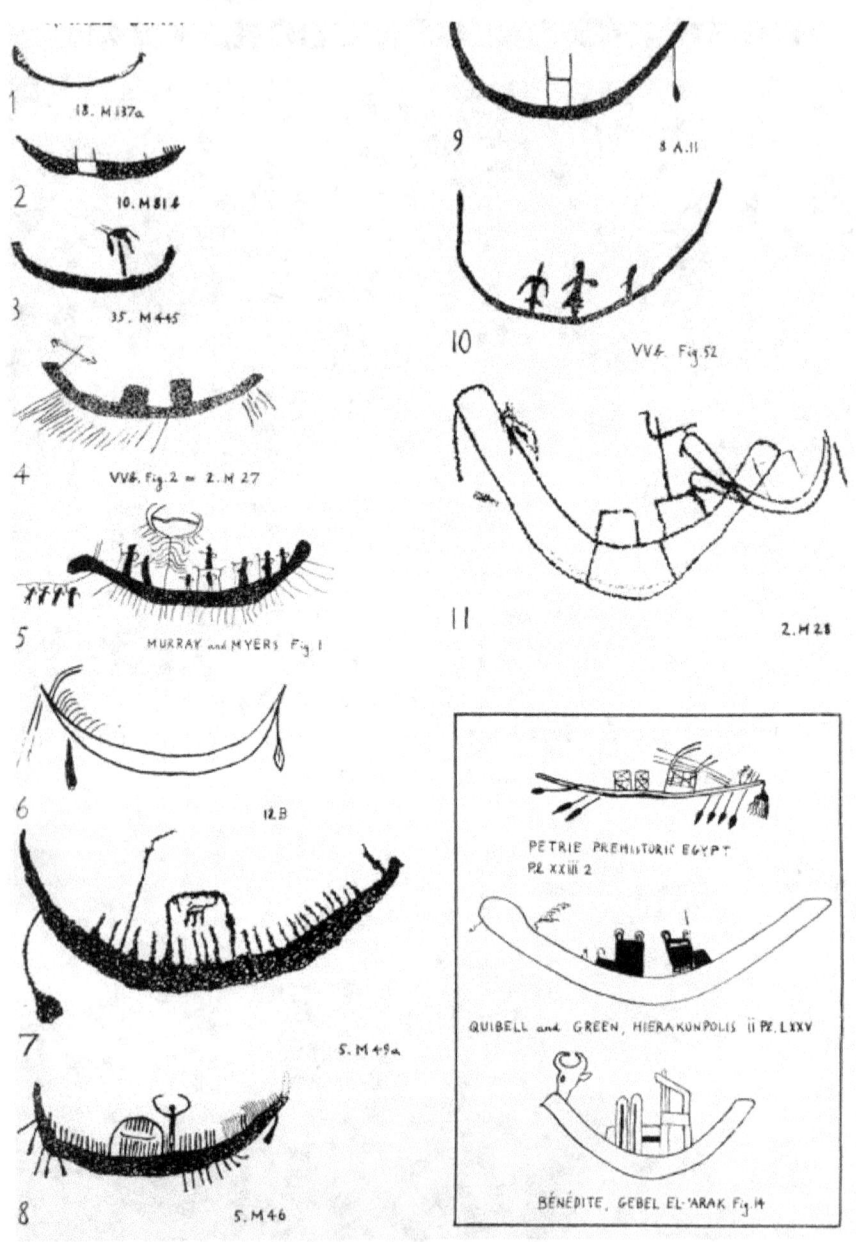

**Black History Extravaganza - Photo - El Bersheh II -** Sickle Boats with examples of Prehistoric, from Hierakonpolis and Gebel el-Arak.

# BLACK HISTORY EXTRAVAGANZA HONORING DR. BEN-JOCHANNAN

**Black History Extravaganza - Photo -** Within Mentuhotep's Deir el Bahari Temple beside that of Hatshepsut, built some 500-years later, from this prototype. Notice the column stumps and their arrangement.

In developing their medical knowledge, in practice of medicine, diseases of the abdomen, bladder, rectum, eyes and skin were studied. Methods of detecting illnesses based on the visible parts of the body such as the skin, hair, nails and tongue were known. While they practiced surgery, and listened to the heart, they also knew of the blood circulation. Further, these medical specialists, who were generally priests, treated gallstones, gout and arthritis. Individual priests specialized in treating one area of the human body and never trespassed on another's area of specialty. They also extracted medicine from plants and minerals. Animal parts and sinews were part of their pharmacopeia.

The gods were considered good to Egypt and they were constantly worshipped and ritualized. In the $5^{th}$ Dynasty Pyramid of King Unas the "Pyramid Text" was inscribed on the walls. This Egyptian "Bible" represented the development and codification of Egyptian religious

# FREDERICK MONDERSON

beliefs and methods of religious expression that were thousands of years old in pre-inscriptional form or oral practice. This lasted for thousands more, thanks to the work of a dedicated priesthood. These were a powerful group who studied the sciences, the arts and made progress in these respective disciplines. In this endeavor, that body was responsible for conducting various religious and social ceremonies and in helping to ensure the administration of justice, the manifestation of truth in the aspiration for righteousness. Even though they were tax exempt, they themselves also collected the state's taxes especially from the farmers and then doled out payments and rewards, especially to the bureaucracy who administered the state.

**Black History Extravaganza - Photo -** Kwesi Ashra (left) and Greg Hardy (right) share a lighter moment at Dr. Ben's affair in the Cemetery.

# BLACK HISTORY EXTRAVAGANZA HONORING DR. BEN-JOCHANNAN

**Black History Extravaganza - Photo - Stele.** Male figure paying homage to Osiris with two goddesses "watching the God's back."

# FREDERICK MONDERSON

**Black History Extravaganza - Tomb of Sennufer -** The Nobleman sits with his wife.

During the inundation or overflowing of the river, boundary marks of property were washed away. So, the priests provided surveyors who

# BLACK HISTORY EXTRAVAGANZA HONORING DR. BEN-JOCHANNAN

mathematically re-surveyed the land and determined where the boundary marks should be placed. By studying the behavior of the river, they also predicted the harvest yield. Taxes were determined based on the height of the Nile and expected agricultural yield. Stern examples were set for those who did not pay their taxes. The priests were also responsible for training all branches of civil administration. They also collected tribute for the temples and taught mathematics, astronomy, geometry, philosophy and the arts, even practiced their medicine in the "House of Life" that also doubled as a "help center."

On the walls of tombs, paintings and drawings depicted daily life during the time of the Old Kingdom. Sculpture in relief and in the round developed. Raised and sunk relief showed man, his culture and nature very plainly. This was an age of colossal, or huge, human portraiture. The hieroglyphics depicted drama in the afterlife.

**Black history Extravaganza - Tomb of Sennufer -** Servants bring goodies to their Lord.

# FREDERICK MONDERSON

**Black History Extravaganza - Papyrus -** Nefertari in full-regal splendor wearing the Queen-Mother Crown with the vulture holding a ring in its talon. The necklace is equally devastatingly beautiful as a cobra pierces the ear.

In politics, the power of the nobles increased and threatened the central administration by the end of the $6^{th}$ dynasty. This resulted in political discontent. Pharaoh Pepi II ruled for 94 years. This is the

# BLACK HISTORY EXTRAVAGANZA HONORING DR. BEN-JOCHANNAN

longest reign in history. At his death ending the 6$^{th}$ Dynasty, the Old Kingdom came to an end. Disorder, anarchy, and civil war broke out in the assertion of who would rule and this state of affairs led to the First Intermediate Period or Dynasties 7 through 10. Some scholars believe in the latter stage of this period foreigners invaded from Asia and comprised the 8$^{th}$, 9$^{th}$ and 10$^{th}$ Dynasties. This is not altogether agreed on but admonitions and instructions paint a gloomy picture of the terrible state the nation had descended into. The whole system of the society was overturned in the chaos, robbery and illicit behavior became rampant and the poor became rich and the rich became poor. He who had lost all and he who had none gained much. There was treachery throughout the land. So much so, a prophet predicted the coming of a "Messiah" who would change all that.

**Black History Extravaganza - Ceramic Art -** The "Eye of Horus."

# FREDERICK MONDERSON

"Before the fall," trade was expanded by land and by sea. Again, merchants exchanged food, crafts, technology, ideas and even exported religion beliefs. They were in contact with the Levant and Nubia where they exchanged gold, ivory and other products. Industry bloomed with beautiful and delicate vessels, pottery jars, tables and dishes. The materials they worked included slate, rock crystal, faience, basalt, marble, alabaster and diorite. Such trades as flint-work, papyrus making, jewelry, metalwork, weaving, woodwork, bone and ivory carving and faience, show these Nile Valley Africans expertly working, planning for the future, even building and also engaged in carpentry. Agriculture included the swidden or shifting method of cultivation. Improved methods of irrigation, ploughing and hoeing helped tremendously in raising sometimes two or three crops per year based on location or proximity to the river. They planted barley, corn, wheat, and cereals. These crops were harvested and placed in storage facilities or grain silos. They kept domestic animals of cows, oxen, pigs, sheep and goats. The shaduf, turned by bulls, horses or donkeys helped move water to higher ground. The canal moved water further inland. The canal was also used for light boating and movement of goods. There were essentially two main parallel canals on both sides of the Nile. There were additional perpendicular canals that in turn further distributed water in smaller criss-crossed canals. Essentially, a checkerboard pattern distributed water further inland from the Nile. Thus, while the Inundation reached certain prime farm-land, "uplands" where the water could not reach was irrigated by the shaduf and other small canal means. Today practically every farmer has a water pump supplied by the government that lifts water, whether from the Nile or any of the extending canals that further aids agricultural growth manifesting in the perennial greenery contrasting the dry, desert-like surroundings one observes in transit across the land.

# BLACK HISTORY EXTRAVAGANZA HONORING DR. BEN-JOCHANNAN

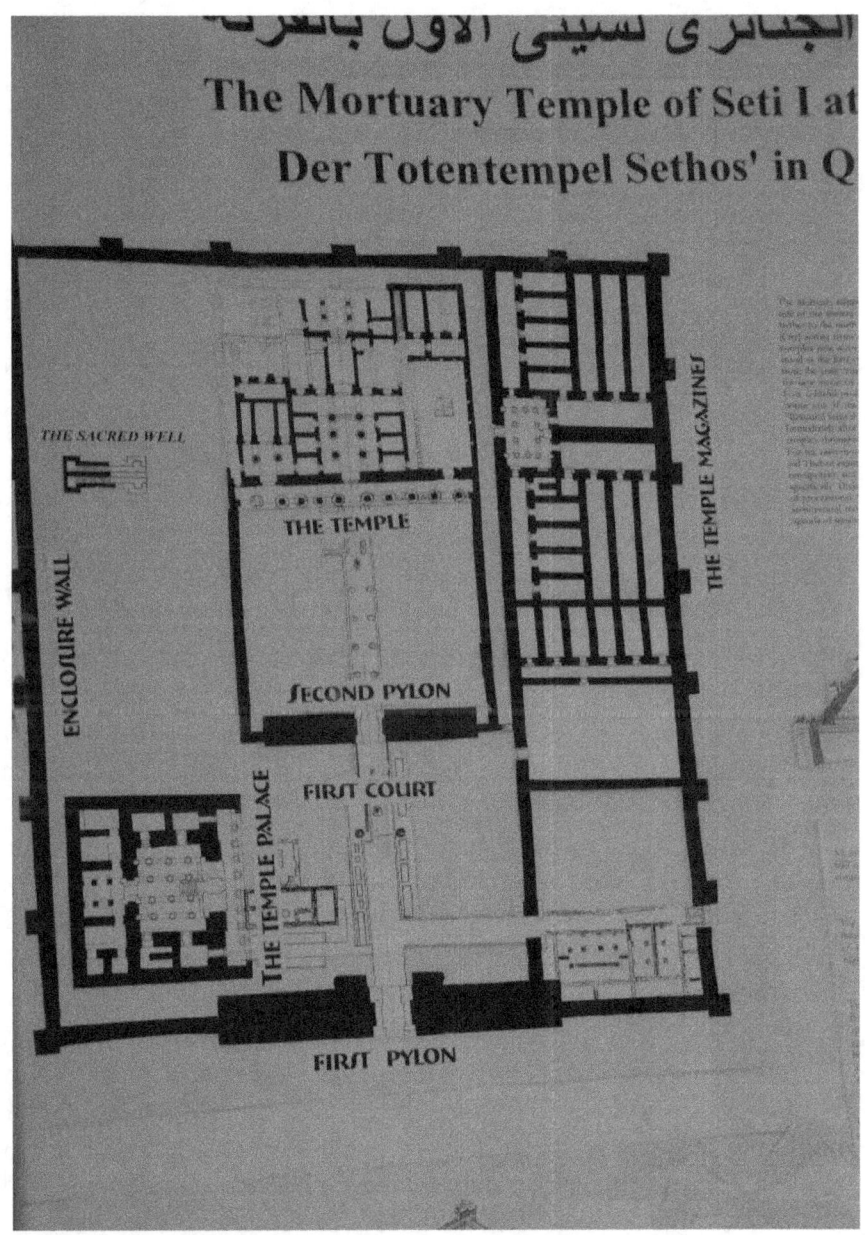

**Black History Extravaganza - Photo -** Plan of the Temple of Seti I at Qurneh.

# FREDERICK MONDERSON

**Black History Extravaganza - Photo -** Dromos entrance to the Temple of Seti I at Qurneh.

Food meats included mutton, beef, goats and gazelles. Birds eaten were geese, ducks, quail, pigeons or squab, and later chickens. Vegetables included lentils, beans, radishes, onions and garlic. Fruits grown were figs, dates, grapes, raisins, pomegranates and melons. Bakers made bread, cakes and pies. Animals provided ingredients for milk, cheese and butter. The fermented juices were wine from grapes, beer from barley and arrack from dates. All this made life bearable for the well-to-do, especially. Meanwhile, the peasants or fellaheen continued to provide agricultural labor, pay taxes and be buried in shallow graves in cemeteries along the desert edge. It was hoped their intelligent sons would "Be a Scribe," the "intellectual of their day," to escape the dread of agriculture life or even become a craftsman who could boast of producing some form of artistic masterpiece.

# BLACK HISTORY EXTRAVAGANZA HONORING DR. BEN-JOCHANNAN

**Black History Extravaganza - Photo -** Seti kneels to make a Presentation to enthroned Ra-Horakhty, with a vulture with outstretched wings below their feet.

**Black History Extravaganza - Photo -** Ark of the god lies "at rest" while within smaller arks and figures attest this is a temple since Uraei hover overhead and standards are stationed below.

# FREDERICK MONDERSON

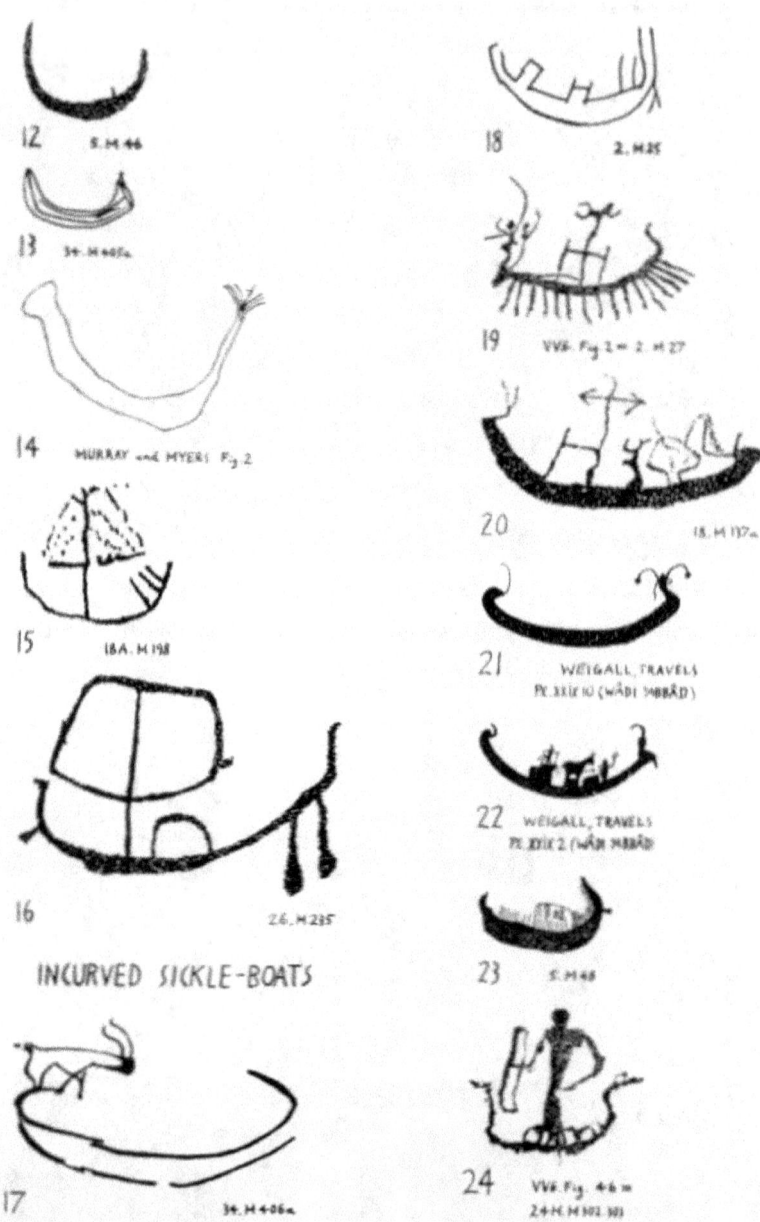

**Black History Extravaganza - Line Drawing -** Boats of various sizes and shapes.

# BLACK HISTORY EXTRAVAGANZA HONORING DR. BEN-JOCHANNAN

In summary, these were some of the accomplishments these Northeast Africans, Nile River dwellers, made some 5000 years ago. Thus, today's African-American youth and adults should recognize, reclaim and speak proudly of their ancestors from the Nile Valley on the African continent, in North-East Africa.

## The Middle Kingdom

The accomplishments of the Old Kingdom were soon lost as the nobles gained more power and a state of political instability ensured. Pepi II of the Sixth Dynasty rule for 94 years and this allowed the increased power of the nobles to threaten the monarchical system. During this pristine and inventive age, all Egyptians wanted to be buried in the shadow of the pharaoh's pyramid. However, with the expanding power of the nobles they shifted alliances and expectations and chose to be buried closer to their nomes and this generated conflict in the threatened society and social order. Therefore, the whole system of government that depended upon their support collapsed at the end of the Sixth Dynasty, around 2240 B.C. The civilization thus entered the First Intermediate Period of dynasties seven through ten. This first "Dark Ages" or rather first age of disruption, clouded the glitter of classical Egypt.

**Black History extravaganza - Photo -** Looks like the "Full Panoply of the Rotunda" as the two "Holy Men" confer at the Podium to the right.

# FREDERICK MONDERSON

**Black History Extravaganza - Photo -** Before a sumptuous "Table of Offerings," Seti I incenses the Bark of the God lying at rest.

The ensuing anarchy of the First Intermediate Period came to an end when the kings of the south again mobilized their forces. These southern dynasts of Thebes were united under a single noble family. This unity assured, they then headed north to subdue and unify the entire land again as Narmer or Menes had done to begin the First Dynasty. Once again Egypt became a united country, thanks to Thebes, "the fighting province." Thus, the pharaohs Intef and Mentuhotep restored order, founded the Eleventh Dynasty and began the Middle Kingdom. Some scholars believe as he grew in stature after each success he may have changed his name so the Mentuhotep I, II, III, may be the same person who built the magnificent Deir el Bahari temple with its new architectural features. This temple served as transitional architecture from the Old Kingdom to the New Kingdom forming the prototype of Hatshepsut's nearby masterpiece that has retained much of its magnificent luster even after some 3500 years. Nevertheless, Mentuhotep bequeathed the succeeding twelfth dynasty a united country, reorganized and the powerful nobles either fully in check or about to be.

# BLACK HISTORY EXTRAVAGANZA HONORING DR. BEN-JOCHANNAN

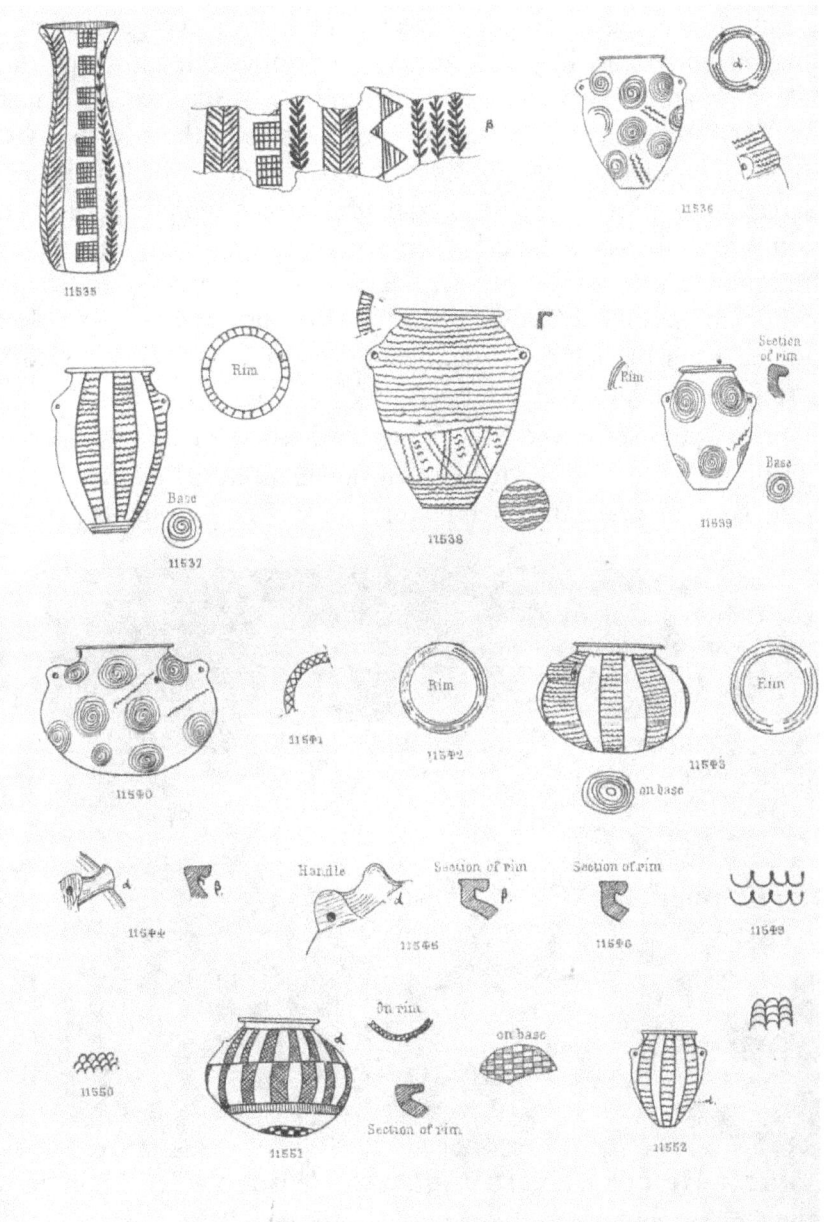

**Black History Extravaganza - Line Drawing -** Various decorated vessels.

# FREDERICK MONDERSON

Thus, the Middle Kingdom was a period of reorganization and expansion of the Egyptian state. The kings Mentuhoteps of the eleventh and Sesostrises and Amenemhats of the twelfth dynasties restored the greatness of Egypt. Sesostris II of the twelfth dynasty broke the power of the nobles in a sort of "buy in or lose what you have" strategy and so he restored internal peace and prosperity. These kings from the south choose Thebes as the cultural, administrative and religious capital of Egypt. During this period, many Africans from Nubia to the south of Egypt further entered the country. Many fought in the wars of liberation, unification and expansion. An incoming group of Nubians called "Pan Grave" people were buried in a new type of grave, some say in the pre-dynastic contracted or fetal position. Their heads were placed to the north and their faces to the east or west. Goods of the grave included pottery, jewelry and weapons.

**Black History Extravaganza - Photo -** Seti I mingle with the Gods as enthroned figure wears horns and disk.

As is known, Mentuhotep II of the Eleventh Dynasty, united the two lands and founded of the Middle Kingdom. He is one of several

# BLACK HISTORY EXTRAVAGANZA HONORING DR. BEN-JOCHANNAN

pharaohs who left evidence of his "black flesh." His statue is in the Cairo Museum. He seemed to make a special effort to portray his "blackness." Later Egyptians linked his name with Menes and Ahmose as unifiers of Egypt. During Mentuhotep's reign, the patron deity of Thebes, Amon, rose to prominence and became identified or fused with Ra - becoming Amon-Ra, the sun god. Thereafter, Amon or Amun, Amen, became head of the Egyptian pantheon of gods. Interesting, Menes, Mentuhotep and Ahmose, all Thebans, were unifiers of Egypt and no other group of pharaohs or region could boast of any such comparative achievement or distinction. It is interesting that Flinders Petrie describes the king of the Seventeenth Dynasty as "coming from Nubia, held Thebes as its capital." One has to query when did this influence begin. What is the relationship of Menes and Mentuhotep to Nubia? To what extent did Nubia and Egypt in the south differ? Given did Upper Egypt extended from its southern border to the Delta tip, how different was the ethnicity of the occupants of Lower Nubia and Upper Egypt? Why is this not given prominence by Western scholars?

Nevertheless, a vigorous foreign policy was pursued in the Middle Kingdom. Expeditions were sent into Africa in Nubia and beyond, Libya, Sinai and Palestine. Western Asia was also attacked. Gold and other wealth poured into Egypt with Thebes as its capital. Trade was pursued extensively. It was a time of great achievements. This period saw many buildings erected and tremendous intellectual growth and unsurpassed artistic achievements attained. It was called the period of classical literary accomplishments. Many tales emerged from this period. Paintings and sculpture depicted the culture in life and death.

# FREDERICK MONDERSON

**Black History Extravaganza - Photo -** Yes, "We're all here for our Hero and Champion."

# BLACK HISTORY EXTRAVAGANZA HONORING DR. BEN-JOCHANNAN

**Black History Extravaganza - Photo -** "Hama and Chama," or "Memnon;" two colossal seated statues of Amenhotep II still stand before his Mortuary Temple destroyed in an earthquake.

**Black History Extravaganza - Tomb of Sennufer -** Servants bring vessels.

# FREDERICK MONDERSON

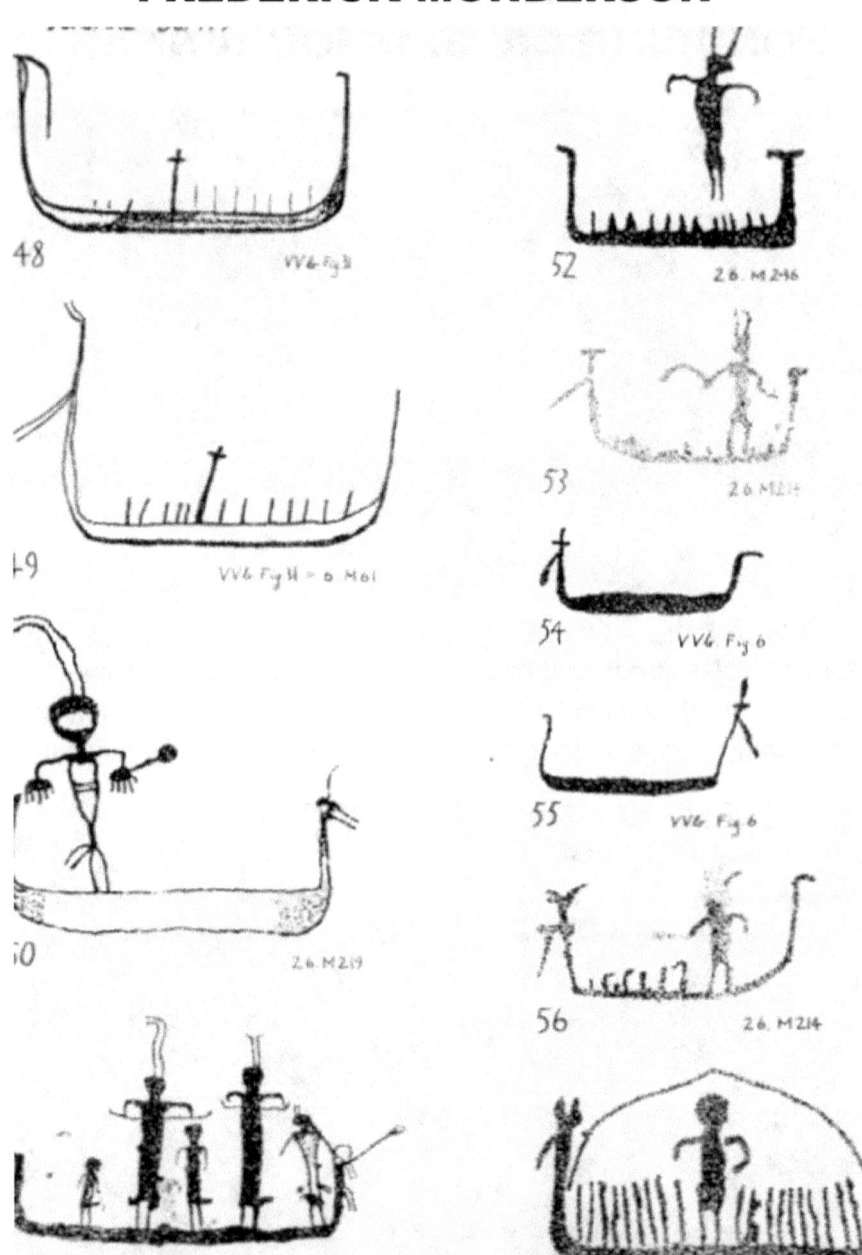

**Black History Extravaganza - Line Drawing -** Of Boats and with human figures.

# BLACK HISTORY EXTRAVAGANZA HONORING DR. BEN-JOCHANNAN

The Hieroglyphic language of Middle Egyptian was further developed during this period. It set the stage for even greater literary feats bequeathed to the New Kingdom. Many literary works and ideas from the old period were copied. Several texts record the exploits and works of the Middle Kingdom, particularly the 12$^{th}$ Dynasty. They tell of the fortresses built to protect trade routes from inner Africa to Upper Egypt. They also recount punitive expeditions to secure peace in that area and elsewhere. Expeditions were also sent to the quarries and mines were opened in the Sinai. Lastly, the diplomatic relations with Western Asia were recounted.

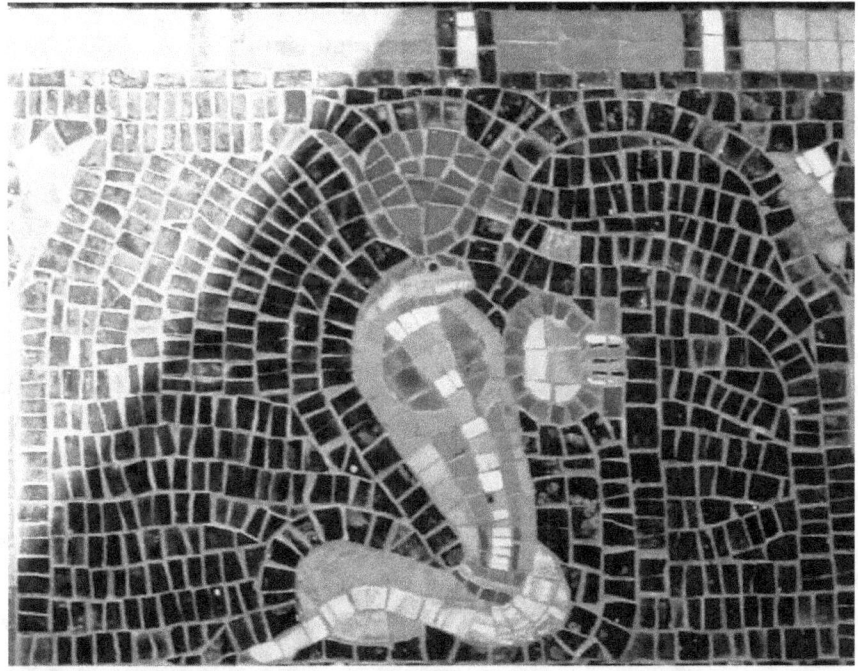

**Black History Extravaganza - Ceramic Art -** Colorful Uraeus with Horns and Sun-disk.

Soon the Twelfth Dynasty ended. Egypt again failed to continue the tradition of fielding strong and vigorous rulers. The Thirteenth Dynasty stepped in but could not continue the policies and works of their predecessors in maintaining vigorous policies of strength and

# FREDERICK MONDERSON

creativity. We do know the remains of at least one Sobekhotep was considered Negro or black and this is not surprising this dynasty, based at Thebes was a continuation of the previous one. Notwithstanding, the Thirteenth and Fourteenth Dynasties were weak. Egypt entered the Second Intermediate Period. The country once again became a divided land. It was thus easy for Hyksos foreigners to entrench themselves in the north as they found the Fifteenth and Sixteenth Dynasties. They contributed little, destroyed much and so, essentially the state stagnated. The Thebans, however, while they recognized these conquerors as overlords and then paid tribute still sought to maintain a state of continuity and readiness.

**Black History extravaganza - Tomb of Sennufer -** Oh, to be out there sailing with the Missus in one's own boat in the Afterlife and to be attended by servants fore and aft.

# BLACK HISTORY EXTRAVAGANZA HONORING DR. BEN-JOCHANNAN

**Black History Extravaganza - Photo -** At the Ramesseum, Mortuary Temple of Rameses II, native Egyptian Guide Showgi Abd Rady stands beside a fallen head of a colossal statue of the king.

# FREDERICK MONDERSON

**Black History Extravaganza - Photo -** From the South, Showgi stands before columns of the Hypostyle Hall.

## The New Kingdom

In this Second Intermediate Period, the nobles again fought each other in claim to be pharaoh. Agriculture, trade, arts and religion suffered. Asiatic invaders called Hyksos attacked the weak and divided nation. This was another bleak time in the glorious history of the Nile River civilization of Egypt, called Kemet, the "Black Land," by early Egyptian and classical writers.

Forming the $15^{th}$ and $16^{th}$ Dynasties, the Hyksos introduced little, absorbed much and destroyed greatly. Yet still, while they controlled the north there was a workable but unstable alliance with the south that recognized the Hyksos as overlords, paying a required tribute. After a lengthy period of occupation and strange enough, the Hyksos King Apophis sent a message to the Thebans complaining that the hippopotamuses grazing the Nile at Thebes made so much noise, though 600 miles away in the Delta, he could not sleep. So, "Shut-up your hippos!" Like all conquerors their arrogance knew no boundaries!

# BLACK HISTORY EXTRAVAGANZA HONORING DR. BEN-JOCHANNAN

To individuals of the 17<sup>th</sup> Dynasty identified as "coming from Nubia," proximate with Thebes in Upper Egypt as their capital, such was "insulting war talk" and the "fighting Thebans" were admonished by Amon to punish these upstarts so they mobilized and went to war.

In "Egyptian Religion" in Hastings *Encyclopedia of Religion and Ethics*, vol. 5, 1912 (236-250), Flinders Petrie, in describing the make-up of the Theban Triad, writes (1912: 247) regarding its principal god, betrays a closely guarded fact. "Amon was the local god of Karnak. He was probably connected with Min, the god of the neighboring desert of Koptos; and a late legend points to Min being the earlier and Amon being a variant, as Isis is said to have divided the legs of Amon, who could not walk before, but had his legs growing together. Min is always shown with the legs joined, Amon with the legs parted. Moreover, Amon is often shown in the ithyphallic form of Min. Had the princes of Thebes not risen to general dominion, probably Amon would have been as little known as many other local gods; but the rise of the XIth and XIIth dynasties brought Amon forward as a national god; and the "XVIIth dynasty from Nubia, holding Thebes as its capital," entailed that Amon became the great god of the most important age of Egypt - the XVIIIth - XXth Dynasties. He thus became united with Ra of Heliopolis, the greatest god of the Delta; and Amon-Ra became the figure-head of the Egyptian religion, king of the gods, and 'lord of the thrones of the earth.'"

# FREDERICK MONDERSON

**Black History Extravaganza - Photo -** Showgi Abd Rady stands before the colossal Osiride figures of the Ramesseum, Mortuary Temple of Rameses II, 19th Dynasty.

**Black History Extravaganza - Photo -** People at work but beyond, columns of the Ramesseum's Hypostyle Hall.

# BLACK HISTORY EXTRAVAGANZA HONORING DR. BEN-JOCHANNAN

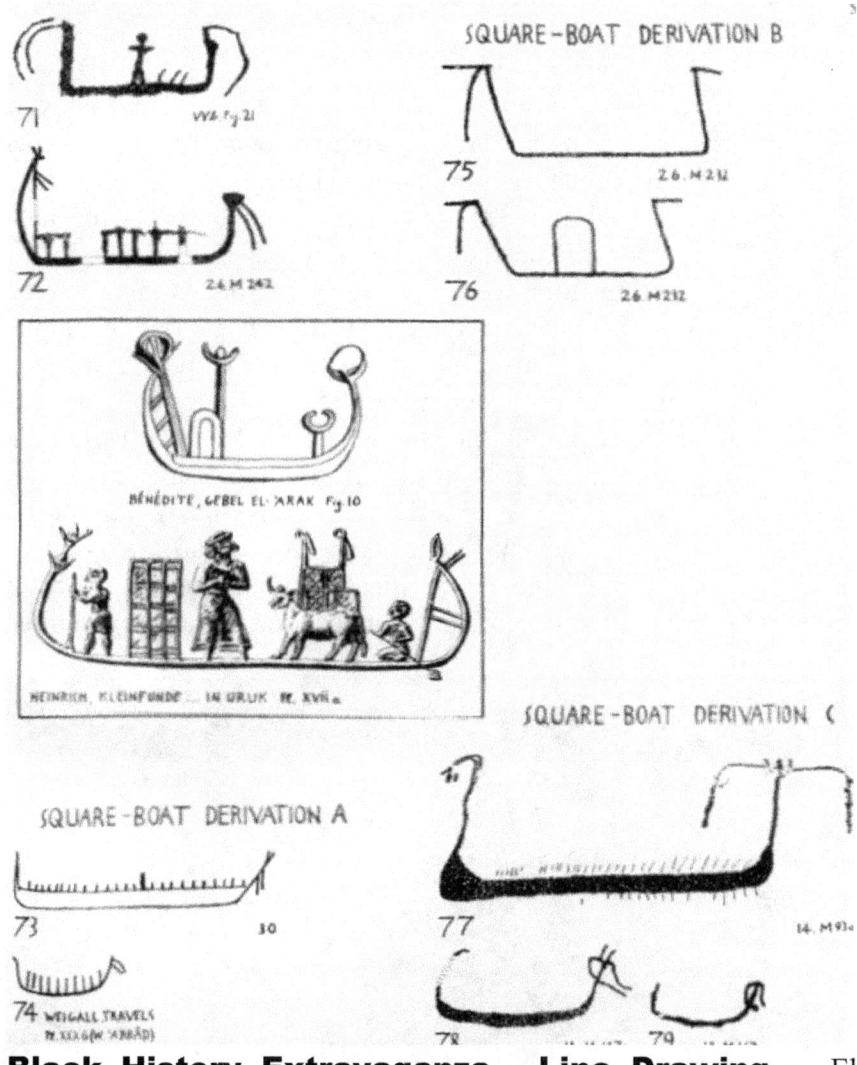

**Black History Extravaganza - Line Drawing -** El Bersheh - Square Boats Derivation A, B, C.

This insight into the origin of the 17th Dynasty, notwithstanding, the admonition from Amon to punish the upstart foreigners empowered the 17th Dynasty who waged a protracted war of liberation that ultimately expelled the invaders, founded the continuing 18th Dynasty and New Kingdom, and begun imperial expansion into Asia and

# FREDERICK MONDERSON

Nubia. The New Kingdom extended into the 19$^{th}$ and 20$^{th}$ Dynasties. After this, a Third Intermediate Period was ushered in between the 21$^{st}$ and 24$^{th}$ Dynasties. In that "age of chaos" the Ethiopians conquered Egypt and founded the 25$^{th}$ Dynasty. The 26$^{th}$ Dynasty came from Sais in the North. This was the last local dynasty before the Persians, Assyrians and again Persians conquered again. Then after these, the new invaders were the Greeks and finally the Romans. Byzantine rule lasted from 395 to 640 A.D. From 640 A.D. onwards, Arabs, Turks, then Mamelukes and finally the French and British ruled Egypt, before rule reverted to native Egyptians under Nasser after World War II. At the end of the Eighteenth Century, Mohammed Ali decimated the Mamelukes and began placing native Egyptians in important positions in his government. Several things could thus be said about Egypt, regarding the Nile River, the Sun, the Desert and permanence of its social and political institutions that characterized this ancient land. All that was developed previously was further crystallized, before the end came. The arts, crafts, agriculture, religion, science, medicine, mummification, quarrying, all got better and this is what attracted foreigners as conquerors and as admirers down through the ages.

**Black History Extravaganza - Tomb of Userhat -** While others are at work, the individuals present a bouquet of flowers and a Table of Offerings to the enthroned Lord and his wife.

# BLACK HISTORY EXTRAVAGANZA HONORING DR. BEN-JOCHANNAN

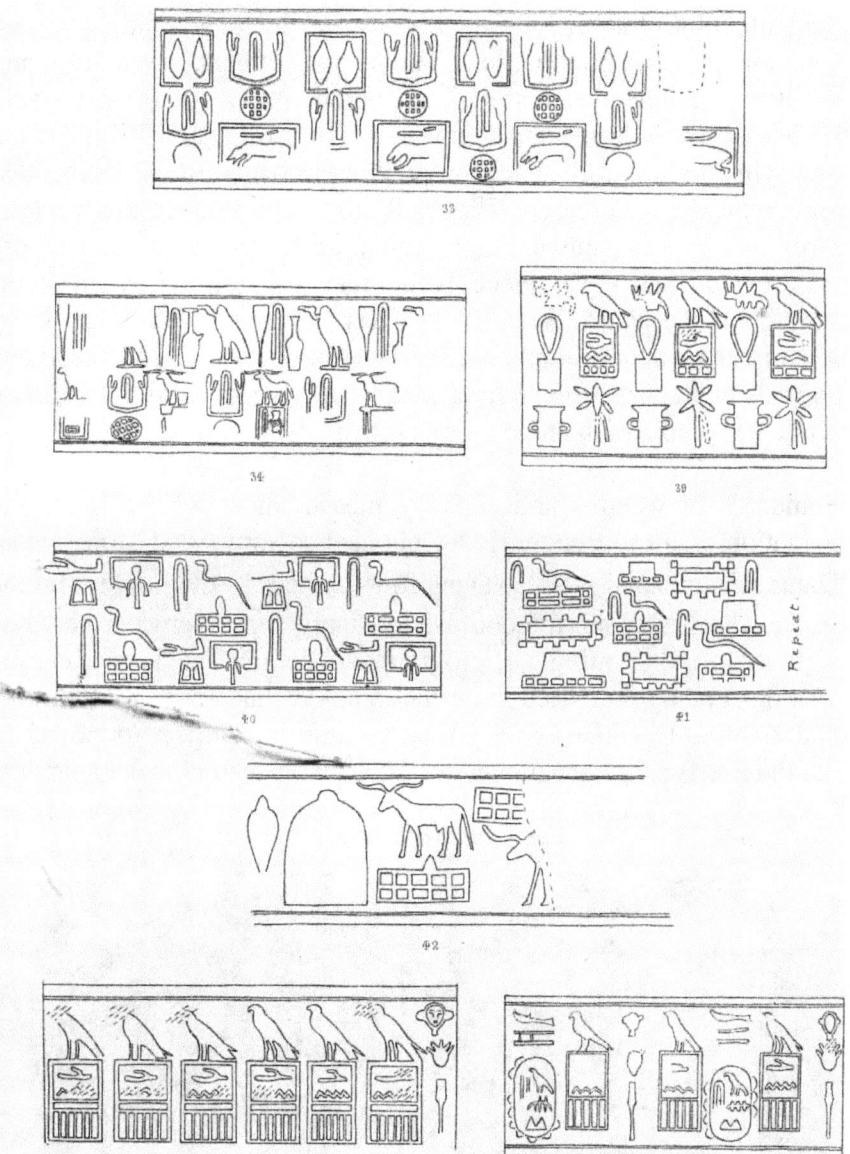

**Black History Extravaganza - Line Drawings -** Archaic Dynasty markings of kings represent some early forms of Hieroglyphs.

# FREDERICK MONDERSON

In the arts, schools from different regions of the country competed in the realm of sculpture, painting, pottery making, boat building, cotton weaving, basketry and matting. The paints, pigments, dyes, inks, and varnishes became even better. More and bigger boats and ships were built to ply the Nile and adjacent waterways. Boring and drilling aided quarrying, gold mining, and iron production while iron use expanded and metal work increased. They still, however, retained use of stone tools in some capacities. Gold and jewelry making became more expert and such masterpieces can today be admired in museums throughout the world. Woodwork, silver and lead production, pottery making, tools and weapons became more pronounced. Domesticated animals and cultivation of food plants improved, as did the culinary arts, their preparation and preservation.

Standards of weights and capacity measurement were refined and irrigation was more extensively pursued to move and store water. Dams, cisterns and wells, water-lifting devices as the shaduf and the water-wheel were put to good use to supply domestic water needs as well as to aid farming. Hieroglyphic, Hieratic and later Demotic writings greatly increased in perfection. Alas, the once great, mighty and creative Egyptian society finally could not project its power or defend itself and so was moved from the pinnacle of global leadership.

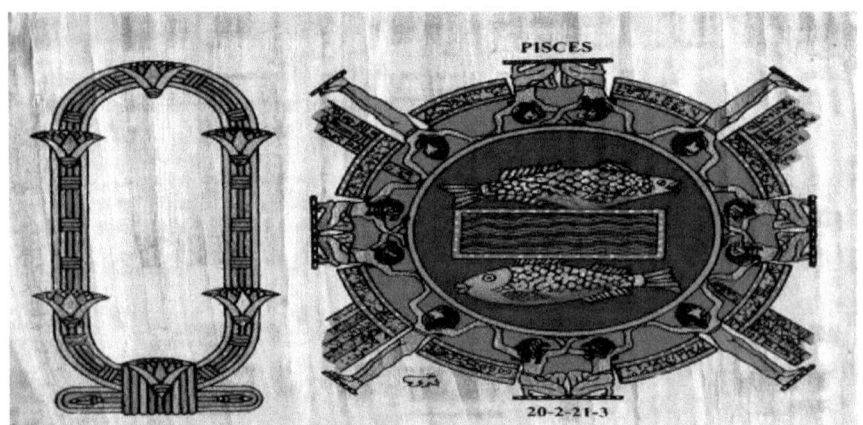

**Black History Extravaganza - Papyrus -** A Blank Cartouche beside the Astrological sign for Pisces.

# BLACK HISTORY EXTRAVAGANZA HONORING DR. BEN-JOCHANNAN

**Black History Extravaganza - Photo -** In the Ramesseum, Mortuary Temple of Rameses II, workers demonstrate how the great stones were moved.

**Black History Extravaganza - Tomb of Userhat -** Workers are similarly engaged in gang-work, this time, tending the animals, etc.

# FREDERICK MONDERSON

**Black History Extravaganza - Photo -** Native Egyptian Guide Showgi Abd Rady points to a spot holding something very ancient.

# BLACK HISTORY EXTRAVAGANZA HONORING DR. BEN-JOCHANNAN
## The Four Principal Gods and Regions

Egyptian religion has intrigued many people as well as been a subject of much discussion, particularly because of the multiplicity of deities in its pantheon. However, this can be easily explained even though it seems rather difficult. While graves of the Prehistoric Period give indication of religious beliefs, the Pyramids offer the first examples of the permanence of the belief in the Afterlife and the utility of the "house of eternity." The Step-Pyramid built by Imhotep for Pharaoh Zoser of the $3^{rd}$ Dynasty, was the first tangible and philosophic concept of ascending to the heavens and the Kingdom of the Sun. The "True Pyramids" at Ghizeh followed and then was added the adjacent mortuary temple that administered to the cult of the dead King. For the much heralded later period, Geoffrey Parrinder in *World Religions* (1975) (1985: 136) explained how New Kingdom tombs in the Valley of the Kings at Thebes were built and decorated to reflect: "The nocturnal journey of the sun-god through the underworld until dawn brings his emergence in the world above. The dead king was believed to accompany the sun-god and to emerge with him in a new dawn - clearly a guarantee of his survival after death."

**Black History extravaganza - Tomb of Userhat -** This time the workers are supervised.

# FREDERICK MONDERSON

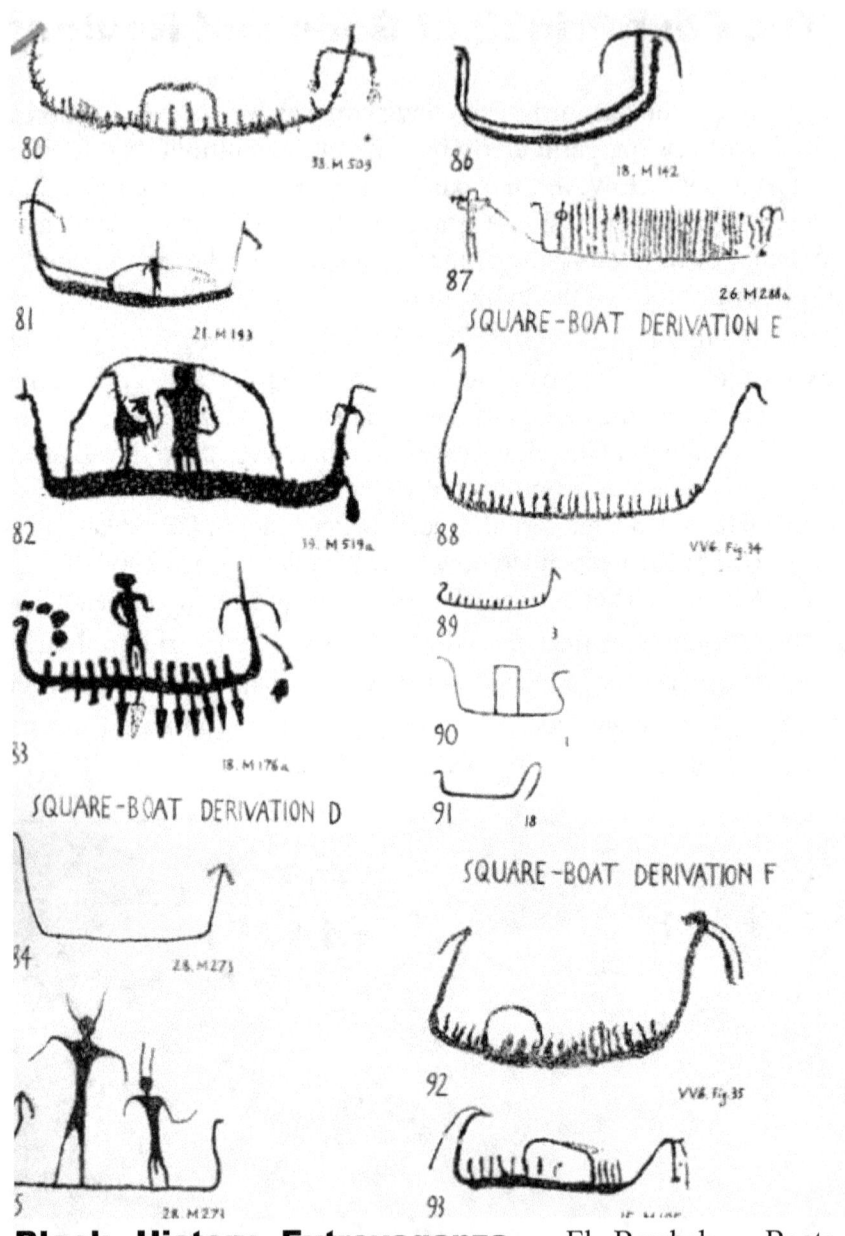

**Black History Extravaganza** - El Bersheh - Boats - Derivation D, E, F.

# BLACK HISTORY EXTRAVAGANZA HONORING DR. BEN-JOCHANNAN

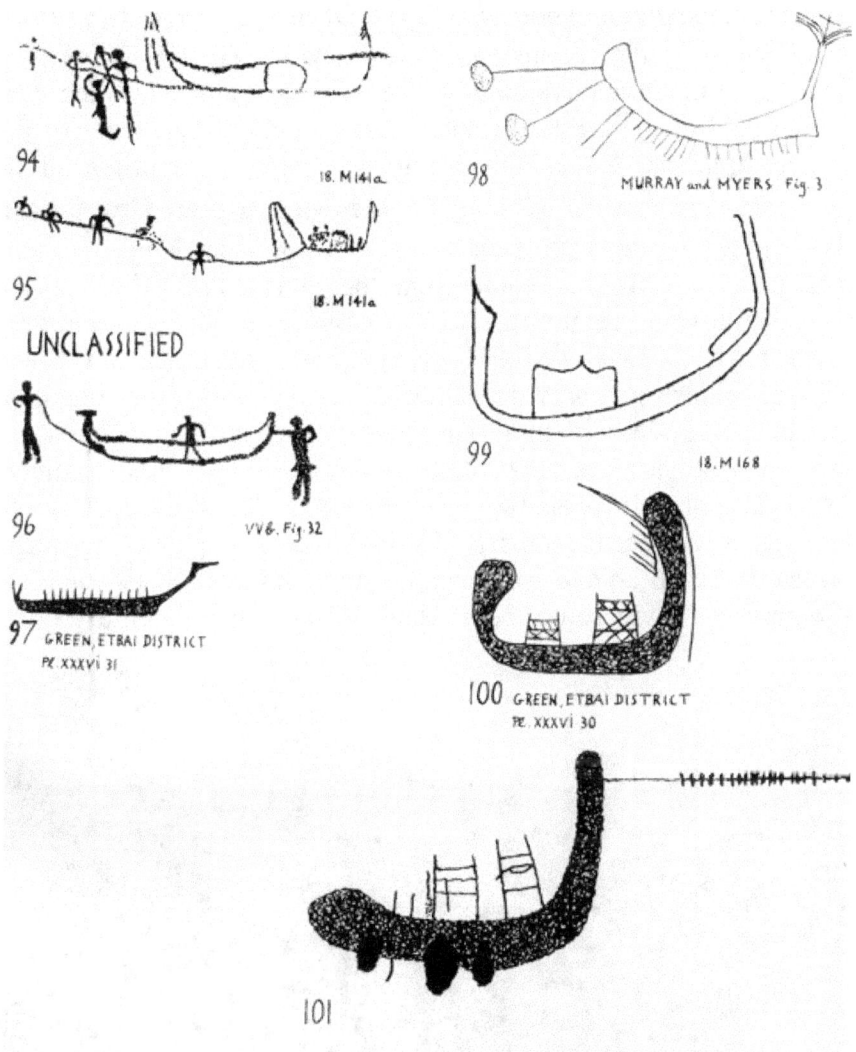

**Black History Extravaganza - Line Drawing -** El Bersheh - Unclassified square and other forms of boats.

As such, the four principal centers of worship with their cosmogonies and theogonies and belief systems were Ra at Heliopolis, Ptah at Memphis, Osiris at Abydos and Amon, later Amon-Ra at Thebes manifesting in his principal temples at Karnak and Luxor. Khnum,

# FREDERICK MONDERSON

who made man on his potter's wheel, resided on Elephantine Island, at Aswan, the southern border of Egypt. Of course, Amon-Ra was also worshipped in the "Mansions of Millions of Years" or mortuary temples of the respective kings of the New Kingdom across the river in the land of the west at Thebes. Cosmogonies are stories of the origins of the universe and theogonies are stories of the origins of the gods. However, when we study the **Geography of the Gods**, interesting questions are posed. Osiris came from Nubia. Wallis Budge tells us Hathor came from the Sudan, and Horus was a blacksmith who "went north." We know the metal age began very early in Africa. Later we see Horus as "Chief of the Blacksmiths" and Hathor as husband and wife. On the *Narmer Palette*, the conqueror has both divinities with him. The Question then is 'Why would he, as a Theban, not be associated with these African Gods?' Like so much, we must apply critical analysis to every aspect of Egyptian history and culture, to correct the grossly distorted record implanted by racist Western, European and American historiography in the 19th and 20th Century that is vigorously being challenged in the 21st Century.

**Black History Extravaganza - Photo -** In the First Court of Medinet Habu, Mortuary Temple of Rameses III (20th Dynasty), round columns and pillars with Osiride statues.

# BLACK HISTORY EXTRAVAGANZA HONORING DR. BEN-JOCHANNAN

**Black History Extravaganza - Photo -** More of the Round Columns and pillars with Osiride Statues (left and right) in the Court of Rameses III's Mortuary Temple at Medinet Habu.

Heliopolis' doctrine featured the creator-god Atum who was identified with the sun god Re or Ra. Parrinder (1985: 138) also noted: "Atum was said to have emerged from a chaos of waters, called Nun, and to have appeared on a hill; he procreated, without a consort, the deities Shu (air) and Tefnut (moisture), the former of whom separated the sky from the earth, so that Geb (earth) and Nut (sky) now came into being. A natural procreation was here envisaged, and the same is true of the children of Geb and Nut, the gods Osiris, Isis, Seth and Nephthys, although their cosmic import is initially less clear. Together the nine gods formed the Ennead of Heliopolis, a concept that was afterwards applied to other local groupings and sometimes extended to include more than nine deities. That the physical creation began with the emergence of land from water would seem to be an idea which came naturally to the inhabitants of the Nile Valley, who sometimes saw islands of mud appearing in the Nile." That is, after the Inundation.

# FREDERICK MONDERSON

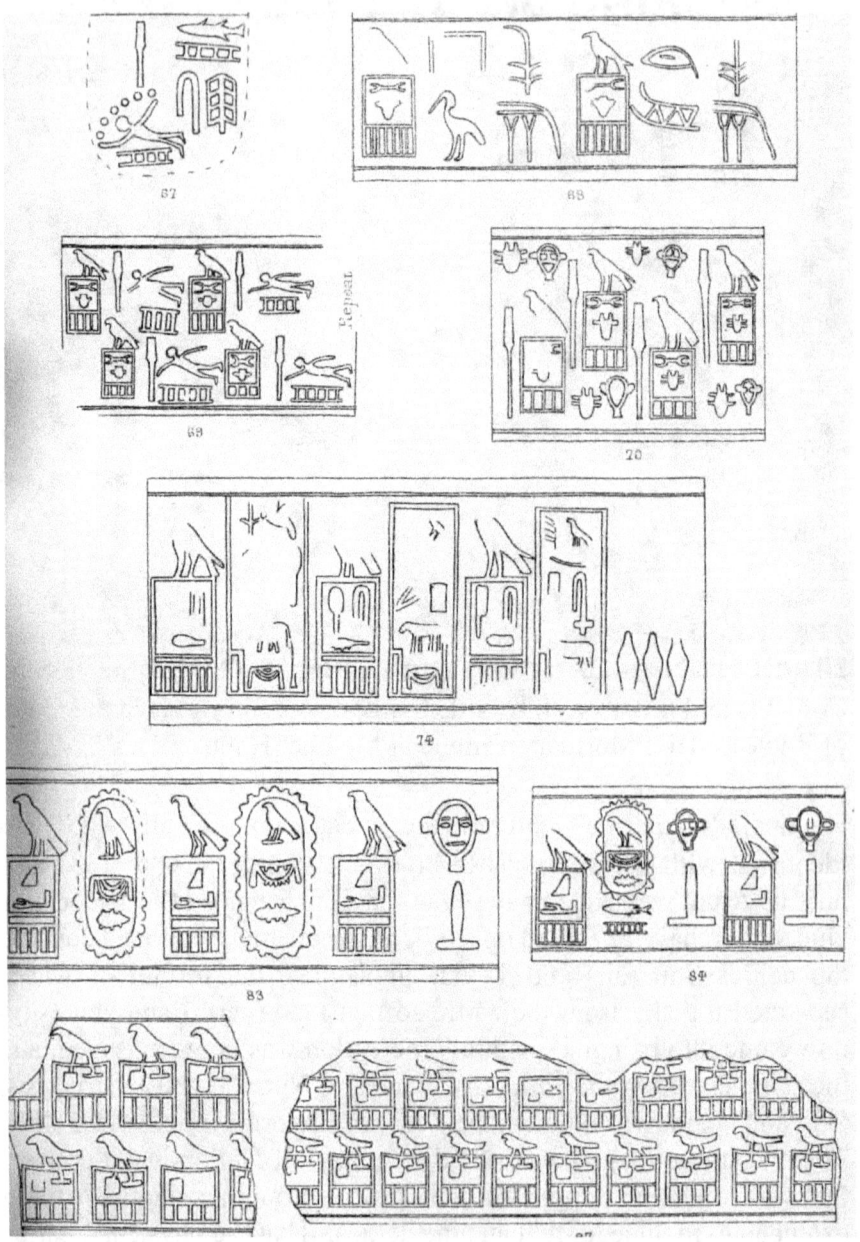

**Black History Extravaganza - Line Drawing -** More of Archaic Dynastic kingly iconography.

# BLACK HISTORY EXTRAVAGANZA HONORING DR. BEN-JOCHANNAN

The Doctrine of Memphis is somewhat different. This Old Kingdom Memphite Theology featured Ptah as the creator-god, who was bisexual for he is both father and mother as creator. Accordingly, Parrinder (1985: 139) wrote: "The creation of the world is here said to have been planned by the god's intelligence and to have been implemented by his spoken word - a striking anticipation of the much later Greek doctrine of the divine logos. At Hermopolis, on the other hand, the theology of creation had some affinities with the Heliopolitan teaching. Thus creation began; it was said, with the emergence of a primeval hill from the waters of chaos. Four pairs of deities were associated with cosmic qualities - Nun and Naunet with the waters of chaos, Huh and Huhet with endlessness, Kuk and Kauket with darkness, Amun and Amaunet with invisibility. This Ogdoad consisted of marital couples in which the males and females were conceptually un-discriminated; perhaps four bisexual deities were the original forms. Amun was the head of the Ogdoad, and his name translates as 'The Hidden One.'"

**Black History Extravaganza - Photo -** Vulture figures with outstretched wings decorate a ceiling area of one of Rameses II's Pylons between the First and Second Court at his Mortuary Medinet Habu Temple.

# FREDERICK MONDERSON

**Black History Extravaganza - Photo -** Usr-Ma'at-Ra Cartouche of Rameses III at his Medinet Habu Mortuary Temple.


Osiris was a king whose complete history, his life, death and resurrection is known. Accordingly, he was murdered by his evil brother Seth who cut up his body into 13 pieces and scattered it across the land, burying each piece at a particular spot that later became venerated. His head was buried at Abydos and his heart was buried at the Temple of Isis on Philae Island, later in modern times moved to Agilka. He arose from death and became judge of the dead and lived in the underworld. His son Horus took his place on earth and ruled as king before the mortal kings who became sons of Horus, his successors.

# BLACK HISTORY EXTRAVAGANZA
# HONORING DR. BEN-JOCHANNAN

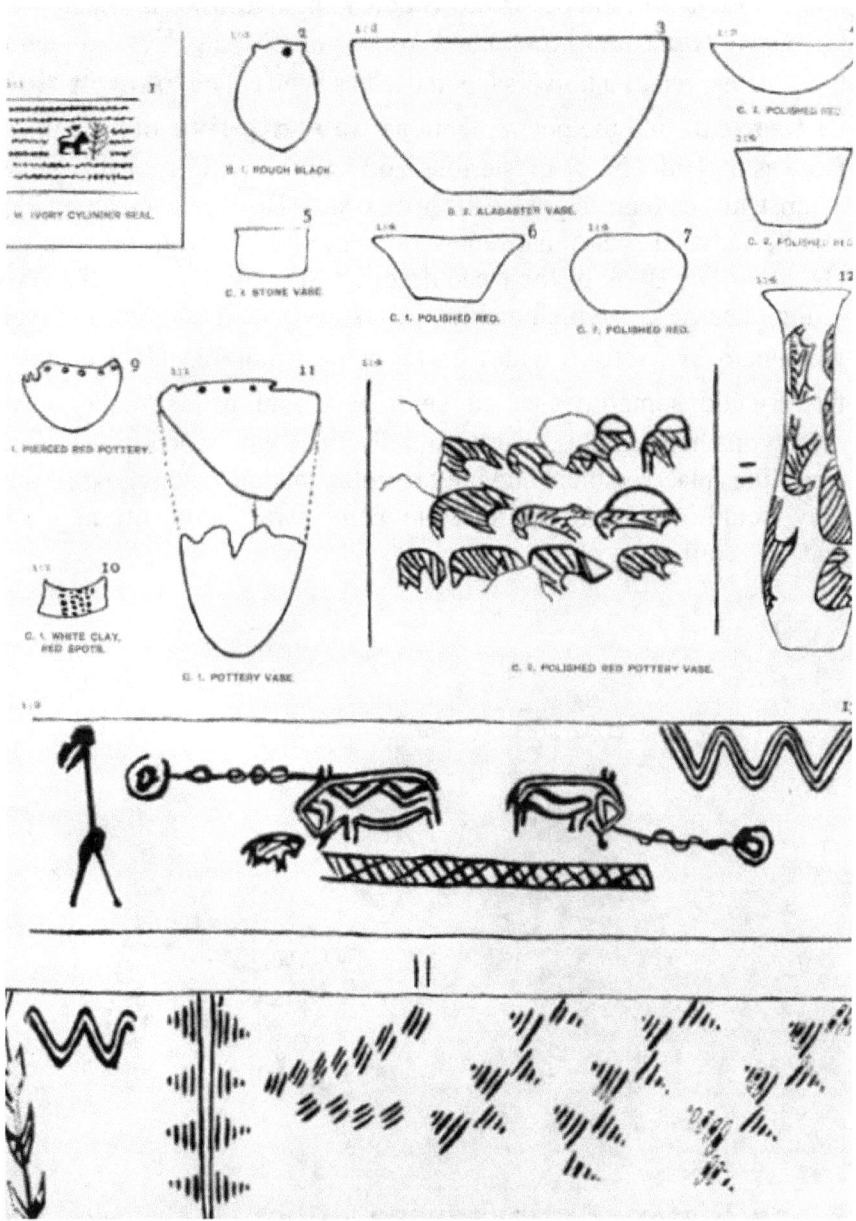

**Black History Extravaganza - Line Drawing -** El-Mahasna and Abydos **-** Various objects from graves.

# FREDERICK MONDERSON

Amon rose to prominence in the Middle Kingdom when his name was associated with four kings named Amenemhat. By the New Kingdom he had emerged as a universal god. He has been called **"Amon rich in names"** and the poem mentions **seventy-five** of his names. He was a "Hidden" or mysterious god and the rattling of the winds against his feathers signaled he was near. He was a creator God, manifested as a snake that renewed itself, and is said to precede the Ogdoad. The Book of the Dead describes him as 'eldest of the gods of the eastern sky,' which makes him a solar god. This is further seen when he is syncretized with Re to become Amon-re. He was also a fertility god, sometimes called Amon-Min, 'bull of his mother.' All these gods had temples, priests and disciples who worshipped them. The Kings placated them and built temples and made donations so that they would in turn provide these monarchs with good fortune I war and statecraft.

**Black History Extravaganza - Photo -** The author, Dr. Fred Monderson (left) joins Showgi Abd Rady and friends on the West Bank at Luxor, Egypt.

# BLACK HISTORY EXTRAVAGANZA HONORING DR. BEN-JOCHANNAN

**Black History Extravaganza - Photo -** Showgi Abd Rady and friends on the West Bank.

**Black History Extravaganza - Photo -** More of Showgi Abd Rady and friends.

# FREDERICK MONDERSON

In another aspect, writing evolved from the earlier slate palettes and culminated in the *Pyramid Texts* on the walls of 5 pyramids during the 5th and 6th Dynasties. Starting with that of Kings Unas and Teti, this began to enshrine this early theology, ritual and mythology. During the Middle Kingdom, the *Pyramid Texts* became transformed into the *Coffin Texts*, because they were written on the inside and outsides of the sarcophagus or coffins of the dead kings and even nobles. Parrinder again (1985: 137) explained: "From the beginning of the New Kingdom it became customary to give the benefits of such writings to the deceased in quite a different form: the text was written on a roll of papyrus and inserted in the tomb. As compared with the *Pyramid Texts*, both the *Coffin Texts* and the *Book of the Dead* are much wider in their application, for they proffer their privileges to non-royal persons. The use of papyrus as a medium also led to a further innovation: the text was often illustrated with beautifully colored vignettes, as in the papyri of Ani and others. Much of Ancient Egypt's religious literature is thus funerary in character."

**Black History Extravaganza - Tomb of Userhat -** Workers under supervision and doing different tasks.

# BLACK HISTORY EXTRAVAGANZA HONORING DR. BEN-JOCHANNAN

**Black History Extravaganza - Photo -** Presenting two ointment jars to enthroned Ra-Horakhty wearing sun-disk.

# FREDERICK MONDERSON

**Black History Extravaganza - Photo -** Presenting a plant to enthroned Ra-Horakhty.

These then are some of the fascinating features that characterized the History of Egypt in ancient times when east was east but there was no

# BLACK HISTORY EXTRAVAGANZA HONORING DR. BEN-JOCHANNAN

west until much later. We now turn to a poem to Osiris to end this chapter.

**Black History Extravaganza - Photo -** This Brother came to Praise and Pay Respects to Dr. Yosef A.A. Ben-Jochannan (left); while other wonderful folks followed him to the Cemetery to be sure he got on is way.

## POEM TO OSIRIS

O Osiris, great immortal with attributes part divine and part human, you are Lord of Being with many names.
Great God, you are the promise of eternity, for the just and those who live by Ma'at's law of right and truth.
Lord of Abydos, you suffered the indignity of death and decapitation, being victimized by conspirators filled with envy.
When the righteousness of your cause reached to heaven, father god Ra dispatched his emissaries to rescue you from the perdition you did not deserve.
They came to shed light on the First among the Westerners, the One God Living in Truth.
You are the Father and Mother of Mankind, Everlasting Soul.
Lord of the Horns with tall Atef-Crown, of good memory in the God's Palace.

# FREDERICK MONDERSON

**Black History Extravaganza - Photo -** Stairs lead to the Hypostyle Hall at Rameses II's Mortuary Temple the Ramesseum, 19$^{th}$ Dynasty. Notice the colossal Osiride Statue to the right.

Presider over the West, your brother Seth and his evil cohorts plotted your death to seize your throne and legacy, Glorious, Good God!

# BLACK HISTORY EXTRAVAGANZA HONORING DR. BEN-JOCHANNAN

They entrapped your body through guile and trickery, and into the Nile they discarded your coffin.

The dastard deed done, the doers of iniquity rejoiced, claiming your legacy, mummy, crown, scepter and whip, great warrior, King of Upper and Lower Kemet/Egypt, King of All the Gods.

When Ra rises every day and comes to the Under-world, in order to survey this land and also the Countries, you sit there also as he.

The Majesty of Thoth stands near unto you, in order to execute the commands, which proceed from your mouth.

You are king of the Illuminated, prototype of the Dead man, King of Eternity.

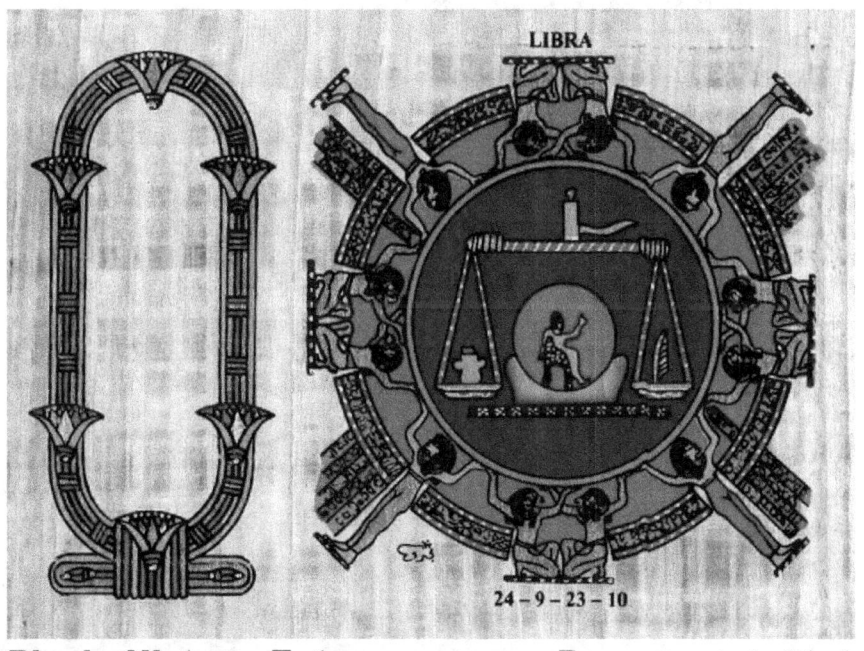

**Black History Extravaganza - Papyrus -** A Blank Cartouche stands beside the Astronomical sign for Libra.

Lord of Rosta, greatly loved on earth, Isis the faithful and loving wife searched the land untiring, for your remains out of honor and duty.
With her sister Nephthys, their lamentations echoed throughout and reached the heavens, triumphant.

# FREDERICK MONDERSON

Thoth, the personification of intelligence and scribe of the gods, with Anubis assisted the search, Great One contained in Sokhen.
You were great of strength when you overthrow the adversary, Powerful of arms when you slew the foe.
Shining noble at the head of nobles, permanent in high rank, stablished in your sovereignty, you are the beneficent power of the company of the gods, the Lord to whom praises are sung.

**Black History Extravaganza - Photo -** Showgi Aby Rady, Native Egyptian Guide leaves Dendera Temple of Hathor.

**Black History Extravaganza - Tomb of Sennufer -** The Brothers stand tall.

# BLACK HISTORY EXTRAVAGANZA HONORING DR. BEN-JOCHANNAN

**Black History Extravaganza - Photo -** Goddess Nuit giving birth to the Sun in the morning and swallowing it at eveningtime, as depicted in a small chapel with its own Court in the Temple of Hathor at Dendera.

You put your fear in the enemy and reached the boundaries of them that plotted mischief. Out of fear of reprisal, Seth decapitated and scattered your body in thirteen locations; Beneficent Spirit in the Land of Spirits.
O Noble One with mysterious ceremonies in the temples, the Celestial Ocean Nun offered you water and the sky created air for your nose for contentment of your heart.
Source of the Nile, the north wind journeys southward to you, the plants grow according to your desire and the fields created its food for you.
Lord of the great house in the city of the eight gods, celestial food, you are the beneficent soul among spirit souls.

# FREDERICK MONDERSON

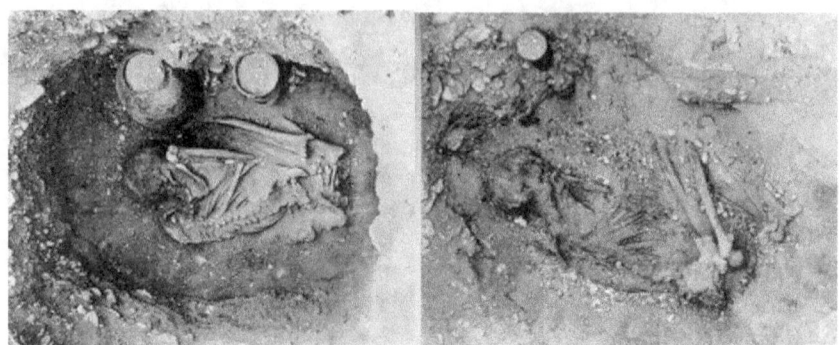

**Black History Extravaganza - Photo -** Various forms of Burial with some "Goods of the grave."

**Black History Extravaganza - Photo -** Brothers from all distances and persuasions came to salute and pay respects to a Champion of African history, culture and empowerment educationally, socially and economically.

# BLACK HISTORY EXTRAVAGANZA
# HONORING DR. BEN-JOCHANNAN

**Black History Extravaganza - Photo -** Sacred instruments form the "Crypt" at Hathor's Temple at Dendera.

# FREDERICK MONDERSON

**Black History Extravaganza - Photo -** Horus as a sacred item in the "Crypt" at Hathor's Temple at Dendera.

# BLACK HISTORY EXTRAVAGANZA HONORING DR. BEN-JOCHANNAN

**Black History Extravaganza - Photo -** Doing a wonderful musical rendition from the heart (left) and the indomitable and profusely eloquent Queen Mother Adelaide Sanford.

**Black History Extravaganza - Photo -** Greg Hardy who frequently made the trip to the Bronx Nursing Home to comfort and show respect to Dr. Ben-Jochannan, was visibly shaken by loss of his longtime friend.

Mighty One, who appeared in greatness at Abydos, your body was lying as Corpse under the Earth.

# FREDERICK MONDERSON

August Being, Isis recovered parts at every site and Temples were erected to worship the Just King murdered by evil and jealousy.
Now aided by divine wisdom, One of Many Names, you're the king who guides the land to prosperity, Ruler of Eternity, Eternal Master, Great God of Abydos.
You are very awful in Shashotep, Osiris, King of Gods.
Justified before the entire Ennead, a slaughtering was made for you in the great hall at Herwer.
Before you, the great mighty ones were in terror; these great ones rose from their mats.

**Black History extravaganza - Tomb of Ramose -** The Funeral Procession carrying the coffin on sleds and wailing women and other individuals portray a graphic picture of this moving experience of funeral and transition.

# BLACK HISTORY EXTRAVAGANZA HONORING DR. BEN-JOCHANNAN

**Black History Extravaganza - Photo -** With Professor James Smalls having performed the crucial **"Opening of the Mouth Ceremony"** and the final goodbyes said, not it's the preparation for the Afterlife journey.

**Black History Extravaganza - Photo –** This Imam came to pay respect to his brother and African nationalist fighter.

# FREDERICK MONDERSON

**Black History Extravaganza - Photo -** Dust to Dust, yet we must make sure this Great Man gets on his way.

**Black History Extravaganza - Photo -** Remembering a Great African who loved his people above all else. The people are her to authenticate such a claim for they have seen his **good works**.

# BLACK HISTORY EXTRAVAGANZA HONORING DR. BEN-JOCHANNAN

**Black History Extravaganza** - Hathor in her various moods at the Temple of Dendera.


Stablisher of truth throughout the two lands, perfect of power in every word, you are Lord to the end of the earth.
Lord of Kerer, with Nephthys, Thoth and Anubis as witnesses Isis performed the ceremony Revivification of Osiris.
Your son Horus at the Heliopolis Bar of Judgment was adjudged your rightful heir and successor.
He assumed the throne reigning as king of the two lands to fulfill the mission of his divine father, to Fill the Land with Excellent Laws.
Powerful leader of every god, you became Governor of Amentet to judge actions of men guided by Ma'at's laws, Ruler of the West.
You are a venerable God, Lord of the Great Dwelling in Sesennou, Lord of Tazoser.

# FREDERICK MONDERSON

**Black History Extravaganza - Photo -** Hathor again in her various moods at her Temple at Dendera.

God of all gods, most excellent glorified one; your head was buried at Abydos, your heart at Philae; and you established truth in Kemet/Egypt.
Ceremonies celebrate your birth, life, death, resurrection, and after life, as god who can invest his Body with All Forms as He Wishes.
Throughout Egypt you were worshiped, Prince of Peace, first Cristos, wonderful spirit.
Men found salvation in your example and purpose for you lived as father, husband, king, betrayed, mutilated, died, revivified, resurrected as deity with power to maintain life indefinitely.
Kings and commoners, worshiped and praised your name, nature, spirit, soul, and divine body while the gods of the provinces are your forms, Primeval God Residing in Tattu, Soul of Ra.

# BLACK HISTORY EXTRAVAGANZA HONORING DR. BEN-JOCHANNAN

**Black History Extravaganza - Photo -** What an interesting Trio. Sister Naya Arinde of the *Amsterdam News* being interview by Minister Clemson Brown, Master Media specialist; and Brother Basir Mchawy paying his respects to one who taught him much.

**Black History Extravaganza - Ceramic Art -** Variations of the Ankh, "Symbol of Life."

# FREDERICK MONDERSON

Master of the Gods, Abydos, throne of your power, is the world's first pilgrimage site, for all seeking your immortality, serene one.
The Great Ennead praised you; the Lesser Ennead loved you, Everlasting King.
All realized there's no empty space on your back.
For millennia adherents imbibed and practiced the Osirian drama recreating your experiences.
Many chose burials near the staircase of the god, or they erected stelae or made pilgrimages for votive offerings as the last rites.

**Black History Extravaganza - Photo -** Further images of the Goddess in her Temple at Dendera.


Your holy site immortalized by ten temples, span the duration of dynastic rule.
Still Seti I's mortuary temple and Osireion at Abydos, birthplace of the sun is a wonderfully magnificent art and architectural testament praising you as God, Lord of the Length of Times in Abydos. This

# BLACK HISTORY EXTRAVAGANZA HONORING DR. BEN-JOCHANNAN

work of majesty recognized and saluted predecessor kings buried in the desert of his temple in your name.

Holy One of the White Wall you have twin souls, bodies and natures. With the power to be born again you rise on the horizon.
Principles of Abundance in On, Creator of the World, the Heavenly Nile derives its water from you.
Soul of the Sun, the Gods Are Joyous at the arrival of Osiris.
The Earth lies upon your arms and its corners upon you even unto the Four Pillars of Heaven.
You stir yourself, the Earth trembles and the Nile comes forth from the sweat of your hands.
Because you rise and stand up, everything whereby man lives, trees and herbs, barley and wheat, is of divine origin, and comes from you. Lord of the World, you made men and women to be born again.
Lord of the Seker Boat and the Neshmet boat, these vessels bore your beauty.

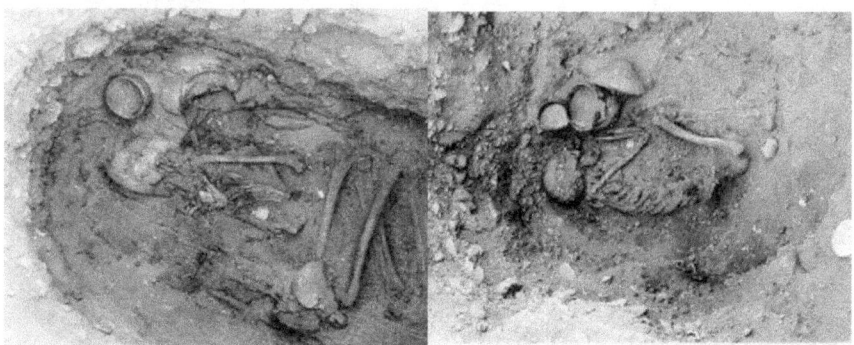

**Black History Extravaganza - Photo -** More evidence of the early forms of burials.

# FREDERICK MONDERSON

**Black History Extravaganza - Photo - Tomb of Sennutem -** Standing before the gods at the final moment can be an awesome experience.

# BLACK HISTORY EXTRAVAGANZA HONORING DR. BEN-JOCHANNAN

**Black History Extravaganza - Photo -** Oh what a story these Eyewitnesses can tell as they make sure Dr. Ben-Jochannan is on his way to the Promised Land so as to prepare a place for us all.

# FREDERICK MONDERSON

Governor of the two companies of gods, praised by your father Keb, beloved by your mother Nut, you established right and justice in Ma'at throughout the two riverbanks.

Admirable in command, heir of Keb in kingship of the two lands, your father entrusted you to lead the two lands to good fortune.

Revered in Ehnas, mighty in Tenent with a great estate in Busiris, you appear on the throne of your father like Ra when he arises on the horizon to give light to those in darkness.

Lord of Eternity in Abydos, Lord of the Great Hall in Hermopolis, abundant in sustenance in Letopolis, the imperishable stars are under your authority.

The height of heaven and earth are open to you, praises are sung in the southern heaven and thanks given in the northern heaven.

Great Mighty One residing in Thinis, Lordship given in Heliopolis, future resurrection, Brother, many found fertile promise in your example.

In the resurrection and ascension men and gods shout for joy in the southern sky and adore you in the northern sky.

Thus, with hope of everlasting life, you have the Right to Command in the place of Double Justice, God of the Birth-house, your form is hidden in the temples.

**Black History Extravaganza - Photo -** Setting up the Tet of Osiris at Seti I's Temple to the god at Abydos.

# BLACK HISTORY EXTRAVAGANZA HONORING DR. BEN-JOCHANNAN

**Black History Extravaganza - Photo** - Osirian drama at the Temple of Abydos with the Tet erected.

Beneficent One, you are the mighty one of possessions in the shrine.
Good God martyred by malice and greed, resurrected, incorruptible, you judge the dead, Mysterious Soul.
Salvation of mankind rested within your bosom, for you possess power to unite bodies and souls.
Another gift of Africa to the world, born again and possessing knowledge, power, and mystery; the father sacrificed, the Black Madonna and Child forever forgiving, salvation is still attainable, Prince of Princes.

# FREDERICK MONDERSON

**Black History Extravaganza - Papyrus -** A Blank Cartouche and a goddess holding his hand, offers ankh to the King.

**Black History Extravaganza - Photo -** Dr. Falu, Dr. Ben's Biographer (left) and another Sister at the podium lavishing praises on Dr. Ben for a life of selfless devotion to African people's welfare.

# BLACK HISTORY EXTRAVAGANZA HONORING DR. BEN-JOCHANNAN

**Black History Extravaganza - Photo -** Everyone feels it an honor to be there to wish Dr. Ben-Jochannan fondest farewell on his **Transition** to becoming a **Revered Ancestor in the Black Pantheon**.

# FREDERICK MONDERSON

# XV. CONCLUSIONS/FURTHER REFERENCES

**Black History Extravaganza - Photo -** Further evidence of early Egyptian burial in excavated graves.

What more can be said about Dr. Yosef A.A. Ben-Jochannan other than he played his hand well. He educated untold numbers. He was a stern and straightforward Pan-African nationalist who worshipped the Black Woman, especially his beloved Gertrude and placed all others on a high pedestal while admonishing the Black man to love and respect the Black Woman because she has done something he can never do.

Dr. Ben helped many Africans worldwide and they recognized his contributions to the upliftment of Africa and her sons and daughters. Along with his research companion George Simmonds they bequeathed a tremendous body of work that provides the basis for African intellectual upliftment and enlightenment of all persons in search of truth. It is a measure of a man, when at his "Passing" persons

# BLACK HISTORY EXTRAVAGANZA HONORING DR. BEN-JOCHANNAN

come from disparate regions to sing him praises and testify to his contributions to uplift humanity. This and more Dr. Ben-has done well and we recognize his contribution and willingly admonish all persons of goodwill to look deep into the truths he revealed and work to make this world a better place within the philosophic construct of the fatherhood of god and the brotherhood of man.

Further Reading can be gleamed from the Index.

**Black History Extravaganza - Photo - Deity** enthroned in a small temple in the Desert at El-Kab Mountains.

**Black History Extravaganza - Photo -** Dr. Ben-Jochannan always loved and respected Black Women, pretty as they alwaysare.

# FREDERICK MONDERSON

**Black History Extravaganza - Photo -** Again, deities enthroned in a small temple in the Desert at El-Kab Mountains.

**Black History Extravaganza - Photo -** Harvesting grapes in a small Temple in the Desert at El-Kab Mountains.

# BLACK HISTORY EXTRAVAGANZA HONORING DR. BEN-JOCHANNAN

**Black History Extravaganza - Photo -** It is quite an individual who can garner such outpouring of love and sympathy; but Dr. Yosef Ben-Jochannan did much to earn that respect and admiration of Africans worldwide.

# FREDERICK MONDERSON

**Black History Extravaganza - Photo -** Showgi Abd Rady with two friends on El-Kab Mountain; and again, Showgi in a small temple on El-Kab Mountain.

**Black History Extravaganza - Photo -** Get me there by whatever means!

# BLACK HISTORY EXTRAVAGANZA HONORING DR. BEN-JOCHANNAN

**Black History Extravaganza - Photo -** Prof. James Smalls, Master of Ceremonies and Great Friend of Dr. Ben-Jochannan.

**Black History Extravaganza - Photo -** Gathering of Elders to Pay Tribute to One of Their Own.

# FREDERICK MONDERSON

**Black History Extravaganza - Photo -** Gathering of Elders to Pay Tribute to One of Their Own.

**Black History Extravaganza - Photo -** Gathering of Elders to Pay Tribute to One of Their Own.

# BLACK HISTORY EXTRAVAGANZA HONORING DR. BEN-JOCHANNAN

**Black History Extravaganza - Photo -** The Crowning Glory of a life lived in defense of a people as Dr. Yosef A.A. Ben-Jochannan has demonstrated for decades.

**Black History Extravaganza -** The Brother with his Gourd really laid it down for Dr. Ben and deserves to be remembered here!

# FREDERICK MONDERSON

**Black History Extravaganza - Photo -** Finally the well-wishers get their last glimpse of an outstanding service of testimonials in praise of a Giant who lived and worked among US; constantly, and for a lifetime, defending and praising African people as he took on the world in pursuing his conviction and finally receiving the accolades and respect of a grateful people, here, there and everywhere!

# INDEX

African American Scholars 250
Aldred, Cyril 339
    *Egyptian Art* (1980) 339, 355-356, 378
Amratian 650-651
*Antiquarian Quarterly* 352
    "Early Dynastic Art and Archaeology" (1925) 352
    "Egyptian Art of the Second Theban Age" (E.A.K) (1926-1927) 352, 409-410
Archaic Period 659-660
Aristotle
    **Physiognomy** 183
Arnett, William 143
    *The Predynastic Origins of Egyptian Hieroglyphs* (1982) 143, 152-153
Asante, Molefi 47
    *Kemet, Afrocentricity and Knowledge* (1990) 47
Badarian culture 644-645, 646-647, 648-649
Badawy, Alexander 450
    "Egypt" in *Dictionary of Art* (1969) 450-451
    *A History of Egyptian Architecture*: *The Empire* (1968) 469, 471
Baldwin, John D. 149
    *Prehistoric Nations* (1898) 149
Bauval and Brophy 34
    *Black Genesis* (2011) 34, 152, 272
Ben-Jochannan Dr. Yosef A.A. 12. 13, 76, 143, 611
    Letters:
        Endorsing Dr. Frederick Monderson 90-91
        Recognizing Dr. Frederick Monderson 93-94
    **Trilogy** 35-36, 58, 74
    **Books**
    *Black Man of the Nile and His Family*     6
    *African Origins of the Major Western Religions*     16
    *The Black Man's Religion - Volume* I
    *A Position Paper*     23

A Chronology of the Bible    27
Africa: Mother of Western Civilization    32
Brother of the Craft and Sisters of the House:    56
Heaven Is Between a Black Woman's Legs
In Pursuit of George G.M. James' Study of    60
African Origins of Western Civilization
We the Black Jews    70
The Black Man's North and East Africa    73
Blacks and Jews: An Old Confrontation    102
The Black Man or the "negro" Bicentennial Year    118
of ??? from 1619-20 to 1976 C.C.: Black Mental
Illness and the Bicentennial - Volume I
Abu Simbel to Ghizeh: A Guide Book and Manual    135
Understanding the African Philosophical Concept    140
Behind the "Diagram of the Laws of Opposites"
The Saga of the "Black Marxist" versus the    154
"Black Nationalist" - A Debate Resurrected
Our Black Seminarians and Black Clergy Without    164
A Black Theology
Tutankhamon' African Roots haley, et. al.    178
Overlooked
The African Called Rameses ("The Great") II and    191
The African Origin of "Western Civilization"
The Black Man's Religion Volume II    211
Africa's Nile Valley, People, Culture and History:    219
A Major Problem for the ADL's Hit Squad
The Black Man's Religion - Volume III    252
Extracts and Comments from Sacred Scriptures
of the Holy Black Bible    273
They All Look Alike! All?!    Volume III and IV    291

Berlin conference 52
Birch, Samuel 50
    *Records of Egypt and Assyria* 1876-1888 50
Black Literary Production 321-322
Blackman, Aylward 131
Blackman, Aylward M and H.W. Fairman.
    "The Consecration of an Egyptian Temple According to the Use of Edfu" (1946) 105-109

"The Opening of the Mouth in Ancient Egypt and Babylonia" (1924) 110-112
"The House of the Morning" (1918) 112-113
"The King of Egypt: Grace Before Meat" (1945) 115-116
"Sacramental Ideas and Usage" (1918) 132
Boahen, Adu 52
    *Topics in West African History* (1975) 52
Boardman, John 334
    *The World of Ancient Art* (2006) 334, 338-339, 353
Boat of Ra defenders 263
Bonwick, James
    *Egyptian Ideas and the Afterlife* (1983)
**Book of the Dead** 40
Breasted, James Henry 45, 218
    *A History of Egypt* (1905) 51
    *Ancient Records of Egypt* (1906-07) 51
    *Development of Religion and thought in Ancient Egypt* (1912) 46
    *Ancient Times* (1916) *51*
    *Conquest of Civilization* (1926)*51*
    *The Dawn of Conscience* (1933) 45, 47, 51, 142, 437-438
Bratton, Fred Gladstone 289
    *A History of Egyptian Archaeology* (1968) 289-290
**British School of Archaeology in Egypt, Publications** 300-301
Brooks, Lester 160, 162
    *Great Civilizations of Ancient Africa* (1971) 160
Browder, Anthony 146
    *Nile Valley Contributions to Civilization* (1992) 146
Brown, G. Baldwin 394-395,
    "The Monumental Art of Egypt" (1915-16) 394-395, 399
    (1903) 434
Brugsch-Bey, Karl Heinrich 197
    *Egypt Under the Pharaohs* (1902) 197
Brunton, Paul 460
    *A Search in Secret Egypt* (1935, 1980) 460
Budge, E.A. Wallis 46
    *Egyptian Literature* (1912) 46

  *Gods of the Egyptians* 204
  *The Mummy* 204
  *Egyptian Magic* 204
  *Egyptian Hieroglyphic Dictionary* 204
  *Egyptian Religion* (1900, 1991) 492-493
  *From Fetish to God in Ancient Egypt* (1934) 556, 562, 565
  *Egyptian Heaven and Hell* (1905, 1996) 549
"Cachette Court" 8
Capart, Jean 297-298
  *Egyptian Art: Introductory Studies* (1923) 297-298
Carruthers, Jacob H. 47, 52, 59, 166
  *Intellectual Warfare* (1999) 47, 59
  *Mdr Ntr: Divine Speech* (1995) 513
  *Essays in Ancient Egyptian Studies*
Carruthers, Jacob and Leon Harris 48
  *African World History Project* (1997) 48
Centers of Worship 707-708
Champollion 287, 347-348
  *Description of Egy*pt 287

**Chronology of Ancient Egypt** 621

Churchward, Albert 277
  *Signs and Symbols of Primordial Man* (1993-1994) 277-278, 541
Clarke, John H. 5, 26, 58, 87, 145, 146, 147, 150, 152
  Review: "The African Origins of Civilization: Myth or Reality" 138
Clarke, J.H. and Y. Ben-Jochannan 58
  *New Directions in African History* 58
Clarke, Sommers and R. Engelbach 385-386
  *Ancient Egyptian Construction* (1990) 385-388
Coffin Texts 40
Conway, Sir Martin 453
  "The Beginning of Egyptian Style of Architecture" (1902-03) 453-454, 457
Creation notions 709
  Heliopolis 709
  Memphis 711
  Hermopolis 711

Abydos and Osiris 712
Amon of Thebes 714
Crowns of Egypt 277
Cumont, Franz
"The Religion of Egypt" (1910) 597-598-603
**Daily Temple Ritual** 542
"Damn" Dam 126
Davidson, Basil 148
"The Ancient World and Africa: Who's Roots" (1987) 148 - 149
Denon, Baron Vivant 187
*Travels in Upper and Lower Egypt* (1803) 187
Description of the Egypt 245
Diop, Cheikh Anta 4, 42, 142, 143, 161, 167, 190, 611
*Civilization or Barbarism*: *An Authentic Anthropology* (1981, 1991) 42, 58, 59
*The African Origin of Civilization*: *Myth or Reality* (1974) 42, 58, 59, 307
*The Cultural Unity of Black Africa* (1958, 1987) 47, 58, 59
Doxey, Denise M. 575
In *The Oxford Encyclopedia of Ancient Egypt* vol. 3 (2001) 575
DuBois, W.E.B. 58
*Black Folks*: *Then and Now* (1903) 58, 227
*The Negro* (1905) 58, 227
*The World and Africa* (1946) 228, 227
Dungee, Drusilla 58
*The Wonderful Ethiopians* (1926)
Edwards, I.E.S.et al.
*Cambridge Ancient History* (1970) 644, 648
Egypt as a Black Civilization 285
**Egypt Exploration Fund** 50, 299
**Egypt Exploration Fund Publications** 302
**Egypt Exploration Society** 50
**Egyptian Research Account, publications** 300-301
Emery, Walter
*Archaic Egypt* (1961) 202
*Encyclopedia Britannica* (1910) 495-496

Engelbach, R.
 *Introduction to Egyptian Archaeology* (1961) 310, 546-547
Erman, Adolf. 47
 *Life in Ancient Egypt* (1894)
 *The Handbook of Egypt Religion* (1907) 486-487, 490, 524-525, 526-527, 530, 532, 556-557, 560, 562, 563, 568-569, 571, 574-576, 576
 *The Literature of Ancient Egypt* (1927)
**Erman colors Amon Black** 566
Fagan, Brian 57, 168
 *The Rape of the Nile* (1975) 57
Fairman, H.W. 106-107
 "Worship and Festival in an Egyptian Temple" (1954) 106-107
Finch, Charles S. III 48
 *The Star of Deep Beginnings* (1998, 2007) 48
Food on the Nile 683
Foster, Herbert J. 138
 "The Ethnicity of the Ancient Egyptians" 138, 139, 141
Foucart, George 147-148
 "King" in *Encyclopedia of Religion and Ethics* 7 (1914)
Frankfort, Henri 335, 236, 511
 "On Egyptian Art" 335
 *Ancient Egyptian Religion* (1946, 1961)
Gann, Lewis H. and Peter Duignan 58
 *Africa and the World* (1972)
Garvey, Marcus 87, 166
 *Philosophy and Opinions* 87
Gebel Arak knife 275
Geography of the Gods 708
Gerzean or Naqada I and II 654
Gliddon, George 149
 *Ancient Egypt: The New World* (1843)149
Goodwin, C.W. 552
 "The 115th Chapter of the Turin Book of the Dead" (1871) 552, 553
**Graeco-Roman Branch Publications** 303
Gundlach, Rolf 125

"Temples" in The Oxford Encyclopedia of Ancient Egypt (2001) 125
Harris, J.E. 228
   *Pillars in Ethiopian History* 228
Harris, John R. 348
   *The Legacy of Egypt* (1971) 348
Hastings - *Encyclopedia of Religion and Ethics* 51
Hereen, A.H.L.
   Politics, Intercourse and *Trade of the Carthaginians, Ethiopians, Egyptians* (1883) 150
Hawass, Zahi 312
Herodotus 182-183
   *The Histories* - Euterpe - 182
Hertzler, Joyce O. 47
   *The Social Thought of the Ancient Civilizations* (1936) 47
Hobson, Christiane 18
   *The World of the Pharaohs: A complete Guide to Ancient Egypt* 18,
   "The Frist Occasion" 18
Huggins, John and John Jackson 58
   *Introduction to African Civilizations* (1936) 58
Imhotep 393
*Instructions of Amenemope* 38
*Instructions of Ani* 13
Jackson, John 229
   *Introduction to African Civilization* (1970) 229
James, George G.M. 48
   *Stolen Legacy* (1954) 48
James, Leonard 26, 52, 310
July, Robert 223
   *A History of the African People* (1970)
   *Colonial Africa* (1975)
Junker, Herman 5, 52
Kamil, Jill 279
   *The Ancient Egyptians* (1976, 1984) 279
   *Luxor: A Guide to Ancient Thebes* (2nd Edition) (1973, 1976)
Kas of the Sun-God **Ra 258**
Karenga, Maulana 47

*Maat: The Moral Ideal in Ancient Egypt* (2004)
*The Book of Coming Forth by day: The Ethics of the Declarations of Essence* (1990)
Karenga, Maulana and Jacob Carruthers 48
*Kemet and the African World view* (1986) 48
Kemp, Barry
*Ancient Egypt: Anatomy of a Civilization* (1989, 1993) 341, 343
King 15
King Lists 617

Kush, Indus 148, 347-348, 349, 351
*The Missing pages of "His-Story"* 347-348
Leakey, Mary 170
*"East African Stone Age Art"* 170
Legge,
*The Slate Palettes* 615
Lepsius, Karl 195, 295
*Discoveries in Egypt, Ethiopia and the Peninsula of Sinai in the Years 1842-1848* 195
*Denkmaler* 295
*Egyptian Chronology* (1849) 295
*Book of the Kings of Egypt* (1850) 295
L'Hote, Henry
*"Tassili Frescoes"*
Ma'at 43, 45
Mann 120
*Sacred Architecture* 120-123
Maspero, Gaston 148, 229, 254, 256, 258
"Place cards" in the Cairo Museum 229
On Mahepra "Negroid but not Negro" 174
*Art in Egypt* (1912) 381, 382
"Creation by Voice and the Ennead of Heliopolis" (1881) 577-578
Massey, Gerald 57
*A Book of the Beginnings* (1881) 57
*Natural Genesis* (1898) 57
*Ancient Egypt: Light of the World* (1907) 57

Maxim 39
Maxims of Ptah-Hotep 38
Medicine 673
Mentuhotep II 25, 29, 171
Michalowski, Kazimierz
    *Art of Ancient Egypt* (1968) 362, 366-367
Middle Kingdom 686-688, 689-690, 693
Min (the Black God) 25, 517
Moore, Richard B.
    *The Name Negro: Its Origin and Evil Use* (1960) 193
Mosso 79
    *Foundations of Mediterranean Civilization* 79
Murdock, George Peter 223
    *Africa: Its Peoples and Their Culture History* (1959) 223
Murnane, William J.
    *The Penguin Guide To Ancient Egypt* (1983) 177
Murray, Margaret 157-158
    *The Splendor That Was Egypt* (1949) 157-158
    "Burial Customs and Beliefs in the Afterlife" (1956) 369
    *The Temples of Egypt* (1931) 541
Murray - *Handbook for Egypt* (1888) 182
Myer, Isaac 46
    *Oldest Books in the World* (1900) 46
Narmer 276-277
Naville, Edouard 210
    "African Origin of Civilization" 210
Need for reconstruction in African historiography 248
Neferhotep's "Double Statue" 8
**Negative Confessions** 522-523, 587
Nelson, Harold H. 98
    "The Egyptian Temple: The Theban Temples of the Empire Period" 98
New Kingdom 696, 700, 702
Obenga, Theophile 17
    *African Philosophy:*
    *The Pharaonic Period* 2780-330 B.C. (2004) 17, 18, 38, 42, 43, 47, 64-65
    "Four Acts of Ra" 18-20

    *Ancient Egypt and Black Africa* (1992) 47
O'Connor, David 169, 227
Old Kingdom 660-661, 662-663, 664-665, 679-681
"Origin of the Egyptian Race" 208
Osei, G.K.
    *African Contribution to Civilization* (1983) 510
Paint Factory in *The New York Times* 170
Paints and pigments 702
"Painted Black for the Funerary Ceremony" 170, 320
Paleolithic sites in Egypt 267
Palettes 615, 656
Peet, T. Eric 86, 334
    "The Problem with Akhenaten" 86, 223
    "The Art of the Predynastic Period" (1915) 373, 377
Petrie, Flinders 25,581
    **Sequence dating at Naqada** 296-297
    *Religion and Conscience in Ancient Egypt* (1898) 46
    "Egyptian Religion" in *Encyclopedia of Religion and Ethics* vol. 15 (1912), 142, 487-488, 521
    *Six Temples at Thebes* (1896)
    *Wisdom of the Ancient Egyptians* (1938) *358*
    "*The Sources and Growth of Architecture in Egypt*" (1901) 444, 482-483
    *Religious Life in Ancient Egypt* (1924) 590
**Physical Characters of the Egyptians** 309-310
Poem to:
    Ra- the Sun God 256-263
    Thoth 323-327
    Ptah 419-
    Amon-Ra 621-638
    Osiris 719-739
"Prince of the City" 471
Predynastic Period 655-656
Principal Gods and Regions 705
"Publish or Perish" 2
Pyramid Complex 462, 667-668, 669
Pyramid Texts 40
Pyramid Text, Coffin Texts and Book of the Dead 716

Rawlinson, Canon George 206
    *The Story of the Nations: Egypt* 206, 544, 545-546
Redford, Donald 61
    "Egyptian Religion" in *The Encyclopedia of Religion* (1987) 61
Richardson, G.H. 603
    "The World's Debt to Egypt" (1914) 603-605, 606-608
Robins, Gay
    *The Art of Egypt*
Rogers, Joel A. 58
    *Sex and Race* (3 Volumes 1967) 58, 230-231, 232
    *World's Great men of Color* (2 volumes 1972) 58
Rosellini the Italian 288
    *Description of Egypt* 288
Ross, E. Denison 332
    *Egyptian Art Through the Ages* (1931)332, 392, 595
Sarton, George 50
Scorpion king 658
Seligman, C.G.
    *The Races of Africa* (1030) 223
**Seven Wonders of the World** 159-160
Seventeenth Dynasty 697, 200
Shafer, Byron E. 99
    *Temples in Ancient Egypt* (1998) 99-102
Shaw, Ian
    *The Oxford History of Ancient Egypt* 616,
Shaw, Ian and Paul Nicholson
    *The British Museum Dictionary of Ancient Egypt* (1995, 2003) 591
    Shorter, Alan W. *The Egyptian Gods: A Handbook* (1937, 1981)
Siliotti, Alberto 151
    *Abu Simbel and the Nubian Monuments: Egypt Pocket Guide* (2000) 151
Simpson, William Kelly 47
    *The Literature of Ancient Egypt* (2003)
Smith, G. Elliot 25
    *The Royal Mummies* (1905) 25, 30,

*The Ancient Egyptians and Their Influence upon the Civilization of Europe* (1911) 212
Smith, Stuart Tyson "Race" in *The Oxford Encyclopedia of Ancient Egypt* 201
Smith, W. Stephenson 29
*The Art and Architecture of Ancient Egypt* (1959) 29, 57, 153, 317, 319, 368, 463
Snape 96
Steindorff, George and Keith C. Seele 51
*When Egypt Ruled the East* (1942, 1971) 51
Stirlin, Henri
*Architecture of the World: Egypt* (ND) 447-448
"Strongly curled hair" found by Randall-MacIver at El-Amra 652
Teeter, Emily 9
*Religion and Ritual in Ancient Egypt* (2001) 9
Temple, Egyptian 96
    "Consecration of the Egyptian Temple" 96
    "Opening the Mouth" 96
    "Liturgy of the House of the Morning" 96
    "Bringing the Foot" 96
    "Episodes in the Temple Liturgy" 96
Temple, Father Placide 86
*Bantu Philosophy* 86
Temples of the Gods 102-103
Tombs at Sakkara 394
Tutankhamon 29
**UNESCO** 1974 Conference 146, 232, 611, 613
Van Sertima, Ivan 47
*Great African Thinkers: Cheikh Anta Diop* (1986, 1987) 47
*Egypt: Child of Africa* (1994, 1995) 47, 234
*They Came Before Columbus* (1976) 59
*Egypt Revisited* (1989) 59, 143, 232
*Nile Valley Civilizations* (1985, 1986) 59
*Great Black Thinkers: Ancient and Modern* (1988) 198
*Uncovering the African Past: The Van Sertima Papers* 59 (Runoko Rashidi) 2015
Volney, Count 55
*Ruins of Empire* (1787) 55, 150, 156, 285

Von Reben 412-414, 415
    *History of Ancient Art* (1902) 412-414, 415
Waters 20-21
Weigall, A.E.P.B. 29, 216, 308
    *Flights Into Antiquity* 216
    *The Antiquities of Upper Egypt* (1910) 216
Wiedemann, Alfred 46
    *Popular Literature of Ancient Egypt* (1902) 46
    *The Religion of Egypt* (1898) 486
Wilkinson, Alix 383
    *Ancient Egyptian Jewelry* (1975) 383-384
Wilkinson, Garner 296
    *The Manners and Customs of the Ancient Egyptians* (1850) 296
    *Wilkinson, Richard H.* 346
        *Reading Egyptian Art* (1996) 346
Wilkinson, Toby 35
    *Genesis of the Pharaohs* (2004) 35, 156, 272, 517
Williams, Bruce 151
    "Evidence of the Earliest Monarchy Found in Nubia" 151-152
Williams, Chancellor 613-614
    *Destruction of Black Civilization* (1962) 613-14
Wilson, J.A. *The Culture of Ancient Egypt* (1951, 1971) 51
    Winkler, Hans A. *Rock Drawings of Southern Upper Egypt* I (1938) 368
Woldering, Irmgard 337
    *The Art of Egypt: In Time of the Pharaohs* (1963) 337
Woodson, Carter G. 57-58
    *The Miseducation of the Negro* (1932), 228
    *The Education of the Negro* (1933) 228,
    *The African Background Outlined* (1936) 58, 228
Woodson, carter G. and Charles H. Wesley 58
    *The Negro in Our History* 58
"World's Earliest Monarchy" 129
Wortham, David 143
    *Origins of British Egyptology* (1971) 143
Yoyote, Jean 372
    "Egyptian Art" (1971) 37, 407-409

www.ingramcontent.com/pod-product-compliance
Lightning Source LLC
Chambersburg PA
CBHW061946300426
44117CB00010B/1244